THE BRITS ARE COMING!

A HISTORY OF BRITISH FOOTBALL CLUBS IN EUROPE

Paul Avenell

THE BRITS ARE COMING

Paul Avenell

Cover image courtesy of Shutterstock

ISBN 9781914615474

A CIP catalogue record for this book is available from the British Library

Published 2022 Tricorn Books
Aspex Portsmouth
42 The Vulcan Building
Gunwharf Quays
Portsmouth PO1 3BF

Printed & bound in the UK

CONTENTS

Foreword

I have always loved football, but not in the customary, tribal context associated with the vast majority of football followers. The only football team I ever showed any specific allegiance to is the Chelsea team of the late 1960s and early 1970s, the team of Osgood, Hudson and Cooke. This was a team glittering in its fashionable King's Road association, a team studded with the aforementioned charismatic individuals, but a team not without its 'journeymen' and 'hard man' contributors, Hollins, Harris and Webb. A football team by necessity comprises nuts and bolts of all varieties – but it was the flamboyant Osgood and Hudson who left the biggest mark on this impressionable teenager.

As a postman during the 1990s, the noughties and the teenies and beyond, I have worked with many men whose allegiance to their clubs blinds them completely to the qualities of other club's players. Not for me this carelessly oblivious stance, this entrenched intransigence. When I first became a postman, an old school friend, a now colleague, took great delight in informing my new workmates that I had followed a fickle path in my allegiance to football clubs, switching from Chelsea to West Ham United to Queens Park Rangers. He missed the point. I am glad, despite the obvious claims by others of my disloyalty, that I did not follow the tribal path of my peers. For me it has always been about the game, about the technical ability of football players; the tactical nuances and strategies of teams; about the characters, their charisma, the moments produced on a green field where timeless memories are created.

My childhood was spent kicking a football on local streets, pullovers for goalposts on each pavement, in the long-lost days of quiet traffic-free roads in the 1960s. The only reason for ever moving the 'goalposts' was if the Mr Whippy or Tony Fresko ice cream vans came around, their melodic fanfares heard in nearby streets alerting us of their proximity. The other vans pervading the streets of my council house neighbourhood were those selling carbonated, bottled Corona drinks. I can still taste the extraordinary cherry and lime flavours to this day. Now Coronavirus has created ghost-like streets in Britain in 2020, making it feel as if society can never be the same again.

While not self-isolating (we've both been working normally), my wife and I have been responsibly observing social distancing. The quieter times we are experiencing have, in a strange way, led me to recall my football-obsessed youth. Between the ages of eight and 12 I received the *International Football Book*, edited as I recall by Brian Glanville, every Christmas as a present. Reading this book every yuletide triggered two avenues of interest that have permeated my life ever since – a love of foreign/international football, and an eternal love of language. Through reading about the exploits of Fachetti, Mazzola, Riviera and Riva in Italy; the stylish wing play of Dragan Dzajic in the old Yugoslavia; the game-changing tactical roles and nous of Beckenbauer in Germany and Cruyff in Holland; a lifelong interest and passion for overseas football sewed its seeds in me. I was introduced to the seedier side of football too through the writings of the *Sunday*

Times football correspondent and editor of that wonderful *International Football Book*, Brian Glanville. Glanville wrote in an elegant and eloquent prose at all times. He also lifted the lid on countless corrupt schemes taking place in Italian football in the *World Soccer* magazine I went on to read in my late teens and early 20s.

Above all, what reading these books and magazines imprinted upon me was, peculiarly, a means of learning language. There existed no educational background or interest in learning within my own immediate family, yet I possessed an uncanny ear from an early age for pronouncing foreign names. At the age of 14, I captained the local YMCA football team; at the age of 15 a neighbour who was a kit man for Guildford City semi-professional team put me forward for a trial. A previous trial with Aldershot (then in the Football League 4ᵗʰ Division) saw me foolishly attempt to emulate one of my boyhood heroes, Alan Hudson, in a 'pulling the strings' midfield role. My Guildford City trial – in my more familiar left-wing position – was an unmitigated 15-minutes disaster, hooked from the field of play to save me from any further embarrassment. The pace of the game took me by surprise. I'd also been pitted against young men who'd been brought up playing organised team football, something I'd not experienced properly myself. Any individual technique or talent kit-man Ron had seen in me was lost as the ball fizzed ferociously around me. I was hopelessly out of my depth. A late developer, I went on to play village football at a moderate level. I have many cherished memories. Many people spoke kindly of me, but the harsh words of an observer while I was playing five-a-side in a local sports centre (a form of football I was quite adept at) still ring shrilly in my ears: "He's not as good as he thinks he is." The stern reality for me was when I attempted to play football at a higher level the pace of the game was challenging indeed. The boyhood dream of being a professional footballer inhabited by thousands of like-minded individuals was gone, an unrealistic shot in the dark.

What I firmly believe I should have been is a football commentator or journalist. As a young boy in the front room of my parent's council home, I would formulate my own football matches, using Eighth Army green soldiers and Africa Korps German soldiers as my players; a small white Lego piece as my football. My imagination took flight; my games received their own personal commentary – and these forms of personalised football matches were so much more realistic than the finger-flicking Subbuteo football game that was in its heyday. In my teens I possessed a photographic memory, a vast knowledge of British and international football. It is this passion and knowledge that I hope to put into practice as I recall the successes and failures; the joyous moments and the disasters; the 'heads in the sand' attitude of British football, fortunately counteracted by the astute, open-to-all-ideas management and coaching staff, in particular at Liverpool FC.

The extraordinary revival by Liverpool in April 2019, overturning a 3-0 defeat at the Nou Camp against Barcelona, winning 4-0 at Anfield to reach the 2019 Champions League Final acted as a catalyst for my coverage of British teams in the three European competitions, the almost forgotten Cup Winner's Cup (played in by the teams who won their main domestic cup competition – the FA Cup in England), the UEFA Cup, now the Europa League, and the European Cup, now the Champions League. It's a story of adventure, discovery, of tragic loss, of triumph, and as in life, the hard reality that sometimes we're just not good enough.

Part 1: European Cup Winners Cup

BRITISH WINNERS/FINALISTS

Launched in 1960, domestic cup winners were each country's entrant unless the same team had won that country's domestic league. In this instance, the country's league runners-up would partake in the competition.

1961: Two-Leg Final: Glasgow Rangers 0 v 2 Fiorentina – Glasgow, 80,000
 Fiorentina 2 v 1 Glasgow Rangers – Stadio Communale, Florence, 50,000
1963: Tottenham Hotspur 5 v 1 Atlético Madrid – De Kuip Stadium,
 Rotterdam,49,143
1965: West Ham United 2 v 0 TSV Munich 1860 – Wembley Stadium, 97,974
1966: Borussia Dortmund 2 v 1 Liverpool – Hampden Park, Glasgow, 41,657
1967: Bayern Munich 1 v 0 Glasgow Rangers – Frankenstadion,
 Nuremburg, 69,480
1970: Manchester City 2 v I Górnik Zabrze – Prater Stadium, Vienna, 7,968
1971: Chelsea 2 v 1 Real Madrid – Karaiskakus Stadium, Piraeus, 66,000
1972: Glasgow Rangers 3 v 2 Dinamo Moscow – Barcelona, 24,701
1973: AC Milan 1 v 0 Leeds United – Salonika, 40,154
1976: Anderlecht 4 v 2 West Ham United – Heysel Stadium, Brussels, 58,000
1980: Valencia 0 v 0 Arsenal (Valencia 4-2 on penalties) – Heysel Stadium,
 Brussels, 40,000
1983: Aberdeen 2 v 1 Real Madrid – Gothenburg, 17,804
1985: Everton 3 v1 Rapid Vienna – De Kuip Stadium, Rotterdam, 38,500
1991: Manchester United 2 v 1 Barcelona – De Kuip Stadium, Rotterdam, 45,000
1994: Arsenal 1 v 0 Parma – Parken Stadium, Copenhagen, 33,765
1995: Real Zaragoza 2 v 1 Arsenal – Parc des Princes, Paris, 42,424
1998: Chelsea 1 v 0 VFB Stuttgart – Rasunda Stadium, Stockholm, 30,216

The European Cup Winners Cup was disbanded in 1999. It was regarded as the third most important of the European football competitions. British record in this competition was quite good. The most startling statistic is the appearance of Glasgow Rangers in the final three times, evidence of the strength of Scottish football in the 1960s and early 1970s.

Total British wins: 10
Runners-up: 7

The team that has won the competition most: Barcelona, four times between 1979 and 1999

1961 EUROPEAN CUP WINNERS CUP FINAL
Fiorentina 4 v 1 Glasgow Rangers (aggregate score)
Ist Leg: Rangers 0 v 2 Fiorentina (Glasgow, 80,000)
2nd Leg Fiorentina 2 v 1 Rangers (Stadio Communale, Florence, 50,000)

The first final was a two-legged affair, played in Glasgow and Florence. To reach the final, Rangers defeated the Hungarians Ferencváros 5-4 on aggregate, and the West Germans Borussia Möenchengladbach by a staggering 11-0 aggregate margin. In the semi-finals, Rangers overcame a strong English rival in Wolverhampton Wanderers by three goals to one over two legs to reach their first ever European final.

The all-British semi-final is best remembered for the astonishingly passionate support of the Glasgow Rangers fans. Eighty thousand supporters were present at the first leg, only 1,000 of them supporting Wolves. Wolves, 1959/1960 FA Cup winners in England, were a strong, physical side at this time. It was their misfortune to be missing the English international Peter Broadbent for the first leg in Glasgow, a skilful inside forward whose footwork was admired by none other than George Best. In 14 years with Wolves, he scored 127 goals, winning three league titles. He also played seven times for England, scoring twice, appearing in the 1958 World Cup. He would be sorely missed by Wolves in these two ties. On top of this, defender Harold Davis pulled a muscle in his leg in the early part of the game, carrying on in these days of no substitutes with a heavily strapped thigh. Davis performed heroically, moving to the right wing to alleviate his impaired importance to his team. Alex Scott opened the scoring for Rangers after half an hour, and a mistake in the 84th minute cost Wolves dearly, Ralph Brand adding a second. Brand was Rangers' third highest scorer post-war and helped himself to a hat-trick against the hapless Möenchengladbach earlier in the competition.

The second leg was played four days after England defeated Scotland 9-3 at Wembley, a game in which the inimitable Jimmy Greaves scored a hat-trick. In contrast to the Wolves fans' apathy – or lack of money – Rangers fans congregated at Molineux to the tune of 10,000 to enjoy a rain-ravaged game. Scott appeared to put the tie to bed with a goal just before half-time. Wolves rallied, equalising midway through the second half, but were unable to break through again. Rangers were inspired on the night by Davie Wilson, one of three Rangers players in the heavy defeat at Wembley for Scotland four days earlier. The Rangers' fans flooded on to the pitch to congratulate their team at the end of the game – what a contrast to later finals when segregation became a prerequisite. Local Midlands police (the Wolverhampton Constabulary) were lenient towards the fans in these days before the appalling scenes seen in the 1970s. In winning, Rangers became the first British team – technically – to participate in a major European club competition. Birmingham had reached the 1959/1960 Fairs Cup Final, but were a representative team of cities who had hosted trade fairs.

Wolves appeared to hold all the cards going into the semi-final. Managed by Stan Cullis, the only player to refuse to salute the German side in Berlin in 1938 (at Adolph Hitler's behest), they were a force to be reckoned with in the English game in the 1950s. Three-times League winners – 1953–54, 1957–1958, 1958–1959 – captained by England captain and then-record caps holder Billy Wright (the Bobby Moore of his day, as a calm and elegant defender), surely Wolves were favourites to beat Rangers in this semi-final? The strength of the club during this era is exemplified by their victory over the 'unbeatable' Real Madrid side in a 1957–1958 two-leg friendly fixture. Real, five-times European Cup winners from 1956 to 1960, lost to Wolves in matches that held a certain prestige in the 1950s and 1960s. Wolves also defeated Hungarian side Honved, a side containing several players who had put England to the sword 6-3 at Wembley in 1953. Wolves were also runners-up in the English league in 1959–1960 and 1960–1961. Wright retired two years before the inception of the European Cup Winners Cup, his legend ensured. Wolves had a prolific goalscorer in Jimmy Murray (166 goals in 299 games). They had Ron Flowers, part of Alf Ramsey's 1966 World Cup squad in 1966. They almost won the double in 1960, beating Blackburn Rovers 3-0 in the FA Cup Final, lost the League to Burnley by just one point, two years before Tottenham Hotspur became the first club to achieve the feat in the 20th century. None of this bothered Rangers, who had quality players of their own. Besides, when it came to playing English clubs during this era, passionate rivalry came strongly to the fore.

Unfortunately for Rangers they came up against an Italian side, Fiorentina, in the final, blessed with one of the world's outstanding footballers of this era, the Swede Kurt Hamrin. Hamrin is the eighth all-time top goalscorer in Italy's Serie A with 190 goals – not bad for a right winger! Fast, creative, technically gifted, an excellent dribbler, Hamrin appeared in the 1958 World Cup Final for Sweden, a final lost 5-2 against Brazil with the 17-year-old Pele scoring twice.

In goal for Fiorentina, 'Ricky' Albertosi, played in the 1966 and 1970 World Cups for Italy. He was praised to the skies for his part in the 'game of the century' at the 1970 World Cup, a semi-final 4-3 victory over West Germany. I remember this game vividly as I watched the entire World Cup competition that year as a 14-year-old schoolboy. 1-1 at 90 minutes, there were five goals in extra time at the Estadio Azteca in Mexico, a record for goals scored in extra time at a major tournament. Albertosi was criticised for being inconsistent, but he was a strong, athletic goalkeeper. Over a 26-year career he won the European Championship with Italy in 1968, adding the Serie A title with two different clubs, Cagliari (who also featured the robust striker Luigi Riva) in 1969–1970, and AC Milan in 1978–1979. The 10th highest appearance holder in Serie A, Albertosi's career lasted, incredibly, between 1958–1984, encompassing three decades.

Fiorentina were managed by the early 1950s legend, the Hungarian Nandor Hidegkuti. Hidegkuti's claim to fame is in establishing the role of the deep-lying centre-forward, a role replicated for England in the 1950s by Don Revie, later famous as the manager of Leeds United's greatest side. Hidegkuti scored a hat-trick in the famous 6-3 demolition of an England side who thought they were invincible at Wembley in 1953. Hamrin, naturally, scored the second goal for Fiorentina in the second leg in Florence. The other goals in the two games were scored by Luigi Milan.

Rangers, managed by Scott Symon, reached the semi-final of the European

Cup in 1960. Their star player, Jim Baxter, famously (and cheekily) sat on the ball at Wembley when Scotland defeated England's World Cup-winning team at Wembley in 1967. Baxter also audaciously played keepie-uppies, juggling the ball in mid-air during the same game. Jimmy Miller, Rangers' top scorer, missed the first leg through injury, returning in the second leg. After their heroics against Wolves in the semi-final, Alex Scott's consolation goal in Florence seemed scant reward. Rangers would come good again.

1963 EUROPEAN CUP WINNERS CUP FINAL
Tottenham Hotspur 5 v 1 Atlético Madrid (De Kuip Stadium, Rotterdam)

Two football matches stood out for me as a boy, watching the highlights of the monochrome BBC recordings. The first was the 1960 European Cup Final between the great Real Madrid and Eintracht Frankfurt from Hampden Park in 1960. Their fifth consecutive European Cup triumph saw Real in their pristine all-white strip put on a display of demonstration football, dominated by their two imports, Ferenc Puskás and Alfredo Di Stéfano. The Hungarian Puskás, known as the 'Galloping Major', was all deft touches and tactical nous. Equally visionary was the dynamic Di Stéfano, astute and explosive in equal measure. These two wonderful players scored all seven goals for Real (Puskás 4, Di Stéfano 3), who triumphed 7-3 in a game blazing with attacking brio. In the era before Pele's pomp, surely these two were the greatest players in the world? Their dominance of proceedings almost overshadowed the fact that Real also possessed a quite thrilling left-winger in Francisco Gento, whose piercing runs contributed to many of the goals seen that night.

The second black-and-white game from that long lost, misty time was Tottenham's trouncing of Atlético Madrid in this 1963 European Cup Winners Cup Final. Atlético went into this final as holders of the competition, but Tottenham, full of self-belief, swept them aside with a marvellous team of their own, again winning with creative attacking play of the highest order. It could be argued that Tottenham's marvellous side of the early 1960s (the century's first double-winning team) had crested the wave of greatness, but they had one majestic performance left in them. What a time to produce your best form, in a major final.

Spurs' great team of '63 included the incomparable Jimmy Greaves, still in my book the greatest English goalscorer I have ever seen, the only player from this team who would feature in the club's next trophy win in 1967, the defeat of Chelsea in the FA Cup Final. I remember being devastated as Chelsea had become my team as an 11-year-old – but Spurs were the better side. Most of this Tottenham '63 side had retired or transferred by 1967. The '63 side, as the great 61-62 double-winning side, were captained by the whimsical, articulate Northern Irishman, Danny Blanchflower. You shouldn't be fooled by Blanchflower's whimsical manner – he read the game like the proverbial book. Alongside Blanchflower was the tragic figure of Scottish international John White. Tragic, because White was killed, aged 27, during a thunderstorm at Crews Hill Golf Course, Enfield, Essex in 1964, cut down in his prime by a freak bolt of lightning as he sheltered under a tree with his golf umbrella. He left behind a 22-year-old widow and two young children. White scored 40 goals for Spurs in 183 appearances and played 22 times for Scotland. Considered frail, but White distinguished himself as a cross-country runner in the army. His stamina clearly deceptive, White possessed a fine touch, passed the ball beautifully, and proved a useful scorer, notching 18 in the double-winning season. Wise counsellors Dave Mackay and Danny Blanchflower recommended White to Spurs supremo Bill Nicholson. White was known as 'The Ghost' for his uncanny positional sense, making him the forerunner at Spurs to Martin Peters.

On the wings (it almost sounds quaint given the context of modern football) were Welshman Cliff Jones on the right, and Terry Dyson on the left. Jones scored 135 goals for Spurs in 318 appearances – and very much lagged behind the strikers in this team on the goal front! It was an impressive return for a winger. Jones also scored 15 goals for Wales in 58 appearances. He played in all Wales's 1958 World Cup games, the Welsh eventually vanquished by Brazil and a goal by the already great 17-year-old Pele. Jones could happily play on either wing (something I could not, being considerably more effective on the left), and was highly regarded abroad, Juventus offering a then-world record fee for him in 1962. Jones even recovered from a broken leg to become a crucial part of Tottenham's early 1960s teams.

Terry Dyson – now here's a story. I watched him play for my hometown semi-professional club, Guildford City. Short of stature – he was the son of a jockey – Dyson was a typically gritty Yorkshireman. You could see he still 'had it' when playing for City at the end of his playing days. The five-feet-four-inches Dyson is not remembered in the same light as some of his more illustrious teammates in the glory days of Tottenham in the 60s, but was hugely instrumental in this Cup Winners Cup Final. He also bagged a very respectable 55 goals in 209 games for Spurs.

Tottenham were blessed with not one but two outstanding strikers in this team. Greaves needs no introduction as the swift shorter half of the attacking duo. His co-striker Bobby Smith was made from different stuff. A powerhouse of a striker, a battering ram in the traditional mould of strikers, Smith scored 176 goals in 271 appearances for Spurs, and 13 in 15 starts for England, a tremendous record, yet played second fiddle in the goal stakes to the miraculous Greaves. Greaves, like Bobby Charlton and George Best at Manchester United, simply glided across the turf. Like Charlton and Best, he made the game look easy with natural talent. Smith's strength and aerial ability made him the perfect foil to Greaves. Smith top-scored in the double-winning season with 33 goals in 43 appearances. He scored in both the 1961 and 1962 FA Cup-winning matches for Spurs, and lies second only to Greaves in Spurs' all-time scoring charts, though Harry Kane will no doubt pass his tally.

Spurs put out the impressive Glasgow Rangers side in the first round of this year's (1962/63) competition, overturning a 3-2 away defeat to move through to the next round with an impressive 5-2 victory in the second leg at White Hart Lane. Attendances for the two games were 80,000 at Ibrox in Glasgow, and 58,000 at White Hart Lane in the return leg.

THE FINAL

Tottenham opened the scoring in the first half in the 16th minute when Cliff Jones broke down the right wing and crossed to the left-hand side of the penalty area. Greaves ghosted in from the left wing to rifle home instinctively. Dyson, an effective and busy presence in this final, subsequently laid back Greaves' right-wing cross into the path of White, who slammed in the second. Greaves showed here he was not just about being a goal-hanger, a penalty-box poacher. How lucky were Spurs over the years to have both Greaves and, later, Gary Lineker, in this mould? Spurs turned around two goals to the good, but Atlético swiftly reduced the arrears with a penalty early in the second half. Only in the last quarter did Tottenham run away with proceedings. Dyson's first goal of the match in the 79th minute owed a little to fortune, but he earned his luck with his quick feet to evade an Atlético defender. Dyson's cross then sailed over the Atlético keeper who badly misjudged the flight of the ball. Dyson was at it again soon afterwards, crossing for Greaves to slide in a simple fourth. The irrepressible Dyson then rifled in a glorious fifth – the goal of the match – when following a slaloming run controlling the ball with both feet he fired in a terrific 25-yarder. Ultimately, Tottenham's attack proved too much for Atlético, the Spurs' players running at the Spaniard's defence at will.

Dave Mackay was forced to sit out this final with a stomach injury. The combination of Mackay's power and leadership, along with Blanchflower and White's innate subtlety, were integral to Tottenham's successes in the early 1960s.

Incidentally, the commentator for this match was the great Kenneth Wolstenholme. I grew up admiring the immeasurable clarity in Wolstenholme's voice, and still regard him as the best commentator I have ever listened to. Brian Moore too, possessed this same clear diction in the 1970s.

1965 EUROPEAN CUP WINNERS CUP FINAL
West Ham United 2 v 0 TSV Munich 1860 (Wembley Stadium, 95,974)

In what seemed like a golden era for British football, both at club level and international level, two years after Tottenham's first British victory in the Cup Winners Cup, an English club further enhanced the home nation's standing in the European game. West Ham could count on the triumvirate of Bobby Moore, Martin Peters and Geoff Hurst in this game, though strangely the trio could not bring the Hammers further domestic success thereafter as the Manchester clubs, Liverpool, Leeds United and even the 'glory boys' of Chelsea, thwarted their every turn.

West Ham beat Belgian, Czech and Swiss teams to reach the semi-finals of this year's competition, defeating the Spanish club Real Zaragoza 3-2 on aggregate in the semi-finals. TSV Munich 1860 (they don't have names like that anymore) defeated the Italians of Torino in a semi-final play-off.

THE FINAL

The trio of Moore, Peters and Hurst were justifiably lauded, but the other player I recall from my youth was the young, fair-haired left-winger (I related to wingers)

John Sissons. Sissons looked glamorous in a younger Bobby Moore vein, immaculately turned out – which brings me to Geoff Hurst. Hurst was tagged the 'Brylcreem boy' back in the day, as he was always smartly turned out, upright in stature and polite and correct when interviewed. Ditto the immaculate Moore. This was post-war, only 20 years on, and Peters, Sissons and goalscorer on the night Alan Sealey all possessed perfectly groomed hair. A goalless first half gave way to a stronger performance in the second period from West Ham. Sealey slammed the first goal from the right-hand edge of the penalty area. The second goal came when Brian Dear chased Bobby Moore's penalty area cross (Moore would repeat the feat in the following year's World Cup Final when his equally quick thinking saw Geoff Hurst head England's first goal) and was felled by the German's goalkeeper Radenski. Sealy was on hand to apply an easy finish as the ball squirted into his path.

A fine accomplishment for this West Ham team whose strong, robust physical presence in Geoff Hurst and Dear belied manager Ron Greenwood's tactical nous and belief in technical excellence. When English football started to look backwards a little in the 1970s (aside from Liverpool), Greenwood was one of the few coaches in our game who seemed to understand that other European countries were beginning to overtake us, to understand the importance of technique over traditional coaching methods. One of the abiding memories of the end of this 1965 European Cup Winners Cup Final was in hearing the Hammers fans 'I'm Forever Blowing Bubbles' ringing out around Wembley Stadium. There wouldn't be too many more opportunities over the years!

1966 EUROPEAN CUP WINNERS CUP FINAL
Borussia Dortmund 2 v 1 Liverpool (after extra time), Hampden Park, Glasgow, 41,657

In winning this Final, Dortmund became the first (West) German team to win a European trophy. This was the beginning of the first great Liverpool team in my living memory. At right back, Liverpool featured Chris Lawler. In the late 1970s I played with his older brother Joe – he once described me as a greyhound – he could have been referring to the legendary American bus company! Inside Chris Lawler stood the towering presence of the Scottish international Ron Yeats. Manager Bill Shankly built a team around Yeats – literally, Shankly thought, such was Yeats's imposing physique – and his fellow Scotsman Ian St. John. The signing of the two Scots in the early 60s– Yeats from Dundee United, St John from Motherwell, was the catalyst for the future generation of Liverpool successes in Shankly's eyes. Shankly considered Yeats a man-mountain who could frighten the life out of rival teams. Shankly was a wonderful character in the great library of British football managers. Shankly it was who insisted in placing in emphatic large letters THIS IS ANFIELD pitch-side as opposing sides made their entrance on to the hallowed turf at Liverpool. Shankly, with his dry Scottish wit, also felt you needed to walk round Ron Yeats in a wide arc in the Anfield changing room. He had a marvellous way of making his players feel ten feet tall, feel they played for the greatest club in the world. "The two greatest teams in the world are Liverpool, and eh, Liverpool reserves," he once famously said. Marvellous. Under Shankly, with Yeats as his captain, four trophies preceded this European final: a 2nd Division Championship in 1961–62 ended an eight-year absence from the top tier; the 1st Division was claimed in 1963–64 and 1965–66, the FA Cup won in 1965, won with a flying header from St John in one of the first FA Cup Finals I recall.

What ever happened to wingers? Liverpool had two masters of the position in this final, Ian Callaghan on the right, Peter Thompson on the left. They were precursors to another marvellous pair in their 70s team, Brian Hall and Steve Heighway. Growing up, every team seemed to play with a right- and left-winger. How football has changed! This method would now be considered far too gung-ho. After 1970 came tactical revolutions: total football, wing-backs, defensive organisation par excellence. One of the finest games I ever played in came with a teammate and I terrorising the opposition from our respective wing positions. We lost the game 4-3, but it didn't seem to matter as it was such an exhilarating game to play in. Thompson was right-footed, coming in off the left wing, a man after my own heart. Callaghan was fast and tricky. Both played for England, both were recognised for their prodigious work-rate and provision of chances for others, rather than for their own goal-scoring exploits.

In Tommy Smith, Liverpool had one of the 1960s/1970s most feared 'hard men'. Chelsea had Ron 'Chopper' Harris, who hilariously chased the elusive, twinkling, George Best 70 yards down the pitch attempting to scythe him down at Stamford Bridge in one game. Undeterred, riding every rough challenge, Best, naturally, went on to score. Leeds had Norman Hunter – although this team were full of 'hard men' (Jack Charlton, Billy Bremner and Johnny Giles). Moustachioed, dark-haired 'gringoesque', Smith's pock-marked face was the epitome of grit and steel. Shankly claimed he "wasn't born, he was quarried". Yet Smith was a fine player whose ruggedness and warrior status masked great versatility and technical prowess. Smith moved from his original position of inside left to right half, a position requiring more defensive than offensive nous. A mark of Smith's all-round ability is revealed by his also playing full-back and centre-half when required. Smith spent 16 years at Anfield, even marking his time with the club with a fine goal in the 1977 European Cup Final victory.

What a pair of attackers Liverpool had here in St John and Roger Hunt. St John scored 96 times for Liverpool in 336 games. Like Denis Law at Manchester United, St John was a dynamic, athletic forward. He scored 21 goals in the club's title-winning season of 1963–64. Hunt's scoring record for Liverpool was phenomenal: 245 goals in 404 games. Hunt famously kept Jimmy Greaves out of the 1966 World Cup-winning team after Greaves injured himself in the group games. It seemed cruel at the time as Greaves was undoubtedly his generation's finest goalscorer, but Hunt was a tremendous finisher in his own right. Ramsey was extremely lucky to have Hunt, Greaves and Hurst to call upon in 1966. Hunt's goals tally at Liverpool is only surpassed by Ian Rush. In the 1961–62 2nd Division Championship-winning season, Hunt scored an incredible 41 goals in 42 games. In the 1st Division title wins that followed, Hunt scored 31 and 29 goals respectively in seasons 1963–64 and 1965–66. Hunt also scored the first ever televised goal on *Match of the Day* in August 1964. Capped 34 times for England, scoring 18 times, Hunt was a lethal finisher, strong, fast, direct, like Harry Kane in 2022, possessing an unerring eye for goal.

To reach this final, Liverpool had to overcome Italian giants Juventus in the first round, 2-1 on aggregate. The Reds lost 1-0 in Turin, but won 2-0 at 'Fortress Anfield' with goals from defenders Chris Lawler and Geoff Strong (both England internationals). Similarly, Liverpool beat Glasgow Celtic 2-1 on aggregate in their semi-final, losing to a Bobby Lennox goal at Celtic Park in the first leg, before turning it around at Anfield with goals from Strong again, and Smith.

Dortmund defeated the previous year's winners West Ham in their semi-final, denying the chance of an all-English final. Ron Greenwood was fulsome in his praise of the West German club's Siggi Held, one of those who would attempt to undermine England's trophy conquest in the World Cup soon after this final.

THE FINAL
In unison with the Hammers fans the year before, English fans' wholehearted singing could be heard ringing around Hampden at the beginning of this occasion, this time the Liverpool chant of 'You'll Never Walk Alone', fresh in people's minds from the Gerry and The Pacemakers chart rendition. Shankly felt that his "fish and chips" Hunt and St John combination up front would hold sway at Hampden, but it was the "salmon and chips" pairing of Held and Lothar Emmerich as Ron Greenwood termed them, key players in West Germany's 1966 World Cup team, who were the shining lights.

Liverpool, untypically, carelessly conceded possession in midfield in the first half, Emmerich and Held combined beautifully on the counter and Held half-volleyed in the first goal. West German national goalkeeper Hans Tilkowski proved an agile opponent to Liverpool in the Dortmund goal. Thompson, predictably, crossed, and Hunt, equally predictably equalised. Over-enthusiastically, Liverpool fans invaded the pitch. The police had to move the offending fans from the field of play. Thankfully, there were no serious repercussions. Liverpool pressed, Smith going close with a long-range drive; another England international midfielder of the time, Gordon Milne, headed narrowly wide. Hunt and St John also narrowly failed to score. Callaghan and Thompson were constantly used as sources of attack, Liverpool keen to use the width of the pitch. Dortmund, a major attacking threat in their own right, fought back. Held was thwarted by Liverpool keeper Tommy Lawrence after breaking through, the ball squirmed out to the right wing and Reinhard Libuda, awake to the opportunity, swept a 35-yard-long chip shot into the far corner of the net. Liverpool challenged again, St John won many headers from his wingers' constant crosses, but unfortunately for Liverpool they were too tame and were comfortably saved by Tilkowski. St John was excellent in the air, given that he was not especially tall, but the tactic proved too predictable. Liverpool were beaten on the night. They would be back again in the European Finals, and would learn from this defeat.

1967 EUROPEAN CUP WINNERS CUP FINAL
Bayern Munich 1 v 0 Glasgow Rangers (after extra time), Frankenstadion, Nuremburg, 69,480

The measure of the quality of Scottish football at this time is shown once more by Rangers defeating holders Borussia Dortmund in the second round of this year's competition – a feat beyond Liverpool in the preceding year's final. Following a goalless draw in Germany, Rangers eclipsed Dortmund 2-1 at home. Peculiarly, a Bayern team containing three greats who were the equivalent of our own Bobby Charlton, Moore and Banks – goal-machine Gerd Müller (the only striker I saw play who may have topped Jimmy Greaves as a pure goalscorer), the imperious Franz Beckenbauer, and goalkeeper Sepp Maier, could only beat Irish team Shamrock Rovers by a 4-3 aggregate score in the same round.

Rangers were desperate for parity with their fierce Glasgow rivals Celtic, who, coining the term 'The Lions of Lisbon', had won the senior European Cup only six days earlier, defeating Inter Milan. Should they have adopted a more positive approach I wonder, given that their centre-forward on this night, Roger Hynd, was a defender deployed as a makeshift striker? Ironically, Hynd it was who had a goal disallowed in normal time as Bayern squeezed past their Scottish rivals in extra time.

The Rangers team included their great leader John Greig – like Billy McNeill at Celtic he 'led from the front', his passion and leadership skills inspirational to those around him. Greig, nominally a strong, forceful midfielder, latterly played in defence for Rangers. In 498 appearances for Rangers Greig scored 87 goals. In tandem with the times Rangers played with two wingers, Willie Henderson (known as 'Wee Willie') and Willie Johnston. Both were skilful, tricky and fast. Johnston scored 89 goals in 211 appearances for the Ibrox club from the left wing. Quick of pace, quick of temper, Johnston liked to showboat – like his friend and teammate Jim Baxter, he sat on the ball in a game later in his career. Johnston recovered from a broken ankle earlier in the season to play in this final.

THE FINAL

I could find only grainy British Pathé footage of this final. The newsreel footage did at least reveal the Beckenbauer I vividly remember from my youth. Shortly after the 1966 World Cup and the forging of Beckenbauer's reputation as a world-class talent, the young German is seen skipping gracefully away from attempted tackles. This man was a class act on the football field. Employed by West Germany in the 1966 World Cup as a foraging midfielder (and excellent he was too in this role), the switching of Beckenbauer to the sweeper role cemented his place in world football legend. Class players always appear to have so much time on the ball. Beckenbauer was the cream of the crop on this count. Only the AC Milan libero Franco Baresi came anywhere close to matching *'Der Kaiser's'* quality in future years. Bayern won on the night with a header from Roth in extra time, a goal giving them their very first European trophy, the first of many as it turned out.

This is a side I remember well. Not necessarily fondly, but undoubtedly the first team I have written about that I had first-hand experience of watching. I saw Manchester City play twice in seasons 1970–71 and 1971–72 at Stamford Bridge. There were many fine sides permanently etched in my mind from this era: Tottenham Hotspur, Manchester United, Leeds United come to mind. Leeds United possessed men of steel and all-round skill. They were admired and loathed in equal measure. Tottenham, Manchester United and the Chelsea team I followed during this period all had special triumvirates within their teams. United had the incomparable Bobby Charlton, George Best and Dennis Law; Tottenham had Jimmy Greaves, Alan Gilzean, Martin Chivers; Chelsea had Peter Osgood, Alan Hudson, Charlie Cooke. This Manchester City team had their own 'Holy Trinity' of Colin Bell, Mike Summerbee and Francis Lee. In Bell they had a silky greyhound patrolling the midfield as if he owned it, all fluidity, grace and liquid skills allied to consummate athleticism. Summerbee always seemed to me to be a player who'd been around the block, full of tactical nous, capable of excellent wing play in the traditional sense, but also capable of switching to a central role equally adeptly. So too Lee, a fiery powerhouse of a player with a tremendous shot, happy also in wide or central positions.

In this final, the only European final City have won to date (2022), they were without the influential Summerbee, who was suffering with a leg injury. Mick Doyle and Neil Young are two more players I recall vividly from my youth, both tall, dark-haired, imposing physical specimens. Doyle shared Summerbee's streetwise nature, a sturdy, no-nonsense central defender, and sometime midfielder. In the mould of Tommy Smith at Liverpool and Ron Harris at Chelsea, Doyle took no prisoners. Young, of slightly slenderer physique than Doyle played as a left-wing-cum striker, and scored City's FA Cup-winning goal in 1969 against Leicester City.

City's team was captained on this night by Tony Book. Book's story is inspirational, almost fairy-tale like. He started as an inside forward, did his National Service in the army, converting to full-back only when signed to Manchester City. Chelsea neglected to sign him despite a recommendation by his army teammate and Chelsea legend Frank Blunstone, a decision they would come to rue, judging by the occasions I saw Chelsea play City in the early 70s. Book played non-league football for Bath City for seven years. Only when Malcolm Allison became Bath manager did Book's fortunes look up. Allison took Book with him to Toronto in Canada, then back to England with Plymouth Argyle, only signing for City when he'd already passed the age of 30. Book then captained City to the Division 1 league title in 1968, the 1969 FA Cup Final victory and subsequently this first and only European triumph over their Polish opponents Górnik. It's quite a story.

Colin Bell's legendary stamina saw him dubbed 'Nijinsky' after the famous racehorse of the time. Bell also scored 117 goals for City in 394 appearances, an excellent return for a midfielder. His England appearances were restricted by the many talented players at Alf Ramsey's disposal at this time – Alan Ball, Alan Mullery, Bobby Charlton and Martin Peters – although he did feature in the ill-fated 1970 quarter-final defeat at the hands of West Germany. Summerbee's off-field reputation was as renowned as his outstanding on-field exploits. A practical joker and great friend of George Best, Summerbee was as well known around the Manchester club scene as Peter Osgood was in the King's Road 'set'. Lee thought Summerbee a fiery on-field competitor, ironic given his own on-field set-tos, feeling that Summerbee was the kind of player to get in his own retaliation first! Summerbee scored 20 goals in City's 1967–68 title-winning season.

Francis Lee, a ferocious competitor in his own right, scored 112 goals in 294 games for City, also scoring 10 in 27 for England. Like Bell he was denied more England caps by the quality of strikers in English football at that time – Hurst, Hunt, Chivers, Allan Clarke and Kevin Hector. Lee would be City's top scorer for five consecutive seasons. In the 1971–72 season he notched 35 goals, 15 from the penalty spot. He acquired a reputation for diving to win most of these penalties. My own feeling is that any striker with pace and Lee's directness is going to draw fouls from his opponents.

Lee is remembered for two incidents specifically: the set-to with Norman Hunter in 1975 having transferred to Brian Clough's Derby County in a match against Leeds United, and his thunderous goal against his old club Manchester City for Derby. The Hunter scenario came about as Lee had his lip cut by a punch thrown by Hunter caused by the ring Hunter was wearing – these were the days when you did not have to have rings removed or taped up. Hunter felt Lee had dived earlier in the game to win his team a penalty. Initially stunned, Lee suddenly let fly at Hunter with hands like flailing windmill sails. The two players were sent off, the fight by all accounts continuing beyond the touchline as they left the field into the Derby County clubhouse after the game had finished. Secondly, memorably on a pure football account, his thunderous drive for Derby against City that was accompanied by Barry Davies's memorable commentary, "Just look at his face!" The ball, struck after coming inside from the left wing, absolutely rocketed into the far corner of the net. Lee left City somewhat reluctantly in 1975, this goal seemed especially cruel to his former club.

City's manager for this Cup Winners Cup Final in 1970 was the great Joe Mercer, who lost much of his own playing career to the Second World War. A sergeant major in the army, Mercer looked like a man from another era (even in 1970) with his slicked-back Brylcreemed hair. He also seemed to me to be a man of integrity. The contrast between him and his successor, the cigar-smoking, fedora-wearing Malcolm Allison, could not have been greater. A footnote here, when Malcolm Allison managed Crystal Palace later in the 1970s, his captain and centre-half was Ian Evans, who also captained Wales. Fast forward to 1990 and a village match in which I played. To my teams' utter astonishment, Evans stepped out on to our awkwardly sloping pitch with its downhill left-side camber. Our right back opened the scoring with an astonishing 40-yard drive. It was my fortune to score the second with the cutest of athletic lob-volleys – when you've had two hip replacements you've only got your memories! The match ended in a

3-3 draw, Evans toe-poking the equaliser in a goal-mouth melee in the very last minute with a leg that could be described as ludicrously telescopic. During the match I remember sprinting past him only for one of those legs to snake out and retrieve the ball from me although I seemed to be well past him.

Joe Mercer's Manchester City side were a side to be reckoned with, full of talented players. They made short work of Spain's Athletic Bilbao, Belgium's Lierse and the Germans Schalke 04 by aggregate scores of 6-3, 8-0 and 5-2 respectively, en route to the final. Only the Portuguese of Academica Coimbra caused City concern, the Manchester club only winning their quarter-final tie 1-0 after extra time following two goalless 90 minutes.

Górnik Zabrze too comfortably beat Olympiakos of Greece and Glasgow Rangers in the early rounds, before finding Bulgaria's Levski Spartak and the Italians Roma equally obstinate opponents in the quarter-finals and semi-finals. Górnik had every reason to believe they might win this match with City. Prior to this final they'd played six seasons in the premier competition, the European Cup. In Wlodzimierz Lubanski, their number 10, they had a man who scored 48 goals in 75 appearances for Poland, second only to the modern goal-scoring machine that is Robert Lewandowski in Polish football history.

THE FINAL
City were victorious thanks to an early goal from Neil Young and a penalty from the effervescent Lee in the first half. Francis Lee was a real handful in the final. A flicked self set-up saw his close-range volley saved by Kostk in the Górnik goal early on. He then twisted and turned on the left, seeing his fierce shot parried and turned away, the onrushing Young able to turn the rebound into the net. It was entirely fitting that Lee should score the second goal – from the penalty spot. A rain-ravaged night saw the Poles claw one goal back through Oslizlo, but City held on for another Manchester glory night just one year after United had won the senior European Cup competition. City played in their change strip of red and black stripes on the night, a psychological ploy by Mercer's number 2 Allison to make the team feel like the mighty AC Milan, a team Allison aspired to emulate. He needn't have worried – this City team could handle themselves admirably and had quality aplenty of their own.

1971 EUROPEAN CUP WINNERS CUP FINAL
Chelsea 1 v 1 Real Madrid, Karaiskakis Stadium, Piraeus, 66,000
Replay: Chelsea 2 v 1 Real Madrid, Karaiskakis Stadium, Piraeus, 20,000

Chelsea were my team as a young boy, but it has always been about the game, the players, for me, as opposed to any obsessive allegiance to a club. I simply loved the game for all its wonderful nuances. I admired players with flair, natural technique, players with character and personality. It should be no surprise then that Peter Osgood became my first football hero. Tall, elegant on the ball for a big man, he possessed exquisite touch – and he was good-looking. He was everything that I was not. As time passed by it became evident to me that Osgood had a 'side' to him (all players in the professional game must possess a mean streak in order to survive at the highest level). Famously, Leeds United's doughty centre-half, Jack Charlton, claimed to have a little black book listing the players he would be looking for in his career. I always thought that Osgood might be high up on that list when witnessing their on-pitch confrontations.

Attracted to strikers and goalscorers as role models, my hero before Osgood was Chelsea's prime goalscorer in the early-mid 1960s, Bobby Tambling, who held Chelsea's record for goals scored for 47 years. Only in 2013 did Frank Lampard supersede it. Tambling scored 164 goals in 302 appearances for Chelsea. I can still recall watching the football results come through on the teleprinter on the BBC one afternoon in 1966 relating Tambling's feat of scoring five goals in a 6-2 victory at Aston Villa. That was really something to me to score five goals in a game. I managed the feat myself twice in local village football, but five goals in top-flight football? I was wowed. I admired Tambling, but Osgood had personality plus. He was also a bit of a lad if press accounts can be believed.

My only other hero as a player was Alan Hudson who Osgood appeared to take under his wing in the early 70s. Hudson was a playmaker of the kind now so tangibly absent from our national football team. Hudson wanted the ball all the time, he pulled the strings for Chelsea for the early part of the era following the 1971 European Cup Winners Cup. Many clubs had players in the Hudson mould in this period – Leeds United had Johnny Giles, whose silky skills were allied to that club's particular devilment in the darker arts; Sheffield United had Tony Currie, a hugely talented central midfielder with flowing locks that were de rigeur in the 1970s. Hudson would come deep, collect the ball from Peter Bonetti in the Chelsea goal and immediately seek to instigate attacks from deep. A wonderful technician, he was only surpassed by the great German midfielder of the time Günter Netzer. Netzer produced a masterclass when West Germany defeated England 3-1 at Wembley in 1972. Happily, I was present in 1975 when England avenged the defeat, winning 2-0 in one of Hudson's two appearances for England, with the Chelsea man at the helm. Hudson produced a virtuoso performance, dominating play in the manner of his Chelsea form, purring like a Rolls-Royce in the midfield. Why did he not play more often for England? His friendship with Osgood and their love of the King's Road lifestyle may have been a factor. When I trialled with one of my local town teams, Aldershot, in 1971, I foolishly opted to play in midfield, seeking to emulate the mercurial Hudson who was only five years older than myself. I proceeded to play local football for 20 years, chiefly as a left-winger who liked to get into the box and score. It was a poor decision on my part, and I proved far too lightweight for the professional game anyway.

In goal for Chelsea, Peter Bonetti bore the nickname 'The Cat' due to his agility, athleticism and spectacular saves. Sadly, Bonetti died in April 2020. I greatly admired Bonetti, thinking at the time – through rose-tinted eyes – that he was better than Gordon Banks. Hindsight tells me that I was wrong. It's a shame that Bonetti is remembered for making mistakes in the 1970 World Cup quarter-final against West Germany when he replaced the sick Banks, as he was an incredible servant to Chelsea, playing over 600 times for the club. At five feet ten inches, Bonetti was short by modern goalkeeping standards. His astonishing reflexes more than compensated for his lack of height. Peter Bonetti was the only professional player I had an autograph from. My father, a groceries delivery driver, delivered to the garage Bonetti's father ran, near Worthing. An autograph was arranged for me from the man who played seven times for England.

At right-back for Chelsea, and captaining the side, was the redoubtable Ron Harris, a player affectionately known as 'Chopper', and apparently chiselled from concrete. Ron revelled in his image of a tough-tackling player. The image of Ron valiantly chasing the Northern Irish genius while Best toyed with him lingers in my mind. Yet Harris, like the other 'hard-men' of this era, could play a bit too. In a team replete with characters, David Webb played alongside John Dempsey at centre-back. When Chelsea found themselves without a goalkeeper when Ipswich Town visited Stamford Bridge in 1971, Webb played between the sticks. I remember him hanging off the crossbar to entertain the home fans as Chelsea dominated possession. Many years later, my wife and I were in an Italian restaurant in Poole when Webb came in with his wife and some friends and sat at a nearby table. I felt too long in the tooth for autographs by this time.

Another favourite of mine played on the right wing for Chelsea, the Scottish international, Charlie Cooke. Cooke was a mesmerising dribbler, only denied more Scottish caps by the presence in the same era of Celtic's irrepressible 'Jinking' Jimmy Johnstone. Cooke was Chelsea's equivalent of George Best. He loved to take players on, check back inside and set up opportunities for the sublimely talented Osgood, for whom the game came easily, restraining from the King's Road lifestyle less so.

The Chelsea team were completed by the 19-year-old Hudson, John Hollins, Keith Weller and Peter Houseman. Hard-working players all, Weller scored his share of goals for Chelsea for a time; Houseman was renowned for his dislike of fuss and fought shy of the press, unlike the personable Osgood. Yet Houseman's cultured left foot was the provider of many of Chelsea's goals in the late 1960s and early 1970s. He was the most underrated player in this Chelsea side, often the butt of the Stamford Bridge crowd's displeasure, but his teammates were in no doubt of his value to them.

John Hollins was a workaholic right midfielder, another player to have a player in front of him denying him more international opportunities. That player: Manchester United's Nobby Stiles, the tough-tackling toothy foil to the creative players around him in England's 1966 World Cup-winning team. When Stiles's star faded, the equally energetic Alan Mullery blocked Hollins's path. I recall one game at Stamford Bridge – against Arsenal – in the mid-late 1960s when Hollins struck the bar from 25 yards out. The ball rebounded so forcefully it shot past him. Without breaking stride, Hollins chased backwards, spun and half-volleyed the ball back into the Arsenal net. The goal summed up the indefatigable spirit of John Hollins. John lived in the neighbouring estate to my own when I was growing up, just three-quarters of a mile away. His son Chris many will know as a winner of *Strictly Come Dancing*, the 2000's Saturday night entertainment phenomenon.

The manager of Chelsea at this time, Dave Sexton, was like a precursor of Arsene Wenger. An articulate man with a professorial demeanour, the total opposite of his predecessor Tommy Docherty, the passionate Scot who'd set the King's Road Chelsea ball rolling with the Tambling and young Osgood side in the early 60s, a side also containing a young Terry Venables, a shrewd operator even then. Venables instigated many different approaches to free kick taking long before they became a regular part and parcel of modern-day football. A canny player, he went on to grace the Tottenham Hotspur side of the mid to late 60s. Sexton – a marvellous coach – infused his teams with an emphasis on attacking football, the reason I was attracted to following his Chelsea team.

Sexton's Queens Park Rangers team of the mid-1970s extended the stylish attacking play he had implemented at Chelsea. My Chelsea allegiance disavowed, I followed QPR with great intent over two or three seasons, thrilled by their 'front five' of Dave Thomas, Gerry Francis, Don Givens, Don Masson and Stan Bowles. What a player Bowles was, cut from the Osgood cloth with his love of a good night out, although Bowles's vice was more gambling than drink. QPR had previously been blessed with another stylish maverick, Rodney Marsh. Bowles took up the baton, but the imagination and hard running of Gerry Francis was also crucial to this team. Sexton also introduced his old trusty players John Hollins and David Webb from Chelsea, and the vastly experienced ex-Arsenal defender Frank McLintock into his defence and midfield, giving the team a lovely balance. QPR missed out on winning the 1975–76 league title in only the last game of the season as Liverpool scored three late goals to overturn a 0-1 deficit at Molineux against Wolves. Seems inconceivable now, doesn't it?

What a shame from Sexton's point of view that when he managed Manchester United later in the decade it proved an unhappy marriage. His tenure at Old Trafford was blighted by a downturn in United's fortunes. Ironically, Sexton took over from Tommy Docherty at United. Docherty championed bright attacking football with wingers Steve Coppell and Gordon Hill, but the golden days of the 1950s and 1960s proved difficult to live up to for Sexton.

Sexton did have a problem handling the stars of the Chelsea team, Osgood and Hudson. Eventually Osgood was sold to Southampton, Hudson to Stoke City. Osgood won the FA Cup for a second time at Southampton in 1976 where he, Jim McCalliog and Mick Channon used all their guile and experience to upset favourites Manchester United. Even Tommy Docherty before him at Chelsea struggled with the emerging superstars at The Bridge. Sexton appeared to be a better coach than manager. He was to my mind a master tactician who did a wonderful job at Chelsea and QPR. Sexton also won the UEFA Under-21 Championship as England's national U-21 coach. He was clearly good with young players. His Achilles heel lay in his dealings with difficult players, but for ten years Dave Sexton produced some of the best football seen in the English league prior to the inception of the Premier League and the influx of foreign talent that followed.

In the early rounds of this year's competition, Chelsea despatched Greek club Thessaloniki 6-2 on aggregate, the Bulgarians CSKA Sofia 4-2 (although extra time was required in the second leg). Chelsea had to overcome the holders Manchester City in the semi-final. Chelsea triumphed 1-0 in both legs, no mean feat. Chelsea at this time were capable of beating anybody, but could equally fail to 'turn up' on occasions. One game sticks in my mind from the 1969–70 season when Leeds United visited Stamford Bridge and gave the Blues a football lesson, winning 5-2. City, formidable opponents, were undone by a lengthy injury list. Both teams fielded under-strength sides due to injuries, Chelsea being without Osgood at Maine Road, but it was City who fared less well as a result. Nineteen-year-old Ron Healy, in goal for City, deputising for Joe Corrigan, was deceived by Keith Weller's extraordinary swerving free kick that crept in at the near post as Chelsea made the final the hard way, winning the away leg of the semi-final. City fielded no less than six teenagers on the night. City applied huge pressure, the ultra-competitive Francis Lee a constant threat, but the Blues were equally dangerous on the counter-attack.

Real Madrid defeated the Dutch cup winners PSV Eindhoven to reach the final against Chelsea.

THE FINAL
The final ended in a 1-1 draw, Peter Osgood opened the scoring with a left-foot volley in the 56th minute. This was a particular talent of Osgood's I recall. For a tall man, Osgood possessed delicate technique. One exquisite right-foot volley (he was adept on both sides) he scored against Arsenal in an FA Cup quarter-final in 1973 is permanently etched in my mind – it won the BBC Goal of the Season award. Surprisingly, Osgood only scored 103 goals in 279 appearances for Chelsea although he remains one of a handful of players to score in every round of the FA Cup in the season 1969–70. Heartbreakingly for Chelsea, Real equalised in the 90th minute. Extra time failed to separate the two teams.

When I knew Chelsea would be playing the great Real Madrid in the final I did not rate their chances, but this was not the all-conquering Madrid team of the 1950s and early 1960s. By this juncture, Real were going through something of a transitional phase. The great Francisco Gento remained on the left wing from the 50s side, a swift and highly skilled raider. Gento holds the record for the most European Cup Final appearances – eight – alongside the equally legendary Paolo Maldini of AC Milan.

THE REPLAY
The replay was a curious affair indeed. When it was decided to replay the final in Piraeus on the Friday following the first Wednesday match, the attendance for the game naturally took a sharp nosedive, a shade under 20,000 in attendance. The majority of Chelsea fans had flown home to London after the first game. A handful stayed on in Piraeus, some sleeping rough in the streets, desperate to see their club claim European glory. Chelsea took the lead in the 32nd minute, another tall, lean player, the Irish central defender John Dempsey, seeing his own initial header blocked, following up with a striker's finish with the rebound. The cultured Dempsey was the perfect foil for the somewhat raw presence of David Webb at the heart of Chelsea's defence. Osgood it was who sealed victory, his crisply struck low drive displaying all his fine technique. Real pulled a goal back in the second half through Fleitas, but Chelsea held on to win their first European trophy.

Third time lucky for Rangers. Victory eluded them in 1961 and 1967, but finally the trophy was theirs, the formidable captain John Greig a particularly deserving winner. The wing wizard Willie Johnston played on the left again in this final. Rangers could also call upon an excellent centre-forward in Colin Stein, a gifted inside-forward in Alfie Conn, and the redoubtable Sandy Jardine at right-back.

Rangers, too, had to overcome the mighty Bayern Munich on a 3-1 aggregate score in the semi-final, further evidence of the strength of Scottish football in this era, as Bayern had Sepp Maier, Franz Beckenbauer, Gerd Müller and Dieter Hoeness in their ranks. Extraordinarily, Rangers appeared to have been knocked out earlier in the competition, in round two. Dutch referee Laurens van Raavens failed to recognise that Rangers had scored three away goals against Sporting Club de Portugal (better known today as Sporting Lisbon). Rangers lost the ensuing penalty shoot-out, only for manager Willie Waddell to point out the rules to UEFA. The referee was overruled, the result overturned, and Rangers went on to defeat the Italians Torino 2-1 on aggregate in the quarter-finals. Rangers' opponents in this final, Dynamo Moscow, were the first Soviet team to reach the final of any European competition.

The Rangers captain, John Greig, grew a beard after the Sporting victory, claiming the beard was a lucky omen. He decided not to shave it off until Rangers exited – or won – the competition. The semi-final triumph over Bayern Munich is remembered as, arguably, the finest victory in the history of Glasgow Rangers football club. Bayern fielded seven of the team that would go on to win the 1974 World Cup for West Germany. As well as the world-class talents of Franz Beckenbauer and Gerd Müller, Bayern included another great midfielder in Paul Breitner, Sepp Maier in goal, George Schwarzenbeck at the back, and Dieter Hoeness in attack. This was a seriously good German team.

In Munich, Breitner scored for the Germans. Having weathered a storm for an hour, Colin Stein's driven cross was deflected in, an own goal being Rangers' riposte. Somehow Rangers salvaged a draw from a game they were seriously overwhelmed in. Sandy Jardine related after the match that Rangers did not only not get out of their own half for the duration of the 90 minutes, they scarcely got out of their own 18-yard box, so good were Bayern in the first match. At Ibrox in the return leg, Jardine scored in the very first minute. Rangers were missing the influential Greig for this match, out with a foot injury we now know as a metatarsal problem. Youngster Derek Parlane came into the team as Greig's replacement and as so often happens on these occasions, he became an unlikely hero, scoring the second, conclusive goal.

THE FINAL

Sandy Jardine had played as a midfielder or forward previously, but his form became revelatory when manager Willie Waddell converted him to right full-back in season 1970–71. Pacy, Jardine loved to join the attack, his athleticism making him a prototype for the modern wing-back. Jardine played 38 times for

Scotland, captaining his country on nine occasions.

Another player forced to convert to a defensive role in this team – due to the excellence of Colin Stein in his preferred centre-forward position – was Derek Johnstone. After Stein retired, Johnstone returned to the central striking position, scoring 38 goals in 1977–78. In this game, Johnstone played at centre-half. How useful to have a player who could excel in two positions at the heart or core of a team.

On the right wing, Rangers had another tricky winger, Tommy McLean. With Willy Johnston on the left, Rangers followed the pattern of the time in British football of playing with two wingers. The game of football always seemed to be more attacking to me in the 1960s and 1970s. My sons, who all played as defenders, the total opposite of their old man, are inclined to say that teams were not so good defensively in this era. I think it would be wrong to say that the likes of Harris, Hunter, Jack Charlton, Bobby Moore and Ray Wilson couldn't defend – I prefer to think it was a question of emphasis in play. I could not disagree with my sons in that teams today are more organised and tactically astute, less gung-ho in their approach. Johnston, as previously mentioned, was an extraordinarily audacious player – and his return of 89 goals in 211 appearances for Rangers was a fine return for a winger. In this final he scored twice, playing more as an additional striker off the shoulder of the traditional striker Stein. A fiery character, Johnston was famously sent home from the 1978 World Cup in Argentina following a positive test for the banned stimulant Reactivan, a medication prescribed to him for hay fever. Sent off playing for Scotland in a friendly against Argentina in 1977, the country proved an unhappy destination for Johnston.

The inside-forward Alfie Conn scored 23 goals in 93 games for Rangers, later scoring a hat-trick on his debut for Tottenham Hotspur. What I remember about Conn, apart from his obvious ball skills, were his flowing locks. This was the era of perms, Conn's mass of hair mirrored by the perms of the Liverpool stars Kevin Keegan and Terry McDermott.

Colin Stein only played for Rangers 112 times, but scored 60 goals. He also netted nine times for Scotland. Stein was a centre-forward in the traditional mould, strong, powerful, good in the air, with a great shot. Tragically for Stein, he is remembered for his equalising stoppage-time goal against Celtic in the 'Old Firm' derby at Ibrox in 1971 that triggered the collapsing of barriers, causing 66 people to die. This was the worst such occasion in British football until the horrors of Hillsborough in 1996.

Stein's goal in this final came as he rampaged clear of the Dynamo defence to fire in a fierce shot. Johnston's first goal was a smart glancing header as he moved stealthily ahead of the Russian's defence to take advantage of Davie Smith's cross. Johnston rode his luck with his second, winning goal after half-time. Dynamo's defenders inexplicably stood off him, allowing the devilish forward a free run and shot on goal. Credit to Johnston though, for springing the offside trap. Skilled in the forward positions, Rangers had also been expertly drilled by coach Jock Wallace whose fitness regime apparently bordered on the fanatical.

Greig deservedly got his hands on this European trophy, but not in the conventional manner. Rangers' fans mistakenly thought they heard the final whistle and invaded the pitch a minute before the end of play. Due to the necessity of peacefully escorting the fans from the pitch on the part of the Spanish police, the presentation of the cup took place not on the pitch, but inside stadium buildings, a strange anti-climax to the night that Stein, for one, felt marred the occasion.

1973 EUROPEAN CUP WINNERS CUP FINAL
AC Milan 1 v 0 Leeds United, Salonika, 40,154

For all the past successes of AC Milan and the talismanic presence of Gianni Rivera, Leeds United might have expected to have won this trophy – this was arguably an inferior Milan side to those who'd gone before, and certainly not of the outstanding standard of those to come in the late 1980s and 1990s. Leeds were missing key men in the final, but were still able to field many of their classic side of this era: Paul Reaney (captain on the night), Paul Madeley, Norman Hunter, Peter Lorimer, Mick Jones. Reaney was disciplined, a fierce competitor. An athletic footballer, Reaney amassed 750 appearances for Leeds 1962–1978. Ironically, in a team passionately proud of their Yorkshire roots, Reaney was a Londoner.

One of the best left-backs I saw play around this time was Terry Cooper. Cooper's linking play with the silky footed Scotsman Eddie Gray was a source of great discomfort to the Chelsea team I watched regularly in the seasons 1969–70 and 1970–71. Cooper loved to forage forward from his defensive position, his style again a forerunner to the modern wing-back. A broken leg suffered by Cooper in April 1972 against Stoke City saw manager Don Revie buy Trevor Cherry as cover from Huddersfield Town. Was Cooper the same after the broken leg? I don't know, but he was an awesome player before the injury. Revie could also play the multi-skilled Paul Madeley in virtually any position on the pitch (certainly in defence or midfield). Impossibly versatile, Madeley played in every position from numbers 2 to 11 in his Leeds career, even declining Alf Ramsey's invitation to be part of the 1970 World Cup squad in Mexico, feeling he would be little more than a 'stand-in'. Madeley played at centre-back alongside Norman Hunter in this final.

Trevor Cherry, the player replacing Cooper in this final had been bought not only to cover his dynamic predecessor, but as a centre-back with Jack Charlton's imminent retirement in mind. Another player who could fill in at left-back or left-midfield was Eddie Gray's younger brother Frank, selected at number 10 in this final. Although a fine player in his own right, receiving 32 caps for Scotland, Frank suffered a little for being in the shadow of Eddie.

The cultured left-footer, Eddie Gray, was voted Leeds United's third best ever player, behind only centre-forward legend John Charles from the 1950s, and the man he played alongside, his fiery, ultra-competitive captain, Billy Bremner. How Leeds did not win the 1970 FA Cup Final amazed all who saw it as Gray led poor David Webb the merriest of dances in the first game at Wembley. Gray was another who suffered injury keeping him out of this Cup Winners Cup Final. Leeds would miss the mercurial Scotsman greatly.

All of the above players were excellent team men, but it was in the forward positions that Leeds seemed especially strong. On the opposite flank to the wizard Gray, wearing his customary number 7 shirt, appeared another great Elland Road servant and Scotsman, Peter Lorimer. Lorimer possessed a thunderbolt shot, bettered only in his day by the peerless Bobby Charlton. Lorimer was also another master technician and exemplary team player. He also holds the club's record for goal scoring, netting 168 goals in total, 151 1962–1979, and a further 17 upon returning to the club from a stint in Canada in the mid-1980s.

The partnership Mick Jones formed with Allan Clarke in the late 1960s and early 1970s was one of the most feared in top-flight football. 'Sniffer' Clarke it was who revelled in the limelight as a natural goalscorer, but the tall, elegant Jones was his natural foil. Jones was technically proficient, mobile and no mean striker and scorer of goals himself. Jones partnered a young Joe Jordan in this final, but a season later debilitating knee problems forced him to retire prematurely from the pro game at the age of 30. Fiercely competitive, strong in the air, Jordan was a more traditional centre-forward than Jones. Jordan won 52 caps for Scotland.

Leeds United were still a force to be reckoned with in 1973, but my memory informs me that the side containing Welshman Gary Sprake in goal, Jack Charlton, Bremner, Johnny Giles, Clarke and Eddie Gray was a stronger unit than the side in this final with added skill factor – the absent Giles and Eddie Gray were sublime technicians.

AC Milan was one of the early 60s great teams – even if their team on this night was a notch down from that side. Central defender Roberto Rosato played in two World Cups, being part of the beaten finalists in 1970, and also part of the country's 1968 European Championship-winning team. Rosato was a strong defender, but also notably adept technically as you would expect of an Italian defender.

The tough-tackling, moustachioed, defensive midfielder Romeo Benetti has an excellent track record in Italian football, not only victorious here, but winner of two Coppa Italia (the Italian Cup) medals with Milan. Transferring to Juventus in 1976, he won two Serie A titles. Upon transferring to Roma, Benetti won two further Coppa Italia winners medals. Benetti was successful wherever he played. An iconic Italian player, Benetti was not for nothing nicknamed 'Panzer' (the tank), 'El Tigre' (the tiger) and 'Roccia' (the rock). Benetti was capped 55 times by Italy.

Milan were captained on this night by one of THE great players of the 1960s and 1970s, Gianni Rivera. Rivera was not always loved by his national team managers, but as a player of superior technical ability and sublime vision he had many admirers. Rivera received 60 caps for his country. Like Rosato, he was a winner of the European Championships in 1968, and a beaten finalist with Italy in Mexico at the World Cup in 1970. Like Bobby Charlton in England, Rivera was known for his classy on-pitch demeanour. He played in four World Cups – 1962, 1966, 1970, and 1974. Dubbed 'the Golden Boy' by the Italian media, Rivera won three Serie A titles with Milan, captained the team for 12 years, and won the senior European Cup twice.

Offensively, Milan relied on the attacking midfielder Alberto Bigon, who scored 56 times for the club, in addition to Luigi Chiarugi, their scorer in this final. Chiarugi could play right across the front line, either wing or in the centre. Known as 'Corrallo Pozzo ('Crazy Horse') due to his impetuous nature, Chiarugi was the Cup Winners Cup's leading scorer in 1972–73 with seven goals.

THE FINAL

A controversial match led to the Greek crowd turning on their own 'national', referee Christos Machos. The Greek fans felt Machos favoured Milan on the night, resorting to hurling projectiles at the celebrating Milan side during their lap of honour. Machos would later be banned from refereeing for life for match-fixing although this particular match was not scrutinised by UEFA. Leeds protested, believing Machos made several questionable decisions on the night, but UEFA refused an enquiry.

With Clarke suspended and Giles out with a hamstring injury, Leeds made light of their misfortune, starting the final brightly, knocking the ball around with their customary ease and composure, but after only five minutes Madeley was perceived to have committed a foul – it looked very dubious – and Chiarugi drove a left-footed penalty into goal off the post, the ball narrowly evading second-choice goalkeeper David Harvey's grasp.

Despite plenty of possession, the aforementioned dubious refereeing decisions combined with AC Milan's notorious defensive organisation to deny Leeds a breakthrough. I first came across 'catenaccio' (translating as 'the spider's web') in the 1960s. Inter Milan were Italian's first proponents of 'catenaccio' in that decade. It always seemed back then that if an Italian team took the lead, the game was dead.

1976 EUROPEAN CUP WINNERS CUP FINAL
Anderlecht 4 v 2 West Ham United, Heysel Stadium, Brussels, 58,000

Manchester City, Chelsea, Glasgow Rangers, Leeds United, four years running British teams graced the final of the European Cup Winners Cup. It would be another three years before West Ham became the next British team to contest the final. I know nostalgia tends to kick in, but I do believe British football enjoyed a 'golden era' 1966–1973. European club football changed conclusively after the great Ajax team won the European Cup three years consecutively 1971–73. Ajax and the Dutch national team introduced 'Total Football', the first great modern tactical innovation. There would be no turning back, and it seems to have taken England's national team almost five decades to remotely play 'catch-up'.

West Ham were undone in a high-scoring match by two goals apiece from Francois Van der Elst and Robbie Rensenbrink. Van der Elst would go on to play for the Hammers 1981–1983. A skilful player, Van der Elst appeared 44 times for Belgium, scoring 14 international goals. Rensenbrink was one of a pair of talented Dutch internationals in this Anderlecht side, the other being Arie Haan. Rensenbrink's talents included a penchant for dribbling as befits a winger; a nerveless eye for goal, and, reflecting a calm temperament, he missed only two penalty kicks in his entire career. Nominally a left winger, it was his misfortune to play in the same position as the immaculate Johan Cruyff, one of the few

28

players for whom the word genius would not be an overstatement. A considerable talent, Rensenbrink played in the 1974 and 1978 World Cups.

Arie Haan, like Rensenbrink, played in the 1974 and 1978 World Cups. Haan was physically strong, like all the Dutch players that came through in the 1970s a consummate technician, and had a happy knack of scoring extraordinary long-range goals. One from 40 yards against Italy in the 1978 World Cup was simply stunning. Haan repeated the feat from a marginally shorter distance against West Germany in the same competition. Haan's club record too was exemplary, helping Anderlecht to win the European Cup Winners Cup again in 1978. With Anderlecht, he helped the club win the Belgian Cup in 1975–76 and the Belgian Championship in 1980–81. Upon moving to Standard Liege, he helped the club win the Belgian Championship twice, the second title being accompanied by the Belgian Cup. Haan had also been a regular performer in the outstanding Ajax side that won three European Cups from 1971 to 1973.

West Ham, then, were not favoured to win this trophy. In Billy Bonds and Frank Lampard (senior) they had two players who could have been dyed claret and blue, tremendous club servants with no little skill. Lampard had a sweet left foot, a club of an instrument he used to score the occasional blockbusting goal from left-back. Billy 'Bonzo' Bonds was the ultimate warrior in a West Ham shirt, the kind of player all footballers at all levels love to play with. Bonds was Mr 110% every time he pulled on a West Ham shirt, committed, passionate and driven. Bonds spent 27 years with the club as player and manager, playing 663 times, chipping in with 48 goals from midfield. Bonds started as a right-back, played at times as a centre-back, but it was his energy as a midfield player that I recall best.

The Hammers had useful players in midfield and attack in Graham Paddon, Billy Jennings and Keith Robson, but the player who appealed most to my sensibility was the immaculate Trevor Brooking. One of my favourite players of all time, Brooking's casual elegance may have seemed to some like a player who was coasting. In this respect Brooking was highly deceptive. Like the great players of the decade before him – Bobby Charlton, George Best and Jimmy Greaves – he simply made the game look easy, drifting around the pitch as if on air. Brooking's standing at West Ham is reflected by the fact he was club player of the year on four occasions. Brooking appeared 528 times for West Ham, scoring 88 goals, and for a player some thought a little lightweight at times, it is interesting that astute football management judges Tommy Docherty (Chelsea), Brian Clough (Derby County) and Bill Nicholson (Tottenham Hotspur) all wanted to sign him between 1965 and 1974.

Brooking played the game in a gentlemanly manner, like another favourite of mine, Bobby Charlton. At international level, Brooking developed a near-telepathic understanding with Kevin Keegan, which could have led to greater success for England at the 1982 World Cup in Spain, but for injury restricting the pair to limited time together at the tournament.

West Ham were managed by the personable John Lyall, a fitting successor to the highly respected Ron Greenwood when he took over the reins in 1974. Lyall would manage the club for 15 years – Arsene Wenger anybody? Lyall's reign would see West Ham overcome favourites Arsenal in the 1980 FA Cup

Final, courtesy of the deftest of headers from Brooking (not Trevor's forte normally). Lyall also held the reins when the Hammers challenged gallantly for the 1st Division title in 1985–86 thanks to 53 goals between Scottish striker Frank McAvennie and his London-born strike partner Tony Cottee.

THE FINAL
West Ham took an early lead in the final when Pat Holland nipped on to a Bonds headed lay-off to slide a close-range goal. It proved to be the calm before the storm. Lampard's under-hit pass let Anderlecht in for a smartly taken equaliser. Van der Elst linked with Rensenbrink, cut in on his right foot and rifled a left-foot drive into the top right-hand corner of the goal. Suddenly West Ham were behind. West Ham rallied briefly, central defender Tommy Taylor thumping a 25-yarder that seemed bound for goal but the Belgian's keeper was equal to it. Brooking's beautifully flighted ball to the near post (the old West Ham staple from the Greenwood/Hurst /Peters years) saw Bryan 'Pop' Robson head the equaliser. Wave after wave of Anderlecht attacks followed. Haan, Rensenbrink and Van der Elst tore the Hammers' defence to shreds as the game went on. Rensenbrink was felled in the area, got up and restored Anderlecht's lead from the spot. Ultimately Rensenbrink's footwork and passing ability, Haan's passing and vision, Van der Elst's pace, trickery and finishing, were just too much for West Ham. The pass from Rensenbrink for Anderlecht's fourth goal bisected the Hammers' defence. Van der Elst checked one way, then the other, completely deceiving the covering defenders and Mervyn Day in the West Ham goal for a splendidly decisive final goal. Before the rampant Belgians (and their magician-like Dutchmen) ran away with the game in the final 17 minutes, Brooking flighted another delightful ball into the box which Jennings headed narrowly over, but it was blowing against a gale, a gale that justifiably won the trophy for Anderlecht.

1980 EUROPEAN CUP WINNERS CUP FINAL
Valencia 0 v 0 Arsenal (Valencia win 5-4 on pens), Heysel Stadium, Brussels

This was a vastly experienced Arsenal team playing against a Valencia team containing 1978 World Cup-winning Mario Kempes, a genuine superstar, and the German stalwart Rainer Bonhof for Valencia. You felt that the Gunners experience should have carried them over the line. Pat Rice and Sammy Nelson at full-back, David O'Leary at centre-half, the hard-working Brian Talbot alongside Graham Rix in midfield – not forgetting Liam Brady, one of Arsenal's greatest ever players with a left peg to die for. They had Frank Stapleton and Alan Sunderland in attack. In the end it mattered not as Valencia won by the smallest of whiskers.

In goal on the night for Arsenal, Pat Jennings was the best British goalkeeper I saw play outside of the legendary Gordon Banks. Jennings had enormous hands that replicated shovels. He played 472 games for Tottenham Hotspur before transferring to the Gunners. He played a further 237 times for Spurs' North London rivals. In February 1983, Jennings became the first player to make 1,000 senior appearances, celebrating by keeping a clean sheet in a match for Arsenal versus West Bromwich Albion. Jennings, a calm and commanding presence between the sticks, also played 119 times for Northern Ireland.

Pat Rice, captain for the evening, was almost a one-club servant throughout his playing, coaching and managing career. Only at the end of his career, following 397 appearances for Arsenal, did he play 112 games for Watford. When Peter Storey was switched to midfield in the 1970–71 season, Rice became Arsenal's first choice, ever-present right-back. Rice had been part of the Arsenal side that became only the second in the 20th century (after Tottenham Hotspur) to complete the double back in 1971. Another dependable presence appeared at left-back in Sammy Nelson. Nelson, another Northern Irishman, and Rice boasted 100 caps between them for their country.

Arsenal had another great servant in David O'Leary (capped by the Republic of Ireland 68 times) at centre-back. Tall, strong, athletic, O'Leary was an elegant defender who read the game supremely well. He played 558 games for the club, only losing his regular first team place when the great Arsenal central defensive pairing of Tony Adams and Steve Bould came together under George Graham.

In midfield, Brian Talbot, a player's player who would run through proverbial brick walls offered further reliability. Having won the FA Cup with Ipswich Town in 1978, Talbot transferred to Arsenal the following season and repeated the feat with his new club. Talbot scored a creditable 40 goals in 254 appearances for Arsenal, a fine achievement for an essentially destructive midfielder.

Liam Brady remains, alongside the outstanding Dutchman, Dennis Bergkamp, one of the greatest technical footballers to lace boots for Arsenal. He scored 43 goals in 253 appearances for the club, but it is his sweet left that could conjure up sublime passes and goals of the highest quality that Brady is best remembered for. Brady would transfer to Italian giants Juventus after this final – doubtless Juventus had been mightily impressed by the impish skills of Brady when losing to the North Londoners in the semi-finals of this competition. Brady was chosen as Arsenal's club player of the season three times, and represented the Republic of Ireland 72 times. Brady won the Italian Serie A title in two consecutive seasons with Juve, but when the club sought to retain Michael Laudrup for season 1982–83 it was Brady who moved on, despite his success in Turin. Rather than being touted as another British failure in Italian football, Brady continued playing with Sampdoria, Inter Milan, and Ascoli for another five years in Italy, leaving with his reputation firmly intact to join West Ham United in 1987.

Graham Rix was another player with a skilful approach to his game, though he was the sorcerer's apprentice here in the shadow of the maestro Brady.

In attack, Arsenal boasted two fine strikers in the quick-footed, skilful Alan Sunderland and industrious Frank Stapleton. None of Sunderland's 55 league goals will be remembered as fondly as his 1979 FA Cup Final injury-time winner, nor his celebration. Sunderland also possessed the archetypal 1970s permed hairstyle allied to a three-Musketeers-styled moustache. Strike partner in Brussels, Frank Stapleton was a highly regarded centre-forward-cum number 10, a model professional, revered by his peers, hard-working, plucky, good in the air and smart 'on the deck'. He scored 75 goals in 225 appearances for Arsenal.

Stapleton came to the fore in season 1976–77, forming a lethal strike pairing with another central striker, Malcolm Macdonald. The latter I saw score five goals for England against Cyprus in 1975. In the only vet's game I played in, aged 41, in 1997, I played against one of the Cypriot midfielders from that evening. The game ended in defeat, but I had the consolation of scoring and winning a penalty for my team. Stapleton played 71 times (scoring 20 goals) for the Republic of Ireland, captaining his country at the 1986 World Cup in Mexico. As you can see, the Arsenal team was replete with Irishmen – a nod to their indomitable spirit I would suggest. When Stapleton moved to Manchester United in 1981, he scored a further 60 goals for the Mancunians in 223 appearances.

The Arsenal team on this evening in Brussels was managed by ex-player (241 apps) Terry Neill – a Northern Irishman of course. He clearly trusted the Irish character, personality and psyche. His trusted ally and coach was Don Howe. Howe's reputation as a coach was unparalleled at this time. He was known as a disciplinarian, instilling in Arsenal an organised ethos that was his trademark. Howe also coached England 23 times in the late 1950s. Howe attempted management with West Bromwich Albion and Arsenal among others, but like Dave Sexton at Chelsea he is better regarded for his coaching abilities.

In a strong year for the Cup Winners Cup, Arsenal defeated Juventus 2-1 on aggregate in the semi-final, winning 1-0 in Turin, after being held to a draw at Highbury. In the first game, Juve scored first from the penalty spot – Jennings saving the penalty, but was unable to keep out the rebound. Then a rarity happened – a headed own goal by the legendary Italian striker Roberto Bettega levelled matters. Arsenal became the first team in 25 years to win in Turin. A tight game with defences reigning supreme produced a surprising fairy-tale outcome. Terry Neill sent on 18 years old striker Paul Vaessen 15 minutes from the end. Anybody remember him? Two minutes from time, Vaessen headed the only goal of the game past the veteran, legendary Juve keeper Dino Zoff, courtesy of Brady's run and chipped cross to the far post.

Glasgow Rangers managed to hold Valencia to a draw in Spain in the second round, only to come unstuck 1-3 at Ibrox. Barcelona proved Valencia's sternest opponents in the quarter-finals in an all-Spanish tie, Valencia ousting the Nou Camp giants 1-0 away and 4-3 at home.

THE FINAL

As stated, Valencia's two stand-out players were the goal-scoring hot-shot Mario Kempes, and the German midfielder Rainer Bonhof. It was to Arsenal's credit that they prevented Kempes from scoring in this final as the Argentinian's record from 1970 to 1984 is quite extraordinary. In a career spanning 555 games Kempes scored 300 league goals. One hundred and twenty-six of these occurred in two stints with Valencia, 95 1976–1981, and following a season in which he returned to Argentina to play for River Plate, he scored a further 21 goals in 42 games 1982–1984. Kempes scored 126 goals in 184 games for Valencia – some feat. Kempes had the look of a rock-star/playboy about him with his long, flowing, dark locks. He was tall, rangy, lightning quick, and a phenomenal scorer. He liked to receive the ball outside the area and run at defenders, something no defender likes. What more could you ask for in a striker? Kempes also scored 20 goals in his 43 internationals for Argentina, his crowning glory coming in 1978, scoring seven goals as the Argentinians swept to World Cup victory on home soil. This same year, 1978, saw Kempes awarded the accolade of South American Football Player of the Year at the age of 23. In 1980, when facing Arsenal here, Kempes was in the prime of his career.

Rainer Bonhof may have been in the shadow of the imperious Franz Beckenbauer, Günter Netzer and Paul Breitner when one recalls the great West German midfielders of this era, but his record of 67 goals from 371 Bundesliga appearances and nine goals in 53 internationals is none too tawdry. What did Bonhof offer the (West) German national team? He could not match the magisterial Beckenbauer, who having been an attacking midfielder par excellence, became the best sweeper I have ever seen on a football field (only Franco Baresi comes close); he could not control the play in the manner of the playmaker Netzer; he may have been a shade shorter in dynamism and forcefulness than Breitner. What Bonhof gave West Germany – and Valencia – was a hard-running style in alliance with the usual consummate German technique, and a vital ability to score goals from free kicks. One 60-yard scamper almost resulted in a goal in this final, thwarted at the last by Jennings' outstretched leg.

A resolute Arsenal defence here of Jennings, Rice, O'Leary, Scottish international Willie Young and Nelson could scarcely be bettered – until George Graham instigated the combined ruthlessness of Lee Dixon, Tony Adams, Steve Bould and Nigel Winterburn in the 1990s. My sons and I had the dubious pleasure of watching six Boxing Day fixtures in this decade at the old Highbury in the Graham era, five ended in 0-0 draws, the only goal we saw scored in these games coming from Paul Merson, earning a 1-0 victory. Thank goodness for 'Mers'! Graham's defence of this period gave a whole new meaning to mean!

A predictably tight final produced few clear-cut chances. The match went to extra time and penalties. Jennings even saved the first penalty, taken by Kempes. Sadly for Arsenal, their talisman, Brady, also missed his kick. With the scores tied, it fell to Graham Rix to be chief miscreant, missing the vital sixth penalty kick. Perhaps his little shimmy as he approached the ball did him no favours. Defensively unbeatable, Arsenal could not find that one spark of magic at the other end to win the final.

1983 EUROPEAN CUP WINNERS CUP FINAL
Aberdeen 2 v 1 Real Madrid (after extra time)

Manager Alex Ferguson's first major title! It's very rare indeed that one would discuss a manager before his players. In all the time I have watched football – from the early-mid 1960s – only two other managers have matched Alex Ferguson for sheer force of personality and charisma, Bill Shankly and Brian Clough, and although I preferred Clough's humour, surely Alex Ferguson has been the greatest club manager in British football. Like Clough, Ferguson knew how to man-manage and handle players of differing character. Like Clough with his 44-day debacle at Leeds United, Ferguson had his moments with players who were strong-minded (Gordon Strachan and David Beckham come to mind), but by and large Ferguson's iron will and insatiable desire to win mark him out as the most successful British football club manager of all time.

It was not always thus that Ferguson was held in such regard. Both at Aberdeen and later at Manchester United, where he created several dynasties, Ferguson suffered stuttering starts. His much-documented background as a plater's helper in the Clyde shipbuilding industry gave Ferguson a tough start in life, an insight into the minds of the working classes, a breed of individual forming the majority of playing staff at professional football clubs. After scoring 171 goals in 317 games for six different Scottish clubs (a record mirrored, ironically, by Clough whose output as a striker was even more prolific) including Glasgow Rangers, Ferguson stepped into management at the relatively tender age of 32. He garnered an instant reputation for being a strict disciplinarian, in addition to having a fiery temperament that could cause rifts with some players.

At St Mirren, Ferguson's second club, he won the Scottish 1st Division in 1977, building a swift reputation for bright, attacking football. Having left St Mirren under something of a cloud, claiming wrongful dismissal after the club sacked him, Ferguson took up the reins at Aberdeen in June 1978. Aberdeen had only won the Scottish top tier once – in 1955. Ferguson would rectify this in style, but only after a testing start. Being only marginally older than some of his players proved an obstacle initially. Fourth place in the league in 1978–79 was followed by a 1979–80 Scottish League Cup defeat to Dundee United. Ferguson, famous for his 'us against the world' mentality when he managed Manchester United, instilled the same siege mentality at Aberdeen, informing his players that the Scottish media favoured the giant Glasgow clubs Rangers and Celtic over his team. Season 1979–80 brought Aberdeen their first league title for 25 years, the team following this with victory in this 1983 European Cup Winners Cup final, and further championship successes in 1983–84 and 1984–85. The team's league fortunes dipped in 1985–86, although the winning of both the Scottish Cup and Scottish League Cup was substantial consolation. Tottenham Hotspur and Arsenal sought his services at this time, but it was to Old Trafford and Manchester United that Ferguson moved in November 1986. The rest is history.

Ferguson was perhaps fortunate to take on Aberdeen at a time when the club were on the up and inherit a fine team with a core of excellent players. Goalkeeeper Jim Leighton would play 300 league games for the club in addition to turning out 91 times for Scotland, including appearing as first choice goalkeeper at three World Cups, 1986, 1990 and 1998. Despite his success with Aberdeen – and later Hibernian in Scotland – Leighton failed to transfer his form in a less happy spell under Ferguson when moving to Manchester United in 1988.

Alex McLeish was, in my recollection, arguably the best central defender to play for Scotland other than the revered Billy McNeill or the elegant, sophisticated, ball-playing Alan Hansen. McLeish was not unlike McNeill as a player, tall, rock-like, a centre-half in the traditional mould, strong and good in the air. McLeish, who played in three World Cups, 1982, 1986 and 1990, receiving 77 caps for his country, formed a formidable centre-back pairing with Willie Miller. Miller, captain for the night in Gothenburg, played 65 times for Scotland. After being loaned out to Peterhead in the Highland league as a striker as a 16-year-old,

Miller returned to his parent club Aberdeen and was converted to the central defender/sweeper position by coach Teddy Scott. A centenary poll in 2003 saw Miller named the greatest player in Aberdeen's history. The combination of Miller's positional sense, pace and awareness, and McLeish's traditional centre-back strengths gave Aberdeen a very strong core indeed.

The player Alex Ferguson had the most problems with in this Aberdeen side was the feisty Gordon Strachan, a man who was prepared to speak his mind and stand up to Ferguson's tyrannical disposition. A right-sided midfielder, Strachan's deceptive strength and tenacity – for a player standing only five feet six inches high – marked him out as a successor to Billy Bremner in the Scottish national team. Apart from a spell later in his career at Coventry City, Strachan scored goals wherever he played – a useful attribute for a midfield player, and his contribution as a team player was substantial. Strachan played 635 times in Scottish and English football, retiring only at the age of 40 while still a Premiership player at Coventry City. He scored 55 goals in 183 appearances for Aberdeen, 33 at Manchester United 1984–1989, and 37 at Leeds United 1989–1995. Strachan's peak years were the seasons 1981–82 and 1984–85, encompassing the Aberdeen glory years and his first season at Manchester United, four years in which as an attacking midfield player he scored 77 goals. Strachan helped Manchester United to win the 1985 FA Cup Final, 1-0 against Everton, before moving on to Leeds United, Ferguson apparently feeling that the Scotsman's star was waning. At Leeds, Strachan won the FWA Footballer of the Year Award in 1990–91 when Leeds returned to the old English 1st Division having won the 2nd Division title in 1989–1990. Strachan then joined forces in a new Leeds midfield comprising Gary McAllister, David Batty and Gary Speed, and promptly captained Leeds to the League title in England, the last season before the top league became the Premiership. Leeds' cause was aided in no little manner to this title by a certain Eric Cantona. Debilitating sciatica hampered the seemingly indestructible Strachan as age finally caught up with him. Gordon Strachan represented Scotland at the 1982 and 1986 World Cups.

In attack, Aberdeen paired Mark McGhee with Eric Black. McGhee's professional career began at Greenock Morton in 1975. A short spell with Newcastle United blighted by managerial changes at the club (nothing new there) was followed by McGhee's most successful period as a centre-forward with Aberdeen 1979–1984, a period in which he scored 63 goals in the Scottish League. McGhee had all the attributes of a traditional centre-forward being strong in the air, direct, mobile. Talented enough to be awarded Scottish PFA Player's Player of the Year in 1982, McGhee's reputation was further enhanced by his role in this Cup Winners Cup Final, Hamburg in Germany securing his transfer. Although he scored seven times in 30 appearances for Hamburg, injury tainted his one-season spell in Germany.

McGhee's partner in attack, Eric Black, was just 19 years old on this famous night in Gothenburg. For a while, Black proved fairly prolific for Aberdeen, scoring 70 goals in 180 appearances. Athletic, good in the air, Black's stature in the game also brought about a foreign transfer, in this instance to French club Metz between 1986 and 1991. Black suffered chronic back problems – an injury manager Ferguson attributed to too much junior football – and was forced to retire very early in the professional game, aged only 27. Black and McGhee formed an impressive, all too short-lived striking partnership.

Neil Simpson, Neale Cooper and Peter Weir joined the effervescent Strachan in a hard-working Aberdeen midfield. Hard-working – a key facet for Ferguson. All Ferguson teams thereafter possessed a thirst for hard work, instilled in them by a manager who never forgot his Clydeside roots.

Once again in a major European final it must be said that Real Madrid were not the force in 1983 that they had been in the early years of the European Cup in the 1950s, nor anything like the star-filled 'Galactico' team of the 21st century. Having said that, the Spaniards were able to call on the international talents of Germany's Uli Stielike and Holland's Johnny Metgod. Metgod's name may be a little unfortunate – the only Dutch players I recall having 'met God' are Johan Cruyff, Ruud Krol, Johan Neeskens, Marco Van Basten, Ruud Gullit, Dennis Bergkamp and Marc Overmars! Metgod's ability was enough to earn him transfers from AZ Alkmaar to Real Madrid, and later Nottingham Forest and Tottenham Hotspur. Tall, cultured in style in the typical Dutch manner, Metgod also took a mean free kick.

Stielike was a player I remember none too fondly in his confrontations with British clubs, and as an awkward opponent for the English national team. Stielike had a 'happy knack' of breaking up play around his own penalty area, never afraid to make a challenge that might concede a free kick, but rarely conceding penalties. Stielike was what you might call a 'knowing' player. For a defensive midfield player, Stielike's return of 41 goals in 215 appearances for Real Madrid is impressive. At first club Borussia Möenchengladbach, Stielike won three successive Bundesliga titles and the 1975 UEFA Cup. His first three years in Madrid garnered three successive La Liga titles. In 1980 and 1982, Real won the Spanish Cup, the Copa del Rey. A second UEFA cup triumph followed in 1985. Whatever my reservations about Stielike's style of play, the man was clearly a serial winner, and a player of considerable talent. He helped Germany to victory in the 1980 European Championship, appearing 42 times for his country. Spanish fans loved him so much he was awarded Best Foreign Player in La Liga for four successive seasons 1978–1981. Upon moving to Neuchatel Xamax, Stielike promptly won two successive Swiss Super League titles in 1987 and 1988. Clearly Stielike offered his clubs a vital component – the steel in Stielike remains vivid in my memory.

The native Spaniards in the Real side included José Antonio Camacho at left-back, a man indelibly linked with Spanish football. He played over 500 games for Real Madrid, helping the club to win 19 major titles, nine of these La Liga championships. Camacho also played 81 times for his country, appearing in the 1982 and 1986 World Cups, going on to manage the Spanish national team 1998–2002. A sturdy defensive player, Camacho even overcame a serious injury in 1978 to help Real win two UEFA Cups (1985, 1986).

In attack, Juanito Gonzalez offered a definite goal threat to Aberdeen with his dribbling ability. It would be Juanito who netted Real's penalty in this final. On a wider stage, Juanito scored 85 La Liga goals for Real 1977–1987. Tragically,

Juanito died in a road accident at the age of 37. The main goal threat for Real came from centre-forward Santillana, a great header of the ball. Santillana amassed 186 goals in 461 appearances in La Liga for Real, and a further 15 in 56 appearances for Spain, 1975–1985.

Aberdeen's sternest opponents en route to the final were Bayern Munich in the quarter-finals. A splendid 0-0 draw in Germany set Aberdeen up for a 'shock' win at Pittodrie. Bayern, using all their nous and feeling of superiority led 2-1, but Strachan's trickery and a barrage of aerial balls into the Bayern penalty area enabled an Aberdeen recovery and a 3-2 win that gave the Scots the impetus to go on and lift the trophy in Gothenburg. Real too overcame one of the games' European giants in Inter Milan by the same 3-2 aggregate in the quarter-finals.

THE FINAL

Heavy rain prior to the match saw the pitch covered with a tarpaulin in an effort to make it playable. After a pitch inspection, referee Gianfranco Menegali gave the game the go-ahead. Black opened the scoring early on for Aberdeen when Real keeper Agustin failed to hold on to McLeish's header from Strachan's corner-kick. Black pounced on the error swiftly. Real soon equalised after McLeish's back pass failed to reach Jim Leighton in the Aberdeen goal, Santillana being fouled. Juanito netted the penalty. Metgod and Stielike shone for Real for the rest of the first half with their imaginative probing of the Dons' defence.

Aberdeen – doubtless stung by Ferguson's words at half-time – revived after the break. Peter Weir, playing one of his finest games, continually asked questions of the Real defence from the left flank. Despite two openings created by Weir, 90 minutes came with stalemate resulting. Weir again it was who fed a delightful ball to McGhee on the left edge of the 18-yard area with just eight minutes remaining of extra time. McGhee made strides and flighted a fine ball into the centre for substitute John Hewitt to glance a winning header into the Real net. Ferguson's finest hour with Aberdeen – even grander European nights beckoned in Manchester.

1985 EUROPEAN CUP WINNERS CUP FINAL
Everton 3 v 1 Rapid Vienna, De Kuip Stadium, Rotterdam, 38,500

Everton dominated this final, but were unable to defend their title due to the sad events at the Heysel Stadium before the 1985 European Cup Final between Liverpool and Juventus (39 people died after Liverpool fans breached a wall in the stadium, most of the victims were Italian/Juventus fans). The ensuing ban on English clubs deprived Everton of their shot at the senior European competition the next season as English Football League champions 1985–86. How like Aberdeen this Everton side were (if one discounts the talismanic Strachan from the equation) with their ultra-strong team ethic. For Everton it was all about the unit.

Everton did have a quite marvellous goalkeeper in Welsh international Neville Southall, FWA Footballer of the Year in this season of 1984–1985. The goal he conceded to Bayern Munich's Dieter Hoeness in the semi-finals was the only one he conceded in the whole of this competition up to the final. Southall played 578 league games for Everton 1981–1998. When he left, Southall drifted around countless lower league clubs and semi-professional teams, only turning out for Torquay United with any sort of regularity. It was as if nothing could compare for Southall with his Everton experiences, indeed nothing in his career came anywhere near his successes at Goodison Park.

Right-back Gary Stevens earned 46 caps for England, playing in the 1986 and 1990 World Cups. Upon leaving Everton in 1988 he won six successive Scottish Premier Division titles with Glasgow Rangers. In his six years at Everton he played 208 league games. Stevens, a determined, athletic, resolute defender, epitomised the doggedness and spirit of this Everton team.

At centre-half, Everton fielded Welsh captain Kevin Ratcliffe (capped for his 59 times for his country) and the tall, moustachioed Derek Mountfield. Ratcliffe, like Southall, bled the Everton royal blue, appearing in 359 league games for the club, 48 appearances at nearby Chester City and Welsh capital club Cardiff City his only other significant football league commitments. Like Stevens, Ratcliffe adopted a no-nonsense, hard-tackling approach to his football. He only scored twice for Everton, but given that one was a 30-yarder at rival Merseyside club Liverpool's Anfield ground, I'm sure he won't mind this low goal return!

Mountfield, though capped at U-21 level by England, was this side's only player not to achieve full international recognition, not that this stopped him forming a formidable partnership with Ratcliffe. Mountfield's 19 goals for Everton indicate his stronger aerial threat in the opposition's penalty area. Upon joining Aston Villa in 1988 when Dave Watson's arrival limited his first team chances, Mountfield helped Villa come desperately close to usurping Liverpool in the 1989–1990 title race.

Pat Van Den Hauwe completed Everton's back four. Van Den Hauwe's senior professional appearances were split almost equally between Birmingham City, Everton and Tottenham Hotspur. Van Den Hauwe's nickname of 'Psycho Pat' tells you all you need to know about the rugged nature of Everton's left-back on this night, yet clearly he could play a bit as he garnered 13 caps for Wales, having turned down offers to play for England and Belgium as a player with British citizenship born outside the UK.

Both of Everton's wide midfield players were highly skilled. Trevor Steven on the right offered width, discipline, excellent crossing ability, and key defensive qualities. Steven played 210 times for Everton in the league, scoring 48 goals. He also appeared 36 times for England. Steven formed a highly effective link-up with right-back Gary Stevens, giving commentators something of a linguistic problem. Kevin Sheedy on the left was the more naturally gifted footballer, blessed with a wand of a left foot, yet once again fitted into the Everton ethos with his work-rate. In 274 league games for Everton he scored 67 times. Sheedy became a free-kick specialist for Everton, scoring more top-flight free kicks in the old First Division than any other player. Sheedy's skills were recognised by his fellow professionals, being selected in the PFA team of the Year in Everton's title-winning seasons of 1985 and 1987. Sheedy also played 46 times for the Republic of Ireland, notching nine goals.

In the centre of midfield Everton had two extraordinarily hard-working players. Neither player was of the playmaker style of a Netzer or Hudson, suggesting that Everton relied largely on the skills of their wide players for goal supply, but goodness me Peter Reid and Paul Bracewell were grafters. I always felt that the super-talented but inconsistent Glenn Hoddle needed Peter Reid as his 'workhorse' to play effectively for England. The pair didn't play together as often for England as I would have liked due to the all-round skills of Manchester United's Bryan Robson denying Reid more international opportunities. It would have been my ideal England national scenario for the gritty Reid to win the ball, give it to the gifted Hoddle and allow the Tottenham man to unlock international defences. Reid, a defensive midfielder, still had enough talent to be voted PFA Player's Player of the Year in 1985, a season in which he also finished fourth in the *World Soccer* Player of the Year Award, only behind Michel Platini, Preben Elkjaer and Diego Maradona – not a bad list to be on! Reid's contribution to this Everton team can be highlighted by the fact that they were only denied a treble by Norman Whiteside's extra-time winner in for Manchester United in the 1985 FA Cup final. Reid only played 13 times for England, but was a pivotal player in the 1986 World Cup team that was only denied a semi-final place by Diego Maradona's sublime skill and dubious key moment in the last eight game.

Paul Bracewell only played 95 games for Everton, playing more top-flight football for Stoke City and Sunderland. Bracewell's work ethic made him an important cog in this team. It was the midfielder's misfortune to miss out on a place in the 1986 World Cup squad after breaking a leg. Bracewell also holds a most unfortunate record of losing the four FA Cup finals he played in with his professional clubs.

Everton had two excellent, doughty, central strikers on the pitch in Graeme Sharp and Andy Gray. Both could lead the line well, Sharp, an excellent all-rounder, Gray possessing a salmon-like leap in the air. During Everton's hugely successful 1980s era, Graeme Sharp was a mainstay of the club and a regular scorer. In 322 appearances he scored 111 goals in the league, 159 in all games. Sharp thrived under former Everton great and then-manager Howard Kendall from 1981–82. Sharp's best season, as so many of this team, was the 1984–85 season, when he scored 30 goals in 54 matches. Only the 1930's legend 'Dixie Dean' has scored more goals for Everton. Sharp also appeared 12 times for Scotland.

Andy Gray only appeared in 49 league games for Everton, scoring 14 goals. Gray had really established himself in England (after scoring 36 goals in 62 apps for Dundee United north of the border 1973–75) with Midlands clubs Aston Villa and Wolverhampton Wanderers, amassing 92 goals in 246 league appearances across the two teams. He was only 19 years of age when he moved to Aston Villa in 1975, but quickly became a crowd favourite. His 29 league goals for Villa in 1976–77 saw him jointly win English football's Golden Boot with Newcastle United's Malcolm MacDonald. He also played in the first two games of the 1977 League Cup Final against Everton (drawn 0-0 and 1-1), although missed Villa's eventual 3-2 triumph in the third match. Gray garnered the PFA Young Player of the Year and PFA Player's Player of the Year awards in the 1976–77 season, a feat repeated by Christiano Ronaldo and Gareth Bale in later seasons. Not bad company to be in.

Popular with the fans once more at Everton, Gray's departure at the end of this 1985 season drew an angry response from the Goodison supporters. His replacement: a certain Gary Lineker. Gray, like Sharp, only featured fitfully for Scotland, appearing 20 times and scoring seven goals. Gray's spirit and humour were keystones of his enduring popularity wherever he played, so much so that it's difficult to believe that this cult hero only played one season at Goodison.

Manager Howard Kendall was another for whom Everton seeped into his bloodstream. As a player he had a distinguished spell with Preston North End 1963–67, becoming the youngest player to play in an FA Cup final in 1964 against West Ham United, aged 17 years and 345 days, since James Princep of Clapham Rovers in the 1879 final. When Kendall – formerly a defender – joined Everton in 1967 he formed a 'holy trinity' midfield with Alan Ball and Colin Harvey. These are players I remember well – Kendall and Harvey were stylish players, Ball literally a ball of energy. The trinity helped Everton to win the 1969–1970 1st Division title.

Kendall stepped in as player-manager at Everton in 1981 (although he only picked himself four times) – the club's most successful era was about to begin. Two titles and the European Cup Winners Cup were won between 1985 and 1987. In between they were runners-up in league and cup to arch-rivals Liverpool. When Gray was controversially replaced in 1986, Lineker promptly scored 38 league goals. A good judge of players and their fitness, Howard Kendall.

Rapid Vienna were heavily dependent at this time on their own superstar striker, Hans Krankl. Krankl's record with the club is astonishing. During his first spell with Rapid 1970–78, Krankl scored 160 goals in 205 appearances. Upon transferring to Spanish giants Barcelona in 1978 Krankl netted 34 goals in 46 league appearances. At the Nou Camp Krankl won the Copa del Rey and the European Cup Winners Cup in his first season in Spain (1978–79), topping the La Liga goal-scoring charts with 29 goals. Returning to Rapid Vienna, Krankl scored a further 107 goals in 145 league games for the club. As player manager with his next club Wiener Sport-Club he scored 40 goals in 60 league games, 1986–88. A career record of 392 goals in 518 league starts is quite staggering. Hans Krankl was a goal-scoring machine. For his country – Austria – Krankl scored 34 times in 69 appearances, once every two games. He was also named Austrian Player of the Year a record five times. That Everton restricted Krankl to Rapid's only goal in this final is testament to Kendall's supremely disciplined side.

To reach this final, like Aberdeen, Everton had to overcome German greats Bayern Munich. Dieter Hoeness's smart goal at Goodison drew first blood for Bayern, but an aerial bombardment began to disturb the German's defence. First Sharp headed an equaliser from Gray's flick-on, and then Gray slotted a second. Sharp's heightened team awareness was evident as his slick pass enabled Trevor Steven to drive in a third, conclusive goal. The Munich sides of this era contained many great players: Hoeness, Lothar Matthäus, Karl-Heinz Rummenige, Paul Breitner. Everton and Aberdeen's achievements in knocking this great club out of the 1985 and 1983 European Cup Winners Cup competitions are magnified by the fact that Bayern twice won the premier European Cup during this period (1982, 1986), and the UEFA Cup in 1984 – and the Cup Winners Cup was always regarded as the third tier of the three European trophies at this time.

THE FINAL

Everton, in their absolute pomp in 1985, turned this final into a demonstration of their superior class on the night. Kevin Sheedy's brilliance was luminous in the early stages, a brilliant one-two conjured with his left foot, resulting in a right-foot shot being saved. Gray had a goal disallowed as Sharp strayed offside to head another delightful cross from Sheedy into his path. The only surprise at half-time was that Rapid had somehow stalled Everton's onslaught to turn around level. The inevitable goal for Everton arrived in the second half when Sharp intercepted a poor back pass and unselfishly laid the ball back for Gray to volley in. Paul Bracewell, a lively presence, fed Steven, who turned magnificently only to fire over. Weak defensive cover by Rapid from a right-wing corner allowed Steven to score at the far post. Everton were now completely in control – but the ever-alert Krankl took advantage of a clever back-heeled pass to round Neville Southall and pull a goal back during Rapid's best spell of the game. Fittingly it was left to the outstanding Sheedy to round off a comfortable victory for Everton with an emphatic left-foot finish. What might Everton have achieved in the 1986 European Cup?

1991 EUROPEAN CUP WINNERS CUP FINAL
Manchester United 2 v 1 Barcelona, De Kuip Stadium, Rotterdam, 45,000

This was the first season in which English clubs were allowed to re-enter European competitions following the 1985 Heysel disaster. It was also United's first European triumph of any description since the fondly remembered 1968 European Cup win at Wembley.

United's route to the final was fairly comfortable, dispatching Montpelier of France and Legia Warsaw of Poland by two-goal margins in the quarter-final and semi-final. Opponents Barcelona had a seriously tougher time of things in the same rounds, beating Ukrainians Dynamo Kiev 4-3 and Italians Juventus 3-2 on aggregate scores.

I always remember this final as the Mark Hughes final, not just because he scored both United goals. Hughes – formerly of Barcelona – was a bullish, vigorous front-runner with considerable talent and technique to boot, and proved positively inspired on this evening. Hughes seemed to take it upon himself to inspire United to victory, hell-bent on a personal mission. It's also worth recording that Alex Ferguson was beginning to make his mark on United by this juncture.

Goalkeeper Les Sealey only played 33 league games for United. Sealey was on loan in 1990 when he replaced the unfortunate Jim Leighton in the FA Cup Final replay victory over Crystal Palace. Sealey's chequered career saw him taken on permanently by United, transferred to Aston Villa, where he took pole position in goal, only to be ousted by Nigel Spink in the 1991–92 season. He returned again to United as cover for the imperious Peter Schmeichel – in my mind and most critic's minds the best Premiership keeper ever – in the 1993–94 season, but did not play. A popular player with the fans, Sealey's contributions to the 1990 FA Cup Final victory and this splendid triumph over Barcelona mean Sealey's ultra-short United career is still remembered by Old Trafford diehards.

What a remarkable full-back Denis Irwin was. Right-back here, but equally at home in the left-back berth, Irwin, ultra-dependable, unfussy, but extremely difficult to beat if you were a forward, was simply one of the stand-out defenders of the 1990s, a certainty for any best British X1 of the decade. Ferguson regarded him as the ultimate professional, and arguably his best ever signing. Irwin had already helped unfashionable Oldham Athletic to the semi-finals of the 1990 FA Cup and the final of the 1990 League Cup when Ferguson signed him in 1990. Irwin would go on to play 368 league games for United, also representing the Republic of Ireland 56 times in the 90s. Irwin was a free-kick and penalty-kick specialist, and such was the consistently high standard of his performances that the younger Phil Neville could not stake a regular place for United over Irwin even when the Irishman was in his mid-30s.

The centre-back partnership of Steve Bruce and Gary Pallister was a key element of United's resurgence under Alex Ferguson. Like McLeish and Miller at Ferguson's former club Aberdeen, they complemented each other perfectly. Geordie Bruce was the traditional stopper centre-half; Pallister had something of the great Alan Hansen about him, being more comfortable on the ball. Both centre-backs liked to join the attack (particularly at corner-kicks); both scored crucial goals for United at times. For a player who failed to win any international caps for England, Bruce's record with United is impressive. Something of a talisman at Norwich City, Carrow Road fans loved Bruce's whole-hearted approach to the game. In nine seasons at United, Bruce won the Premiership three times, the FA Cup three times, one League Cup, and this European Cup Winners Cup Final among 12 trophy successes. What Bruce lacked in pace he made up for in spades with courage and spirit, scoring 36 league goals for United in 309 league appearances, an excellent return for a centre-back.

Pallister made his name at Middlesbrough, having moved to County Durham at an early age. He helped Boro to 2nd and 1st Division promotions in 1987 and 1988, earning a £2.3 million transfer to United in 1989, a then-record British fee for a defender. Pallister was the elegant, poised, stylish foil to Bruce, scoring fewer goals (12 in 317 league apps) than his partner, but oozing a commanding presence at the core of this United defence. Pallister won four Premiership titles with United (1993, 1994, 1996, and 1997) and succeeded in representing England, where Bruce did not, on 22 occasions.

Clayton Blackmore and Mike Phelan gave United versatility – either could play in midfield or at full-back. Here they were full-backs. Phelan is best remembered for being Alex Ferguson's right-hand man during a ten-year spell that brought United three Premiership titles and two Champions League Final appearances, losing to Barcelona, and defeating Chelsea on penalties.

The flair factor in United's midfield here in Rotterdam was provided by wide player Lee Sharpe. Sharpe was essentially a left-winger, or at least he would have been ten or 20 years earlier when wingers were still in fashion. Circa 1991 teams had begun to play a highly disciplined game compared to the gung-ho attacking game of United teams of yesteryear in the 60s and 70s with their wing wizards, George Best, Willie Morgan, Steve Coppell and Gordon Hill. With this in mind, the talented Sharpe would be asked to 'tuck in' on occasions, although his attributes leaned towards those of a traditional wide player.

Sharpe rose to fame with a scintillating display against Arsenal at Highbury in 1990, scoring a hat-trick in a 6-2 League Cup fourth round demolition, a game not fondly remembered by Highbury diehards. Sharpe was talented enough to play eight times for England, but despite being prodigiously skilful, often found the lightning quick Andrei Kanchelskis and the sublimely gifted Ryan Giggs blocking regular turn-outs for United. Sharpe even filled in at times as a left-back when Irwin was asked to cover at right-back due to injury to Paul Parker. At international level, Sharpe found John Barnes denying him opportunities as a left-winger. Injuries also took their toll on him. Sharpe's skill set deserves greater recognition.

The pairing of Bryan Robson and Paul Ince in the centre of United's midfield in this team gave them passion, purpose, power and strength. Both players were almost unnaturally possessed with a tremendous will to win. Although the 'Dutch master' Ronald Koeman was in direct opposition to the pair on this evening, Robson and Ince would not be denied. Robson gloried in the tag of 'Captain Marvel' and was generally regarded as the finest all-round midfield player in English football since the ill-fated Duncan Edwards, so tragically lost to English football in the 1958 Munich air crash. A powerhouse of a player, Robson lost many crucial matches for United and England due to his insatiable desire to win, to be the best. Older devotees of Manchester United's illustrious history would claim that Edwards would have gone on to be the greatest player ever seen at the club and in an England shirt, but Robson was still voted United's greatest ever player in a 2011 poll of former Reds players. Bobby Robson, his namesake and 1990 World Cup international manager, felt that Bryan, alongside Alan Shearer and Ipswich stalwart Kevin Beattie, were the finest players he ever worked with. It is perhaps no surprise that these three players possessed power and drive far beyond the average footballer.

The curse of injury afflicted Bryan Robson before he ever played for Manchester United and England. He twice broke his left leg and subsequently his right ankle while playing for first club West Bromwich Albion. When Albion manager Ron Atkinson left to manage Manchester United in 1981, Robson soon followed, leaving behind an Albion career record of 40 goals in 198 league appearances. At United Robson scored a further 74 goals in 345 league appearances. Robson became a United legend, his pride in wearing the shirt fiercely tangible to United supporters and football followers across the country. His United career spanned 13 years, 1981–1994. In 90 appearances for England Robson contributed 26 goals. Bryan Robson was simply the heart and soul of the United team in the 1980s and early 1990s. In 1983 Robson tore his ankle ligaments in a semi-final League Cup victory over Arsenal. In 1986 he dislocated a shoulder.

A barren spell for United ended in 1990 when the club lifted the FA Cup following a 1-0 replay victory over Crystal Palace (after a thrilling 3-3 Ian Wright-inspired first game draw). Robson became the first United captain to lift the FA Cup three times. In all competitions, 'Captain Marvel' scored 99 goals for Manchester United – if any player deserved to reach the century mark it was Bryan Robson.

Paul Ince played for United for six years 1989–1995. The feisty Ince would enjoy (or endure) a fractious relationship with Alex Ferguson despite his attributes of ferocious tackling and commitment. Ince would win all the domestic trophies of League, FA Cup and League Cup during this time, in addition to this European triumph. Ince moved to Inter Milan in 1995, spending two seasons in Italy, garnering a reputation for being one of the better British exports to Italian football. When he returned to England it was to play 65 games for Liverpool. Whatever the differences between Ince and Ferguson you don't get to play for Manchester United, Liverpool and Inter Milan without having something about you. Ince also played 53 times for England, suggesting he had character in abundance.

Mark Hughes's strike partner in Rotterdam was the Scotsman Brian McClair, a player I always enjoyed watching. McClair seemed to possess a natural instinct for the game of football. Some players have a happy knack of being in the right place at the right time; a knowledge of space on a football field; and a technical ability to take advantage of that space. Brian McClair was one such player. Initially a midfielder at Motherwell, then manager Jock Wallace converted McClair to a striking role, seeing the player score five goals against Rangers and Celtic in 1983. Billy McNeill liked what he saw, signing McClair for Celtic in May 1983. In his first season at Celtic Park McClair scored 32 goals. One hundred and twenty-six goals in all competitions and four seasons later McClair signed for Manchester United. In 355 league games for United, McClair scored 88 goals, but it was not just a natural goalscorer's instinct that marked out his time at United as successful, but his team awareness, his overall contribution to the club's success. His first season at Old Trafford brought rich personal gain with 31 goals in all competitions (1987–88), but silverware eluded United. Surprisingly, McClair scored only twice for his country.

Mark 'Sparky' Hughes had a point to prove in Rotterdam on this evening. A disappointing spell at Barcelona saw the passionate Welshman score only four goals in 28 games. Hughes wanted to show his former employers what they had missed out on – and how he achieved his mission with a barnstorming display. In two separate spells with United, Hughes scored 120 goals. Highly regarded around Europe, Hughes's frustrating time at Barcelona was followed by a short, positive spell at Bayern Munich. Not especially tall for a professional striker at 5 feet 11 inches, Hughes possessed a powerful physique. For Wales, Hughes scored 16 times in 72 games. Post-United in 1995 he also enjoyed a successful short stint with Chelsea in the Premiership, scoring 25 times. Hughes's impact at United in his first spell at the club saw him split the Frank Stapleton/Norman Whiteside pairing, Irishman Whiteside reverting to a midfield role he excelled in.

After Hughes's dalliance with European giants Barcelona and Bayern Munich, he returned to United for season 1988–89 and was promptly voted PFA Player of the Year, a feat he repeated in season 1990–91. Hughes was not a prolific goalscorer in the mould of an Alan Shearer or Gary Lineker, but his all-round skills and combative style endeared him to manager Alex Ferguson. At Chelsea, Hughes would be instrumental in FA Cup Final victories and a further European Cup Winners Cup triumph. By winning the FA Cup with Chelsea, Hughes became the only player in the 20th century to win the competition four times. Mark Hughes was no respecter of reputations, scoring 17 minutes into his Welsh national team debut, ensuring victory against England.

In goal for Barcelona this evening was Carlos Busquets – name sound familiar? It should, as he is the father of Sergio, the defensive midfielder in the incomparable Barcelona team of the 21st century. Carlos tended to be support goalkeeper during his time at the club as national keeper Andoni Zubizaretta was first choice.

The aforementioned Ronald Koeman was one of the stars of this Barcelona side, though a villain in my eyes for feigning injury and winning a free kick from which he scored to help the Netherlands defeat England in a crucial game, I recall. Koeman has a tremendous goal-scoring record for a man who played either as a defender or midfielder for club and country. This was partly down to his proficiency as a penalty and free-kick taker. Starting in Holland with FC Groningen in 1980, Koeman scored 23 times in 94 league appearances over three seasons. Controversially signing for big rivals PSV Eindhoven, Koeman went on to score 51 goals in 98 league appearances for the club. Clearly his was a talent that the circling vultures of Europe's big clubs couldn't ignore.

In 1989 Koeman duly signed for Barcelona, rejoining his former Ajax coach Johan Cruyff. This 'Dream Team', as they were coined, contained the great individual stars Bulgarian Hristo Stoichkov, Brazilian Romario, Dane Michael Laudrup, and recent Manchester City manager Pep Guardiola. Koeman helped Barcelona win the Spanish La Liga in four consecutive seasons 1991–94. Koeman would score in this match against United, repeating the feat a year later to make Barcelona European Cup winners for the first time in their history. Plenty more success followed for Barca. In the 1993–94 season Koeman scored eight goals in the Champions League, an astonishing feat for a man who did not play in attack.

Internationally, Koeman enjoyed one great success – he could hardly fail as part of a team that also contained Ruud Gullit, Frank Rijkaard and Marco Van Basten. Glorious victory came versus Russia in the 1988 European Championships (having knocked out hosts West Germany in the semi-final). For a team with such multiple talents however, the Netherlands continued in the vein of their great 1970s sides, unable to add another international trophy to their tally. Koeman did manage to score 14 goals in his 78 games for his country. Koeman's composed style of play was allied to his other attributes, the capability of deft, curling free kicks or free kicks of awesome power; the Dutchman also had an eye for the long ball in the manner of our own Bobby Charlton, Glenn Hoddle and Steven Gerrard.

At right back, Barcelona had Albert Ferrer, tough-tackling, quick, obdurate. Ferrer would go on to play 76 games for Chelsea 1998–2003, but here he was a key player in the Barca 'Dream Team', key for his commitment among a team of great individuals. Ferrer played over 200 times for Barcelona and 36 times for Spain.

In midfield, Barca had José Bakero, a skilful Basque who began his career with Real Sociedad, scoring 67 goals in 233 appearances 1980–88. Joining Barcelona, Bakero scored a further 72 times in 260 league games for the Catalan side. Bakero also played 30 times for Spain, scoring seven goals. An adept technician – aren't all Spanish players – Bakero, though short in stature, possessed great passing ability, a lethal right foot, and was surprisingly good with his head for a man standing 5 feet 8 inches. Bakero, known for his leadership skills, won 17 titles in his 17-year career.

At centre-forward Julio Salinas was a lanky, ungainly player with a useful scoring record – 60 goals in 146 league appearances for Barcelona. Salinas scored over 200 goals for five different Spanish clubs 1981–1996, belying his awkward physique. He also scored 22 times for Spain in his 56 appearances, a respectable return at international level. Between 1986 and 1996 Salinas represented Spain at three World Cups and two European Championships.

Another Basque-born player representing the Catalonian Barcelona on this evening was the current (2020) Manchester City director of football Txiki Begiristain (surely the most tongue-twisting, linguistic nightmare for commentators of European football in the 1990s). Begiristain played as a wide left-forward in this match. Begiristain would retire from professional football an eight-time title winner with Barcelona, four La Liga titles and the 1992 European Cup among them. Starting with Real Sociedad (like Bakero), Begiristain transferred after 187 appearances and 23 league goals with the Basques. At Barcelona he was more prolific, netting 63 times in 223 appearances. He also managed to score six times in 22 international games for Spain. Begiristain's link with Pep Guardiola is strong, their bond reformed since Txiki became Manchester City's director of football in 2012. City's resurgence since that time has been marked by the pair's insistence on a Barca-style passing game and a passionate belief in the importance of technique and possession football – no bad thing. At my own lowly level, I used to tear my hair out when defenders lumped the ball forwards aimlessly – I wanted the ball at my feet, so that, hopefully, I could inflict damage on the opposition.

Pre-Hristo Stoichkov and Romario, THE 'Dream' player for me in this Barcelona side was the exquisitely talented Dane, Michael Laudrup. Laudrup's effortless skill always made me sit up in my seat. 24 goals in 38 league games for Danish side Brondby in season 1982–83 alerted all of Europe's top professional clubs. A silkily smooth forward, Laudrup spent the next 13 years of his career with the top clubs in Italy and Spain, firstly with Lazio and Juventus; latterly with Barcelona and Real Madrid. In the notoriously disciplined, defensive-minded Serie A, Laudrup netted nine times for Lazio and 16 times for Juventus. In the more attack-minded La Liga he managed 52 goals for the two Spanish giants, performing most effectively for Barcelona (40 goals in 167 league appearances). Laudrup also scored 37 times in 104 appearances for Denmark. In 1999 Laudrup was voted the Best Foreign Player in Spanish football encompassing the preceding 25-year period. He ended his professional career with a season at Ajax in Holland

(1997–98) netting 11 goals in 22 games. How many players play for so many of Europe's top teams?

At Barcelona, Laudrup was an integral part of the 1991–94 team, winning four consecutive La Liga titles. Upon transferring to Real Madrid he promptly won La Liga for the fifth year running. Like Bobby Charlton, Laudrup never received a red card in his entire career. Michael Laudrup was my kind of player, a player of great individual talent, a player who was most effective as an attacking midfield player; he could also play off the front man as an extra forward. The great Michel Platini thought Laudrup too unselfish – but if you're putting the team first that has to be right, doesn't it? Graceful, stylish, supremely talented, Michael Laudrup was a joy to watch. Denmark's surprise European Championship victory in 1992 only came about after they replaced Yugoslavia who were omitted from the tournament due to war in their country. Laudrup thought his country's chances of success so low he declined to play in the competition. This must be the only black mark on his illustrious career, as the Danes overcame all odds to defeat Holland in the semi-finals and favourites Germany in the final. Danish football's finest ever player missed out on his country's crowning glory. Laudrup's sublime solo goal in the 1986 World Cup 6-1 thrashing of Uruguay remains his defining international moment.

THE FINAL
Winning this final was quite a personal coup for United manager Alex Ferguson. Barca's opposite number was none other than the legendary Johan Cruyff, one of the greatest players I have ever seen grace a football field. Cruyff's management record wasn't bad either. Cruyff was intent on implementing his 'total football' ideas into his teams, choosing to play with mobile footballing defenders, usually with three at the back (a system favoured by Glenn Hoddle in English football). Ajax won the European Cup in 1995 with a Cruyff-inspired team formation. Implementing an attacking style with Barcelona, success came swiftly. The team defeated Italians Sampdoria in the 1989 European Cup Winners Cup Final, defeating the same opponents in the 1992 European Cup Final.

McClair sliced badly over the crossbar in the first half when clean through on goal – he'd scored in every previous round of the competition. Half-time came with the score goalless. Sensing the game was edging their way, Hughes started to bring all his force to bear in the second half. First he lobbed over the bar, and then drove fiercely over the goal. Steve Bruce climbed highest from a free kick to head goal-wards, the lurking Hughes making sure by prodding the ball over the line. Whose goal? Hughes is credited with it. The second goal was an absolute peach. Hughes was driven wide by the advancing Busquets in the Barcelona goal but powerfully drove the ball into the goal from the 18-yard penalty area angle with the outside of his right boot. Koeman – predictably– retrieved a goal with a strong free kick that slipped under Les Sealey's grasp at the near post. Barcelona were very threatening as the game wound down. Bakero 'equalised' but was given offside. There was still time for McClair to drive narrowly wide with a shot from the left, and the rampant Hughes was not finished. Bursting past two defenders, Hughes was checked by Nando who received a red card for his pains. Laudrup side-footed past Sealey but Clayton Blackmore cleared off the line. United breathed a sigh of relief and Hughes celebrated a golden night for Alex Ferguson's side.

1994 EUROPEAN CUP WINNERS CUP FINAL
Arsenal 1 v 0 Parma, Parken Stadium, Copenhagen, 33,765

Perversely, football followers other than Arsenal diehard fans forget this victory, remembering only defeat a year later for the Gunners and David Seaman's unhappy misjudgement of Nayim's high steepling ball. Yet Arsenal were finalists two years running in this competition during a fine spell for the North London club under manager George Graham. How my own family recall well the meanness of this Arsenal team. I took my four sons six years running during the Graham era to watch the club's Boxing Day fixture (third son Simon supports Arsenal, and at that point Premiership tickets were readily available at Highbury, where some other London club's tickets were more difficult to obtain). Over six festive games we witnessed five 0-0 draws and a 1-0 victory (thank goodness for Paul Merson's goal in the latter one). Was this the effect of festive food on Christmas Day; the apathy of the players to play during the Christmas period; the necessity of rotating players in overloaded Premiership fixture pile-ups; or simply testament to Graham's organisation of the best, most obstinate defence seen in British football over the last 30 years? Whatever the reason it was hard not to admire the resolute defending of Seaman, Lee Dixon, Steve Bould, Tony Adams and Nigel Winterburn. Winterburn simply would not use his right foot, curiously. I always thought it strange that a player at this level was so one-footed. It didn't matter, the balance of this back four was impeccable – two tough-tackling full-backs and two tall (they looked as big as the nearby London skyscrapers), imposing centre-backs.

Graham's impact on Arsenal defensively is recognised by the club's fans singing '1-0 to the Arsenal' throughout this Copenhagen evening. George would surely have made a splendid manager of Italian clubs in the 1960s! Conversely, Graham was a cultured, technical midfield player himself, a model of the composed, skilful footballer that I tend to admire. As a manager he certainly knew how to organise a defence!

Arsenal won their way through to the final in typical fashion, beating Odense of Denmark, Torino of Italy, and Paris Saint-Germain of France by one-goal aggregate margins. By a quirk of fate they thumped Belgian opposition 10-0 over two legs in the second round. Parma needed to overcome traditional European giants Ajax and Benfica in the quarter-finals and semi-finals.

In goal for Arsenal, David Seaman appeared for the club in 405 league games. Good enough to appear 75 times for England, Seaman's consistency over nearly 20 years of professional football is 'marred' by the memory of two pieces of misfortune that colour the career of many a fine goalkeeper. Firstly the Nayim incident a year on from Copenhagen, and then a similar losing of the flight of the ball when Ronaldinho famously scored from a free kick for Brazil against England in the quarter-final of the 2002 World Cup. It is the goalkeeper's lot, the curse of being remembered for the occasional costly mistake. Mostly at Arsenal, Seaman was 'Mr Consistency'. The best keeper I ever played with could make the odd mistake from time to time, but what I remember most keenly was his absolute command of the penalty area, his commitment to come and collect high balls flung into the penalty box, his calmness under pressure, and his consummate ability to talk to our defence – and he was a quiet man off the pitch. Seaman didn't do too badly – he played in two World Cups, two European Championships, he won the double of league and FA Cup twice with Arsenal, winning eight titles in all. Not bad for a keeper unfairly remembered for two calamitous moments.

Lee Dixon made his name with Potteries club Stoke City, but went on to play 458 league games for Arsenal. Quick, hard in the tackle, but above all, defensively astute, Dixon has become an accomplished football pundit, especially of top European games. Dixon holds the record of having played at 91 of the 92 football league grounds – amazingly he never played at Fulham's Craven Cottage. Dixon usurped Seaman's record of three League Championships, winning four. Conversely, Dixon was a three-time FA Cup winner compared to Seaman's four. Dixon signed for Arsenal alongside Steve Bould, the pair's performances for Stoke earning them transfers for a combined fee of £765,000, a bargain when compared to modern-day transfer fees. For all Dixon's defensive nous, he also liked to join the attack – modestly he claims that with Adams, Bould and Winterburn covering for him, any personal deficiencies were disguised. It is a fact that 'the unit' is worth more than the individual – never was there a case of a unit being as well-prepared and formidable as this Arsenal back four. Dixon played 22 times for England, but was unfortunate to be around at the same time as Everton's Gary Stevens and Manchester United's Paul Parker.

Nigel Winterburn, as stated, was all left foot, which makes it all the more curious that with Kenny Sansom holding down the left-back position, Winterburn broke into the Arsenal first team as a right-back. Like Dixon, Winterburn was 'Mr. Dependable', if a little less inclined to join the attack than his opposite full-back partner. Winterburn would play 440 league games for Arsenal over a 13-year spell with the club, helping to forge the tightest defensive unit I've seen in British football.

What can you say about Tony Adams? He was a magnificent captain, and leader of the team, with an unquenchable spirit. How sad that alcohol had such a detrimental effect upon him (along with teammate Paul Merson). Adams played 504 league games for Arsenal, surprisingly netting only 32 goals in that time given his menace at corners. Adams spent 22 years with Arsenal from 1980–2002, never playing professional football for any other club. Tony Adams bled Arsenal through and through. Who can forget the 1988–89 title-decider when Arsenal's never-say-die spirit enabled them to snatch the league title from under Liverpool's noses with a decisive, second 92nd-minute goal? Adams marshalled his troops superbly that evening. Despite his much-reported battle with alcoholism, Adams (under Arsene Wenger's supportive, sure-handed guidance) would go on to captain Arsenal to two double league and cup-winning seasons in 1997–98 and 2001–02. Adams is the only player in English football history to captain title-winning teams in three decades. Not especially quick, Adams compensated for this with his aerial ability, reading of the game, and his total commitment to the team. He also turned out 66 times for England.

Adams' centre-back partner here in Copenhagen was the immovable force that was Steve Bould. An inch taller than Adams (no wonder we Avenells thought they were taller than the nearby Islington tower blocks), Bould helped form a 'they shall not pass' core in the centre of Arsenal's defence. Giants in the centre of defence, secure, dependable full-backs flanking them. This really was some Arsenal defence.

Arsenal had several splendid players of ethnic origin during this period – David Rocastle and Michael Thomas starred in that famous 1989 title snatch. On this night, Paul Davis maintained the standards of his predecessors stylishly. Denied opportunities by the consistency of Kevin Richardson and Thomas's drive, Davis possessed a cultured left foot and silky passing ability when given his chance in the team. Despite not always being a regular in the team, Davis managed to accrue 447 league appearances for Arsenal.

Stephen Morrow and Ian Selley joined Davis in midfield, the former a solid performer who won 39 caps for Northern Ireland; the latter a skilful player who hails from Chertsey, a few miles up the road from my hometown of Guildford. Only 20 on this evening, Selley broke his leg against Leicester City in 1995, compounding the agony with a second leg break playing for Fulham in 2000. For one blessed with natural ability, Selley is remembered for another reason during his tenure with a local semi-professional club in my vicinity, Woking, for receiving ten yellow cards in his first season at Kingfield!

The star of the Arsenal midfield was the ridiculously talented Paul Merson, like Adams tormented by alcohol addiction. It is difficult for me to associate Merson with any other club than Arsenal, yet he went on to play for Middlesbrough, Aston Villa and Portsmouth with reasonable degrees of success, and even captained the latter two clubs despite his alcohol and gambling problems. Over 11 years 1985–1997 Merson racked up 78 league goals in 327 apps for Arsenal. In the Boxing Day fixtures that my sons and I watched at Highbury we always felt that Merson would be the one player, if any, to unlock opposition defences. In the fabled 1988–89 title-winning season Merson was voted the PFA Young Player of the Year. Deft of touch, Merson was largely utilised by Arsenal as an attacking midfield player, though he could play as a second striker off the centre-forward. Merson was an entertainer, always willing to run at players, yet capable of performing his duty for the team. His obvious talent earned him 21 caps for England – it might have been considerably more but for his personal problems.

Merson's versatility restricted the appearances of one of the two co-strikers on this evening, Kevin Campbell. Campbell had power and pace aplenty, and he was a fine striker of the ball to boot, but he lacked Merson's natural technical ability. The addition of Ian Wright in 1991 (suspended for this final) further restricted Campbell's opportunities at Arsenal. Despite the signings of John Hartson and Dennis Bergkamp post-1994, Campbell would score 60 goals in his 224 games for the North London club.

Alan Smith was generally first-choice centre-forward for Arsenal during his time at the club, 1987–1995. A tall, gangly striker with a technique that belied his deceptively awkward frame, Smith could be relied upon both to score important goals and link up play as a target man with fellow players. At his former club, Leicester City, Smith reaped 76 league goals in 200 appearances, forming a fine partnership with Gary Lineker for a while. Smith it was who scored the only goal of the game here in Copenhagen. He top-scored for Arsenal in four consecutive seasons, amassing 86 goals in 264 league appearances. He was also a very fair player, receiving only one yellow card throughout his entire professional career.

Arsenal's Italian opponents on this evening, Parma, fielded a team with several outstanding international players. At number 6, Argentina's Roberto Sensini was a multi-functional player capable of playing at full-back, centre-back or as a central midfielder as a defensive shield. Technically proficient, tactically astute, rugged in the tackle, Sensini was very much the archetypal South American footballer. Playing in more than 160 games for Parma, Sensini would win two UEFA Cups and two Italian Cups with the club. Moving to Lazio in 1999 he immediately helped the capital city team to title success and an Italian Cup victory in his first season with the club. Internationally, Sensini played in the 1990, 1994 and 1998 World Cups during his 60 caps for Argentina.

The man wearing number 7 on this evening, Tomas Brolin of Swedish extract needs no introduction to followers of the English national team. Brolin struggled with weight issues throughout his playing time, and a broken bone in his foot during a 1996 European Championship qualifier in Stockholm led to five months out of the game in November 1994, meaning he never lived up to the rich promise he showed in the early stages of his career. With a relatively fit and firing Brolin in his early 20s, Sweden finished third at the 1994 World Cup, and reached the semi-finals of the European Championships in 1992. Parma also came into this final as holders of the European Cup Winners Cup from 1993. Deceptive due to his tubby physique, Brolin's technical gifts more than compensated for his appearance. Brolin's natural ability meant that he could be accommodated in the Parma team as a midfield player if other forwards were considered a greater goal threat. Brolin's three goals for Sweden at Euro 1992 (he joint-top scored with Henrik Larsen, Dennis Bergkamp and Karl-Heinz Riedle) included a brilliant effort to help defeat England. He went on to score three more crucial goals at the 1994 World Cup for Sweden, a year in which he scored nine international goals for his country. Not a prolific goalscorer at club level, Brolin's record of 27 goals in 47 matches for his country suggests a man whose patriotic fervour was high.

Every English football fan knows the pocket genius who was Gianfranco Zola, wearing number 10 in this game for Parma. The back-heeled volley for Chelsea at Stamford Bridge against Norwich City in a 2002 FA Cup tie, arriving at the near post to meet a right-wing corner is one of the greatest goals ever seen at the ground. In 2003, fans voted Zola Chelsea's greatest-ever player – no mean feat given that Roy Bentley, Bobby Tambling, Peter Osgood, Charlie Cooke et al all came before him. The diminutive Zola generally played as a forward, but could be utilised as an attacking midfield player.

Zola's first top-flight experience came in Serie A with Napoli as an understudy to Diego Maradona. Maradona was elated that Zola was even shorter than himself! Short in stature but huge in talent, Zola was able to score important goals for Napoli as they won Serie A in 1990 – his only league title win in a 21-year playing career. Everywhere he played Zola scored goals – 32 league goals for Napoli, 49 for Parma, 59 for Chelsea (at 229 league appearances his longest stint with any one club), 22 at Cagliari in Serie B. With Zola in their team, Parma would play a third consecutive European final in 1995, winning the UEFA Cup. Upon joining Chelsea in November 1996, Zola found himself playing in the same team as other greats Ruud Gullit and Gianluca Vialli. At the end of the 1996–97 season Zola was awarded the FWA Player of the Year title despite not playing a full season in the Premier League. Zola also scored ten times in 35 appearances for Italy, but generally found international selection difficult with the likes of Alessandro Del Piero and Roberto Baggio ahead of him in the pecking order.

Wearing the number 11 shirt for Parma was the extraordinary Colombian international Faustino Asprilla, remembered fondly at St James' Park, Newcastle. Like Brolin, Asprilla did not score prolifically in club football. Quick, agile, skilful, creative, Asprilla could also be frustratingly inconsistent. Thirty-five goals in 78 games for his Colombian club Atletico Nacional of Medellin brought the gifted Asprilla to Parma's attention. Asprilla scored four times in his eight games during the successful 1993 Cup Winners Cup run, including two against Atlético Madrid in the semi-final. Injury put paid to him appearing against Royal Antwerp in the final. Asprilla would be unable to influence the final, but came good again two years later as Parma lifted the UEFA Cup against great Italian rivals Juventus.

Moving to Newcastle in 1996, Asprilla continued to frustrate, his temperament questioned, his performances erratic. He helped Newcastle to two consecutive second-placed seasons in the Premiership in a multi-talented Tyneside outfit featuring Alan Shearer, Les Ferdinand and David Ginola, although he saved his greatest individual performance for the 1997–98 season when Ferdinand had moved to Tottenham Hotspur and Shearer was sidelined by a serious injury. Playing at home against the mighty Barcelona, Asprilla scored a hat-trick in a 3-2 victory, taking the game against the Catalan giants firmly into his own hands. Despite this momentous occasion, a return of nine goals in 48 Premiership league games was a poor reflection of Asprilla's undoubted talent. With Parma, the Colombian enigma netted 25 times in 84 initial league appearances, returning to Parma after his Newcastle sojourn, netting only once, but winning the UEFA Cup again in the 1998–99 season.

Both Arsenal and Parma squeezed through narrowly in the latter stages of the 1994 European Cup Winners Cup, Arsenal defeating Torino 1-0 in the quarter-finals on aggregate and Paris Saint Germain 2-1 in the semi-finals. Parma defeated Ajax 2-0 in the last eight and Benfica on away goals after drawing 2-2 on aggregate in the last four.

THE FINAL
Parma started the final brightly with a flying header from Brolin narrowly clearing the crossbar. Sol Campbell glanced a header wide at the other end, though Brolin's shot that hit the post could just as easily have gone in. Against the early flow Alan Smith chests down, pouncing to steer a left-foot shot inside the near post for the

only goal of the game. Cue the Highbury faithful's constant chanting of '1-0 to the Arsenal' throughout the remainder of the match, and sure enough George Graham's highly organised, defensively resolute side stifled Brolin, Zola and Asprilla and held on to become the fourth London side after Tottenham, West Ham and Chelsea to win this competition. Parma applied concerted pressure in the second half – the jinking Zola turned and fired over, Dixon was lucky not to concede a penalty, Parma had the ball in the net but it was clearly offside. There was no way past the 'Graham wall' and Arsenal secured only their second European triumph.

1995 EUROPEAN CUP WINNERS CUP FINAL
Real Zaragoza 2 v 1 Arsenal (after extra time), Parc des Princes, Paris, 42,424

Arsenal, like their opponents Parma in the previous year, returned in an attempt to retain this European trophy a year later. Like Parma they failed, on this occasion in dramatic fashion, losing to a 120th minute extra-time goal by Nayim. Arsenal's team showed six changes from 1994. Leading scorer Ian Wright was able to play this time, partnered in attack by Welshman John Hartson. Andy Linighan partnered Tony Adams in the centre of defence. Martin Keown wore the number 7 shirt – giving the Gunners three centre-backs in their team, a curious decision by interim manager Stewart Houston (following the departure of George Graham). Graham's tenure of nearly nine years at Arsenal will forever be associated with a near impregnable defence. Houston, as caretaker manager, picked his team here in the manner of his former boss, prioritising defence. The addition of Ray Parlour to Arsenal's midfield gave the team high energy. The final change in personnel came in the shape of Swedish international midfielder Stefan Schwarz.

This team, in my eyes, were slightly inferior to the '94 team, missing Bould's authority and assurance, Davis's silky technique, and Smith's all-round know-how. Linighan, a solid, dependable centre-back played 119 league games for the club, tended to be fourth choice behind Adams, Bould and Keown in Arsenal's conveyor belt of top-quality central defenders. Keown was a warrior, a fiercely competitive centre-back whose very appearance seemed to intimidate some attackers, and was blessed with a sturdy physique to boot. Injured in 1994, by 1995 Keown had ousted the imperious Bould from the starting line-up through sheer force of nature. When Arsenal won the double of league and FA Cup twice in 1998 and 2002, Keown was a vital cog in the centre of defence, strong, quick and indefatigable. Keown played 43 times for England, winning favour with some international managers, but not others. His commitment to Arsenal was unquestionable, his 310 league appearances far and away the most he played at any club – although he proved a key player at Aston Villa and Everton before joining Arsenal.

John Hartson played only 54 league games for Arsenal, scoring 14 Premiership goals. Hartson it was who scored for the Gunners on this evening, although he arguably became a more talismanic attacker when joining West Ham United in 1997, scoring 33 goals in 73 games at Upton Park. Hartson's greatest success came afterwards upon joining Glasgow Celtic in 2001. In Glasgow, Hartson became a hero, netting 88 times in 146 appearances, winning the Scottish Football Writer's Association Player of the Year in 2005. His fiery temperament betrayed him at times; his battles with weight problems and fitness ultimately bringing about his retirement in 2008. Hartson played 51 times for Wales, scoring 14 times. A year after retiring from the professional game, John was diagnosed with testicular cancer that had spread to his brain. Fortunately treatment prevailed and the Welshman fought the disease off, in the way that he fought off his opponents, with enormous courage and spirit.

The relentless energy of Ray Parlour in Arsenal's midfield was a bonus in Paris on this evening. Ironically nicknamed 'the Romford Pele' due to his no-nonsense style, Parlour always gave his all for the cause. His wavy fair locks gave him the appearance of a more charismatic player, but Ray's attributes lay in his non-stop running and never-say-die spirit. He did score the occasional fine goal, but it was his commitment and his inexhaustible 'engine' that endeared him to Arsenal fans. For a man living in the shadow of the great Patrick Vieira and Emmanuel Petit, Parlour's 339 league appearances speak volumes about his desire. He also played ten times for England. A better player than he was given credit for, Ray Parlour – three Premier League titles and a League Cup inform you of that.

The captain of the opposition here, Real Zaragoza, Miguel Pardeza, was part of a lauded group of five Spanish players who came through the Real Madrid youth academy together, and were all part of Spain's 1990 World Cup squad. 'La Quinta del Butre' ('Vulture's cohort') gained their name from the group's most famous player, Emilio Butragueno. Pardeza, all 5 feet five inches of him, made his name at Zaragoza, playing 221 league games, scoring 71 times in these fixtures.

The irony behind Arsenal's nemesis in this game, Mohamed Ali Amon, better known as Nayim, lies in the fact that in 123 league games for Zaragoza he scored only five times. No one who supports Arsenal will ever forget his 120th-minute winner here. Nayim had even played 112 league games for Arsenal's arch-rivals Tottenham Hotspur over six seasons, always proving an adept technical player, but rarely troubling opponents in their penalty area (he did net 11 times for Spurs). Curiously, among goals scored by Nayim for Spurs was a 'Goal of the Month' competition-winning volley, and a hat-trick against Manchester City. Nayim could do the spectacular, just not very often. How Arsenal rued the fact that he chose this evening to score from 45 yards.

Zaragoza's main striker on this evening was Juan Esnáider, an Argentinian whose aerial prowess was his main strength. Like Nayim, he was not a prolific scorer (29 goals in 61 league games) for Zaragoza; like Nayim he scored a crucial goal on this evening. Further irony for the Gunners came in having this season's leading scorer in the European Cup Winners Cup competition in Ian Wright – Wright failed to score in this final. Esnáider's form in Spain won him a transfer to Italian giants Juventus in 1999. The notoriously difficult Serie A league brought him a zero goal return in 16 matches. It's not only English strikers who've historically failed to hit the mark in Italian football. Esnáider did enjoy successful spells later with Atlético Madrid and Espanyol.

The best-known player to English fans (latterly) in this Zaragoza team was the Uruguyan Gustavo Poyet. Usually employed as a wide left midfielder, Poyet's excellent technique was matched by an impressive goal return for a midfield player. In 115 league games in his home country of Uruguay Poyet netted 36 times. His return for Zaragoza was outstanding, 63 goals scored in 239 league games. His form alerted English clubs, the Uruguyan transferring to Chelsea where he found the net 36 times in 105 league appearances. Moving to North London to join rivals Tottenham Hotspur, Poyet added another 18 goals in three seasons at White Hart Lane. A tall man for a midfielder at six feet two inches, Poyet was popular with teammates and fans alike. Only a cruciate ligament injury prevented Poyet's time at Spurs being more successful. Poyet also represented Uruguay 26 times, helping his country win the Copa America (South American Football Championship) in 1995. To win this competition means defeating the likes of Brazil and Argentina. Poyet was named the tournament's best player in his position. An impressive player, Gus Poyet.

En route to the final, both teams experienced tough semi-finals. Sampdoria, managed by Sven-Göran Eriksson, were defeated by Arsenal, but only after both ties ended 3-2 in favour of the home teams, Arsenal squeaking through on penalty kicks. Zaragoza had to beat Chelsea in their semi-final denying an all-English final, winning through 4-3 on aggregate, 3-0 at home, losing 3-1 at Stamford Bridge in a game that Chelsea just couldn't quite find enough in their locker to overcome the tricky Spanish outfit.

THE FINAL

He didn't score in this final, but Ian Wright's willingness to take players on, his nuisance value, were a definite plus for Arsenal. From the first minute, Wright caused Zaragoza defence problems. The first half ended goalless as Zaragoza negated Arsenal's goal threat and continually frustrated their favoured opponents. In the second period David Seaman blocked Higuera's shot at one end before Hartson's diving header was cleared off the goalline. A sensational turn and volley from Esnáider left Seaman rooted to his spot as Zaragoza took the lead. The plucky Hartson slipped the ball past the Zaragoza keeper to equalise. Dixon's lunging tackle provided another borderline penalty decision that went in Arsenal's favour.

In the first period of extra time, Seaman made a great save, diverting a header on to the post. Seaman's luck then ran out when Nayim's 'hit and hope' shot from 45 yards dipped under the crossbar in the last minute of extra time. Seaman got his hand to it, but credit Nayim for realising Seaman was off his line. Wright, an emotionally invested player at all times, was in tears as the game ended. Zaragoza proved awkward opponents – technically excellent as all Spanish teams are, courageous, united as a team in their desire to deny Arsenal.

This Chelsea team seems like something of an interim team now, between the 'King's Road playboys' of 60s lore – Osgood, Hudson, Cooke et al – and the 'super' team of the new millennium – Terry, Lampard, Drogba. This may be a little unfair on this 11 who contained several outstanding players from foreign shores: Romanian Dan Petrescu, Italians Roberto Di Matteo and Gianluca Vialli, and the Norwegian Tore Andre Flo. Curiously the man of the match award went to the diminutive dynamo Gianfranco Zola, who only entered the fray in the 71st minute, scoring the only goal of this final almost instantaneously. Zola of course had played for Parma in the 1994 final against Arsenal. Another returning finalist for Chelsea on this evening was the Uruguayan Gus Poyet, a finalist and winner with Real Zaragoza in 1995. Two players whose fates were intertwined with the European Cup Winners Cup, and two players who were crucial to any success Chelsea had in the 1990s.

Another player whose career has been largely associated with Chelsea was Scottish full-back Steve Clarke. After completing 200 league appearances for St Mirren, Clarke transferred south of the border to Chelsea in 1987, going on to enjoy an 11–year spell with the King's Road club, playing 330 league games. Clarke's later career saw him gain high respect as a coach at Chelsea as assistant to José Mourinho 2004–07, a period in which Chelsea won two Premiership titles, an FA Cup, and two League Cups. In 2022 he held the post of Scotland national team coach.

At centre-back, Frank Leboeuf was one of the iconic players in this team. Leboeuf was a tall, classy defender, good enough to play for France 50 times. Leboeuf stepped in for the suspended Lauren Blanc in the 1998 World Cup Final won by France 3-0 against Brazil; he was also part of the French 2000 European Championship-winning squad. For Chelsea, Leboeuf played over 200 games, scoring 24 goals, mainly from penalties and set pieces. Leboeuf's classy style and appearance extends to his off-field activities as he has become an actor, emulating Eric Cantona's move into this field after leaving Manchester United.

Arguably the best all-round player in this Chelsea side was the Romanian Dan Petrescu. Petrescu played 95 league games for his native Steaua Bucharest, appearing in the 1989 European Cup Final (a game he'll want to forget as the Romanians were ripped apart by a Ruud Gullit/Marco Van Basten-inspired AC Milan). Petrescu played for Foggia and Genoa in Italy before transferring to Sheffield Wednesday in 1994. Petrescu's performances in Yorkshire won him a place at Chelsea for the beginning of the 1995 season. Dan Petrescu became the epitome of the modern wing-back at Chelsea over the next five seasons. In tandem with Graham Le Saux in the left wing-back position, Petrescu perfected this modern role of dual rampaging attacker and adept defender. I don't think I've seen a better wing-back pairing in British football. The equivalent today is the pairing of Alexander Trent-Arnold and Andy Robertson at Liverpool. It could be argued that the Liverpool duo play in a more traditional 4-2-4 system (although this is clearly fluid), whereas Petrescu and Le Saux played in a 3-5-2/5-

3-2 system. Dutch fans will tell you that none of this is new, as their 70's 'total football' style was entirely dependent on players rotating positions/filling in for one another. Petrescu's form for Chelsea was never less than excellent, playing 152 league games for the club. He was also capped 95 times for Romania, scoring the crucial winning goal against England in the 1998 World Cup, a result that fatefully pitted the English against Argentina in the knock-out stages.

Has there ever been an English player in recent football history to make the absolute maximum of his talent than Dennis Wise (Kevin Keegan excepted)? Short in stature, but huge in spirit, Wise made his name at Wimbledon, helping the 'Crazy Gang' defeat red-hot favourites Liverpool in the 1988 FA Cup Final. Wimbledon were unable to compete in the 1988–89 European Cup Winners Cup due to the Heysel ban – their one chance of European football cruelly denied. Wise played 135 league games for Wimbledon. An unfashionable club, Wimbledon. It came as a surprise to some when Wise transferred to the eminently fashionable club Chelsea in 1990. Wise proved any doubters massively wrong over the next decade. In his first season at Stamford Bridge, he netted 13 times; in his second he scored 14 goals. Wise swiftly became a fan's favourite. A 'cheeky chappie' character endeared him to supporters; his tenacity did not go unnoticed; even more so from within the club as incoming manager Glenn Hoddle made him club captain.

Dennis Wise was not simply tenacious. He scored some wonderful goals for Chelsea (53 in total in the league) and allied perceptive passes to his unquenchable spirit. Wise had issues – an assault on a taxi-driver resulting in a three-month prison sentence that was overturned on appeal; three red cards in the 1988–89 season that followed this European triumph. No one could ever question Dennis Wise's commitment to the cause. Chelsea players and fans alike adored him; twice he won the club's Player of the Year. Wise played 21 times for England, though invariably found himself down the pecking order of international managers that even included his old club boss Glenn Hoddle.

Wise's impact on the team was significant, but the multinational influence on Chelsea circa 1998 was undeniable. In contrast to Wise's in-your-face physicality, the Italian Roberto Di Matteo alongside him was all silky skills. Yet, like Wise, he possessed a ferocious shot when the occasion called for it. Born in Switzerland to Italian parents, Di Matteo played for three Swiss clubs, the first of which was his hometown of Schaffhausen, before joining Lazio in Italy in 1993. Moving to Chelsea in 1996, Di Matteo swiftly became another crowd favourite at Stamford Bridge. A sweeper in youth football, a deep-lying midfielder with Lazio, Di Matteo built his reputation at Chelsea on fine passing ability and his capacity to score important long-distance goals – a 30-yarder after a mere 42 seconds set Chelsea on their way to their 2-0 victory over Middlesbrough in the 1997 FA Cup Final. Di Matteo twice more scored crucial goals in League Cup and FA Cup wins for Chelsea. He came alive in a Wembley final. A classy player, Di Matteo played 34 times for Italy, including appearances in the 1996 European Championships and the 1998 World Cup.

The presence of Italy's Gianluca Vialli and the towering Norwegian international Tore Andre Flo meant no final place this time for the impressive

Mark Hughes. The pairing of Vialli and Flo gave Chelsea a multitude of attacking options. Vialli built a major reputation in Italy before joining Chelsea in 1996. Scoring nearly 150 league goals in Serie A with Cremonese, Sampdoria and Juventus is no mean feat – ask Ian Rush or Jimmy Greaves. Vialli's form struck gold with Sampdoria where he formed an intuitive strike partnership with Roberto Mancini. At Sampdoria, Vialli won Serie A, three Italian Cups, and the European Cup Winners Cup. At Juventus he won Serie A, the Italian Cup, the UEFA Cup, and the Champions League.

Moving to Chelsea with his career ostensibly past its peak, Vialli subsequently scored 21 league goals in 58 appearances for the club, winning a League Cup, an FA Cup and this Cup Winners Cup trophy. Gianluca was a serial winner. He is the only forward (among nine professional players) to have won all three European trophies, the Cup Winners Cup, the UEFA Cup and the Champions League. For Italy he scored 16 goals in 59 games, playing in the 1986 and 1990 World Cup competitions, and the 1988 European Championships. At Chelsea, Vialli, a strong presence in the Chelsea squad with much experience, did not always see eye to eye with his initial incumbent manager Ruud Gullit, leading to his omission from the side at times. Vialli didn't need to worry about personal disagreement on this night as he had become player-manager for the side! Vialli was a fine all-round striker, an adept target man, an aware team player. The only aspect missing from his armoury, preventing him being a ten-out-of-ten striker was a lack of lightning pace, but many quick players lack his all-round skills.

Tore Andre Flo stood six feet four inches, his gangling physique enough to upset many a central defender. Like so many tall strikers (Peter Crouch is a point in case) his apparent awkwardness belied a fine touch – and Flo had a habit of scoring goals wherever he played. Flo came from a family of footballers, playing for his first professional club Sogndal with brothers Jostein and Jarle. Sixty-seven league goals in Norway with Sogndal, Tromso ND Brann saw Flo earn a transfer to Chelsea in 1997. In three seasons with Chelsea, Flo scored 50 goals in all games. A hat-trick against Tottenham in his first season with the club was followed by an important brace against Real Betis in the quarter-finals of this competition. Nineteen goals in his final full season at Stamford Bridge were not enough for him to retain his starting position when the 2000–01 season began with Jimmy Floyd Hasselbaink and Eider Gudjohnsen preferred as first-choice strikers. Unhappy at playing second fiddle, Flo moved to Glasgow Rangers where he scored 29 goals in 53 appearances. In his short time with Chelsea, Tore Andre Flo proved a handful indeed for Premiership defenders.

The Stuttgart side in opposition had few players well known to English supporters. The best-known was arguably central defender Thomas Berthold, who had been part of the Germany World Cup-winning side in 1990. Captain of the side, Freddie Bobic, played 37 times for Germany, scoring ten times, and, unsurprisingly given his surname, was of Slovene and Croatian descent. Bobic's main career was spent with VFB Stuttgart and Borussia Dortmund between 1994 and 2002, a period in which he scored 86 Bundesliga goals, top-scoring in the league with 17 in 1996.

The attacking midfielder Krasamin Balakov at number 10 for Stuttgart was part of the Bulgarian team who finished fourth at the 1994 World Cup, regarded as the second-best player of his generation behind the venerated Hristo Stoichkov. Appearing in 236 Bundesliga games for Stuttgart, Balakov scored 54 goals.

The loss of Brazilian striker Giovane Elber to Bayern Munich at the end of the 1997 season was felt keenly here by Stuttgart. Elber had scored 41 goals for Stuttgart, and would over double that tally with Bayern, scoring a further 92. Bobic, Balakov and Elber were considered to be the 'magic triangle' for Stuttgart. Bobic and Balakov remained to threaten Chelsea on this evening, but Chelsea would win out – but no German opposition in a final is a 'gimme'.

If one had to be critical, it could be argued that the standard of teams in this final year of the European Cup Winners Cup did not match that of previous years. In a snow-bound trip to Tromso in Norway in the last 16 of this year's competition, Vialli displayed uncanny balance to score twice. In the last eight, two excellent goals from the big man Flo in the away leg helped Chelsea to a 5-2 aggregate victory. Vicenza of Italy were beaten 3-2 over two legs in the last four. These matches featured a superlative header from the talismanic Zola, and a defiant (given his omission from the starting line-up in the final) strike from Mark Hughes. Hughes turning of the last defender and his lashed half-volley into the far corner were a reminder of the Welshman's determination and excellent technique.

Stuttgart's path was even less onerous, defeating Slavia Prague 3-1 on aggregate in the quarter-finals, and Lokomotiv Moscow by the same score in the semi-finals.

THE FINAL
Naturally Stuttgart proved typically obdurate German opposition. The game was typical of many a final, tactical, cagey, with Stuttgart not remotely overawed by Chelsea's team of multinational stars. Chelsea's dominance of possession in the second half of the game finally produced the moment of glory. Dennis Wise's cleverly dinked pass over the Stuttgart defence sailed into the path of Zola. The Italian genius, only on the pitch for less than a minute as a substitute, latched on to the ball and struck a wonderful rising half-volley past startled Stuttgart goalkeeper Franz Wohlfahrt. Even the sending off of Dan Petrescu failed to deny Chelsea, who became the first British team to win this trophy twice.

Arsenal had a really good stab at winning this trophy, being finalists three times, but winning only once. Glasgow Rangers were also finalists twice. The European Cup Winners Cup seems like an anomaly now, a competition completely forgotten, a competition deemed unnecessary and invaluable in the history of European football. Yet this denounces the importance of a domestic cup win in football across the continent of Europe. Other European countries may view their domestic cup competitions with less fervour than I, but for me the FA Cup in England remains important. Growing up, those first memories of our European-trophy hunters in Europe are fresh in my mind. Tottenham's attacking talents of Greaves, White and Dyson; the Ron Greenwood ethos of playing stylish football at West Ham in the manner of the great European sides abroad; and the flamboyant talents of Osgood, Cooke and Hudson at Chelsea shine brightly in my memory. To win in 1971 Chelsea had to defeat the legendary Real Madrid. To even qualify for the 1971 European Cup Winners Cup Chelsea had to overcome a superhuman Leeds United side who largely outplayed them over two games in the 1970 FA Cup Final and replay. For these reasons – and all those valiant efforts through the 1980s and 1990s – the European Cup Winners Cup will always have a place in my heart.

Part 2: UEFA Cup Europa League

UEFA CUP
LIST OF BRITISH WINNERS AND FINALISTS
TWO-LEG FINALS

1971–72 – Wolverhampton Wanderers 1 v 2 Tottenham Hotspur, Molineux, 45,000.
Tottenham Hotspur 1 v 1 Wolverhampton Wanderers, White Hart Lane, 54,000.
Tottenham Hotspur, 3-2 on aggregate.

1972–73 – Liverpool 3 v 0 Borussia Möenchengladbach, Anfield, 41,169.
Borussia Möenchengladbach 2 v 0 Liverpool, Bokelbergstadion, 35,000.
Liverpool, 3-2 on aggregate.

1973–74 – Tottenham Hotspur 2 v 2 Feyenoord, White Hart Lane, 46,281.
Feyenoord 2 v 0 Tottenham Hotspur, De Kuip Stadium, Rotterdam, 59,000.
Feyenoord, 4-2 on aggregate.

1975–76 – Liverpool 3 v 2 Club Brugge, Anfield, 56,000.
Club Brugge 1 v 1 Liverpool, Olympiastadion, Bruges, 32,000.
Liverpool, 4-3 on aggregate.

1980–81 – Ipswich Town 3 v 0 AZ Alkmaar, Portman Road, 27,532.
AZ Alkmaar 4 v 2 Ipswich Town, Olympisch Stadium, Amsterdam, 32,000.
Ipswich Town, 5-4 on aggregate.

1983–84 – Anderlecht 1 v 1 Tottenham Hotspur, Constant Vanden Stoot, Brussels, 40,000.
Tottenham Hotspur 1 v 1 Anderlecht, White Hart Lane, 46,205.
Tottenham Hotspur, 2-2 on aggregate, 4-3 on penalties.

1986–87 – IFK Göteborg 1 v 0 Dundee United, Nya Ulevi, Gothenburg, 42,548.
Dundee United 1 v 1 IFK Göteborg, Tannadice Park, 20,911.
IFK Göteborg, 2-1 on aggregate.

The first single leg final took place between Inter Milan and Lazio at the Parc des Princes, Paris at the end of season 1997–98 season with Inter Milan triumphing.

UEFA CUP
LIST OF BRITISH AND WINNERS AND FINALISTS
SINGLE-LEG FINALS

1999–2000 – Galatasaray 0 v 0 Arsenal, Parken Stadium, Copenhagen, 38,919
Galatasaray, 4-1 on penalties.

2000–01 – Liverpool 5 v 4 Alaves, (after extra time), Westfalenstadion, Dortmund, 48,050.

2002–03 – Porto 3 v 2 Glasgow Celtic, Estadio Olympico de Sevilla, 52,972.

2005–06 – Sevilla 4 v 0 Middlesbrough, Philips Stadium, Eindhoven, 33,100.

2007–08 – Zenit St Petersburg 2 v 0 Glasgow Rangers, City of Manchester Stadium, Manchester, 43,878.

In the last competition in the guise of the UEFA Cup in season 2008–09, Ukraine's Shakhtar Donetsk beat Germany's Werder Bremen in Istanbul.

EUROPA LEAGUE
LIST OF BRITISH WINNERS AND FINALISTS

2009–10 – Atlético Madrid 2 v 1 Fulham, Hamburg Arena, Hamburg, 49,000.

2012–13 – Chelsea 2 v 1 Benfica, Amsterdam Arena, Amsterdam, 46,163.

2015–16 – Sevilla 3 v 1 Liverpool, St.Jacob Park, Basel, 34,429.

2016–17 – Manchester United 2 v 0 Ajax, Friends Arena, Solna, Sweden, 46,961.

2018–19 – Chelsea 4 v 0 Arsenal, Olympic Stadium, Baku, Azerbaijan, 51,370.
9 British winners – (Liverpool the most, three times).
7 British runners-up.

Spain is the country who has won the competition most times, combined UEFA Cup/Europa League, England second on the list alongside with Italy. For all my reservations about English football loitering on the international stage, at club level England's record is impressive.

The seeds of the UEFA Cup (which became the overblown, extended Europa League in season 2009–10), began with the Inter-Cities Fairs Cup. Technically the competition is not recognised with regard to its successor, the UEFA Cup. Yet the idea of European cities playing in a competition outside of the European Cup (league title-winning teams of each European country, now known as the Champions League) was born. The Inter-Cities Fairs Cup began in season 1955–56, the idea being to promote international trade fairs. Hence the first curiosity of matches in 1955 between a London XI and Barcelona, held at Stamford Bridge and the Nou Camp. While the London side held its own in England's capital, they were trounced 6-0 in the second leg. The competition could only be played in by one club from any one city. This first competition did not finish until 1958, as it was intended to coincide with each country's trade fairs.

Birmingham City fared no better representing the Midlands in the 1958–1960 competition, drawing at home, but losing conclusively to Barcelona in the Nou Camp. These sprawling competitions owed their longevity to the domestic leagues' reluctance to interfere with the core league fixtures of each country.

From 1960–61 the competition was played in one season only, Birmingham again losing, this time to the Italians Roma. Only in season 1964–65 did the Fairs Cup expand to something akin to the latter-day UEFA Cup and Europa League, 48 teams competing in a competition won by the Hungarians Ferencvárosi. The Hungarians – surprisingly some might say – defeated Italians Juventus 1-0 in the final in Turin. It has been Juventus's misfortune too often to be the bridesmaids in European competitions down the years. Any suggestion that Ferencvárosi were fortunate winners would be in denial of the stature of Hungarian football in the 1950s and 1960s. While Hungarian club sides were not as truly special as the 1954 national breed of Puskás, Hidegkuti and Kocsis, many fine players plied their trade in Hungarian football in 1965: Florian Albert, Ferenc Bene, Janos Farkas – outstanding forwards all. Albert was a legend at Ferencvárosi, and was such a wonderful all-round centre-forward that he became European Footballer of the Year in 1967. This Ferencvárosi team were also good enough to defeat a Manchester United side containing George Best, Bobby Charlton and Denis Law in the 1964–65 semi-final.

Leeds United made it to the Fairs Cup Final in season 1966–67, succumbing to the Yugoslavs Dynamo Zagreb 2-0 on aggregate. This was a period of near-dominance of English football by Leeds – only a surfeit of games surely prevented them from winning more trophies. While they might have been expected to beat Dynamo Zagreb, context is put in to place by the fact that Yugoslavia would be finalists in the European Championships of 1968, only beaten after a replay by host nation Italy. Leeds did remedy their defeat in 1967–68, becoming the first British club to win this competition, overcoming Ferencvárosi 1-0 on aggregate thanks to an Eddie Gray goal.

The following season, 1968–69, Newcastle United won the final in stirring fashion, handsomely defeating the other excellent Hungarian side of this era, Újpest Dózsa, 6-2 on aggregate. That other Hungarian 'master' (after Albert) of the 1960s, Ferenc Bene, scored four goals over the two legs of the semi-finals. He could manage only one in Budapest in the second leg of the final against Newcastle, outscored by the rock of a central defender, Scotsman Bobby Moncur, who hit the net three times over the two-legged final. The strikers for Newcastle did not manage a single goal of the six over the two games, but Welsh centre-forward Wyn Davies and the elusive 'Pop' Bryan Robson were a splendid twin strike force for Newcastle United. Newcastle –as has been much documented in recent times – have not won a trophy of any real consequence since this competition (unless one counts the defunct Anglo-Italian Cup in 1973, the defunct Texaco Cup in 1974 and 1975, and the UEFA Intertoto Cup in 2006).

Continuing a spell of fruitful success for English clubs, Arsenal overturned a 3-1 deficit from the first leg in Brussels against Anderlecht, winning the return leg 3-0 at Highbury in 1969–1970. A domestic double of league and cup beckoned for this strong Arsenal side in 1970–71, making them only the second club (after fierce rivals Tottenham Hotspur) to win the double in English football in the 20th century. This Arsenal team featured a fine centre-forward in John Radford, and a co-striker in Ray Kennedy who would be transformed into a midfielder par excellence at Liverpool. Arsenal, pre-George Graham management, had already begun to forge an impressive reputation as a strong team unit. Ironic then that wearing the number 11 shirt for the double-winning team was none other than Graham himself. A back four of Peter Storey (another of the late 60s/early 70s 'hard man' brigade), Frank McLintock, Peter Simpson and Bob McNab with Bob Wilson behind them in goal had shades of the later Seaman, Dixon, Adams, Bould, Winterburn quintet about them. The mercurial Charlie George gave the Gunners much-needed flair in attack. There were many flair players of George's ilk in this era: Tony Currie at Sheffield United, Alan Hudson at Chelsea, Rodney Marsh at Queens Park Rangers and Manchester City – they made watching football a constant delight for someone in his early-mid teens.

The Italian giants Juventus were once again the bridesmaids in the last season of the Fairs Cup in 1970–71, beaten by Leeds United (their second victory in the short-lived competition in four seasons), although the two ties could not have been closer. A 0-0 draw in the Stadio Communale in Turin was followed by a 1-1 draw at Elland Road. A play-off match took place, this time in Turin, Leeds winning the trophy by dint of superior away goals in a 2-2 drawn game. For Leeds, their crucial home goal came from Alan 'Sniffer' Clarke whose nickname draws parallels with the likes of other great English finishers Jimmy Greaves and Gary Lineker. Three great Italian players scored over the three games for Juventus: centre-forward Roberto Bettega, co-forward Pietro Anastasi, both prolific scorers for the Turin-based club; and one Fabio Capello, a robust midfield enforcer who tended to score a greater ratio of goals for his country than he did for his club. Capello would later 'enjoy' a five-year tenure as England international manager 2007–2012.

As two-time winners, Leeds were then invited to play a trophy play-off match against three-time winners Barcelona in 1971 to decide which club would retain the Fairs Cup outright. Barcelona – predictably given Leeds' wretched run of luck in big games – won the match, played in the Nou Camp, 2-1.

THE UEFA CUP

Although forgotten now, the abandoned Inter-Cities Fairs Cup acted as an important staging post for the new competition that evolved in 1971–72. The practice of one club, one city long discarded, teams qualifying for the new UEFA Cup had to finish high in their respective leagues, whether that be top two, three, four or five, depending on the quality of each European nation's leagues. As I remember well from my youth, British football seemed to be in a particularly good place circa 1966–1977. Only from the latter 70s onwards did England and Scotland's teams falter for a decade or two as Dutch 'total football' revolutionised the European scene, and the newly unified Germany produced a string of extraordinarily difficult-to-beat teams. Italy's fortunes on the international stage continued to hold sway; Spain would foster club teams in Real Madrid and Barcelona that were virtually unmatched in European football history.

1971–72 UEFA CUP FINAL
1st Leg: Wolverhampton Wanderers 1 v 2 Tottenham Hotspur
2nd Leg: Tottenham Hotspur 1 v 1 Wolverhampton Wanderers
Tottenham Hotspur 3-2 on aggregate

In 1971–72, English football was on something of a high (Celtic and Rangers too remained strong in European club competition). This brings me to the very first UEFA Cup Final, Tottenham Hotspur versus Wolverhampton Wanderers. Watching Chelsea over two seasons as a teenager at Stamford Bridge, there were three teams that visited southwest London that I always feared. They were not the northwestern powerhouses Liverpool and Manchester United that came to dominate English football in the 1970s, 1980s and 1990s. They were the Manchester City team of Bell, Summerbee and Lee; the fearsomely competitive Leeds United team managed by Don Revie, and the Tottenham Hotspur team, now lacking former Chelsea man Terry Venables, and the man I still regard as the greatest English goalscorer of all time, Jimmy Greaves. Instead the Tottenham team of 1971–72 came to the Bridge with Pat Jennings in goal (for all Peter Shilton and David Seaman's merit, the best goalkeeper I've seen in British football other than Gordon Banks – he had hands like shovels!); the relentless driving force that was Alan Mullery in midfield; the silky, stealthy Martin Peters alongside him; and a tremendous striking partnership of Martin Chivers and Scotsman Alan Gilzean.

Route to the Final
I once played in a game where my team were beaten 15-1; I also played in games that my teams won 12-5 and 12-2. These sorts of results tend to be confined to Sunday league football. In the first round of this season's UEFA Cup, Tottenham beat the hapless Icelandic team IBK Keflavik 15-1 on aggregate, 6-1 away and 9-0 at home. I recall the ridiculously skilled, annoyingly good-looking, God-like Peter Osgood (I wasn't at all envious!) scoring five times against Luxembourg's Jeunesse Hautcharage in a Cup Winners Cup tie won by Chelsea by a European aggregate record score of 21-0. The home tie in which Osgood scored five, Chelsea won 13-0. Tottenham's ex-double-winning skipper Danny Blanchflower was less than complimentary about Chelsea's feat given that it came against a Luxembourg 'village' team containing four brothers, one player over 40 years of age, and a one-armed striker (I was present, I've never forgotten it). The fact that a 'village' with a population of between 300 and 800 (depending on which figures you believe) had won their nation's domestic cup was quite a feat in itself, although indicative of the quality of Luxembourg football in 1971.

Returning to Tottenham's passage to the first UEFA Cup Final, a relatively undemanding route ensued until the semi-finals when Spurs played Italy's AC Milan. 'Mr. Tottenham', Steve Perryman, scored twice as Tottenham won the home game 2-1; Mullery's early goal in Milan was enough to secure a precious draw in the return leg.

Wolverhampton Wanderers were also among the goals in their first-round tie, beating the Portuguese club Academica de Coimbra 7-1 on aggregate, the talismanic Northern Irish centre-forward Derek Dougan scoring a hat-trick in Portugal. The Dutch team Den Haag were similarly dismissed 7-1 in the second round; the East Germans Carl Zeiss Jena 4-0 on aggregate in the third round. To reach the final, Wolves then beat Juventus and the Hungarians Ferencvárosi (Albert was still banging in the goals) in the last eight and the last four. Dougan again scored the decisive, winning goal against 'Juve' at Molineux in the quarter-final second leg. An Albert goal in Budapest couldn't deny Wolves, the Midlands club claiming a 2-1 home win and an overall 4-3 aggregate victory.

In goal for Wolves, Phil Parkes played 303 league games 1964–1978. Parkes saved two penalty kicks in the semi-final ties against Ferencvárosi. Centre-back Frank Munro, scorer of two goals in the Ferencvárosi semi-final ties, played 296 league games for Wolves, receiving nine international caps for Scotland. Munro began his career as a centre-forward with Chelsea – hence his striking prowess. Munro was also the scorer of Aberdeen's first-ever European goal in the 1967–68 European Cup Winners Cup competition. Signed as a midfielder with an eye for goal, Munro converted to centre-back upon signing for Wolves in 1968. He obtained a winning medal in the 1974 League Cup Final when Wolves beat a Manchester City team beginning to decline 2-1.

The captain of Wolves was a very fine player indeed. Scottish midfielder Jim McCalliog signed for Chelsea in 1963, but played only seven times for the London club. McCalliog gained his revenge, scoring in an FA Cup semi-final victory for his next club Sheffield Wednesday over Chelsea in 1966. Wednesday lost the final, one of my earliest TV football memories, a tremendous comeback by Everton from 2-0 down with 20 minutes remaining, winning 3-2. McCalliog then transferred to Wolves in 1969. It would be McCalliog who scored Wolves goal in the first leg of this UEFA Cup Final at Molineux. Injuries hampered McCalliog's later time as a Wolves player, but he enjoyed a last hurrah as part of a Southampton side that stunned Manchester United in the 1976 FA Cup Final. Remembered as the 'Bobby Stokes' final, make no mistake, the brains behind this fondly recalled FA Cup shock were the veterans McCalliog, Peter Osgood and the unquenchably enthusiastic Mick Channon. McCalliog also played five times for Scotland 1969–1971, his misfortune being around at the same time as so many great Celtic and Rangers players palpable.

Kenny Hibbitt was another talented midfield player in this Wolves side. Hibbitt only needed 15 games in the old Division 4 with Bradford Park Avenue to arouse Wolves' interest in him. Hibbitt went on to play a total of 544 games for Wolves in all competitions, scoring 114 times. Hibbitt scored in the 1974 League Cup Final.

What a central striking partnership Wolves had here in Derek Dougan and John Richards – and what a contrast in styles. Richards was a swift, mobile, intuitive striker, a scorer of 194 goals in all games for the club. Richards scored a total of 36 goals in season 1972–73; the winning goal in the 1974 League Cup Final; was club leading scorer in six of seven seasons during the 1970s. His tally of goals was only bettered by Steve Bull later, but Richards was the better all-round player. Faced with the competition of Osgood, Channon, Chivers, Kevin Keegan, Derby County's Kevin Hector, and Allan Clarke during this era, Richards was unfortunate to win only one cap for England.

Dougan, by contrast, was a towering six feet three inches, a rugged, traditional centre-forward, but with no little skill, and an absolute menace in the air. Dougan was old enough in 1972 to have played for Northern Ireland in the 1958 World Cup, but he remained an intimidating opponent for centre-halves in the early 1970s. He made his name in English football with Blackburn Rovers, scoring 26 goals in 59 league appearances. Transferring to Aston Villa he scored 19 goals in 51 appearances, a period blighted by injury. A car crash left Dougan with arm and head injuries. A fellow passenger died in the crash. Dougan dropped down to the old Division 3 to play for Peterborough United, his career apparently damaged irrevocably. At Peterborough he scored 38 goals in 77 league games, earning a transfer back to the top flight with Leicester City in 1965 where he scored 35 goals in 68 league games. A free spirit, Dougan endured a troubled relationship with Leicester manager Matt Gillies. Dropping down again to Division 2, Dougan helped Wolves win promotion to the top flight in his first season at Molineux. Initially he formed an excellent partnership in attack with Ernie Hunt, but Hunt was sold to Everton in September 1967, swiftly annulling their allegiance. Forming another excellent partnership with Peter Knowles, brother of Tottenham's left-back Cyril, this union came to a sudden and surprising end when Knowles Junior became a full-time Jehovah's Witness at the age of 24, one of the 1970's startling football stories. Dougan, signed by Ronnie Allen to Wolves, suffered another personality clash with the new incoming manager Bill McGarry. Despite their differences, Dougan scored 95 goals in 258 appearances with Wolves, only succumbing eventually to further injury problems as his career drew to a close. Dougan played 43 times for Northern Ireland, but even George Best's presence in the same team couldn't enable the Northern Irish to qualify for a World Cup following their 1958 appearance.

On the left wing Wolves had Dave Wagstaffe to occupy the attentions of Tottenham's Joe Kinnear. Wagstaffe's talent was enormous, but his goals rare in 404 league appearances for Wolves. A 35-yarder won him goal of the month against Arsenal in 1971, and he scored Wolves' goal at White Hart Lane in the second leg of this final.

Pat Jennings was such an unassuming individual that he comfortably switched between North London's top clubs, Tottenham and Arsenal, with scarcely a whisper of dissent from supporters. A calm, yet commanding presence in goal, Jennings played 591 times in all competitions for Tottenham 1964–1977. As if a 13-year career in top flight was not enough, Jennings switched allegiances from White Hart Lane to Highbury, holding on to the number 1 jersey with Arsenal for another eight years. A supremely competent goalkeeper, he was comfortable with crosses, one-on-ones, and shot-stopping. In short he was the complete goalkeeper. He also, sensationally, scored with a long downfield punt in the 1967 Charity Shield match that skipped over a startled Alex Stepney in the Manchester United goal. Jennings won the 1973 Football Writer's Association Footballer of the Year award, following this in 1976 with the PFA's equivalent accolade. The only other goalkeeper to win the latter was Peter Shilton. At Arsenal, Jennings helped Tottenham's rivals to four cup finals in his first three seasons with his new club – they won only the FA Cup Final in 1979 (this following an FA Cup victory, two League Cup wins and this UEFA Cup with Spurs). On 26 February 1983, Jennings became the first player to make 1,000 senior appearances at West Bromwich Albion's Hawthorns ground, fittingly keeping a clean sheet. Jennings also holds the record for international appearances as a goalkeeper for Northern Ireland, 119 caps received. Jennings played 472 league games for Tottenham; 237 for Arsenal during a time when his senior career was deemed to be coming to an end. Internationally, Jennings played in six World Cup qualifying campaigns. Only Gordon Banks in British football should be held in higher esteem than Pat Jennings in the goalkeeping stakes.

At right-back, Joe Kinnear was as tenacious a tackler as he would become an ebullient manager. The game was essentially about defending for Kinnear, a facet he employed supremely at Tottenham in 196 league appearances over ten years, retiring at the age of 30. Kinnear was capped 26 times by the Republic of Ireland.

A cultured, elegant, accomplished footballer, Cyril Knowles played on the left side of Tottenham's defence. With his natural poise, it comes as no surprise that Knowles started out as a left-winger. Rejections from Manchester United, Blackpool and Wolves made Knowles question his future. First club Middlesbrough converted him to left-back, consequently Tottenham came calling. Knowles would make over 400 league appearances for Spurs, his crossing ability a natural attacking outlet for the team in an 11-year stay with the club. Regular knee problems forced his retirement at the age of 31.

Captain for the evening, Alan Mullery, would have played more than 35 times for England, but for the 'toothy' terrier Nobby Stiles being Alf Ramsey's go-to defensive midfielder. Mullery was actually a better offensive player than Stiles, but Ramsey valued Stiles's man-marking ability. Mullery could play the defensive midfield number 4 role, but his energy and shooting ability gave Tottenham an added dimension. In addition to these attributes, Mullery's goal in the second leg of this final came from a header. A great all-rounder, Alan Mullery. Either side of his 312 league games for Tottenham (and 25 crucial goals) Mullery played 364 league games for Fulham, adding another 37 goals.

Mike England at centre-half was another Tottenham stalwart of this era. Tall at six feet two inches, he was commanding in the air, strong in the tackle. England's career began with Blackburn Rovers. Following 165 league appearances in the north-west, England completed 300 league games for Spurs. He also played 44 times for Wales. Phil Beal alongside England could play equally well at full-back. Beal played 333 league games for Spurs.

What else could you call Steve Perryman other than 'Mr Tottenham'? Perryman played a staggering club record 866 games for Spurs in all competitions, largely as a midfield player, latterly as a defender. He didn't score many times (31 to be precise), but critically, scored the two goals in the home victory in this year's UEFA Cup semi-final first leg. Seventeen years with one club is some feat. His peers admired his energy and drive; the Football Writer's Association awarded him their 'gong' of Player of the Year in 1982 in recognition of his sterling service and commitment to Tottenham in the wake of a second successive FA Cup victory at Wembley. Despite playing 17 times for England U-23s, Perryman played only once as a substitute for the full England team. A lack of pace, maybe? You certainly couldn't fault Steve Perryman's endeavour. Gary Mabbutt offered similar qualities to the 1990s Tottenham team.

Martin Peters was a wonderful footballer, athletic, an intelligent reader of the game, and a World Cup winner from 1966. Forging a reputation as the complete midfield player with West Ham United, the elusive Peters, known for ghosting into the penalty area, scored 81 league goals for West Ham in 302 appearances. The West Ham side during Peters' time with the club was admired greatly for the Moore/Peters/Hurst triumvirate, but club silverware eluded this trio after the 1964 European Cup Winners Cup triumph.

Moving to Tottenham Hotspur after an 11-year stint with the Hammers, if anything Peters became an even better player. Peters scored 76 goals for Spurs in his overall total of 260 games, his all-round game making a massive mark on his new club. At Spurs, Peters won the League Cup in 1971, this 1971–72 UEFA Cup, and the 1973 League Cup. 1974 brought another UEFA Cup Final, but victory eluded Spurs, Feyenoord of Holland their vanquishers.

Having begun his career in 1959 as a 16-year-old with West Ham (his all-round ability may have been something to do with playing schoolboy football as a centre-back or full-back), Peters was not even finished by the time of his Tottenham departure in 1975. Moving to Norwich City, Peters helped the East Anglian club gain a foothold in the top flight as a newly promoted club, winning the club's Player of the Season award two years running in 1976 and 1977. In 207 appearances Peters scored 44 league goals for Norwich. In 1978 while still playing in the 1st Division (the equivalent of today's Premiership) Peters was awarded an MBE for services to football. A great technician on the football field; a proud ambassador for English football. A class act, Martin Peters.

Peters scored against West Germany in our never-to-be forgotten 1966 World Cup victory, typically arriving in the penalty area at the right moment to steer home Geoff Hurst's deflected shot. He scored again against the same opposition in the 1970 World Cup quarter-final. When England appeared to be coasting at 2-0 with 20 minutes remaining, Alf Ramsey committed the cardinal sin of substituting Peters and Bobby Charlton, presumably saving his best players for a potential semi-final. The rest is history as Franz Beckenbauer, Gerd Müller et al had the last laugh. Amazingly, Peters (like Hurst a late addition to Ramsey's first choice XI in 1966) only played 67 times for England. Twenty goals tell you everything about the prowess and instinct of this immaculate footballer.

Ralph Coates could play on either wing. Coates's appearance, balding with a wisp of hair on top, belied his tremendous work-rate and energy. Coates covered an awful lot of ground on the pitch. Similar to Chelsea's John Hollins in this respect, Coates utilised his skills in the wide positions where Hollins's domain was the middle of the park. A Burnley stalwart 1964–1971, Coates transferred to Tottenham when Burnley were relegated at the end of season 1970–71. Coates played over 300 games for Spurs 1971–78. He wasn't a prolific scorer, although he scored the winner in the 1973 League Cup Final. What Ralph Coates had in spades was a huge heart.

Solid and sound at the back and in midfield, it was in the attacking positions that this Tottenham side excelled. Perhaps the solidity of those behind them gave Spurs' attacking talents the platform to hurt opponents going forward. One of the great unsung players of this era wore the number 7 shirt on this evening. Alan Gilzean, despite his numbered shirt, was not a winger at all. Gilzean was a player of immense guile and cunning, blessed with a splendid touch, and one of the best headers of a ball I witnessed during the early 70s. Before even joining and enjoying a stellar career with Spurs, Gilzean had scored goals for fun at his first senior club, Dundee. An unbelievable return of 169 goals in 190 league games for Dundee showed the Scotsman's mettle. Such was Gilzean's impact at Dundee that the club reached the semi-finals of the 1962–63 European Cup, only bowing out to eventual winners, super-club AC Milan. Gilzean scored the winning goal in the home leg of the semi-final.

Sadly, Dundee were vanquished 5-1 in the first leg at the San Siro.

Gilzean initially formed a splendid partnership with Jimmy Greaves at Tottenham. When Martin Chivers was signed from Southampton in 1968, Gilzean's place was under threat, but Gilzean was a player who was simply too good to leave out. It was Greaves, at the end of his career, who moved on to West Ham United in 1970. Gilzean promptly formed another impressive partnership with Chivers. When I saw these two in action at Stamford Bridge in 1969–1970 and 1970–71 I was all too aware of their power (Chivers) and finesse (Gilzean). A hugely intelligent footballer, Gilzean also played 22 times for Scotland, scoring 12 goals. Strangely, Gilzean claimed he didn't enjoy professional football. I once heard the Liverpool 'hard man' Tommy Smith say that his career was "just a job", but how could one as naturally talented as Gilzean not have enjoyed playing football? "It's a funny old game" as his former colleague Greaves once famously stated. Gilzean scored 93 goals in 343 league appearances for Spurs.

Martin Chivers built his reputation at first club Southampton, scoring 96 goals in 175 league appearances for his hometown. Yet Chivers played second fiddle to Welsh international Ron Davies when Southampton were promoted from Division 2 to Division 1. The only reason Saints were prepared to let Chivers leave was the knowledge that Mick Channon was emerging as the perfect replacement. Chivers transferred to Tottenham in January 1968, for a then club record fee of £125,000. Only when Greaves departed for West Ham did Chivers firmly establish himself. Perhaps he needed to feel he was the team's main striker, as on the occasions I saw him he was hugely impressive. A broad-shouldered, barrel-chested man, his power, pace and explosive shot made him a constant threat to opposition defences. In season 1970–71 Chivers scored 34 goals in 58 games, including two in a League Cup Final victory over Aston Villa. In season 1971–72 he surpassed these figures, scoring 44 times in 64 appearances. Seven goals in seven League Cup ties from Chivers took Spurs to a semi-final which they duly lost to Chelsea (I was present at Wembley to see an experienced George Eastham/Peter Dobing/Gordon Banks-inspired side deny Chelsea's glamour boys the trophy). Banks had been an immovable force over two legs of Stoke's semi-final against West Ham United, confirming my belief that he is the best goalkeeper ever seen in British football.

Thirty-two goals for Chivers followed from 61 appearances in season 1972–73. Chivers scored eight goals in the UEFA Cup this season, only to see final glory snatched from Tottenham by Liverpool on the away goals rule. Six more goals followed in the 1973–74 UEFA Cup campaign. Chivers appeared to be one of the main scapegoats of England's 'shock' 1-1 draw with Poland at Wembley in 1973 (England subsequently failed to qualify for the 1974 World Cup). That 'failure' was put into context by Poland finishing third in the 1974 World Cup, a tournament in which Holland's 'total football' and West Germany's refusal to bow to them enthralled football supporters the world over. Chivers scored 13 goals in 24 appearances for England – some scapegoat.

Incredibly, a decade after Tottenham's history-making first English double of League and FA Cup, Bill Nicholson remained as Tottenham Hotspur manager. Nicholson had been a mainstay of Tottenham's 1950–51 'push and run' league-winning side. Nicholson's teams, like Matt Busby's at Manchester United, always played with style. In Nicholson's first game as Tottenham manager in 1964, Tottenham defeated Everton 10-4, the bulldozing centre-forward Bobby Smith scoring four times. Nicholson was old school. Disenchanted with the hooliganism he witnessed when Tottenham lost the 1973–74 UEFA Cup Final to Feyenoord, and disheartened by the team's poor start the following season, Nicholson resigned. Along with Busby and the inimitable Bill Shankly, Nicholson was one of THE great managers of the 1960s and 1970s.

THE FINAL
Two goals for Martin Chivers secured a 2-1 away victory in the first leg of the final, the first a fine header, the second an explosive 25-yarder with only three minutes of the game remaining.

In the second leg the gifted Alan Gilzean somehow lifted the ball over the crossbar from two yards out. The quick-thinking Peters atoned for Gilzean's rare aberration, spotting Mullery arriving late in the penalty area, the industrious ex-Fulham man sneaking in front of Parkes in the Wolves goal to head Tottenham into an early lead. Wagstaffe, not a frequent scorer, shuffled the ball on to his left foot from a wide right position and sent a rocket of a shot into goal via the far post to equalise. Even the impeccable Jennings couldn't stop this one. Tottenham held on, repelling dangerous Wolves attacks to win this first all-English European Final.

1972–73 UEFA CUP FINAL
1st Leg: Liverpool 3 v 0 Borussia Möenchengladbach
2nd Leg: Borussia Möenchengladbach 2 v 0 Liverpool
Liverpool 3-2 on aggregate

Here began the true beginnings of a sustained period of Liverpool dominance in English football. The tone had been set by the twinkly Scotsman Bill Shankly, manager of the Merseyside club in the 1960s and early 1970s. Shankly remained at the helm here, and although the Hansen/Souness/Dalglish/Rush team of the 1980s was arguably an even better team, this Liverpool team boasted an outstanding strike pairing of Kevin Keegan (at his regal best in the 1970s) and John Toshack; a midfield dynamo of insatiable enthusiasm in Emlyn Hughes; wonderful wide players in Ian Callaghan and Steve Heighway – not forgetting one of the country's safest goalkeepers in Ray Clemence.

Curiously, Liverpool defeated three other German clubs en route to the final, one from West Germany, Eintracht Frankfurt, and two from East Germany, Dynamo Berlin and Dynamo Dresden. In the semi-finals the Reds overcame holders Tottenham Hotspur from England by the narrowest of margins, by virtue of an away goal from Steve Heighway at White Hart Lane, the tie ending 2-2 on aggregate. Extraordinarily, Möenchengladbach scored goals for fun on their way to the final, netting an incredible 34 goals in their five two-legged ties. They too defeated two (West) German sides to reach the final, 1. FC Köln and 1. FC Kaiserslautern. In the semi-finals, Möenchengladbach comfortably dispatched the Dutch team FC Twente, 5-1 on aggregate. Liverpool were 1st Division champions in 1972–73; Möenchengladbach finished only fifth in a German Bundesliga invariably dominated by Bayern Munich. Liverpool, technically, held an edge over their German rivals, but this was German opposition in an era of high achievement in German football.

Heavy rain in Liverpool during the week before the first leg of the final (does it always rain in England's northwestern corner?) resulted in the first attempt to play the Anfield first leg of this final being abandoned after 27 minutes. It became impossible to pass the ball to a teammate in the quagmire conditions. Replayed the following evening, Liverpool learnt enough in those 27 minutes to formulate a game plan going in to the match.

Ray Clemence in goal for Liverpool was one of England's very best keepers. It was Ray's misfortune to be in competition with Peter Shilton for the England goalkeeping position. This didn't prevent him collecting 61 caps for his country, additionally enjoying stellar careers with Liverpool – 470 league appearances – and Tottenham Hotspur – 240 league appearances. Like the rock-steady Pat Jennings, Clemence's career peak appeared over after leaving premier club Liverpool, only for Clemence to prove his doubters wrong in a second, excellent club career in North London. Clemence's worth in this two-leg final was illustrated by saving a penalty at Anfield, enabling Liverpool to have a three-goal cushion in Germany for the second leg. With Liverpool, Clemence won five league titles, one FA. Cup, one League Cup, three European Cups and two UEFA Cups. An impressive haul. Moving to Tottenham, Clemence won a further FA Cup and UEFA Cup in the early 1980s, although injury prevented him actually appearing in the latter final. Much respected within football, Ray Clemence has also been a goalkeeping coach for the England national team, head of the FA's Head of Development Team with a responsibility to oversee the progress of teenage players through to the U-21 national team. He was appointed an MBE in the Queen's 1987 Birthday Honours. Clemence is still regarded as Liverpool's best-ever goalkeeper.

Chris Lawler played at right back in these games, although he was best known as a key player in Shankly's 60s teams. Chris played 406 league games for Liverpool, with a useful return for a full-back of 41 goals. Over seven seasons in the 60s, Chris missed just three games. He was dependable, reliable, a class act. A bit like his older brother Joe, who I played with who I recall matched his slick, dark hair with slick passing ability and a typically streetwise scouse demeanour. In my late teens at the time, I was hopelessly naive. Still, we live and learn, don't we?

Centre-backs at Anfield for the first leg were another dependable, rock-like pair: Larry Lloyd and Tommy Smith. Lloyd didn't necessarily look like a footballer at all times in his career, such was his portly physique. But you don't win a UEFA Cup and two European Cups (the latter with Nottingham Forest) without being a proper footballer. Lloyd's career at Liverpool was short-lived. Signed to replace the 'man-mountain' Ron Yeats, Lloyd played 150 league games for the club 1969–1974, ultimately losing his place following injury to the 'up and coming' Phil Thompson who was preferred by Shankly's successor Bob

Paisley. Lloyd switched to Coventry City for two seasons, catching the eye of Brian Clough's right-hand man, Peter Taylor. Lloyd became another of Clough's inspired signings of so-called 'journeymen' players: Frank Clark, Kenny Burns and John McGovern, all of who played their best football under the irascible master man-motivator. Like Chris Lawler, Lloyd played four times for England.

Tommy Smith partnered Lloyd in the centre of defence for this final, but as stated before, Smith could also make an uncompromising full-back or midfield player.

Emlyn Hughes was a tremendous athlete; a magnificent competitor; a tireless worker in the centre of midfield, and able to fill in at centre-back or left-back when required. Hughes earned the nickname 'Crazy Horse' because of his rampaging sorties up-field – and the occasional wild tackle that he committed. A fall-out with 'hard man' teammate Smith did not affect their performances in a Liverpool shirt, and Hughes captained Liverpool and England too on many occasions during his 62 appearances for his country. Hughes appeared for England in three separate decades, the 60s (1969), the 70s and the 80s – the company he keeps here includes Stanley Matthews, Bobby Charlton and Peter Shilton.

In all, Hughes played 665 games for Liverpool, scoring 35 league goals, some of these spectacular long-range efforts. After a barren first four years at the club, Hughes ultimately won four league titles, an FA Cup, two European Cups, and two UEFA Cups. He won the Football Writer's Player of the Year in 1977. Upon leaving Liverpool for Wolves, he promptly won the only title that eluded him in a red shirt, the League Cup, in his first season at Molineux. Post-football he became one of the most loved, best-remembered team captains on the BBC's institutional *A Question of Sport* programme, his natural exuberance even extending to a very informal bantering session with Princess Anne on one programme, putting his arm around her, ignoring royal protocol.

On the right side of Liverpool's attack was local lad Ian Callaghan. Toxteth-born, the tricky Callaghan worked tirelessly, ostensibly as an old-fashioned right winger, but was eminently capable of tracking back to help teammates defend. An exceptional crosser of the ball, the all-action Callaghan played a total of 857 games for Liverpool 1960–1978, scoring 50 league goals (his assists were too numerous to record). Callaghan – weirdly – also played four times for England like Lawler and Lloyd. He was named the FWA Footballer of the Year in 1974. Moving to Swansea in 1978 to play for old teammate John Toshack, Callaghan helped Swansea to a second successive promotion to the old 2nd Division in 1979. He played his last game for Crewe Alexandra in the old fourth tier at the age of 40 in 1982. Ian Callaghan was a two-time European Cup winner and a two-time UEFA Cup winner. Some pedigree. Callaghan was also part of Alf Ramsey's 1966 World Cup squad, appearing in the 2-0 victory over France in the group stages.

On the other flank was one of my favourite players of this era (as a nominal left-winger myself). Steve Heighway delighted my eye with his traditional wing wizardry. Dublin-born, the rangy Heighway tormented full-backs in the traditional manner of a winger. Tricky, athletic, Heighway had something of the greyhound about him in an era when top-tier teams retained wingers as an attacking source, a constant supply from wide positions for traditional centre-forwards lurking in the penalty area. Heighway also appealed to my sensibility as an intelligent man who educated himself to a higher level than your average footballer, attaining a degree in economics and politics while waiting for his big break in football at a senior level. Along with future teammate Brian Hall (another academic), Heighway garnered the nickname Bamber (Gascoigne – not Paul!), Steve was coined 'Big Bamber', Hall being called 'Little Bamber'.

Strangely for a player coming into top-flight football from Skelmersdale United at the ripe age of 23, Heighway adapted to life with Liverpool as if to the manor born. Heighway played 34 times for the Republic of Ireland in the 1970s and was always a joy to watch.

It's not very often in football that you see two players so obviously on the same wavelength. Kevin Keegan and John Toshack were so remarkably in tune on the football pitch they could have been joined at the hip. Keegan and Toshack's telepathic understanding was one of the early 1970's strongest memories for me. To Liverpool fans, the pair's understanding reaped rich rewards – if you supported another club you were doomed to be repeatedly frustrated by their uncanny bond.

I always felt that Keegan could not truly be compared with the other greats of this era, the Cruyffs, Beckenbauers of the world clearly had superior technique to the Doncaster-born Keegan. But how Keegan worked at his game to make himself the very best player he could be. Keegan's relentless energy and enthusiasm, his desire to reach ever-greater heights made him, arguably, English football's most iconic player of the 1970s.

Bought by Bill Shankly from Scunthorpe United as a wide midfield player, Keegan soon found himself partnering Toshack up front after scoring four goals in a firsts against reserves match as a striker. Keegan scored 12 minutes into his top-tier debut against Nottingham Forest, swiftly being idolised by the home fans in the Kop. In 1974 I worked for S.R. Jeffery & Son Ltd, a peerless family-run sports retailer. The owner of the company decided to place a television within the sports department (the shop's repertoire also included camping and walking, fishing and a popular gun department). The day was so busy that the FA Cup Final between Liverpool and Newcastle United completely passed me by. It was a day when Keegan produced a memorable performance, scoring twice in a 3-0 victory.

Keegan continued to produce performances of sustained vigour and energy, his passion sometimes betraying him. Months later in the 1974 Charity Shield match at Wembley, Leeds United set out their stall to frustrate the man they clearly saw as the biggest threat to victory. Fouls on Keegan by Johnny Giles and Billy Bremner went unchecked by the referee. Keegan finally reacted, punching Bremner. Bremner and Keegan were both sent off, leaving the field of play shirtless in protest in one of the 70s most iconic football moments.

Keegan's emotional approach to the game served him better in his last season with Liverpool as the club came agonisingly close to a treble of league championship, FA Cup and the UEFA Cup, only thwarted by a Manchester United side at Wembley that were talented, while not being of the ilk of the 1968 European Cup winners or Alex Ferguson's mighty ensembles of the 1990s.

Keegan's reputation grew and grew until in 1978 he sought pastures new as European clubs clamoured for his signature. Moving to Hamburger SV, Keegan's performances were such that he was named European Footballer of the Year in 1978 and 1979, making him English football's finest export since John Charles at Juventus in the 1950s. In his first season with Hamburg, he helped the club win the German Bundesliga. In 1980 Hamburg reached the European Cup Final where Brian Clough formulated a game plan to stop the human dynamo Keegan.

Keegan then returned to England for further seasons, two with Southampton, two with Newcastle United, becoming a folk hero on Tyneside. At Southampton Keegan teamed up with Peter Osgood, Alan Ball, Mick Channon and Charlie George. This plethora of experience and flair enabled unfashionable Southampton to sit at the top of the 1st Division in April 1982 only to falter at the death and finish seventh. Oh to be a spectator at The Dell in that season! Keegan did receive the PFA Player of the Year award as a personal consolation. The goals were not drying up either as he netted 30 times to win the Golden Boot for top scorer in the league. Keegan also received an OBE for services to football in 1982.

England's best chance with Keegan in their ranks came at the 1982 World Cup when he enjoyed a similarly telepathic understanding to the one he enjoyed with Toshack; on this occasion his soulmate was West Ham's Trevor Brooking. Suffering with a troubling back injury, Keegan was only able to appear as a last-ditch substitute in a 0-0 draw with Spain. England, having failed to qualify for the 1974 and 1978 World Cups during a barren spell internationally, were eliminated from this 1982 tournament without losing a game. Keegan, for a player of immense vigour and purpose, a player who made things happen on the football pitch, surprisingly won only 63 international caps, scoring 21 goals. At club level Keegan scored 88 league goals for Liverpool, 32 for Hamburg, 37 for Southampton, and 48 for Newcastle.

As a manager Keegan is best remembered for the near-miss with his beloved Newcastle United (his ancestors from Ireland settled in Newcastle) in season 1995–96. A team containing David Ginola, Faustino Asprilla, Robert Lee, Peter Beardsley and Les Ferdinand illuminated that season with the greatest attacking football seen in English football until the recent Manchester City and Liverpool-dominated seasons. Sadly for Newcastle, they lacked the defensive nous of the modern maestros in Manchester and on Merseyside. The title should have been theirs – in January 1996 Newcastle led the table by 12 points from Manchester United, yet on the final day of the season the teams were equal on points. It was widely felt that United's wily old fox Alex Ferguson played mind games with Keegan, playing on Keegan's legendary emotional nature.

No one can deny the passion and enthusiasm Kevin Keegan had for football. Ironically, no other player in English football has matched his intensity of feeling – and emotion – other than his Liverpool teammate Emlyn Hughes.

Keegan's foil in attack, John Toshack, was an altogether different physical specimen. Although only five inches taller, Toshack's long, gangly frame made him appear bigger still than the squat, stocky Keegan. Chalk and cheese, black and white, the pair could not have been more different, yet how they dovetailed together. Toshack started out at Cardiff City, scoring 74 league goals, a tally he exactly replicated in the top tier upon transferring to Liverpool. Toshack's aerial ability allowed Keegan to feed off countless knockdowns as the pair formed their famous partnership from 1972 onwards. The signing of Ray Kennedy from Arsenal in 1974 made their pairing short-lived, yet the memories linger of Toshack winning headers and Keegan devouring his lay-offs. Kennedy was switched to a midfield role he excelled in (did anyone at the time see that one coming?) and Toshack won back his place. Sadly for Toshack, a number of injuries began to curtail his impact on the team, and the Welshman took the decision in 1984, after five seasons with Swansea City, to retire and plunge headlong into management. His management career has been long and varied, bringing periodic success. Clubs queued for his experience and know-how – he has managed Sporting Club and Deportivo in Portugal; Real Sociedad, Real Madrid and Real Murcia in Spain; Besiktas in Turkey; Catania in Italy; and managed the Macedonian national team, and the Welsh national team (the latter twice). In Spain he was awarded La Liga Coach of the Year twice, in 1989 and 1990.

In opposition. Borussia Möenchengladbach did not ostensibly offer the severe threat of Bayern Munich, but fielded several outstanding German internationals. What should be borne in mind is that Möenchengladbach won the Bundesliga five times in the 1970s: 1970, 1971, 1975, 1976 and 1977, in a period prior to Bayern's true dominance of German football. This gives you an idea of Borussia's level.

What baffles me is the decision to play two of that generation's best midfield players, Rainer Bonhof and Günter Netzer in defence for the first leg of this final at Anfield. Only the April before in 1972 Netzer pulled the strings in an exquisite manner in midfield as West Germany defeated England 3-1 at Wembley in a European Championship quarter-final game. How I rejoiced when one of my old heroes Alan Hudson (in one of only two internationals he played) emulated Netzer's performance, controlling a friendly match which England won 2-0 at Wembley in 1975 while I was in attendance.

Bonhof, later to star with Valencia in Spain, was the consummate athlete, able to play wing-back, defensive midfield, with energy to burn. Netzer, as stated, produced one of THE great individual performances that night at Wembley in 1972. His range of passing was astonishing; a technically gifted playmaker, Netzer was voted Footballer of the Year in Germany in 1972 and 1973, before moving on to Real Madrid. For a player who liked to control the game from midfield, Netzer scored an impressive 108 goals for Möenchengladbach, which further begs the question why on earth did he feature in defence at Anfield in the first leg of this final? Joining Real Madrid – along with another superstar of German football, Paul Breitner – Netzer won La Liga in 1975 and 1976, and the Copa del Rey in 1974 and 1975. Curiously, Netzer played only 37 times for West Germany 1965–1975, scoring six times. The problem for Netzer lay in the fact that Wolfgang Overath (1. FC Köln) played in the same central position in midfield, the feeling persisting that the two players were too similar in style – Steven Gerrard and Frank Lampard anyone? Netzer liked to be the pivotal player in the team. However good two players are, playing them both sometimes spoils team shape if they are too similar. Netzer's crowning glory internationally came with West Germany's 3-0 dismissal of the Soviet Union in the 1972 European Championship Final held in Belgium.

Netzer's management record wasn't bad either – as general manager at Hamburger SV he oversaw three Bundesliga title wins in 1979, 1982 and 1983, and a European Cup victory in 1983.

One-club man Herbert Wimmer – as was Overath at 1. FC Köln – scored the second goal in the European Championship Final victory of 1972. Wimmer earned the nickname 'Iron Lung' for his defensive midfield displays. Someone had to win the ball and distribute it to the conductor Netzer! Unshowy, yet crucial to the team, Wimmer appeared 366 times for Möenchengladbach 1966–1978, scoring 51 goals – and a mark of his selflessness came in being chosen in the team of the tournament in Belgium in 1972 – Netzer, predictably, was also chosen.

The player who truly represented German defensive qualities at their very best was Berti Vogts. Tigerish in the tackle, Vogts garnered the nickname '*Der Terrier*' in a long career – one-club again – with Möenchengladbach 1965–1979, playing 419 times for the club. Vogts it was who subdued the super-talented Johan Cruyff in the 1974 World Cup Final, West Germany triumphing over Holland 2-1. Fearless and tenacious, Vogts fared less well when he became national team manager, winning only one tournament for his country. Guess which one? Euro 1996, the oft-revered near miss for Terry Venables' England team when Germany beat England on penalties in the semi-final. Sound familiar?

Möenchengladbach's main striker during this golden period for the club was Jupp Heynckes, the fourth highest goalscorer in the history of the Bundesliga with 220 goals. Gerd Müller (the greatest goalscorer I have ever seen in world football, marginally ahead even of our own Jimmy Greaves) heads that table with 365 goals. Third in this table is Bayern Munich's recent shooting star, the Pole Robert Lewandowski with 235 as of June 2020. Heynckes suffered unfairly for having played in the same era as the metronomic Müller. Heynckes scored twice in the 1971–72 European Cup drubbing of Inter Milan. An astonishing 7-1 victory was annulled because of a drinks can being thrown on to the pitch, striking Inter's Roberto Boninsegna. The replayed match ended 0-0 and Möenchengladbach were eliminated!

Heynckes would have his own personal moment of European glory in 1975 when Möenchengladbach defeated Dutch side Twente Enschede 5-1 in that year's UEFA Cup final, scoring a hat-trick in Holland after missing the home match. Heynckes also scored 12 times in this 1972–73 UEFA Cup campaign. Heynckes' long association with Möenchengladbach ensured he became manager of the club in 1979, but success was not forthcoming until he became manager of Bayern Munich in 1987. Bayern won the 1988–89 and 1989–1990 Bundesliga titles with Heynckes at the helm. In 1998, Heynckes succeeded in winning the European Cup when managing Real Madrid. In doing so, Heynckes returned the trophy to Madrid for the first time since 1966. In 2006, Heynckes returned to Möenchengladbach only to oversee his old club's relegation from the Bundesliga. Returning to Bayern Munich, Heynckes' fortunes remained fraught as Bayern finished second in the Bundesliga, lost the German Cup Final – the DFB Pokal – to Borussia Dortmund 5-2, a match in which Lewandowski scored a hat-trick – he would be earmarked as a Bayern signing, then lost the Champions League Final to Chelsea. Better fate smiled upon Heynckes the following season as Bayern swept all before them in the Bundesliga, won the DFB Pokal final against VFB Stuttgart, and defeated Borussia Dortmund at Wembley in the Champions League Final. Pep Guardiola replaced him at the end of that season. Jupp Heynckes is a highly respected figure in German football, despite his chequered managerial career.

Substitute for this final, Allan Simonsen, had stronger days to come. Simonsen would ultimately play and score in the final of all three European competitions. On this occasion the Dane had to be content with a mere eight-minute cameo at Anfield. The more experienced Henning Jensen was preferred as the right-sided attacker in these two games. Jensen's profile was higher than Simonsen's at this stage in their careers, his talent enabling him to win top-tier titles in Germany with Möenchengladbach, with Real Madrid in Spain, and with Ajax in Holland.

THE FINAL – 1ˢᵗ Leg
The combination of Toshack and Keegan proved lethal at Anfield – when the game finally took place, following the first match abandonment. Preferred to Brian Hall in the starting line-up, Toshack's aerial presence reaped almost instant rewards. His headed lay-off in the 21ˢᵗ minute presented Keegan with a diving header of his own that I recall as one of this era's defining images. The two combined again 12 minutes later, Toshack, with his back to goal, heading the ball to Keegan who volleyed Liverpool 2-0 up. In between, Keegan missed a penalty – he could have had a first half hat-trick. Larry Lloyd headed a third after half-time from a corner-kick, but there was still time for Ray Clemence to save Heynckes' penalty kick and ensure a 3-0 safety net for Liverpool going into the second leg.

THE FINAL – 2ⁿᵈ Leg
Torrential rain, this time in Germany, made for a slippery surface in the Bökelbergstadion, Möenchengladbach. Liverpool appeared to be in trouble as relentless attacking from the Germans reaped the reward of two Heynckes goals by the 40ᵗʰ minute. The Germans eventually ran out of steam, Liverpool kept their cool and ran out winners 3-2 on aggregate, their first European trophy, and the first English club to win their domestic league and a European competition in the same season. The end was nigh for Bill Shankly, but Liverpool went from strength to strength in the 1970s and 1980s.

1973–74 UEFA CUP FINAL
1ˢᵗ Leg: Tottenham Hotspur 2 v 2 Feyenoord
2ⁿᵈ Leg: Feyenoord 2 v 0 Tottenham Hotspur
Feyenoord 4-2 on aggregate

I have stated on these pages before what a splendid side Tottenham Hotspur were in the early 1970s. Evidence of this comes with Spurs' second UEFA Cup final appearance in three seasons. Unfortunately fortune failed them on this occasion, and they were beaten semi-finalists in this competition in the interim season of 1972–73. The strength of German football during this period was borne out by the appearance of two West German clubs and one East German club in this year's quarter-finals. Tottenham dismissed the 1. FC Köln team of Wolfgang Overath 5-1 on aggregate in the last eight, following this with a 4-1 aggregate victory over the East Germans Lokomotiv Leipzig in the last four. Feyenoord, Holland's second-best team after the all-conquering Ajax team of the early 70s, triumphed 4-3 over two legs of the semi-finals against West Germans VFB Stuttgart.

Tottenham's team showed a few changes from the 1971–72 side. Sorely missed were Alan Mullery, Alan Gilzean and the full-backs Joe Kinnear and Cyril Knowles. The latter pair arguably made Tottenham more resilient in defence. Gilzean's subtlety would be a major deficit to any team. Feyenoord could not boast the world-class Ajax players Ruud Krol, Johan Neeskens and Johan Cruyff. Instead, they boasted another three of the tremendous 'total football' Dutch national side of the time, Wim Rijsbergen, Wim Jansen and Willem Van Hanegem. Rijsbergen looked more Scandinavian than Dutch with his blond locks. Ostensibly a right-back – he wore the number 2 shirt – like his Dutch teammates of the time he popped up all over the pitch, interchanging positions at will. Rijsbergen only played 28 games for Holland, yet seemed integral to the great Dutch national sides of 1974 and 1978.

Wim Jansen played over 400 games for Feyenoord, acting as a key anchor man/defensive midfielder. Jansen won four league championships with Feyenoord, one Dutch Cup, this UEFA Cup Final, and the ultimate club achievement when lifting the European Cup in 1970. Transferring to Ajax later in his career – upon recommendation from Cruyff – did not sit well with Feyenoord fans. Jansen played 65 times for Holland 1967–1980.

Van Hanegem I recall as a feisty character. His goals haul for Feyenoord is impressive – 88 in 247 appearances. A fine technician, his bandy gait enabled him to strike the ball with a wicked curve – and he loved a tackle. Van Hanegem went on to manage Feyenoord, winning both league and cup; he also assisted the Dutch national team as a coach.

THE FINAL – 1ˢᵗ Leg
Tottenham twice led the first-half match at White Hart Lane through Mike England's far-post header and an own goal, but Van Hanegem's wicked free kick that clipped the crossbar on its way into the net was followed by a precise through ball by Van Hanegem enabling Theo De Jong to strike a second equaliser with his left foot.

THE FINAL – 2ⁿᵈ Leg
Tottenham's great 'P's – Peters and Perryman – were prominent early on for Tottenham in the return leg in Rotterdam, the latter narrowly missing from a smartly taken free kick by the former. Tottenham even had a goal disallowed during a bright start. Sadly, this game is notable for Tottenham supporters rioting when Rijsbergen opened the scoring for Feyenoord with a rare header courtesy of an equally rare Jennings' handling error. It was a soft goal that led to a poor

reaction from the English supporters. A goal down shortly before half-time, the rioting continued into the second half in a shameful era for English hooliganism. Feyenoord scored a second to run out 2-0 winners on the night and 4-2 overall victors. Rijsbergen, a fine athlete, unselfish, team-first player, set up Ressel for the concluding goal. You forget what a fine team this Feyenoord side were due to the glittering exuberance of Ajax in this era. The spectre of hooliganism in connection with English football weighed heavily over the 1970s. *The Daily Mail* ran the headline 'Rioting Fans Shame Britain' the following day.

1975–76 UEFA CUP FINAL
1st Leg: Liverpool 3 v 2 Club Brugge
2nd Leg: Club Brugge 1 v 1 Liverpool
(Liverpool 4-3 on aggregate)
Route to the Final

Liverpool progressed comfortably after a slight scare in the first round. Drawn against Scottish club Hibernian, Liverpool lost the first leg in Edinburgh 1-0. A John Toshack hat-trick at Anfield secured a 3-1 home win, the Reds squeaking through 3-2 on aggregate. Being drawn against Scottish rivals, the 'auld enemy', is akin to being drawn against another English club, ensuring a derby-style game, often the worst possible draw a British club could have in European competition as the teams tend to cancel each other out, their knowledge of each other too comprehensive.

Not until the quarter-finals and semi-finals were Liverpool challenged as sternly again, the Reds inching past Dynamo Dresden of East Germany and Spanish giants Barcelona, 2-1 on aggregate on both occasions. Keegan was on the mark at Anfield against the East Germans; Toshack scored the only goal of the game in the Nou Camp to seal an impressive 1-0 away win against Barcelona.

All of Club Brugge's victories en route to the final were close affairs. Ipswich Town under Bobby Robson, in the throes of building their own UEFA Cup-winning team further down the line, trounced the Belgians 3-0 at Portman Road in the second round. Astonishingly, Brugge trumped this feat, winning the return leg 4-0. Roma were beaten 2-0 on aggregate next; the quarters and semis produced 3-2 and 2-1 aggregate victories over high quality opposition, AC Milan and Hamburger SV respectively.

These were the beginnings of a prolific period of achievement in Belgian football. Club Brugge were the country's first representative in a major European final. By 1980, Belgium's national team would be strong enough to contest the European Championship Final in Italy against West Germany, running out narrow 1-2 losers.

For Liverpool, a smooth transition had occurred at right-back from previous seasons. Replacing Chris Lawler, Phil Neal came from Northampton Town, going on to play 455 league games for Liverpool, and 50 times for England. Neal is the only player to have appeared in all of Liverpool's 1970s and 1980s European finals. He amassed eight 1st Division titles, four League Cups, four European Cups and one UEFA Cup during his time at Anfield. Steady, dependable, energetic, disciplined, Neal was everything a right-back should be.

Phil Thompson had been pushing for a starting place before Larry Lloyd's departure – now was his time. A supporter on the terraces at Anfield as a boy, Thompson, bled, lived and breathed Liverpool FC. Physically he was a completely different specimen to predecessors Lloyd and Ron Yeats. Lean, tall, gangly, Thompson could win the ball in the air, but read the game well on the ground too. With Emlyn Hughes moving to Wolves in 1979, Thompson became club captain. Partnering him in defence as the 80s approached was the elegant, ball-playing Alan Hansen. Together they would form a tight and talented centre-back pairing. After 340 appearances at Liverpool and 42 appearances for England, Thompson spent a brief stint at Sheffield United, only to return to Anfield as a coach in the late 80s.

Ray Kennedy was spotted playing youth football in his native north-east by an Arsenal scout. The Gunners had gone to look at Kennedy's strike partner Ian Watts, but ended up signing Kennedy who was considered too slow at one point to play at professional level. Kennedy's lucky break at Highbury came when the unfortunate Charlie George broke his ankle in the opening game of the 1970–71 season. Kennedy became John Radford's regular strike partner and at the end of the season Arsenal became only the second club to win the double of League and Cup in the 20th century. One of the most iconic footballing moments of the 70s arrived when Kennedy scored a late header against North London rivals Spurs to deprive the unlucky Leeds United of the title.

Suffering with loss of form and weight problems, Kennedy transferred to Liverpool in the close season of 1974. He'd played 158 league games for Arsenal, scoring 53 goals. What did Liverpool see in him? Kennedy initially formed a fine relationship with Kevin Keegan in Liverpool's attack, but when Toshack forced his way back into the side, Liverpool's coaching staff had a light bulb moment. Kennedy dropped back into midfield where his vision and distribution reinforced an already excellent part of the team. His former nous as a striker enabled him to support the attack as evinced by his return of 51 goals from 275 league appearances with the Anfield club. Bob Paisley thought Kennedy was one of Liverpool's finest-ever signings.

What to say about the enigmatic David Fairclough? The red-haired striker tended to be used as a substitute by Liverpool, earning the nickname 'Supersub' as he affected matches in the latter stages countless times. With Toshack and David Johnson ahead of him in the pecking order as strikers, Fairclough appeared only 98 times in the league for Liverpool over seven seasons, scoring 34 times. In his latter days at Anfield, Fairclough could not forge a place in an attack comprising Kenny Dalglish and Ian Rush. Little wonder! Fairclough made a rare start in this UEFA Cup Final at number 8.

Incredibly, the evergreen and ever-industrious Ian Callaghan wore the number 11 shirt, having played his first game for Liverpool in 1959! Among the substitutes were future stars Jimmy Case and Terry McDermott.

In midfield for Club Brugge, Julien Cools made his name on the back of hard-running and the occasional crucial goal for the club. Cools helped Club Brugge to the Belgian league title three years running – 1975, 1976, 1977 – and to victory in the Belgian Cup in 1977. Cools' crowning glory came when he played in all four of Belgium's games at the 1980 European Championships.

At centre-forward, Raoul Lambert was another one-club man, playing 373 league games for Club Brugge. His goal-scoring return for the club was exemplary, 216 goals in the league, 270 in all competitions. Lambert also scored 18 times in 33 internationals for Belgium. Liverpool would know where the goal threat came from, but it was Belgian football's eye for organisation that made its impact in the 1970s and 1980s, unlike the flair-filled team of the 21st century.

The left-winger of Club Brugge, the Dane Ulrik Le Fevre, possessed a fierce shot. Winner of the Bundesliga twice with Borussia Möenchengladbach, Le Fevre found himself ousted by Henning Jensen and moved to Belgium. Le Fevre scored 34 goals in five seasons at Club Brugge.

THE FINAL – 1st Leg
Early in the game, Neal, starting on the left side of the defence (he was better at right-back) headed a back pass that fell short of Clemence in the Liverpool goal and Lambert scored with a cute lob. Cools' sweet left-foot volley gave Club Brugge a roaring start at Anfield. 2-0 down, could Liverpool recover against a strong Belgian outfit? Liverpool in the 70s were made of stern stuff. Resilience was their byword. The second half substitution of Jimmy Case for Toshack proved an inspired move. Case should have scored from a wide right position in the penalty area, but drifted his shot wide. Keegan drove a shot against the goalkeeper's legs as a typical Anfield siege ensued. Keegan's energy infected the team as the Anfield icon slid the ball into the path of Heighway on the left. Heighway, my kind of player, always an intelligent footballer, laid the ball carefully into the path of Kennedy who lashed the ball left-footed into the far corner. These three players were also involved in the last two goals. Keegan's smart turn away from his marker when there appeared to be no space freed him to tee up Kennedy. Thwarted by a last-ditch tackle, Kennedy's shot trundled against the post only for Case to follow in and tap over the line. Heighway then beat his man on the left edge of the penalty area and was brought down. Keegan sent keeper Birger Jensen the wrong way with an emphatic penalty kick. Three goals in six minutes – the legendary Anfield hothouse pressure worked the trick on this night, one of the early indications of Liverpool as a force in Europe.

THE FINAL – 2nd Leg
An early penalty for Lambert after Tommy Smith was adjudged to have handled the ball gave Brugge the one goal they needed to win the Cup, having scored twice at Anfield. The lead lasted just four minutes. Phil Thompson rolled a short free kick to Keegan and the latter drove a firm low shot past Jensen in the Brugge goal. Club Brugge applied fierce pressure after the break, Lambert hitting the post. Cools was denied by a diving Clemence as the game closed out. If any British club have grasped what it takes to win European club football over the years it is Liverpool. They have always had immaculate conditioning to enable fitness levels that will last 90 minutes; they have always possessed a discipline and organisation of the highest class; and perhaps most importantly they have always

been prepared to learn from continental teams when some British teams carried an unwarranted superiority complex. When you add technical accomplishment to the mix you have an elixir for success at the very highest level of club football.

1980–81 UEFA CUP FINAL
1st Leg: Ipswich Town 3 v 0 AZ Alkmaar '67'
2nd Leg: AZ Alkmaar '67' 4 v 2 Ipswich Town
Ipswich Town 5-4 on aggregate

Route to the Final
The headline story of Ipswich Town's journey to the 1980–81 UEFA Cup Final belongs to Scottish midfielder John Wark. Long-haired, hair dark in colour, moustachioed, Wark was a swashbuckling bandit-imaged player, the kind of all-action player every team yearns for in midfield. Wark scored an astonishing 14 goals in total during this season's European campaign – bear in mind he was a midfield player, not a striker!

In the first round, Ipswich played the Greek side Aris Salonika. A bad-tempered home leg at Portman Road saw Ipswich awarded three penalties, all of which Wark converted. He then scored a fourth goal. Paul Mariner added a fifth as Ipswich ran out 5-1 winners. A 3-1 defeat in Salonika proved irrelevant to Ipswich's progress in the competition. Wark scored twice more in the second round as Bohemians of Prague were seen off 3-0 at Portman Road. Again a 0-2 defeat in Prague failed to deter the 'Tractor Boys'. Wark scored a hat-trick in the next round as the Poles of Widzew Lodz were beaten 5-0 at home. Wark loved playing at Portman Road. A Saint-Étienne team containing the immaculate Michel Platini and one of the great Dutch players of the 70s, Johnny Rep, were beaten 4-1 away in one of Ipswich's greatest performances in the quarter-finals, Wark scoring only once on this occasion. Naturally he scored again in the 3-1 home return game. In the semi-finals, Ipswich beat the Germans 1. FC Köln 1-0 in both legs, Wark, predictably, scoring the goal in the home tie.

AZ Alkmaar '67's route to the final only became truly testing in the quarters and semis as they overcame near-neighbours in Belgium's Lokeren 2-1 in the last eight, followed by a 4-1 two-leg victory against the French side Sochaux in the last four. Going into the final, AZ '67' had defeated Feyenoord to win the Dutch Eredivisie league title with six games to spare, so this was a team in a rich vein of form. Fortunately the same could be said of Bobby Robson's fine Ipswich team.

One of the most impressive players I saw play live was Kevin Beattie. He was tremendously powerful, tremendously quick, a great tackler, possessing a hammer of a left foot. Sadly, Beattie's later career was ravaged by injury, particularly to his knees. This proved to be his last season at Ipswich Town, and although he scored a thunderbolt free kick against Bohemians in the second round, and played in the 4-1 trouncing of Saint-Étienne, Beattie was not selected for this final. When I saw him play at Loftus Road against Queens Park Rangers in 1976, a game which Ipswich won 1-0, Beattie was mightily impressive, a rock-like, imposing central defender.

At five feet 11 inches, Paul Cooper was not especially tall for a goalkeeper, but in over 500 games for Ipswich Cooper proved to be a highly reliable and agile keeper. In 1979–1980, Cooper saved eight of ten penalty kicks he faced, a record for a goalkeeper in English top-flight football. Cooper was named Player of the Year by Ipswich supporters at the end of this 1980–81 season. He was unfortunate to be the only player in this team not to achieve international status. The reason: Peter Shilton and Ray Clemence were his rivals to the national goalkeeping position.

At right full-back, Mick Mills was one of the outstanding servants to this Ipswich Town team. Born in Godalming four miles from my home (I played against his brother back in the 1970s), Mills was capable of playing in either full-back position. He was strong in the tackle, consistent, unflustered, the latter characteristic a good one for a defender. Bobby Robson appointed Mills captain of his team in 1971 five years after the Godalming-born player started his career with Ipswich. Mills would play only one more season after this, completing a 16-year stay with the Suffolk club. The most successful period for Mills and Ipswich came between 1977 and 1982. Surprise winners of the 1978 FA Cup in 1978, beating Arsenal 1-0, Ipswich finished in the top five of the league in five successive seasons. Aged 33, Mills found himself surplus to Robson's requirements in 1982, joining Southampton. He continued to play consistently in over 100 games for The Saints, but Ipswich Town were his team, a fact proven by over 600 appearances in all competitions for them. Mills also played 42 times for England.

Terry Butcher was simply a tower of strength in the centre of Ipswich Town's defence. A big man, he was utterly heroic at times, fearless and a great leader on the pitch. Butcher played 271 league games for Ipswich. Ipswich were pipped for the 1st Division title in 1981 by Aston Villa, a year in which the traditional Manchester, Liverpool and London 'powerhouses' were made to play second fiddle. Upon leaving Ipswich, Butcher joined an exodus of English players joining Glasgow Rangers in Scotland. Butcher's passion on the pitch in Scotland occasionally spilled over into disputing referee's decisions, but the supporters loved him for his undying passion. Butcher played 77 times for England during the 1980s, his international career ending in 1990. The image of Butcher's blood-soaked, bandaged head in a 1989 World Cup qualifying game with Sweden is as vivid today as the blood that poured from his wound. Russell Osman was Butcher's centre-back partner, a player good enough to win 11 England caps, but what a shame Beattie's injury-blighted career prevented his appearance here.

What an outstanding asset to Ipswich Town John Wark was. Wark's affinity with the club proved so deep that he played for them not one, not twice, but three times, making 266, 89 and 154 league appearances (totalling 509) between 1975 and 1997. Wark scored 94 league goals during these three spells. The Scot moved to Liverpool in 1984, staying at Anfield for four seasons, scoring 28 league goals in 70 appearances. In between his last two spells at Ipswich, Wark played 32 league games for Middlesbrough, but clearly the Scotsman had a long-running love affair with Ipswich. Wark's achievement of scoring 14 goals in this UEFA Cup season equalled the record held by José Altafini of AC Milan from the 1962–63 European Cup campaign. Wark helped Ipswich to two successive second-placed finishes in the 1st Division in 1980 and 1981, behind Liverpool and Aston Villa respectively. Wark was so highly regarded at Portman Road that he won the club's Player of the Year award four times. He won the respect of his fellow professionals too, winning the PFA Player of the Year award in this 1980–81 season. Astonishingly, Wark scored 36 goals from midfield in all competitions in 1980–81. He also scored 20 goals in his final season at Portman Road in 1982–83.

Signed by Liverpool, Wark even outscored the prolific Ian Rush to become the club's leading scorer in 1984–85. An ankle injury, followed by an Achilles heel injury denied him more game time at Anfield, and when John Barnes signed for Liverpool from Watford, Wark returned to Ipswich for his second spell at Portman Road. In 1988–89, Wark was equal top scorer at Ipswich with strikers Dalian Atkinson and Jason Dozzell. Two seasons back at Ipswich, and Wark won Player of the Year in both seasons.

Wark played 29 times for Scotland, scoring seven goals. Perhaps the reason he didn't score more often for his country was due to the fact he was sporadically chosen as a defender. Wark's goal-scoring record, his professionalism and commitment, make him one of the greatest ever Ipswich Town players. Wark had the happy knack, as Martin Peters had before him, and Bryan Robson had after him, of arriving late in the penalty area to score vital goals.

What a midfield this Ipswich side had. Alongside Wark in the centre of the park were the two 'Dutch masters', Frans Thijssen and Arnold Mühren. In a period of the highest quality Dutch football, kick-started by Johan Cruyff's imperious Ajax side of the early 1970s, neither Mühren or Thijssen played that many times for their national team. Yet how they shone in this Ipswich team. There seemed to be a greater inherent understanding of the game of football in the Netherlands during the 1970s and 1980s; a shrewder tactical acumen, an infinitely superior technical level – and this was before the second wave of 'Dutch masters' Gullit, Van Basten and Rijkaard came along.

Thijssen's performances were terrific in his short three-season-plus stint at Portman Road, combining technique and supreme athleticism. In this 1980–81 season his standout skills won him the English Footballer of the Year award. He scored in both legs of this UEFA Cup Final. Transferring to Brian Clough's Nottingham Forest in 1983, Thijssen's form dipped. A personality clash, I wonder? Frans Thijssen played just 14 times for Holland, but what a stirring cameo he provided at Portman Road 1979–1983.

Arnold Mühren was a Dutch player in the classical mould. A cultured, stylish player, Mühren began his professional career with Volendam in Holland, before swiftly signing for older brother Gerrie's Ajax. Gerrie had won the European Cup three years running. There is a footballing pedigree in the Mühren family. The younger Mühren's class is evinced by his being one of a handful of players to have won all three European competitions; the European Cup in 1973; this UEFA Cup in 1981; and the European Cup Winners Cup upon returning to Ajax in 1987. A quality player, Arnold Mühren. His first spell at Ajax ended in 1974 when he transferred to Twente Enschede, his new club winning the KNVB Cup (the Dutch equivalent of the English FA Cup) in 1977. Prior to this success, Twente reached the final of the UEFA Cup in 1975, losing that game to Jupp Heynckes' extraordinary hat-trick at the Diekman Stadion, Enschede. Interestingly, the classy Mühren was only a substitute in the home leg of this 1980–81 UEFA Cup Final, where Thijssen, his former Twente Enschede teammate, played in both games.

Mühren moved to Manchester United, winning two FA Cup trophies in 1983 and 1985, although for the latter game he lost his starting position to the Dane Jesper Olsen. Mühren played only 23 times for Holland, but his crowning glory came, aged 37, when he helped his country win the 1988 European Championships, defeating hosts West Germany 2-1 in the semi-finals, then beating the Soviet Union 2-0 in the final in Munich, the game in which Marco Van Basten volleyed THAT goal from an oblique angle. Mühren retired the following season, aged 38. Like the great Cruyff, watching Arnold Mühren was a reminder that football can be an art form, a thing of beauty.

With orthodox wingers gradually being cast aside, Bobby Robson's Ipswich Town, ironically, bore more of a mark of the great Ajax side of the early 70s with the likes of Mühren filling in to the wide positions, and Mills and left-back Steve McCall being asked to overlap when the occasion arose. Without traditional wide men, Ipswich were happily graced with three excellent 'front men' on this occasion, Eric Gates, Alan Brazil and Paul Mariner.

Gates played 345 games for Ipswich, scoring a total of 96 goals in all competitions. He began his Ipswich career in 1973 as an 18-year-old, ending his time at Portman Road in 1985. County Durham-born, Gates then moved to the north-east to join Sunderland, scoring a further 55 goals in 219 games, maintaining his average of one goal every four games. A determined, tricky player, Eric Gates won two caps for England. This 1981 UEFA Cup Final was the pinnacle of his career.

Alan Brazil, the stockily built, guileful Scotsman was at six foot, taller than he first appeared. Difficult to dispossess, smart on the turn, Brazil's average goal-scoring record for Ipswich was even better than that of Gates, scoring 80 goals in 210 games 1976–1983. Like Gates, Brazil's importance to this Ipswich team cannot be underestimated. The season after this UEFA Cup triumph, Brazil's 22 league goals placed him second in the 1st Division scoring list, behind only the evergreen and ever-industrious Kevin Keegan at Southampton. Moving to Tottenham Hotspur, Brazil's impact was comparatively subdued, although he scored four times in the club's run to the 1984 UEFA Cup Final. The Scotsman moved again at the end of the 1984 season, but a recurring back injury restricted his appearances over his two-year stay with Manchester United – and he faced stiff competition for a starting place from Mark Hughes, Frank Stapleton and Peter Davenport for striking roles. Alan Brazil played 13 times for Scotland. Latterly, Brazil has become a much-listened-to sports media pundit on Talk Sport Radio, following stints on GMTV and Sky Sports television.

Paul Mariner worked hard to overcome the view that he was 'just an old-fashioned centre-forward'. Fifty-six goals in 135 games for Plymouth Argyle won him his contract at Ipswich Town. Mariner gave and took plenty of stick with opposing centre-halves, gradually improving technically under the guidance of Bobby Robson at Portman Road. Mariner won the Man of the Match award in the 1978 FA Cup Final against Arsenal. His improving performances for Ipswich saw him achieve international recognition. In 35 games for England he scored 13 times, a creditable return. Mariner scored six times during this UEFA Cup run. Not a prolific goal-scoring centre-forward, Mariner's attributes as a target man compensated for this minor blemish on his record. Ultimately he did score 96 goals in 260 league appearances for Ipswich and formed an excellent triumvirate with Gates and Brazil. Transferring to Arsenal as a player in his 30s, Mariner made a good start to his Highbury career, but managed only 17 goals in 80 starts for his new club. Mariner is best remembered as an integral part of Bobby Robson's successful Ipswich Town side. Internationally, Mariner lost his place as the more mobile and technical Gary Lineker and Peter Beardsley (a magical pairing at times for England) came to the fore.

AZ '67' were led from the front in this two-legged final by Johnny Metgod, the Dutchman whose form subsequently led to transfers to Real Madrid, Nottingham Forest and Tottenham Hotspur, and Feyenoord. Metgod's specialism, the free kick, was best witnessed during his time at Forest's City Ground. In goal for AZ, Eddy Treijtel had won this UEFA Cup competition in 1974 with Feyenoord. In the centre of defence, Ronald Spelbos played 241 league games for AZ, earning 21 caps for Holland. Only a knee injury prevented him playing part in Holland's 1980 European Championship triumph. Centre-back and captain Hugo Hovenkamp suffered the same cruel injury setback as Spelbos, only earlier, as he was forced to withdraw from Holland's 1978 World Cup squad. Like Spelbos, his appearance record is almost totally in synch with his teammate, playing 239 league games for AZ. Hovenkamp was chosen 31 times for Holland.

In midfield, Jan Peters also appeared 31 times for Holland, most famously scoring the two goals that earned the Dutch a 2-0 victory against England at Wembley in 1977. Peters' performances for AZ (32 goals in 120 league appearances) won him a transfer to Italy where he spent four seasons playing with Genoa and Atalanta.

At number 9, Kristen Nygaard, a Danish striker who scored 11 times in 36 appearances for his country, comprised one part of AZ's spearhead in this UEFA Cup competition. Nygaard scored 104 times in 363 league games for AZ during his ten years at the club. Partnering Nygaard, Dutch striker Kees Kist was even more prolific. Kist scored 196 goals in 323 league appearances for AZ in a similar ten-year spell at the club. There appears to be a certain symmetry about AZ '67' as a football club! Overall Kist scored 259 goals in 441 games in all competitions for AZ – Kist was a serial goalscorer, fourth in the all-time Eredivisie Dutch League scorers list. At number 11 on this evening, Kees 'Pier' Tol scored over 100 goals in the Eredivisie, 86 of these in 238 league appearances for AZ. Clearly there were goals in this AZ team.

THE FINAL – 1ˢᵗ Leg
Frans Thijssen shone brightly in this match. Hovenkamp handled in the penalty area, allowing Wark to send Treijtel the wrong way with his penalty kick. In the 46ᵗʰ minute, Thijssen added a second, following up his own blocked shot to head a second at a crucial time in the game, giving Ipswich impetus. A lovely turn and

cross from Brazil allowed Mariner to notch a third. Thijssen, unsurprisingly, was named Man of the Match.

THE FINAL – 2ⁿᵈ Leg

Ipswich started brightly, Thijssen lashing a magnificent volley to give the English club an overall, apparently unassailable 4-0 aggregate lead. AZ were not lying down meekly however. Two headed goals from Metgod and Welzl brought the fighting Dutch club back into the tie. A fine angled volley by Wark made the aggregate score 5-2, but AZ laid siege to the Ipswich goal. Further strikes from Tol and a fierce, deflected free kick from Jos Jonker brought the tie back to 4-5 in favour of Robson's team. Ipswich managed to hold on in the face of the AZ storm, winning their one and only European trophy by the tiniest of margins.

1983–84 UEFA CUP FINAL
1ˢᵗ Leg: Anderlecht 1v 1 Tottenham Hotspur
2ⁿᵈ Leg: Tottenham Hotspur 1 v 1 Anderlecht
Tottenham Hotspur 4-3 on penalties

Now this is a final that is indelibly etched in my mind. Tottenham's days as a league-winning team (the 50s and 60s) were long behind them, but they were then, and to some extent, remain a magnificent cup team. Winners of the FA Cup in 1981 and 1982 when blessed with World Cup winners Ossie Ardiles and Ricky Villa in their side, Tottenham's spirit, especially in the home leg of this final at White Hart Lane was immense. Belgian football was in the middle of a purple period and how Anderlecht made Tottenham work for this memorable English victory. Victory sounds a little over-exultant in a way as both ties were drawn and extra time at White Hart Lane could not separate the sides, but what a match the second leg was, full of incident and an atmosphere I would suggest unmatched in any other British team-involved UEFA Cup Final I have ever witnessed. My wife and I were fortunate indeed to be present at 'Super Saturday' in 2012 during the London Olympics. A work colleague happened to be present at White Hart Lane for this 'Super Spurs' triumph – he felt the noise might have matched our experience in the Olympic Stadium. It sounded awesome in 1984 – it must have been some atmosphere if it any way matched 2012.

Route to the Final

Tottenham drew the Irish team Drogheda United in the first round – and won 14-0 on aggregate! A splendid 6-2 aggregate victory over Feyenoord saw them through the second round, Steve Archibald and Tony Galvin each scoring twice in a 4-2 home win, Galvin scoring again as Tottenham impressively won 2-0 in Rotterdam. Tottenham's biggest scalp of the competition came in the third round with the defeat of Bayern Munich. Tottenham lost in Germany to an 86ᵗʰ-minute Michael Rummenigge goal, but triumphed in the return leg at White Hart Lane courtesy of goals from Archibald and Mark Falco, the deciding goal coming just three minutes from time. In the quarter-finals the former Ipswich hero Alan Brazil scored both home and away as Tottenham defeated Austria Wien 4-2,

Archibald again scoring in the home leg. The Croatians Hajduk Split proved an altogether harder nut to crack in the semi-finals. Spurs were beaten 2-1 in Split, despite an early lead established by Falco. In the return, Micky Hazard's sixth-minute goal was enough to see Tottenham into the final on away goals.

Anderlecht had a series of closer games in order to reach the final, their biggest challenge coming from Brian Clough's Nottingham Forest in a semi-final contest (the second leg at least) that was mired in controversy. Anderlecht were awarded a dubious penalty converted by Kenneth Brylle, and in the last minute, Forest had a goal disallowed. Two late goals from England international Steve Hodge had given Forest a two-goal advantage going into the second leg. Ultimately, Erwin Vandenbergh's 88th-minute goal in Brussels denied Forest a tilt at Tottenham in an all-English final. To this day, Forest feel they were wrongfully denied that opportunity.

Curiously, the away team scored first in each leg of the two final ties near the hour mark. Equally oddly, the equaliser came four or five minutes from the end from each home team in each tie. Neat symmetry. These teams literally could scarcely be separated over 210 minutes of gripping cup-tie football.

Between the posts for Tottenham for these two ties, Tony Parks only played because the unflappable Ray Clemence was injured. Parks would make his mark in memorable fashion in the second leg of this final. Parks played for 15 different clubs in a 250 league appearances career, only playing for Tottenham 37 times in an eight-year career at the club. Ask a Tottenham fan if they remember Tony Parks and 1984 will flood straight into the mind. Parks played 24 times during this 1983–84 season. The only other season he played anywhere near this amount of games came in 1987–88, when he played 19 times.

A Tottenham favourite, Chris Hughton played at left-back, while on the right was Danny Thomas. Hughton played over 300 games for Spurs during a 13-year stay at the club. Hughton was equally adept in defence or as an auxiliary attacking full-back, his attacking sensibilities stemming from his career beginnings as a winger. Injury blighted his later time with Tottenham, but during the early 1980s Hughton became an integral part of Tottenham's teams that often enjoyed cup successes (FA Cup winners 1981, 1982, League Cup runners-up to Liverpool when Steve Archibald's goal left them only three minutes from another victory, only for Ronnie Whelan to equalise, score again in extra time, Ian Rush sealing matters later on). Hughton played 53 times for the Republic of Ireland, becoming the first mixed race player to play for the country. Latterly Hughton managed Newcastle United, Birmingham City, Norwich City and Brighton and Hove Albion, the last club with a degree of success, earning The Seagulls a place in the Premiership for the first time in the club's history in 2017.

What a career the indefatigable Graham Roberts had. Released as a schoolboy by Southampton, Portsmouth gave him a chance but sold him to non-league Dorchester Town. Local rivals Weymouth stepped in to sign him, and after 29 games on the Dorset coast, Tottenham Hotspur decided to give him an opportunity in the professional game in 1980. From this moment in time, Roberts played for Tottenham, Glasgow Rangers, Chelsea and West Bromwich Albion – he must have had something about him. That something was an inner steel, a never-say-die spirit. He also earned six caps for England. Roberts it was who scored Tottenham's goal in the second leg of this UEFA Cup Final. Roberts never knew when he was beaten. An iconic image remains of Roberts in the FA Cup Final of 1981, the player missing three teeth, but refusing to leave the field. Roberts played 209 league games for Spurs, scoring 23 goals, playing generally as a central defender, although he could be deployed as an uncompromising defensive midfielder with licence to join the attack. At Chelsea, Roberts helped the club win the old 2nd Division title in 1989–1990 by a handsome margin. Alongside Roberts for Spurs on this evening, Paul Miller played a similar amount of league games for the club (208), again crucially notching the only goal in the first leg of this final.

Gary Stevens (not to be confused with the Everton defender) played 147 league games for Spurs, winning seven England caps during his time at White Hart Lane. Versatile, Stevens could play either in defence or midfield, his role in these two games as a right-sided midfield player. Stevens bookended his professional career on England's south coast, with Brighton and Portsmouth, scoring the second equaliser for Brighton in the 2-2 drawn 1984 FA Cup Final, only for Manchester United to trounce The Seagulls 4-0 in the replay. A cultured player, Stevens was chosen for the 1986 World Cup Squad, making two substitutes appearances. Everton's Gary Stevens was also in the squad – confusing for manager Bobby Robson!

The terrific servant Steve Perryman, whose industry and appetite for the game were unquenchable, was joined in midfield by the talented Micky Hazard and specialist wide man Tony Galvin. Hazard was spotted playing for his school team in Sunderland by a Tottenham scout. He trained with the club from the age of 14, becoming apprenticed at Tottenham aged 16. Hazard suffered serious homesickness. Pining for the north-east, he returned home six times in his early life at Tottenham. He played only 91 league games for Spurs before transferring to Chelsea. Hazard provided the assists for both of Tottenham's goals in this UEFA Cup Final. A silky ball player, he was perhaps unfairly compared to the outrageously talented Glenn Hoddle at Tottenham 1978–1985. At Chelsea he played 81 league games, and like Roberts, played a significant part in the club's 2nd Division title win in 1989–1990. Moving to Swindon Town to play under Hoddle in 1990, Hazard's influence in midfield was tangible, helping the Wiltshire club into the Premiership for the only time in 1993. The experience proved to be a sour one for Swindon, conceding 100 goals and suffering instant relegation back to the Championship.

Ostensibly Tony Galvin was a left-winger, though his role at White Hart Lane demanded he played as much as a wide left midfield player capable of tracking back to help his defence whenever required. A physically strong player with a good touch, Galvin literally galvanised Tottenham to great effect 1978–1987. Born in Huddersfield, Galvin qualified to play for the Republic of Ireland through parentage, having already played for England schoolboys. He played 29 times for the Republic, playing in all three 1988 European Championship games. By this stage of his career, Galvin had joined Sheffield Wednesday, but it is his appearances for Spurs that linger in the memory (over 200), scoring on

31 occasions. Interestingly, like the immaculate Steve Heighway at Liverpool, Galvin was academically gifted, attaining a degree in Russian before joining Spurs, and latterly teaching in a London college.

A prolific scorer in junior football in the London borough of Hackney, Mark Falco signed for Tottenham in 1978, playing in a total of 236 games for the club, scoring 98 times in all competitions. Tall, muscular, good in the air, equally adept on the ground, Falco enjoyed a successful eight-year spell at Tottenham. Latterly he played for Watford, Glasgow Rangers, Queens Park Rangers and Millwall, scoring goals wherever he played.

Alongside Falco in attack, the Scotsman Steve Archibald could have passed as a Scandinavian with his fair hair and Vikingesque beard. Archibald certainly pillaged his fair share of goals in an illustrious career at home and abroad in a span of 22 years. Yet Archibald began his career as a midfield player with Clyde north of the border in the Scottish 1st Division. Billy McNeill, then-manager of Aberdeen, bought him to play in the Scottish first tier, converting him to striker where he scored 29 league goals in 76 games. Archibald won the Scottish Premier Division title in 1980, playing under Alex Ferguson. When Tottenham came hunting at the end of that season, Archibald ventured south of the border. In his first season 1980–81 Archibald topped the English 1st Division scoring list and Tottenham won the FA Cup, a feat repeated in 1982. Archibald then won this UEFA Cup trophy in 1984. The Scotsman scored 77 goals in 189 total appearances for Spurs. A new challenge beckoned at the end of the 1984 season. Transferring to Barcelona, Archibald helped the Nou Camp club win their first La Liga title in 11 years in his first season. In 1986 Barca reached the European Cup Final only to be denied by the Romanians Steaua Bucharest on penalties. Archibald played 27 times for Scotland, scoring four times 1980–86. A fine finisher, Archibald's time at Tottenham is cemented in the memory for his strike partnerships with Falco and Garth Crooks, the latter pairing particularly memorable. Crooks was an unused substitute in these two 1984 UEFA Cup Final ties.

Belgian football, firmly in the ascendancy during the late 1970s and early 1980s, was always going to provide Tottenham with the sternest of tests. Anderlecht, one of Belgium's foremost clubs throughout the decades, happened to be managed by a man who was legendary himself in Belgian football. Paul Van Himst was such a scoring threat during his own career (233 goals in 457 league games for Anderlecht) that he was constantly targeted by opponents by fair means or foul. Van Himst won the Belgian league title an astonishing eight times with Anderlecht. Van Himst also scored 30 goals in 81 appearances for Belgium. He won the Golden Shoe for Belgian best player in a season four times. In 2003, Van Himst was named the Golden Player by the Belgian FA as their most outstanding player of the previous 50 years. Some pedigree, Paul Van Himst. Could the 1984 Anderlecht team live up to their manager's reputation?

The answer: Anderlecht made an almighty good fist of enhancing their manager's hallowed status. Georges Grün at right back had been part of the 1983 UEFA Cup-winning team, the Belgians overcoming Benfica of Portugal 2-1 on aggregate. With Anderlecht, Grün went on to win the Belgian league title three years running. Joining Italian club Parma Grün was part of their Coppa

Italia cup-winning team in 1992, and their European Cup Winners Cup-winning team of 1993. Grün played in three World Cups for Belgium – 1986, 1990, 1994, appearing for his country 77 times. Grün could be deployed as a man-marker at full-back or centre-back, but was stylish enough to bring the ball out of defence and play the perfect pass.

The stand-out player in Anderlecht's defence was the Danish libero/sweeper Morten Olsen. After 40 games in his home country with B1901, 1970–72, starting out as a right-winger, then central midfielder, Olsen transferred to Cercle Brugge in Belgium. He would spend the next 14 years of his career – his peak years – playing his club football in Belgium. At Brugge, Olsen played in every position except goalkeeper. Little wonder the Dane was so comfortable on the ball. This was a truly accomplished footballer, a master technician. Yet Olsen did not win his first trophy until moving to Anderlecht in 1980–81. Eventually Olsen would captain Anderlecht. Following Anderlecht's UEFA Cup triumph in 1983, Olsen was named Danish Player of the Year. Olsen, aged 36, joined 1. FC Köln in Germany, spending his last three years of professional football there. Given the start to his career as a winger, Olsen did not score many goals for clubs or country, but under Danish team manager, the German Sepp Piontek, Olsen was given licence to bring the ball out of defence and supplement the attack. Supremely skilful, Olsen sits only marginally beneath the great central defenders Franz Beckenbauer, Ruud Krol and Franco Baresi. Olsen's star shone brightly prior to Denmark's finest hour (the 1992 European Championship win), but a total of 102 international caps reflects his standing in Danish football. He won the Danish Player of the Year award again in 1986 following an impressive World Cup campaign. As a manager of his country, Olsen also coached over 100 games, without the overall success of his own playing career.

In the midfield, another foreign export excelled for Anderlecht. Belgian-born to Sicilian parents, Enzo Scifo earned the nickname 'Little Pele' in youth football, scoring 432 goals in four seasons as a junior. For the best part of the 1980s and 1990s, Scifo was rightly regarded as one of the most talented midfield players in the world. Only 18 years old at the time of this UEFA Cup Final, Scifo's precocious skills earned him a transfer to Inter Milan in 1987. Like so many star players in their own country, Scifo struggled a little in Italy initially. Transferring to Bordeaux in France, and hampered by injuries, Scifo's career again stalled. A spell at Auxerre in France revived his fortunes, 25 goals in 67 league games bringing about a return to Italy with Torino. A further UEFA Cup Final appearance in 1992 transpired (Torino losing out on away goals to Ajax), a Coppa Italia win occurring in 1993. Scifo returned again to France, winning the French Ligue 1 with AS Monaco in 1997. Returning for a second spell with Anderlecht, Scifo won a fourth Belgian title with the club in 1999–2000.

Internationally, Scifo was the youngest-ever player (at that time) to play in the European Championships of 1984, aged 18. He went on to play in the next four World Cups for Belgium, 1986, 1990, 1994 and 1998, being named the best young player in the 1986 tournament. Likened to the Italian greats Gianni Rivera and Giancarlo Antognoni, Scifo was sometimes berated like these Italian idols for perceived lack of work-rate, but no one could doubt his technical abilities, his touch, his vision, his dribbling ability. Scifo played 82 international games for Belgium, scoring 18 times.

René Vandereycken actually spent more time at Club Brugge, playing 233 league games there, whereas he only played 94 league games for Anderlecht. The midfielder scored 63 times for Club Brugge, 13 in his time at Anderlecht. Vandereycken was capped by Belgium 50 times, going on to coach the national team 2006–09.

Wearing number 11, Kenneth Brylle Larsen kept the better known (in Britain) Frank Arnesen out of the starting 11. At Vejle Boldklub in his native Denmark Brylle scored enough goals to attract Anderlecht's interest. Moving to Belgium in 1979, Brylle scored a respectable 50 goals in 122 league games for the Belgian club in a five-year spell. After stints with PSV Eindhoven in Holland and Marseille in France, Brylle returned to Belgium, winning the Belgian championship with Club Brugge, scoring 49 goals in 101 matches in all competitions. Brylle played 16 times for the Danish national team.

Trumping Brylle as Anderlecht's main spearhead and goalscorer, Erwin Vandenbergh topped the scoring lists in Belgium six times across three clubs: Lierse, Anderlecht and Gent. In 1980, Vandenbergh was the top goalscorer in Europe with an impressive return of 39 goals from 34 games. He also notched 20 goals in 48 appearances for Belgium.

In a team packed with goal threat, the other striker in this Anderlecht 11, Alex Czerniatynski, had a long 22-year career in Belgian football, scoring over 200 goals. His peak years were 1982–1993, scoring 43 goals in 87 league games for Anderlecht, following this up with 46 for Standard Liege, and 45 for Royal Antwerp. Czerniatynski also scored six goals in 31 games for Belgium. Tottenham were to be subjected to a serious attacking barrage over these two ties.

Among the subs for Anderlecht was the other Dane, Frank Arnesen, who would get the nod over Brylle for the second leg of this final. Arnesen's record is again impressive, winning the Dutch Eredivisie three times as an Ajax player (1977, 1979, 1980). Ajax also reached four KNVB Cup Finals (the Dutch equivalent of the English FA Cup) but won on only one occasion. At Ajax, Arnesen scored 75 times in 205 league games. A short spell with Valencia in Spain reaped 13 goals. 50 league games with Anderlecht produced a further 15 goals. Returning to Holland, Arnesen won the Eredivisie three years in a row with PSV Eindhoven (1986, 1987, 1988). Arnesen also notched 14 goals in 52 games for his country, Denmark. A talented player, Frank Arnesen. Latterly he has coached under Bobby Robson at PSV, 1991–93, and been Sporting Director at both Tottenham Hotspur and Chelsea. Arnesen is credited as a coach for discovering the Brazilian Ronaldo, as well as Dutch stars Jaap Stam, Ruud Van Nistelrooy and Arjen Robben. Clearly the Dane had an eye for talent.

Another of the substitutes in the first leg, Franky Vercauteren, spent 12 years at Anderlecht, amassing 367 league appearances, scoring 93 league goals. Vercauteren won four Belgian league titles, two Belgian Cups, two European Cup Winners Cups, and the 1983 UEFA Cup. Quite a handy substitute. Vercauteren also played for Belgium 63 times, scoring nine goals. 'The Little Prince' as he was known, captained the side in the second leg at White Hart Lane.

Anderlecht could replace their main three strikers with three of virtually equivalent quality. The Icelandic forward Arnór Gudjohnsen scored 40 goals in 139 league games for Anderlecht in a seven-year spell with the club. Gudjohnsen came on as a substitute at White Hart Lane. It was his misfortune to be the player whose final penalty kick was saved by Tony Parks to give the English club the trophy. Arnor is the father of the former Chelsea striker Eider Gudjohnsen. Arnor played 73 times for Iceland, scoring 14 goals. Extraordinarily, father and son almost played international football together, Eider (17) coming on to replace his father (34) against Estonia in 1996. A missed opportunity!

THE FINAL – 1st Leg
The first match, by its very nature as the opening tie, lacked the sheer drama of the White Hart Lane return. Paul Miller headed Tottenham ahead from a right-wing corner. Morten Olsen took advantage after Parks failed to hold on to a shot from long range to restore parity.

THE FINAL – 2nd leg
Olsen was again instrumental in Anderlecht taking the lead at White Hart Lane, his clever through ball with the outside of his right boot setting Czerniatynski clear to lift the ball over Parks. Tottenham piled the pressure on the Anderlecht goal, but were always vulnerable to the Belgian side's splendid array of attackers on the break. Spurs, seeking a psychological lift in this toughest and tightest of finals, were wearing the all-white strip made famous by Real Madrid. Ossie Ardiles came on as a sub. Archibald had a shot saved; Ardiles somehow contrived to hit the crossbar from two yards out – but the irrepressible Roberts scored in the very next attack, the plucky warrior squeezing between two defenders to guide the ball in from three yards. The last six minutes were insufficient to separate two wonderful football teams in this incident-packed game. Tottenham's players were exhausted at the end of the 90 minutes. Ardiles had been a key player for Tottenham in preceding seasons, but having left the club because of the Falklands War he'd lost a regular starting place. Tottenham also had to play without Glenn Hoddle in these two games due to injury. Hoddle it was who'd inspired the 6-2 aggregate defeat of Feyenoord earlier in the competition following criticism of him by the great Johan Cruyff. It can be argued that Tottenham won this UEFA Cup without their two most influential, creative players playing a full part.

Even more exhausted after a further 30 minutes failed to separate the two teams of matadors, Tottenham found a way to win through sheer willpower and a massive desire to win. A penalty shoot-out never fails to provide drama, but the high-quality events of the previous 120 minutes made any loser of this game unlucky in the extreme. Morten Olsen's kick was saved by Parks. Roberts and Falco scored comfortably. Gary Stevens sent the Anderlecht keeper the wrong way. 3-1. Scifo repeated Stevens' feat to make it 2-3. Archibald, socks rolled down in typical fashion, made it 4-2. Vercauteren sent Parks the wrong way. The noise level when looking at TV footage is audible; the tension as taut as a tightrope. Danny Thomas's penalty was saved and Anderlecht revived to 3-4. Roberts and Archibald consoled the distraught Thomas. Gudjohnsen's penalty kick arrowed into the corner, but Parks leapt to save magnificently. Parks had saved a kick into each corner of his goal.

Somehow Tottenham found enough creative spark and unquenchable team spirit without Hoddle at all, and Ardiles for the first part of this match, to overcome an Anderlecht team replete with firepower. This was one of the most memorable British European trophy-winning matches I can recall. Tottenham, ostensibly without their match-winning players, won against all the odds.

1986–87 UEFA CUP FINAL
1st Leg: IFK Göteborg 1 v 0 Dundee United
2nd leg: Dundee United 1 v 1 IFK Göteborg
IFK Göteborg 2-1 on aggregate

An unlikely final of a major European competition on paper this one, yet Göteborg had previously won the competition in 1982. This proved to be Dundee United's only European final. Göteborg's captain Glen Hysen would later play 72 league games for Liverpool.

Route to the Final
Dundee United beat Lens of France 2-1 on aggregate in the first round, Universitea Craiova of Romania 3-1 in the second round, Hadjuk Split of Croatia 2-0 in the third round, claiming their biggest scalp in the quarter-finals by beating the mighty Barcelona home and away (3-1 on aggregate). In the Nou Camp United stunned Barcelona with two goals in the last five minutes to reach the semi-finals. The Germans of Borussia Möenchengladbach were dispatched 2-0 in the last four, the Scots once again defying the odds by winning by two clear goals in Germany after a 0-0 stalemate at Tannadice Park.

IFK Göteborg enjoyed an untroubled run to the quarter-finals beating Czech, German and Belgian opposition before a run-in with the Italian giants Inter Milan in the last eight. A 0-0 draw in Gothenburg was followed by an impressive 1-1 draw in Milan, the Swedes progressing on away goals. Another surprising semi-finalist awaited them, Swarovski Tirol of Switzerland, IFK duly dismissing the Swiss 5-1 on aggregate, a 4-1 win in Gothenburg in the first leg making the outcome a formality. Aside from Inter, Barcelona and Möenchengladbach, Torino, Napoli, Atlético Madrid, Feyenoord and Bayer Leverkusen were among the other competitors in this 1986–87 UEFA Cup season. It was an impressive feat for Dundee United in reaching the final. Sadly, they could not take the final step.

Whatever happened to Scottish football? The halcyon days of Celtic and Rangers' European trophy glory happened in the misty, long-lamented days of the late 60s and early 70s. Alex Ferguson's Aberdeen revived Scottish European success with their 1983 European Cup Winners Cup win. A year later Dundee United, Scottish League champions from 1983, almost reached the premier European competition's final, losing out to Roma, despite claiming a 2-0 advantage in the home leg at Tannadice – Roma trumping that score with a 3-0 victory in the Olympic Stadium. One of the outstanding players from this Dundee United team, Richard Gough, moved to Tottenham Hotspur at the end of the 1985–86 season. Dundee United's defence still contained two excellent defenders in Maurice Malpas and David Narey. The long-serving one-club man Malpas played a total of 830 competitive games for Dundee United in a 21-year spell. With Malpas at right-back, Dundee United reached five Scottish Cup Finals in nine years. Only in the last of these did Malpas finally taste success with a 1-0 victory over Rangers in 1994. Malpas was the Scottish Footballer of the Year in 1991 and was rewarded for his loyalty to Dundee United with two testimonial matches in 1991 and 2000. He received 55 caps for Scotland.

Captain and centre-back in these two ties, David Narey, also enjoyed a near-lifetime of football with Dundee United, playing over 600 games in a 21-year spell. An outstanding athlete, Narey could play in defence or as an attacking midfielder. Leaving Tannadice in 1984, Narey had the misfortune to play in four losing Scottish Cup Finals, missing out on the 1994 success. Narey played 35 times for Scotland, scoring his only international goal with a sensational long-range shot against Brazil at the 1982 World Cup – if this is to be your only goal for your country, what a memorable way to achieve it.

In the centre of midfield, Jim McInally became a key defensive midfielder during his nine-year spell at Tannadice. His career had stuttered somewhat prior to his time with Dundee United, although he won the Player of the Year award in the 1984–85 season at Nottingham Forest. McInally's most productive time in football came in his first spell at Tannadice, a period in which he won ten caps for Scotland.

Alongside McInally, Billy Kirkwood appeared in nearly 400 games for the club, scoring 44 league goals. Starting out at Tannadice as a striker, Kirkwood top-scored for the club in 1976–77 and 1977–78. Kirkwood later managed the club, overseeing relegation from the top flight, and then promotion back to the top tier. Kirkwood proved to be the club's most offensive midfielder, David Bowman's solidity complementing him. Bowman joined Dundee United in a double transfer with McInally from Nottingham Forest, their careers intertwined as the two had briefly played together at Coventry City.

The final piece of Dundee United's midfield jigsaw was Eamonn Bannon, whose career encompassed Heart of Midlothian, Chelsea, Dundee United and a return to Hearts in Edinburgh. Once again Bannon's most productive form came at Tannadice where he scored 72 goals in 290 league games. Bannon played 11 times for Scotland.

Probably the best-known player in the Dundee United team was the livewire striker Paul Sturrock. Not an imposing physical specimen, Sturrock negated any perceived lack of strength with his positional play and lightness of touch. Sturrock knew where the goal was too. In two years of amateur football 1972–74 Sturrock scored over 150 goals, earning him a contract with Dundee United under manager Jim McLean in the summer of 1974. The skilful Sturrock didn't prove quite as prolific in the professional game as he had in 'junior' football, but netted 109 times in 385 league games for Dundee United. He jointly holds the record of scoring five goals in a game (against Greenock Morton in 1984) in the Scottish 1st Division, a record he shares with Marco Negri, Kenny Miller, Kris Boyd and Gary Hooper. Sturrock played 20 times for Scotland, scoring three goals. He went on to manage St Johnstone and Dundee United in Scottish football, moving south of the border to manage Plymouth Argyle to two promotions, followed by spells managing Southampton, Sheffield Wednesday and Swindon Town among others.

Ian Redford played in attack alongside Sturrock in these two ties. Redford enjoyed spells with Dundee, Rangers and then Dundee United in Scotland, his most prolific time as a goalscorer in top-flight football coming at Dundee with 35 league goals, adding 23 with Rangers and 20 with Dundee United. Redford scored a vital goal in the victory over Borussia Möenchengladbach in this season's semi-final.

Glen Hysén enjoyed a multinational playing career, beginning with IFK Göteborg in his home nation Sweden in 1978, transferring to PSV Eindhoven in Holland in 1983, returning for this successful trophy win for the Swedes for a stint lasting until 1987. He then moved to Fiorentina in Italy for two seasons until 1989. Hysén played three seasons at Liverpool in England, acquiring a reputation as a stylish defender, uncompromising in defence, but useful as an auxiliary attacker. Hysén forged a fine partnership with Alan Hansen at Anfield, Hansen's late career injuries forcing Hysén into a new centre-back pairing with Gary Ablett. The latter pairing prospered, but Hansen's were big shoes to fill. Two outstanding displays for Sweden against England in World Cup qualifying games ensured English interest in Hysén, Manchester United also keen to sign the Swede. Hysén was an integral part of the last Liverpool team to win the Premiership (or 1st Division title) in England in 1990 until the recent Liverpool champion side of 2020.

The Göteborg side did not contain many players well known to British football followers. What the Swedish sides had back in the 1980s and 1990s – and continue to have to the present day – is an abundance of unity. This is best exemplified by the fact that this particular Göteborg team contained two brothers, Tord and Tommy Holmgren. The best-known player outside of Hysén was probably the striker Stefan Pettersson. After 78 league games for Göteborg1984–88 (and 31 goals) Pettersson signed for Ajax of Amsterdam, substantially improving on his goal return with 99 goals in 195 league games. Returning to Göteborg after six seasons in Amsterdam, Pettersson scored a further 28 goals in 84 league games, making him noticeably Göteborg's biggest goal threat in this 1987 UEFA Cup Final. With Ajax, Pettersson won the Dutch league twice, the Dutch Cup once and triumphed again in the 1992 UEFA Cup Final (he scored again from the penalty spot), winning on away goals after a 2-2 aggregate draw with Torino of Italy.

Among the substitutes for Göteborg, Roland Nilsson enjoyed a fine spell with Sheffield Wednesday after making 124 league appearances for the Swedish club 1983–89. Nilsson played 151 league games for Wednesday, gaining vast popularity with the Hillsborough fans who felt he was the club's greatest-ever right-back. It makes it all the more surprising that Nilsson was only a substitute in the first leg of this final, especially as he won 116 caps for his country. Nilsson helped the Yorkshire club win the 1991 League Cup, the team finishing runners-up in both FA Cup and League Cup in 1993. Nilsson's finest hour with Sweden came when the Scandinavians surprised many by finishing third at the 1994 World Cup.

In the second leg of this UEFA Cup Final, Kevin Gallacher featured in attack for Dundee United. Gallacher scored 26 goals in 131 league games for the Scottish team 1983–1990, but his greatest achievement came as part of Blackburn Rovers' Premiership-winning side in 1994–95. Gallacher proved more effective in front of goal at Ewood Park, scoring 46 times in 144 league games. Two broken legs (one occurred at Highbury in those Arsenal Boxing Day games my family saw) marred his time at Blackburn. On the international scene, Gallacher contributed nine goals in 53 games for Scotland.

THE FINAL – 1st Leg
Both legs of the final were closely fought. United could make little headway against a resilient Swedish defence in Göteborg and left Scandinavia trailing by a solitary goal headed in from a left-wing corner-kick by Stefan Pettersson.

THE FINAL – 2nd Leg
Commentary of the second leg speaks of the 'Tannadice Roar'. Bright orange flags illuminated the ground. The Tannadice crowd chant "We shall not be moved". The decibel levels were huge, but no amount of Scottish passion could lift the players sufficiently to defeat the obdurate Swedes. Nilsson broke clear on the left, cut in and drove the ball in at the near post. Half-time and the Scots trailed 2-0 on aggregate. The roar of the crowd lifted the Dundee United players in the second half, John Clark scoring a consolation goal with a left-foot drive that entered the goal via a post. The Scots' effort cannot be denied, but Göteborg held on comfortably to deny Dundee United the ultimate glory that Celtic, Rangers and Aberdeen enjoyed before them.

THE SINGLE LEG FINALS
The first final to be decided by the course of a single match occurred in season 1997–98, an all-Italian final seeing Inter Milan defeat Lazio at the Parc des Princes in Paris. The Brits would have to wait a further two seasons before having a (beaten) finalist.

UEFA CUP FINAL 1999–2000
Galatasaray 0 v 0 Arsenal
Galatasaray 4-1 on penalties after extra time

After Dundee United's near-miss it took British teams another 13 years to reach a final of the UEFA Cup – and the end result was a goalless draw. This season's UEFA Cup Final brought together two teams who entered the 1999–2000 Champions League at the first time of asking, each team finishing third in the group stage of the premier European competition. Cue protests from teams that entered the UEFA Cup as high-placed clubs within their domestic leagues with the potential to win the trophy, only to be denied the opportunity by teams entering the UEFA Cup by the 'back door' route, reducing the chances of the teams starting out in the competition's inception of actually winning the thing. Such are the vagaries of qualification for the modern-day UEFA Cup, or Europa League as it is now called.

This was Galatasaray's first-ever European Final appearance, and Arsenal's first-ever UEFA Cup Final appearance. For Galatasaray, their 4-1 penalty triumph after a goalless 120 minutes formed part of a treble in this season, as they had already won the Turkish league and cup.

Route to the Final

Arsenal finished behind Barcelona and Fiorentina in their Champions League group, entering into the UEFA Cup at the third round in accordance with the rules. Arsenal defeated Nantes of France at this stage 6-3 on aggregate, the underrated Ray Parlour scoring a hat-trick in the away leg. Deportivo Coruna of Portugal were beaten by the same aggregate score in the next round. Werder Bremen of Germany were beaten by a similar overall score of 6-2 in the last eight. In the semi-finals, Arsenal defeated French club Lens 3-1 on aggregate.

Galatasaray met with stiff opposition in the third and fourth rounds, narrowly beating Bologna of Italy and the Germans Borussia Dortmund. Real Mallorca of Spain were dispatched 6-2 on aggregate in the quarter-finals. There could have been an all-English final, but Leeds United faltered at the last, beaten by the Turkish side 4-2 on aggregate in the semi-finals.

Arsenal went into this final as marginal favourites, their side containing the core of the defence built by George Graham: Seaman, Dixon, Adams and Keown. The only change if you discount the Adams/Bould axis (one could argue anyway that the Adams/Keown axis was just as strong) came with the Brazilian Sylvinho taking the place of Nigel Winterburn at left-back. Sylvinho played 55 league games in two seasons at Arsenal. Sylvinho's popularity with Arsenal fans was based on his raiding runs and the occasional spectacular goal. I would argue that Winterburn at his peak gave Arsenal more solidity at the back. Having said this, Sylvinho went on to play for Barcelona for five seasons, winning the Champions League twice in 2006 and 2009. At Arsenal, Sylvinho found himself replaced ultimately by another outstanding left-back, Ashley Cole.

What made Arsenal favourites for this UEFA Cup Final was the composition of its midfield and attack. It was a 'front five' to use archaic football parlance, of outstanding individuals, all of whom contributed fully to the team ethic. A 'front five' of international stars, nay, superstars. Alongside the tireless Ray Parlour in midfield were the French World Cup-winning stars Emmanuel Petit and Patrick Vieira. These two marvellous players remain the best individuals to grace the Arsenal midfield in recent memory. Petit, fair-haired, pony-tailed, rock star in appearance, belied his looks with endless energy and superlative technique. Manager Arsene Wenger knew what he was getting with 'Manu' Petit. Wenger managed AS Monaco 1987–1994, Petit's first professional club. When Wenger became Arsenal manager in 1996, Petit was instantly on his radar. Petit played 222 league games for Monaco 1988–1997, largely as a central or left-sided midfielder, winning the Coupe de France at the club (the French equivalent to the FA Cup). Monaco lost to Werder Bremen in the 1992 European Cup Winners Cup Final. Petit signed off his Monaco career by captaining the club to the French Ligue 1 title.

Joining Arsenal, Petit was switched to a defensive midfield role, allowing Patrick Vieira to be the one who surged forward to assist the attack. The power, poise and sheer skill of this awesome duo gave Arsenal the platform for much success in the early years of Wenger's Arsenal managerial career. Petit's presence helped Arsenal to win the English domestic league and cup double in his first season at the club, 1997–98. Moving to Barcelona in 2000, Petit suffered a series of niggling injuries. In conjunction with being asked to play in defence at the Nou Camp, it was not a happy time for the Frenchman. Returning to England, Petit played three seasons at Chelsea in south-west London. Although forming another impressive midfield partnership with Frank Lampard, Petit will always be remembered for his dynamic pairing with Vieira at Arsenal.

Patrick Vieira was quite simply the driving force in this era of Arsenal's great domestic success – and near-misses in European competition – under Arsene Wenger. The Senegalese-born Vieira, two inches taller than Petit, powered through challenges, his natural athleticism and energy, his highly competitive nature, making him one of the great modern box-to-box midfield players. Interestingly, Manchester United had their own variant of a box-to-box midfield payer in Roy Keane. Keane may have been noticeably shorter than Vieira, but my goodness how supercharged were their confrontations.

One season in 1994–95 at Cannes in France was enough to inspire AC Milan to sign Vieira. Sadly, Vieira's one season at the San Siro was virtually written off by injury. Wenger signed Vieira in 1996, so beginning a nine-year stint that ensured greatness for the Senegalese-born, French international in the pantheon of English football. Vieira played 279 league games at Arsenal. He didn't score that often (29 league goals) but his impact on the club was monumental. Firstly with the double of league and cup in 1997–98, secondly with another double triumph in 2002. In between times, Vieira suffered a rash of red cards. His disciplinary record did not deny him admirers. Alex Ferguson wanted to sign him for Manchester United. Petit's transfer to Barcelona along with Marc Overmars left Vieira feeling Arsenal had been noticeably weakened. When Tony Adams retired, Wenger made Vieira captain in an attempt to make him feel wanted at a time of dissatisfaction for Vieira, who also felt referees were biased against him in terms of his style of play. He also suffered periodic racial abuse during his time with Arsenal. Despite his misgivings, Vieira stayed with the club, his reward coming as part of Arsenal's 'Invincibles' side who won the 2003–04 Premiership without losing a single game, a record of 26 wins and 12 draws.

Petit and Overmars were gone, but fellow Frenchman Robert Pires starred for Arsenal; Sol Campbell formed the next generation of outstanding Gunners centre-back pairings with Kolo Touré; Ashley Cole was firmly established as the country's premier left-back; Gilberto Silva proved to be Vieira's best midfield ally since the almost irreplaceable Petit; Freddy Ljungberg provided mobility and goals from midfield; and Arsenal could boast the peerless Thierry Henry, regarded as Arsenal's best-ever striker, and lauded by his fellow professionals as the best foreign striker ever seen in the Premiership; and alongside Henry, Dennis Bergkamp was all silky touch and vision. In his final season with Arsenal, Vieira scored the winning goal in the 2005 FA Cup Final against Manchester United.

United laid siege to Arsenal's goal throughout the game. Arsenal resisted stoutly, took the game to extra time, and won the penalty shoot-out with Vieira scoring the crucial final penalty kick.

Vieira moved to Italy for the 2005–06 season, helping Juventus win the Italian Scudetto (Italian top-tier league), only for the title to be removed later due to a match-fixing scandal. Automatic relegation for Juve transpired. Ironically, Vieira played in the 2006 Champions League quarter-final against Arsenal, losing to his former club 2-0 on aggregate. Arsenal reached the final in that season without Vieira, losing 2-1 to Barcelona. Vieira promptly signed for Inter Milan for the 2006–07 season. At Inter Milan, Vieira won four successive Scudetto league titles. A persistent groin injury marred his later career in Milan. Returning to England in 2010, Vieira won the FA Cup with Manchester City. Once again disciplinary problems bedevilled Vieira, but his impact on top-flight European football over a 17-year period was undeniably significant.

On the international stage, Vieira won 107 caps for France, playing in the 1998 and 2006 World Cup Finals. He came on as a substitute in the 1998 final, setting up Petit for the third goal as France overcame Brazil 3-0. He started the 2006 final against Italy, leaving the field injured as France succumbed on penalties after a 1-1 draw. Vieira was also an integral part of France's triumph in the Euro 2000s, won by David Trezeguet's golden goal against Italy.

Pace, power, tackling ability, leadership, technique, vision, aggression, aerial prowess. Patrick Vieira had the lot. He was the complete midfield package; his only fault his suspect disciplinary record (he maintained he was being singled out by referees because of his athletic, aggressive style). If you wanted 'a soldier in the trenches', Patrick Vieira was your man.

Marc Overmars provided the width for Arsenal on the left in this 2000 UEFA Cup Final. The flying Dutchman was a major success story for Ajax prior to joining Arsenal, helping the Amsterdam club win three successive Eredivisie Dutch titles. In 136 league games for Ajax, Overmars scored 36 goals. Overmars was part of the young 1994–95 Champions League-winning Ajax team that defeated favourites AC Milan. Typical of Dutch footballers, Overmars possessed impressive technique allied to his bewitching pace and trickery. Yet his Arsenal career began fitfully. Pundits were not convinced initially, but by the end of the 1997–98 season Overmars won all doubters over, his winning goal against fierce rivals Manchester United an abiding memory. Overmars also scored the first goal in the 1998 FA Cup Final as the Gunners completed the double.

A nasty knee ligament injury curtailed Overmars' progress at Ajax. It was considered a risk Wenger buying Overmars because of the severity of the injury. Ultimately the quality of Overmars's play over 100 league games and a return of 25 goals made the Dutchman one of Arsenal's most effective players in his three seasons at the club.

Flattered by interest from Barcelona, Overmars was thrilled to move to the Nou Camp in the dual transfer with Manu Petit in 2000. Persistent knee problems blighted Overmars's time in Catalonia, preventing his dream move from being more successful. Barcelona failed to win any silverware in Overmars's three seasons with the club.

Overmars played 86 times for Holland, scoring 17 goals, a useful return for a winger. He featured in four major tournaments for Holland: the 1994 and 1998 World Cups, and the 2000 and 2004 European Championships. At five feet eight inches, Marc Overmars was relatively short, but physically strong, mobile, a player of pace and poise. Gary Neville rated Overmars his most difficult opponent in the Premiership. Sadly, persistent knee problems caused the Dutchman to retire after returning to Holland from Spain.

King of Arsenal's attacking riches, Thierry Henry graced the club's attack to the tune of 174 goals in 254 league appearances. While at Arsenal, Henry was twice runner-up in the World Player of the Year award, finishing behind France's Zinedine Zidane and the Brazilian Ronaldinho respectively. He was also named the PFA Player's Player of the Year twice, and the FWA Footballer of the Year three times. Scouted in a game in which he scored all six goals by Arsene Wenger's Monaco, Henry, aged 13, came under his mentor's wing very early on. Initially Henry played as a winger due to his natural speed, control and balance. It was always in Wenger's mind that Henry could play as a centre-forward. At Arsenal, Henry habitually cut in from the left before placing shots into the far corner of the goal even as a central striker. Opponents knew what was coming – they simply couldn't stop him.

At Monaco, Henry was named the French Young Footballer of the Year in 1996; in 1997 he helped the team win the French Ligue 1. Like so many high-profile youngsters, Henry transferred to Italy, joining Juventus, only to find the serial defensive disciplinarians of Serie A the toughest of opponents. Unsettled, Henry moved to Arsenal to play once again under his professional mentor Wenger, this time with stunning success. In his early games at Arsenal, Henry started in the wide left position, but Wenger's supposition that he could play effectively down the middle proved startlingly accurate. Eight goalless games raised eyebrows at Wenger's decision, but Henry ended his first season at Arsenal with 26 goals. In his first two seasons at Arsenal the club finished second each year behind Alex Ferguson's Manchester United; lost this UEFA Cup Final in 2000; and lost the 2001 FA Cup Final to Liverpool. Finally in his third year with the club, 2001–02, Arsenal won the Premiership and completed the double beating Chelsea 2-0 in the FA Cup Final. He finished the 2002–03 season as the leading goalscorer in the country with 32 goals in all competitions, but proving he wasn't just a one-trick pony, provided an astonishing 23 assists for teammates' goals. Arsenal won the FA Cup Final again, beating Southampton 1-0.

In the 'Invincibles' season of 2003–04, Henry scored 39 goals in all competitions, winning the European Golden Boot Award as leading scorer in European football. Despite losing out to Chelsea in the 2004–05 Premiership race, Arsenal once again won the FA Cup, this time without the injured Henry, and fortuitously on penalties against a Manchester United team who had dominated the game.

In season 2005–06, Henry became Arsenal's all-time record goalscorer, surpassing Ian Wright's 185, also breaking Cliff Bastin's long-standing tally of 151. Henry ended the season in style, scoring a hat-trick against Wigan Athletic in the last-ever match played at the old Highbury stadium. In the absence of the departed Patrick Vieira, Henry had become club captain. A fine season personally ended on a disappointing note as Barcelona proved too steep an obstacle in the final of the Champions League.

Henry had signed a new four-year contract in 2006, then suffering his most frustrating season, marred by hamstring, foot and back injuries. Barcelona came knocking in 2007 and Henry surprisingly left Arsenal, the club he'd come to love. Henry cited the departure of director David Dein as the main reason for leaving. In my former days as a sports retailer, I was interviewed by Mr Dein with the view to managing Arsenal's souvenir shop. The job didn't materialise, but I too was impressed by David Dein's gentlemanly manner.

In a poll in 2008, Arsenal fans voted Henry the club's best-ever player. Henry left the club having scored 228 goals in all competitions. Despite being used primarily as a left-winger at the Nou Camp, Henry top-scored in his first season with Barcelona, netting 19 times. The following season he surpassed this with 26, again from the left wing. In this second season for Barcelona the club won an historic treble, beating Athletic Bilbao 4-1 in the Copa del Rey Final, following this with the La Liga title and a Champions League victory, 2-0 over Manchester United. Henry, Samuel Eto'o and the incomparable Lionel Messi scored 100 goals between them in this season.

Thierry Henry sampled life in the American Major League 2010–14 having lost his place in his last season at Barcelona to the emerging Pedro, a player who performed impressively for Chelsea in the second decade of the 21st century. In the middle of his American spell, Henry was loaned back to Arsenal for a brief four-game return. He scored the only goal of the game in an FA Cup tie against Leeds United, and then fittingly scored his last Arsenal goal in his last appearance, an injury time winner against Sunderland.

Internationally, Henry played 123 times for France, finishing as his country's all-time leading scorer with 51 goals. Henry top-scored for France at the 1998 World Cup, despite being an unused substitute for the final against Brazil; he top-scored again in the trophy-winning European Championship team of 2000. Most controversially, Henry handled the ball before crossing for William Gallas to score the decisive goal in the 2010 World Cup qualifiers. The referee gave the goal, ensuring France appeared at the 2010 World Cup in South Africa. Opponents Republic of Ireland lodged a formal complaint, requesting a replay. FIFA declined. Justice was done when France were eliminated at the group stage of the 2010 World Cup, beaten by hosts South Africa. It was an unfortunate end to Henry's previously illustrious international career. Henry's reputation at Arsenal football club remains untarnished. His lightning pace, eye for goal, and overall team contribution retain a place forever in the hearts of Arsenal fans.

Alongside Henry in this UEFA Cup Final, for me, Dennis Bergkamp was arguably an even better player. Not a prolific score like Henry, there was a grace, an elegance, touch, vision and awareness that made Bergkamp my kind of player.

Following five years in the Ajax youth team, Bergkamp made his senior debut as a 17-year-old in 1986. He appeared 23 times in the 1986–87 season, Ajax winning the European Cup Winners Cup in the seasons' finale, beating Lokomotiv Leipzig 1-0, Bergkamp coming on as a substitute. As Bergkamp became a fixture in the Ajax side, the team's success increased accordingly, winning the Dutch Eredivisie in 1990, exorcising a five-year league drought. The following season, Bergkamp top-scored alongside the great Brazilian Romario with 29 goals in 36 games. Ajax won the 1992 UEFA Cup beating Torino on away goals. Bergkamp top-scored in the Eredivisie three years running, 1991–93. He was Dutch Footballer of the Year in 1992 and 1993.

Alerting all the top European clubs with his ability, Bergkamp transferred to Inter Milan in 1993. Like many others he found the organised, disciplined Serie A teams a tough nut to crack. Despite struggling in the Italian league, Bergkamp scored eight times in the 1994 UEFA Cup as Inter won the trophy, beating Austria Salzburg in the two-legged final. A difficult two-season stay in Milan ended when Bergkamp moved to Arsenal.

Another difficult first season evolved at Highbury under then-manager Bruce Rioch, the talented striker scoring a relatively meagre 11 goals in 33 appearances. Much more than an out and out striker, Bergkamp's creativity was invaluable the following season (1996–97) as he provided 13 assists to the team. In his third season at the club with new manager Arsene Wenger looking to Bergkamp to guide the team's offensive play, the Dutchman top-scored for Arsenal with 22 goals. In this season, Bergkamp scored a goal against Leicester City that is still remembered to this day, an instant touch, a dink over Matt Elliott, and a shot into goal, the goal exemplifying his exquisite control of a football. Interestingly, Bergkamp admired Glenn Hoddle's softness of touch as a young player looking for role models. In 1998 Bergkamp became only the second non-British player to win the PFA Players Player of the Year (after Eric Cantona in 1994).

In 1999 I attended the semi-final FA Cup replay at Villa Park with a work colleague and my third son Simon, a die-hard Arsenal supporter. I have never forgotten the atmosphere, the coloured balloons of the two clubs soaring into the night sky before kick-off. The huge drama of the evening did not sit so well with Dennis Bergkamp. A memorable game between England's two premier sides at that time was drawing to a close (literally with the teams tied) when Arsenal were awarded a penalty kick, Bergkamp's penalty attempt was saved by the Premier League's best-ever keeper, Peter Schmeichel – Bergkamp never again took a penalty kick. The rest is history. In extra time, United, a man down after Roy Keane's sending off (predictably the Irishman had been immense), won the match in adversity with Ryan Giggs's extraordinary solo goal and even more extraordinary shirt-twirling bare-chested celebration that followed.

The departure of Manu Petit and Marc Overmars disenchanted Bergkamp, but he stayed with Arsenal as Frenchmen Thierry Henry and Sylvain Wiltord supplemented the team. Runners-up three seasons running in the Premiership, Arsenal finally triumphed in the 2001–02 season, pipping perennially successful Manchester United in the league to win the double after beating Chelsea 2-0 in the FA Cup Final. Bergkamp was a member of the 'Invincibles' team that won the league with its unbeaten record in 2003–04, the first English team to achieve the feat in over a century, and particularly creditable in the modern game where Premiership clubs are eminently capable of all beating each other on any given day.

Dennis Bergkamp was so highly regarded among the Highbury faithful that he was granted a 'Bergkamp Day' on 15 April 2006 in commemoration of his service to the club, a day when fans were given commemorative orange 'DB 10' shirts. His last game with Arsenal came as an unused substitute in the 2-1 Champions League Final defeat to Barcelona in 2006. He scored 87 league goals for Arsenal in 315 appearances, but his style, the quality of some of his goals, his team contribution, will never be forgotten.

For Holland, Bergkamp scored 37 times in 79 internationals. At the European Championships in 1992 the Dutch were surprisingly beaten on penalties by eventual winners Denmark. Bergkamp scored three times in the competition. In the 1994 World Cup, Bergkamp scored five times in qualification, then three times in the competition proper. Three more goals followed at the 1998 World Cup, including another breathtaking last-minute winner against Argentina in the quarter-finals, killing Frank de Boer's long ball with his customary deft touch, feeding the ball through Roberto Ayala's legs and volleying the ball into the net with the outside of his right boot. Holland lost the semi-final on penalties to Brazil. The Ajax 'school of football' served Dennis Bergkamp well, each player playing in every position on the field to give them an understanding of the team's requirements. He began his career as a midfielder, but his sublime touch clearly dictating his eventual placement in the Ajax team as a striker. At Arsenal, Bergkamp was able to play as the perfect 'second striker' with first Ian Wright, Nicolas Anelka and ultimately Thierry Henry as his partner and main striker in attack. Fleet of foot, quick of mind, a hugely intelligent player, Dennis Bergkamp gave Arsenal fans and British football followers in general a treasure trove of memories between 1995 and 2006.

Such was the wealth of attacking riches available to Arsenal on this evening that two of their attacking substitutes were the hugely talented Croatian Davor Suker and the languid, occasional match-winning Nigerian Nwankwo Kanu. Suker was only at Arsenal for this one season. Richly gifted, his touch only marginally inferior to that of Bergkamp, Suker enjoyed greater personal success with Sevilla and Real Madrid in Spain between 1991 and 1999, scoring well over 100 La Liga goals. At the 1998 World Cup, Suker won the Golden Boot, scoring six goals in seven matches, enabling Croatia to finish third. He scored eight times in his 22 appearances for Arsenal. Kanu scored 44 goals in his 197 games in all competitions at the club, often proving to be a game-changing substitute. Kanu was named African Footballer of the Year twice in 1996 and 1999, and was a star of Nigeria's 1996 Olympic-title-winning team.

Strasbourg-born Arsene Wenger changed the face of English football irrevocably. After winning the French league with Monaco in 1988 and the Coupe de France in 1991, Wenger spent a season with Japanese club Nagoya Grampus Eight in 1995–96. His appointment as Arsenal manager was met with disdain by some – Arsene who? being the reaction to his arrival at Highbury. The Brits soon found out who as Wenger introduced better diets, curtailed the drinking culture at Arsenal that cursed Tony Adams and Paul Merson, placed emphasis on youth, and perhaps most pertinently, brought quality players into the set-up due to his innate knowledge of French football. The great shame for Arsene Wenger came in his latter years at Arsenal when shorn of the likes of Petit, Vieira, Henry, Pires and Wiltord, Arsenal's core grew weaker by the year and Wenger's attacking philosophy failed to win Arsenal further silverware. Wenger was also lucky to have the Brazilian midfielder Gilberto Silva, and the flying Dutchman Marc Overmars, and Dennis Bergkamp – who didn't like air travel – and the dynamic Swedish midfielder Freddie Ljungberg under his auspices during his time as Arsenal manager. Recent years' Arsenal 'groups' have lacked the pace, power and purpose of this purple period in Arsenal's history. Wenger's height, bespectacled face and professorial demeanour all made him something quite unique in English football. His impact and the fierce rivalry engendered with Manchester United during his early tenure are vivid illustrations of his undying passion for Arsenal football club.

A formidable football club, Arsenal, circa 2000. So why didn't they win the 2000 UEFA Cup Final? They were firm favourites with many outstanding individuals and an outstanding team ethic. This reckoned without the fierce patriotism of their Turkish opponents Galatasaray, allied to the inclusion of four richly gifted 'foreign' players in their ranks: Brazilian national goalkeeper Cláudio Taffarel, Brazilian right-back Capone, Romanian centre-back Gheorghe Popescu, and one of the outstanding footballers of his generation, the diminutive Romanian wizard, Gheorghe Hagi.

For a player who earned 101 caps for his country, the keeper Taffarel acquired a reputation as an inconsistent, if brilliant, custodian between the posts. His 89 appearances for Galatasaray 1998–2001 were the most at any one club he played for. He also played 80 games for Parma in Italy during two separate spells with the club. In his home country of Brazil, Taffarel played 73 times for Atlético Mineiro 1995–98 before transferring to Galatasaray. Agile, with excellent reflexes, Taffarel's weakness lay in dealing with crosses. This didn't stop him being a World Cup winner with Brazil in 1994.

Captain for the night, Bülent Korkmaz, was a one-club servant to Galatasaray, appearing in 430 league games during his 19-year senior career with the club, winning eight league titles, six Turkish cups, and this UEFA Cup Final. In all, Korkmaz played 102 times in all European competitions, also appearing 102 times for his country. Heroically, Korkmaz played on in this final having dislocated his shoulder, refusing to leave the pitch. The injury caused him to miss out on Turkey's appearance at UEFA Euro 2000. In 2002 Korkmaz was part of the Turkish squad which surprised many by finishing third at the World Cup.

The star striker in the Galatasaray team was Hakan Sükür, who played 392 league games for the club during three spells, 1992–95 and 1995–2000, a failed stint with Italian club Torino bridging the first two spells. Sükür tried his hand briefly in Italy again with Inter Milan and Parma, spending an even briefer spell in England with Blackburn Rovers 2000–2003, but didn't really settle anywhere other than Galatasaray, where he accumulated 217 league goals during those three spells. Sükür played 112 times for Turkey, scoring 51 goals. Scoring goals was not a problem in his homeland, or for his country.

Sükür and Borkmaz notwithstanding, the outstanding footballers in this Galatasaray team were the Romanians, Gheorghe Popescu and Gheorghe Hagi.

Ironically, Popescu was Hagi's brother-in-law. Not blood related, but both players excelled in the best Romanian national team in living memory. Popescu was highly rated for his tactical acumen, positioning and general defensive qualities. He began his senior career with Universitea Craiova in Romania, appearing in 103 league games (with a useful return of 22 goals for the sweeper, centre-back, defensive midfielder), was then loaned to Steaua Bucharest in 1998, helping the club to the European Cup semi-finals. Popescu transferred to PSV Eindhoven in Holland in 1990, playing 109 league games (24 goals), before moving to Tottenham Hotspur for a short-lived spell in 1994. Upon transferring to Barcelona in 1995, Popescu became the Catalan club's captain, helping them win the Copa del Rey in 1996 and the European Cup Winners Cup in 1997.

Turning to Galatasaray in 1997, Popescu stayed four seasons, scoring the final penalty in the penalty shoot-out of this final. In the seasons 1989–2001, Popescu was always in the top four ranked players in the Romanian Footballer of the Year awards. Popescu appeared 115 times for Romania (his country's third most capped player), scoring 16 goals, appearing in the 1990, 1994 and 1998 World Cups, and at the 1996 and 2000 Euros.

Gheorghe Hagi was simply one of the best players in the world during the 1980s and 1990s, earning the nickname the 'Maradona of the Carpathians'. This was perhaps a little unfair – Hagi was short at five feet nine inches, but not as diminutive as Maradona, and an outstanding, visionary footballer in his own right. Deployed as an attacking midfielder, Hagi was adept at dribbling, close control, short and long passing, and possessed an unerring eye for the spectacular goal. Hagi tended to play as an advanced playmaker. He was clearly the brains of the Romanian national team during his golden years, drifting behind the strikers, maximising his wonderful technique for the benefit of the team,

After playing 223 league games in his home country, 97 with Steaua Bucharest (76 goals), 1982–1990, Hagi formed a spectacular career abroad with Real Madrid (16 goals in 64 league games), 1990–92, Brescia in Italy (14 goals in 61 league games), 1992–94, and Barcelona (seven goals), 1994–96, before moving to Galatasaray in 1996. In five seasons with the Turkish club, Hagi became a hero, scoring 59 goals in 132 league appearances. With Galatasaray, Hagi helped the club win four league titles, two Turkish cups and this UEFA Cup Final. At international level, Hagi is the second most capped player in Romania, and the joint highest scorer (with Adrian Mutu) with 35 goals in his 124 appearances. Hagi was named Romanian Footballer of the Year seven times, being selected in 2003 by the Romanian Football Federation as their most outstanding player of the past 50 years.

THE FINAL

Gheorghe Hagi's weakness – if he had one – was a lack of discipline at times. Tangling with Tony Adams as the final entered extra time, the super talented Romanian received a straight red card, Adams receiving a yellow during the altercation. Despite losing their talisman, the plucky Turks refused to be cowed, still creating chances of their own, even with only ten men on the pitch. Extra time came about due to Galatasaray's absolute determination not to be second best to this star-studded Arsenal team. This wonderful Arsenal team had ridden their luck at times as the Turkish team gave every bit as good as they got in the 90 minutes.

In the penalty shoot-out, Davor Suker, on as a substitute, struck the inside of the post and the ball stayed out from Arsenal's first penalty kick. Hakan Suker, cool as you like, scored for Galatasaray. Ray Parlour made no mistake with his kick, but Patrick Vieira's thundering shot struck the underside of the crossbar. Arsenal ended up losing convincingly 4-1 on penalties. Sadly, match-day violence flared, supporters of the two clubs embroiled in fights that were attributed to the death of two Leeds United fans a month earlier in the semi-finals. In all, 19 injuries were incurred during riots on the morning of the game in City Hall Square, Copenhagen. A group of 300 Arsenal fans also targeted Turkish restaurants in Finsbury Park, Islington, North London, after the match. The game itself reflected the passion of both teams, chances created throughout at both ends of the pitch. Arsenal may have been favourites, but this was no one-sided encounter.

2000–2001 UEFA CUP FINAL
Liverpool 5 v 4 Alaves (after extra time)

What a contrast this final was to the previous year's goal drought. The highly skilled, proficient defences of Galatasaray and Arsenal were banished from the memory in a 2001 final that was frankly, loose and disorganised defensively. Instead, these two teams served up a goal feast, defensive prowess the least of their concerns, it seemed. Alaves of Spain were a surprise finalist, appearing in the UEFA Cup Final for the first and only time to date. In contrast, Liverpool were challenging for the trophy for the third time.

Route to the Final
All of Liverpool's two-legged ties were close-fought affairs, especially from the fourth round onwards when they beat Roma 2-0 away, courtesy of two Michael Owen goals, suffering a rare 1-0 home defeat, but securing a 2-1 aggregate victory. In the quarter-finals and semi-finals Liverpool reverted to type, winning the ties at 'Fortress Anfield' thanks to 2-0 (Owen again and Danny Murphy) and 1-0 (a Garry McAllister penalty) margins over Porto and Barcelona respectively, holding out for goalless draws in Portugal and Spain.

Alaves's toughest opponents were Inter Milan in the quarter-finals, a 3-3 home draw with the Italians seemingly jeopardising their dreams of reaching the final, only for the Spaniards to upset the odds by winning 2-0 at the San Siro. Alaves scored freely throughout the competition, four or five goals in every round, but no one could have foreseen the manner in which they dismissed the Germans Kaiserslauten 9-2 on aggregate in the semi-finals, 5-1 at home (three from the penalty spot) and 4-1 away.

The face of British football had changed conclusively by the year 2001. The litmus paper for this change was the forming of the Premiership League on 27 May 1992. The inaugural 1992–93 season saw Alex Ferguson's team triumphant;

Blackburn Rovers with the famous Shearer/Sutton axis were a surprise winner in 1994–95. Apart from Leicester City's 'fairytale' triumph in 2015–16, the Premier League has been dominated by Manchester United, Arsenal and Chelsea, Manchester City and Liverpool, the latter after a 30-year hiatus breaking the stranglehold in recent years. What changed most drastically during this 27-year period is the influx of foreign players into British football. Initially these foreign imports tended to be at the end of their careers, until the financial lure of recent years brought the likes of Kevin De Bruyne and Mo Salah into the fold, playing their prime years in English football, bucking the early trend. The upside of foreign players honing their skills in British football comes from their often superior technique manifesting itself and influencing younger British players. The downside has seen a restriction of opportunities for young British footballers. Lack of opportunity means a lack of growth in British footballer's careers and a stunting of their capacity to compete against Europe's best in the elite competitions.

A look at the make-up of Liverpool's team for this 2001 UEFA Cup Final reveals the impact of foreign players in British football. The team was a multinational one, Dutch, German, Swiss and Finnish players in the starting line-up; French and Czechs among the substitutes. Naturally this cosmopolitan make-up of a team gave Liverpool the best of all worlds: players blessed with excellent technique, tactical nous, fighting spirit, players of all temperaments and abilities.

In goal for Liverpool, Dutchman Sander Westerveld had to play second fiddle for his country behind Edwin van der Saar (he won six international caps). Westerveld's crowning glory at club level came in this 2000–01 season, Liverpool winning a treble of the FA Cup, League Cup and this UEFA Cup.

Right-back Marcus Babbel won the UEFA Cup firstly with Bayern Munich in 1996. Babbel built his senior career with the Bavarian club, but swiftly moved to Hamburger SV in 1992, playing 60 league games there before returning to Bayern. A further 170 league appearances for Bayern, Babbel, a model of consistency, attracted Manchester United's attention. A proposed deal fell through, allowing Liverpool manager Gérard Houllier to snatch Babbel from under the nose of Liverpool's great north-western rivals on a Bosman (Babbel, without a contract, moved to Anfield without Bayern receiving a fee). This freedom of movement contract allowed Houllier to include more foreign players in his team as long as they were EU state members.

Babbel's Liverpool career was cruelly curtailed by his suffering with Guillain-Barre syndrome, a muscle weakness caused by the immune system weakening the peripheral nervous system, triggering sensations of pain in the back. Babbel recovered sufficiently to be loaned to Blackburn Rovers. He moved back to Germany to play for VFB Stuttgart in 2004, but was forced to retire in 2007. Babbel played 51 times for Germany 1995–2000. England players will remember him well as part of Germany's victorious Euro 1996 team.

A player who made the reverse switch – from Blackburn Rovers to Liverpool – was Swiss international Stéphane Henchoz. Ironically, where Babbel's proposed transfer to Manchester United foundered, Henchoz could have signed for Alex Ferguson, opting for Ewood Park instead. Henchoz formed a solid partnership with Sami Hyppiä after transferring to Liverpool in 1999 when Rovers were relegated to the Championship. Henchoz received 72 caps for Switzerland.

Sami Hyppiä is very fondly remembered at Anfield. At six feet four inches a towering presence in the heart of Liverpool's defence, Hyppiä was a surprisingly elegant and technically adept player for such a tall man. Obviously good in the air, Hyppiä was no slouch with ball at feet. Interestingly, not only was Hyppiä's father a professional player, but his mother played as an amateur goalkeeper. Hyppiä played ice hockey as a teenager – my youngest son Daniel, a life-long Liverpool supporter, whose wife Heidi is Finnish, met Hyppiä in recent years at an ice hockey match in Helsinki – but football was Hyppiä's first-choice sports career. Former iconic captain from the 1960s Ron Yeats felt Hyppiä was a bargain buy, one of the best transfers Liverpool ever made when the Finn came to Anfield from Dutch club Willem 11, having made 100 league appearances there. A natural leader, Hyppiä swiftly assumed captaincy duties, a role he shared with Robbie Fowler and Jamie Redknapp during this 2000–01 season. Hyppiä would go on to forge another impressive defensive partnership with Jamie Carragher during the 2004–05 season, a partnership so dependable the team won that year's Champions League trophy. Hyppiä lies second only to the mercurial Jari Litmanen as Finland's highest capped player, appearing 105 times for his country. Curiously, Litmanen, a wonderfully talented player who won the Champions League in 1995 with Ajax, played just one season at Liverpool in 2001–02, Hyppiä having given Houllier glowing references of him. I recall Litmanen's exquisite touch, but wrist and ankle injuries prevented him having the same impact Hyppiä had at Anfield.

What a character Jamie Carragher was. A one-club man, Liverpool through and through (yet an Everton supporter as a boy), my abiding memory of Carragher is hearing his chirping voice ringing out at Selhurst Park in a match against Crystal Palace I attended with my sons back in the late 1990s. Carragher simply never stopped talking all game! Clearly he'd taken it upon himself to be the defence's organiser-in-chief, and anyone who's played football knows the value of a player talking to you – as long as it's constructive! Carragher always seemed to be just a whisker away from being a regular for England (he made 38 appearances), but no one could deny his passion for his 'hometown' club, a passion that saw him play 735 times for Liverpool. Carragher also holds the all-time appearance record at Anfield for playing in European games with 149 outings. Initially a more than competent full-back, Carragher's best years at Liverpool came when new manager Rafael Benitez switched him to centre-back in 2004. Carragher won two FA Cups, three League Cups, this UEFA Cup, and the icing on the cake, the Champions League in 2004–05. Three times voted Liverpool Player of the Year, Carragher may have been a blue-shirted Everton supporter as a boy, but no Anfield attendee could ever doubt his full-blooded commitment to Liverpool's cause.

What can one say about Liverpool's talisman Steven Gerrard, a player who (most unfairly) carried Liverpool's hopes and dreams so squarely on his shoulders in the latter years of his career. My son Daniel and I watched a 19-year-old Gerrard spray 70 yard balls all over Anfield on a day when the team defeated Leeds United

3-0 back in the late 1990s. Gerrard had only just broken into the team, but it was evident that day what an awesome talent was on view. Internationally, Gerrard and the equally talented Frank Lampard often seemed unable to integrate their undoubted talents in the 'golden generation' era of England midfielders. Perhaps the biggest problem was that Gerrard and Lampard both succeeded with their clubs as the team's offensive midfielder. When you think the England team these two played in also included David Beckham, Paul Scholes and Wayne Rooney, England definitely under-achieved in these 'golden years'. Pertinently, football teams are all about finding the right balance, not necessarily the best players – Alf Ramsey and Jimmy Greaves' exclusion from England's 1966 World Cup-winning team the best example of that.

Steven Gerrard's career at Liverpool is simply stellar. The only player to score in a League Cup Final, an FA Cup Final, a UEFA Cup Final and a Champions League Cup Final – and be on the winning side in each game, Gerrard was rated by none other than Pele and Zinedine Zidane as the best all-round footballer in the world in 2009. A 2018 documentary film reveals the prodigy Gerrard as a schoolboy footballer, how he raced through opposition teams to score goals at will – yet he never played for the England schoolboys' team.

Gerrard trialled with Manchester United, but signed for Liverpool on a YTS contract, before signing professional at Anfield in 1997. Gerrard's early career at Liverpool only hinted at the impact he would have on the club later on. Struggling to find his best position, and weighed down by expectation and late growth spurts, Gerrard came more into his own following this UEFA Cup victory. By 2004 Chelsea were attempting to lure him away from Anfield, but Gerrard resisted the temptation to move to London. The result: the epic recovery from 3-0 down at half-time in the 2004–05 Champions League final against AC Milan, a game when Gerrard seemed to single-handedly drag his teammates back from the brink of defeat. Football is, of course, not about one player, but Gerrard's efforts certainly inspired those around him. In the 2006 FA Cup Final Gerrard scored twice against West Ham United, including a thumping 35-yarder to bring Liverpool back into the game. Liverpool eliminated Gerrard's persistent suitors Chelsea in the 2006–07 Champions League semi-final, only to lose out in the final to AC Milan. In December 2007, Gerrard became the first player since John Aldridge to score in seven consecutive games for Liverpool – and this feat achieved as a midfield player, where Aldridge was an out-and-out striker. By now Gerrard had established himself as captain of the team, but his cherished dream of winning the Premiership continued to elude him. In the twilight of his career in the 2013–14 season it seemed the Liverpool dream might finally be realised. Spurred by a superlative trio of strikers in Luis Suarez, (a fit) Daniel Sturridge and a young Raheem Sterling, Liverpool appeared on the verge of becoming champions, leading the table with five games remaining. Football has a habit of being cruel to even the most illustrious however. Gerrard, receiving the ball in the centre of the field, slipped, lost the ball and Demba Ba escaped to score a crucial goal for Liverpool's opponents. The opposition: Chelsea of course! The wily José Mourinho, renowned for 'parking the bus', dented Liverpool's hopes as Chelsea won 2-0 at Anfield, Liverpool losing the title to Manchester City.

Steven Gerrard lies sixth in Liverpool's all-time record goalscorer's list, heading even the multigifted Kenny Dalglish. He won the 2009 Football Writer's Association Footballer of the Year Award; captained Liverpool over 400 times. At international level, Gerrard played 114 times for England, scoring 21 goals, making him the fourth most capped player of all time for his country. Stylistically Steven Gerrard was an all-action player, capable of striking great goals from distance, a superb passer of the ball whose vision allowed him to play deeper as age and injuries began to take their toll, but most of all, his ability to lift the players around him is what he is best remembered for.

Since retiring, Gerrard has begun the difficult task of reclaiming glory for Glasgow Rangers in Scotland. His task: to get Rangers back on an equal footing with recently all-conquering Glasgow Celtic. To date, it's Celtic who have continued to hold sway in the Scottish league, but Gerrard, as one would expect, applies himself to the full, tackling the task head-on. What else would one expect of Steven Gerrard? A I write, the Covid-19-disrupted 2020–21 season sees Rangers with a 20 plus points lead over Celtic. It seems Gerrard the manager has achieved the longed-for Rangers revival.

One of the stalwarts of this successful 2000–01 Liverpool team was the German midfielder Dieter 'Didi' Hamann. Hamann played 105 league games for Bayern Munich 1993–98, a time of internal conflict for the club. Despite switching roles from right wing to defensive midfielder, and not always being a regular, Hamann's time in Munich garnered a 1996 UEFA Cup Final victory, two Bundesliga titles and a German Cup Final victory. After playing for Germany at the 1998 World Cup, Hamann signed for Kenny Dalglish's Newcastle United. His form on Tyneside earned him his transfer to Liverpool in 1999, signed by Gérard Houllier. Hamann played 191 league games for Liverpool, 1999–2006, establishing himself as ultra-reliable, a supreme technician and a great team player. He was also a typically composed Germanic player, scoring crucial penalties in the 2005 Champions League Final and the 2006 FA Cup Final. A trusted player for Liverpool, Hamann was 'Mr Dependable'.

Hamann played 59 times for Germany, his finest achievement being in the side that reached the 2002 World Cup Final, losing 2-0 to Brazil in Yokohama, Japan. What makes Hamann's success all the more remarkable is that before gracing the shirts of Liverpool and Newcastle United in England he suffered a stroke early in his career in Germany, making a subsequent full recovery. A stroke is a shock at any stage in a human being's life, but for it to happen in your 20s must be devastating.

Gary McAllister had already won the title with Leeds United in its old guise of the 1ˢᵗ Division (its last season before becoming the behemoth that is the Premiership). This Leeds side also contained Eric Cantona, pre-Manchester United. Either side of his 231 league games for Leeds, McAllister played for Midlands clubs Leicester City and Coventry City, playing 201 and 119 league games respectively. McAllister only played 55 league games for Liverpool, coming to a 'glamour' club rather late in his career. McAllister was a highly respected player among his peers, solid, technically proficient, a fine passer of the ball. A leader on the field, McAllister captained Leeds for two seasons in addition to captaining Scotland over a four-year period.

McAllister earned an MBE in 2001 in recognition of his outstanding contribution to football. In total, McAllister played 709 league games in Scotland and England. He also played 57 times for Scotland. Aged 35 when he played for Liverpool, Gérard Houllier described the evergreen McAllister as his most "inspirational signing". Like a fine wine, McAllister matured with age, his performances consistently high as his career reached its zenith.

Danny Murphy played 170 league games for Liverpool, scoring 25 goals. Tactically astute, Murphy specialised in long-range goals and free kicks. Murphy signed for Liverpool in 1997, having begun his senior career with Crewe Alexandra. Often forced to play wide in midfield to accommodate the outstanding duo of Gerrard and Hamann, Murphy sometimes sailed under the radar a little. A brief spell at Tottenham Hotspur where he failed to hold down a regular place was followed by a longer stint with Fulham, helping the Thameside club to their one and only UEFA Cup Final, a 2-1 defeat to Atlético Madrid. Murphy captained Fulham during that 2009–10 season. Astonishingly, the Cottagers knocked out Juventus, defending champions Shakhtar Donetsk from the Ukraine, and Wolfsburg and Hamburg from Germany en route to the final. Murphy played nine times for England. Unsung perhaps, but good enough to keep Nicky Barmby and Czech internationals Patrick Berger and Vladimir Smicer on the bench for this 2001 UEFA Cup Final.

In attack, Liverpool possessed a fabulous combination of the 'mighty' Emile Heskey and the 'mighty mouse' Michael Owen. Heskey, a quiet character, never seemed to realise just how good he was. Always a useful scorer, Heskey's power and pace made him a constant threat to opposing teams. Starting his professional career at Leicester City, Heskey scored 40 goals in 154 league games at Filbert Street. The conundrum for Heskey was that the game was never simply about scoring – he was almost too unselfish at times as a striker, but the likes of Tony Cottee at Leicester and Owen and Robbie Fowler at Liverpool certainly benefited from Heskey's unselfishness.

Heskey transferred to Liverpool in 2000 for a then-record £11 million fee. He scored 22 goals in all competitions during this 2000–01 season. Even when faced with the competition for his place from Fowler, and later, Milan Baros, Heskey continued to offer Liverpool a more direct option and was often chosen ahead of his rivals and teammates. Heskey later played for Birmingham City, Wigan Athletic, and Aston Villa, always contributing massively to the team, despite his often criticised low goals per games ratio. Heskey was good enough to play 62 times for England, scoring seven goals, often paired in attack with the quicksilver Michael Owen.

Michael Owen's professional career began in sensational style. At five feet eight inches Owen was on the short side for a striker, but his searing pace in his early years as a professional often made the difference for Liverpool and England. Sadly, persistent hamstring injuries hampered the longevity of his career as a top player – although this didn't stop Real Madrid signing him in 2004. Owen also possessed an unerring eye for goal – but for his recurring hamstring problems Owen would surely have helped an underperforming England team achieve better things in the 2000s. Owen's clinical finishing made him top scorer for Liverpool every season 1997–2004. In total, Owen scored 158 times in 297 appearances in all competitions for Liverpool. Owen is the youngest player to reach 100 goals in the Premier League. 1997–98 was a special season for Michael Owen. Aged just 17 as the season began, Owen won the PFA Young Player of the Year at the climax of the season, and finished third behind Dennis Bergkamp and Tony Adams for the senior award. He even finished second behind the irrepressible Zinedine Zidane in the World Player of the Year Award following his exploits at the 1998 World Cup. He also won the Premier League Golden Boot as top scorer, a feat he repeated in 1998–99. Unfortunately, by 1999 Owen was already incurring repeated problems with hamstring injuries. The jet-heeled pace that was Owen's byword would sadly be his undoing.

The 2000–01 season culminated with Michael Owen being named European Footballer of the Year, the first Englishman to attain the honour since Kevin Keegan in 1979. Two late goals in the 2001 FA Cup Final from Owen made Liverpool victorious when defeat appeared to be staring the club in the face. Triumphs in the Charity Shield and the UEFA Super Cup (added to the League Cup, FA Cup and the UEFA Cup) made Liverpool the first English club to win five trophies in a calendar year. Injuries continued to blight Owen's Liverpool career, but a persistent Real Madrid finally signed him for £8 million in 2004. After constantly chasing Owen during Houllier's reign as Liverpool manager, Real then used the speedster sparingly. Owen was generally found warming the substitute's bench. Despite this relative inaction in Madrid, Owen scored 16 goals in 45 appearances. A year later Owen surprisingly returned to England signing for Newcastle United when a return to Liverpool seemed more likely. How did Owen start his Newcastle career? With a thigh injury incurred pre-season, followed by a broken metatarsal in December 2005. Owen followed this with an anterior cruciate ligament injury in the first minute of a World Cup match against Sweden in 2006. Once seen as the 'saviour' of both Liverpool and England, Owen now seemed thoroughly cursed by injuries. Between 2005 and 2009, Owen scored 26 goals in 71 league appearances for Newcastle, but the thigh injury resurfaced again in 2007. Another surprise (free) transfer followed – to Manchester United, Liverpool's fierce rivals. This move came way too late in Owen's injury-wrecked career for Alex Ferguson to reap the benefit of Owen's lightning pace and clinical finishing. Owen stayed three seasons with United 2009–12, but clearly his best days were behind him.

Michael Owen's goal record for England bore comparison to his best days with Liverpool, scoring 40 times in 89 appearances. He appeared at the 1998, 2002 and 2006 World Cups, and at the 2000 and 2004 European Championships, but post-1998 injuries – particularly to his hamstrings – deprived Owen of making the impact that his scintillating late teenage form had richly promised. Who can forget the exhilarating run and shot in scoring against Argentina at the 1998 World Cup? It is one of the competition's most iconic moments – not bad when you consider those provided by Pele, Cruyff, Maradona et al. On the back of this golden moment, Owen became 1998 BBC Sports Personality of the Year. Owen also memorably scored a hat-trick in England's astonishing 5-1 victory over Germany in Munich during the qualification for the 2002 World Cup (the unfairly vilified Heskey also scored on the night), arguably the nation's greatest ever away win. What might Michael Owen have helped England achieve had he been blessed with better fitness? His initial impact with England – along with the equally injury-cursed Wayne Rooney (at or before major international competitions) is the most vivid in recent memory.

Liverpool's bench for this UEFA Cup Final provided a veritable wealth of attacking riches – ironic when you consider Alaves' Jordi Cruyff (son of Johan) had accused Liverpool pre-match of being a team who could stifle opponents defensively (how wrong his words proved to be given that Liverpool shipped four goals in this final, yet emerged as victors). The aforementioned Patrick Berger and Vladimir Smicer were established Czech internationals. Berger a dynamic, explosive player with an eye for goal, scored 28 league goals in 148 games at Liverpool, scoring a further 18 for his country in 42 appearances. Less flamboyant, but all subtlety and finesse, Smicer played 121 league games for Liverpool 1999–2005. Smicer scored in the dramatic Champions League Final against AC Milan in 2005, also scoring the decisive penalty kick in the shoot-out finale. Smicer played 80 times for the Czech Republic, scoring 27 times. Smicer replaced the much-loved Steve McManaman at Anfield when 'Macca' moved to Real Madrid. These were big shoes to fill, but Smicer deserves to be remembered with affection for his part in a seismic time in Liverpool FC's history.

Unfortunately both Berger and Smicer's Anfield careers were affected by injuries – why should it be only England's 'boy wonder' Owen? What with Owen's cruel misfortune with injuries, Berger and Smicer's injury-blighted Liverpool careers, it seems appropriate to relate that one of the other substitutes, Nicky Barmby, also suffered his share of ill fortune during his short spell at Anfield 2000–02. A pity, as I enjoyed watching Barmby play enormously. A successful start to his professional career at Tottenham saw Barmby score 21 goals from 89 league starts. An attacking midfielder, Barmby, was a bright, inventive player who constantly sought to play the killer ball from his position behind a team's main strikers. Another fine spell at Everton led to Barmby switching Merseyside allegiances, but by now Barmby too had become a little injury-prone, appearing in only 32 league games for Liverpool, scoring just twice. A shame, because he was better than that. Twenty-three appearances for England and four goals prove the point.

At five feet nine inches, Robbie Fowler was only an inch taller than Michael Owen, and only an inch behind Owen in the goal-scoring stakes. Fowler, as a Toxteth-born Liverpudlian, was widely loved by the fans at Liverpool. Fowler scored 183 goals in all competitions for the club 1993–2001. Fowler's deadly eye in front of goal is borne out by scoring 16 goals in one schoolboy game for Thorvald; and by scoring all five goals in a League Cup tie against Fulham in 1993. In the 1994–95 season Fowler scored a hat-trick in four minutes and 33 seconds against Arsenal. The emergence of Owen overshadowed Fowler slightly, yet for a period in the 1990s Fowler was rated the best finisher in the Premier League, scoring over 30 goals in a season in three consecutive calendar years. In this season of 2000–01 Fowler scored 17 goals, but found himself sidelined often as manager Houllier preferred the 'little and large' combination of Heskey and Owen. Despite being third-choice striker, Fowler captained the team when he did play. Further spells at Leeds United and Manchester City saw Fowler continue to score vital goals, but it's at Liverpool he's best remembered. Fowler played 26 times for England, scoring seven times.

The free-scoring Alaves team were completely unknown to English football fans in 2001. Far and away their best-known player, Jordi Cruyff, played 41 league games for Barcelona, the club his father Johan graced, scoring 11 goals 1994–96. His form at the Nou Camp alerted Manchester United. Jordi spent four seasons at Old Trafford, four seasons once more blighted by injury. He played only 34 league games for United, scoring eight times. My memory tells me that Cruyff junior struggled to make an impact at the club, often being on the fringes of play, but clearly his fitness betrayed him at times. Jordi Cruyff enjoyed his most successful time in the Basque region of Spain with Alaves, playing 94 league games, scoring seven times, helping the club to their one and only European final. Jordi Cruyff played nine times for Holland. Perhaps his downfall was in not playing in a regular position during his career. He played mostly as a midfield player, sometimes in an attacking role, at times in a more defensive role. He even played as a central defender for Metalurh Donetsk in the Ukraine 2006–08. That's the downside of Dutch 'total football' – Dutch players are so technically proficient that they can play anywhere on the pitch, and what price being the son of one of the greatest players in world football in any era?

THE FINAL

Alan Hansen, the ex-Liverpool centre-back, commentating for the BBC, hailed this match as "the best final ever". Finals are often low key, cat-and-mouse, closely contested affairs with defences dominant. Not on this occasion. The experienced Gary McAllister proved an outstanding asset for Liverpool, creating three goals and scoring one himself. Liverpool started strongly, Marcus Babbel heading in after only three minutes. Owen fed Gerrard soon afterwards, the latter looking so young with a crew-cut hairstyle, driving home at the near post. Two fine headed goals from Alaves were sandwiched by Owen rounding Alaves's keeper Herrera only to be brought down. McAllister, the epitome of cool, scored comfortably from the spot.

In the second half, Alaves, refusing to go quietly, made it 3-3 when Javi Moreno's free kick scudded under Liverpool's defensive wall and deceived Westerveld in the English team's goal. Scorer of the second expertly guided header for Alaves, Moreno had his second goal of the evening. The pick of the goals on the night came from Robbie Fowler, on as a substitute for Heskey, he burst into the penalty area and drove a fine goal. The scales tipped even further in Liverpool's favour when Magno hauled down Smicer and was sent off. A man light, Alaves somehow contrived a fourth equaliser in the 88th minute when Jordi Cruyff was allowed a free header from a corner – the six feet four Hyppiä unable to prevent the goal. Three headed goals against them on the night suggested Liverpool suffered an aerial weakness at the heart of their defence.

Extra time and the final was decided on the 'golden goal' rule in the first period of the extra half-hour. The irrepressible McAllister sent over a pinpoint free kick from the left, the ball deflecting off the head of an Alaves defender into the far corner of the net. Liverpool's curious sharing of the captaincy during this season was evinced as Fowler and Hyppiä held the trophy aloft at the end in unison.

2002–2003 UEFA CUP FINAL
Porto 3 v 2 Glasgow Celtic

Whatever happened to the halcyon days of Scottish football? Growing up, Scottish players of genuine class abounded in the 1960s and 1970s: John Greig, Billy McNeill, Jim Baxter, Jimmy Johnstone, Alan Gilzean, Archie Gemmill, Alan Hansen, Kenny Dalglish, Graham Souness. The glory days of Glasgow Celtic and Glasgow Rangers competing on equal footing for the European Cup and European Cup Winners Cup had long gone by 2003. Alex Ferguson's interim Aberdeen in the 1980s provided Scots with genuine hope for bigger things from Scottish football, but the formation of the Premier League, and the general influx of European players to England kept Scottish football at a lower level, their top teams generally equivalent in standard only to English Championship sides.

In recent years, Scottish clubs have acquired international players of repute, the most recognisable, Virgil van Dijk at Celtic, but as a rule Scottish football has trailed in the wake of the behemoth that is the Premiership.

In 2003 Celtic were blessed with an outstanding central striking pairing of Chris Sutton (Premiership title-winner with Blackburn Rovers) and the prolific Swede Henrik Larsson. Celtic's team for this final was a multi-ethnic mix of Swedes, a Belgian, a French-born Guinea international, a Bulgarian and two Celtic stalwarts, Scotsman Paul Lambert and the Northern Irish manager (2020) of the club, Neil Lennon. The mix of multinational players was there, even if the quality was slightly inferior to that seen in the Premiership. Unfortunately for Celtic, the opposition on this evening, Porto, were a rising force in Portuguese and European football with one genuinely world class player in their ranks in Deco. Managing the two clubs: Martin O'Neill, European Cup winner with Nottingham Forest, fiery, wily, experienced, no-nonsense, ultra-professional. His opposing coach on the evening was none other than the less experienced (at the time) José Mourinho.

Two extraordinary facts about this game: It was the first to use the 'silver goal' rule, as opposed to the 'golden goal' rule. Where a 'golden goal' in extra time ended a match instantly, a 'silver goal' meant a game would end at half-time of extra time if a team had taken the lead. Over-complicated or what! The second, even more extraordinary circumstance came with the fact that 80,000 (!) Celtic fans converged on Seville in Spain for this match. A well-behaved Scottish contingent subsequently won a FIFA Fair Play Award – a welcome change from some of the horror stories of hooliganism rife in the 70s, 80s and 90s.

Route to the Final
Ironically (with Sutton in their side) Celtic put out Blackburn Rovers 3-0 on

aggregate in the second round. Away goals victory over Celta Vigo of Spain and a narrow 5-4 aggregate victory over VFB Stuttgart of Germany placed Celtic in opposition to Liverpool in the quarter-finals. Celtic's best performance in the competition saw off the Merseysiders 3-1 on aggregate. In the first leg at Parkhead the arch poacher Larsson put Celtic ahead. A driving run and deft pass from left full-back John Arne Riise set up Emile Heskey for a fine equaliser. Early pressure from Liverpool in the second leg at Anfield brought long range shots by Dieter Hamann and Steven Gerrard that only narrowly failed to give the Liverpudlians the lead. Celtic then threw a spanner in the works with two marvellous strikes, an Alan Thompson free kick, followed by a 25-yard stunner from another injury-cursed player, John Hartson. Celtic were able to see off one Portuguese side, Boavista, 2-1 on aggregate in the semi-finals, but found Porto a step too far in the final.

Porto's route to the final was somewhat more comfortable, a tricky quarter-final against the Greeks of Panathinaikos surmounted 2-1 after extra time in the second leg. Surprisingly Porto then dispatched the Italians Lazio more serenely to the tune of 4-1 on aggregate in the semi-final.

Celtic's back three for this final were all foreign players. The Swede Johan Mjällby began his pro career with AIK Stockholm in 1989, appearing in 135 league games, mainly as a tough-tackling midfielder. Only at Celtic did he cement a place as a central defender. With Celtic, Mjällby played 144 league games, contributing 13 goals. A popular player with the Celtic Park crowd, Mjällby earned the nickname 'Big Dolph' as he resembled the Swedish actor Dolph Lundgren. Mjällby switched to midfield again when John Barnes held the reins at Celtic, but returned to defence when Kenny Dalglish took over. Under Martin O'Neill, Mjällby took the left side role of the defensive three. Mjällby played 49 times for his country. An injury-ravaged 2003–04 season steered Mjällby towards refusing a one-year extension on his contract.

Bobo Baldé, the French-born Guinea international (he appeared 52 times for Guinea) was another popular player with the Celtic fans. Transferring to Celtic from Toulouse in France in 1999, Baldé went on to play 161 league games for the Glasgow club. Baldé's popularity saw him pick up the Celtic Player of the Year award at the end of season 2002–03. A committed all-or-nothing player (hence his popularity with the fans), Baldé received a yellow card in each of the first six games of the 2004–05 season. A sometimes over-zealous tackler, Baldé missed the start of the 2006–07 season with a recurring stomach injury, and then broke his leg in a fixture on Boxing Day. Baldé won the Scottish League five times while at Celtic. I think it's a shame that what was once a two-horse race for the Scottish league had become a one-horse race in recent years. Thankfully, Rangers appear to be on the up under Steven Gerrard, but oh for a stronger Aberdeen, Hibernian or Hearts to challenge the Glasgow clubs.

Completing Celtic's three-man international defence, Joos Valgaeren plied his trade with Mechelen in Belgium and Roda JC in Holland, his performances with the latter earning him a transfer to Glasgow in 2000. Valgaeren played 116 league games for Celtic 2000–05, helping the club to a domestic treble of League, Scottish Cup and Scottish League Cup in his first season. Injuries again took their toll towards the end of his Celtic tenure, although upon returning to Belgium he won the Belgian Cup with Club Brugge in 2007.

Frenchman Didier Agathe tended to be used as a right wing-back by manager O'Neill. After seven years in French football, followed by a year with Raith Rovers and Hibernian in Scotland, Agathe joined Celtic in 2000, enjoying six seasons in Glasgow. Agathe suffered with a suspect knee, but O'Neill took a chance on him anyway, and not until his last season with the club did his errant knee catch up with him.

The Bulgarian Stiliyan Petrov is best known by followers of English football for the sadness of his contracting leukaemia while at Aston Villa. Prior to this the consistent Petrov enjoyed two lengthy spells at Celtic and Aston Villa, having arrived in Scotland from CSKA Sofia in 1999. A teenager in Glasgow, Petrov was initially homesick, but with John Barnes departed, Petrov thrived under the stewardship of Martin O'Neill, being the first foreign player to win the SPFA Young Player of the Year award. In the 2004–05 season, Petrov won the Celtic Player of the Year award. Petrov played 312 games in all competitions for Celtic over seven seasons, scoring 55 goals. Petrov rejoined then-departed manager O'Neill at Aston Villa in 2006, initially suffering inconsistent form. In the 2008–09 season Petrov's form recovered sufficiently enough for him to be made Villa captain. In this season the Bulgarian was named supporters' Player of the Year and the Player's Player of the Year. Petrov played 105 times for Bulgaria, scoring on eight occasions. Petrov announced his retirement on the pitch at Villa Park, doing a lap of honour with his family as a thank you for their support while he was in remission from leukaemia.

Alan Thompson's career at the top of the game was largely split between Bolton Wanderers 1993–98 and Celtic 2000–07, making 157 and 158 league appearances respectively at those clubs. It was Thompson's piledriver that opened the scoring at Anfield when Celtic upset the odds to defeat Liverpool in the quarter-finals of this UEFA Cup competition. He also scored the decisive goal a year later when Celtic knocked out Barcelona in the last 16 of this same tournament. On the downside, Thompson managed to get himself sent off three times in the 'Old Firm' derbies against Rangers!

Augmenting the midfield five on this evening were the two Ls, Lambert and Lennon. L by name, but certainly not by 'L plates', Paul Lambert and Neil Lennon were tough-tackling, constructive players, possessing excellent tactical brains to the point where they became outstanding coaches/managers. Lambert starred as a 17-year-old for St Mirren, winning the Scottish Cup in 1987. He played 227 league games for the club, following this with 103 at Motherwell. At the latter club he helped them finish runners-up in the Scottish League in the 1994–95 season, the club's best finish since 1933–34. Lambert played against Borussia Dortmund in the 1994–95 UEFA Cup season. In the 1996 season, Lambert won the Supporters' Player of the Year Award at Motherwell.

Leaving under the Bosman rule, Lambert had trial spells with PSV Eindhoven and Borussia Dortmund. Signing for Dortmund at the same time as the Portuguese Paulo Sousa, Lambert experienced fierce competition for a place at the German club, but cemented his place in the team during the 1996–97 season. It was a season in which Dortmund won the Champions League, defeating Juventus 3-1 in the final. Lambert was integral to the victory in that he quelled the threat of the richly talented Zinedine Zidane in his defensive midfield role. Lambert became the first British winner of the Champions League since its restyling from the original European Cup in 1992. Lambert then joined Celtic in 1997, staying in Glasgow until 2005. During this time, Lambert played 193 league games for Celtic. He won four League titles, two Scottish Cups and two Scottish League Cups at Celtic, also winning the Scottish Football Writer's Player of the Year award in 2002. Lambert won 40 caps for Scotland, captaining the side 15 times. Paul Lambert's managerial career takes in Livingstone in Scotland, Wycombe Wanderers, Colchester United, Norwich City, Aston Villa, Blackburn Rovers, Wolverhampton Wanderers, Stoke City and Ipswich Town. He is best remembered for sealing two successive promotions at Norwich City in 2009–10 and 2010–11.

Neil Lennon started out as a player with Glenavon in Northern Ireland, joined Manchester City as a trainee, subsequently signing for Crewe Alexandra in 1990. In between 1990–96 Lennon played 147 league games with the Gresty Road club, his intelligence and consistency making him the first Crewe player to win an international cap for 60 years. Signing for Leicester City, Lennon promptly won the League Cup in 1997, his team defeating Middlesbrough in a replayed final.

Lennon's attachment to Celtic is a long-standing one. He supported the club as a boy (despite being Northern Irish) and in signing for Martin O'Neill in 2000 Lennon achieved his dream move. Between 2000–07 Lennon racked up 214 league appearances, becoming captain of the club when Gordon Strachan took over from O'Neill in 2005. Ironically, Lennon played the same total of 40 games (as Lambert) for his country. Lennon became first-team coach at Celtic in 2008, becoming caretaker manager upon Tony Mowbray's departure in 2010. Made first team manager in June 2010, Lennon's first decision was to shed over a dozen players, claiming the existing incumbents lacked hunger and desire. One of the players he would bring into the club was goalkeeper Fraser Forster, who went on to set a new SPL record for clean sheets. Lennon's own passion was such that he tended to court controversy at times, receiving touchline bans for disputing referee's decisions. Lennon transformed Celtic's domestic trophy aspirations until he departed in 2014, but success in European football did not follow as the might of the likes of Juventus and Barcelona put the quality of Scottish football into clearer perspective.

The fiery Lennon spent the next two seasons as manager of Bolton Wanderers before returning to help Hibernian win the Scottish Championship title (equivalent to the English Championship) in 2017. When Brendan Rogers took over at Leicester City in February 2019, Lennon returned 'home' to Celtic Park. A record third domestic treble at Celtic followed under the auspices of Lennon.

Henrik Larsson enjoyed the best spell of his professional career at Celtic. He scored goals for fun at Celtic Park (an astonishing 175 in 221 league games) which begged the question at the time why wasn't he playing for a bigger club, or in the Premiership in England? Larsson answered the question himself ultimately by joining one of the European giants, Barcelona. Larsson played for Hogaborgs BK and Helsingborg IF in his native Sweden 1989–1993 before joining Feyenoord in Holland. Between 1993 and 1997 Larsson won two KNVB Cups with Feyenoord. Transferring to Celtic in 1997 Larsson suffered the ignominy of scoring an own goal in his first European game for the club. It was a minor blip. In his second season with Celtic he scored 38 goals, ending the season top-scorer in Scotland. Despite his exploits, Celtic were pipped to the title by Rangers. Larsson's consolation came in the shape of winning SPFA Player's Player of the Year, SWFA Footballer of the Year and Swedish Footballer of the Year.

In October 1999 Larsson suffered a career-threatening leg break in a UEFA Cup tie against Lyon. Having excelled in collusion with Slovakian playmaker Lubomir Moravcik under then-manage Jozef Venglos, Larsson returned after fears of a more debilitating fracture to thrive once more in the 2000–01 season under Martin O'Neill. Excelling in a new strike partnership with English Premiership-winning Chris Sutton, Larsson scored 35 goals in 38 league games, becoming SPL top scorer and winner of the European Golden Shoe (top scorer in all European competitions). In all competitions in this season Larsson scored 53 goals. Scoring in each leg of the semi-final of this 2002–03 UEFA Cup enabled Larsson's Celtic to reach their first European final since 1970. Having tasted defeat in this 2003 UEFA Cup Final, Celtic then suffered the bitter fate of losing the Scottish league title to Rangers by a single goal difference having attained the same points total.

Larsson was top scorer five times in his six seasons in Scottish football; he is the top scorer for Celtic in UEFA European competitions. When Celtic fans voted for the greatest-ever Celtic team in 2002, Larsson was the only non-Scot selected. Joining Barcelona in 2004, Larsson endured a chequered couple of seasons at the Nou Camp due to injuries. He still managed to net 13 times in 40 league games. More conclusively, upon entering the field as a substitute in the 2006 Champions League Final against Arsenal, Larsson provided the assists for both Barca goals that turned the final on its head. Larsson played 106 times for Sweden, scoring 37 goals. He was part of the Swedish squad who finished third at the 1994 World Cup.

Chris Sutton, a classical centre-forward in the best British tradition, enjoyed three very successful spells in British football, with Norwich City, Blackburn Rovers and Celtic – and that disregards a short stint with Chelsea, where his one league goal does not reflect the contribution Sutton always made to the team ethic. Sutton actually started life as a centre-half before Norwich manager Dave Stringer switched him to centre-forward. Sutton was part of the Norwich team that famously eliminated the all-powerful Bayern Munich from the 1993 UEFA Cup. Sutton scored 25 times in that Premiership League season after an indifferent goal-scoring start to his life as a striker. Sutton subsequently became the most expensive player in English football when transferred to Blackburn Rovers in July 1994. In Sutton's first season at Ewood Park he formed the 'SAS' partnership with Alan Shearer, scoring 15 times to Shearer's 34.

Sutton, always a trier, didn't necessarily fit into Chelsea's style of play upon moving there in 1999. At the end of that season Sutton swiftly regained form upon joining Celtic. Having scored 35 and 47 goals respectively with Norwich and Blackburn, Sutton superseded this with 63 for Celtic in 130 league games. Sutton may have struggled for goals at Stamford Bridge, but he positively relished European competition, scoring crucial goals for Celtic against Ajax, Juventus, former club Blackburn Rovers and VFB Stuttgart. With John Hartson also in the Celtic ranks, Sutton sometimes returned to his old centre-half role while at Celtic. Hartson, plagued by a back injury, did not appear in this UEFA Cup Final.

Celtic manager for the evening, Martin O'Neill, won the Champions League twice in 1979 and 1980 with Brian Clough's Nottingham Forest. O'Neill, sadly, had to resign as Celtic manager in 2005 to care for his wife who had contracted lymphoma. O'Neill set a new standard during his reign as Celtic manager 2000–05, being the club's most successful boss since the imperious Jock Stein. A feisty, compelling, interesting man, O'Neill has made an excellent pundit on football programmes over the years – like Roy Keane and Lee Dixon recently – with his sharp observations. Like these two, O'Neill knows what he's talking about.

In opposition, Porto's manager José Mourinho may have been in his novice years compared to the experienced O'Neill, but his Porto team were packed with experience. In goal Vitor Baia played for the club over 400 times in two stints at Porto. He also played 80 times for Portugal. In between his two spells at Porto, Baia won the Cup Winners Cup with Barcelona. At right-back, Paulo Ferreira played only 62 league games for Porto 2002–04, going on to play for Chelsea for nearly ten years from 2004. Ferreira also played 62 times for Portugal, being a runner-up at Euro 2004, his country losing 1-0 to Greece in one of the great international upsets.

Captain for the night, Jorge Costa, played 251 league games for Porto in 15 seasons with the club. Revelling in the nickname 'bicho' (animal), the physical Costa played 50 times for Portugal. The other centre-back on this evening, Ricardo Carvalho, also later joined Chelsea, where he is fondly remembered for his cultured, committed performances. A stylish player for a defender, Carvalho nevertheless deployed the dark arts if called upon. At the end of the 2003 season Carvalho was named Portuguese League Footballer of the Year. The following season, Porto went one better than this UEFA Cup victory, winning the Champions League 3-0 against Monaco in the final.

With Mourinho transferred to the hot seat as manager of Chelsea in 2004, Carvalho joined his former boss at Stamford Bridge. The classy Carvalho helped Chelsea to two consecutive Premiership titles 2004–05, 2005–06. Alongside John Terry he formed a formidable central defensive unit. Carvalho followed Mourinho again when his manager took on the reins at Real Madrid. Real had been tracking Carvalho for years, only able to secure his transfer when Mourinho became their manager. Carvalho played 89 times for Portugal.

The left-back, Nuno Valente, played 33 times for Portugal, reinforcing the strength and experience at Mourinho's disposal – and this was just the team's defence.

What a player the attacking midfielder Deco was. In his 148 league games with Porto, Deco scored 32 goals. Deco is a two-time Champions League winner with Porto and Barcelona. His performance in the 2004 Champions League Final against Monaco won him the Man of the Match Award. He also won the

UEFA Best Midfielder Award while at Porto and Barcelona. Deco only qualified as a Portuguese following five years residence in the country. Born Anderson Luis de Souza, he actually hails from Sao Bernardo do Campo, Brazil. Upon leaving Porto in 2004 for Barcelona, Deco was expected to be eclipsed by the multi-talented Brazilian Ronaldinho, instead of which Deco was named Barcelona's Player of the Year in season 2005–06. Deco's tactical nous, deft passing and vision, allied to a healthy work rate, surprised his new employers. Deco then signed for Chelsea in 2008, playing under Brazilian manager Luiz Felipe Scolari. Deco played 43 league games for Chelsea 2008–2010, often being instrumental in the club's victories, although injuries hampered regular appearances. He did play a vital part as Chelsea won the double of League and FA Cup in the 2009–2010 season. It's an anomaly how many London clubs have won the double (Tottenham, Arsenal, Chelsea) given the overall domination of the northern powerhouses Liverpool and Manchester United over the last 50 years in British football.

With Brazil possessing the riches of Ronaldinho, Rivaldo and Juninho in midfield, Deco did not receive an international call from his home nation. Ironically, upon receiving Portuguese residency, his first Portuguese cap came against Brazil. You can't script these things, can you? Guess what? Deco scored the winning goal from a free kick as Portugal ran out 2-1 winners. Another irony: the great Luis Figo was less enamoured than some of the Brazilian-born Deco playing for Portugal. You wonder whether this caused problems within the Portuguese camp as for a few years prior to the arrival of goal machine Cristiano Ronaldo, Figo and Deco were undoubtedly Portugal's two world class players – unless you bracket Carvalho as a third top-notch player. A great dribbler, a player with outstanding technique, elusive, tactically aware, Deco was one of the great players in international football of the last 20 years. He played 75 times for Portugal.

The defensive midfielder, Costinha, Lisbon-born to an Angolan father, transferred to Porto from Monaco in 2001. At Monaco he was part of a team that knocked Manchester United out of the Champions League in 1998. Over four seasons Costinha played 109 league games for Porto, scoring 13 goals (a fair return for a 'holding' midfield player). Costinha played 53 times for Portugal.

The central midfielder Maniche appeared for Benfica, Portugal's other senior club 1999–2002, before transferring to Porto. Maniche played 80 league games for Porto 2002–05, scoring 16 goals. In Lisbon, Maniche played as a winger, his goal-return therefore not entirely unexpected. Maniche's most successful venture abroad came at Atlético Madrid, where he played 64 league games 2006–09, scoring seven goals. He also scored seven times in 52 internationals for Portugal.

The Russian attacking midfielder Dmitri Alenichev scored in both this 2003 UEFA Cup Final and the 2004 Champions League Final, although he was not always a first-choice player. Despite irregular selection (or being the first player to be substituted), Alenichev chalked up 84 league appearances for Porto 2002–04. He played 55 times for Russia, six goals.

On the left side of an attacking duo, Capucho played 130 league games for Sporting Club de Portugal of Lisbon and Vitoria Guimaraes from whom he transferred to Porto in 1997. The best spell of his career came at Porto as he played 188 league games 1997–2003, scoring 32 goals. Capucho also played 34 times for Portugal, often deployed as a defensive midfielder, curiously.

The Brazilian Derlei completed Porto's line-up in attack. In three seasons with Porto he played 57 league games, scoring 19 goals. Upon transferring to Dynamo Moscow in 1995, Derlei scored 20 goals in his two seasons in Russia. This short time period encapsulated Derlei's best form and performances. With Porto he helped the club win eight major titles. Extraordinarily, the sporadic-scoring Derlei found the net 12 times in 13 UEFA Cup appearances 2002–03.

José Mourinho, Porto's manager 2002–04, has established himself in the 21st century as a football management legend. Yet his beginnings were not the traditional route-finding into management of football clubs. Feeling he lacked the necessary physical power to play top professional football as his father had done, Mourinho enrolled at the Technical University of Lisbon to study sports science (a course one of my sons attained a degree in – though in Chichester, not Lisbon!). Mourinho attended courses held by the English and Scottish Football Associations, Andy Roxburgh, the Scottish Football Association's Director of Coaching noting Mourinho's drive and attention to detail. Mourinho went from being a school coach, to being a youth team coach at Vitoria de Setubal in the early 1990s. He then turned his hand to interpreting, assisting Bobby Robson at Sporting Lisbon as an English translator. Robson moved to Porto and Mourinho went with him, all the while discussing tactics and players. Mourinho moved again with Robson to Barcelona, then when Robson departed, new manager Louis Van Gaal entrusted Mourinho with the coaching of the Barcelona B team. Moving to Benfica to be assistant manager Mourinho became manager when Jupp Heynckes departed in October 2000.

Mourinho asked for a contract extension at Benfica when the club defeated city rivals Sporting Lisbon 3-0 in the derby – Mourinho was refused by club president Joao Vale e Azevedo. He resigned and took the management position at little known Uniao de Leivia, enabling his new club to complete on a level playing field with Porto and Benfica in the 2001–02 season. Porto, impressed with this new maverick manager, made Mourinho first team manager in January 2002. The 'maverick' signed Nuno Valente and Derlei from Uniao de Leivia, Paulo Ferreira from Vitoria de Setubal, Maniche from Benfica, and Jorge Costa after he'd been loaned to Charlton Athletic in England – a missed opportunity for the South Londoners surely.

In this UEFA Cup-winning season Mourinho employed a high-pressing game to pressurise opponents into losing possession. In recent years, Mauricio Pochettino and Jürgen Klopp especially have perfected this style of play in England. Mourinho was utilising the plan 20 years ago. This UEFA Cup victory was merely the beginning for Mourinho. His wild celebrations when Costinha scored a decisive 89th-minute goal at Old Trafford in the Champions League in the 2003–04 season are etched in the minds of Mancunians particularly. This moment encapsulated José Mourinho in a nutshell – some loved him, others loathed him. There's no sitting on the fence with Mourinho.

After his two European triumphs at Porto, Mourinho arrived at Stamford

Bridge as Chelsea's new manager in 2004, declaring himself 'the special one'. Bankrolled by the Russian oligarch Roman Abramovich, Mourinho signed Carvalho and Ferreira from Porto, midfielder Thiago from Benfica, Michael Essien from Lyon, Didier Drogba from Marseille, and Mateja Kezma from PSV Eindhoven. At a stroke Mourinho transformed the fortunes of West London's 'sleeping giant' club. Along with the excellent Chelsea stalwarts John Terry and Frank Lampard, Chelsea now had a side to compete with Manchester United and Arsenal, the two teams dominating English football at this time.

In the 2004–05 season, Mourinho's Chelsea won the League Cup, defeating Liverpool. The Reds turned the tables in the Champions League semi-final, depriving Mourinho of another tilt at the premier European trophy. Undaunted, Chelsea promptly won the Premiership with a then-record 95 points total. The title was retained in 2005–06. A 'two-season wonder' nickname was beginning to haunt Mourinho, who seemed to pull things together impressively over a two-year span, but ruffled feathers and fell out with club owners in the process. The signing of Andriy Shevchenko, a splendid striker who Roman Abramovich knew personally, caused friction behind the scenes, especially as Mourinho preferred Drogba as his main striker. Frankly, Drogba more than earned his stripes under Mourinho. The number of times the powerful Ivorian put the frighteners on Arsenal in league games were numerous, and Drogba became key to Chelsea's imminent European success.

Mourinho, somewhat predictably, would not be around to enjoy the fruits of the Drogba-Terry-Lampard inspired Chelsea team. Mourinho left, bestowed with the honour of being Chelsea's most successful manager ever, having won the 2007 FA Cup Final in his last 'first' spell with the club. With relations with owner Abramovich at a peak, Mourinho moved to Inter Milan in June 2008. He immediately signed Diego Milito, Thiago Motta and Wesley Schneider. In his first season at the San Siro, Inter won Serie A, the Italian title, but were knocked out of the Champions League by Manchester United. Equally predictably, Mourinho became embroiled in squabbles with high-profile Italian managers Carlo Ancelotti and Claudio Ranieri. In the 2009–10 season Inter knocked Mourinho's former club Chelsea out of the Champions League, going on to win the trophy, defeating Bayern Munich 2-0 in the final, a match Bayern were favoured to win, and a game that was testament again to Mourinho's organisational skills and tactical nous.

The big European rivals to Inter were clamouring now for Mourinho's services as manager. On 28 May 2010, Mourinho took the reins as Real Madrid manager, again as previous manager of a Champions League-winning team (Inter Milan). Mourinho once more signed big players with the view to winning the Champions League again in Spain: Sami Khedira, Mezut Ozil, Ricardo Carvalho, Angel Di Maria. A fierce rivalry was instantly established with major Spanish rivals Barcelona. Mourinho seems to have instilled an 'us against the world' policy at all the clubs he has managed. Barcelona were beaten in the Copa del Rey Spanish Cup Final, ending an 18-year hunt for the trophy, but Barcelona exacted their revenge, knocking Real out of the 2010–11 Champions League semi-finals. The Champions League continued to elude Real under Mourinho's stewardship, as

Bayern Munich beat the Spaniards at the same semi-final stage in 2011–12, but Mourinho's Real won La Liga at the end of the season, their first title triumph for four years. For the third year running the semi-finals were reached in the Champions League, this time Borussia Dortmund were Real's conquerors. After losing the Copa del Rey to city rivals Atlético Madrid, Mourinho left Real by mutual consent.

They say you should never go back – I think it's true – but Mourinho then signed a new four-year contract at former club Chelsea in 2013 after spending five years on the continent. His first season back at 'the Bridge' resulted in a third-place finish in the Premiership, and another semi-final defeat in the Champions League at the hands of Atlético Madrid as the club entered a period of transition. His second season was a chequered one indeed: shock defeat to Bradford City at Stamford Bridge in the FA Cup; victory over Tottenham in the League Cup Final; defeat on away goals in the last 16 of the Champions League against Paris Saint-Germain; and another Premiership title at the end of the season. Yet by December 2015 Mourinho left Chelsea again by 'mutual consent' after a run of nine defeats in 16 Premier League games.

On 27 May 2016 José Mourinho signed a three-year contract as manager of Manchester United. Mourinho and Manchester United were never a comfortable fit. United as a club have a history of playing stylish football – rather like Tottenham. United's great teams of the 60s and the 90s, even the less great team of the 70s, always played with two wide players of innate skills. In the 60s it was Willie Morgan and George Best; in the 70s it was Steve Coppell and Gordon Hill; and in the 90s it was the speedster Andrei Kanchelskis and the multi-gifted Ryan Giggs. Throughout the years – even when the game became considerably more tactical and organised – Manchester United stood for a certain way of playing the game of football. The five youngsters who represented United's 'Class of 92', Gary Neville, Nicky Butt, Paul Scholes, David Beckham and Giggs, oozed talent as well as a burning passion for Manchester United. Mourinho's desire to play a more defensive game sat very uncomfortably with Manchester United. Mourinho attempted his customary strengthening of a side with the signings of Romelu Lukaku, Victor Lindelof and Nemanja Matic, but it was no surprise to see him part company with United in December 2018.

A serial winner, is Mourinho now living on past glories? As manager of Tottenham Hotspur from November 2019, Tottenham remained trophy-less under his tutelage at the end of the 2019–20 season. Mourinho is a great believer in midfield strength as the key to a winning team. One of Tottenham's best players in recent years, Christian Eriksen, decided to vacate that midfield and move to Inter Milan following Mourinho's appointment. Super-intelligent, tactically astute, Mourinho's impact on the modern game is unquestionable. It remained to be seen whether his winning ways would bring Tottenham their longed-for trophy.

THE FINAL

At the beginning of Mourinho's glory years he could do no wrong. Exquisite skill from Deco almost brought Porto the first goal of this final, a juggle of the ball and a sharp turn, only for the little maestro's shot to hit the side-netting. The opening goal came very shortly afterwards, Derlei finishing after seeing his first shot saved. Deco's awareness was acute as he toe-ended a subtly perfect through ball for the second goal. In between, Henrik Larsson scored a majestic looping header that entered the net via a post from a right-wing corner-kick. Larsson, noted as much for his mobility and fine technique and awareness on the ground, scored a second fine header to equalise. Derlei again took advantage of sloppy defending after Celtic failed to clear an attack. The sending off of Baldé for a wild challenge in the first half did not help Celtic's cause, but in truth the Glaswegians were second-best to this skilful Porto outfit. Only a near miss in the second half when Chris Sutton fired over the bar, threatened an unlikely comeback.

Footnote: Neil Lennon lost the Celtic management job on 24 February 2021. As Steven Gerrard's Rangers ran away with the Scottish League Championship, Lennon paid the price of failing to halt Gerrard's 'runaway train' on the other side of Glasgow. Success must be instant in football in the 21st century, not one of the modern game's more endearing traits. At least the managers are paid well – and they know what they are letting themselves in for when they accept a job in the high-octane world of modern professional football.

2005–2006 UEFA CUP FINAL
Seville 4 v 0 Middlesbrough

Two English clubs rather surprisingly reached the UEFA Cup Final during the first part of the 21st century. Their appearances were on a par with the surprise Scottish finalist, Dundee United, in 1987. The first of these English clubs to rail against the odds were from the north-east, Middlesbrough. Middlesbrough have never been spoken of as one of the giants of the north-east in the same breath as Newcastle United and Sunderland, which is ironic given the struggles of these Tyne and Wear clubs over the past 50 years.

Route to the Final
After topping an initial group stage, Middlesbrough navigated their way through a minefield of classy European teams in order to reach the final. Beating VFB Stuttgart and Roma (both on away goals), then Swiss side Basel 4-3 on aggregate in the quarter-finals, and Romanians Steaua Bucharest 4-3 in the semi-finals was no mean feat. Boro's home wins in the latter two ties, 4-1 and 4-2 were particularly impressive.

A quick look at Boro's line-up for the final reveals four notable players. Captaining the side was none other than Gareth Southgate. Playing wide left, Stewart Downing's form was sufficient to see him included in England's squad along with Southgate. Most impactful were the dual attacking spearhead of Mark Viduka and Jimmy Floyd Hasselbaink who offered plenty of goal threat.

In goal for Boro, the six feet four inch Australian Mark Schwarzer offered an imposing presence. Regarded as one of the best goalkeepers to play in the Premier league, Schwarzer played 367 league games for Boro 1997–2008, following this with a further 172 appearances for Fulham. He would represent the Cottagers in the 2010 UEFA Cup Final.

Southgate never played for the top clubs in English football, but gave sterling service to Crystal Palace (152 league apps) and Middlesbrough (160 league apps). A classy, elegant footballer, Southgate began life at Palace as a right-back before being redeployed as a central midfielder. He captained Palace to the 1993–94 1st Division title. Once at Villa Park, Southgate moved to a centre-back position, a position he is best remembered for. Leaving Villa in an attempt to further his career in 2001, Southgate became captain again at Middlesbrough, finally winning some elusive silverware as Boro beat Bolton Wanderers to win the 2004 League Cup. 2006 proved to be an unfortunate ending to Southgate's professional playing career. Boro found themselves outclassed by Seville in this UEFA Cup Final, then came Euro '96 and THAT semi-final. My memory tells me England were marginally the better side in that game, but this was Germany we were playing, and when it came to penalties, the cool, clinical Germans won out and the unfortunate Southgate, who at least had the courage to step up and take a sudden-death penalty kick, saw his shot saved and England and Terry Venables's adventure was over.

Southgate played 57 times for England and deserved a better finale to his playing days. In mitigation Southgate has remodelled the English national football team as manager, encouraging the side to play a brand of possession football that every continental side imposed upon our country for the decades leading up to his appointment. I at last feel that the lessons of the past are being learnt and the heads in the sand attitude of previous England teams are no more. An intelligent player, Southgate is recreating his England team in the manner of his own stylish playing days. An amusing footnote: Southgate's decision to wear waistcoats at the 2018 World Cup saw Marks and Spencers' sales of this apparel soar by 35%! Southgate is a man who appears to lead by example – in April 2020 he agreed to take a 30% salary cut due to the Covid-19 pandemic. In 2019 Southgate was awarded the OBE for services to football, no doubt due to the excellent performance of England in reaching the semi-finals of the 2018 World Cup.

Stewart Downing started his professional career with Middlesbrough in 2001. Downing began as an old-fashioned winger, being transformed into an attacking midfielder as the modern game developed into one where the midfield numbers earned superiority for a team and wingers became virtually obsolete. As one who spent all but a few games of my village/local football-playing days as a left winger I find this incredibly sad. In the semi-final of this season's UEFA Cup the talented Downing provided three assists in Boro's decisive home win against Steaua Bucharest. Downing's talent was never in question – some felt that he did not impact enough on games at times. What was always evident was Downing's cultured approach to the game. When Boro were relegated in the 2008–09 season, Downing transferred to Aston Villa, being Martin O'Neill's first signing as new manager at Villa Park. Downing showed enough at Villa Park in two seasons for Liverpool to track his progress. In July 2011, Downing made the move to Anfield. In February 2012, Downing helped his new club win the League Cup, but his form was patchy and with Liverpool beginning to rebuild under Brendan Rogers, Downing moved to West Ham United in 2013. Strangely for such a naturally gifted player, Downing was never a prolific scorer, yet in August 2010 he scored the Goal of the Season playing for Aston Villa against West Ham. When Downing did score it was often from distance, and usually spectacular. For Villa, Liverpool and West Ham, Downing played more than 60 league games at each club, but it is Middlesbrough for whom he played a total of 404 games in all competitions that Downing is most associated. Good enough to play 35 times for England, you feel Stewart Downing could have made more of his career – he'll be remembered more for his creativity than for what surely should have been a greater goal return.

Mark Viduka, the Croatian/Australian striker, scored four goals in the Champions League during his career, more than any other Australian international player. Beginning his playing days with Melbourne Knights in Australia, Viduka alerted the wider professional football world with 40 goals in 48 league appearances in Melbourne 1993–95. In 1995 he signed for Dinamo Zagreb in Croatia, repeating the 40-goal trick 1995–98. He helped Dinamo to three league and cup double successes, and won the Best Foreigner Football Award while in Zagreb. In December 1998 Viduka signed for Glasgow Celtic. Despite his time in Glasgow being less than settled, Viduka scored 30 goals in 37 league appearances, including 27 in all competitions in his one and only full season.

Moving again in 2000, Viduka enjoyed a much happier and fruitful association with Leeds United in England. Signed by manager David O'Leary to link up with Michael Bridges and Harry Kewell, injuries to these players meant Viduka forged successful strike partnerships with Alan Smith and Robbie Keane instead. Viduka, an excellent target man, brought more to the table than mere goals (although these were plentiful), his link-up play benefiting those playing off or around him. In four seasons at Leeds, Viduka scored 59 goals in 130 league games, netting 22 times in all competitions in both 2001–02 and 2002–03. In the 2002–03 season Viduka was top scorer at the club, but with Leeds mired in financial difficulties, Viduka was sold at the end of the season to Middlesbrough.

With Middlesbrough, Viduka was frustrated by injuries initially, but in his second season 2005–06 he was on fire, assisting the club in cup campaigns in the FA Cup (quarter-finalists) and League Cup (semi-finalists), and this UEFA Cup Final. Especially impressive in Europe, Viduka helped Boro overturn three-goal deficits in the quarter-finals and semi-finals. In his final season with Boro, Viduka netted 19 times in all competitions. Managed by Southgate by this juncture, Viduka was offered a new contract, but moved on to Newcastle United after scoring 42 league goals for Boro. Sadly, injuries prevented his Newcastle venture being as successful as his forays at Celtic, Leeds and Middlesbrough. On the international scene, Viduka won his first cap as an 18-year-old against South Africa in a friendly, going on to score 11 goals in 43 internationals, captaining the side in later matches.

Viduka's strike partner, Jimmy Floyd Hasselbaink, was an entirely different forward proposition. Four inches shorter than Viduka, stocky in build, Hasselbaink was quick, with a powerful shot. The two complimented each other well. Another very useful scorer, Hasselbaink was born in Surinam, his family moving to Holland where he began playing – as a goalkeeper. On the professional stage, Hasselbaink played three seasons in Holland with Telstar and AZ Alkmaar 1990–93, before moving to Campomaiorense in Portugal in 1995. A year later he joined Boavista. Thirty-two league goals with these clubs earned him a transfer to Leeds United in 1997. From this point his career truly kicked on, winning the Premier League Golden Boot Award in 1999 with 34 goals (jointly with Michael Owen and Dwight Yorke).

A contractual dispute saw the Surinam-born Dutchman move again, this time to Spain, signing for Atlético Madrid. Hasselbaink stayed only one season, with a return of 24 goals in 34 league games, scoring twice against Real Madrid at the Bernabeu to ensure Atlético won the Madrid derby for the first time in nine years. Atlético were surprisingly relegated at the end of the 1999–2000 season – it's unthinkable now. A clause in Hasselbaink's contract allowed him to leave after only one season. This time he moved to London to enjoy four excellent seasons with Chelsea, scoring 69 goals in 136 league games. At Stamford Bridge, Hasselbaink forged a productive strike partnership with the Icelander Eider Gudjohnsen. Only when Gianfranco Zola arrived did Hasselbaink play fewer games for Chelsea, but he continued to score vital goals. In the 2003–04 season the arrivals of the Romanian Adrian Mutu and the Argentinian Hernán Crespo made life even more difficult for Hasselbaink. His response – he top-scored for Chelsea, scoring 17 goals in all competitions. In 2004 he opted for a free transfer move to Middlesbrough, signing a two-year contract. This 2006 UEFA Cup Final appearance proved to be Hasselbaink's last game for the club after a further 22 goals in 58 league games and countless important cup goals. Hasselbaink played 23 times for Holland, scoring nine goals in the process. The stumbling block for him internationally was the presence of Patrick Kluivert, the exquisitely talented Dennis Bergkamp, and wingers Boudewijn Zenden and Marc Overmars.

There was plenty of experience on the bench for Boro on this evening. Cover at centre-back was provided by ex-Aston Villa stalwart Ugo Ehiogu. Cover in midfield came in the shape of the tigerish Lee Cattermole, only 18 years old at the time, and the vastly experienced Ray Parlour (in the evening of his career, Parlour remained an unused substitute). It's difficult to associate Parlour with any other club than Arsenal, although he made 46 league appearances for Boro 2004–07. Attacking cover came from international exports Massimo Maccarone and Yakubu. The Italian Maccarone sparkled initially at the Riverside Stadium, but his form tailed off. Despite this he scored three crucial goals against Basel and Steaua Bucharest in the quarter-finals and semi-finals of this UEFA Cup competition (two in the latter tie after coming on as a substitute). Yakubu – 'The Yak' – hails from Nigeria. An archetypally powerful African player, Yakubu enjoyed nine seasons in English football with Portsmouth, Middlesbrough, Everton, Leicester City (on loan) and Blackburn Rovers. He scored goals everywhere he played in England, a total of 107 at these clubs in league football. His goal return with Boro was 25 from 73 league games. His scoring record for Nigeria is equally respectable, 21 from 57 games.

Evidence of the multi-ethnic nature of 21st-century football came in the nature of Boro's starting line-up for this match. Other players included French left-back Frank Quedrue, Dutch midfielder Gorge Boateng, and Brazilian midfielder Fabio Rochemback.

Boro were managed on this evening by Steve McLaren, assistant to Alex Ferguson at Manchester United 1999–2001, two seasons in which United won the Premiership. His stock was high, and he did an excellent job at Middlesbrough over five seasons. Less successful was his time with England as manager when defeats against Russia and Croatia and consequent failure to qualify for the 2008 Euros meant his international managership tenure was a brief one. With the likes of John Terry, David Beckham, Steven Gerrard and Frank Lampard at his disposal, McLaren might have expected better fortune with England.

What of Boro's opponents Sevilla on this evening? British football followers knew little of them – unless as Sky subscribers you had access to La Liga matches. For Sevilla this was the beginning of an epic journey. A journey that would see them win this competition six times in 14 seasons. It's as if Sevilla believe they have a divine right to win the UEFA Cup; as if they believe the competition belongs to them – and let's face it if you can't win the crème de la crème of European football – the Champions League – you might as well be the winner of Europe's second tier competition. Sevilla have accorded the UEFA Cup the respect it deserves. I don't always feel English clubs have approached the competition with the same intensity, or desire to win it. The Premiership is everything now in England – to players, to managers, to fans. There are too many games and something has to give. Sadly this mantra even extends to some player's desire to represent their country. Surely there is no higher accolade than to play for your country? On the contrary, the money in modern football dictates that the Premiership is king.

Sevilla have undergone several changes of personnel during the past 14 seasons, but their desire to win the UEFA Cup – or Europa League as it is now known in its ludicrously over-bloated form – has not wavered since 2006. This first UEFA Cup-winning team was a cosmopolitan mix of players, highly skilled, some of whom went on to even greater things. Prominent among them was the Brazilian right (wing) back Dani Alves who following splendid service with Sevilla went on to multiple trophy-winning success with Barcelona. Indeed Alves lays claim to being the most decorated player in football history with 43 trophies to his name; he is also equal with the great Italian Paolo Maldini as the most honoured defender in European competition football.

Having won two UEFA Cups and a Copa del Rey with Seville, Alves excelled himself at Barcelona, winning the treble in his first season at the Nou Camp. Alves ultimately left Barcelona on a free transfer in 2016 with five La Liga titles and two Champions League winners medals under his belt. In his one season at Juventus in Turin, Alves won the double of Serie A and the Coppa Italia – this despite breaking a leg in November 2016. Juve also reached the final of the Champions League in this season. In 2017 Alves joined Paris Saint-Germain, winning a treble in his first season in France. Internationally Alves has been capped 118 times (circa 2020), being a member of two World Cup squads and five Copa America tournament squads (the latter the South American Football Championship, the equivalent of the Euros). Brazil won the Copa America twice with Alves participating in 2007 and 2019.

Alves almost went to Anfield at the end of the 2006 season, but Liverpool would not meet Sevilla's £8 million transfer demand. What an opportunity missed! A player of great pace and stamina, Alves may not have been the biggest at five feet eight inches, but his energy, sublime technique, and fine passing ability made him a constant menace to the left flank of any opposing team.

Sevilla's captain for the night, Javi Navarro, was an imposing figure, at the heart of the defence during the club's first two UEFA Cup triumphs in 2006 and 2007. He played 168 league games for Sevilla 2001–09, missing many more games through injury. Partnering him at centre-back, the Frenchman Julien Escudé formed a formidable core in Sevilla's defence, although he too would suffer his own injury problems in 2007–08 with a nagging groin problem.

Jesús Navas is well known in British football for his performances at the Etihad Stadium for Manchester City. Prior to his transfer there, Navas played over 550 matches in all competitions for Sevilla 2003–2013, only scoring 23 league goals, but setting up scores more for his appreciative teammates with his dribbling ability, crossing and countless assists. The speedy Navas tended to play on the right, making Alves's attacking forays more measured if the two played together. At Barcelona, Alves had plenty of opportunity to harness his attacking threat potently. Navas, for his part, reduced many a defence to jelly – if only he scored more often! At Manchester City, Navas played a further 123 league games 2013–17 before returning 'home' to Seville where he played over 100 games in all competitions post-2017. Navas has played 44 times for Spain, scoring five times.

Another player to move on to Barcelona, again Brazilian, Adriano played wide left in this UEFA Cup Final. Appearing for Sevilla in 157 league games 2005–2010, he scored 11 times in these games. At the Nou Camp, Adriano would generally play second fiddle to French international Eric Abidal. Adriano played 17 times for Brazil.

Keeping the Brazilian connection going in attack, Luis Fabiano carried a massive goal threat for Sevilla. Joining the club from Porto in 2005 after a troubled season in Portugal, Fabiano took to life in Spain without rancour, scoring 72 goals in his 149 league appearances for Sevilla 2005–2011. He also scored 28 goals in only 45 games for Brazil. Powerful, skilful, Fabiano sometimes allowed his physicality to overshadow his ability.

Alongside Fabiano in attack, the Argentine Javier Saviola was a completely different physical specimen. At five feet six inches, seven inches shorter than Fabiano, the pair formed a South American 'little and large' combination. Saviola won league titles in Argentina, Spain and Greece before scoring 45 goals in 86 league games for River Plate. Saviola, nicknamed 'El Conejo' ('the little rabbit'), started senior football with River Plate in Argentina, winning the 1999 South American Footballer of the Year Award, aged only 18. He was seen as an heir to the throne of Diego Maradona. Only 19, Saviola moved to Barcelona, but with Carlos Rexach, swiftly followed by Louis Van Gaal, Radimir Antic and Frank Rijkaard as head coaches at the Nou Camp, Saviola suffered a little after an excellent first season, when he scored 17 goals. He ended his time with Barcelona having scored 49 goals in 123 appearances.

Surplus to Rijkaard's requirements, Saviola went on loan in 2004 to Monaco, then again to Sevilla in 2005. In essence, Saviola was only a loan player in this UEFA Cup-winning side – he scored nine goals in 29 games for the club. Despite his obvious natural ability, Saviola continued to be farmed out to other clubs, joining Real Madrid for two seasons 2007–09; a more successful three-year term followed at Benfica, where he helped the Lisbon club win the Portuguese title for the first time in five years, scoring 24 goals in his 69 games for the club. Single seasons followed at Malaga (Spain), Olympiakos (Greece) and Verona (Italy), suggesting a restless spirit. Finally, in 2015, Saviola returned to River Plate after a 14-year absence. Saviola played 39 times for Argentina, netting 11 times. They say size doesn't matter if you've got the ability, but I think it does. Obviously if you're mentality is tough it shouldn't be an insurmountable obstacle (think Alan Ball, England World Cup-winner, 1966), but one wonders whether Saviola's diminutive size prevented him from becoming one of the world's greatest players as Argentinians hoped back in 1998 when he was a 'wonderkid'. For a time, his quick-wittedness made him a very dangerous player in his second-striker role.

One of the substitutes for Sevilla – he came on and scored – was Frédéric Kanouté. Kanouté's record as a goalscorer at Sevilla is very impressive, a total of 89 league goals coming in 209 appearances 2005–2012, a record that makes him the Spanish club's highest-ever foreign goalscorer. Kanouté, French born, but with a Malian father, is well known in England for his stints with West Ham United and Tottenham Hotspur. An intermittent scorer at these clubs (29 league goals for the Hammers, 14 league goals for Spurs), Kanouté went on to be a successful and integral player for Sevilla, winning two UEFA Cups and two Copa del Reys 2005–2012. After not being selected for France between 2000 and 2004, Kanouté opted to play for Mali for whom he scored 23 goals in 39 appearances.

Sevilla's manager Juande Ramos built a strong reputation thanks to the two UEFA Cup-winning seasons of 2006 and 2007. This earned him the position of manager at White Hart Lane for the 2007–08 season. Unfortunately for Ramos, Tottenham Hotspur were in the midst of a period of inconsistency (it's a perennial problem!), their defence particularly vulnerable. Ramos managed to lift Spurs mid-term, the club eventually going on to win the League Cup in 2008, defeating a strong Chelsea team after extra time. A poor start to the new 2008–09 season sowed the seeds of Ramos's demise at Tottenham. This didn't prevent Real Madrid appointing him as successor to Bernd Schuster, but failure to halt the Barcelona juggernaut cost him his position at the end of the 2008–09 season. Sevilla's early UEFA Cup exploits remain Ramos's career highlights.

THE FINAL
Sevilla took the lead after 27 minutes when Fabiano superbly headed Dani Alves's right-wing cross past Mark Schwarzer in the Boro goal. Alves's constant probing on the right was simply too much for the Boro defence. Smart interplay, fast counter-attacking, Alves tied Boro's defence in knots, the English team's back four never quite sure where Alves was coming from next. Italian midfielder Maresca then took centre stage, scoring a second after Kanouté's shot was blocked. Maresca made it 3-0 with a 20-yard shot. The same player's shot from

the right was parried into the path of Kanouté, on as a substitute, and the Malian made no mistake to complete the scoring. On the night, Middlesbrough were blown away by Sevilla. McLaren took a risk by sending on Yakubu, a striker, for the injured defender Frank Quedrue. The decision backfired as Sevilla's fast-breaking team scored three of their goals after the substitution in the last 12 minutes of the game.

2007–08 UEFA CUP FINAL
Zenit St Petersburg 2 v 0 Glasgow Rangers

This was the last time a Scottish team reached a final of any European competition. One can't help but hark back to the halcyon years of Celtic and Rangers 1967–1972, a time when Scottish football belonged at the pinnacle of the European game with the likes of Celtic's 'jinking' Jimmy Johnstone, and then throughout the 70s and 80s when Scottish football produced top players like Hansen, Souness, Dalglish and Archie Gemmill.

The Rangers team here didn't contain too many players known south of the border in England. Manager Walter Smith's 4-1-4-1 formation suggested a cautious approach to this final in Manchester. Rather a shame for the 200,000 Rangers supporters who descended upon the English north-west, the largest travelling support of any club known in football history for a final. Both teams started the season in the senior Champions League competition, Rangers finishing third in their group behind Barcelona and Lyon; Zenit finishing third behind Everton and Nurnberg, both clubs consequently being relocated to the UEFA Cup.

Route to the Final
Rangers' route to the final reflects their manager's cautionary nature – Panathinaikos beaten on away goals in the last 32, Werder Bremen 2-1 in the last 16, Sporting Lisbon 2-0 in the quarter-finals (a notable 2-0 away victory here), and Fiorentina beaten 4-2 on penalties after two 0-0 games in the two legs of the semi-finals.

Zenit fared similarly in the last 32 and last 16 (while scoring more goals), beating Villareal of Spain and Marseille of France on away goals. Credit should be given to the Russian side for the manner in which they won their quarter-final and semi-final matches. In the last eight, a fine 4-1 away win against Bayer Leverkusen of Germany confirmed their last four place despite a 0-1 home defeat. In the semis the Russians beat the formidable Bayern Munich 5-1 on aggregate (4-0 in St Petersburg).

During this 2007–08 season Rangers scored only 16 goals in the two European competitions they were involved in, conceding 11 in 18 matches. This tight, disciplined, defensive approach revealed the shrewd tactical mind of manager Walter Smith. One of the stalwarts of his defence, David Weir, chalked up 606 league games north and south of the border, 133 for Falkirk, 76 for Heart of Midlothian, 235 for Everton on Merseyside, and ultimately 162 for Rangers 2007–2012. Weir captained Everton at times 1999–2007, and then Rangers from 2009. Weir would win three league titles with Rangers, the last as a 41-year-old in

134

2011. A fallow period followed for Glasgow's joint senior club thereafter as Celtic dominated the league in Scotland. Weir, utterly dependable and solid, the perfect traits for a centre-back, won 69 caps for Scotland.

Alongside Weir in the heart of the defence, the Spaniard Carlos Cuéllar enjoyed just one stellar season with Rangers 2007–08. Playing 65 games in all competitions, Cuéllar forged a fine partnership with Weir and was awarded the Scottish Premier League Player of the Year at the end of the season. Which makes it more of a mystery that his subsequent career failed to flourish, despite 94 league appearances at next club Aston Villa. Cuéllar appeared classy at times, inconsistent at others.

What Rangers did possess in abundance in midfield were hard-working players. On the right side of Smith's bank of four midfielders, Stephen Whittaker provided both a foraging attacking threat and sound defensive cover having previously been deployed as a full-back. Whittaker began his senior career in Scotland with Hibernian, playing 141 league games for the Edinburgh-based club, before switching to Glasgow, playing a further 150 league games for Rangers. He transferred to Norwich City in England when Rangers went into administration in February 2012. Whittaker played 31 times for Scotland.

Captaining Rangers on this evening, Barry Ferguson was an integral member of the club during two spells, 1997–2003, and 2005–09, totalling 431 games and 60 goals in all competitions. A treble for Rangers in 2003 helped Ferguson win the SFWA Footballer of the Year Award – he'd already won the award in 1999. In all, Ferguson won the Scottish Premier League, Scottish Cup and Scottish League Cup five times apiece. In between these periods Ferguson played 36 league games for Blackburn Rovers, where he was also made captain by Graham Souness, who probably saw something of the fighter in himself in Ferguson, a fellow Scot. A fractured kneecap and a feeling that the Premiership or Lancashire derbies couldn't match the 'Old Firm' Glasgow derby saw Ferguson move back to Rangers. A fall-out with manager of the time, Paul Le Guen, saw Ferguson temporarily discarded, but Ferguson was swiftly reinstated as captain of the side under caretaker manager Ian Durrant when Le Guen departed.

In April 2009 Ferguson was stripped of the captaincy of club and country following incidents in matches against Holland and Iceland that were deemed 'unacceptable'. A committed, competitive, feisty player, Ferguson's desire to win sometimes led him to be outspoken if he felt a situation warranted it.

Joining Birmingham City in 2009, Ferguson promptly became the club's Player's Player of the Year for the season 2009–2010. A broken rib suffered by Ferguson in the final didn't prevent this perennial winner from aiding Birmingham City to a surprise League Cup victory over favourites Arsenal. When Birmingham were relegated at the end of this 2010–11 season, Ferguson's wages made him an obvious target for Birmingham to reduce their wage bill. Ferguson joined Championship club Blackpool, swiftly succeeding Charlie Adam as club captain. A born leader, Ferguson took over as caretaker manager of Blackpool in January 2014, following Paul Ince's dismissal. Despite a record of only three wins in their last 20 matches, Blackpool somehow staved off relegation under Ferguson's tutelage.

Ferguson's scoring record in England was dismal, although his role as a midfielder was largely that of a ball-winner. For Scotland, Ferguson played 45 games, scoring three goals. It's Rangers for whom Ferguson's career is best remembered, appropriate as his family supported the club from their South Lanarkshire home, 12 miles south-east of Glasgow. Barry Ferguson is the all-time Scottish record holder of appearances in European competition football, his total of 82 games surpassing David Narey and Kenny Dalglish.

Alongside Ferguson in the Rangers midfield resided another fiercely hard-working player, the Northern Irishman Steven Davis. Davis is a player well known to English football fans. Starting out professionally with Aston Villa in the 2004–05 season, Davis was named Young Player of the Year at the end of his first year at Villa Park, in addition to being Fans Player of the Year and Player of the Year. In 102 games in all competitions for Villa up to 2007 Davis scored nine goals. One season at Fulham resulted in a loan period in Glasgow that became a four-year permanent move in August 2008. Three consecutive Scottish League titles followed 2009, 2010, 2011. Like Ferguson, Davis's inspiration was allied to copious perspiration. Fans and players alike always admire a player with a big engine, a player who is always seen to give 110%. From being a temporary captain at Rangers in 2011, Davis was another player who exercised his right to leave as a free agent when Rangers went into administration in 2012. Davis subsequently played 193 league games for Southampton 2012–19, becoming captain in his later years at St Mary's.

In 2019, Davis returned to Rangers, first on loan, then on a permanent transfer under manager Steven Gerrard. Davis is the most capped midfield player in British football, his 119 caps for Northern Ireland surpassing David Beckham's 115 for England. Davis was appointed an MBE in the 2017 Birthday Honours for services to football.

In attack, Jean-Claude Darcheville was asked to plough a lone furrow against Zenit. Darcheville's form with Lorient and Bordeaux in France earnt the French Guianese a transfer to Rangers in 2007. Between 2007 and 2009 Darcheville scored 13 goals in 38 league games for the Glasgow club, but his selection as a lone striker gave him little opportunity to shine in this final. His selection for this match seems odd to me, with goal machine Kris Boyd on the bench. Boyd scored 25 goals in this season alone. In December Boyd would score five goals in a 7-1 demolition of Dundee United. Between 2006 and 2010, Boyd scored over 100 goals for Rangers. Boyd would often be used as a substitute with question marks hanging over his team contribution. If you've got a goalscorer in your ranks, for heaven's sake play him! I did once play up front with a striker who scored 52 goals to my 17, but my frustration with his 'selfishness' at times was tangible – but I have to acknowledge his finishing ability was invaluable to the team that season. Boyd played 18 times for Scotland, scoring seven goals. He knew where the goal was. Presumably the pacy Darcheville gave more to the team in Walter Smith's eyes.

Another of the substitutes, the Spaniard Nacho Novo, also had a fine goal-scoring record with Rangers, netting 47 goals in 179 league games. Another sub, Lee McCulloch, scored over 50 goals in his 200-plus appearances for Rangers. The defensive-minded Smith certainly had options to call upon from his bench.

Smith also had fine athletes and technicians in reserve in Christian Dailly and Charlie Adam, the latter a particularly good technical player whose free-kick expertise has been witnessed at clubs in England: Blackpool, Liverpool and Stoke City. You've got to be a very good footballer indeed to play for Liverpool, even if Adam played only one season at Anfield (2011–12).

Walter Smith's managerial record at Rangers is unquestionably impressive. Smith oversaw 13 trophy wins in seven seasons, 1991–98, including seven successive league titles in the era before Celtic dominance in the early 21st century. Another eight trophies followed when Smith returned to Rangers, 2007–2011. In the interim, Smith managed Everton for four seasons and provided a mini-revival in his country's fortunes as Scotland manager, 2004–07. One cannot question Smith's winning achievements. I only wonder whether a more positive outlook may have borne fruit against Zenit St Petersburg.

Very little was known on these shores about Zenit going into this final. Clearly the Russians possessed firepower, their goal ratio en route to the final indicated this. Who were their star players? Man of the match on this night in Manchester was Andrey Arshavin, whose star rose substantially in the subsequent 2008 Euros when Russia reached the semi-finals. Only five feet eight inches, but sublimely talented, Arshavin scored 51 goals in 238 league games for the St Petersburg-based club 1999–2009. His outstanding displays in this final and the 2008 Euros earnt a transfer to North London (Tottenham and Barcelona also wanted him), joining Arsenal. Something of an enigma at the Emirates, Arshavin's individual crowning glory came in scoring all four goals in a 4-4 draw with Liverpool at Anfield. Arshavin also starred when Arsenal finally defeated their nemesis Barcelona 2-1 in the Champions League last 16 of 2011. In all, Arshavin scored 23 times in 105 league games for Arsenal. Frustratingly inconsistent at times, Arshavin remains arguably the most talented Russian player of the last two decades.

The captain of Zenit, the Ukrainian Anatoliy Tymoschuk, a defensive midfielder or centre-back, had an impressive career with Shakhtar Donetsk 1998–2007, two seasons with Zenit, and then a fine spell with Bayern Munich, 2009–2013. The consummate professional in the eyes of Zenit's then-manager, Dick Advocaat, Tymoschuk also captained Shakhtar and the Ukrainian national team, for whom he played a record 144 games.

In midfield, Zenit possessed players in Konstantin Zyranov and Igor Denisov who would both win more than 50 caps for Russia, but Rangers and British football followers in general knew little of them.

Zenit's manager Dick Advocaat was already vastly experienced come this final, having managed five teams in Holland including PSV Eindhoven, and also the Dutch national team 1992–94. Advocaat was very well known to Rangers' fans having held the reins at Ibrox Park 1998–2001. During his spell with Rangers, Advocaat won a domestic treble, a feat emulated by Walter Smith. Advocaat then managed Borussia Möenchengladbach in Germany, and the United Arab Emirates and South Korean national teams before going head-to-head with Smith in Manchester for this UEFA Cup trophy. Advocaat's managerial CV post-2008 is even longer, stints in Belgium, Holland, England (with Sunderland in 2015), Serbia, and Turkey took him up to 2019 when he managed Feyenoord in Holland.

THE FINAL

Glasgow Rangers – no European win since 1972. Arshavin would deny them victory in this final. The enigmatic Russian spurned the first chance of this final from wide on the left. Darcheville, starved of ball by Smith's team selection, almost equalised after Steven Davis found him on the left. Darcheville escaped the last defender on the right side of the penalty area, but his shot was blocked. Full-back Aleksander Anyukov produced the next meaningful action, his long-range drive saved by Rangers' keeper Neil Alexander. The first half ended goalless. In the second half, Arshavin came to the fore, not as a scorer of spectacular goals as he came to be remembered at Arsenal, but with his persistent probing of Rangers' defence. First he teed up Denisov for the opening goal in the 72nd minute. Shortly afterwards, substitute Nacho Novo blasted the ball high and wide for Rangers, but Arshavin had the last word, bisecting Rangers' defence again to allow Radek Sirl to overlap and leave Zyranov a simple chance to net for 2-0. My fading memory tells me that Zenit were the better technical side on the night and merited their victory.

THE EUROPA LEAGUE FINALS

2010 EUROPA LEAGUE FINAL
Atlético Madrid 2 v 1 Fulham (after extra time)

At the time, neither of these clubs had serious European competition football history. Atlético won the European Cup Winners Cup in 1962 – the season before being humbled by the magnificent Tottenham Hotspur team including the great Jimmy Greaves. Fulham were playing only their second season in European football. It is a great tribute to the Cottagers that they ever made this final, defeating the Ukrainian holders of the trophy, Shakhtar Donetsk, along the way. Atlético's record since 2010 when they have fought tooth and nail with their illustrious Madrid rivals Real, makes Fulham's achievement seem even more remarkable now.

Route to the Final

Fulham finished second in their Europa League group stage behind a very strong Roma team. This qualified the Craven Cottage-based club for the round of 32 in which they defeated Shakhtar Donetsk 3-2 on aggregate. Better was to come. Having lost, predictably, 3-1 to Juventus in Turin in the last 16, Fulham produced one of the great nights in the club's history, beating Juve 4-1 in the return leg. VFL Wolfsburg were beaten 3-1 on aggregate in the quarter-finals; the team hosting the 2010 UEFA Cup Final, Hamburger SV were denied a presence in their own showpiece by Fulham after a 0-0 draw in Germany was followed by a tight 2-1 win at home for the south-west London team.

Atlético finished third in their Champions League group in 2009–2010, denied progress by a rampant Chelsea, and the Portuguese European specialists Porto. This saw the Madrid club allocated a place in the last 32 of the newly founded, UEFA Cup-originated, Europa League. Atlético's route to the final was even more tortuous than Fulham's: Galatasaray of Turkey beaten 3-2 in the last 32; Sporting CP of Lisbon on away goals in the last 16; Spanish rivals Valencia on away goals in the quarter-finals; and denying the opportunity of an all-English final, Liverpool on away goals after extra time in the semi-finals (1-0 at home 1-2 at Anfield).

In goal for Fulham on the night was Mark Schwarzer, Middlesbrough's keeper from the 2004 final, he of the long career and even longer physique. Schwarzer's 172 league appearances for Fulham are only superseded by his 367 appearances for the Boro. Schwarzer's timespan and form for Fulham 2008–2013 made Arsene Wenger want to sign him in the twilight of his career for Arsenal. Arsenal had never – may still not have – properly replaced David Seaman post-2004.

Many of the names of Fulham's players on this evening do not trip off the tongue, but they were established top-level players, some of whom were internationals. At right-back, Chris Baird began his professional career with Southampton, establishing himself as a regular under the stewardship of the former (classy) Ipswich full-back George Burley. Fulham's bid for Baird proved successful in 2007. Baird played 127 league games for Fulham 2007–2013, initially struggling to attain regular football as he had at Southampton. Baird gained a foothold in the team during this 2009–10 season. A player who could play centre-back or defensive midfield, it is at right-back he seems to have succeeded in achieving regular first-team football at the highest level. Baird played 79 times for Northern Ireland.

Baird's fellow Northern Irishman, Aaron Hughes, played centre-back in this final, although he too could also be deployed as a full-back. Hughes was firmly established as a top-flight player, having played 205 league games for Newcastle United 1997–2005 and 54 for Aston Villa 2005–07. For Fulham, Hughes played over 200 games in all competitions 2007–2014. He also represented his country 112 times, captaining Northern Ireland from 2003–2011, finishing his international career as the second highest capped player behind Tottenham and Arsenal's great goalkeeper Pat Jennings.

The other centre-back, Brede Hangeland, played 217 league games for Fulham 2008-2014. As with Schwarzer, Hangeland was linked with Arsenal, but remained at Craven Cottage having forged a strong career initially with Viking Stavanger in Norway (a Norwegian Cup-winner in his first season 2000–01) and Copenhagen (two-time Danish Superliga winner 2007 and 2008). In a team replete with natural leaders (their leadership skills, if not their obvious individual brilliance indicates the reason Fulham made it to this final), Hangeland also captained Norway in 48 of his 91 appearances for his country.

At left-back Paul Konchesky received numerous plaudits for his performances with first club Charlton Athletic. Konchesky's natural talent was not necessarily matched by a physicality that seems paramount in modern-day football. A loan period to Tottenham Hotspur in 2003 didn't materialise into a permanent move. Instead West Ham United took a chance on him. Konchesky scored in the famous 2006 FA Cup Final for the Hammers, the game remembered specifically for Steven Gerrard's rasping long-range goal for Liverpool. After a total of 70 games in all competitions for West Ham, Konchesky signed a four-year contract at Craven Cottage. Konchesky played over 100 games for Fulham, 2007–2010, his natural ability earning him a move to Liverpool for the season 2010–11. It was an ill-fated switch, with Konchesky struggling to establish himself at Anfield. After being loaned out to Nottingham Forest, Konchesky re-established himself at left-back for Leicester City 2011–16 where he played the most league games of his career (138) other than at Charlton Athletic (149). Konchesky played twice for England.

Fulham's midfield for this match were a talented, diverse group. The Nigerian Dickson Etuhu gave the side physical presence. David Moyes signed him from first pro side Manchester City in 2002. Etuhu subsequently played 134 league games for Preston North End, but his form fluctuated during his time at Deepdale. A loan period at Norwich City became a permanent move 2005–07, followed by a season with Sunderland 2007–08. Etuhu signed for Fulham in August 2008 on a three-year contract. He played 91 league games for Fulham 2008–2012. He also played 33 times for Nigeria. Etuhu's physical presence made him perfect as the team's defensive midfielder. The players around him in the centre of the park were all slighter, all with more obvious technical skills.

Simon Davies, scorer of Fulham's goal in this final, often flattered to deceive. Clearly a very good technical player, Davies, like Konchesky, suffered at times from a lack of physicality at this elevated level. Davies began his career at Peterborough United. His obvious natural talent earned him a move to Tottenham Hotspur along with Matthew Etherington to White Hart Lane in 2000 after three seasons in the lower leagues. Davies's skill was there for all to see and in the rarefied atmosphere at Tottenham Davies thrived for a while. A few niggling injuries halted his time with Spurs, but Davies completed 154 games in all competitions, scoring 24 times. Davies then spent two seasons with Everton without reproducing his Spurs form. In January 2007, Davies returned to London, joining Fulham as a replacement for the popular Craven Cottage icon Steed Malbranque. He proceeded to play the most top-flight games of his career at Fulham. Craven Cottage fans admired his pace and skill, Davies winning Player of the Year at the end of his first full season with the club, 2007–08. Knee and hip injuries curtailed what had been a promising start to Davies's Fulham career. Davies equalled his league goals tally of 13 at Tottenham while with Fulham. A skilful player, Davies was recognisable by his wavy brown locks. He played 58 times for Wales, scoring six goals, and was named Welsh Footballer of the Year in 2002.

Davies tended to play wide right at Tottenham and Fulham. Playing wide left here for Fulham was the super-talented and extremely industrious Republic of Ireland international, Damien Duff. Duff's work-rate was prodigious – one wonders whether this contributed to the many injuries he incurred. Not tall – the same height as myself being a little shy of five feet ten inches – Duff's stocky physique helped him withstand the many vigorous, occasionally dubious, challenges a winger/wide player has to endure during the 90 minutes plus of a football match. But how much did these tackles take their toll? The Ballyboden, Dublin-born Irishman began his pro career with Blackburn Rovers, helping the Lancashire club to a League Cup win in 2002, beating Tottenham 2-1 in the final at the Millennium Stadium. In his last season at Ewood Park, Duff helped Blackburn qualify for the 2003–04 UEFA Cup.

Signing for Chelsea in July 2003, Duff was among the first raft of big signings by manager Claudio Ranieri following the takeover of Chelsea by Russian businessman Roman Abramovich. Abramovich did not stand on ceremony in his early tenure as the new owner of Chelsea. Ranieri would be sacked at the end of the season despite Duff assisting Chelsea to a second-place finish in the Premiership in 2003–04, their highest finish for 49 years. Ranieri's sin: failure in the Champions League, losing their semi-final to AS Monaco, matches Duff missed through injury. The following season, Chelsea, now linked with all the world's top players due to Abramovich's financial clout, signed the mercurial, extravagantly gifted Arjen Robben. Duff's place on the left seemed under threat. Instead the hard-working, talented Duff forced his way into Chelsea's starting 11 as a right winger/right wide midfield player. The dual threat of Duff and Robben made Chelsea in 2004–05 an unstoppable force at domestic level, the club winning the Premiership by 12 points from second-placed Arsenal, and winning the League Cup.

Duff scored 14 goals in 81 league games for Chelsea, but moved again in July 2006 to Newcastle United where he stayed three seasons. When Newcastle were relegated at the end of the 2008–09 season Duff moved back to the Premiership, signing for Roy Hodgson's Fulham (Hodgson managed Duff at Blackburn). Duff played 130 league games for Fulham 2009–2014, scoring 14 times. These would be his last games in English football, Duff's final playing days taking place in Melbourne, Australia, and Shamrock Rovers in the League of Ireland's Premier Division. Less obviously gifted than Robben, Duff's work ethic made him an invaluable player in the Premiership and in Europe. His first-class attitude, allied to a considerable level of craft and skill, made Damien Duff a wonderful player for teammates to play alongside. Duff was capped by the Republic of Ireland 100 times, scoring eight goals. Unsurprisingly, Duff was named Ireland's Player of the Tournament at the 2002 World Cup.

Fulham's midfield was completed by a player well known in the modern English game due to his excellent punditry with the BBC, Danny Murphy. Chester-born Murphy began his pro career with his 'local' club Crewe Alexandra, playing 134 league games in the lower divisions. Murphy's technique and excellent ball retention earned him a transfer to Liverpool in 1997. Initially he struggled to hold down a regular place as the central midfield positions were held by Steven Gerrard and Dieter Hamann. Murphy tended to play as a wide midfield player as a result, when he broke into the Liverpool first team. Coach and former player Phil Thompson thought Murphy was Liverpool's most tactically aware player. The fans appreciated Murphy too, his performances earning him the supporters' Player of the Year for the season 2002–03. In Murphy's 170 league games for Liverpool he scored 25 goals, including three winning strikes against Manchester United. After seven seasons at Anfield, Murphy moved to Charlton Athletic, staying for two seasons 2004–06, followed by a year of fitful form under Martin Jol at Tottenham Hotspur.

Murphy rediscovered his mojo when moving to Fulham under Roy Hodgson in 2007. Despite being constantly linked with other clubs, Murphy remained at Craven Cottage until 2012, playing 169 league games, and captaining the club in this final. Mark Hughes replaced Hodgson as manager in the 2010–11 season, Hughes praising Murphy's contribution to Fulham's successful battle against relegation. In 2011–12 Murphy played 49 games at Fulham – ironically now managed by Martin Jol. Murphy created more goals than any other player in the Premiership during this season. One season at Blackburn Rovers followed before Murphy called time on his playing career. Murphy played nine times for England 2001–03.

Playing 'in the hole' behind striker Bobby Zamora, Hungarian international Zoltan Gera proved a highly successful addition to Fulham 2008–2011. Making his mark at Ferencváros in Hungary 2000–04, Gera won Hungarian Footballer of the Year in 2002, 2004 and 2005. He won the Hungarian title in 2001 and 2004, and the Magyar Cupa (the Hungarian Cup) in 2003 and 2004. Gera moved to West Bromwich Albion in 2004, playing 135 league games for the Hawthorns club, scoring 21 goals. His time in the Midlands was largely successful, although hampered by injuries. Gera helped WBA to win a Premiership place in his last season, 2007–08, but opted to join Fulham in June 2008. Gera's input in the run to this final was profound. He scored two goals in a man-of-the-match performance as Juventus were trounced 4-1 in the last 16 second leg at Craven Cottage. Gera scored the winning goal against Hamburger SV in the semi-final, and provided the assist for Fulham's goal in this final.

Under Mark Hughes, Gera did not play regularly. His 86 league game run at Fulham consequently ended, the Hungarian returning to WBA 2011–14. Surplus to WBA's requirements at the end of the 2013–14 season, Gera returned to Ferencváros. In 2015–16, Gera was part of another title success for Hungary's premier club, not bad for a player deemed 'past it' in England! Zoltan Gera was capped 97 times for his country with a very respectable goal return of 26. Gera's impact in English football with WBA and Fulham was considerable, his technique, vision and tactical awareness making his role behind the main striker a very useful asset to his clubs.

Centre-forward Bobby Zamora had taken a circuitous route to arrive at Fulham. Like Simon Davies, he had played for Tottenham Hotspur, albeit for only 16 games in the 2003–04 season. Zamora made his reputation with Brighton and Hove Albion 2000–03, scoring 83 goals in 136 games in all competitions on the south coast. His goals went some way to ensuring Brighton won successive promotions from the lower divisions. Zamora's ill-fated move to White Hart Lane saw him score only one goal, a goal that knocked West Ham United out of the League Cup in October 2003. West Ham it was who took a chance on Zamora in January 2004. Zamora's form picked up with the Hammers, the striker scoring 40 goals in 152 appearances in all competitions. Zamora joined Fulham in July 2008, struggling initially to score the goals he had been bought for. Zamora had a return of 20 goals in 91 league games for Fulham, but proved useful in the European games of 2009–10, scoring against Juventus and Wolfsburg en route to the final. Sadly for Zamora his fitness was less than 100% for Fulham's tilt at this UEFA Cup Final. In 2012 Zamora signed for Queens Park Rangers but surgery on a hip injury was the beginning of the end for the striker. He returned to Brighton and Hove Albion in 2015, but was forced to retire in December 2016. Zamora promised much – indeed he won two England caps, but his best days were in his first spell at Brighton and arguably, at West Ham.

The most interesting of Fulham's substitutes was the American Clint Dempsey. Dempsey signed for Fulham from American club New England Revolution in January 2007, staying at Craven Cottage for five seasons, scoring 60 goals in all competitions. The American came on as a substitute in the last 16 against Juventus, scoring a memorable chipped goal from the edge of the penalty area to seal victory. Coming on as a substitute against Atlético Madrid in this final, Dempsey became the first American football player to appear in a European final. Fulham fans voted the American their Player of the Year in the subsequent 2010–11 season. Dempsey moved to Tottenham Hotspur in August 2012, scoring a further 12 goals in all competitions for Spurs. Two of these goals came in a Europa League quarter-final against the Swiss side Basle, but they were not enough to prevent his new club losing on penalties.

Dempsey played an astonishing 141 matches for The United States, with a very healthy goal return of 57, an equal top-scoring record with Landon Donovan. Dempsey played either as an out-and-out striker, or in his preferred role just off the main striker. Among Fulham's other substitutes were Norwegian striker Erik Nevland and the experienced ex-Manchester United, Middlesbrough and West Bromwich midfielder Jonathan Greening.

A curious aspect of Fulham's 2010 UEFA Cup Final opponents Atlético Madrid is how many of their team went on to play in the English Premiership. Indeed David De Gea and Sergio Agüero continued to play in the Premiership in 2020. De Gea was only 19 years old when he appeared in this final. He made 57 league appearances for Atlético 2009–2011 before signing for Manchester United in June 2011. De Gea has subsequently played over 300 games for United. His reputation has faltered in recent times, suffering it seems with the typical goalkeeper's curse of the occasional lapse of concentration. At his best, De Gea has proved himself a consummate shot-stopper.

'Kun' Agüero has established himself as one of the Premiership's greatest ever strikers. Aged only 21 in this final, Agüero amassed 74 goals from 175 league games for Atlético 2006–2011. The 20 league goals he scored in the 2010–11 season led to his transfer to Manchester City. Agüero's winning goal in the dying moments of the final game of the 2011–12 season against Queens Park Rangers confirmed Manchester City as Premiership champions for the first time, the first time City had won England's top-tier title since the halcyon days of Bell, Sunmmerbee and Lee in 1968. The goal, scored in such dramatic fashion in injury time, continues to be shown today.

Agüero has gone on to score 180 Premiership goals (up to 30-09-20). When Agüero's second goal entered the net against Bournemouth on 25 August 2020, it was his 400th professional goal. Agüero is quite simply a goal machine. He scores goals with both feet; his head; he scores typical striker's penalty-box goals; but he can score the spectacular also. He is arguably the deadliest striker ever seen in the English Premiership. With Manchester City, Agüero is a four-time Premiership winner (2011–12, 2013–14, 2017–18, 2018–19), an FA Cup winner (2018–19), and a five-time League Cup winner (2013–14, 2015–16, 2017–18, 2018–19, 2019–20). Agüero has played 97 times for Argentina, scoring 41 goals (up to 30-09-20).

Sergio Agüero – along with Thierry Henry – is the best overseas striker to grace the English Premiership. Yet his thunder was stolen in this final by his Uruguyan co-striker Diego Forlan. Ironically, Forlan played for Argentinian club Independiente prior to Agüero (1997–2002). Agüero then played for Independiente 2003–06. Forlan is best known on these shores for his stint with Manchester United 2002–04. At Old Trafford, Forlan's form was less than consistent. His talent was unquestionable, but his 37 goals in 80 league games for Atlético were not matched by his ten in 63 for United. He did win the Premier League in 2002–03 and the FA Cup in 2003–04 with United, but in terms of goals it took a move back to Spain to resurrect his fortunes.

Joining Villareal in 2004, Forlan went on to score 54 league goals in 106 appearances. In his first season in Spain, Forlan shared the European Golden Boot with Arsenal's Thierry Henry. Villareal reached the semi-finals of the Champions League in 2005–06, only to be beaten at the last gasp by Henry's Arsenal. Joining Atlético in time for the 2007–08 season he was united in attack with Agüero, the pair forming a fearsome strike force. Forlan came back to haunt the English clubs in this 2009–2010 UEFA Cup campaign. In the home leg semi-final against Liverpool, Forlan scored the only goal. At Anfield Forlan scored again, the crucial away goal enough to see Atlético through at the Merseysiders' expense. Two more in the final against Fulham saw Forlan complete the 2009–2010 season with 28 goals, six of which came in the UEFA Cup. Forlan scored a total of 74 league goals for Atlético in 134 games 2007–2011.

The big European teams were knocking at Forlan's door. He moved to Inter Milan in Italy, but stayed only one season, his form affected by being played out of position. An inveterate traveller, Forlan then played for Internacional in Brazil, Cerezo Osaka in Japan, back to Uruguay to play for Penarol, on to Mumbai City in India, finally playing with Hong Kong Premier League team Kitchee. Forlan retired from the professional game in August 2019. He played 112 times for Uruguay, scoring 36 goals, being his country's highest ever scorer until overtaken by Luis Suarez. Forlan often looked physically lightweight at Manchester United, but there's nothing remotely lightweight about his stellar career in Europe and South America. His apparent lack of physicality didn't stop the Uruguayan impressing greatly with his pace, technique, awareness, vision and all-round team play.

Completing the quartet of well-known players in this Atlético Madrid side was the tragically departed José Antonio Reyes. Reyes first inspired Sevilla 2002–04, scoring 21 goals from the wing. He was only 16 when he broke into the Sevilla side. Arsenal signed him in February 2004. Within days, Reyes scored an own goal against Middlesbrough in the League Cup, but he swiftly redeemed himself, scoring twice against Chelsea to knock the King's Road team out of the FA Cup. Reyes was part of the Arsenal team that ultimately went unbeaten all season earning the tag the 'Invincibles'. Reputedly homesick, Reyes agitated for a return to Spain. He was still around for the 2005 FA Cup Final, but was sent off for a second yellow offence. Somehow Arsenal held on, defeating Manchester United (who had been infinitely the brighter side) on penalties after extra time. Reyes came on as a substitute in the 2006 Champions League Final against Barcelona, but chose to return to Spain on loan for the 2006–07 season. It was the last Arsenal fans would see of the talented winger.

Reyes suddenly found himself switching clubs in Madrid, his loan at Real replaced by a permanent move to Atlético in 2007. Reyes continued to be an enigma – another loan period with Benfica in Portugal followed, before he returned to Atlético, finally finding his feet with some success. Reyes played 103 league games 2007–2012 at Atlético, scoring outrageous goals at times, but only in the club's more fruitful times finding greater consistency. In January 2012 he returned to Sevilla and helped the club to win the UEFA Cup again in 2015, his night being crowned by captaining the team.

Reyes played 21 times for Spain, scoring four goals, his international opportunities restricted by the talents of David Silva and Santi Cazorla (players equally well known to supporters of Manchester City and Arsenal). While travelling between Utrera and Seville in Spain on 1 June 2019, Reyes tragically died in a car crash. He is remembered fondly at Arsenal for his electric pace, great touch and his eye for goal.

THE FINAL
Fulham returned to Hamburg for the final having beaten the host club in the semi-final. Fulham fought tooth and nail to compete with their gifted Spanish opponents, but it became swiftly evident that Forlan was on fire on this evening. Early on, Agüero fed Forlan on the left, the Uruguyan's shot sweeping across goal and off the outside of the post. Reyes, displaying his electric pace, broke free on the right, his long crossfield ball finding Agüero, whose half-hit shot was followed in by Forlan who diverted the ball into the net. Unbowed, Fulham equalised when Simon Davies crashed a fine half-volley past de Gea at the far post. Sadly for Fulham, the dynamic duo of Forlan and Agüero were a constant threat throughout the game. Early in the second half Forlan burst past the Fulham defence on the left, but the Cottagers somehow averted the danger. Davies had a shot smartly saved by de Gea at the other end; Damien Duff struck a hopeful shot wide. In extra time, Agüero chased a ball down the left-hand side, crossed and the ever-alert Forlan deflected his cross past the helpless Schwarzer. Forlan was deservedly named Man of the Match, while strike partner Agüero contributed both assists.

2012–2013 EUROPA LEAGUE FINAL
Chelsea 2 v 1 Benfica

Chelsea's win here made them the first English club to win all three European titles – only Juventus, Ajax and Bayern Munich have equalled this feat. The Stamford Bridge club joined exalted company.

Route to the Final
Chelsea began the season in the Champions League, joining the Europa League at the round of 32 after finishing third in their group of the premier European

competition. In the last 32, Chelsea beat the Czech Republic team Slavia Prague 2-1 on aggregate. In the last 16 they defeated the Romanians Steaua Bucharest 3-2 on aggregate. In the quarter-finals a higher-scoring affair still only resulted in a one goal winning margin for the Blues, the Russians Rubin Kazan beaten 5-4 on aggregate. A fine Basle team were beaten soundly 5-2 over two legs in the semi-final, the Swiss side having beaten Tottenham Hotspur in the last eight.

Benfica, who also entered the competition in the round of 32 having finished third in their Champions League group, beat the Germans Bayer Leverkusen with a 3-1 aggregate score at this stage. Bordeaux of France were defeated 4-2 over two legs in the last 16. English club Newcastle United surpassed themselves by reaching the last eight only to succumb 4-2 over two games against the Lisbon giants. Benfica then edged past the Turkish side Fenerbahce 3-2 on aggregate to reach the final against Chelsea.

This is a Chelsea side that still lingers in the memory. A percentage of the players brought into the side by José Mourinho – and some that he inherited – remained. For a few years Mourinho's side were a physically imposing, powerful, multi-talented outfit. While John Terry and Didier Drogba were not in this side, and the slippery, skilful Eden Hazard missed the final through injury, Chelsea's team were a hybrid of multinational delights.

In goal, Petr Cech had established himself as the best goalkeeper, save for Peter Schmeichel, seen in the Premier League's almost-30-year history. At 19 years of age – like de Gea in the 2010 UEFA Cup Final – Cech had established himself as first-pick custodian for the Czech Republic team Sparta Prague. At Sparta he went a record 903 minutes in matches without conceding a goal. A transfer to Rennes in France followed where he played 70 league games in Ligue 1 2002–04. Upon signing for Chelsea in July 2004, Cech became the most expensive goalkeeper in Chelsea's history at that time. Cech displaced the unfortunate Carlo Cudicini – who suffered an elbow injury – and promptly set a new Premiership record 1,025 minutes without conceding a goal in March 2005. A tribute to Cech's prowess at this time is witnessed by the fact Chelsea conceded only 15 league goals all season – an astonishing record. In 2005–06 Chelsea conceded only 22 league goals in the season, retaining their Premiership title. Cech was named the International Federation of Football History and Statistics Goalkeeper of the Year for 2006.

On 14 October 2006 Cech sustained a serious head injury against Reading at the Madejski Stadium. Uncannily, Cudicini replaced him, was also knocked unconscious, leaving John Terry 'between the sticks' for the remainder of the game. Cech suffered a depressed skull fracture – the fractious Mourinho less than impressed by Stephen Hunt's challenge that led to the injury. Cech returned against Liverpool in January 2007, after recuperating for three months in line with medical advice, wearing a rugby-style head guard that became his signature headwear. It could be argued that Cech did not command his penalty area in quite the same way thereafter, but he remained one of the top players in his position in the world, and even went 810 minutes without conceding a Premier League goal after losing 2-0 in his return match with Liverpool.

In 2010–11 Cech was awarded the Chelsea Player of the Year. Calf, shin and knee injuries were not helping the indefatigable Cech's cause, but he came good in the 2011–12 season, helping Chelsea to their first Champions League win, saving former teammate Arjen Robben's extra-time penalty, then two more subsequent penalties in the penalty shoot-out against Bayern Munich – yes, an English club defeated a German club on penalty kicks!

In the 2014–15 season, the Belgian keeper Thibaut Curtois ousted Cech as Chelsea's first choice custodian. A year later Cech moved across London to join Arsenal. One of Cech's first acts was to keep a clean sheet for his new club as they beat his former club in the 2015 Community Shield. At the end of the 2015–16 season, Cech was named the Premier League Goalkeeper of the Season by football journalists. At the start of the 2017–18 season Arsenal again defeated Chelsea in the Community Shield with Cech 'between the sticks', this time courtesy of an extra-time penalty shoot-out. On 11 March 2018 Cech became the first Premier League keeper to keep 200 clean sheets. In the game against Watford on this date, Cech saved Troy Deeney's penalty kick. Cech's final game for Arsenal would come in the 2019 Europa League Final with former club Chelsea exacting handsome revenge for those two Community Shield defeats, to the tune of 4-1.

Internationally, Cech proved his worth early on in his career. As a 20-year-old in the 2002 U-21 European Championships he performed what would become his customary heroics, letting in only one penalty in the shoot-out, earning the Czech Republic their first title at this level. At the 2004 Euro tournament held in Portugal, Cech was named as the goalkeeper of the tournament. The Czech Republic almost made the final, losing out in the last four to eventual surprise winners Greece. Petr Cech is the most capped player in his country's history, winning 124 caps.

Cech's dominance of his penalty area, his decision-making, and leadership skills rightly make him one of the greatest goalkeepers seen in British football. He won the Premier League with Chelsea four times (2004–05, 2005–06, 2009–2010, 2014–15); the FA Cup with Chelsea four times (2006–07, 2008–09, 2009–2010, 2011–12); the League Cup three times (2004–05, 2006–07, 2014–15); the Champions League just once in 2011–12 – although Chelsea were beaten in their only other appearance in 2008 on penalties in the all-English final against Manchester United; and this UEFA Cup win against Benfica in 2013. How about this for a footnote: Cech appeared in 2019 as a goalkeeper for my local hometown ice hockey team Guildford Phoenix. What happened on his debut on 13 October 2019? He saved two penalties in a shoot-out victory, and was named the man of the match. Hugely respected by his peers within the game of football; quite a defender of his goal, Petr Cech.

Truly a multinational side, Chelsea's first 11 contained only three English players. Two of these played in defence. Gary Cahill's route to the top was not textbook, but long, measured, with top teams constantly reviewing him but resisting signing him until later in his career. Cahill spent the years 2004–08 ostensibly at Aston Villa, but was loaned out in 2004–05 to Burnley, and in 2007–08 to Sheffield United. Only upon signing for Bolton Wanderers in January 2008 did Cahill begin to make his way in the game. Cahill played 130 league games for Bolton before Chelsea took the plunge in signing him in January 2012 at the age of 27. In his first season at Stamford Bridge, Cahill won the Champions League – not a bad late entry into life with one of England's premier clubs! At first rotated with other central defenders John Terry, David Luiz and Branislav Ivanovic (who could also play equally adeptly as a marauding right-back), Cahill played regularly in the 2014–15 season, ultimately being named in the PFA Team of the Year. The six feet four inches Cahill combined the archetypal centre-back's traits of being a good stopper, good in the air, with useful technique and passing ability for a big man.

Following the departure of Chelsea stalwart Terry to Aston Villa in the 2017–18 season, Cahill became club captain. Now in his early 30s Cahill moved to Crystal Palace for the 2019–20 season where he continued to show his worth as a Premiership central defender. Cahill played 61 times for England. His aerial presence at set pieces meant he scored 13 goals apiece for Bolton Wanderers and Chelsea, and a further five for England.

Ashley Cole, the other Englishman in the team's defence, proved himself at Arsenal and Chelsea to be one of the world's very best left backs. Starting in the professional game with the Gunners, Cole played 228 games in all competitions, scoring nine goals with the North Londoners. He won the Premier League twice with Arsenal, 2002 and 2004, and the FA Cup three times: 2002, 2003 and 2005, a period of high dominance for the club. Ironically, the only time Arsenal did not win the FA Cup in this four-year period was in the season of their 'Invincible' team of 2004.

Cole left Arsenal in acrimonious circumstances, Chelsea being accused of 'tapping up' the player – Cole left with the tag 'Cashley' ringing in his ears from Arsenal fans in the summer of 2006. Whatever the rights or wrongs of the situation, Cole went on to play 229 league games for Chelsea, only confirming his status as the best player in his position in Britain, and drawing praise worldwide for his performances. Cole was twice awarded Chelsea's Player's Player of the Year in his time with the club 2006–2014, only leaving when current Chelsea incumbent the Spaniard César Azpilicueta took his place. Cole spent a year with Roma in Serie A, curtailed his contract in Italy to play for LA Galaxy in the American Major Soccer League 2016–18, playing nine games for old teammate Frank Lampard at Derby County in the Championship as his career ran to a close. Cole retired in August 2019.

For England, Cole received 107 caps, winning a fan's poll as England Player of the Year in 2010. Curiously for a player who loved to forage forward to link up with his attackers, Cole never scored for England. The defensive side of Cole's game improved as he matured. A no-nonsense player, Cole's ability to avert danger by reading situations was a particular forte.

Chelsea's defence on this evening was completed by the aforementioned Azpilicueta and Ivanovic. Azpilicueta is a tough-tackling, swift defender who can play in either full-back position, or even as an emergency central defender. A technically adept and tactically aware player, Azpilicueta began with Osasuna in Spain as a forward or midfield player, reflecting his all-round capability. After four years with Osasuna, Azpilicueta spent two seasons at Marseille, swapping the sunshine of Southern France for the attraction of south-west London in 2012. He has since played nearly 300 league games for Chelsea (2020–21), his adaptability allowing Chelsea to sell Cole in 2014. When Cahill departed in 2019, Azpilicueta became the new Chelsea club captain. The versatile Pamplona-born (the home of bull-fighting, a metaphor for his combative style perhaps) Azpilicueta has played 25 times for Spain (2020).

The Serbian-born Branislav Ivanovic is a powerfully built player who switched as required by Chelsea between the right-back and centre-back positions. Ivanovic played four seasons in Serbia professionally before joining Russian club Lokomotiv Moscow in 2006. He won the Russian Cup with Lokomotiv in 2007. With AC Milan, Inter Milan, Juventus and Ajax circling, Chelsea pipped the European giants for his signature. Ironically, Ivanovic's fitness betrayed him initially. Only after Brazilian manager Luiz Felipe Scolari departed did Ivanovic begin to play regularly under his successors Gus Hiddink and Carlo Ancelotti. Even then he did not always find favour under Hiddink. Ivanovic's crowning glory came in this final as he headed the winning goal in the third minute of stoppage time. He was awarded the Man of the Match for his performance. Next Chelsea manager (they seemed as frequent as the English rain under Abramovich's club ownership) José Mourinho tended to play Ivanovic regularly – perhaps his chopping and changing of positions betrayed Ivanovic's cause. Personally, I preferred him at full-back, his perceived weakness there being the temptation to get caught too far forward at times, losing his defensive position and consequently affecting the team's shape.

The Serb became Chelsea's vice-captain for the 2015–16 season, deputising as captain many times as John Terry continued to suffer with injuries. Ivanovic eventually lost the full-back position to Victor Moses in the 2016–17 season, and signed for Zenit St Petersburg in February 2017. Surprisingly the Serb returned to the Premiership on a one-year contract with West Bromwich Albion in 2020. His teammate Frank Lampard lauded his performance in this final; Raheem Sterling claims he is one of the "scariest" players he's played against – all of which makes his stuttering start to his career at Stamford Bridge more difficult to comprehend. Ultimately Ivanovic won three Premier League titles at the Bridge, three FA Cups, one League Cup, one Champions League, and this Europa League Final.

I recall Ivanovic as part of a very physically powerful Chelsea team. In the period he played 261 league games for Chelsea 2008–2017, he scored 22 goals in the Premiership. He was part of a team that contained other 'beasts' or strong physical specimens: Cech, Terry, Lampard, Drogba. This perception downplays Chelsea's technical prowess in the period 2004–2017, but the Blues were undoubtedly an unflinching opponent to Liverpool, Manchester United, Arsenal, Tottenham and Manchester City during this spell. Ivanovic also played 105 times for Serbia, scoring 13 goals for his country.

The only other Englishman in the side on this evening was Frank Lampard, soon-to-be Chelsea manager until his dismissal in 2021. Lampard's record as Chelsea's all-time leading goalscorer is an incredible tribute to his talent given his 211 goals in all competitions came from a midfield position. I grew up loving the hunger for goals shown by Bobby Tambling; the silky smooth skills of Peter Osgood. Those players were strikers and expected to score goals. Lampard overtook the tallies of these Chelsea heroes from midfield for heaven's sake!

Frank Lampard began his pro career at West Ham United, the team his father excelled for as a left-back in the 1960s, 1970s and 1980s. His father possessed a crushingly powerful shot when joining the attack. Lampard Junior could strike a ball vehemently too, but I'm sure his father wouldn't mind admitting that his son was a more rounded player. Lampard junior loved to attack, he was the epitome of a box-to-box midfield player, and he was a fine passer of the ball to boot. In his six seasons with the Hammers, Lampard junior played 148 league games, scoring 24 times. His move to Chelsea in 2001 was the making of him. Surrounded by better players, Lampard became the fulcrum of the Chelsea team until he departed in 2014, his goal-scoring feats reaching new heights. Of the players who have scored 150 plus Premiership goals, unsurprisingly, Lampard is the only midfield player. Technically adept with both feet, Lampard's stock in trade soared in the 2004–05 season as he scored goals in victories over European giants Barcelona and Bayern Munich. Having beaten the cream of Europe that season, Chelsea were thwarted in the semi-finals of the Champions League by fellow English club Liverpool. With Terry suffering a back injury in the 2006–07 season, Lampard filled in as Chelsea captain. Despite Chelsea losing the 2008 Champions League Final to Manchester United on penalties, Lampard was named the UEFA Club Midfielder of the Year.

Captain of the side on this evening, 2011–12 proved an especially fruitful year for Lampard. He provided the assist for Didier Drogba's winner in the club's 2-1 FA Cup triumph. Captaining the side against Bayern Munich in the Champions League Final, Lampard lifted the trophy after the game ended 1-1, Chelsea winning 4-3 on penalties. There's always a twist in football though. Lampard subsequently missed Euro 2012 with England courtesy of a thigh injury. Too much football?

Lampard surprised many by taking out a loan period with Manchester City until January 2015. Typically, Lampard scored his first goal for City against Chelsea, ending his former club's winning streak at the beginning of the 2014–15 season. In 2015 Lampard signed a two-year contract with New York City in the American Major Soccer League. Despite appearing alongside Spanish great David Villa and Italian maestro Andrea Pirlo, the team failed to make the end of season play-offs.

Frank Lampard played 109 times for England, scoring 29 goals. In his first major competition for his country at Euro 2004, Lampard scored three times in the four matches England played, finding himself named in the UEFA Team of the Tournament. He was voted England Player of the Year by fans in 2004 and 2005. In 2006, the England team were knocked out of the World Cup in the last eight against Portugal (repeating their defeat at the Euros in 2004), losing on penalties. Lampard was one of those who missed his penalty kick, yet his record with Chelsea was excellent. In 2010 – crucially perhaps – Lampard's first-half shot bounced off the crossbar, crossed the line, but a goal was not given. This would have tied their World Cup last 16 game with Germany at 2-2. Instead England crumbled, Germany went on the rampage, and the game was lost 4-1. 2014 brought further elimination for England as they finished bottom of their

World Cup group behind surprise group winners Costa Rica and Uruguay. The nation managed only one point, two less than third-placed Italy. While English clubs had reasonable success in European club football, the English national team reached a new low point in 2014.

In this 2013 Europa League Final, Lampard sat deeper alongside David Luiz, with Ramires, Juan Mata and Oscar employed in front of them, forming a bank of five in midfield, very much in tune with modern football tactical formation. An excellent dead-ball taker of free kicks and penalties (2014 an exception on the latter), a fine passer of the ball, an astute dictator of the pace of the game – Lampard was the complete midfield player. Lampard's employment deeper in midfield later in his career might have negated his goal-scoring prowess – it didn't impact that greatly. I just wish England could have derived more from four of the best midfield players seen in this country over the last two decades: Lampard, Gerrard, Scholes and Beckham. They just didn't seem to gel as a unit, despite them all being high-class international players.

Turning to management, Lampard guided Derby County to the Championship play-offs in his first season as a manager. Placing an emphasis on youth, Lampard marginally failed to elevate County into the Premiership in that 2018–19 season, Aston Villa beating them 2-1 in the Play-Off Final. Tactically astute, unafraid to give the youngsters their head, and always emphasising the attacking game he excelled at himself, he'd done enough to earn a return to Chelsea as manager in July 2019. Chelsea finished fourth in his first management season at Stamford Bridge, behind only the new 'super-powers' Liverpool and Manchester City, and only a whisker behind third-placed Manchester United. Lampard appeared to be becoming a fine manager as well as an outstanding player. One of the greatest successes of his Chelsea team of recent times is Mason Mount, in his early 20s, a young player Lampard brought with him from Derby County, who has played 31 times for England (July 2022). Mount is an attacking midfielder, somewhat in the image of his boss. What greater tribute for Frank Lampard?

There were three Brazilians in this Chelsea 2013 UEFA Cup-winning side: Ramires, Oscar, David Luiz. What can one say about the enigmatic Luiz? Is the Brazilian's best position at centre-back or in midfield? More often than not he has played at centre-back – if he plays in a three he can be vulnerable. Playing in a four alongside the likes of Terry or Cahill gave him defensive cover and solidity. An obviously gifted ball player, do his technical qualities make him better suited to playing in midfield? It's an eternal argument with Luiz. You do not play for Benfica, Chelsea, Paris Saint-Germain and Arsenal without being a top, top player. I have seen Luiz excel in the really big games – a Champions League Final for example. Yet Luiz and his teammates in the Brazilian national side were absolutely torn apart by Germany in the 2014 World Cup semi-final, losing 7-1, the type of scoreline unheard of at that level in the modern game. I've seen Luiz resort often to the dark arts when exposed one-on-one with a striker. Enigmatic, charismatic, by all accounts an excellent leader within a team, Luiz is hugely talented, flawed, a mystery to many observers.

Joining Benfica in 2007 from Salvador (north-east Brazil) club Vitoria, Luiz was voted Portuguese Player of the Year in 2009–10. He transferred to Chelsea in January 2011. With his rock-star looks, his long, curly hair, Luiz stands out on a football pitch. If you're going to look like David Luiz you'd better be able to play. It seems his every error is magnified, his appearance meaning there is no hiding place on the pitch. Luiz's first spell at Chelsea 2011–14 brought 81 league appearances and six goals. The latter small tally seems inconceivable because when Luiz did score it tended to be of the spectacular variety. Luiz scored in both legs of the semi-final of this 2013 Europa League competition against Basle.

When Luiz departed for Paris Saint-Germain in June 2014, his £50-million transfer was a world record fee for a defender. Before he'd even laced his boots in a competitive match for PSG Luiz suffered the horrors of THAT World Cup semi-final versus Germany. Yet the Brazilian's flair saw him included, surprisingly. In the FIFA World Team of the Year at the 2014 Ballon d'Or Awards – this did occur six months before his nightmare evening against the Germans. In March 2015, Luiz returned to Stamford Bridge in a last 16 Champions League tie. Predictably, he scored as PSG went through on away goals. At the end of his first season in Paris, PSG won the domestic treble of Ligue 1, the Coupe de France, and the Coupe de la Ligue. The feat was repeated the following year. Luiz was making his mark in Paris, albeit in a league some thought inferior to the Premiership, the Bundesliga, Serie A and La Liga. To be fair, French football has delivered a massive renaissance in recent years, culminating in France's 2018 World Cup triumph.

Luiz returned to Chelsea in August 2016. At the end of the 2016–17 season Luiz was included in the PFA Team of the Year. In his second stint back at the Bridge, Luiz played 79 league games, scoring five goals. As younger blood began to force its way into the Chelsea team, Luiz's perceived vulnerability made him surplus to requirements. In August 2019 Luiz moved across London, joining Arsenal with the theory promoted that he was past his best. Initially Luiz committed a few errors suggesting the pundits may be right. Always a paradoxical character, Luiz later turned in some excellent performances. On the one hand, Luiz conceded five penalties during the 2019–20 season, the most of any single player in any single season in the Premiership. In contrast, Luiz played a leader's role in helping Arsenal defeat old club Chelsea in the 2020 FA Cup Final. David Luiz really does give his teammates, his managers, the watching fans the full 'Clint Eastwood treatment': 'The Good, the Bad, and The Ugly'.

Luiz has played 57 times for Brazil (October 2020), his games including an own goal, an outstanding goalline clearance, notable absences of positional play, great goals, fine passing. There's never a dull moment with David Luiz.

Neither Oscar nor Ramires were anywhere near as colourful as Luiz, which seems a harsh critique, as both these Brazilians in midfield proved their worth. I particularly liked the fluid, elegant Oscar. In his home country of Brazil, Oscar played only 11 games for Sao Paulo before being caught up in a contractual wrangle as he moved to Porto Alegre club Internacional. At Internacional his first season in 2010 was marred by injury. Ultimately Oscar played only 36 league games for the club, scoring 11 goals. His lack of game time did not deter Chelsea, who signed him on a five-year contract in July 2012. His first game for Chelsea could not have been tougher – a home tie in the Champions League against Turin's mightiest, Juventus. He marked his debut with a deflected shot and a curled second to give Chelsea a 2-0 lead. The Italians clawed their way back to draw 2-2, but Oscar won the Man of the Match Award. Under manager Roberto Di Matteo, Oscar formed a creative triumvirate with Juan Mata and Eden Hazard. When Di Matteo was replaced as manager by the more cautious Rafael Benitez, Oscar was not always considered first choice. Benitez was replaced by the returning José Mourinho. Oscar, along with Didier Drogba and Cesc Fàbregas, was pilloried by Chelsea fans when Mourinho was ousted from the club after a run of poor form.

Oscar, Ramires, and latterly Willian, do not seem to have been appreciated as much as they should have been by supporters. My only reservation about selecting these gifted players is the old one: it has restricted opportunities for young talented English players. The consequence: lack of exposure at the highest club level hinders England on the international stage. Oscar completed over 200 games for Chelsea in all competitions, scoring 21 league goals – a player with his natural gifts should arguably have scored more. On the international stage, Oscar has scored 12 goals in 48 appearances for Brazil, a better reflection of his undoubted talents. At Chelsea, Oscar was moved around positionally, playing in wide positions, behind the strikers, as a playmaker – once again it could be a lack of regularity in a role preventing more consistent performances.

Ramires was a completely different animal, a box-to-box midfield player, hard-running, energetic – a modern Brazilian player, not at all in the mould of the individually gifted midfield players of the 70s and 80s: Gerson, Rivellino, Socrates and Zico. After two seasons with Cruzeiro in Brazil 2007–09, Ramires joined Benfica in Portugal, starring as the Lisbon club won their 32nd league title in 2009–10. Benfica also won the Taca da Liga (the Portuguese League Cup) in Ramires's only season with the club. In August 2010 Ramires signed a four-year contract with Chelsea. He would go on to play 160 league games for Chelsea, scoring 17 goals. Ramires scored the decisive away goal in the second leg semi-final of the 2011–12 Champions League in the Nou Camp against Barcelona, a goal that took Chelsea through to the final they ultimately won against Bayern Munich on penalties. His fellow players voted him Player's Player of the Year at the end of that season.

When Gus Hiddink replaced Mourinho at Chelsea, Ramires was used more sparingly. Often employed on the right side of midfield, Ramires's energy and work-rate made him particularly dangerous on the counter-attack. He played 52 times for Brazil, appearing in all of Brazil's seven 2014 World Cup matches, making him one of those who suffered the humiliating semi-final defeat against Germany.

Completing the midfield for Chelsea in the 2013 Europa League Final was the diminutive Spaniard, Juan Mata, a player I feel has not always been recognised sufficiently for his impact on a match. In the modern game of six foot plus powerhouse players, Mata's slighter physique and height (five feet seven inches) sometimes work against him, but this is a player with a lovely eye for the telling pass. Occasionally chastised – under Mourinho at Chelsea this occurred – Mata has the perfect response: along with Fernando Torres he became the first player after this 2013 Europa League triumph to hold winner's medals in the Champions League, the Europa League, the World Cup, and the European Championships simultaneously. Not a bad collection, although the unassuming Mata does not seem the type to flaunt his glittering haul.

After starting out in 2006 with Real Madrid Castilla (Real's reserve team who play in Segunda Division B-Group 1), Mata joined Valencia in 2007, becoming an integral part of the club's midfield 2007–11, playing 129 league games and scoring 33 goals. In his first season at Valencia he won the Copa del Rey, beating Getafe in the final. Mata scored the opening goal. Fans and players voted Mata Player of the Year at the end of 2007–08. In his second season, Mata's 11 goals and 13 assists left him behind only Barcelona legend Xavi statistically. In his last two seasons with Valencia the club finished third in consecutive seasons – it's difficult to dislodge Real Madrid and Barcelona from the top two in Spain.

In August 2011 Mata signed a five-year deal with Chelsea, following advice from Fernando Torres. With Roberto Di Matteo at the helm, Mata switched from wide midfield to a central midfield role, allowing the creative Spaniard to bisect opposing defences with his clever passing. At the end of the 2011–12 season Mata was voted by Chelsea fans as Player of the Year. His 14 assists for goals lay second only to Manchester City's David Silva, a fellow Spanish international. It was Mata's corner-kick in this 2013 Europa League Final that led to Ivanovic scoring the winning goal. For the second year running Mata won Chelsea's Player of the Year, in addition to being Player's Player of the Year for 2012–13.

The incoming José Mourinho preferred Oscar as his playmaker, bringing about an early end to Mata's contract in 2014. In 135 appearances in all competitions Mata scored 33 goals for Chelsea, and, crucially, provided 58 assists for his teammates. Unfortunately for Mata the managerial merry-go-round continued unabated.

Under Louis van Gaal at new club Manchester United, Mata didn't always find favour despite a strong start to his career at Old Trafford. In the 2016 FA Cup Final, although substituted, he scored United's opening goal in a match won 2-1 after extra time against Crystal Palace. Ironically, Mourinho then took over from van Gaal. Once again Mata's defensive nous was questioned by Mourinho, a man for whom work-rate, team shape, fitness, and spirit override all else. In and out of the team under Mourinho, Mata's forte – his ability to find his teammates with a killer pass – did not falter. In 180 league games to date Mata has scored – eerily – 33 goals (2020). He helped United win the Europa League Final in 2017 but could not prevent old club Chelsea from defeating the Red Devils in the 2018 FA Cup Final. United also finished second in the Premiership 2016–17.

On the international stage, Mata's successes came early as Spain won the 2006 European U-19 Football Championship, the midfielder scoring four goals in the tournament. In 2011 Spain won the UEFA European U-21 Championship, Mata being included in the UEFA Team of the Tournament, being named individually as the tournament's Golden Player. In the senior UEFA Euro 2012 tournament, Mata came on as a substitute and scored the fourth goal as Spain trounced Italy 4-0. In all, Mata has scored ten goals for Spain in 41 matches. A player of his quality would surely have played more often for his country had he not been down the pecking order behind Spain's 'golden generation' of midfielders: Xavi, Iniesta, David Silva and Busquets. Clearly Mata's perceived deficiency comes in his lack of physicality and tackling prowess, but what a fine distributor of the ball Juan Mata is. His nimble feet, deft technique and superlative passing compensate for his short, slight, stature.

Chelsea opted to play the modern formation of a packed, fluid midfield in this final, meaning only one place for an out-and-out striker. If you're going to play a lone striker – and I'm not a fan – your striker might as well be Fernando Torres. Imagine being a lone striker with four or five defenders surrounding you every time you receive the ball. I understand that in the modern game if you don't flood the midfield you tend to be outnumbered, but one up front is a negative tactic in my book. As a striker you thrive on having someone assisting you in attack to feed off, whether that be a fellow striker, a deep-lying striker (false nine), or attacking wide players. Torres, to his eternal credit, was a willing workhorse up front for Chelsea, exploiting his pace, ball control and slick finishing to good effect.

The Chelsea years were certainly not Torres's golden years, although he helped the Blues win a Champions League and this Europa League in his time at the Bridge. The peak of Torres's powers were witnessed with first senior club Atlético Madrid, and sensationally, at Liverpool. Torres scored 82 goals in 214 league appearances for Atlético 2001–07, departing for Liverpool as Diego Forlan moved from Villareal to wear the red and white stripes of Atlético. Chelsea had already expressed interest in signing Torres in 2005, but it was to Anfield that Torres moved in July 2007. It might have appeared as if Torres had moved to the second English club of interest to him, but he fitted like a glove into the Anfield 'machine'. In 102 league games at the Anfield club Torres scored 65 goals 2007–11. He scored a hat-trick against Reading in the League Cup in September 2007; he scored two hat-tricks at Anfield in successive games in 2008 against Middlesbrough and West Ham United, the first Liverpool player to do so since Jack Balmer in 1946.

Torres's first season with Liverpool ended with a tally of 29 goals in all competitions, superseding Michael Owen's record for goals scored in a season. Torres was named in the 2007–08 PFA Team of the Year, and finished second to Cristiano Ronaldo in the FWA Footballer of the Year Award. Torres scored in eight consecutive games in the 2007–08 season, equalling a record set by Liverpool's England World Cup-winner Roger Hunt. He also surpassed Ruud van Nistelrooy's total of 23 goals in a season to be the highest-scoring foreign player in an individual season in the Premiership. Torres was also named in the FIFPRO World XI for the season 2007–08.

Chelsea continued to pursue Torres, but it seemed entirely prescient that Torres stay at Liverpool at this time. At the end of the 2008–09 season, Torres was again named in the PFA Team of the Year despite niggling hamstring problems during the season. In December 2009 he was again named in the FIFPRO World XI. After scoring twice against Benfica in a Europa League match in April 2010, Torres missed the season's denouement as he required knee surgery. He still completed the 2009–10 season as Liverpool's top scorer with 22 goals in 32 games in all competitions.

Despite his protestations of loyalty to Liverpool, when Chelsea came calling again in January 2011, Torres put in a transfer request. Liverpool rejected his request, but Torres decided to move anyway, signing for Chelsea on 31 January 2011. Ironically, his first match for his new club took place at the Bridge against Liverpool. Chelsea lost 1-0. After Chelsea's sustained pursuit of this stunning striker, the rest of the season in 2011 proved a massive anti-climax for Torres as he scored only one goal. In 110 league games for Chelsea, Torres would score only 20 goals. It seemed a classic case of a player not fitting a club's style, not being able to adapt to the system employed by that team. In 20 years of playing local football I only failed to gel in one of the four teams I played for. My old next-door neighbour encouraged me to join the club, but I just didn't enjoy playing there, didn't seem to fit with players I had admired when playing against them. By the same token, I asked a former fellow striker from my first club to join my second team – he'd been utterly prolific as a goalscorer at our first club, but he couldn't hold down a place in my new team, not fitting into our pattern of play. It sometimes happens, whatever your ability.

With the powerful Didier Drogba a steam-hammer first-choice centre-forward at Chelsea, Torres would only come on as a substitute in the 2012 Champions League Final against Bayern Munich. He ended his first full season with Chelsea (2011–2012) with 11 goals from 49 games in all competitions, a paltry return for such a fine striker. Torres's form was less than consistent, the goals had dried up.

In the quarter-final of the 2012–13 Europa League versus Rubin Kazan, Torres scored three goals over the two legs. He scored the first goal in this final against Benfica. Torres ended this season with 22 goals in 64 competitive matches, a better return. Many fine players have lost favour and fallen foul of José Mourinho. When Mourinho returned to Chelsea as manager, Torres found himself in and out of the team again. In August 2014 he joined Italian giants AC Milan on a two-year loan. Big clubs continued to vie for his services, but Torres's stay in Milan lasted only ten league games, Atlético re-signing their old talisman in December 2018. Torres scored a further 13 goals in 58 league games back in Madrid, before trying his luck in Japan during the 2018–19 season with Sagan Tosu. It was a muted farewell, the rangy striker scoring five goals in 35 league games.

Torres's return for his country is favourable, 38 goals accumulated in 110 matches. As a youth he won the 2001 UEFA European U-16 Championship, hosted by England, scoring the only goal in the final, top-scoring in the tournament, and being named Player of the Tournament. Spain and Torres repeated that feat in triplicate in the 2002 UEFA European U-19 Championships held in Norway. There seemed no stopping the prodigious talent of the Fuenlebrade-born Torres. Moving up to the senior national side, Torres won the 2008 Euros with Spain, scoring the only goal in the final victory against Germany. He and teammate David Villa were named in the Team of the Tournament. Having undergone knee surgery at the end of the 2010 season, Torres's game-time at the 2010 World Cup was limited, but he came on as a substitute in extra time as Spain defeated Holland 1-0 in the semi-final. Torres was again used as a substitute as Spain defeated Italy handsomely in the final.

Ultimately, a succession of injuries took their toll on Torres, his natural speed reduced by fate. At his peak, the athletic Torres was a player of high spectacle, pacy, skilful, a lethal finisher.

Chelsea's bench for the final contained the now-accepted modern vein of a multinational group of players. Only reserve goalkeeper Ross Turnbull was English. The outstanding right-back Paulo Ferreira received 62 caps for Portugal, completing over 140 league games for Chelsea. The tall, doughty Nigerian Jon Obi Mikel played 249 league games for the club, in addition to 91 games for his country. Much had been expected of the young Mikel and he became a mainstay in Chelsea's midfield for over a decade, only losing his place as Chelsea became ever-ambitious under Abramovich's fiscal control. The Israeli international Yossi Benayoun graced both West Ham United and Liverpool's first teams for several seasons. Though his slight physique was a little at odds with this powerful Chelsea team, he had skill to burn. Another Nigerian, Victor Moses, cemented a place as a right wing-back over coming seasons at Chelsea, enjoying a successful run in the team before a succession of loans after losing favour. In 2020 Moses was on loan at Inter Milan, one of Europe's premier clubs. Like Torres, Moses scored twice in the quarter-final Rubin Kazan ties in this 2013 competition. The Dutchman Nathan Ake, a useful central defender for Bournemouth in recent seasons (and with Manchester City, October 2020) was among the unused substitutes on this evening.

Curiously, in this modern era of multinational teams, Benfica, fielded only one native Portuguese player, the right full-back André Almeida. Their team comprised two Brazilians, four Argentinians, two Paraguayans, and two players well known to English Premiership fans and followers, Spaniard Rodrigo (latterly at Leeds United), and the Serbian Nemanja Matic, a key player for Chelsea themselves 2014–17, and latterly of Manchester United.

When David Luiz switched to Chelsea in 2011, Matic went to Lisbon as part of the swap deal. Matic, a solid, no-nonsense, dependable holding midfielder, is one of those players every team should have. He links play sensibly, rarely loses the ball. In this season of 2012–13 his move to Lisbon resulted in him being awarded Portugal's Primera Liga Player of the Year. It's difficult to know who got the best deal – the flamboyant Luiz, capable of brilliance, but prone to errors, or the rock-steady 'Mr Dependable' Matic. One excites, but frustrates, the other goes distinctly under the radar. In a game of football both have their place. Matic's reward for his consistency with his most recent club, Manchester United, was a new three-year contract. He played 121 league games for Chelsea 2014–17. Here in this 2013 Europa League Final he was an integral part of Benfica's team of worldwide players.

Rodrigo scored 27 goals in 68 league games for Benfica 2010–15. A nationalised Spaniard, Rodrigo was actually born in Rio de Janeiro, making him the third Brazilian in this team. Moving to Valencia for five seasons 2015–20, Rodrigo scored 35 goals in 141 league appearances. He has been capped by Spain 27 times (July 2022) and raised his profile again when signing for Leeds United, newly promoted to the Premiership in 2020, subsequently scoring a fine equalising goal against Manchester City at the start of the 2020–21 Premiership season.

Benfica's main goal threat appeared to come from the six feet four inches Paraguayan centre-forward Oscar Cardoso, scorer of 112 goals in only 175 league games for the Lisbon-based club. His 172 goals in all competitions for Benfica make him the club's highest scoring foreign player. Paraguayan Player of the Year in 2006 and 2009, Cardoso helped Benfica to win the domestic treble in this 2012–13 season – only this Europa League trophy eluded them.

Among Benfica's substitutes was a young André Gomes, known to Everton supporters as a splendid midfield player, and the Argentinian Pablo Aimar. Aimar was considered one of the most gifted players of his generation, excelling at Valencia in Spain 2001–06, helping the club win La Liga for the first time in 31 years in his first full season in Spain. This, after helping Valencia reach the 2001 Champions League Final where they lost to Bayern Munich on penalties. In 2003–04, Aimar helped Valencia win La Liga again, in addition to winning the UEFA Cup. Maradona thought Aimar the best of the Argentine players at this time, although Aimar and even Lionel Messi have struggled to impact on the Argentine national team in the wake of Maradona's retirement. Aimar played 52 times for Argentina, scoring eight goals, but ultimately promised more than he was able to deliver. In his first season with Benfica, teaming up with fellow Argentinians Javier Saviola and Angel di Maria, and the prolific Cardoso, the South American quartet wreaked havoc in the 2009–10 season, scoring a combined total of 78 goals as Benfica won a league and cup double. Sadly for Aimar, injuries meant he would leave at the end of this 2012–13 season, and prevented him even appearing from the substitutes' bench in this 2013 Europa League Final.

THE FINAL
Chelsea were favourites for this final on the back of their Mourinho/Abramovich-inspired revival in the new millennium, but the proud Portuguese/multinational Benfica team fought their corner manfully. Rodrigo failed to convert in a goalmouth scramble in the first half. Lampard responded with a trademark 25-yard drive that Arthur in the Benfica goal tipped over. Torres then did the job he'd been selected for, dancing round Arthur and sliding the ball into an empty net. Azpilicueta handled as Benfica responded in kind, Cardoso converted the penalty kick and the game was 1-1 after 90 minutes, but not before Petr Cech earnt his corn by brilliantly tipping over Cardoso's 25-yard volley. Lampard, always a threat from distance, struck the post with another 20-yard effort. Mata's corner kick was met in the third minute of stoppage time by a massive leap by Branislav Ivanovic and a firm header that gave Arthur no chance. It was a dramatic ending to a final that proved Benfica remain one of Europe's leading clubs, Chelsea having to dig deep into their experienced reserves to quell their opponents.

2015–2016 EUROPA LEAGUE FINAL
Sevilla 3 v 1 Liverpool

Jürgen Klopp's first season as manager of Liverpool and the advent of *'Gegenpressing'* in English football. There were already signs of his influence as the Reds reached the Europa League Final held at St Jacob Park, Basle, Switzerland, the second smallest venue ever chosen for a major European Final. Controversially, Klopp suggested (before backtracking) that Liverpool fans should travel to Basle even if they did not have tickets – presumably to enjoy the atmosphere of a day in the Swiss city, and offer any kind of support to Liverpool that might give them an edge.

Route to the Final
Liverpool's route to the final came through qualifying via the group stages; opponents Sevilla finished third in their group stage of the Champions League behind Manchester City and Juventus, transferring into the Europa League at the round of 32 stage. Ironically, given the choice of a Swiss venue for the final, Liverpool pipped Sion as Group B winners of the initial stage. Alien to how Liverpool performed in subsequent seasons under Klopp, goals were at a premium in the group stage. Only Bordeaux, defeated 2-1 at Anfield, and Russian side Rubin Kazan, defeated 1-0 away, brought definitive victories for Liverpool. All four of their other ties were drawn either 1-1 or 0-0. This goal scarcity continued in the round of 32 as German side Augsburg lost to Liverpool 1-0 on aggregate thanks to a James Milner penalty at Anfield.

At last the goals started to flow when Liverpool met Manchester United in the last 16. A Daniel Sturridge penalty, followed by a Roberto Firmino goal secured a 2-0 home win, while a Philippe Coutinho goal equalised an earlier Anthony Martial penalty for United at Old Trafford. In the quarter-finals Liverpool beat another German side – Klopp's former club Borussia Dortmund. Divock Origi opened the scoring for Liverpool in Germany, Mats Hummels equalising. Two early goals at Anfield from players well known to English football followers, Henrikh Mkhitaryan and Pierre-Emerick Aubameyang, threatened to put the tie beyond Liverpool's reach. Origi reduced arrears early in the second half, but a Marco Reus goal left Liverpool with a mountain to climb. Coutinho's 66th-minute strike revived the Reds, the infamous 'Kop roar' lifting Liverpool to new heights. Mamadou Sakho levelled the tie in the 77th minute. Dramatically, defender Dejan Lovren headed the winner from Milner's cross in stoppage time. This remarkable comeback was a precursor to an even more spectacular revival in the 2018–19 Champions League semi-final against Barcelona.

Spanish side Villareal provided stiff opposition in the Europa League semi-final, a late Adrian Lopez goal stealing a slight advantage for their opponents in Spain. At Anfield an own goal levelled the tie. Further goals from Sturridge (remember him?) and Adam Lallana (after Sevilla central defender Victor Ruiz was sent off) sent Liverpool through to this 2013 final, the club apparently riding the crest of a wave having embraced Klopp's go-to 'Gegenpressing' philosophy, a mantra requiring his teams to adopt a high press, high-octane attacking style whereby players must retrieve the ball instantly if the ball is lost.

Sevilla despatched Norwegians Molde and the Swiss side Basle summarily in the last 32 and last 16, 3-1 and 3-0 on aggregate respectively. In the quarter-finals, Spanish rivalry made for a hotly contested tie, a 2-1 away victory followed by a 2-1 home defeat. Opponents Athletic Bilbao refused to bow easily, ultimately losing to Sevilla by a 5-4 margin on penalties after extra time. The Ukrainian side

Shakhtar Donetsk, one of the more successful European competition teams from Ukraine were defeated 5-3 on aggregate in the semi-finals.

Liverpool's team for this final shows only two of the mainstays of the club's recent hugely impressive standing as one of Europe's premier teams: Milner and Firmino. The style which Klopp insists upon was evident, the personnel has evolved somewhat in Klopp's six years at Anfield. Brendan Rogers, currently (July 2022) Leicester City's manager, deserves credit too for transforming Liverpool's style into more attack-minded mode during his tenure at Anfield. The three S's, Suarez (Luis), Sterling (Raheem), and Sturridge almost secured a first Premiership title in nearly 30 years under Rogers. It would be left to Klopp to realise that long-awaited dream in 2019–20.

In goal for Liverpool, Belgian international custodian Simon Mignolet endured mixed fortunes for the club. He moved to Anfield from Sunderland in June 2013, ultimately playing 155 league games for Liverpool. Clearly a consummate shot-stopper, Mignolet has suffered the goalkeeper's lot of being blamed for occasional errors that are highlighted by being the 'last man standing' (between the posts). At times a goalkeeper is laid bare by those before him – if his defenders are not doing their job, the keeper becomes exposed. When Klopp became manager he tended to favour Loris Karius, a young German goalkeeper, making Mignolet's appearances less frequent. Only when Liverpool signed Brazil's excellent Alisson Becker did Mignolet realise his time at Anfield was up, moving home to play for Club Brugge in 2019. Mignolet had played 35 times for Belgium as I write.

If there is an area Liverpool have noticeably improved under Klopp it is at full-back. The full-backs of 2016, Nathaniel Clyne and Alberto Moreno were of considerable merit, but current incumbents Trent Alexander-Arnold and Andy Robertson have taken Liverpool to another level. Clyne established himself as one of English football's most promising full-backs at Crystal Palace (2008–12) and Southampton (2012–15). In the 2010–11 season, Clyne was awarded Palace's Player of the Year. Over 200 Premier League games under his belt, Clyne signed a five-year contract at Anfield in July 2015. Clyne is another player whose career has been cruelly blighted by injury. A back injury prevented much playing time in the 2017–18 season; an anterior cruciate ligament injury in a 2018–19 pre-season friendly with Klopp's 'old wards' Borussia Dortmund the final nail in Clyne's Anfield coffin.

Left-back Moreno spent three seasons at Sevilla, firstly in the reserves, then in the first team. He was playing in this 2016 final against a club he loved. Moreno gave Liverpool a positive attacking outlet on the left, although defensively he does not match his successor Robertson in the current set-up. Moreno even lost out to 'Mr Consistency' James Milner as one of Klopp's preferred left-back options on occasions. He played over 100 games in all competitions for Liverpool before returning 'home' to Sevilla in July 2019.

James Milner is Liverpool's 'everyman'. Ostensibly a midfield player, Milner's versatility has allowed him to fill in at full-back when called upon. Milner is one of those players who seems to have been around forever, although he is still only 36 (July 2022). His pro career began at Leeds United (2002–04), but it shouldn't be a surprise to know what a fine sports all-rounder he was before adopting football as his career choice. Milner, whose energy level seems insatiable, was a school cross-country champion, a 100-yard sprint champion, played cricket for Yorkshire schools, and represented England at U-15 and U-17 level at football, helping his country win a 2002 nationwide summer tournament against Italy, the Czech Republic and Brazil in the latter age group.

He appeared for Leeds on 10 November 2002, still 16 years old, making him the second youngest debutant in the Premiership at that time. A goal in December against Sunderland made him the youngest goalscorer in the Premiership until Everton's James Vaughan surpassed him in 2005. With Leeds in financial difficulties, Milner was sold – against the club's coaches wishes – to Newcastle United in 2004. Milner played at times as a wide right midfield player-cum winger at St James's Park, but when Bobby Robson departed as manager, Milner's game-time was curtailed by incoming boss Graham Souness. Forty-eight league games at Elland Road; 94 at St James's Park. It was clear to anyone watching that Milner's team commitment and energy were invaluable, but did he suffer like others before him for being almost too versatile? Loaned out to Aston Villa in 2005, the move became permanent in 2008. In the 2009–10 season Milner won Villa Fan's Player of the Year award, in addition to being crowned the PFA Young Player of the Year.

It's an interesting career, James Milner's. Even in 2022 Milner is tagged a 'bits and pieces' player – yet the last ten years have seen his stock soar to higher levels. In August 2010 he signed for Manchester City. Over five seasons with City, Milner played over 150 matches in all competitions, winning the Premiership twice (2011–12, 2013–14), the FA Cup (2010–11) and the League Cup (2013–14). Ultimately Milner was unable to hold down a regular place as City's new financial clout resulted in numerous high-priced and high-quality acquisitions arriving from abroad.

Milner moved again in June 2015 to Anfield, where, finally, his all-action style, his never-say-die attitude, and, naturally, his great versatility, have seen him recognised as one of the top professionals in English football. It didn't take him long to be accepted at Liverpool, as the club made him vice-captain in August 2015. He was named captain for this Europa League Final. To date Milner has played over 200 games in all competitions with Liverpool. He came on as a substitute in the 2019 Champions League win over Tottenham Hotspur. When Liverpool finally shook off their 30-year 'albatross' to win the Premiership in 2019–20, Milner was a highly valued member of the squad. He has since signed a contract to keep him at Anfield until 2022. There's nothing fancy about James Milner – his high energy, good reading of the game, adaptability to the team's needs, make him the complete modern footballer, a player good enough to have played 61 times for England. He doesn't score often, but his assists count is among the highest in the Premiership. A tenacious, dependable team player – every team knows how important is to have a player like James Milner in their side.

Liverpool's centre-backs for this final were the Croatian Dejan Lovren and the Ivory Coast international Kolo Touré. Lovren played the longest spell of his career at Anfield, only losing favour when Klopp brought in the hugely influential Virgil van Dijk. Lovren's family fled fragmenting Yugoslavia to escape the Bosnian

War when Lovren was three years old. Aged 17, Lovren returned to Croatia to play for Dinamo Zagreb. In 2010 Lovren signed for French Ligue 1 team Lyon, winning the Coupe de France (the French equivalent of the FA Cup Final) in 2012. In 2013 Lovren came to England to play for Southampton. He started only 31 league games on the south coast before signing for Liverpool in July 2014. Lovren it was who scored the decisive winning goal in the 4-3 quarter-final victory over Borussia Dortmund in this 2015–16 UEFA Cup campaign. Lovren tended to be played either alongside Joel Matip at times, or one player gave way to the other as the Croat's Anfield career progressed. Ultimately Lovren played 131 league games for Liverpool, his endeavours to establish himself as a first team regular ending when he moved to Zenit St Petersburg in 2020. Lovren has played 70 times for Croatia (four goals, July 2022).

Kolo Touré is the older brother of Yaya Touré (formerly a star of the emergent Manchester City team of the last decade or so, he carved a mightily impressive career of his own). A fee of £150,000 paid to Ivorian club ASEC Mimosas for Kolo seems like peanuts in modern transfer parlance. This was Arsenal's outlay in 2002 for a player who would become one of their 'Invincibles' in 2004. Used by Arsenal initially as a utility player (defensive midfield/full-back), it was Arsene Wenger's decision to employ Touré senior as a centre-back that transformed his Arsenal career. Playing alongside Sol Campbell at the heart of the Gunners' defence the pair's pace, power and leadership created an impenetrable core in the club's undefeated 2003–04 league season.

Yet Kolo found himself competing with Philippe Senderos and Pascal Cygan the following season. With Campbell injured and suffering a loss of form, Touré combined with Senderos as centre-backs as Arsenal reached the 2006 Champions League Final. Kolo captained Arsenal periodically thereafter, but injuries during the 2007–08 season marred his form and in July 2009 he moved to Manchester City having completed 225 league games for Arsenal.

Kolo Touré also captained City at times between 2009 and 2013, although he was used only sparingly when the club won the Premiership in the 2011–12 season. After 82 league appearances for City, Touré moved to Anfield in July 2013. Touré continued to fluctuate between powerful and less consistent performances with Liverpool, playing a further 46 league games over three seasons. Touré's last hurrah in British football came under former Liverpool manager Brendan Rogers' stewardship at Celtic, helping the Glasgow club win a treble of League, Cup and league Cup in his final season in top-flight football in 2016–17. Kolo Touré played 120 times for the Ivory Coast, retiring from international football two years earlier than from club football in 2015.

Emre Can occupied the defensive midfield space beside James Milner in this final. The Frankfurt-born Can played fleetingly with Bayern Munich and Bayer Leverkusen (2012–14) before signing for Liverpool in July 2014. Under Brendan Rogers, Can was often used as a full-back or centre-back. Klopp's arrival saw Can moved back to his preferred midfield position. Injuring ankle ligaments in this 2015–16 campaign in the quarter-final against Borussia Dortmund jeopardised Can's chances of appearing again in that season. Can returned ahead of schedule to play in the successful semi-final against Villareal, duly taking his place in the final against Sevilla. Can's overhead kick against Watford won him the Premiership Goal of the Season the following year.

Can completed 115 league games for Liverpool 2015–18, scoring ten goals. He transferred to Turin giants Juventus in 2018, playing two seasons in Italy before moving back to Germany to play for Borussia Dortmund. Can could have played for Turkey due to his Turkish ancestry but opted to play internationally for Germany. To date (July 2022) he has completed 37 games for Germany. Can's all-round game has seen him used in central defence, central midfield or in the wide attacking full-back positions. Versatile to a fault again, perhaps.

Ultimately, Adam Lallana's Liverpool and England careers have been slightly tarnished by injury. Lallana excelled at Southampton, having joined the renowned Saints Academy as a 12-year-old. Former graduates of the academy include Alan Shearer, Gareth Bale and Theo Walcott. Lallana's slighter than average physique at five feet eight inches made him a 'will o'the wisp' type player, capable of flitting between opponents, his eye for the defence-splitting pass a main characteristic of his game. An attacking midfielder, Lallana helped Southampton to recover their Premiership status with two promotions, scoring 20 goals in all competitions 2009–10 (the first midfielder to do so at the club since Matt Le Tissier in 1994–95). Back in the 'big time' Lallana was named in the PFA Team of the Year in season 2013–14.

Lallana signed for Liverpool in the summer of 2014. In April 2015 Lallana was selected in the Football Manager Team of the Decade (players who featured in the Championship, Leagues 1 and 2 in the English Football League). Playing in the Premiership was a big step up, and Lallana was making a good fist of it, scoring goals against Bordeaux, Sion and Villareal during Liverpool's 2015–16 Europa League run.

Playing in a biennial pre-season friendly tournament, the Audi Cup, staged at the Allianz Arena in Munich, Lallana suffered a long-term injury that prevented him meeting expectations of his career flourishing further. Cursed by injuries, Lallana was named as a substitute in the Champions League Finals of 2018 and 2019. He signed a short-term extension contract at Liverpool in June 2020, but with the club's horizons soaring ever higher Lallana moved back to the south coast again to play for Brighton and Hove Albion. Lallana's form prior to his run of injuries was good enough to earn him the England Player of the Year award in 2016. He has played 34 times for England. A deft, subtle player, capable of bisecting defences with his clever forward movement from midfield positions, injury has meant Lallana not entirely fulfilling his rich early promise.

Two exquisitely talented Brazilians completed the offensive midfield in Liverpool's two-deep, three forward, five-man Liverpool central area of the field in this 2016 Europa League Final. Philippe Coutinho and Roberto Firmino have influenced the Liverpool team greatly over the last decade. For a period of time under Brendan Rogers, Coutinho was one of the shining lights of a Liverpool team threatening to end their near-30 year wait for that elusive Premiership title. Coutinho – in line with all Brazilians – developed his immaculate touch and control playing Futsal (a shorter form of five/six-a-side football where ball control and technique are paramount). The last time I read about Futsal in England there was talk of disbanding the English national Futsal team due to funding issues. It beggars belief – we have continually struggled as a nation to compete with continental/European opponents with glaringly obvious superior technique. Why do we always have our heads in the sand in Britain?

The skills Coutinho developed in Futsal won him a contract with Italian giants Inter Milan, aged only 16. Although Coutinho stayed five seasons at Inter his playing time – unsurprisingly under José Mourinho initially – was very limited. Only when loaned out to Espanyol in Spain did Coutinho begin to truly flourish under Mauricio Pochettino. He returned to Inter and signed for Liverpool in January 2013, then-manager Rafael Benitez describing the five feet eight inches Brazilian as 'world class'. Benitez's judgement proved very sound indeed as Coutinho shone brightly during five seasons, playing 152 league games for Liverpool, scoring 41 goals. All Coutinho's talents came to the fore – his tight ball control, incisive passing, astute reading of the game. Coutinho also proved deadly in dead-ball situations, and scored many stunning long-range goals for Liverpool. Coutinho's mesmerising dribbling skills helped set up countless goals for Luis Suarez and Daniel Sturridge as Liverpool agonisingly missed out on the 2014 Premiership title, their seven-point cushion over Manchester City overturned at the death.

In season 2014–15 Coutinho was the only Liverpool player named in the PFA Team of the Year. The Brazilian narrowly lost out to Eden Hazard and Harry Kane for that season's PFA Player's Player of the Year and PFA Young Player of the Year respectively.

In January 2017 Coutinho signed a new five-year contract at Anfield (these contracts are worthless when a bigger club comes calling). Coutinho became the highest scoring Brazilian in the Premiership, overtaking ex-Middlesbrough star Juninho, when he scored his 30th Premier League goal against Stoke City in 2017. In August 2017 Barcelona bid a staggering £72 million for the hugely gifted Coutinho. The Brazilian consequently put in a transfer request. Despite the unsettling nature of Barca's courting, Coutinho captained Liverpool at times, even scoring a hat-trick against Spartak Moscow in the 2017–18 Champions League group stages. Coutinho appeared to hanker after playing for one of the 'big two' Spanish clubs, Barcelona or Real Madrid. Whether it was impatience or simply following the dream of playing for one of the greatest clubs in European football history, the great irony is that the money that came in upon Coutinho's transfer to Barcelona in January 2018 funded the signing of two of the most influential players in Liverpool's recent successes – Brazilian goalkeeper Alisson Becker and the talismanic Dutch centre-back Virgil van Dijk.

In his first season at the Nou Camp, Coutinho scored goals against Tottenham Hotspur and Manchester United in the Champions League – the latter in the quarter-final. At the end of the season he'd played 54 matches in all competitions, scored 11 goals, and won La Liga with Barcelona. His decision appeared to have been justified. Yet Coutinho was farmed out to Bayern Munich in August 2019 on a season-long loan. Leaving Liverpool – the club were not entirely happy about Coutinho's decision – meant that the Brazilian, ironically, missed out on winning the Champions League in 2019 and the Premier League in 2020.

Coutinho rectified these losses in the 2019–20 season as Bayern won the Champions League in the strange Covid-19 times that signalled a fan-less final. He appeared as a substitute against Barcelona in one of European football's most iconic games, the stunning 8-2 rout in the quarter-finals, scoring the last two goals. He was used as a substitute again as Bayern defeated Paris Saint-Germain 1-0 in the final. The arrival of Ronald Koeman as the new manager of Barcelona saw Coutinho return to the Nou Camp for the 2020–21 season. Sought after by all of Europe's big clubs, could the Rio de Janeiro-born 28-year-old Coutinho confirm his world-class status and finally settle in Spain? The answer was no, as Coutinho rejoined former teammate Steven Gerrard at Aston Villa in 2022, beginning life at Villa Park in thrilling style, although his form has since faltered.

To my mind, only Kevin De Bruyne at Manchester City has made a similar impact to Coutinho as a midfield playmaker of all the foreign imports in the Premiership over the last decade. Pochettino compares Coutinho to Lionel Messi and Ronaldinho; Klopp compares him to the Italian great Alessandro Del Piero with his quick feet and devastating long-range goal-scoring ability. By July 2022 Coutinho had played 68 times for Brazil, scoring 21 goals, although like Messi he has yet to enable his country a World Cup win.

Roberto Firmino continues to go massively under the radar at Anfield, yet nobody at Liverpool is in any doubt about the massive impact the subtly talented Brazilian has had on the team since joining in 2015. Firmino's role as an attacking midfield player/stroke second striker is something of a misnomer. He glides in the spaces between the opposition midfield and defence, his assists for goals far outweighing his own goal return. Jürgen Klopp regards Firmino as the engine that enables Liverpool's passing game and forward creativity to function fully.

Starting out in Brazil with Figueirense 2009–2011, Firmino scored eight goals in 38 league games. His form won him a contract with German club 1899 Hoffenheim in 2011. Firmino stayed in Germany until 2015, scoring 16 goals in the 2013–14 Bundesliga season, and being named as the season's Breakthrough Player. In total Firmino scored 38 goals in 140 league appearances at Hoffenheim.

Firmino began slowly after signing for Liverpool in 2015, but Klopp's masterstroke of playing Firmino as a 'false 9' has seen the Brazilian's influence on the team grow immeasurably. At the end of the 2015–16 season (post-the sensational Suarez/Sturridge/Sterling triumvirate), Firmino was Liverpool's top scorer with ten Premiership goals. The following season Firmino netted 12 league goals, but it was his ability to link with those players in front of him and knit Liverpool's play together that Klopp recognised as truly impacting on the team.

In the 2017–18 season the 'Fab Four' – an obvious Beatles reference applied by the fans at Anfield – of Firmino, Coutinho, Mohammed Salah and Sadio Mané –wreaked havoc, but Coutinho's transfer left a 'Fab Three' who, astonishingly, racked up 91 goals between them by the end of the season. Firmino, not as prolific as Salah or Mané, still equalled Salah's Champions League tally of 11 goals in 2017–18. Unfortunately the multi-talented Real Madrid proved a step too far in the Champions League. 2017–18 was Firmino's most fruitful on the goal front, as he finished with 27 goals in all competitions. Despite missing the games leading up to the Champions League Final of 2019 against Tottenham Hotspur, Klopp valued him highly enough to start him as Liverpool triumphed 2-0. To date (July 2022), Firmino has scored 71 goals in 231 league games for Liverpool. He has also played nearly 55 times for Brazil with a respectable 17-goal return.

Highly regarded by his teammates for his work-rate and unselfishness, Firmino is not regarded in the same light as the more glamorous goal-hunters Salah and Mané, but his team ethic makes him invaluable to Liverpool's cause.

The lone striker for Liverpool in this 2016 Europa League Final, Daniel Sturridge, is something of an enigma, and another player whose career has stalled due to successive injuries, but for a while his link-up with Luis Suarez and Raheem Sterling at Liverpool made the Anfield club an exciting watch, arguably even more so than Pep Guardiola's Manchester City in the modern English game. Following a youth career at Aston Villa and Coventry City, Birmingham-born Sturridge began his senior career at Manchester City in 2006. He became the first player in season 2007–08 to score in the FA Youth Cup, the FA Cup, and the Premier League in one calendar year. A gifted player with a delightful touch, Sturridge has represented England at all levels from boys, to youths, to senior mens level.

In season 2008–09 Sturridge was named Manchester City's Young Player of the Year. When his contract expired in 2009, Sturridge opted to sign for Chelsea. In the 2009–10 season Sturridge top-scored with four goals in the FA Cup campaign, although he was only a substitute as Chelsea defeated Portsmouth 1-0 in the final. With the powerhouse Ivorian centre-forward Didier Drogba blocking his path to regular first team football Sturridge was loaned out to Bolton Wanderers in January 2011. He scored eight goals in 12 games for Bolton, returning to Stamford Bridge for the 2011–12 season. Unfortunately for Sturridge, Drogba prevented him playing any part in the 2012 Champions League Final which Chelsea won in dramatic penalty shoot-out style against Bayern Munich. When Rafael Benitez took over as Chelsea manager, a combination of Benitez's preference for other players and injuries meant Sturridge's time at Chelsea was up.

Moving to Liverpool in January 2013, Sturridge scored in each of his first three games for the club, the first player to do so since Ray Kennedy in 1974. In the 2013–14 season Sturridge scored in seven consecutive league games, the first Liverpool player to do so in the Premier League era. In April 2014 Sturridge was named in the PFA Team of the Year. Sturridge, in the form of his life, still seemed to be held in less regard than his dynamic strike partner Suarez. Sturridge's 21 Premier league goals made him runner-up in the 2013–14 Premier League Golden Boot... behind Suarez.

Sadly, the 2014–15 season marked a downturn in Sturridge's fortunes as he missed almost six months of football with thigh, calf and hip injuries. Further injuries to a knee and a hamstring in 2015–16 hinted at Sturridge's Liverpool career being curtailed. Despite his misfortunes, he scored against Manchester United in the Europa League last 16 in 2015–16, going on to complete 50 goals in all competitions for Liverpool in 87 games, the fourth fastest in the club's history – not bad when you think Liverpool's strikers over the years have included Roger Hunt, Ian Rush, Michael Owen and Robbie Fowler, Clearly the succession of injuries was taking its toll, but goals in the semi-final of the Europa League against Villareal and Liverpool's solitary goal in the final against Sevilla proved his continuing worth to the side. With Suarez departed for pastures new at Barcelona, Sturridge ended the 2015–16 season as Liverpool's top scorer with 13 goals.

Sturridge lasted another 18 months at Anfield, but with Roberto Firmino above him in the pecking order, and injuries denying him full capacity, he tended to be used as an impact substitute during this time. Loaned out to West Bromwich Albion in January 2020 he suffered a hamstring injury in only his third game for the club. Back at Liverpool for the 2018–19 season, Sturridge scored against Paris Saint-Germain, following this up with a sublime equaliser against former club Chelsea in the Premier League. Sturridge signed for Turkish club Trabanspor in August 2019. Crazily, he scored seven goals in just 16 appearances in Turkey. Mired in betting controversies, cursed by continual injury problems, it seemed that Sturridge would not succumb to career closure without a fight.

Internationally, Daniel Sturridge's star shone brightly from a young age. Although England were eliminated at the group stage of the UEFA European U-21 Championships in 2011, Sturridge was named in the Team of the Tournament. Selected for England at senior level later in the year he impressed immediately with his vivid technique, pace and imagination. The cruel spate of injuries curtailed his England career (2011–17), although he scored eight times in his 26 appearances. For a while I felt that with Daniel Sturridge in the England side our country had a player with the technique to compare with any continental striker. His longevity at the top seemed short, his body betraying him.

Jürgen Klopp had plenty of experience at his disposal on the bench for this final: Slovakian national captain and central defender Martin Skirtel; Brazilian midfielder Lucas; Welsh international midfielder Joe Allen; current (2022) captain Jordan Henderson; Belgian forwards Christian Benteke and Divock Origi. None of these could prevent Sevilla from winning the final.

The Sevilla side bore no relation to the side that defeated Fulham in 2010. It was a team of all nationalities and all talents. Crucially, what had changed, and seems not to have changed to this day, is Sevilla's grip on the UEFA Cup/ Europa League competition. The club have developed a desire to win the trophy, a feeling that they have almost a divine right to retain the cup. In defence they boasted a Brazilian Mariano at full-back, a French international Adil Rami alongside Mexican Daniel Carrico as centre-backs. Sevilla's defensive midfield duo comprised Grzegorz Krychowiak, a 60-times capped Polish international who was part of their Europa League-winning teams of 2015 and 2016; and a player known to English football fans, Steven Nzonzi. Nzonzi played nearly 200 league games for Blackburn Rovers and Stoke City prior to joining Sevilla in 2015. He was named Blackburn's fans' Player of the Year for the 2009–10 season. The towering six feet five inches French-born Nzonzi was clearly a fans' favourite, but it remained something of a surprise when he joined Sevilla given that his physical all-round game was slightly at odds with Spanish football's firm beliefs in technical possession football. Initially he struggled to adapt, but his form picked up considerably as Sevilla went on to retain the Europa League Cup against Liverpool. Since 2018, Nzonzi has played for Roma in Italy, before being loaned out to Galatasaray in Turkey and Rennes in France. There is always a place for a player of Nzonzi's imposing strength and athleticism in modern football.

Arguably the standout players for Sevilla were the Captain, Coke, midfield player and Man of the Match in this 2016 Europa League Final, and the forward Kevin Gameiro. Coke helped Rayo Vallecano up into La Liga from Spain's second tier in a seven-season stay 2004–2011, departing for Sevilla in June 2011. Coke was present in the team that defeated Benfica in the 2014 season's Europa League Final, little knowing this would trigger a three-season hat-trick of Europa League wins. The Ukrainians Dnipro were defeated in the 2015 final, then it would be the turn of Liverpool to feel the pride in winning this competition imbued in Sevilla, on this occasion overseen by soon-to-be Arsenal manager Unai Emery. Switching between right back and right midfield, it was in the latter position that Coke effervescently won Man of the Match against Liverpool. After signing for German club Schalke in 2016, Coke suffered a severe cruciate ligament injury to his right knee in a pre-season friendly. His career in Germany was over before it had even started. Coke has since returned to Spain, signing for Levante, but it seems that the 2016 Europa League Final was the pinnacle of his career. Coke played 117 league games for Sevilla, but like so many of his generation he could not dislodge Xavi, Iniesta, David Silva and Busquets from the national side.

Alongside Coke in midfield was the talented Ever Banega, 65-times capped by Argentina, and Man of the Match in the 2015 final, but it was Sevilla's solitary forward Kevin Gameiro who shone almost as brightly as Coke in this 2016 Europa League Final. French-born Gameiro scored 79 league goals in his home country 2005–2013 for Strasbourg, Lorient and Paris Saint-Germain, before signing for Sevilla. In a three-season spell with Sevilla, Gameiro scored 39 goals in 92 league starts. In the 2014 Europa League Final against Benfica, Gameiro came on as a substitute to score the decisive winning goal in the penalty shoot-out. Gameiro's goal that equalised Daniel Sturridge's opener for Liverpool in this 2016 final was his eighth of the 2015–16 Europa League campaign. He has since transferred firstly to Atlético Madrid (scoring 19 league goals in 56 starts) and subsequently to Valencia where he netted 16 goals in 89 league games, before signing for French club Strasbourg in 2021. Gameiro has represented France at international level 13 times.

The most interesting (to Brits) of Sevilla's substitutes was the gangly centre-forward Fernando Llorente, who only played this 2015–16 season with the club (23 league appearances, four goals). The Pamplona-born striker was a massive success with his native Athletic Bilbao 2005–2013, scoring 85 times in 262 league games. Goals in both legs of a 2011–12 Europa League tie helped Bilbao defeat Manchester United. Bilbao went on to reach the final that season only to lose 3-0 to fellow Spaniards Atlético Madrid. Llorente's seven goals in the competition made him the Europa League's highest scorer for 2011–12. Llorente transferred to Juventus in Italy in 2013 where he enjoyed some success, scoring 23 goals in 66 Serie A games, no mean feat in the notoriously defensive-minded Italian top flight. He made a substitutes' appearance in the 2015 Champions League Final, although Juve lost out 3-1 to Barcelona.

A free agent in 2015, Llorente signed for Sevilla. Llorente's goal against former club Juventus in the Champions League was sufficient to enable third-placed Sevilla to enter the 2015–16 Europa League draw for the last 32. He did not come on to the field of play for this 2016 Europa League Final. Another inveterate traveller – like Diego Forlan – Llorente then signed for Swansea City, scoring 15 goals in 33 league starts to help the Swans stave off relegation from the Premiership 2016–17. Llorente then spent an interesting two seasons at Tottenham Hotspur 2017–19, largely being used as cover for 'super striker' Harry Kane. Llorente's rangy six feet four inch frame made him an awkward opponent for centre-halves, a quintessential target man. Perhaps Llorente's biggest impact for Spurs came in the 2019 Champions League semi-final second leg when he replaced Victor Wanyama at half-time with Spurs trailing Ajax 3-0. By the end of the 90 minutes the tide had turned as Tottenham pulled level at 3-3 and qualified for a final against Liverpool. Llorente again came on as a substitute in the final, a 2-0 defeat at the hands of the Merseysiders. Llorente has played 24 times for Spain, scoring seven goals (October 2020). Latterly he joined Napoli in Italy, tending to take the sub's role once more.

Sevilla manager Unai Emery had an unhappy season with Arsenal 2018–19, but nobody can take away from him his huge run of success in the Europa League with Sevilla. Emery would take Arsenal to the 2018–19 Europa League Final, but a heavy defeat against fellow Londoners Chelsea was the straw that broke the camel's back as Arsenal failed to qualify for the Champions League once again. It was Emery's misfortune to take the reins at Arsenal as the first successor to the long-standing Arsene Wenger. Emery has since taken over as manager of Villareal in Spain.

THE FINAL
Liverpool started the final encouragingly, but sadly ran out of steam. An early Sturridge header from Nathaniel Clyne's cross was cleared from the goalline as the Reds sought to establish control over their doughty Spanish opponents. Sturridge's header lacked sufficient power to trouble the Sevilla keeper. Sturridge threatened again in a lively start, his excellent movement denied by the feet of the Sevilla keeper. In response, Kevin Gameiro's overhead kick proved to be a portent of things to come. Sturridge seemed to be on a one-man conquest to score in this final as his exquisite left-foot struck with the outside of his left boot gave Liverpool the lead. Other early chances fluffed, Liverpool paid the price. Mariano marauded down the right flank and provided the lurking Gameiro with a tap-in. Gameiro then mis-kicked when it looked easier to score.

Sevilla came out in the second half a different team. When it had looked distinctly possible that Liverpool might claim the trophy, the second half was one-way traffic as the Spaniards upped the ante. Playing with far greater energy, Sevilla took the lead when Coke stole the ball from a teammate to drive his team ahead. The ball then reached Coke on the right side of the penalty area, his shot was parried by Mignolet, but there was just enough strength on the midfielder's shot to carry it into the net. After a strong opening half-hour, Liverpool faltered and Sevilla ran out deserved winners.

This was United's first Europa League/UEFA Cup Final; it was Ajax's second having beaten Torino of Italy in the 1992 final. United's team were packed with experience in this final; Ajax were a team full of youthful promise – in the end experience told – and no doubt he would tell it, the talismanic José Mourinho reproduced his perennial managerial successful trophy-winning touch.

Route to the Final
United only finished second behind the Turks Fenerbahce in their initial group stage, beating them 4-1 at Old Trafford, but losing 2-1 in Istanbul. Similar results were achieved against Dutch club Feyenoord, a convincing 4-0 home win followed by a 1-0 defeat in Rotterdam. Fortunately, 2-0 and 1-0 victories against Ukrainians Zorya Luhansk were enough to qualify United for the last 32 as Group A runners-up. Saint-Étienne of France were dispatched comfortably enough in the last 32, 4-0 on aggregate; three altogether stickier confrontations followed. Rostov of Russia were beaten 2-1 on aggregate in the last 16 courtesy of a narrow 1-0 win at Old Trafford. It was even closer in the quarter-finals, traditional European over-achievers Anderlecht of Belgium only beaten in extra time at Old Trafford in the second leg, 3-2 on aggregate. The semi-final against Spanish club Celta Vigo ran a similar course – this time a 1-0 away win being followed by a nerve-jangling 1-1 draw at Old Trafford.

Ajax – some might say as a result of qualifying virtually on an annual basis from a less demanding league than the Premiership – started the 2016–17 campaign in the Champions League, losing 5-2 on aggregate to United's eventual Europa League opponents Rostov in their group. Moving into the last 32 draw of the Europa League, Ajax topped a fairly tough Group G comprising Celta Vigo, Standard Liege of Belgium, and Panathinaikos of Greece. Each of their six games were understandably tight, home wins against Standard (1-0), Celta (3-2) and Panathinaikos (2-0), set against a 1-1 draw in Belgium, a 2-2 draw in Spain, and a healthy 2-1 victory in Greece.

The closely contested nature of their draw in the competition continued. In the last 32, Legia Warsaw of Poland were beaten only by a solitary goal in the home tie. The Danes of Copenhagen were beaten 3-2 on aggregate, a 2-1 defeat away followed by a 2-0 home win in the last 16; a 2-0 home win in the quarter-finals against the Germans of Schalke, followed by a 2-0 loss in Germany, ending in a dramatic extra-time winning goal for a 4-3 aggregate victory. A semi-final home win by four goals to one against French club Lyon seemed to set Ajax up for the final, but they suffered a few nerves in France, losing 3-1, but squeaking through to the final 5-4 on aggregate.

Mourinho opted to select Sergio Romero, United's Argentinian stand-by goalkeeper, rather than first-choice David De Gea, as Romero had kept goal in all cup competitions that season. Peculiar really, as Romero had only played seven league games in a five-year career at Old Trafford. Romero – capped 96 times by Argentina – kept clean sheets in the 2016–17 Europa League competition against

Zorya Luhansk, Feyenoord, Saint-Étienne, and Ajax in this final. Why would an established international goalkeeper at a club so long be happy to play second fiddle (to de Gea)? On a humorous level, the six feet four inches Romero is known in Argentina as *'Chiquito'* ('the little one') as he is shorter than his brothers – his professional basketball-playing brother Diego is six feet nine inches!

The captain for the night, Antonio Valencia, the Ecuadorian international, gave United the best years of his footballing life. A great servant to the club for ten seasons, 2009–2019, Valencia's engine at times seemed inexhaustible. His energy, his capacity to get up and down the pitch, bailed United out many a time for a decade, often in defending apparently lost causes, at other times playing almost as an auxiliary winger, providing crucial assists for goals. This latter ability to provide an extra attacking outlet stemmed from playing as a right winger prior to his glory days at Old Trafford.

Curiously, Valencia played only twice in La Liga in three seasons with Villareal, being farmed out on loan to Segunda B (2nd Division) side Recreativo de Huelva. Did Villareal seriously miss a trick? Valencia is one of the most obviously industrious players of the Premier League in my recall. Certainly the Ecuadorian impressed during his first spell as a Premiership player with Wigan Athletic 2008–09, sufficiently so for Real Madrid to court him. Instead Valencia made the move that signalled a spell of sustained success. In short, he found a club that enabled him to fulfil all his promise, a club in which he fitted into the style of play unerringly. Valencia would go on to win two Premier League titles, an FA Cup, two League Cups and this Europa League Cup. Valencia played in the 2011 Champions League defeat to Barcelona. The following season, 2011–12, he won the Matt Busby Player of the Year Award (the Fan's Player of the Year), and the clubs' Player's Player of the Year Award. His teammates were in no doubt of his massive team contribution.

The left-back for United, the Italian Matteo Darmian has since been deemed surplus to the club's requirements. Darmian came through AC Milan's youth system, spent one season at Parma, four with Torino, accumulating 151 starts in all competitions, and was selected in the Serie A Team of the Year for the season 2013–14. Darmian signed for United in 2015 and initially lived up to his early promise. He would play four seasons at Old Trafford, switching between the full-back positions, also appearing occasionally at centre-back. In 2019 Darmian returned to Italy, signing for Parma. In 2020 he joined Inter Milan on a one-season loan. The big clubs in Italy obviously see something in the versatile defender. Darmian had played 36 times for Italy at the end of 2020.

Chris Smalling, one of the centre-backs on this evening, has since taken the Italian route himself, his latest club being Roma. Greenwich-born Smalling started out in semi-professional football with Maidstone United, attracting interest from 'local' professional clubs in the south-east of England: Fulham, Charlton Athletic, Reading and Gillingham. When he turned professional it was to the north Smalling turned at first, but he pined for the south after signing for Middlesbrough and his contract on Teeside was annulled. In June 2008 his professional dreams were realised when he signed for Fulham. At Craven Cottage, Smalling forged a reputation as a stylish, elegant centre-back. In 2010 he signed for Manchester United. Over ten seasons Smalling played over 220 Premiership games for United. At first Smalling, Phil Jones and Jonny Evans were merely backup to one of the Premiership's finest centre-back pairings, Rio Ferdinand and Nemanja Vidic.

In 2015 Smalling gained entry in the Guinness Book of Records when scoring two goals as a first half substitute against Burnley, including the fastest goal as a substitute from the kick-off. Smalling captained United occasionally; he was voted United's Players' Player of the Year for the 2015–16 season. Out of form as the decade wore on, Smalling went on loan to Roma in 2019–20, a permanent contract following in October 2020. Smalling has played 31 times for England, but recently lost out to ball-playing centre-halves Harry Maguire, John Stones and Eric Dier. Smalling, inspired by his wife, has lately turned vegan, feeling the move has aided his health and recovery time from the intensity of high-level football matches.

The other centre-back, Daley Blind, is a product of the world-famous Ajax youth system. The system first came to wider notice with the outstanding Ajax team of the early 1970s, its graduates including Johan Cruyff, Johan Neeskens, and Ruud Krol, three players who would have been chosen in any World X1 at that time. I am an ardent fan of the 'Dutch way', methodology that put paramount importance upon technique. Most Dutch players are highly proficient technically, are comfortable receiving the ball with either foot, and are taught the importance of interchanging positions, covering for their teammates ('total football').

Daley's father Danny was an Ajax player for 13 seasons, receiving 42 caps for Holland. Eventually Daley would surpass his father's international tally, his international caps totalling 92 by July 2022. Blind junior played 102 league games for Ajax 2008–14, helping the club win the Dutch Eredivisie title twice, 2010–11 and 2011–12. Not until the 2012–13 season did he truly establish himself as the team's first-choice left-back however. Firmly established as a regular, Blind was voted Ajax Player of the Year in 2012–13. In 2013–14 he took one step further being named Dutch Footballer of the Year.

Signing for Manchester United in 2014, Blind went on to play 90 Premiership games, but, like Smalling, he didn't convince all his managers – or critics – all of the time, despite clearly being technically adept. Initially used as a centre-back at Old Trafford, Blind lost favour to Phil Jones and the Argentinian Marcus Rojo, perhaps because they were viewed as more natural defenders. Unbowed, Blind won selection in the United team as a left-back. Returning to Ajax in 2018, Blind scored a hat-trick in a home match against De Graafschap as a defender – I've never forgotten playing with a teammate who scored a hat-trick from left-back in a local game! In December 2019 Blind was diagnosed with myocarditis, the inflammation of the heart muscle, the diagnosis leading to the fitting of an implantable cardioverter defibrillator. Did this undetected problem hinder him, one wonders?

The most gifted, yet most frustrating of United's midfield players in this final was undoubtedly the mercurial, enigmatic Frenchman Paul Pogba. There are two sides to the charismatic World Cup-winning Pogba. The rangy, athletic, technically gifted Pogba can turn a game, win a game from nothing. His critics would say that at times he doesn't turn up. It's more likely that, like our own Glenn Hoddle in his pomp (he always played better for England in my eyes when he had the ball-winning Peter Reid of Everton supplying him), Pogba needs to play as the offensive midfielder with a top-class defensive midfielder as his ally. For France, Pogba has the cream of defensive midfield players, N'Golo Kanté, to do the dirty work for him.

Pogba has a strong association with United, having joined the club initially in 2009 from French Ligue 1 club Le Havre. In 2011 Pogba starred as United won the FA Youth Cup, defeating Sheffield United.

In July 2012, Pogba, just 17 years old, and hankering for the first team football he felt Alex Ferguson would not grant him, signed for Italian giants Juventus. In Turin, Pogba came of age. In 2013 he was named Golden Boy, an unfortunate title coined by the journalist who awarded the accolade, one might say, for the Best Young Player in Europe. In 2015 Pogba was named on the 2015 UEFA Team of the Year, as well as the FIFA FIFPRO World X1. In four seasons in Turin, Pogba assisted Juventus in the winning of four consecutive Serie A titles and two Coppa Italias, also helping Juve to the 2015 Champions League Final, their first in 12 years that ended in defeat to a Barcelona team still at the height of their powers.

With this track record, surely Pogba's return to Manchester United in 2016 would be an unqualified success, wouldn't it? Well no, it's been a rocky road for Pogba after a bright enough start. He climbed the very pinnacle of the game in 2018, starring and scoring in France's 4-2 defeat of Croatia in the World Cup Final. In this 2017 UEFA Cup Final he opened the scoring against Ajax. In the modern game of football obsessed by organisation, disciplined marking, fitness and formations, Pogba's maverick style leaves him open to criticism, especially for his laid-back nature and his lack of defensive covering within the team structure.

His form continued to fluctuate wildly. In the 2017–18 season he produced an inspiring display against Manchester City, scoring twice in a 3-2 win. In the 2018 FA Cup Final, United lost 1-0 to Chelsea, Pogba spurning a chance to send the game into extra time. Appointed captain in the absence of Valencia at the start of the 2018–19 season, and designated penalty-taker for the team, Pogba began the new term well. Mourinho, who had defended him stoutly, turned against Pogba as his form floundered once again. With Mourinho removed from the manager's seat, Pogba regained form under caretaker manager Ole Gunnar Solskjaer. He reached a personal best of 16 goals in all competitions during the 2018–19 season, but as United's form slipped in the last 12 games (securing only two wins) Pogba was once again criticised for his inconsistency. Despite his erratic displays, he was named in the PFA Team of the Year. An ankle injury picked up against Southampton in August 2019 hampered him again.

Real Madrid and Juventus continued to be linked with Pogba, but in March 2021 he remained a United player. Finally Juventus took the risk of him returning to their ranks in the summer of 2022. What does the future hold for this enigma? Clearly his peers rate him highly. It just seems perverse to be talking about a World Cup winner as a fitful, inconsistent performer (one could say the same of Mesut Ozil). Maybe Paul Pogba would have fitted more neatly into the 1960s/

early 1970s game I grew up adoring where most teams seemed to have players with real flair. To date (October 2022) Pogba has played 91 times for France, scoring 11 goals.

Talent alone is never enough of course. Man of the Match in this 2017 Europa League Final was Pogba's midfield teammate Ander Herrera. Herrera cannot compete with Pogba's tricks and intricacies, but he never left anything of himself on the football field. Herrera played 132 Premiership games for United 2014–19, winning this Europa League, and an FA Cup and League Cup during his stay with the club. Herrera, essentially a hard-working, dynamic midfield player, happily fitted into United's team positionally, as required. He lacked Pogba's flair, but always gave 100% plus. Between 2009–14 Herrera performed consistently for Real Zaragoza and Athletic Bilbao in Spain. At Bilbao he reached – and lost – Copa del Rey and Europa League Finals. The signing of Nemanja Matic from Chelsea in 2017 limited Herrera's game-time with United, but top French club Paris Saint-Germain saw enough in his combative displays to sign him in July 2019.

As a player I prefer the style of another Spaniard alongside him this evening, Juan Mata. Mata I have spoken of before, his relationship with José Mourinho at Chelsea and Manchester United somewhat chequered. Mata's ability to drift in the open spaces between midfield and attack, his delightful touch, ingenuity and inventiveness, make him my kind of player.

The Manchester United midfield was completed by the awkward, physically imposing, aerial threat of the Belgian international Marouane Fellaini. The six feet four inches, perm-haired Fellaini is one of those players no footballer likes to compete against. He appears ungainly, but he's the kind of player who's always in your face. Born to Moroccan parents near Brussels, Fellaini joined Anderlecht at the age of 18. As a youngster he was also a fine track athlete, his preferred distance the 10,000 metres. After proving himself with Standard Liege in Belgium 2006–2008 (64 league games, nine goals), Fellaini initially rebuffed Manchester United, opting to sign for Everton in England instead. Fellaini became something of a talisman at Goodison Park, noted for his headed goals, and his cussed perseverance in midfield/attack. At the end of his first season with Everton 2008–09 he was voted the club's Young Player of the Year. In December 2012 *The Guardian* newspaper saw fit to name him No. 60 in their 'The 100 Best Footballers in the World' poll.

When David Moyes moved from Everton to take the managerial hot seat from the retiring Alex Ferguson (a tough task to follow the iconic Ferguson), Fellaini followed him in September 2014. For opposing reasons to the mercurial Pogba, Fellaini struggled initially to impress at Old Trafford. The Belgian's raw physicality, his liking of an aerial duel in the opponent's penalty area, were at odds with United's historical status as a fast-raiding, quick-passing, counter-attacking, ball-playing team.

When Moyes departed to be replaced by Dutchman Luis van Gaal, Fellaini found himself deployed as a striker on occasions due to his aerial presence. With van Gaal gone, Fellaini's rugged style suited incoming manager José Mourinho. The Portuguese managerial icon admired the Belgians' fighting qualities, even though Herrera and Pogba often prevented Fellaini's presence in the United midfield. When Solskjaer took over in the 2018–19 season he preferred a more refined approach. In January 2019 Fellaini ended his time with United, moving to Chinese club Shandong Luneng. Fellaini has had the misfortune of being among a handful of footballers to test positive for the Covid-19 coronavirus. Fellaini has played 87 times for Belgium, scoring 18 goals, retiring from international football in 2019, at a time, ironically, when Belgium have become the No. 1 ranked team in world football, a team replete with fine technical players.

Henrikh Mkhitaryan, born in the Armenian capital of Yerevan, has captained his country, earning 88 caps, and scored 30 goals. In the early 1990s the Mkhitaryan family moved to France where Henrikh spent his childhood in Valence in the Auvergne-Rhone-Alps region. He played for the now defunct Valence team, helping them win promotion from the third division to the second division. The family returned to Yerevan where he made his professional debut for Pyunik, aged 17. He won four Armenian Premier League titles with Pyunik, then joined Metalurk Donetsk in 2009; Shakhtar Donetsk in 2010. At Metalurk he became the youngest captain in the club's history, aged 21. With Metalurk he scored 16 goals in 45 matches. At Shakhtar, Mkhitaryan scored 44 goals in 106 appearances, being named Best Player in the club's official website poll in 2011–12. In the 2012–13 season, Mkhitaryan set a Ukrainian league goal-scoring record of 25 and was named the Ukrainian League Player of the Year. He won three domestic doubles of league and cup with Shakhtar, and then joined Borussia Dortmund in Germany for £27.5 million, becoming the most expensive Armenian player of all time.

In his first season at Dortmund, Mkhitaryan scored for the German side as they defeated Arsenal 2-1 at the Emirates in the Champions League. Dortmund ended the season as runners-up in both league and cup, Mkhitaryan's personal haul totalling nine goals and ten assists. He won the DFL Supercup (winners of the Bundesliga and the DFB Pokal – German Cup) in 2014; in season 2014–15 he provided the most assists in the Bundesliga – 15 – the second highest in Europe that season. Mkhitaryan was also voted the Bundesliga's Player's Player of the Season. Upon leaving Dortmund he had amassed 41 goals from 140 Bundesliga appearances.

Moving to Manchester United for £30 million – the first Armenian to play in the Premier League – he won the FA Community Shield, started life with United with a flourish, supplying five assists in his first three matches, and scored the conclusive second goal in this Europa League win with a smart finish, but lost form. He signed for Arsenal in 2018 after his dip at Old Trafford, moving to London in the swap deal that saw Alexis Sanchez move north (if it was any consolation, Sanchez's form at United was arguably worse than the Armenian's). His form continued to waver at the Emirates despite his obvious talent (he supplied three assists in his first match alone, a 5-1 drubbing of Everton), and like Smalling at United he was loaned out to Roma in Italy in 2019–2020, a move made permanent in 2020–21. He scored nine goals in 59 appearances for Arsenal. Armenian Footballer of the Year ten times, the only years Mkhitaryan missed out were 2010 and 2018 since 2009. His father was a striker for FC Aravat Yerevan during the 1980s, tragically dying from a brain tumour when Mkhitaryan was just seven years old. His mother is head of the National Teams Department in the Armenian Football Federation; his sister works at UEFA's headquarters.

Mkhitaryan was centre of a controversial issue ahead of this 2019 Europa League as Azerbaijan and Armenia did not have international relations, Armenians being forbidden entry into Azerbaijan. At Roma, Mkhitaryan scored on his debut as Sassuolo from the Emilia-Romagna region were beaten 4-2. On 5 November 2020 Mkhitaryan scored the fastest ever goal (57 seconds) in the Europa League as Roma defeated Romanian club CFR Cluj 5-0. Three days later he scored a hat-trick as Roma beat Genoa 3-1 in Serie A. A precise passer, a fine dribbler with close ball control, he also works industriously on the pitch, and possesses an explosive shot. Mkhitaryan is a polyglot – he speaks eight languages. This speaks volumes for his willingness to learn. By March 2021 he had scored 20 goals in 54 games for Roma – he may have found his footballing 'home'.

Marcus Rashford, aged 23, literally came of age in 2020. His efforts to ensure child hunger and homelessness were addressed during the Covid-19 pandemic post-March 2020 have led to wide acclaim – but he appeared to have grown up on the football pitch too, looking a more complete team player, until puzzlingly losing form. At the club from the age of seven, Rashford scored twice on his debut for the first team against the Danes of Midtjylland in the Europa League in February 2016. He became the youngest United goalscorer in Europe, a record previously held by the genius George Best. Mason Greenwood has since scored at an even younger age than Rashford in the 2019–20 season. Rashford promptly scored another two goals three days after his dream debut against Arsenal in the Premier League. He scored in his first Manchester derby – the youngest to do so again, dislodging previous incumbent of this record, Wayne Rooney. He also scored on his EFL League Cup and Champions League debuts, and on his England national team debut. Rashford was the youngest player at the Euro 2016 tournament. He's thus far scored 59 goals in 171 Premiership appearances for United, and 12 in 46 for England (July 2022).

Raised in Wythenshawe, Manchester by a single mother from a working-class background, with a grandmother from St Kitts, West Indies, Rashford knows about child hardship. His mother often skipped meals so that the five Rashford siblings always had a meal. His mother took on multiple jobs – ditto my wife and I as we raised four children. Rashford attended Ashton-on-Mersey school – United have sent their academy players there since 1998 as it is located near their Carrington training ground. He played for Fletcher Moss Rangers Boys Club – as a goalkeeper – from the age of five. He trained for a week with Manchester City, while also attracting interest from Liverpool and Everton, at seven years old before joining United's academy. Chosen for Manchester United's Schoolboys Scholars scheme, aged 11, a year ahead of most other candidates, Rashford's potential was evident early on. He played cage football with Paul Pogba, Jesse Lingard and Ravel Morrison to fast-track this potential. He first trained with the first team aged 16 while David Moyes managed United. The signing of Zlatan Ibrahimovic for the 2016–17 season limited Rashford's appearances for a while. There were two sides to this – Rashford could learn from the experienced top-class Ibrahimovic, but his own growth may have been held back. Rashford himself credits the Swedish international star with helping his progress as a young player.

On 23 October 2017 Rashford was voted third in the 2017 Golden Boy Best Young Player award behind French stars Kylian Mbappé and Ousmane Dembélé. Mbappé has since gone on to be the best young player in the world. Mourinho was inclined to play Rashford on the wing, a decision criticised in some quarters. I would rather see Rashford playing as a second striker – although like Thierry Henry there's something to be said for drifting into the penalty area from wide positions and driving towards goal, rather than being caught up in penalty-area traffic. This is Rashford's own preferred position, apparently. Under Ole Gunnar Solskjaer, Rashford has been given more opportunities, now establishing himself as a regular starter in the United team. Solskjaer clearly believed in him, feeling he could become one of the world's best strikers. In the 2019–20 season Rashford scored 16 goals in 20 games, the best scoring run of his career to date. At the season's end Rashford was voted third in the FWA Footballer of the Year poll, receiving in addition the PFA Merit award for his work in connection with the Covid-19 pandemic persuading the government to retain free school meals for children. In October 2020 Marcus Rashford was awarded an MBE.

In a Champions League match in 2020 Rashford scored a hat-trick from the substitutes' bench against RB Leipzig in a 5-1 victory. He was the second United player in the club's history to score three goals from the bench, following Solskjaer, in a Premiership game in 1999. On 26 December 2020 Rashford became the third youngest United player to score 50 Premier League goals. In February 2021 he became the fourth youngest United player to achieve the milestone of 250 appearances.

In his only appearance for the England U-21s, Rashford scored a hat-trick against Norway. In the 2018 Euros Rashford became the youngest ever England player, aged 18, to play in a European Championship, breaking Wayne Rooney's record from Euro 2000 by four days. Rashford equalled a record set by the late, great Jack Charlton (set in 1966) when playing his 16th England game in a calendar year in 2019. Pacy, direct, Rashford appears happy at the moment to rotate between wide and central attacking positions.

United's bench on this evening oozed experience: David de Gea as goalkeeping cover; Michael Carrick (524 appearances for the club), current first-team coach at United and an excellent playmaker in his 12-year playing career at Old Trafford; one of Rashford's mentors, Wayne Rooney, past his best here, but holder of England's national scoring record with 53 goals in 120 appearances, and 183 career goals from 393 appearances with United, cruelly prevented from making an even bigger impact internationally at major tournaments during his peak years 2004–2010 by injury; and younger attacking talents Jesse Lingard and Anthony Martial. The latter two came on as substitutes in this final.

Solskjaer did a fine job as United manager, for all the constant barbs from the media due to his perceived lack of top-flight managerial experience. He may not have possessed Mourinho or van Gaal's back catalogue of success, but United stood by the Norwegian, giving him the chance to rebuild United in the hope of reclaiming former glories – until bringing in the German coach Ralf Rangnick as a temporary replacement in 2022. Coaches/managers need time to establish settled teams playing in their desired manner – this can't be achieved in half a season. Modern football, sadly, rarely allows managers the luxury of several seasons in which to create stability. Mourinho it was who was at the helm in Solna, Stockholm for this 2019 Europa League Final. His experience seemed critical as it turned out, the young Ajax team unable to usurp the old maestro's tactical nous on the night.

The young Ajax team in opposition contained several players who have since transferred to the Premier League: centre-back Davinson Sanchez, a Colombian international who played against England in the epic last 16, 2018 World Cup match. Hakim Ziyech, now plying his subtle skills in Chelsea's midfield (though likely to leave as the football 'merry-go-round' continued its vagaries at the end of the 2021–22 season), and Bertrand Traoré, who is playing fitfully well for Aston Villa. Sanchez was a dominant figure in that 2018 World Cup game, ultra-competitive, fired-up in vain in his quest to ensure his country progressed to the quarter-finals. He has played 49 times for Colombia (July 2022), and over 120 times in the Premier League for Tottenham Hotspur since moving from Ajax in the 2017–18 season. He has yet to find a consistently high level in the Premiership, although he became a regular starting choice at Tottenham.

Bertrand Traoré scored four goals in this 2016–17 Europa League campaign, including two against the club he would move to in June 2019, Olympique Lyonnais of France. Traoré joined Chelsea as far back as August 2010 from Auxerre in France, and was on loan from Stamford Bridge while playing for Ajax in this final. He scored 13 goals in this 2016–17 Eredivisie season, a respectable return. He has thus far netted seven times in the Premier League for Aston Villa (July 2022) but remains a player still seeking to fulfil his early promise. Traoré has represented Burkina Faso internationally since 2011.

Hakim Ziyech looked the best prospect of these three Ajax players from 2017 currently playing in the Premier League. Deft of technique, keen-eyed, a player of penetrating passes into forward areas, a wicked crosser of the ball, he also knows where the goal is himself. Ziyech scored 30 goals in 68 appearances for Twente Enschede 2014–16, 17 in his last season at Twente in addition to ten assists. At Ajax (2016–18) Ziyech scored 38 goals in 112 appearances. In the 2018–19 season Ziyech performed impressively in the Champions League as Ajax reached the semi-finals only to be denied a tilt at Liverpool in the final by an inspired Tottenham Hotspur. Ziyech scored against Sturm Graz of Austria, Real Madrid and Tottenham during the 2018–19 Champions League campaign. He joined Chelsea in the 2020 season for £40 million. It was clear that Ziyech has the touch and talent to succeed at Stamford Bridge. Did he have the consistency to match? He has so far netted six times in 46 Premier League games (March 2021), having scored 49 goals in 165 Dutch Eredivisie games for Ajax. Having opted to play for the country of his birth, Morocco, over the land of his heritage, Holland, Ziyech scored 17 times in 40 starts for Morocco (July 2022).

The stand-out player in this Ajax team was the centre-back Matthias de Ligt. Making his senior debut, aged 17, for Ajax in 2016, de Ligt scored direct from a corner-kick after 25 minutes, becoming Ajax's second youngest ever goalscorer after Clarence Seedorf. In December 2018 de Ligt became the first defender to win Europe's Golden Boy (Best Young European Player). His performances in this 2017–18 season won him a transfer to Juventus in Italy on a five-year contract. Ajax received £75 million for the precociously talented youngster. He promptly won the Kopa Trophy for best performing player aged under 21, organised by France Football. He also became the youngest player to represent Holland in 2017 since 1931. When Davinson Sanchez was sold to Tottenham, de Ligt became a regular starter at Ajax, becoming club captain in 2018. In April 2019 de Ligt scored the winner as Ajax knocked Juventus out of the 2018–19 Champions League quarter-finals. Astonishingly, when de Ligt made his international debut away to Bulgaria in March 2017, he'd only played twice for the senior Ajax team. It was de Ligt's header that defeated England in the inaugural Nations League semi-finals in 2019. Holland lost the final to Portugal 1-0. As with many classic Dutch players before him, de Ligt has played in other areas of the pitch in youth football, in his case as an attacking midfielder. Composed beyond his years, blessed with keen anticipation, excellent ball control, de Ligt is a massive threat from set-pieces. A prominent future seems assured for the precocious de Ligt who has already played 38 times for Holland, aged 22 (July 2022).

Other young substitutes for Ajax on this evening included Frenkie de Jong, Donny van de Beek, and Justin Kluivert, son of Patrick. Frenkie de Jong promised as big a career as de Ligt, transferring to Barcelona in 2019 on the back of highly impressive defensive midfield performances at Ajax. In the 2018–19 season Ajax won the double of Eredivisie and KNVB Cup, reached the Champions League semi-finals, and in addition de Jong was named Eredivisie Player of the Season. When de Jong was selected for the FIFA FIFPRO World X1 in 2019 he was one of three Dutch players chosen, the first time this occurred in five years. Barcelona have played de Jong primarily as a central midfielder. Unsurprisingly, close control is a key component with this Dutch midfield player, a trait also marking him out as the perfect Barcelona player. Like de Ligt, de Jong has played many times for Holland (44, July 2022) from a young age.

What a frustrating player Donny van de Beek has proven to be with Manchester United, for whom he transferred to from Ajax. For Ajax de Beek scored 28 times in 118 appearances. In 27 starts for United he scored just twice, before being loaned out Everton in 2022. Like de Jong, his ball control is tight, he rarely looks like losing the ball, but I yearn for him to play a more incisive pass rather than opting for safety-first at all times. He reminds me of the cruel jibe aimed at Chelsea's former England international Ray Wilkins who earned the nickname 'The Crab' for his sideways passing. Wilkins was better than that, acting as a supreme playmaker for Chelsea. It remains to be seen whether de Beek can reach those heights. The young Dutchman had played 19 times for Holland by July 2022, scoring one more goal for his country than he managed for United.

THE FINAL

United imposed themselves from the start, Juan Mata prominent with his probing play. Mata's cross evaded all his teammates, the lunging Fellaini unable to convert at the far post. Traoré fired a shot straight at Sergio Romero at the other end, but it was a rare foray in those early stages of the game. United took a first-half lead when Mata teed up Pogba whose shot was deflected past keeper Onana. In the second half United put the game beyond the reach of Ajax with a lovely goal from Mkhitarayn. Smalling headed the ball goalwards from a right-wing corner-kick and the Armenian smartly diverted the ball away from Onana with his back to the goal. The forceful Fellaini almost added another with a header. Ajax offered only a tame shot after a smart turn from substitute de Beek on the right side of United's penalty area. Smalling, Fellaini, Pogba and Mata's power and know-how were too much for the largely inexperienced Ajax team. Mata looked very sharp – a reminder to Mourinho of just what a good player he could be. Ajax were largely restricted by a thoroughly professional United team versed in the Mourinho image to shots from long-range.

2018–19 EUROPA LEAGUE FINAL
Chelsea 4 v 1 Arsenal

When I was a young teenager it seemed an extraordinary feat to me for Chelsea to win a European Trophy (the Cup Winners Cup, 1971). Come 2019, Chelsea had been bred to expect to win a European trophy on the back of a raft of foreign-imported players, top-class international managers, and Roman Abramovich's money. The most pertinent additional feature of this game was the introduction for the first time in the Europa League of the sometimes controversial VAR (video assistant referee) system.

This was Chelsea's sixth European final – it's no surprise four of them have come since the arrival of Mr Abramovich. They have appeared twice in each of the three competitions I am writing about. It was also Arsenal's sixth appearance in a European final, their record being a 3-2-1 in respect of the Cup Winners Cup, Europa League and the Champions League. Although they won the 1970 Inter Cities Fairs Cup Final against Anderlecht of Belgium 4-3 on aggregate (the forerunner of the UEFA Cup/Europa League), their only win came in the 1993–94 Cup Winners Cup Final versus Parma, 1-0. A win here for then-Arsenal manager Unai Emery would have seen him surpass Italian legend Giovanni Trapattoni as the most successful UEFA Cup/Europa League manager, but his team never looked like bringing the trophy home from Baku, Azerbaijan. A good season this for English football with Liverpool and Tottenham Hotspur contesting the Champions League Final.

Route to the Final
The group stages of this season's competition were arguably the weakest that English teams had faced in the Europa League. Chelsea topped Group L with 16 points, undefeated across six games against BATE Borisov of Belarus, Vidi of Hungary and PAOK Thessaloniki, Macedonia. Similarly, Arsenal topped Group E with 16 points, only Sporting CP of Portugal offering any serious resistance, while Vorsha Poltava of the Ukraine and Qarabag of Azerbaijan were summarily dismissed.

Both London teams scored hatfuls of goals throughout the knockout stages.

Chelsea beat Malmö of Sweden 5-1 on aggregate in the last 32; Dynamo Kiev were surprisingly beaten 8-0 in the last 16; and Slavia Prague of the Czech Republic could not halt Chelsea's advance in the last eight, the Blues winning out 5-3 on aggregate; Eintracht Frankfurt proved typically obstinate German opponents in the semi-finals, Chelsea winning 4-3 on penalties after extra time following two 1-1 draws.

Arsenal defeated Chelsea's Belarussian group opponents BATE Borisov 3-1 in the last 32; a tough encounter with Rennes of France saw the North London side overturn a 3-1 deficit from the away leg with a fine 3-0 win at the Emirates in the last 16; Napoli of Italy were beaten 3-0 on aggregate in the last eight before Valencia of Spain were hit for seven goals (three conceded) over the two-legged semi-final.

The choice of Baku as the final venue caused consternation among the fans of the two London clubs, the trip involving a near 5,000-mile return trip, and almost ten and a half hours flight time there and back. Baku had been chosen over Seville and Istanbul as the final venue – UEFA looking for votes come election time perhaps? The ongoing conflict between Azerbaijan and Armenia also raised questions as to the wisdom of this choice, Arsenal's Henrikh Mkhitaryan opting not to travel.

Chelsea's team for this final revealed only two players who were present in the 2013 Europa League Final against Benfica: captain for the night César Azpilicueta and David Luiz, although Luiz played at centre-back here, not in midfield as he had done in 2013. Eden Hazard would have been the third player to reappear had he not been injured in 2013.

In goal, Kepa Arrizabalaga hails from the Basque region of Spain (Ondarroa) and was transferred for a world-record fee for a goalkeeper of £80 million from Athletic Bilbao in 2018. Sadly for 'Kepa', as he is colloquially known, his performances have been less than consistent at Chelsea. A fine start (six clean sheets in 12 matches) was followed by error-strewn games that cost him his place to the Senegalese international Edouard Mendy in 2021. Arrizabalaga has been selected by Spain internationally despite his early promise ebbing.

Playing inside Azpilicueta, the young Danish centre-back Andreas Christensen attracted attention from Arsenal, Manchester City, Bayern Munich and Chelsea from a very early age. Son of Brondby IF goalkeeper Sten Christensen, Andreas chose Chelsea because he believed their style of play suited him, after playing for eight years with the Brondby IF Youth team. He joined Chelsea Youth for the 2012–13 season, swiftly being elevated to the senior squad, but a couple of full-back starts were all he mustered in the beginning of his senior career.

Loaned out to Borussia Möenchengladbach 2015–17, the Dane played 62 times in the Bundesliga. Ironically, Christensen was named Player of the Season at Möenchengladbach in 2015–16, ahead of his adversary in this final, the Swiss player, Granit Xhaka who'd captained Möenchengladbach at that time. The German side wanted to retain Christensen, but he returned to Chelsea in 2017–18 As of July 2022, Christensen had played 56 times for Denmark.

David Luiz partnered Christensen at centre-back in this final before moving across London to Arsenal in 2019. At left-back on this evening was Brazilian-born Italian international Emerson Palmieri. Establishing himself in senior football with Italian side Roma 2015–18, an anterior cruciate ligament injury in 2017 may have disrupted his career, given that since joining Chelsea in 2018 he was used intermittently.

Chelsea possessed two outstanding wide midfielders in this final: French international N'Golo Kanté on the right; Spanish international Pedro on the left. At five feet six inches Kanté is one those players who looks and seems innocuous, but his presence as a ball-winner in midfield have seen Leicester City unexpectedly win the Premier League in 2016, France win the World Cup in 2018, and Chelsea win the Premier League, The Europa League, and the FA Cup with Kanté key to these successes.

Born to Malian parents, Kanté played junior football in the French capital city of Paris for a decade. Professionally he played Ligue 2 and 3 football with Boulogne and Caen in France before joining Leicester City for that fateful 2015–16 season. The reason that Leicester bought him is that while at Caen no other player in Europe recovered possession after losing the ball more than Kanté. This became an obvious trait as Leicester startled the Premier League 'big shots' in 2015–16 with a fantastic team ethic, aided and abetted by Kanté's remarkable ball recovery rate and a 'pest' of a goalscorer in former non-league speedster Jamie Vardy. Steve Walsh, Leicester's chief scout had previously scouted Vardy and Riyad Mahrez for Leicester – and while with Chelsea he alerted the club to the talents of Gianfranco Zola and Didier Drogba. Walsh clearly possesses a keen eye for exceptional talents in key positions. Kanté was one of four players from Leicester chosen for the PFA Team of the Year in 2015–16. Incredibly Kanté made 175 tackles and 157 interceptions during the 2015–16 season, topping these statistics in the Premier League by some distance. When he left Leicester City for Chelsea, Leicester declined in 2016–17, unable to replace his style of player until turning to Wilfrid Ndidi, a Nigerian international six inches taller than the diminutive Kanté.

In his first season with Chelsea, Kanté became the first player since Eric Cantona (Leeds United/Manchester United) to win back-to-back Premier League titles with different clubs. *L'Equipe*, the famous French newspaper devoted to sport, named Kanté the sixth best player in the world in 2016. He was also named the PFA Player's Player of the Year, the FWA Footballer (Football Writers) of the Year and the Premier League Player of the Season in 2016–17. He'd begun life with Chelsea with a bang. In May 2018 Kanté was voted Man of the Match by the BBC as Chelsea beat Manchester United 1-0 in the FA Cup Final.

Things were all about to turn sour for Kanté in the Premier League – but not before he'd helped France win the World Cup for a second time, his holding play key in releasing Paul Pogba for attacking forays upfield. First an ankle injury prevented Kanté playing for Chelsea, secondly the Covid-19 pandemic decimated lives across Europe, Kanté choosing to train independently of his teammates at their Cobham training ground, and initially losing his place in the Chelsea team as a result.

Internationally Kanté has played 53 times for France, having declined the opportunity to play for Mali (July 2022). Kanté has proved himself the best player of his type in Europe, or even in world football. He scurries relentlessly around the pitch, winning the ball an inconceivable amount of times for his teammates. Purportedly he doesn't particularly enjoy the role, but believes in its necessity to the team. This selflessness may be his undoing, as injury seems to have held him back recently. Alex Ferguson called Kanté the best player in the world in 2016; Claudio Ranieri thought Kanté ran on batteries. Let's hope N'Golo Kanté's batteries haven't run out.

Pedro, the Spanish left-sided forward wide midfield player, hails from the capital of Tenerife in the Canary Islands, Santa Cruz, making him an islander like Portugal's Madeira-born superstar Cristiano Ronaldo. Pedro began professionally with Barcelona, playing for their C and B teams 2005–08. Breaking into the first team squad in 2008, Pedro became a part of the most successful Barcelona team of all time. Pedro only played 14 times 2008–09 as Barcelona won a treble of La Liga, Copa del Rey and the Champions League. The following season Pedro became the first player to score in six different competitions as he established himself under Pep Guardiola. By 2010–11 Pedro had become a first team regular, scoring the first goal as Barca gave Manchester United a football lesson in the 2011 Champions League Final. Coming on as a substitute in the 2015 Champions League Final, Pedro helped Barca defeat Juventus and become the first club in European football history to win their domestic league, domestic cup, and the premier European trophy twice following their 2009 feat.

Joining Chelsea for the 2015–16 season, Pedro scored on his debut away to West Bromwich Albion, providing an assist for a further goal as the Blues won 3-2. On 23 October 2016 Pedro scored the fastest goal of the season against Manchester United, Chelsea running out 4-0 winners. In 2018 on his 150th Chelsea appearance he scored Chelsea's 1,000th Premier League goal at Stamford Bridge versus south-west London rivals Fulham. Pedro also scored in this 2019 Europa League Final, becoming the fifth player to score in UEFA Cup/Europa League and Champions League finals after Allan Simonsen, Dmitri Alenichev, Hernán Crespo and our own Steven Gerrard.

In August 2020 Pedro signed a three-year deal with Roma in Italy. Pedro amassed 58 career goals in 204 senior appearances with Barcelona, 29 in 137 games for Chelsea, and has since performed creditably for first Roma, then Lazio in Italy. In 65 games for Spain he has scored a highly respectable 17 goals. A hugely talented player, the five feet seven inches Pedro is equally adept at linking play and scoring the occasional quality goal. As with his Spanish peers, Pedro is technically near perfect. Could we have learned something from the Dutch and Spanish pre-Gareth Southgate?

The Brazilian-born Italian international midfielder Jorginho adopted one of the two central midfield spots for this final. Jorginho is a curious player – some managers swear by him. Maurizio Sarri at Chelsea wouldn't have a bad word said about him, but Jorginho's slight physique and lack of pace sometimes betray his passing accuracy, vision and generally dependable penalty-taking. Sarri feels that having brought the player on during his time as Napoli manager in Italy that Jorginho (133 appearances 2014–18) was key as a playmaker who could dictate play. Jorginho approaches 130 games for Chelsea (July 2022). He opted to play for Italy, rather than Brazil, and has received 44 caps as I write. The jury is still out regarding his impact on the Chelsea team.

The player alongside Jorginho in the centre of midfield on this evening gave Chelsea considerably more energy. Mateo Kovacic, the Croatian international, operated as the team's attack-minded midfield player. A player admired by Europe's leading clubs, Kovacic began professionally with Dinamo Zagreb in Croatia, aged 16. He won two consecutive league titles in Zagreb, joining Inter Milan in 2013. Inter were forced to sell Kovacic to Real Madrid in August 2015 due to the financial fair play regulations introduced by UEFA to ostensibly prevent the biggest clubs capturing all the best players. It certainly worked well for Kovacic in Madrid – at least in the beginning under Rafael Benitez. Kovacic discovered – as did Gareth Bale – that it takes a lot to impress Zinedine Zidane when the France World Cup-winner took over as manager. Kovacic won the Champions League in Madrid in 2015–16, 2016–17 and 2017–18, although he only appeared in the team sporadically.

Kovacic joined Chelsea in August 2018 on a one-year loan from Real, his move becoming permanent in July 2019. In August 2020 Kovacic was named Chelsea Player of the Year for the 2019–20 season. Incoming manager Thomas Tuchel restored Kovacic to the team after a sticky patch at the start of the 2020–21 season, but the German has since preferred Mason Mount as his dynamic, energetic midfield player, having N'Golo Kanté, Kai Havertz et al to call on as well. Kovacic is still trying to fully establish himself. Again the jury is out on Kovacic as a long-term Chelsea player. His driving runs and passing ability may yet make him part of the Chelsea tapestry. Kovacic has been capped by Croatia 81 times (July 2022). He has his supporters in Trapattoni, Inter legend Javier Zanetti and ex-Croatian international and long-time AC Milan star Zvonimir Boban.

In attack on this evening, Chelsea paired ex-Arsenal centre-forward Olivier Giroud with the exciting Belgian striker Eden Hazard. Giroud's career began to flourish at Tours in France as he scored 24 goals in 44 Ligue 2 games, earning him a transfer to Montpellier in the French top flight in 2008. He then scored 33 goals in 73 matches for Montpellier – 21 in the 2011–12 season, helping the club to their first ever Ligue 1 title. Moving to Arsenal, Giroud scored 105 goals in 253 games in all competitions for the Gunners.

In his debut season at Arsenal, Giroud scored 17 goals and provided 11 assists in 47 appearances. In the 2013–14 season Giroud was instrumental in Arsenal winning the FA Cup. He scored twice against Everton in a 4-1 quarter-final victory; scored a penalty kick in the semi-final shoot-out against Wigan; and he provided the assist for Aaron Ramsey's cup-winning goal as Arsenal beat Hull City 3-2 in the final. Coming on as a substitute in the 2015 FA Cup Final, Giroud scored Arsenal's final goal in a 4-0 rout over Aston Villa. Two hat-tricks – one against Olympiakos in the Champions League, the other in the final match of the season against Aston Villa in the Premier League – helped Giroud to a total of 24 goals in all competitions in the 2015–16 season.

Despite being used only fitfully in the 2016–17 season, Giroud's 'scorpion-kick' volley against Crystal Palace won him the FIFA Puskás Award for the Goal of the Year. Giroud again came on as a substitute in the 2017 FA Cup Final against Chelsea; again he provided the assist for another Aaron Ramsey winning goal. On 31 January 2018 Giroud transferred to Chelsea. Giroud continued to be used 'as and when' the situation arose, rather than as a regular starter. This, despite scoring 11 goals in the 2018–19 Europa League campaign, the first Chelsea player to achieve the feat. Giroud it was who opened the scoring in this 2019 Europa League Final. The feeling persists that Giroud suits the European games better than the hurly-burly of an English Premier League contest. His 11 goals in this 2018–19 Europa League season broke Néstor Combin's record for a French player in a European competition, a record going back to the 1963–64 season, and Just Fontaine's (the record World Cup scorer in 1958 with 13) ten in the 1958–59 European Cup.

On 2 December 2020 Giroud became the oldest player to score a hat-trick in the Champions League (aged 34) against Sevilla, ending the game with all four goals in a 4-0 win. He also scored in six successive games in the Premier League for Chelsea (the oldest player to do so) in the 2020–21 season. His European form continued to hold up as he scored the only goal of the game against Atlético Madrid in the Champions League last 16 first leg in Madrid.

In 112 games for France Giroud has scored 48 goals (July 2022). His three goals at the 2016 Euros left him as joint second top-scorer in the competition. Giroud's physical presence – he stands six feet four inches – ensured his starting position in all seven games at the 2018 World Cup. He didn't score himself in the competition, but his aerial threat and fine link-up play enabled co-strikers Antoine Griezmann and Kylian Mbappé to score four goals each. He currently lies third in his country's highest goalscorer chart behind only the incomparable duo of Thierry Henry and Michel Platini, two players of the very highest calibre. An ideal target man with a powerful shot, surprisingly agile for such a big man, my feeling with Giroud has always been that if you play him he's likely to contribute or score – he's unfairly tagged at times a 'mere' target man.

Eden Hazard, Philippe Coutinho, Mo Salah, Kevin De Bruyne, David Silva – these players have been the guiding lights for their English clubs in the last decade of the Premier League. Hazard, curiously, like Coutinho, achieved his 'dream' move to a top Spanish club – Real Madrid in Hazard's case – but injuries have thus far prevented the Belgian from revealing his previous glittering form in Spain.

Hazard is rightly regarded as one of the best players of his generation, but remains in the tier below the global superstars Messi, Ronaldo and the 'emperor in waiting', Mbappé. Hazard's star shone brightly from a young age. The son of two former footballers, his brother Thorgan is also a Belgian international, while Eden now captains Belgium. Starting out professionally with Lille in France, aged 16, Hazard was the first non-French player to win Ligue 1 Young Player of the Year Award in 2008–09. In 2009 he won the award again; in 2010–11 Hazard won the senior Ligue 1 Player of the Year Award as Lille won the domestic double of league and cup. He scored 50 goals in 190 appearances in all competitions for Lille.

Hazard signed for Chelsea in June 2012, winning the Europa League in his first season at the Bridge, although injury prevented his appearance in the final against Benfica. Hazard's first season ended with 13 goals in all competitions – a scant return for such a fabulously gifted player, although he provided many assists. Hazard scored his first Premier League hat-trick against Manchester United in February 2014. He won the PFA Young Player of the Year Award at the end of the 2013–14 season, finishing second to Luis Suarez in the PFA Player's Player of the Year poll. He was also rated Chelsea's Player of the Year. At the end of the 2014–15 season Hazard won the PFA Player's Player of the Year Award, won Chelsea's Player of the Year Award for the second season running, joining Juan Mata, Frank Lampard, Ray Wilkins and John Hollins on that particular list. Chelsea lifted the Premier League title at the end of the term, Hazard hugely influential. Hazard had begun to question manager José Mourinho's tactics, feeling Chelsea were essentially set up to counter-attack – Tottenham found the same under Mourinho.

In April 2017 Hazard was named in the PFA Team of the Year for the fourth time in five seasons. An ankle injury while training with Belgium ruled Hazard out for six to eight weeks as the 2017–18 season began, but Hazard ended the season by winning and converting a penalty against Manchester United for the only goal of the 2018 FA Cup Final. In the 2018–19 season, 15 assists made Hazard the Premier League's Playmaker of the Season, joining Thierry Henry, Matt Le Tissier and Eric Cantona on a list of Premier League players notching 15 goals and 15 assists in a single season. Hazard scored twice in this 2019 Europa League Final, a fitting swansong for this richly talented player.

Touted by Zinedine Zidane as one of the greatest young players in the world a decade earlier, the great French/Algerian, a boyhood hero to Hazard, the Belgian achieved his dream move to work under Zidane at Real Madrid in June 2019. Signed for £100 million, Hazard became Real's most expensive player. Unfortunately for Hazard, an ankle injury sustained in November 2019 against Paris Saint-Germain in the Champions League – ironically inflicted by Belgian national teammate Thomas Meunier – stalled his fledgling Real career. Returning from injury in February 2020, Hazard promptly suffered a fibula fracture in his ankle against Levante in La Liga. Restricted to 16 league appearances, Hazard at least had the consolation of a La Liga winner's medal at the end of the season.

Hazard appeared in his first international against Luxembourg, aged just 17. France courted Hazard due to his Lille connection, but the player always preferred Belgium, the country of his birth. With Vincent Kompany injured, Hazard captained Belgium at the 2016 Euros, although Belgium suffered a surprise defeat in the last eight at the hands of a Gareth Bale/Aaron Ramsey-inspired Wales. Hazard had the consolation of providing the most assists – 4- in the tournament alongside Ramsey.

At his scintillating best in a Belgian team of all stars at the 2018 World Cup, Hazard helped his country finish third with a goal against England in the third and fourth place play-off match. He was instrumental in reviving Belgium's fortunes in the last 16 against Japan, and again as Belgium played superbly in defeating Brazil in the quarter-finals. Feted by critics as the most talented all-round team in the world – they are currently ranked No. 1 – the Belgians lost the semi-final to eventual winners France.

Hazard's speed, intricate footwork, ball control and dribbling are a phenomenon. Possessing a sharp eye for a telling pass also, Hazard can play effectively as a '10' as well as exhibiting his electric pace on the flanks. Kylian Mbappé seems like the new 'king of football' in waiting. Have Hazard's cruel injuries consigned him to the second tier of excellence in world football terms? Or would the postponed 2020 Euros or the 2022 World Cup in Qatar see Belgium justify their No. 1 world ranking? No to the first, as Belgium were eliminated by Italy, 2-1, at the quarter-final stage. In 2021 the Belgians dropped to second in the world rankings behind Brazil.

Among the substitutes for Chelsea were Argentine keeper Willy Caballero, Spanish left-back Marcos Alonso, Italian right-back David Zappacosta, the vastly experienced Argentine striker Gonzalo Higuain (an outstanding scorer at his peak, but past his best here), and the Brazilian wide attacking midfielder Willian. Willian played 234 Premier League games for Chelsea, scoring over 50 goals in all competitions. When he signed for Arsenal in August 2020 after seven seasons with Chelsea, he too appeared past his best. The English substitutes for Chelsea included the ever-dependable Gary Cahill, the frustratingly inconsistent, but talented midfielder Ross Barkley, and Conor Gallagher who thrived in West Bromwich Albion's midfield, before switching to Crystal Palace and excelling in Patrick Vieira's midfield.

In goal for Arsenal was former Chelsea hero and idol Petr Cech who went on to play over 100 games for the North London club. Arsenal's Achilles heel – there have been several in reality – in recent years has been a less than watertight defence and a porous midfield. They opted for a back three on this evening with French international and captain for the night, Laurent Koscielny, their best defender. Sokratis Papastathopoulos and Nacho Monreal flanked Koscielny. Monreal played over 200 games in all competitions for Arsenal 2013–19, turning in some decent performances. He's been capped by Spain over 20 times, but current left-back Kieran Tierney looks a sounder prospect, both defensively and offensively. Papastathopoulos has played over 90 times for Greece (April 2021) yet Arsenal released him in January 2021 following several inconsistent performances. At 32 and with a multi-international club career behind him with AEK Athens, Genoa, AC Milan, Werder Bremen and Borussia Dortmund, Arsenal seemed a club too far for Sokratis. He's since returned to play for Olympiakos in Greece.

Arsenal chose to pack their midfield (a modern tactic) with Ashley Maitland-Niles and Sead Kolasinac as wing-backs, Uruguayan ball-winner Lucas Torreira and the hapless Swiss Granit Xhaka, one-time captain of Borussia Möenchengladbach in the centre of midfield. The mercurial Mesut Ozil was asked to sit behind the strikers at the apex of a five-man midfield in order to supply the bullets for the fine front men Alexandre Lacazette and Pierre-Emerick Aubameyang. The system signally failed as Arsenal could not cope on the night with Chelsea's fast-raiding Hazard and Pedro, or their old centre-forward Olivier Giroud.

Maitland-Miles was a product of the Arsenal Academy, joining the club aged six. In 2014 Maitland-Miles became the youngest player to play in a Champions League match for the club against Galatasaray, after Jack Wilshere. He was loaned out to Ipswich Town in the 2015–16 season to gain experience. Returning to Arsenal he broke into the first team for the 2016–17 season. Sometimes used in midfield, but mostly at right- or left-back, Maitland-Miles struggled to lock down a first-team place under current manager Mikel Arteta, being loaned out again to West Bromwich Albion in February 2021. Capped at U-17, U-18, and U-19 level by England, and five times at senior level by the year 2021, Maitland-Miles has yet to fulfil his rich early promise.

The diminutive Torreira starred for Uruguay at the 2018 World Cup, his ball-winning properties integral to Uruguay's progress to the quarter-finals where they lost 2-0 to eventual winners France. After making his mark in Italy with Pescara and Sampdoria, Torreira transferred to Arsenal after his sparkling 2018 World Cup displays for Uruguay. Early indications suggested that the five feet five inches Torreira could be a crucial component in Arsenal's struggling midfield. His promising start stalled with a season-ending ankle injury incurred against Portsmouth in the FA Cup. The Premier League suspension and the Covid-19 pandemic harmed his recovery, and in October 2020 Torreira joined Atlético Madrid on a season-long loan. A lack of height and physicality in a Premier League bossed by powerful physical specimens may have worked against Torreira.

Granit Xhaka continues to be an Arsenal player despite his many critics and a raft of underwhelming performances for the club. At times he's appeared to fit the bill; at others he's been woefully inconsistent. He possesses a fine shot yet doesn't often get into shooting positions. His tackling can be fearsome, though often over-zealous, meaning yellow or red cards are always imminent. He's played over 150 Premier League games for Arsenal but Xhaka always feels like an accident waiting to happen. Yet Swiss national team boss Ottmar Hitzfeld likened his quality to Bastain Schweinsteiger, Germany's outstanding central midfielder.

With Basel, Xhaka won the Swiss Super League Championship in 2010–11, following this with a league and cup double in 2011–12. He started slowly with Borussia Mönchengladbach upon transferring in 2012, but by 2014–15 Xhaka was named in the Bundesliga Team of the Season. Xhaka's volatility is exemplified by his five red cards with the German club.

Moving to Arsenal in May 2016, Xhaka's first goal for the club was a 25-yard rocket against Hull City. It augured well, especially as he followed it with a 30-yarder in the EFL Cup defeat of Nottingham Forest. His first goal in the 2017–18 season was another 25-yard thunderbolt in a drawn game with Liverpool. It's a pity he doesn't have his shooting boots on more often. Not over-popular with the Arsenal fans, Xhaka got into an altercation with them when substituted against Crystal Palace in September 2019. Having been named captain – his commitment cannot be questioned – he was subsequently stripped of the captaincy. Despite his fitful form, Xhaka revived under Mikel Arteta and helped Arsenal avenge their 2019 Europa League humiliation in beating Chelsea in the 2020 FA Cup Final. Xhaka has played over 100 times for Switzerland (you've got to have something to represent your country that many times!), although his Albanian heritage has seen his occasional captaincy of the side questioned by ex-Swiss international and Liverpool legend Stephane Henchoz. His goal ratio for Switzerland (12 in 104 games, July 2022) is considerably better than his Arsenal scoring rate of 10 in 188 games in the Premier League (July 2022).

Xhaka continues to waver between excellent and inconsistent contributions to the Arsenal cause. If only he could temper his occasional reckless tackles by reining in his physical prowess a little. I played with a player in village football who was similar – he could find himself sent off for over-zealous tackles, yet he possessed a glorious left foot. Sometimes there's a trigger in a player, a spark that can be counter-productive to the team if they find themselves a man short.

In talking about Mesut Ozil I should be talking about a player who compares with the all-time greats: Pele, Cruyff, Maradona, Messi, Ronaldo, Platini. Yet the German international of Turkish descent has fallen from grace dramatically in recent times. Outstanding as a playmaker in Germany's 2014 World Cup-winning team, Ozil's application is constantly questioned. The 'King of Assists' as he has been tagged, provided the second highest ever amount of passes for goals (19) in a Premier League season before losing his way.

Ozil played for his hometown team Schalke 04 in Germany 2006–08, winning a transfer to rivals Werder Bremen. At Bremen he played 71 games, scoring 13 goals. He won the DFB Pokal with Bremen in 2008–09. Real Madrid signed him in 2010, and he helped 'Los Blancos' win La Liga in 2011–12, finishing first in assists for three straight seasons (an astonishing 25 in his first season; 17 in 2011–12; 26 (!) in 2012–13. Signing for Arsenal for £42.5 million he became the most expensive German player of all time. At this juncture Ozil seemed assured of world-class status.

Ozil appears to need the assurance of those he is playing for and with. Cristiano Ronaldo felt Ozil was the player who understood his penalty area moves best, the player who could best create opportunities for him. Feeling he was not receiving the necessary backup at Real he began his sojourn at Arsenal in style. In October 2013 Ozil was selected in the UEFA Team of the Year. He had the world at his feet apparently. Ozil is slightly built, although nearly six feet in his boots. One wonders whether the physicality and relentless pace of the Premier league brought about his downfall? He aided Arsenal's two FA Cup triumphs in 2013–14 and 2014–15, yet Premier league consistency eluded him. 2015–16 turned matters around for him, those 19 assists making him Arsenal's Player of the Year.

In 2017 Arsenal won the FA Cup again as Ozil completed the season with 12 goals and 13 assists. Problems with an inflamed knee and a fractured relationship with boss Unai Emery meant the 2016–17 season would be Ozil's swansong at Arsenal in effect. Emery questioned Ozil's work-rate and commitment, and although Ozil played in this 2019 Europa League Final he made little impact. In February 2018 Ozil became the fastest player to reach 50 assists in the Premier League, superseding Eric Cantona before him – but the assists petered out as Emery repeatedly left him out of the side. A further problem existed with Ozil reportedly being Arsenal's highest earner while not even being selected for the team. By 2020–21 Ozil had been left out of Mikel Arteta's 25-man Premier League squad.

On 27 January 2021 Ozil signed a three-and-a-half year deal with Turkish club Fenerbahce. It's too soon to know whether this player – world class in 2014 – can still impact at the highest level (his peak it seems was decidedly over when he moved to Istanbul Basaksehir in 2022). For Germany Ozil excelled between 2012 and 2014. He even scored five goals in qualification for the 2012 Euros as Germany won all ten of their group games, also providing seven assists. Germany would fall at the semi-final stage at these Euros, Ozil scoring from the spot as they lost 2-1 to Italy. Ozil was named in the Team of the Tournament. Ozil, essentially a provider of goals, a playmaker, subsequently top-scored with eight goals in 2014 World Cup qualification. He was absolutely at his peak. At the 2014 World Cup, Ozil was switched to a wide midfield cum-left wing role when Marco Reus was injured in a warm-up game. It proved an inspired move as Ozil scored the winning goal a minute from the end of extra time against Algeria in the last 16. Ozil only provided one assist, but with a sublimely subtle pass, for Sammy Khedira, as Germany astonishingly swept Brazil aside 7-1 in the semi-final. Germany prevented Argentina and Lionel Messi from achieving Messi's long-yearned for World Cup triumph (leaving doubters to say that Messi lies behind Pele and Maradona in the order of best-ever world player), winning 1-0 with an extra-time goal from Mario Götze. Ozil completed the most passes in the final third of the pitch (171) at the 2014 World Cup, surely proving there was no finer creator of chances on the world stage. Germany failed to replicate their form at the 2018 World Cup, but Ozil remained the player who created the most chances at this tournament.

Support for Turkish president Recep Erdogan in the 2018 Turkish general elections caused something of a stir in Germany, Ozil subsequently retiring from international football. Per Mertesacker, his Arsenal and Germany teammate was notable among those who supported Ozil's stance. Quick, agile, intelligent, possessing the most delicate of touches, Ozil at his best could unlock any defence in the world. His passing and crossing, his exquisite left foot, for a while made Mesut Ozil the leading creator/playmaker in world football. At Arsenal Ozil scored 44 times in 254 Premier League games; for Germany he netted 23 goals in 92 internationals. Ozil seems like a 'nearly man' now, his reputation at Arsenal tarnished by his failure to impact on games in his last years at the club – but let's not forget his outstanding impact on the German international team at the 2014 World Cup and beyond. A maestro who needed an arm around his shoulder, Ozil's standing in the game should be higher than it is.

French international Alexandre Lacazette and Gabon international Pierre-Emerick Aubameyang are both fine finishers. Apparently good friends, their close relationship off the pitch hasn't always translated into a close understanding on the pitch. Both Emery and Arteta seemed reluctant to pair them together on the football pitch, perhaps because they both need to be the focal point of the attack. Is it simply the nature of the modern game of football that disallows a two-striker system? Or can these talented players simply not play fluently together?

Alexandre Lacazette made his name with Lyon in France, scoring 100 goals in 203 appearances 2010–17, a very healthy return indeed. The Lyon-born Lacazette excelled in youth football, appearing for France at all age levels. In the 2010 UEFA European U-19 Championship Final, Lacazette scored the winning goal against Spain. In the 2014–15 season Lacazette was Ligue 1 top scorer and won the Ligue 1 Player of the Year. At the end of that season Lacazette had broken

Lyon's Ligue 1 scoring record for a season with 26, surpassing André Guy's tally which stood since 1969. An aborted deal with Atlético Madrid in May 2017 resulted in Lacazette signing instead for Arsenal for £53 million in July 2017.

Lacazette completed his first season at the Emirates Stadium with 14 goals, having missed a number of games through injury. He managed to score important goals in the 2017–18 Europa League season against Dynamo Moscow and Atlético Madrid under his new manager Arsene Wenger. The player's fortunes faltered upon incoming manager Unai Emery's appointment. Despite not always being selected by Emery, Lacazette finished the 2018–19 season with 13 goals, and received the supporter's vote as Player of the Season. His fortunes continued to fluctuate throughout 2020 and 2021, his obvious talent still marred by a lower-than-expected goal count, and spasmodic selection by Mikel Arteta. Ultimately he returned to Lyon in the summer of 2022, only a marginal success at Arsenal.

At international level, France have an abundance of riches once more in the 2020s, attacking talents Kylian Mbappé, Ousmane Dembélé, Antoine Griezmann and even the old war horse Olivier Giroud largely ahead of Lacazette in manager Didier Descamps' thinking. Lacazette's 16 games 2013–17 for France produced three goals.

Even more so than Lacazette, Pierre-Emerick Aubameyang has been expected to provide Arsenal with sufficient goals to keep the club in the elite top four of the Premier League. Four goals in two matches Arsenal were not expected to win, against Manchester City and Chelsea, brought the FA Cup back to North London in August 2020. A new contract rewarded for Aubameyang's streak has since seen his form stutter alarmingly.

Beginning with AC Milan in Italy in senior football in 2008, Aubameyang was immediately loaned out to Dijon, Lille, Monaco and Saint-Étienne in France over the next three seasons. Only after securing a permanent move to Saint-Étienne in 2011 did Aubameyang begin to make his mark. In 2011–12 he became Ligue 1's top scorer with 16 goals. In 2012–13 he netted 19 times, finishing only behind Zlatan Ibrahimovic in the scorer's list. He also provided eight assists, ending the season by being named in the Ligue 1 team of the season, and receiving the Ligue I Player of the Year award.

Now established as a regular goalscorer, the lightning quick Aubameyang joined German club Borussia Dortmund for the 2013–14 season on a five-year contract. Dortmund had narrowly lost the Champions League Final 2-1 to German rivals Bayern Munich in 2012–13. Aubameyang quickly became the focal point of Dortmund's attack. He could not have made a more dramatic impact on his debut, scoring with his first shot in the Bundesliga, ending the game with a hat-trick against FC Augsburg. He ended his first season with 16 goals in all competitions. In the 2014–15 season Aubameyang scored against future club Arsenal in the Champions League.

The 2015–16 season started thrillingly for Aubameyang as he became the first ever player to score in each of the club's first six Bundesliga matches, a record he extended to eight consecutive games. He ended the season with 35 goals in all competitions, 25 of them coming in the Bundesliga – the second highest tally behind the prolific Pole, Bayern Munich's Robert Lewandowski. Aubameyang also scored three goals against Tottenham Hotspur as Dortmund defeated Arsenal's North London rivals 5-1 in the last 16 of the 2015–16 Europa League.

The 2016–17 season saw Aubameyang caught up in an internal dispute with manager Thomas Tuchel (latterly at Chelsea) and temporarily out of the Dortmund team. When he returned he scored four times at Hamburger SV in a 5-2 victory, following this up with the winner against Bayern Munich. He ended the season with 31 Bundesliga goals and scored the winner, a penalty, against Eintracht Frankfurt, in the DFB Pokal Cup Final.

In January 2018 Aubameyang signed for Arsenal for a then-record club fee of £56 million. He quickly became the first player to score five goals in his first six games for his new club. In 13 Premier League starts Aubameyang scored ten goals and provided four assists. Astonishingly, Aubameyang's curled goal against Cardiff City in September 2018 was his first from outside the penalty area in 77 goals scored, suggesting a goal-poacher's penchant for penalty-box action. In scoring a hat-trick against Valencia in the semi-final of this 2018–19 Europa League competition, Aubameyang became the first Arsenal player to do so in a European last four game. At the end of the season, he tied with Liverpool's Mo Salah and Sadio Mané on 22 Premier League goals for the Golden Boot.

In November 2019 Unai Emery gave Aubameyang the captain's armband following Granit Xhaka's altercation with Arsenal fans. As a team Arsenal continued to frustrate, suffering erratic form. The latest debacle for the club came as they lost to Olympiakos of Greece in the Europa League last 32 in February 2020. On 1 July 2020, Aubameyang scored his 50th goal in just 79 league appearances following the resumption of Premier League football after the Covid-19 pandemic's first lockdown. He became the quickest player to reach this target for Arsenal, surpassing even the great Thierry Henry. Once again he ended the season with 22 Premier League goals, only one behind Golden Boot winner Jamie Vardy of Leicester City. The season ended with Aubameyang apparently back with a bang with those four goals against Manchester City and Chelsea and Arsenal's unexpected FA Cup triumph.

Aubameyang seemed set fair for a fine 2020–21 season, yet the goals dried up, and in March 2021 he was omitted from the side against Tottenham in the North London derby. Clearly a fine goalscorer when in the mood, was Aubameyang's time at Arsenal running out? His goals total in the Premier League stands at 68 in 122 games (March 2021) – impressive indeed, yet his future seemed uncertain. For Gabon, Aubameyamg scored 30 goals in 72 games. Transferring to Barcelona – another big stage for the player – Aubameyang scored 11 La Liga goals during 2022. Moving back to London to Chelsea for the 2022-23 season, Aubameyang started soundly with 3 goals in three games. At 33 who knows how much longer Aubameyang can continue scoring goals regularly.

Among the substitutes Arsenal had for this evening two players who have since become integral to Arsenal's first team: German goalkeeper Bernd Leno, and the massively talented left-sided player Bukayo Saka. Saka, along with Emile Smith Rowe, provides the precious creative spark in an otherwise continually inconsistent Arsenal team. Many of the other substitutes have moved on: Alex Iwobi to Everton; Danny Welbeck, an excellent player for England at times, but beset by injuries, to Brighton and Hove Albion; Carl Jenkinson to Championship side Nottingham Forest; Skhodran Mustafi to German club Schalke 04. Eddie Nketiah may yet fulfil his promise; Egyptian international Mohamed Elneny sometimes fits the bill as a midfield ball-winner, but sums up Arsenal's general malaise of inconsistency.

The two managers for the night have since moved on: Unai Emery unable to reproduce his Sevilla Europa League-winning habit returned to Spain to manage Villareal returning to England again in October 2022 to manage Aston Villa after Steven Gerrard's dismissal. Maurizio Sarri's 'Sarri-ball' philosophy grinding to an early halt at Chelsea, the Italian returning home to oversee Juventus's fortunes. Much respected in their own countries, neither was able to stamp their personalities on the Premier League. Were the management positions at Chelsea and Arsenal a poisoned chalice in 2021? Any manager not securing a trophy in double-quick time at Chelsea was likely to be summarily dismissed under Roman Abramovich's trigger-happy ownership. Arsene Wenger himself struggled to reassert Arsenal's former glories in his final years – Emery and Arteta have since discovered how difficult it is to remain in the elite group of Premier League clubs without the financial clout of Chelsea, Manchester City and to some extent, Manchester United and Liverpool. The sparkling new stadium at the Emirates saw money apportioned that has been channelled away from team improvements at Arsenal. The grand stadium has almost become an albatross around the club's neck – Tottenham may find the same occurs to them.

THE FINAL

The controversial choice of venue: the Olympic Stadium, Baku, Azerbaijan. The first chance of the game fell to Arsenal's Lacazette but he was felled by Kepa in the Chelsea goal. No penalty was given. Next Xhaka struck one of those all-too-rare 25-yard shots that clipped the crossbar. At this stage there was no hint of Arsenal's second-half collapse. A lovely Chelsea team move ended with Giroud's shot saved by Cech. It was the shape of things to come in the second half.

After the break, Chelsea upped the tempo and took the game away from Arsenal. Giroud turned the clock back with a beautifully glanced header from a perfectly flighted cross from Emerson. Hazard's pass from the left was smoothly swept home by Pedro. Chelsea were now piling on the pressure and Arsenal had little response. A strong run by Kovacic saw Pedro take the ball off his foot to feed Hazard who was fouled in the penalty area. Hazard sent Cech the wrong way from the spot and the game was up for the struggling Gunners. After an even first half, Arsenal were now falling apart. Iwobi gave Arsenal hope with a right-foot rocket on the volley from the right diagonal of the penalty area, but when Aubameyang lost the ball in midfield Hazard was in the right place at the far post to convert Giroud's cross for 4-1. Substitute Joe Willock had a great chance to reduce the arrears but swept the ball wide when it seemed easier to score. Arsenal's defence were all at sea in the second half when Chelsea showed renewed vigour, their nemeses the unplayable – on the night – Hazard, the experienced Pedro, and their old ally Giroud. Hazard was rightly named Man of the Match, his passing and movement simply too good for the weak Arsenal rearguard.

This was Ole Gunnar Solsjkaer's fourth attempt as manager of Manchester United to win silverware at the semi-final stage and beyond. In the 2019–20 season Chelsea beat United 3-1 in the FA Cup semi-final; Sevilla beat United 2-1 in the Europa League semi-final of the same season. Manchester City were their conquerors, 2-0, in the 2020–21 EFL Cup semi-final. Solsjkaer did enable United to finish second, inevitably, behind Manchester City in the 2020–21 Premiership title race – although a clear 12 points adrift. Solsjkaer re-instilled a little pride in United after the indifferent spells of David Moyes, Louis van Gaal and José Mourinho, re-establishing the United attacking ethos of old, but the ever-critical, at times over-critical media always saw Solsjkaer as a stop-gap manager. No manager since Alex Ferguson has been able to keep Manchester United competing with the super-rich, super-talented Manchester City, Chelsea and Liverpool teams.

Route to the Final
Villareal topped Group I of the 2020–21 Europa League with 16 points. In their first high-scoring match of the group the Spaniards beat the Turkish side Sivasspor 5-3 at home, striker Francisco 'Paco' Alcacer scoring twice. Alcacer was on the scoresheet again as Villareal won their second match against Qarabag of Azerbaijan 3-1. It was Colombian striker Carlos Bacca's turn to score twice next as Villareal soundly beat Maccabi Tel Aviv of Israel 4-0 in their next game. The return game in Israel ended 1-1. Villareal's fifth game ended with a narrow 1-0 victory in Turkey over Visasspor; the Spanish teams' last game against Qarabag in Villareal was cancelled due to their opponents suffering absences because of Covid-19 infections, Villareal being awarded a 3-0 victory.

Manchester United, superficially stronger than their Spanish opponents in this 2020–21 Europa League Final, started the season in the Champions League, but could finish only third in a tight group that saw Paris Saint-Germain and RB Leipzig of Germany pip them by three points at the group stage. This meant 'demotion' for United to the secondary European competition, the Europa League. United therefore restarted their hunt for European silverware in the last 32 of the second-tier Europa League tournament.

United made short work of the Basques of San Sebastian, Spain, in the neutral Covid-19-enforced venue for the first leg in Turin, Italy, winning 4-0 with Marcus Rashford scoring twice. The second leg at Old Trafford was a goalless irrelevance. Drawn against AC Milan in the last 16 meant an altogether tougher ask of United. Ivory Coast winger Amad Diallo gave his team a 1-0 lead (he only started three Premier League games for United), but Danish captain and centre-back Simon Kjaer scored a 92nd-minute equaliser for Milan. At the San Siro in the return Paul Pogba proved his worth with the only goal of the match.

Another Spanish club, Granada, were lambs to the slaughter in the last eight, United winning both legs 2-0 to secure a comfortable 4-0 aggregate victory. Two extraordinary games followed in the semi-finals, giving United genuine hope of winning the competition outright. At Old Trafford A.S. Roma were swept aside 6-2 as United played with a swagger associated with some of their former great teams. The exemplary Edinson Cavani scored twice; Bruno Fernandes also scored twice, Pogba and Mason Greenwood adding the others. Roma fought manfully in the second leg at the Stadio Olimpico, the ex-Manchester City striker, the Bosnian Edin Dzeko scoring as he had done in the first leg, but Cavani's two goals ensured United's safety. Roma won 3-2 on the night, but United prevailed 8-5 on aggregate to win through to the final.

Villareal won through comfortably in the last 32, defeating Red Bull Salzburg of Austria 2-0 away and 2-1 at home, Gerard Moreno scoring both goals in Spain. Their quarter-final too was a procession, Dynamo Kiev of the Ukraine dismissed 2-0 in both games, Gerard again scoring twice as his team gained a 4-0 aggregate victory. Villareal defeated Tottenham Hotspur's conquerors from the last 16, Dinamo Zagreb of Croatia, in two tight games in the quarter-finals. Gerard's penalty won a hard-earned 1-0 win in Croatia; Alcacer and Gerard scoring in Villareal as the Spaniards won 2-1, confirming a 3-1 aggregate victory.

Villareal's opponents in the semi-finals were the English club Arsenal, the scoreline a portent of things to come for Manchester United in the final. Manuel Trigueros and Raul Albiol gave Villareal a two-goal cushion in Spain, a Nicolas Pepe penalty reducing the arrears. Arsenal's young team gave their all in the second leg, but the streetwise defence of Villareal held out for a goalless draw. Arsenal 'reject' Unai Emery had cast his spell over his old club, maintaining his excellent record in the Europa League competition.

United went into this final as marginal favourites. The tag weighed heavily on them as Solsjkaer's attack-minded team were slowly suffocated by Villareal's determined, disciplined Spanish 'underdogs'. United set themselves up in a 4-2-3-1 formation, the in-form Edinson Cavani leading an attack that possessed youthful riches on the flanks in England's Marcus Rashford and Mason Greenwood, the experience of Portuguese international midfielder Bruno Fernandes sandwiching them. Scott McTominay offered solidity behind them. Paul Pogba was supposed to provide the flair. United's back four provided extra width behind Rashford and Greenwood in attacking full-backs Aaron Wan-Bissaka and Luke Shaw.

David de Gea was chosen as United's regular custodian 'between the sticks', his sometimes inconsistent performance level was not an issue on this night. Sadly it was a lack of penalty-taking finesse that let him down on this occasion.

The athletic Croydon-born Aaron Wan-Bissaka earned a Crystal Palace Player of the Year award in the 2018–19 season. A transfer to Manchester United followed in June 2019. By the end of the 2019–20 season Wan-Bissaka had made the highest number of tackles by any player in the Premier League, although United diehards still pine for the days of the reliable Gary Neville who so obviously wore his heart on his sleeve.

Luke Shaw made his name with Southampton 2011–14. Shaw joined The Saints academy, aged seven. Under then-manager Nigel Adkins, Shaw debuted in the 2011–12 season for Saints senior team, helping them achieve promotion to the Premiership. In his last season at St Mary's Stadium, Shaw was named left-back in the 2013–14 PFA Team of the Year.

Transferring to Manchester United in June 2014, Shaw initially struggled to establish himself. As he was beginning to make inroads at Old Trafford he suffered a double leg fracture in September 2015 against PSV Eindhoven in the Champions League. He was out of action for six months. Shaw's form took a while to return, but ultimately he won the club's Player's Player of the Year award and the fans' Sir Matt Busby Player of the Year award for 2018–19.

In recent times Luke Shaw has won the heart of England manager Gareth Southgate, establishing himself as England's regular left-back at the delayed 2020 Euros in 2021. Shaw was arguably England's best player in the 4-0 drubbing of the Ukraine in the quarter-finals. Shaw's second-minute goal gave England the lead in the final only for the savvy Italians to deny Shaw the space he'd enjoyed in previous games. Shaw has 21 England caps to date (July 2022).

United's centre-backs, the Swedish international Victor Lindelöf (50 caps, January 2022) and Eric Bailly (Ivory Coast international, 41 caps, January 2022) are fine defenders, but critics claim the pair lack the consistency of former United central defenders from Alex Ferguson's glory days as manager. Are they as good as Vidic and Ferdinand or even Bruce and Pallister? Probably not, but Lindelöf was good enough to win three Primeira Liga titles with Benfica and two Taca de Portugal (Portuguese Cups and 1 Taca Da Liga League Cup) before joining United in June 2017. This runners-up medal in the 2020–21 Europa League is his only United silverware thus far.

Bailly, ironically, signed for United in June 2016… from Villareal, where he played just one season in 2015–16, Bailly's power and pace were seen as good reasons for future success with United. Sadly a serious knee injury suffered against Chelsea in a 4-0 loss in October 2016 appears to have set him back. In November 2017 he suffered an ankle injury that kept him out for over three months. He is contracted to the club until 2024, suggesting United have not lost faith in him yet.

The six feet four inches Scott McTominay proved to be the standout player for United in this final. Lancaster-born McTominay qualifies to play for Scotland (34 caps, July 2022) through his Scottish father. Formerly a centre-forward he was converted to midfield by then-United coach Warren Joyce. McTominay first impacted in the Champions League in the 2018–19 season with fine performances against Paris Saint-Germain and Barcelona. Injuries since this Europa League final have derailed McTominay's progress a little. What is certain was that his drive, desire, and inspiration exceeded that of some of his more hallowed teammates in this 2020–21 Europa League final.

Partnering McTominay behind Greenwood, Fernandes and Rashford, was the ludicrously talented, ridiculously frustrating Paul Pogba. A World Cup winner with France in 2018, Pogba was sadly unable to make such an extravagant impact on this 2021 Europa League final. Pogba, Greenwood, Fernandes and Rashford; Cavani ahead of them, the excellent Uruguayan seemingly in prime form leading into the final. United couldn't repeat the attacking brilliance of their semi-final first leg destruction of A.S. Roma. Much was expected of Pogba, but maybe United's attacking set-up was imbalanced against a super-organised Villareal team.

Mason Greenwood looks the most natural finisher in the United team since the days of Ruud van Nistelrooy and Robin van Persie. Capped at England U-15, U-17, U-18 and U-21 level, Greenwood's solitary England senior start against Iceland hasn't been repeated as 2022 began. Breaking quarantine guidelines in Iceland along with the highly rated Phil Foden didn't help his cause. Twenty-one goals in 80 Premier League games for United since 2018 (January 2022) revealed a striker of rich promise, a player happy shooting with either foot. His finishing can be explosive. Still only 20, Greenwood has plenty of time to mature into a player United and England could rely heavily upon in the future, but off-field misadventures have stalled his career.

Bruno Fernandes lit up United's attack in the 2020–21 season, having won the Portuguese Cup (Taca de Portugal) 2-2, 5-4 on penalties over Porto in 2019–20. Sporting Lisbon, his club, also won the Taca da Liga (League Cup) in this same 2019–20 season, beating the same opponents in a similar manner, 1-1, 3-1 on penalties. This latter trophy was retained as Sporting had beaten Vitoria de Setubal 1-1, 5-4 on penalties in the 2018–19 season. It was in this season that Fernandes truly announced himself on the European stage, scoring 33 goals in all competitions, becoming the highest scoring Portuguese and European midfielder in a single season.

Since joining United, Fernandes has scored 31 goals in 69 Premier League games (January 2022). United leaned heavily on Fernandes for inspiration and goals in 2020–21. The signing of his friend and Portuguese international teammate Cristiano Ronaldo seems to have dampened Fernandes's own goal-scoring powers in the 2021–22 season. Fernandes won the fans' Sir Matt Busby Player of the Year award in his debut season for United, 2019–20. The 2020–21 season saw Fernandes score 18 Premier League goals, also providing 12 assists for his teammates. At times he seemed like a 'one-man band' as Solskjaer toiled to bring unity to his team of talented individuals. Fernandes has appeared 40 times for Portugal, scoring eight goals (July 2022).

Marcus Rashford flanked Fernandes to the left, his appearance in this final, like so much of his stop-start career, coming after returning from injury. He needs a clear run of fitness to establish whether or not he can be the superstar player he's suggested himself to be at times for Manchester United and England. Thus far, Rashford's pace and (sometimes) erratic finishing have garnered him 59 goals in 204 Premier League games since 2015; a further 12 in 46 internationals for England (July 2022).

The lone striker for United on this evening, Edinson Cavani (133 Uruguayan caps, 58 goals) is an exceptional player whose movement and penalty area nous were exemplary to his younger teammates in this 2020–21 season. A recognised goalscorer wherever he has played, Cavani came to United in the twilight of his career. Playing for Danubio, a Montevideo-based club, in his home country of Uruguay, Cavani scored nine goals in 25 games 2005–07. His professional career really started upon moving to Italy. With Palermo 2007–2011 he scored 34 goals in 109 Serie A games, helping his Sicilian club qualify for Europe in 2009–10. Already dubbed 'El Matador' in Italy for his composure in front of goal, Cavani joined Napoli on loan for the 2010–11 season, the move becoming permanent 2011–13. In Naples he scored 78 goals in 104 Serie A games, an exceptional tally in Italy's notoriously rigorous defensive-minded game. Napoli won the 2011–12 Coppa Italia, beating titans Juventus 2-0 in the final, Cavani scoring the first goal from the penalty spot. He finished the season with 23 Serie A goals. In 2012–13 he top-scored in Serie A with 29 goals. In November 2012 Cavani scored all four goals as Napoli beat Dnipro Dnipropetrovsk 4-2 in the Champions League group stages.

Manchester City and Chelsea expressed interest in signing the prolific Uruguayan. Instead Cavani joined the cavalcade of stars gravitating towards Paris, signing a five-year contract with Paris Saint-Germain. One hundred and thirty-eight goals in 200 Ligue 1 games in France 2013–20 revealed a striker in his prime. Whether the overall intensity of Ligue 1 compares with the overall intensity of the Premier League, LA Liga, Serie A or the Bundesliga is a matter for debate. It seems that winning Ligue 1 for PSG is most akin to Bayern Munich perennially winning the Bundesliga – there don't appear to be too many other worthy adversaries. Having said that, French football has clearly been on the up over the last decade, the 2018 World Cup win for France confirming the fact.

In the 2016–17 season Cavani netted 35 Ligue 1 goals, and was named Ligue 1 Player of the Year. With Brazilian superstar Neymar signing from Barcelona in 2017, along with the emergence of the next great world star Kylian Mbappé, PSG suddenly possessed a wealth of attacking riches. PSG scored 24 goals in the 2017–18 group stages, the highest by any team at this stage of the competition's history. Cavani scored in each of his first three Champions League games, against Celtic, Bayern Munich and Anderlecht. In November 2017 he became only the third player to score 100 goals in two top European leagues (Premier League, Bundesliga, Serie A, La Liga, Ligue 1) after Argentine Gonzalo Higuain and Swede Zlatan Ibrahimovic. Scoring against Montpellier in January 2018, Cavani became PSG's all-time top scorer. Cavani won six Ligue 1 titles with PSG, five Coupe de Frances (French Cups) and six Coupe de la Ligues (League Cups), but the feted, elusive Champions League continued to evade the French giants despite their ever-increasing Qatari-backed wealth. Bayern Munich thwarted French dreams in the 2019–20 final.

Now 34 (January 2022), his 35th birthday imminent, Cavani's time at United has been marred by intermittent injuries. Twelve goals in 41 Premier League games since signing in October 2020 is scant reflection of the Uruguayan's talent. When fit he's looked a class act, a top professional whose movement has made him a template for the promising young strikers at Manchester United. Only since the signing of Cristiano Ronaldo for the 2021–22 season has doubt been cast about Cavani's worth to United, although the player has been reported as being homesick.

At the World Cup in 2010 in South Africa, a Uruguayan team blessed with Cavani, Luis Suarez and Diego Forlan in attack won Group A. Suarez's brace saw off South Korea in the last16; Forlan's goal in a 1-1 draw with Ghana enabled a 4-2 penalty shoot-out victory in the last eight; Cavani and Forlan as strikers took on the Dutch in the semi-finals, the Uruguyans falling at the penultimate hurdle 3-2. In qualification for the 2018 World Cup, Cavani was in outstanding form, scoring ten goals. At the 2018 World Cup proper in Russia, Cavani scored in his country's clinical 3-0 defeat of the hosts in the group stage. In the last 16 his brace of fine goals saw Uruguay overcome Portugal 2-1. Uruguay didn't have enough in the tank to beat France in the quarter-finals, Raphaël Varane and Antoine Griezmann's goals ending their run.

A Christian, an advocate of ballet, Edinson Cavani is not your average professional footballer. His pace, athleticism, excellent positional sense and fine finishing mark him out as one of the very best players in the world in the 21st century.

Manchester United's opponents Villareal set up in a conventional, unfussy 4-3-3 formation. Several of the team and its substitutes had experience of the English Premier League. None of them had been anything other than a moderate success in England. The rest of the Villareal team were largely unheralded, rather like the multi-Europa League winning team previously managed by their manager on this night, Unai Emery. Yet it would be foolhardy to dismiss any Spanish top six or seven team as 'inferior' to our own regular top six finishers in recent years, United, Tottenham Hotspur or Arsenal. In addition, any Spanish La Liga team, even if they are not Real Madrid or Barcelona, will automatically be excellent technically.

Argentine right-back Juan Foyth spent three seasons at Tottenham, 2017–2020, without making himself a regular starter. Tottenham rated Foyth without offering him hope of regular first team football. After just 16 Premier League starts Foyth was loaned out to Villareal in September 2020, going on to win this Europa League title, and earning himself a permanent contract in the summer of 2021. Foyth made 13 starts for Argentina's national team from 2018 onwards, his most notable performances coming in the 2019 Copa America where the Argentinians lost 2-0 in the semi-final to Brazil.

Villareal's central defenders were excellent on this evening. Captain Raul Albiol was doggedness personified, never conceding an inch to United's talented attackers. A highly experienced player, Albiol played 131 La Liga games for Valencia 2004–09; 81 for Real Madrid 2009–2013; 180 Serie A games for Napoli 2013–19; before returning to Spain and Villareal in 2019. In 11 Europa League games in this 2020–21 campaign Albiol scored twice. Albiol won the 2003–04 Europa League with Valencia (the next one was a long time coming, but well worth the wait), beating Marseille of France in the final 2-0. He also won the 2007–08 Copa del Rey against Getafe with Valencia, 3-1. Among the scorers in that game was substitute opponent on this night, Juan Mata. Albiol won La Liga in 2011–12 with Real Madrid, and a Copa del Rey as Real beat Barcelona 1-0 in the 2010–11 final. With Napoli, Albiol won the Coppa Italia against Fiorentina in 2014, diminutive Euro 2020 star Lorenzo Insigne a scorer of two goals in a 3-1 win.

Raul Albiol has played 58 times for Spain (July 2022). Largely overlooked in major tournaments – he had Carlos Puyol and Sergio Ramos contending for the central defensive positions – Albiol's own attributes were exceptional indeed as United found to their cost on this evening. Albiol wore his passion for his shirt clearly, refusing to be on the losing side.

199

Alongside Albiol, Pau Torres's career has been spent largely at Villareal, working up through their C and B teams to play for the first team – apart from a season-long loan at Malaga in 2018–19. Not especially familiar to English fans, Pau was as inspired as Albiol on this evening in rainy Gdansk. Pau has played 19 times for Spain since 2019 (July 2022).

In the centre of the field, the defensive midfielder Étienne Capoue was well known to United fans. The Frenchman played for Toulouse 2007–2013, making 174 Ligue 1 appearances, scoring 13 goals. In 2008–09 he had the mixed impact of receiving 14 yellow cards, and earning a nomination for Ligue 1 Young Player of the Year. On the verge of signing for Cardiff City in July 2013, Capoue instead signed for Tottenham Hotspur.

Between 2013–15 Capoue played 24 Premier League games for Spurs without establishing himself as a regular starter. He transferred to Watford in July 2015 where he finally became a key player in a Premier League team's midfield. One hundred and sixty-seven Premier League games (nine goals) cemented Capoue's reputation. He won Watford's Player of the Year award for 2018–19.

In December 2020 Capoue signed for Villareal. Regarded as a little inconsistent in his time in England, Capoue won the Man of the Match award in this 2021 Europa League final. I'd have given it to Albiol, but the essence of this Villareal performance was their unity – any of their players might have won it. Capoue has played seven times for France (January 2022) but has never been seen as a regular starter with a host of talented players in front of him in his position – not least N'Golo Kanté.

This 2020–21 season was an exceptional one for Gerard Moreno with seven Europa League goals and 23 La Liga goals. He is currently Villareal's all-time top scorer with over 80 goals. Gerard was again faced with exceptional rivals for a national team place in his early years in Spanish football (David Villa, Andrés Iniesta), Moreno has since played 17 times for Spain, scoring five goals (July 2022).

Carlos Bacca, Villareal's Colombian striker, has an excellent scoring record in European football. After scoring 94 senior goals in Colombian football 2007–2011, Bacca signed for Club Brugge in Belgium, debuting in January 2012 against Mechelen. In a season and a half in Belgian football, Bacca scored 28 goals in 45 games, finishing as the top scorer in Belgium in 2012–13.

Bacca moved to Seville in July 2013, signing a five-year contract. In his first spell at the club, 2013–15, he scored 34 times in 72 La Liga games. The Spanish daily sports newspaper *Marca* voted Bacca the best signing of the 2013–14 La Liga season. At the 2013–14 La Liga awards, Bacca was voted the best player from the Americas for the season, ahead of the feted Angel di Maria of Real Madrid and Barcelona's Neymar. Bacca scored seven Europa League goals in 2014–15 as Sevilla retained the trophy beating the Ukrainians of Dnipro Dnipropetrovsk 3-2 in the final in Warsaw, Poland. Bacca scored twice in the match.

Bacca's European journey next took him to AC Milan where he continued his scoring form in the toughest of all European leagues defensively, Serie A. Bacca netted 31 goals in 70 Serie A games. He returned to Spain to Villareal on loan for the 2017–18 season, scoring 15 goals in 35 La Liga matches. The move became permanent in 2018, Bacca finding the net a further 13 times in 75 La Liga games before moving to Granada in sunny southern Spain. Only in recent times has Bacca's star waned somewhat. He has played 52 times for Colombia 2012–18, scoring 16 goals.

Bacca has all the attributes of the quintessential modern striker: pace, power, an eye for goal, excellent touch. If he has a fault it lies with his propensity to play off the shoulder of the last defender, bringing comparisons with Italian striker Filippo Inzaghi. I used to play in this same manner, always seeking to take advantage of the quick through ball. I used to blame the slowness of thought of my midfield players for not seeing the pass early enough! Both Bacca and Inzaghi have been inclined to be caught offside regularly. Bacca has also been accused of failing to contribute to his teams' build-up play, although the diligent Unai Emery managed to get Bacca to observe his defensive duties better than some of the player's other managers/coaches.

Among the substitutes for Villareal were two other players well known to English football followers, the ex-Liverpool left back Alberto Moreno and French midfielder Frances Coquelin, ex-Arsenal. Moreno was a fitful performer at Anfield, a better player coming forward than in his designated left-back defender's role. Coquelin played 105 Premier League games for Arsenal 2008–2018, promising more than he ultimately delivered. He seemed destined to become a star player for Arsenal in the 2014–15 season. Perhaps the knee injury sustained against West Bromwich Albion in the autumn of 2016 spoiled the party for Coquelin.

Spanish clubs were not daunted by Coquelin's inconsistency, seeing as Arsene Wenger had done a player who could perfect the defensive midfield role in their teams, a player with sound continental technique. Valencia signed him in January 2018. Coquelin played 61 La Liga games for Valencia 2018–20; he then joined Villareal in August 2020 on a four-year deal. At Valencia he won the 2018–19 Copa del Rey with an excellent 2-1 final win over Barcelona. Then came this deserved 2020–21 Europa League triumph. Coquelin's career seems to have taken off in Spain.

In 'Paco' Alcácer, Villareal had a worthy striking substitute (he came on in the 77th minute of this final). Like Bacca, Alcácer has played in another top European League – in his case the Bundesliga in Germany. His goal-scoring is less prolific than in his early days with Valencia – 30 in 96 La Liga games 2010–16, but a player who has played for Valencia, Barcelona (ten goals in 37 La Liga games 2016–19), Borussia Dortmund and Villareal, has pedigree.

I have always fought the modern adherence to Sky Sports or BT Sport, knowing that if I subscribed I would probably be as wedded to watching infinite amounts of football as millions of others do. I also think it's important to detach oneself from one's obsessions in order to keep a marriage sane. On this evening I switch on the internet at 7.55 pm and lo and behold I find that the Europa League Final is available free on BT live streaming.

THE FINAL

From the onset of the match it was apparent that Villareal were in the image of all Spanish football teams, extremely comfortable in possession. For decades it's been British clubs' mission to untangle this problem with their often more direct approach. A mix of styles can work the oracle, but United's night was set up by the opening three minutes in which they scarcely touched the ball. The clash of styles was glaringly obvious, United mixing it up, short and long, seeking to counter-attack swiftly; Villareal content to absorb pressure and counter-attack. The Uruguayan Edinson Cavani, in such outstanding form towards the end of this 2020–21season, was in from the start after appearing more often than not as a 'super-sub' in the run-up to the final. United created the first chance, Marcus Rashford cutting in from the left to set up midfielder Scott McTominay, but the young Scotsman dragged his shot wide. At least United had a foothold in the game, beginning to impose themselves on the stylish Spaniards. The bright yellow apparel of the Villareal bench was heightened by a bench full of players and medical staff wearing yellow face masks. Welcome to the world of pandemic-riven football circa 2021.

McTominay had begun to assert himself in this United team at this stage as a key ball-winner. United had struggled to find the right player for this role in recent times. As usual with United, the flair players in midfield were not in such short supply. One of these, the enigmatic, erratic, but occasionally brilliant Paul Pogba, played an exquisite ball to free the Portuguese attacking midfielder Bruno Fernandes on the right side of the penalty area, but Fernandes's shot was lofted high with the outside of his right boot. A team needs all types of midfield players, this is clear. McTominay, Pogba and Fernandes could not be more different, this is equally clear.

The rain slanted down in the Polish port city of Gdansk as the match progressed. The rain in the previous month in the UK had been incessant, only calming down in the 48 hours leading up to the final. Gdansk hadn't noticed – at least United players should be accustomed to the rain coming from the city of Manchester where rain appears to be an everyday staple if watching *Match of the Day* can be believed. Luke Shaw drove a cross in from the left as United struggled with the efficient marking of Villareal. Mason Greenwood narrowly failed to get a touch on it. Villareal – a top six team in La Liga for the last eight seasons – are no mugs. Proving they were not here to be United's 'whipping boys', Carlos Bacca showed great skill but an opportunity went begging as a header cleared the bar at the other end. Rashford, Cavani, Greenwood, Fernandes, United were not short of fine attacking options, but were they too top-heavy in attack on the night? Full-backs Shaw and Aaron Wan-Bissaka were also keen to push up and supplement the attack.

With United in the ascendency, Villareal stunned the English team. A free kick from the left evaded Victor Lindelöf and Gerard Moreno stretched to half-volley past David de Gea. 1-0 Villareal. Gerard (stick an extra 'R' in and you have a famous Champions League winner from England) scored his 30th goal of the season, ironically equalling Villareal's previous seasons' scoring record by a former United player, Giuseppe Rossi. United responded with a lovely lay-off from Cavani that allowed McTominay to burst into space, but he drove the ball over the crossbar. United were having the lions' share of possession but Villareal were a very tight unit, limiting United's chances for all the Red Devils' territorial dominance. Rashford switched flanks, showing exquisite skill, but had a shot blocked. Greenwood drove into the box from the right-hand side but his cross deflected unkindly off Villareal defender Albiol. There was little to cheer for United as the break was reached with Villareal leading 1-0.

A goalmouth mix-up almost led to a second Villareal goal in the 47th minute. Bacca was leading the line well for Villareal as United attempted to reassert themselves, constantly probing, using the width of the pitch to good effect (something I passionately believe in as a former winger), but the Spaniards were defending in numbers. Étienne Capoue – ex-Watford, now playing in a major European final – was booked for Villareal. McTominay battled hard to win a corner for United – it was the youngster's spirit that was in evidence on the night, but they could have done with a moment's inspiration from the likes of Fernandes or Cavani. It arrived from the corner-kick, the ball breaking loose off McTominay's shins from Rashford's driven shot, and Cavani gleefully passed the ball into the net. There was a question mark of offside, but VAR checked it and the goal stood. 1-1. In the next attack, the industrious McTominay swiped at the ball and missed, Fernandes following in behind him to smash the ball wastefully wide. Fernandes's 40 goals in 80 games in the last two seasons made him their great white/red hope. United ramped up the pressure, but Fernandes's divine inspiration evaded him.

Fernandes broke free down the right, crossed to Rashford who missed an open goal, but Rashford's blushes would probably have been spared by Fernandes's suspected offside position. Shaw badly miss-hit a cross that the ever-alert Cavani almost diverted into goal. McTominay continued to drive United on from midfield, but Cavani couldn't get anything on another cross from Shaw.

Ole Gunnar Solskjaer, United's manager, looked lonely and despondent in the dugout. Alex Ferguson and Wayne Rooney were in evidence at the ground, this past 'royalty' willing Solskjaer to win his first trophy after four semi-final defeats in cup competitions since he took over as United manager. In the meantime, Villareal had made three substitutions. By the 87th minute United's 11 was the same as at the start of the match. Rashford and Shaw combined on the left to tee up a header for Pogba that sailed over the bar. In the 90th minute Villareal almost snatched it when defender Pau Torres curled an effort over the bar as United were slow to close him down. 1-1 after 93 minutes. Extra time was required despite United having twice as many goal attempts as their opponents.

Villareal's manager Unai Emery – a mishap as Arsenal manager, but a three-time winner of this competition with former club Sevilla – haunted the touchline, his slicked back dark hair making him look like Christopher Lee from the Hammer Horror 'Dracula' films of the 1960s. His player Alcacer swept the ball over the bar as Villareal started to look the fresher of the two teams. At last United brought on substitutes, but Fred was not an inspiring attacking substitution. Some of the Spanish players were milking some of the tackles made by their tiring United opponents. Fred at least freed up space ahead of him, allowing Fernandes to push up. The hugely talented, but inexperienced Greenwood was sacrificed. The game remained 1-1 after 105 minutes.

The second half of extra time started with the Gdansk rain teeming down. The match was tight, the weather was dour, and United were increasingly frustrated.

The Villareal bench covered their legs with towels as defence against the torrents of rain. From the restart, Lindelöf fired a sharp ball through the middle but Villareal keeper Rulli just beat Cavani to the ball. United, for so long controlling the game, began to lose impetus. Rashford came off after a tussle with the powerful, imposing Albiol. Daniel James, the young Welsh international, came on. The ex-Liverpool full-back, Alberto Moreno, on as a substitute for Villareal, almost worked an opening in combination with Alcácer, but it was McTominay who was back to avert the danger once again. The ball struck Fred in the United penalty area. VAR was checked and Fred escaped – but penalties had been given for this in the Premiership in the 2020–21 season. Emery's team – like his former club Sevilla – had been supremely well organised. The last throw of the dice for Solsjkaer came with the hugely impressive McTominay leaving the field along with Wan-Bissaka. Juan Mata and Alex Telles replaced them, presumably with the penalty shoot-out in mind. Pity the creative Mata wasn't used earlier, his ability to pick the pocket of the tightest of defences might have been crucial.

The penalty shoot-out occured at the end with the Villareal supporters present. Was this sufficient to deter United? Gerard sent de Gea the wrong way, Mata comfortably scored in the corner to equalise. The unfortunate de Gea went the wrong way again, 2-1. Telles, a prolific penalty taker with former club Porto, made it 2-2. Solsjkaer's late extra-time subs were at least justified. A desperate de Gea got a hand to Alcácer's next penalty – he should have saved it, but it's 3-2. Fernandes made it 3-3, but maybe Rulli could have saved this one. Moreno made it 4-3. Rashford shuffled up to the ball – often a dubious ploy, but comfortably made it 4-4. Parejo made no mistake 5-4. Cavani held his nerve, predictably, to make it 5-5.

It was down to the non-penalty takers now. Moi Gómez hit the ball straight down the middle, 6-5. Fred made it 6-6 – the substitutes were not letting Solskjaer down. Albiol coolly rolled the ball into the corner, de Gea guessed wrong again, 7-6. Daniel James sent Rulli the wrong way, 7-7. Coquelin, ex-Arsenal, glided the ball effortlessly into the top corner, 8-7. Shaw squeezed the ball past Rulli. A close call, but it was 8-8. The longest serving Villareal player, Mario Gaspar, made it 9-8. Another late substitute for United, Tuanzebe, coolly emulated Coquelin to make it 9-9. Pau Torres effortlessly made it 10-9. Lindelöf blasted an equaliser, 10-10.

Down to the goalkeepers! Rulli made it look easy – 11-10. For United, de Gea's penalty kick was too soft, Rulli saved, and the 'Yellow Submarine' as Villareal had been tagged all night, had defied the odds to win Unai Emery his fourth Europa League title. United didn't deserve to lose – or win, arguably, but they couldn't find enough creativity on the night to unlock a tight defence marshalled superbly by Pau Torres and Albiol. A cruel night for United, keeping them trophy-less for a fourth consecutive year. Villareal, a city of 50,000 people – less than the 70,000 in my hometown of Guildford, Surrey – defeat the giants of Manchester United, a massive urban city. A fairy-tale win for the seventh placed team of La Liga in 2020–21. Once again it's proven just how difficult it is to win European silverware. It has never been a given.

My wife thinks I suffer with obsessive compulsive disorder! She's probably right as when I approached the completion of my writings for this book, two British teams reached the finals of the Europa League and the Champions League. Naturally I must include these games to bring my treatise up to date. The first of these, somewhat surprisingly, was Glasgow Rangers. If anything the more likely British finalist appeared to be West Ham United, who performed superbly in the last 16 and the last eight in knocking out Sevilla and Lyon. Perennial Europa League winners Sevilla beat West Ham 1-0 in Spain, but a defiant West Ham team equalised through the excellent Czech international Thomas Soucek, before Ukrainian forward Andriy Yarmolenko won the tie for the Hammers in extra time. In the last eight West Ham produced an outstanding result in beating Lyon 3-0 in France to confirm a 4-1 aggregate victory, goals coming from centre-back Craig Dawson, the impressive England midfielder Declan Rice, and new England forward Jarred Bowen. Unfortunately West Ham came up short in the semi-final, losing 2-1 at home to the Germans of Eintracht Frankfurt, then losing 1-0 away with Aaron Cresswell being sent off. David Moyes did not feel West Ham got the 'rub of the green' in the away leg, but once again German opposition confounded their English opponents.

Rangers quietly went about their business, beating decent European opposition at the same stages in Red Star Belgrade in the last 16, 4-2 on aggregate, captain and right-back James Tavernier scoring a penalty in one of the ties; Braga of Portugal were overcome 3-2 on aggregate after extra time in Glasgow, Tavernier scoring twice in the deciding home leg; and in the semi-finals German outfit RB Leipzig were beaten 3-2 on aggregate, Tavernier again scoring. The full-back built quite a reputation leading into this final, but found his opponent on the night, the Serbian international Filip Kostic, quite a handful. Tavernier's career up to this point was a chequered one, mostly spent in English football. He spent years as a youth player with Leeds United 2001–08, spending loan spells thereafter with Newcastle United, Carlisle, Sheffield Wednesday, MK Dons, Shrewsbury Town, Rotherham, Wigan Athletic and Bristol City. Only upon signing for Rangers in 2015 did Tavernier truly settle down, this 'journeyman' player completing 238 appearances for Rangers (May 2022), scoring 57 goals.

The problem for Scottish football in recent years stems from the league having lost its star power of the late 60s and early 70s. Also, the money gravitated towards the Premier League in England from 1992 onwards, feeding down from Sky Sports. Scottish clubs couldn't compete on a level playing field financially. The best players played in England, the next tier of players, whether they be English players like Tavernier who didn't quite make it in England, or second tier foreign exports played in Scotland. The consequence: less joy for Scottish football clubs in Europe. I was surprised Rangers made this final, but all credit to the Glasgow outfit for reaching a pinnacle that proved beyond West Ham United.

John Lundstram partnered Calvin Bassey in the centre of Rangers' defence on the night. Lundstram, like Tavernier, was a much-travelled player in the lower tiers of English football, his most recent club before joining Rangers in 2021 being Sheffield United. Bassey, the Nigerian centre-back (six caps for Nigeria, July 2022) performed manfully on this night. The brother of English popular music rapper Y.CB (Matthew Bassey), Calvin's night was ultimately marred by only one error of judgement, a costly one that led to Rafael Borré's equalising goal.

One of Rangers' brightest players on this night was Ryan Kent, a graduate of the Liverpool academy 2004–15. The lively Kent never played a senior game with the Anfield club, signing for Rangers in 2019 (84 appearances, 19 goals, May 2022). Capped by England at U-18 and U-20 level, Kent's finishing let him down on the night. Similarly, Scott Wright has been capped by Scotland at U-17, U-19, U-20 and U-21 level. He looked lively at times against Frankfurt, only a goal missing from another promising display.

Most emphasising the gap between the very best English and Scottish clubs in 2022, Rangers' sole striker on this evening, Joe Aribo, played semi-professional football for Staines Town, 20 miles down the road from my home before spending four years at Charlton Athletic. Aribo never stopped trying against Frankfurt, but looked like an unfinished article compared to Frankfurt's best player Filip Kostic. Aribo has made his mark internationally, despite the slow start to his career, scoring twice in 20 internationals for Nigeria (July 2022). Southampton saw enough in him to sign him for the 2022–23 season.

Rangers' manager Giovanni von Bronckhorst was experience personified, having played for Rangers, but also twice with Feyenoord in his homeland, and with Arsenal and Barcelona. The Dutchman won 106 international caps – Rangers could have done with him on the pitch against Eintracht Frankfurt!

In opposition, Frankfurt had the Man of the Match on the night in their goalkeeper Kevin Trapp. Trapp, unsurprisingly, for all his excellence here in Seville in this final, has won only six international caps. The reason – one Manuel Neuer imposing a very large obstacle to his path into the German national team. The star player for Frankfurt, the 48 times capped (three goals, July 2022) Serbian left-sided forward Filip Kostic signed for Frankfurt from Hamburger SV in 2018. In 128 appearances for Frankfurt, Kostic scored 18 goals (May 2022). If his goal count seems low, his threat to Rangers was tangible on this evening, as a provider, as well as a potential goal threat. The other danger to Rangers came in the form of the Colombian international Rafael Santos Borré (17 caps, one goal, July 2022). Borré, slight, but skilful, proved to be the match-winner on this occasion. For Frankfurt, after signing from Argentina's River Plate, Borré scored eight goals in 31 appearances (July 2022).

THE FINAL
Watching this final I couldn't help feeling that a fit and firing West Ham United would have beaten either of these teams. Unfortunately for the English club, it was Eintracht Frankfurt who put West Ham out of the competition in the last four after a splendid run in the competition from David Moyes's team. Whether injuries and fatigue caught up with the Hammers, one can only ponder.

The Germans of Frankfurt were on the front foot from the beginning of the final. A lovely turn by Scott Wright almost set up Joe Aribo early on as Rangers valiantly fought for a foothold in the game. Frankfurt conceded a corner-kick, but James Tavernier's kick was poor. Tavernier top-scored in this year's Europa League campaign with seven goals – an impressive total from a full-back, but he would be unable to impose himself upon this match. Tavernier, who likes to play high up the pitch, stayed up in the next attack, but the quality of his direct opponent Filip Kostic made for an uncomfortable night for Rangers' captain.

The most notable moment of the first half occurred when Rangers' ex-Sheffield United player John Lundstram caught the head of Frankfurt's Sebastian Rode. Rode continued after several minutes' delay with blue surgical tape applied to his head, reminiscent of the old warrior Terry Butcher playing for England. Rangers attacked towards a 'white wall' of Frankfurt supporters in the first half, mirroring the famed 'yellow wall' of another German team's supporters, Borussia Dortmund. Messy defending from Rangers led to their goalkeeper Allan McGregor (42 caps, Scotland) producing a comfortable save. Rangers regained some composure at the back as the first half progressed. McGregor produced an even better fingertip save to deny Knauff. At the other end, Lundstram was afforded the freedom of Seville in the penalty box, but miscued badly. The game was even, but Frankfurt were creating more clear-cut chances. Wright again fed Aribo, the ex-Staines Town player, but Aribo curled narrowly wide. There was a gorgeous sunset setting over Andalusia and the Estadio Ramon Sanches Pizjuan Stadium. The heat in the stadium meant a cooling break was taken after 27 minutes – it was hot out there even in the early evening. Frankfurt threatened through Kostic, his thumping volley sailing wide. The Serbian international wide man then drove forward from deep and arrowed a shot wide of the far post. Ryan Kent was fouled at the other end and from the ensuing free kick, Lundstram's header was tipped over by the solid Kevin Trapp in the Frankfurt goal. Aribo set up midfielder Ryan Jack for a rising drive that cleared the bar. 0-0, half-time.

The Frankfurt fans attempted to ramp up the atmosphere as the second half began, flares soaring, white flags fluttering. The flares set off a shroud of smoke, but Rangers remained focused at this juncture. Tuta struck a 30-yarder past McGregor's post, the keeper untroubled. Another deflected shot deceived McGregor but drifted past the post as Rangers had a let-off. Midfielder Ryan Kent looked threatening for Rangers, but didn't have his shooting boots on. The first of two gilt-edged chances for the ex-Liverpool player saw the player slash the ball horribly wide. Rangers were given a second chance soon afterwards. An uncharacteristically poor clearance from Trapp in Frankfurt's goal allowed Aribo to take advantage of a further aberration in the centre of Frankfurt's defence and slid the ball into the net. Out of nowhere, Rangers had the lead. Frankfurt responded almost immediately, the ball hitting Nigerian centre-back Calvin Bassey on the arm. I've seen penalties given for this – Rangers had a lucky break here.

In the 69th minute Rangers' luck ran out. Frankfurt's Colombian striker Rafael Borré scored an opportunist equaliser. Kostic crossed from the left and the Colombian gambled on squeezing between Bassey and Goldson, the Rangers' centre-backs, and poked the ball past McGregor at the near post. It was the first time the Rangers defence had switched off and it proved costly – they should have closed down Borré's space. Thirty-seven-year-old Steven Davis came on as a 74th-minute substitute for Rangers, but it was Hauge for Frankfurt who had the next chance, lifting the ball over the bar. When Tavernier missed a ball that came over his shoulder, Kostic drove the ball left-footed across the goal. Rangers were now living dangerously. There was five minutes injury time, but the sides could not be separated.

Scott Arfield, another ex-English Football League player, came on as a substitute for Rangers and drove a shot over the bar. Kostic remained dangerous for Frankfurt, the tiring Tavernier struggling to keep tight to him. Bassey slipped on the left, Borré bore down on goal, but the Nigerian recovered to concede a corner-kick. In the second half of extra time, Rangers' Croatian defender Borna Borisic blasted a shot goalwards but it was straight at Trapp and he parried. In response, Hauge teed up another Frankfurt substitute, Krusic, and he dragged a left-foot shot wide. Jackic fired another shot narrowly over as Frankfurt continued to take the game to Rangers. With just two minutes left on the clock, Ryan Kent had the chance to win the game for Rangers. Kent failed to anticipate his opportunity quickly enough close to goal and saw his shot deflected into Trapp's arms. This was Rangers' moment, similar to Paul Gasgoigne's excitable miss in Euro 96 against the redoubtable German national team. With 30 seconds remaining, Tavernier curled the ball towards the top of the net at the near post, but Trapp was equal to the task.

Penalties: Taken at the Rangers end after Tavernier won the toss. Frankfurt lost to Chelsea three years previously in these circumstances, but the old German penalty-king mantra kicked in. Tavernier sent Trapp the wrong way, but Lenz repeated the feat against McGregor. Davis fired high into the net to put Rangers 2-1 up. McGregor guessed wrong again and it was 2-2. Arfield rifled his kick into the corner of the net and Rangers led 3-2. Kamada, a Japanese international, made it 3-3 via a post. The Welsh international Aaron Ramsey, a class act and a hero for Wales in the 2016 Euros, on as a substitute for Rangers, then made a hash of his kick, Trapp kicking his shot away. Why is it that the key players often miss penalty kicks in these circumstances? Kostic arrowed the ball into the corner of the net and for the first time in the shoot-out, Frankfurt led. Kemar Roofe hit the net with another shot off a post, 4-4. Rafael Borré, lively throughout, fired high into the net and Frankfurt took the trophy 5-4 on penalties after a 1-1 drawn game. The win was just about deserved, Frankfurt having been the more pro-active team throughout on the night, Rangers playing more conservatively. The only time on the night Rangers lost their shape, Borré punished them. Sadly for Rangers, the game followed almost to a tee the 2020–21 final which Manchester United lost to a marginally better Villareal side. In this 2021–22 final a similar pattern unfurled, Eintracht Frankfurt just shading the win over Rangers. It's always been an uphill struggle for British teams in Europe.

Part 3: The European Cup

THE EUROPEAN CUP
LIST OF BRITISH WINNERS AND FINALISTS

1966–67 – Glasgow Celtic 2 v 1 Inter Milan
Estadio Nacional, Lisbon, 45,000

1967–68 – Manchester United 4 v 1 Benfica (after extra time), Wembley
Stadium, London, 92,225

1969–70 – Feyenoord 2 v 1 Glasgow Celtic (after extra time)
San Siro, Milan, 53,187

1974–75 – Bayern Munich 2 v 0 Leeds United
Parc des Princes, Paris, 48,374

1976–77 – Liverpool 3 v 1 Borussia Möenchengladbach
Stadio Olimpico, Rome, 57,000

1977–78 – Liverpool 1 v 0 Club Brugge
Wembley Stadium, London, 92,500

1978–79 – Nottingham Forest 1 v 0 Malmö
Olympiastadion, Munich, 57,500

1979–80 – Nottingham Forest 1 v 0 Hamburger SV
Santiago Bernabeu, Madrid, 51,000

1980–81 – Liverpool 1 v 0 Real Madrid
Parc des Princes, Paris, 48,360

1981–82 – Aston Villa 1 v 0 Bayern Munich
De Kuip Stadium, Rotterdam, 46,000

1983–84 – Liverpool 1 v 1 A.S. Roma (Liverpool 4-2 on penalties after extra
time)
Stadio Olimpico, Rome, 69,693

1984–85 – Juventus 1 v 0 Liverpool
Heysel Stadium, Brussels, 58,000

THE CHAMPIONS LEAGUE
LIST OF BRITISH WINNERS AND FINALISTS

1998–99 – Manchester United 2 v 1 Bayern Munich
Camp Nou, Barcelona, 90,245

2004–05 – Liverpool 3 v 3 AC Milan (Liverpool 3-2 on penalties after extra time)
Ataturk Olympic Stadium, Istanbul, 69,000

2005–06 – Barcelona 2 v 1 Arsenal
Stade de France, Saint-Denis, Paris, 79,610

2006–07 – AC Milan 2 v 1 Liverpool
Olympic Stadium, Athens, 63,000

2007–08 – Manchester United 1 v 1 Chelsea (Manchester United 6-5 on penalties after extra time)
Luzhniki Stadium, Moscow, Moscow, 67, 310

2008–09 – Barcelona 2 v 0 Manchester United
Stadio Olimpico, Rome, 62,467

2010–11 – Barcelona 3 v 1 Manchester United
Wembley Stadium, London, 87,695

2011–12 – Chelsea 1 v 1 Bayern Munich (Chelsea 4-3 on penalties after extra time)
Allianz Arena, Munich, 62,500

2017–18 – Real Madrid 3 v 1 Liverpool
NCS Olimpiyskiy Stadium, Kiev, 61,651

2018–19 – Liverpool 2 v 0 Tottenham Hotspur
Metropolitano Stadium, Madrid, Madrid, 63,272

2020–21 – Chelsea 1 v 0 Manchester City
Estadio do Dragao, Porto, 14,110

Liverpool, remarkably, have been in nine finals, winning six. Manchester United have won three times, being losing finalists on two occasions. Chelsea have appeared in the final three times with a 2/1 win/lose record. A mark of just how difficult it is to win European football's premier trophy is revealed by the fact that no other British team has appeared in the final more than twice. Nottingham Forest, essentially a provincial club seen as 'lower tier' than the Liverpools, Manchester Uniteds and Chelseas of this world, astonishingly won the European Cup twice under the canny stewardship of the great Brian Clough.

Another English Midlands provincial club, Aston Villa, were surprise winners of the trophy in 1982, Tony Barton overseeing a side largely built by his predecessor Ron Saunders. Leeds United were desperately unlucky losers to Bayern Munich in 1975, albeit to a German side graced by Franz Beckenbauer, Gerd Müller and Sepp Maier. Arsenal made the final in 2006 during Arsene Wenger's glory years at Highbury, but even a side containing the graceful Thierry Henry were no match for a Barcelona team in their pomp. Tottenham Hotspur reached the 2018 final, losing to a superior Liverpool team, unable to do themselves justice on the grandest of stages.

Far and away the team who have left the biggest mark on the European Cup/ Champions League are the Spanish giants Real Madrid, 17 times finalists, and an astonishing 14 times winners. The Ferenc Puskás/Alfredo Di Stéfano /Francisco Gento team of the early years of the competition completely dominated, winning for the first five seasons 1956–1960. The 1960 European Cup final is indelibly etched in my mind. I saw highlights of Real's 7-3 triumph over the German Club Eintracht Frankfurt on the BBC. The match took place in Britain at Hampden Park, Glasgow, and remains the record score for a European Cup Final. My sons are forever telling me that defences in the 60s and 70s were less organised than from the 1980s onwards – and they are right, but I cannot forget the first impression the great Puskás and Di Stéfano made upon me.

The Frankfurt team simply couldn't contain these early geniuses of 'modern' football. I'd read about Puskás's performances in 1953 for Hungary in particular, admiring old newsreel footage of one of his goals in Hungary's 6-3 trouncing of the 'invincible' England team at Wembley. Proving the result was no fluke, the Hungarians won a return game the same year in Budapest 7-1. Puskás, Hidegkuti, Kocsis, are names ingrained in my mind from that team. Hungary should have won the 1954 World Cup with that team. Who defeated them in the final? Why West Germany of course, organised, disciplined, cussed, even back in 1954.

The sleight of foot and skill shown by Puskás and Di Stéfano, the Argentine-born, Spanish nationalised midfield player-cum striker, were a sight to behold for Real Madrid in that 1960 European Cup final. I probably saw the footage retrospectively as a seven- or eight-year-old in 1963 or 1964, but genius makes an impression on a person even at that young age.

AC Milan are second on the list of most final appearances with seven wins and four losses, aided by three wins in five years with the outstanding Dutch superstars Ruud Gullit, Marco Van Basten and Frank Rijkaard in the side, and bolstered by the all-time great Italian defenders Paolo Maldini and Franco Baresi. Next on the list come the German giants Bayern Munich with the same record of 11 final appearances. Three-time winners in the mid-1970s with 'Der Kaiser' Franz Beckenbauer exemplifying the perfect sweeper, and Gerd Müller out-gunning our own Jimmy Greaves as a goal-machine. This was a Bayern team to cherish.

To their great credit, Liverpool and Manchester United are fourth and seventh on the list. Even the superlative Barcelona team of the 21st century lie one place behind Merseyside's finest, in fifth place. The placing of the Dutch maestros Ajax in sixth place is largely due to the 'total football' geniuses Johan Cruyff, Johan Neeskens and Ruud Krol being part of the side that won the trophy three years running in the early 1970s.

Those days seem far way now, and indeed my first memories of the European Cup are vivid green and white hooped ones from the Stadium of Light in Lisbon circa 1967. Celtic shouldn't have won the European Cup in 1967 on paper, but it's often said that you don't win games on paper, and I will never forget how Celtic attacked with abandon the ultra-defensive Italians of Inter Milan from the outset of that 1967 European Cup final. It was literally attack against defence, the Italian game in the mid-late 1960s mired in the system called 'catenaccio', literally meaning the spider's web. Italian clubs, and also the Italian national team in those days tended to take a 1-0 lead and promptly 'shut up shop', enmeshing their opponents in a defensive cocoon. To this day Italian players are master defenders – it's simply part of the Italian psyche. For Italians defending is an art form.

1966–67 EUROPEAN CUP FINAL
Glasgow Celtic 2 v 1 Inter Milan

Route to the Final

Celtic scored goals for fun in the early rounds of the 1967 European Cup, beating the Swiss side FC Zürich 5-0 on aggregate in the first round (rampaging full-back Tommy Gemmell scoring three goals including a penalty), and French side Nantes 6-2 on aggregate in the second round. The finalists only needed to play four ties in order to reach the final in Lisbon. An interesting result in the second-round ties was the 7-3 aggregate humbling of Liverpool by Ajax of Amsterdam, an early indicator of the Dutch club's strength to come in the early 1970s. A young Johan Cruyff scored twice in the 2-2 draw at Anfield. Celtic lost 1-0 to the Serbians of Vojvodina away in the last eight, but turned the tie around in Glasgow, winning 2-0. The Czechs of Dukla Prague, conquerors of Ajax in the last eight, were then beaten 3-1 on aggregate by Celtic in the semi-final.

Inter Milan pulled off the Italian trick of winning 1-0 on aggregate in the first round against the Russians of Torpedo Moscow, thanks to an own goal by Russian international midfielder Valery Voronin. In the last 16 Inter did manage a 4-1 aggregate victory over Vasa SC Budapest. The previous year's trophy holders Real Madrid were seen off 3-0 on aggregate in the last eight. The semi-final proved a sterner test for Inter, two 1-1 draws with CSKA Red Flag of Bulgaria (the Central Sports Club of the Army). This may seem like a surprise result, but the Bulgarian national team performed respectably at the 1966 World Cup.

In winning this 1967 European Cup, Celtic became not only the first British team to win the competition since its inception in 1956, but the first team to win from anywhere in Northern Europe. Previous winners had all been from Southern Europe: Real Madrid, Benfica, Inter Milan. Having won the competition in 1964 and 1965, Inter went into this final as strong favourites. Celtic were also missing striker Joe McBride with a knee injury. McBride scored 35 goals in the 1966–67 season finishing top scorer in Scotland – yet didn't play a match after Christmas Eve 1966 because of his injury! In mitigation, Inter were also devoid of star midfielder, Spanish international and Ballon d'Or winner Luis Suarez (yes there was another before the infamous Uruguayan international of modern lore). The Ballon d'Or was awarded to the Best Player in Europe, Suarez winning the award in 1960 while with Barcelona. Inter Milan were on a treble in this 1966–67 season, but fell short just before this final in the Scudetto (Serie A), and in the Coppa Italia semi-finals. This was their last chance to salvage a trophy from their season – perhaps they were psychologically in the wrong place.

In goal for Celtic, Ronnie Simpson was 36 years old on this evening. This might be construed as a prime time for a goalkeeper (the likes of Pat Jennings, Peter Shilton, Gianluigi Buffon of Juventus have played into their early 40s), but it didn't stop the Celtic players giving Simpson the nickname 'Faither' to Simpson due to his perceived older age. Simpson enjoyed a long career with Newcastle United in the 1950s (1951–1960), winning the FA Cup twice in 1951–52 and 1954–55 – Newcastle United, trophy winners – it seems an awful long time ago! Simpson moved back to Scotland in 1960 to play for Edinburgh-based club

Hibernian, before moving to Celtic in 1964. Standing only five feet ten inches, Simpson was not unlike Peter 'The Cat' Bonetti at Chelsea, compensating for his short stature as a goalkeeper with his agility and unorthodox shot-stopping with his forearms and elbows.

Simpson won this European Cup, four league titles, one Scottish Cup and four Scottish League Cups with Celtic. A dislocated shoulder in 1969 brought about his retirement in 1970. Simpson represented Scotland five times, most famously in the 1967 3-2 triumph over World Cup winners England at Wembley. Reflecting his unorthodox style, Simpson saved a header from Sandro Mazzola in Inter's first attack of this final with his knees.

William 'Billy' McNeill captained Celtic on this memorable evening at centre-back. McNeill's association with Celtic was the very essence of longevity – 60 years as a player, manager and club ambassador. Apart from his early association with Blantyre Victoria (a South Lanarkshire club) in junior football, McNeill never played professionally for another club. He signed for Celtic for £250 in 1957 after then-Celtic reserve team coach, and manager on this evening, Jock Stein, saw him playing for Scotland schoolboys against England. McNeill's father was a soldier in the legendary Black Watch. To this day I recall Billy McNeill as a solid, upright, regimented, disciplined footballer and epic team leader. Look at an image of McNeill today and you see a forthright looking man with a strong jaw. McNeill looked like a born leader, yet Celtic failed to win a trophy in eight years in McNeill's early career with the club. McNeill – and Celtic's fortunes – looked up in 1965 when the club won the Scottish Cup, McNeill scoring the winning goal. This was the first year an award was made for Scottish Footballer of the Year and McNeill became its first recipient.

When McNeill was made captain, Celtic began a period of sustained success, winning nine Scottish Championships in a row, in addition to seven Scottish Cups and six Scottish League Cups. McNeill was not the only reason of course. He simply happened to be the perfect leader of a golden generation of players who've come to be regarded as Celtic's best ever team. McNeill, nearly six feet two inches, was always a threat at set pieces, his last-minute header guaranteeing progress against Vojvodina Novi Sad in this year's quarter-final tie. When he retired in 1975, McNeill had appeared in a club record 822 games for Celtic in all competitions. The fact that he was never once substituted in a Celtic game tells you everything about his character, presence and leadership. Given his outstanding leadership qualities it is surprising that McNeill only played 29 times for Scotland 1961–1972, scoring three times.

In 1977 McNeill took his first steps into football management when appointed by Clyde. Only two months later, after Aberdeen's Ally McLeod took on the management of the Scottish national team, Jock Stein recommended McNeill as the Pittodrie-based club's replacement. McNeill stayed only one season with Aberdeen, the club finishing second in the league and being beaten finalists in the Scottish Cup. One of McNeill's legacies was the signing of two players for Aberdeen who went on to enjoy stellar careers in England, Gordon Strachan and Steve Archibald. McNeill only left because he was asked to manage his first love, Glasgow Celtic, in the 1978–79 season. He immediately guided Celtic to the 1978–79 Scottish Championship title. Celtic won the league three times under McNeill, and won the Scottish Cup and Scottish League Cup once apiece. Unusually during this period, the competition for domestic titles came not from perennial rivals Glasgow Rangers, but from Aberdeen and Dundee United during their golden patches – Aberdeen under the guidance of one Alex Ferguson.

At Celtic, McNeill brought on top young players in Paul McStay and Charlie Nicholas, but when Nicholas was sold to Arsenal against McNeill's wishes he moved to England to manage Manchester City, 1983–85. McNeill endured mixed fortunes in England, restoring City to the top flight in a fallow period for the club. He moved again to manage Aston Villa in 1986, but Villa were relegated in 1987, Graham Taylor replacing the Scot at the helm.

McNeill returned to Celtic once more in 1987–88, the club winning the double of league and cup in this their centenary season. Disappointing seasons followed, and Celtic dismissed McNeill in 1991. He would not return to the club again until 2009 when he became an ambassador for Celtic. McNeill had a brief dalliance with Hibernian in 1997–98 as football development manager, but while Hibs also wore green and white, Billy McNeill was a true Celtic man through and through.

How I remember the rampaging runs of Tommy Gemmell at left-back for Celtic on this evening. A tall player for a full-back, Gemmell was right-footed despite usually playing at left-back (as a left-winger myself I always preferred being able to cut in on my right foot). What I never had in 20 years of playing village football was much of a shot. I wish I'd had half the explosive power of Tommy Gemmell's shooting. He may have been a defender, but Gemmell always seemed like an extra attacker in this inventive Celtic team.

Gemmell signed youth terms with Celtic in October 1961, the same day as another 'local' lad, right-winger Jimmy Johnstone. Gemmell and Johnstone became cornerstones of this great Celtic side, the first British team to win the European Cup. Gemmell ignored Jock Stein's orders to stay back as right-back Jim Craig had already ventured forward in this final. The result: a typically ferocious strike that brought Celtic back into this match in Lisbon. Ironically, Craig it was who squared the ball for Gemmell to drive in the equaliser. Gemmell would also score in the 1970 European Cup final defeat against Feyenoord, making him one of three British footballers to score in two different European Cup finals, the others being Phil Neal of Liverpool and Gareth Bale of Real Madrid.

A mark of Gemmell's importance to Celtic as an auxiliary attacker is shown by his goals tally of 63 in 418 appearances in all competitions, a tally as good as any midfield player. He was helped in no small part by being Celtic's penalty taker, scoring 34 times from 37 attempts. Recognisable by his quaffed hair, prominent nose and chin, and most importantly for his galloping runs, Gemmell certainly impacted on me as an 11-year-old watching this wonderful final. Unfortunately Gemmell suffered sectarian abuse from fans – and even some teammates – as a Protestant playing for Catholic Celtic. Surely what matters at the end of the day is a player's commitment to his team, and Tommy Gemmell's was never in question.

Gemmell played 39 games for Nottingham Forest 1971–73, but his best days were behind him. A short stint in the North American Soccer League with Miami

Toros followed. When it seemed Gemmell's time was up, he returned to Scotland, joining Dundee in July 1973. In his first season with Dundee he won the Scottish League Cup... beating Celtic in the final. Gemmell scored once in 18 games for Scotland, 1966–1971, from the penalty spot. Gemmell also plied his trade as a manager with Dundee and Albion Rovers, but the image of this forceful, foraging defender-cum-attacker on the football field is one of my abiding memories of the 1967 European Cup final.

Jim Craig at right-back and John Clark partnering McNeill at centre-back completed Celtic's defence on this glorious night, but to the 11-year-old watching this first great night for British football it was the midfield and attacking players who caught the eye. A retrospective look at these 'Lisbon Lions', as the Celtic team circa 1967 became known, reveals that many of them did not play as often for their country as one might think – this was a mark of the general strength in depth of Scottish club football in those dim and distant 1960s days. A point in case was right midfielder Bobby Murdoch who enjoyed a lengthy career with Celtic spanning almost 500 games 1959–1973, scoring 100 goals in all competitions. A sign of those times, Murdoch signed for Celtic in 1959 as a part-time player while retaining his day job as a sheet-metal worker.

Murdoch was another player this slight 11-year-old admired for his physical presence, his short, dark hair and smart demeanour, a throwback to post-World War 2 times, a decade before perms took over á la Keegan and McDermott!

Murdoch won eight Scottish league titles, four Scottish Cups and five Scottish League Cups in his time at Celtic. It was Murdoch's shot in this 1967 European Cup final that led to Steve Chalmers' deflected winner. Murdoch was redeployed by Jock Stein when the manager took over in 1965 from an old-fashioned inside-right to the deeper-lying right-half position, a switch made in order for the team to benefit from the player's long-passing ability.

A stockily built player, Murdoch struggled with his weight as he got older, and injuries impacted on his previous form come the early 1970s. He remained influential enough to be voted Scottish Footballer of the Year in 1969, but became new Middlesbrough manager Jackie Charlton's first signing in 1973 on a free transfer. Murdoch helped Boro win promotion from the old Division 2 to Division 1 in his first season, proving a useful resource of knowledge and information to his young teammate Graeme Souness. Murdoch retired in 1976, having won only 12 caps for Scotland, but the competition in his position internationally included Glasgow Rangers' gifted Jim Baxter and Leeds United legend Billy Bremner.

Alongside Murdoch in the centre of the park, Bertie Auld started with Celtic in 1955. Auld began as a full-back, became a winger, and started this game in Lisbon as a central midfielder, giving one an idea of his versatility. Auld was sold to Birmingham in 1961, in time to appear in the 1960–61 Inter Cities Fairs Cup (the precursor to the UEFA Cup/Europa League) against A.S. Roma, the Midlands club losing 4-2 on aggregate.

Auld returned to Celtic in 1965 when Jock Stein took over the reins. In the tunnel before this game Auld instigated a version of 'The Celtic Song', a song played over the PA system at Celtic Park, a song part-derived from the 1879 Gilbert and Sullivan comic opera *The Pirates of Penzance*. The Inter Milan players would have been mystified and cowed in equal measure by this comic song regaling their ears. Auld played a total of 176 league games in his two spells at Celtic, scoring 53 league goals, and was capped three times by Scotland.

In an era where wingers were commonplace, Celtic possessed one of the very best in Jimmy Johnstone on their right flank. As a follower of the 'King's Road Playboys' at Chelsea in the late 1960s, I could not understand why the tricky Charlie Cooke did not play more often for Scotland. The reason was 'Jinking' Jimmy Johnstone. The Northern Irish had the cream of the crop in George Best, who would only have to wait 12 months for his moment of European glory, but in Johnstone, Celtic had the second-best winger in British football in 1967. The respect with which Johnstone's tantalising dribbling skills were held came in 2002 when Celtic fans voted the 'wee' man – he was five feet four inches – the best Celtic player of all time. Johnstone was also voted in third place in the 1967 Ballon d'Or for best European player. In 515 appearances for Celtic Johnstone scored 129 goals in all competitions and made goodness knows how many more while reducing defences to quivering wrecks.

Johnstone dribbled round milk bottles as a boy to hone his skills; took a leaf out of Stanley Matthews' book by wearing miner's pit boots to strengthen his calves, a ploy that 'Jinky' thought would add three yards to his pace. Johnstone first became involved with Celtic as a ball boy thanks to his PE teacher Tommy Cassidy's connections with the club. Playing for his local Boys Guild team in the late 1950s, the team travelled to Manchester United to play their boys team. For those old enough to remember, can you imagine a Manchester United team with Jimmy Johnstone on the right and George Best on the left? The idea was mooted at the time – United would have been unplayable.

Johnstone began his playing days at Celtic ignominiously, debuting in a 6-0 defeat at Kilmarnock. It wouldn't happen today, would it? In this debut season of 1963 Johnstone appeared in the Scottish Cup final against Glasgow Rangers, having a goal disallowed in a 1-1 draw. Celtic lost the replay 3-0, Johnstone omitted from the side. In the 1963–64 season Johnstone became a regular in the first team, Celtic reaching the semi-final of the European Cup Winners Cup. Johnstone scored in a 3-0 home win against MKT Budapest. Celtic seemed assured of a final appearance, but in an era of fine Hungarian players, lost the return in Hungary 4-0.

When Jock Stein became manager in 1965, he harboured doubts about Johnstone's individualism, but was eventually won round by Johnstone's pure skill. The 1965–66 season saw Celtic win their first Scottish title in 12 years with Johnstone in the team; once again they lost in the semi-final of the Cup Winners Cup, this time to Liverpool 2-1 on aggregate.

Johnstone scored 82 league goals for Celtic 1962–1975. Upon leaving Celtic he played for San Jose Earthquakes in America, at Sheffield United, Dundee, Shelbourne in Dublin and Elgin City back in Scotland, but by his own admission his motivation and inner drive had departed. Surprisingly, the magical Johnstone played only 23 times for Scotland 1963–1974, scoring four goals, and is remembered more for an offshore boating incident when he was rescued by the Coastguard at Largs, Ayrshire, than for his incredible dribbling skills, and his ability to open up the toughest of defences. In 2008 a bronze statue of Johnstone created by sculptor Kate Robinson was unveiled at the main entrance to Celtic Park. In this era of many highly skilled individualists, Jimmy Johnstone had his doubters and critics, but those who witnessed him grace the green and white hooped shirt first hand only recall a 'pocket genius'.

On the other wing Bobby Lennox was another fine player with a greater pedigree as a goalscorer, another who was voted by Celtic fans into their greatest-ever team. Lennox scored 301 goals in all competitions for the club 1961–1981, winning 11 league titles, eight Scottish Cups and five Scottish League Cups. Pacy, Lennox was tagged by Celtic fans as 'Buzz Bomb'.

After a brief sojourn in America with Houston Hurricane in the NASL – the North American Soccer League – Lennox returned to Celtic in 1978, helping the club to the 1978–79 league title and subsequently the Scottish Cup in 1980. Lennox even managed to score ten goals in these last 42 appearances for the club despite being in his late 30s. Lennox was among the scorers in Scotland's famous 3-2 win over England at Wembley in 1967, but played a meagre ten times for his country, scoring three times. Players of the stature of Bobby Charlton and Alfredo Di Stéfano thought Lennox was the equal of the mercurial Jimmy Johnstone. Lennox was the last of the 'Lisbon Lions' to retire from the professional game.

Another to play just a handful of games for Scotland was striker Willie Wallace, nicknamed 'Wispy'. Wallace had the initial misfortune to step into the shoes of 'Golden Vision' Alex Young at Heart of Midlothian, the 'golden boy' having been sold to Everton in 1961. After a tricky start, Wallace became Hearts' top scorer for four successive seasons, helping the club win the Scottish League Cup in 1962. His form dipped as the top Scottish clubs circled him, but his return of 131 goals in 248 games in all competitions at Hearts was highly respectable.

Wallace, expected to sign for Rangers by the Scottish media, signed instead for Celtic and Jock Stein just six months before this great Lisbon night. Wallace went on to score 140 goals in 239 games for Celtic in all competitions, winning the league title four seasons running, in addition to three Scottish Cups and two Scottish League Cups between 1966 and 1971. Clearly Wallace was a reliable goalscorer. Another shortish player at five feet eight inches, Wallace played seven times for Scotland.

Wallace's co-striker in Lisbon, Stevie Chalmers, began life with the RAF, doing national service at RAF Stradishall near Bury St Edmunds in Suffolk. Returning to Scotland, Chalmers signed professional forms with Celtic in 1959 and went on to become one of the club's greatest goalscorers. Ending his career with Celtic in 1971, Chalmers scored 155 league goals in 263 appearances, scored the winner in this final, and won six league titles, three Scottish Cups and four Scottish League Cups. A broken leg in the 1969–70 season caused Chalmers to miss the 1970 European Cup Final defeat against Feyenoord of Rotterdam. He is the fifth highest score in the Celtic's history, and represented Scotland five times 1964–66, scoring three goals.

In the 60s players were more highly regarded than managers (pre the iconic managers of the 2000s like Ferguson, Mourinho, Guardiola, Klopp et al). Jock Stein acquired iconic status in British football thanks to this first British success in European football. Only Matt Busby at Manchester United and Bill Shankly at Liverpool come close to the regard with which Stein was held at this time.

Like Ferguson with his docker's background, Stein knew how the working class grafted, 'earning his keep' as a young man as a coal miner while playing part-time football with Blantyre Victoria and Albion Rovers. Stein turned professional with Welsh club Llanelli Town in 1950, returning to Celtic to captain a Celtic team that won the league and cup double in 1953–54. Stein played at centre-half, hence knowing a good number 5 when he saw one in Billy McNeill. Persistent ankle injuries meant Stein had to retire early from playing in 1957, but Stein learnt from his experiences. In particular, Celtic players attended the match at Wembley in 1953 in which Hungary humbled England 6-3; Stein too soaked up the opportunity given him by Celtic to attend the 1954 World Cup in Switzerland. Stein absorbed the poor preparation Scotland had for the tournament in comparison to the superior approach of teams such as Hungary.

In June 1957 Stein was appointed coach of Celtic reserves, but as a Protestant it seemed unlikely that he would ever become first team manager. In March 1960 Stein became manager of Dunfermline. His first trophy with Dunfermline came in a Scottish Cup final replay, winning 2-0 against... Celtic. In the 1961–62 season Stein took Dunfermline to the last eight of the European Cup Winners Cup. In the 1962–63 Fairs Cup, Stein's Dunfermline beat Everton, then recovered a four-goal deficit against Spanish side Valencia, only to lose the play-off game.

Stein moved to manage Hibernian in Edinburgh in March 1964, the club's bigger base theoretically bringing him greater opportunities. Stein gained considerable kudos when inviting Real Madrid to play a friendly in Edinburgh which Hibs won 2-0 against a team who had dominated the early years of the European Cup. Hibs won the 1964 Summer Cup, but otherwise remained trophy-less under Stein despite his win percentage rate being the highest of any Hibernian manager.

In March 1965 Jock Stein became Celtic's first-ever Protestant manager, and, incredibly, only the fourth manager in Celtic's club history at this juncture. Celtic immediately won the Scottish Cup under Stein, beating his old club Dunfermline in the final. Stein's one major signing for the 1965–66 season, Joe McBride from Motherwell, repaid the manager's faith with 43 goals. Celtic won the Scottish League Cup, beating city rivals Rangers in the final, but were controversially beaten by Liverpool in the European Cup Winners Cup semi-final, Bobby Lennox's 'goal' that would have put them through on away goals disallowed for offside. The 1966 league title came Celtic's way as compensation for losing the Scottish Cup Final to Rangers. The rivalry between these two clubs was intense in the 1960s. In those halcyon days for Scottish football there wasn't more than a hair's breadth between the country's two strongest clubs, the standard of their players the equal of any of those in the upper reaches of the old England top-flight 1st Division.

Stein had imprinted the belief in his players that they could win everything in 1967. He seemed to have the Midas touch and it was apparent that he was a master motivator before Alex Ferguson ever claimed the mantle. Celtic beat Aberdeen 2-0 to win the 1967 Scottish Cup Final. A 2-2 draw in the final game of the

1966–67 season with great rivals Rangers secured the Scottish league title. With the League Cup also under their belt, this European Cup triumph meant Stein became the first manager in British football history to win every competition his club entered in a single season.

In 1967–68 Celtic won the League and Cup double for the third year running. In 1968–69 they won a second domestic treble in three years. The team were absolutely in their pomp but could not win the European Cup for a second time in 1970, losing out to Holland's second-best club of the time, Feyenoord. This was the beginning of a period of sustained quality in Dutch football. Despite losing the final, Celtic had overcome Benfica and Leeds United to reach the top European club game in Milan. Manchester United were keen to take Stein from Celtic but Stein remained loyal to Celtic. In 1970 Stein received a CBE, that would have been an OBE but for a notorious Intercontinental match against the Argentines of Racing Club, a game that saw four Celtic players sent off. The Argentines had not forgotten the sending off of their country's captain Antonio Rattin at the 1966 World Cup in the quarter-final at Wembley.

Stein completed nine successive Scottish League titles with Celtic, equalling the world record at the time jointly held by MKT Budapest in Hungary and CSKA Sofia in Bulgaria. Such was Celtic's dominance of Scottish football in this period – the early 70s – that the Scottish Football League reconstructed its format in 1975. After a serious car crash in 1975 when Stein nearly died, he returned to oversee a tenth league and cup double in 1976–77 but was asked to stand down in 1978 after a season of struggle.

Stein moved to manage Leeds United in August 1978. Infamously, Brian Clough only lasted a month after attempting to replace the man the Leeds players admired and respected, Don Revie. The players were happier about Stein's appointment, but the team were in decline and when Ally MacLeod resigned as Scotland manager, Stein stepped into the breach. Ironically, Stein, like Clough, managed Leeds for only 44 days, but left without the rancour surrounding Clough's departure.

Stein believed that the Scottish national team played with too much emotion, a trait that saw them lose games they might win with a more detached approach. Scotland lost to Belgium twice in the European Championship qualifiers, failing to reach the 1980 tournament. These losses were put into context by Belgium reaching the final, only to lose to West Germany. Stein did enable Scotland's qualification for the 1982 World Cup finals in Spain, his only major tournament appearance as a manager. A 5-2 win over New Zealand was followed by a 4-1 defeat against a super-talented Brazil side, despite the Scots taking an early lead courtesy of a thunderous strike from David Narey. In a final group game requiring victory to progress the Scots drew 2-2 with the Soviet Union, departing the tournament on goal difference. Scotland played well enough to get through, but at world level there always heightened challenges.

Tragically, Jock Stein died while in charge of the Scottish national team. Scotland pulled level with Wales 1-1 at Ninian Park, Cardiff, in 1986, securing a play-off qualification. The intensity of the occasion, coupled with Stein's abstaining from taking medication for heart disease led to the great man's sad demise. Alex Ferguson, his assistant manager, led Scotland to victory in the play-off match against Australia, and into the 1986 World Cup finals, but Stein's death came as a great shock. Jock Stein had a massive physical presence and aura; he transformed players' careers with his man-to-man motivational skills. A giant of a man, and a giant in the pantheon of Scottish football, Stein's loss was felt enormously in British football as a whole.

The Inter Milan team were captained by Armando Picchi, playing at the rear behind three further defenders. This new role in the modern game became known as the 'libero', or sweeper system. Picchi started out as a forward, became a central midfielder, then a right-back, but was switched to libero by then-incumbent manager, the Argentine Helenio Herrera. The libero suited Herrera's nod to the *'catenaccio'* system, the 'spider's web' that enmeshed opponents and ensured many a 1-0 victory for Inter. Picchi's influence spread to those in front of him, players such as Tarcisio Burgnich and Giacinto Facchetti, players who would feature in a strong Italian national team who went on to win the 1968 European Championships, and were beaten finalists against the great Brazilian team at the 1970 World Cup in Mexico.

With Picchi revelling in this libero role, Inter won three Scudettos (Serie As), the European Cup in 1964 and 1965, and two Intercontinental Cups. Ironically, Picchi was deemed too defensive-minded by Italian national coach Edmondo Fabbri to be chosen for the 1966 World Cup squad. When Ferruccio Valcareggi replaced Fabbri as head coach, Picchi won call-ups for the national team. He played 12 times for Italy 1964–68, but a fractured pelvis denied him the opportunity of appearing in the successful 1968 European Championship-winning team. Picchi set the template for the sweepers who followed him in Italy, most famously Franco Baresi at AC Milan. Picchi was small at a shade under five feet eight inches, but he was quick, read the game well, and led the team by example with his swift interceptions at the back. Sadly the Livorno-born Picchi contracted cancer soon after beginning a coaching career. He died, aged 35, in 1971, his final role in football being that of Juventus coach in the 1970–71 season.

Tarcisio Burgnich featured on the right side of Inter's defence on this evening, as he would for Italy's successful national team during this period, but 'La Roccia' (the Rock) as he was dubbed by Picchi, could play equally well as a centre-back or in Picchi's own sweeper role. Burgnich was the consummate defender, quick, strong, able to supplement the attack, but obdurate defensively.

Burgnich appeared in almost 500 Serie A games, initially with Udinese, Juventus and Palermo, but found his feet when transferring to Inter Milan in 1962, where he stayed until 1974. Burgnich won Serie A with Juventus in 1960–61, but Inter provided him with the platform to win the title four more times. Controversially sold to Napoli in 1974, Burgnich won the Coppa Italia in 1976 in the sunset of his career. He played 66 times for Italy 1963–1974, scoring twice, one of those famously in the 1970 World Cup semi-final 4-3 victory against West Germany that was tagged 'The Game of the Century'. Burgnich thought Pele was just 'skin and bones' like any other player – but conceded he was wrong after Pele orchestrated Italy's downfall in the 1970 World Cup Final. Outwitted he may have been by the great Edson Arantes do Nascimento (Pele), but Burgnich forged a rock-like stature at the heart of a sterling Italian rearguard over the course of a decade in the 60s and 70s.

On the left side of Inter's supremely organised defence, the tall majestic Giacinto Facchetti was one of the great Italian players of this era. The six feet three inches Facchetti was exceptionally tall for a full-back, but like Burgnich he could adapt to play as a centre-back. The quality of Facchetti's defending is vindicated by his selection in second place for the 1965 Ballon d'Or. Facchetti also supplemented the attack to considerably greater effect than Burgnich. In 634 games for Inter in all competitions Facchetti scored 75 goals. Facchetti followed Picchi as captain of Inter, also captaining Italy for several years.

Born in Treviglio, Bergamo, in Lombardy, Northern Italy, Facchetti started out with Trevigliese, his hometown club, as a pacy forward with exemplary technique and a great shot. It was Herrera again who converted him to the left-back position, encouraging him to attack whenever the situation allowed it. Facchetti is considered one of the first attacking full-backs in the vein we now term wing-back. Facchetti's stamina was great which meant his defensive prowess was rarely compromised. He held the record for goals scored by a defender in Serie A (ten in 1965) until it was broken by Marco Materazzi in 2000–01. Facchetti's compensation comes in his 59 goals in Serie A, making him the top-scoring defender in the history of the Scudetto.

Capped 94 times by Italy, scoring three goals, he wore the captain's armband 70 times. He was chosen in the Team of the Tournament at the 1968 European Championships; played at the 1966, 1970 and 1974 World Cups, captaining the team at the latter two tournaments. He was also named in the 1970 World Cup Team of the Tournament. An outstanding technician renowned for his pace, anticipation and power, Facchetti's sportsmanship was generally highly regarded, being sent off only once in a near-20 years career. Pele thought Facchetti was one of the top 125 greatest living footballers in FIFA 100th anniversary celebrations in 2004; in 2015 Facchetti was posthumously inducted into the Italian Football Hall of Fame. Perhaps most pertinently, Internazionale posthumously retired the number 3 shirt in his honour. A massively talented, classical defender with an attacking threat to boot, Giacinto Facchetti was one of the icons of 1960s and 1970s European football.

Alongside Burgnich and Facchetti, Aristide Guarneri was also regarded as a 'gentleman of the game' due to never being sent off, preferring instead to apply his tenacity and reading of the game to winning the ball without recourse to illegal play. Guarneri played 21 times for Italy 1963–68, completing a seriously strong Inter defence on this evening.

In the absence of Luis Suarez, Inter's star man on this evening was, ostensibly, Sandro Mazzola. In the event Celtic managed to stifle Mazzola's threat by dint of their own desire to attack the Italians come what may. Mazzola was regarded as one of Europe's greatest talents in 1967 due to his speed, technical ability, creativity, and eye for goal. Like Facchetti, Mazzola was a one-club man, playing 417 Serie A games, scoring 116 goals. Mazzola's father Valentino also played as an attacking midfielder-cum-forward. Tragically, Valentino died in the Superga air disaster of 1949 that took the lives of the entire Torino team, a forerunner to the equally awful air crash that decimated the Busby Babes in 1958.

Signing for Inter in 1960, Mazzola became central to Inter's success in the 60s, the team becoming known as Grande Inter. He was initially a little in the shadow of Suarez, Herrera's general, who came from Barcelona with him, but Mazzola possessed sufficient skill of his own to become one of the team's brightest talents. In the 1964 European Cup final Mazzola scored twice as Spanish giants Real Madrid were beaten 3-1 in Vienna. Inter retained the trophy in 1965 by beating Benfica. In 1966 Real Madrid avenged the defeat by Inter, winning the semi-final contest between the clubs. Mazzola gained his own personal glory in the 1965–66 season by finishing Serie A top scorer with 17 goals. Mazzola opened the scoring from the penalty spot in this 1967 European Cup final. Inter reached the final again in 1972, only to lose to an imperious Johan Cruyff-led Ajax 2-0. In 1971 Mazzola finished second in the Ballon d'Or behind… Cruyff.

Like his peers at Inter, Mazzola won Serie A four times with this 'Grande Inter' team: 1963, 1965, 1966 and 1971. Mazzola played 70 times for Italy 1963–1974, scoring 22 times. He was part of the Italian team that were pelted with tomatoes upon returning home after an early exit from the 1966 World Cup. On a happier note, he was named in the Team of the Tournament as Italy triumphed on home soil in the 1968 European Championships.

Opinion was deeply divided in Italy in 1970 as to who should play in the attacking midfielder's role: Mazzola or AC Milan's hugely gifted Gianni Rivera. Coach Valcareggi did not feel the two 'superstars' could play together – Gerrard and Lampard for England in the 2000s? Mazzola was quicker; Rivera the more influential playmaker who could dictate the tempo of the game. Valcareggi controversially deployed the pair in the quarter-finals one half at a time – Mazzola in the first half, Rivera in the second when the tempo of the game slowed in the Mexican heat. With Rivera influencing the defeat of West Germany massively in the semi-final, Mazzola was not included in the starting line-up for the 1970 World Cup final.

In 1974 the two players played together at the World Cup, but an ageing team were eliminated in the first round. Mazzola's forte was his speed and athleticism. He was almost balletic in style as a slim player in an era before players became behemoths, huge physical specimens. For a period of time in the mid-1960s Sandro Mazzola's technical and tactical prowess, his close control, and reading of the game made him one of the world's best players.

One of the players who'd caught my eye as my interest in world football grew through reading Brian Glanville's *International Foot*ball books was the lively right-winger Angelo Domenghini. Once again, as a wide player myself, I was drawn to a team's right- and left-wingers (in old parlance).

Domenghini won the Coppa Italia with his first professional club, Atalanta from Bergamo, Lombardy, in 1963, scoring a hat-trick in the final against Torino. Moving to Inter Milan under Herrera in 1964, Domenghini played 164 games in all competitions 1964–69, scoring 54 goals. Transferring to Cagliari in 1969, Domenghini immediately assisted the Sardinian side to his third Serie A title (two with Inter), forming an attacking triumvirate par excellence with Luigi Riva and Sergio Gori. Domenghini scored 18 goals in 99 Serie A matches with Cagliari.

He spent a season with A.S. Roma in 1973–74, and then moved to Verona in Serie B, immediately helping the team rise to Serie A in 1975. Domenghini played 33 times for Italy 1963–1972, scoring eight goals, the most important an equalising free kick in the 80th minute of the 1968 European Championship final against Yugoslavia to snatch a 1-1 draw. Italy went on to win the replay 2-0, claiming their first ever European Championship title, and Domenghini was named in the Team of the Tournament. Quick, agile, technically adept, Domenghini was my kind of player.

On the left-wing in Lisbon, Mario Corso was something of a legend in Italy. He played for Internazionale 1957–1973, appearing in 413 Serie A games, scoring 75 goals. Corso was credited with possessing 'God's left foot' due to his outstanding crossing ability and free-kick skills. Strangely, for such a highly rated player, he never played tournament football for Italy, despite receiving 23 caps, and scoring four goals. Largely ignored by his country, FIFA saw fit to play him in an all-star international team playing a prestige friendly against Spain in 1967. The reluctance to select Corso more frequently for Italy seemed to stem from his free-spirited approach to the game, his undoubted technical ability undermined by a perceived lack of tactical discipline. Corso believed the ball should do the work. It's difficult to deny this belief if the end product is there.

Helenio Herrera, Buenos Aires-born, was one of the most famous managers in the world in 1967. Managing Atlético Madrid 1949–1952, he won La Liga twice in Spain; at Barcelona 1958–1960 he won the title twice more. At loggerheads with Hungarian star László Kubala at Barcelona – he left him out of the 1960 European Cup semi-final which Barca lost 6-2 to Real Madrid, Herrera was subsequently removed from his position as manager, and Kubala was restored to the team. Herrera moved to Inter Milan in 1960, enjoying an eight-year period of constant success. It was his 'Verrou' door-bolt system, later tagged 'catenaccio' that ensured Inter's dominance in Italy and Europe in the middle 1960s. At first Herrera combined his duties at Inter with managing the Spanish national team 1960–62. The 'catenaccio' system not only stifled opponents' attacking threat, but was supplemented to allow greater flexibility to counter-attack. This became Inter's mantra in the 1960s, a method even adapted for home games, when in England and Scotland the onus would be on the home team to attack.

In 1968 Herrera moved to Roma, becoming the highest paid manager in the world. The age of the 'superstar manager' had arrived. In his first season in Rome the Coppa Italia was won, but erratic results cost Herrera his job the following season. Herrera took the reins at Inter Milan for the 1973–74 season, but a heart attack meant he needed to choose a quieter life thereafter.

Helenio Herrera was the first international manager to use psychology to motivate his players. Slogans around his training grounds were commonplace, such as 'Class+ Preparation+Intelligence+Athleticism'. Herrera encouraged his players to chant these slogans during training sessions. He also preceded Arsene Wenger's influence in England by around 30 years by controlling diets. Herrera's attitude towards the game was the antithesis of Barcelona's 'tika-taka' football, decrying the obsession with ball possession, feeling the ball moved quicker in a counter-attacking system. To this end, Herrera's swift, strong, attacking full-backs at Inter, Burgnich and Facchetti, became key players. The addition of the deeper-lying playmaker with great passing ability, Luis Suarez, ensured Herrera's years at Inter Milan were hugely successful.

THE FINAL

This European Cup final, more than any other in living memory, is best known for attack triumphing over defence. Inter's '*catenaccio*' system was legendary going into the game. Jock Stein promised before the game that Celtic would attack at all times. How he kept his word. Despite going behind early on to an Inter team tuned to 'shutting up shop' and closing down games, Celtic attacked in waves, their sheer will-to-win and desire to play the game 'the right way' making this a final that has come to be regarded as a triumph for football.

Mazzola's header was saved in an early attack by the redoubtable Ronnie Simpson's knees. Mazzola kept his nerve when Inter were awarded a penalty, sending Simpson the wrong way to give Inter a 1-0 lead. All onlookers knew what was supposed to occur from here on. Inter would defend the lead as if their lives depended on it. Celtic duly had 90% possession in the first half alone.

The second half was a relentless wave of green and white hooped attack, an equaliser finally coming when Tommy Gemmell's rocket shot beat Sarti in the Inter goal all ends up. Seven minutes from time ,Bobby Murdoch drove the ball goalwards and Stevie Chalmers reacted to divert the ball past Sarti. Gemmell felt Inter played into Celtic's hands by playing so many men behind the ball. I remember on the night the relentless Celtic pressure, the seeming inevitability that attack would win out over defence in the end. The Lisbon stadium is known as 'The Stadium of Light', and how the sun shone that evening in 1967. Jock Stein looked resplendent in sunglasses. It was an emotional evening, and I for one, though not Scottish, was a proud 'Brit' as Celtic became the first British team to win the European Cup with some style.

1967–68 EUROPEAN CUP FINAL
Manchester United 4 v 1 Benfica (after extra time)

Twelve months on from the 'Lisbon Lions' and I was an even prouder English 'Brit'. Manchester United had been on a ten-year quest to purge the awful horror of the 1958 Munich air disaster, a plane crash that left manager Matt Busby's life hanging by a thread. Busby appeared on the touchline at Wembley in 1968 at the helm of a fine United team possessing the world-class talents of Bobby Charlton and George Best. It could be argued Busby's team on this night was a comparative hotchpotch compared to the sadly unfulfilled promise of the Busby Babes, many of whom perished at the end of an ice-bound runway in Bavaria. The world would never know after that tragic, catastrophic night in 1958.

Route to the Final

Celtic, the proud holders of the European Cup from 1967, found themselves eliminated in the first round in 1967–68 at the hands of the Russian team Dynamo Kiev. Manchester United comfortably beat Hibernians of Malta 4-0 on aggregate, before squeezing through three further rounds by one-goal margins. Busby's '68 team were not going to make the winning of this long yearned for trophy easy. In the second round, United beat Sarajevo from Bosnia 2-1 on aggregate; in the last eight the Poles Górnik Zabrze were beaten by the same score.

In the semi-finals United beat Real Madrid 1-0 at Old Trafford thanks to a George Best goal. The return at the Bernabeu Stadium was a real roller-coaster ride. Three first half goals for Madrid from star players Pirri, Francisco Gento (the wonderful left-winger from the great 1950s side was still playing in 1968) and Amancio, gave Real the ascendancy, United replying with an own goal from Zoco. For much of the game it seemed United would lose out on the much longed for Busby quest to reach the final. With time running out and United's spirits rallying manfully with one last valiant cry, two goals came from unlikely sources: utility/midfield player David Sadler in the 73rd minute, and centre-back Bill Foulkes, heroically one of the survivors of the 1958 Munich air crash, in the 80th minute. United's never-say die spirit and commitment (as with Celtic the previous year) to attacking football saved the day, United progressing 4-3 on aggregate after this courageous 3-3 draw in Madrid against all the odds.

Benfica reached the final with European superstar Eusébio as the tournament's top scorer with six goals. Gento and Amancio scored five and four respectively for Real Madrid, Best and Sadler accumulated three each by the tournament's end. Surprisingly, the celebrated Benfica team, winners of the European Cup in 1961 and 1962, but arguably past their peak in 1968, only drew 1-1 on aggregate with Northern Irish side Glentoran in the first round, winning thanks to a very late 86th-minute away goal from Eusébio in Antrim in the first leg. Benfica then narrowly beat the French team Saint-Étienne 2-1 on aggregate in the second round, before despatching Vasa Budapest of Hungary 3-0 in the last eight. Having endured a tricky passage to the semi-finals, Benfica raised their game considerably in the last 4 by beating Italian giants Juventus 2-0 at home, and 1-0 away, Eusébio scoring in both games.

Although this would be Benfica's fifth European Cup final (it helped their cause considerably that in Eusébio they had arguably the second-best player in the world at that time after Pele), and Manchester United's first, United were strong pre-match favourites with the final being played in England at Wembley. The choice of Wembley was considered advantageous to United, making the game more like a home tie. It seemed that not just all of Britain, but the entire world wanted United to win the trophy as scant recompense for the dreadful loss of lives in Munich on that snowy night in Munch in 1958. The only thing that could deny United their win would be an over-emotional approach to the game – but how could this have been anything other than a hugely emotional evening?

Sadly for United, one of their fearsome attacking triumvirate, Denis Law, had undergone a knee operation the weekend before the final. In goal for United, Alex Stepney initially failed a trial with Fulham, ending up with Tooting and Mitcham United in the semi-professional game. Millwall signed Stepney as an amateur in 1963, swiftly elevating him to their professional ranks. Playing 158 games in all competitions for Millwall, Stepney earned 3 U-23 England caps while at The Den.

In May 1966, in a curious transfer, Stepney was signed by the great character Tommy Docherty at Chelsea for £50,000. The turbulent Scot Docherty intended alternating Stepney with Peter 'The Cat' Bonetti, but Stepney played only once for Chelsea before Manchester United signed him in August 1966. It was to be the beginning of Stepney's longest and happiest association in professional football. Stepney had to step into the boots of another Munich 1958 hero and survivor, Harry Gregg, who famously went back into the wrecked plane to haul out other survivors including Bobby Charlton and Matt Busby. Gregg's career came to an end due to injury.

The 1967–68 season started inauspiciously for Stepney. In the Charity Shield against Tottenham Hotspur at Wembley, Stepney was deceived by Pat Jennings's long down-field punt, conceding a goal to his opposing goalkeeper! This put United 2-0 down. He was fortunate to have Bobby Charlton (two goals) and Denis Law (one) in his team as the game ended a 3-3 draw.

A highly capable keeper, Stepney remained down the pecking order for England custodian behind Gordon Banks (Stoke City), Bonetti, Everton's Gordon West and Sheffield Wednesday's Peter Springett. Stepney won his one and only full international cap a mere week before this European Cup final, in a victory over Sweden.

When United were relegated in 1974, their European Cup-winning team having aged as much as their 1968 opponents Benfica, Stepney had the last laugh on his old adversary Pat Jennings. Under new manager Tommy Docherty (life is full of delicious ironies), Stepney scored twice from penalty kicks as United bounced straight back up to the top flight as 1974–75 Division 2 champions.

Alex Stepney created his own history by being the last player from the 1968 European Cup-winning team to play under Matt Busby before the great man (Busby) retired in 1971. Stepney played 546 games in all competitions for United, playing his last game for the club in April 1978. United reached the FA Cup Final in both 1976 and 1977 with Stepney in goal, losing the first to Southampton 1-0, but winning the second against Liverpool 2-1. The vagaries of football are revealed by the fact that United were strong favourites in 1976, and underdogs in 1977. Never attempt to predict the outcome of a football match. Stepney kept 175 clean sheets in those 546 games, an impressive record, especially in the pre-Ferguson era when United were better known for their attacking proficiency, and lacked the class of defender Ferguson would enjoy having in his teams: the Pallisters, Bruces, Irwins, Stams, Vidics, Ferdinands and Gary Nevilles. Alex Stepney is best remembered for being a great organiser and talker at the rearguard of his team, a top trait in a goalkeeper.

United's full-backs in Lisbon were a pair of Republic of Ireland internationals, Seamus 'Shay' Brennan, and Tony Dunne. Brennan actually played his first game for United in an FA Cup match against Sheffield Wednesday in 1958, the very first game after the horrific Munich air disaster. Brennan, right-back on this evening, played as a left-winger against Wednesday on that day in 1958, scoring twice. Brennan replaced the departed legend-in-the-making David Pegg, and the injured Albert Scanlon, casualties of the air crash.

Brennan was born in Manchester, but qualified for the Republic of Ireland through his Irish parents, the first player to qualify for the Republic in this way. Brennan enjoyed a long career with United, playing 359 games 1957–1970, helping the club to the league title in 1965 and 1967. Brennan became the first member of the '68 team to die, suffering a heart attack while playing golf near Waterford, Munster, in 2000. His death preceded that of George Best by five years. Brennan played 19 times for the Republic of Ireland.

Dunne joined United in 1960 after winning the Football Association of Ireland Cup with Shelborne in his second year in senior football. Moving to United, he stayed at Old Trafford for 13 years, making over 500 appearances in all competitions. After being released by United in 1973, Dunne played a further six seasons with Bolton Wanderers, helping the club win the old 2nd Division in 1977–78. Dunne won the FA Cup in 1963, United beating Leicester City 3-1, as well as sharing Brennan's title successes in 1965 and 1967. Dunne did well to make this 1968 European Cup Final at all, having ruptured his Achilles tendon in the quarter-finals against Górnik Zabrze.

Internationally, Dunne represented the Republic of Ireland 33 times, captaining his country on four occasions. He was named Irish Footballer of the Year in 1969. Short in stature, smartly turned out with his dark hair, Dunne seemed to me to be the epitome of a 60s full-back, unlikely the lanky, statuesque Facchetti from Inter Milan the previous year.

Speaking of archetypal players, no player in this '68 United team better epitomised the post-World War 2 footballer than centre-back Bill Foulkes. Foulkes looked like your granddad in a team that contained 60s fashion icons in the shape of Best and Law. Foulkes had short back and sides hair, looked rugged, and was heroic on the scale of teammate Harry Gregg in assisting teammates in the wrecked debris of the Munich airplane in 1958. Foulkes's rugged looks may have come from his father who captained St Helens rugby league team and played 'league' for England.

The mid-1950s were very different days. Foulkes was another who continued working his 'day job' (as a miner at Lee Green Colliery) while playing junior football. By 1954 Foulkes played his one and only game for England and was firmly established as a professional player with Manchester United. Only then did he cease working down the mines. Foulkes enjoyed a near-20-year career at United, 1951–1970. His first goal – of nine – came against Newcastle United from 45 yards out – quite a feat for a defender – in the 1953–54 season. In 1955–56 United won the title with Foulkes in the side. At the end of this season Foulkes was called up for national service, temporarily losing his place in the United team. Buckling down upon his return, the committed Foulkes regained his place in the first team.

The Football League did not want English clubs to partake in the early seasons of the European Cup, feeling European commitments would be a distraction from the serious matter of domestic football. Did we always have our heads in the sand?

In Matt Busby, United had a pro-active manager who could see the value of confrontation and competition with the best club teams in Europe. United consequently went against Football League feeling in entering the 1956–57

European Cup. Early signs were good for the Busby Babes, as their young starlets of the mid-late 1950s had already been tagged, as they thrashed Belgium's Anderlecht 10-0. This remains a record victory in the annals of Manchester United's history. In a season of rich promise for the 'Babes', United lost out in the semi-finals of the European Cup to the all-conquering Puskás-Di Stéfano -Gento-led Real Madrid 5-3 on aggregate. United then lost the FA Cup Final 2-1 to Aston Villa, but found solace in a second successive league title.

After defeating Red Star Belgrade of Yugoslavia 5-4 on aggregate in the 1957–58 quarter-finals (Bobby Charlton scored three of the goals, two on the tragic night when United drew 3-3 in Belgrade), United's plane stopped off to refuel in Munich. The British Embassy in Belgrade gave United's successful players a bottle of gin each to take home with them. Their take-off twice aborted on the snowy runway in Munich, Foulkes remained angry for years afterwards that a third attempt came to grief with the loss of two-thirds of the Busby Babes team. It was clear to Foulkes that take-off should not have been considered, partly because of boost-surge problems with the plane, partly because of the appalling weather conditions. Ironically, Foulkes's bottle of gin, placed above him in the overhead rack, hit him on the head upon crashing. It was the only injury Bill Foulkes suffered.

Following the air crash, Foulkes took over the captaincy of United from the sadly deceased Roger Byrne. United struggled, understandably, with younger players promoted from the junior ranks, in addition to players brought into the club courtesy of the goodwill of other English Football League clubs. The semi-finals of the 1957–58 European Cup took place as per the rules and regulations, a weakened United side somehow defeating AC Milan 2-1 at Old Trafford, but the return in the San Siro resulted in a 0-4 defeat. United would have to wait a decade for another European Cup Final opportunity.

United finished second in the 1958–59 league season, a creditable achievement with a dramatically changed team, but fell away badly thereafter, finishing 15th in the 1961–62 season. They fared even worse in 1962–63, ending in 19th place, narrowly avoiding relegation, yet won the FA Cup, defeating Leicester City 3-1. Foulkes was struggling with his weight, but he was struggling psychologically as well as physically. Only in the 1963–64 season did he begin to enjoy his football again, a season in which United finished second in the league. By now the mercurial George Best had arrived at the club. In 1964–65 United won the league, Foulkes now regularly playing as a centre-back rather than as a full-back. Foulkes and Bobby Charlton were the only Munich 1958 survivors. When Foulkes aided United's 1966–67 league triumph it was his fourth league title. No other United player would compete with this feat for another 32 years.

When United won the European Cup on this emotional evening at Wembley in 1968, Foulkes was 36 years old. Foulkes felt that winning the trophy helped to cast aside some of the demons he'd been living with since 1958. Retirement was foremost in Foulkes's mind now, but Busby persuaded him to stay at Old Trafford until he was 38, even though appearances in the first team were very limited. At this juncture – 1970 – Foulkes held United's record appearances with 688, although Charlton superseded him a year later, eventually completing 758 appearances. Only Ryan Giggs and Paul Scholes have since passed Foulkes's total, making the 'old warrior' fourth in United's all-time appearance list.

In retirement Foulkes remained as a youth team coach at Old Trafford until 1975, completing 25 years unbroken service. In May 2008 Foulkes attended the Champions League Final in Moscow (United winning on penalties against Chelsea), one of five players still living after the 1958 Munich air disaster. Bill Foulkes (he passed away in May 2013) should be remembered – despite his protestations – for being as much of a hero as Harry Gregg for his selflessness in assisting the injured in the wrecked plane on the Munich airfield in 1958.

David Sadler wore the number 10 shirt on this late May 1968 evening, but played alongside Foulkes at the heart of United's defence. Sadler was a player in the mould of Leeds United's Paul Madeley, a utility player capable of playing as a defender, midfield player or even as an emergency striker. A throwback in appearance with his short, smart hairstyle, Sadler played elegantly too. Born in Yalding, Kent, Sadler played semi-professionally with Maidstone United before signing for Manchester United in 1963. For a player from such modest beginnings, Sadler fared well, playing four times for England 1967–1970. In 272 league games Sadler scored 22 goals.

It was in midfield and attack that United excelled in 1968, their defence considered a little vulnerable. On the right side of midfield, the Scotsman Pat Crerand, a Glaswegian of Irish descent, was a cultured player, a fine passer of the ball who also never shirked a tackle. In short, Crerand was the archetypal midfield player. Crerand lost his father when he was just two years old, Crerand senior the victim of a German air raid on John Brown's shipyard in Clydebank, Glasgow. The memories of World War 2 remained stark and vivid in 1968.

Crerand began his professional career with Celtic in 1958, playing 120 times in Glasgow, before signing for United on the fifth anniversary of the Munich air disaster on 6 February 1963. The timing of the signing indicates another player, along. with Foulkes and Charlton, who felt it was a personal crusade to win the European Cup for Matt Busby and his surviving colleagues. George Best, reputedly looked around for Pat Crerand when opponents dished out the rough stuff on the football field. The pugnacious Crerand would invariably be right by Best's side. United would be Crerand's only other professional club after Celtic.

Ultimately Crerand played 401 times for United in all competitions, scoring 19 goals. In an era of gifted Scottish midfielders, Crerand played 16 times for Scotland 1961–65. He was another who remained at United as a coach when his playing days ended in 1971.

United's midfield in 1968 certainly didn't lack for grit. Wearing number 6, Norbert 'Nobby' Stiles suffered somewhat by comparison to the richly talented Charlton-Law-Best triumvirate, but we're talking about a World Cup-winner here. Stiles could play, but given a man-to-man marking job he would carry it out to the letter. Stiles had already marked Eusébio out of the 1966 World Cup semi-final, and by and large, he duly achieved the same at Wembley in 1968. Yes, Eusébio had chances in this game, but they were restricted by the ferocity of Stiles's tackling and his relentless close-marking of the great Mozambique-born superstar.

Nobby Stiles's career is largely associated with Manchester United, although after his time at Old Trafford he spent further spells in the north of England with Middlesbrough and Preston North End. Another 'war baby', Stiles was born in the cellar of his family home in Collyhurst, Manchester, during an air raid in 1942. Evidence of the skill Stiles possessed that is largely ignored by his destructive midfield qualities came early as he represented England Schoolboys aged 15. Short in stature at five feet six inches, short-sighted (he wore contact lenses on the field), gap-toothed, Stiles didn't replicate the perceived idea of the natural footballer, but he belied this with his fearsome character.

When Stiles won the ball, he'd usually look for Charlton or Best to give the team forward momentum. Peter Reid later perfected this holding role for Howard Kendall's successful 1980s Everton side. Every team needs a holding player and Stiles knew his limitations, while understanding how much he gave the team in other ways. Stiles's style didn't always sit comfortably with the attack-minded Busby – he left him out of the 1963 FA Cup Final team, but later came to realise that you needed a Stiles in your team if you were going to nullify a player of the class of Eusébio.

Stiles eventually completed 395 matches for United, scoring 19 goals. At Middlesbrough Stiles played 57 league games 1971–73, before signing for Preston North End (as did David Sadler) for a further two seasons. Stiles only played 28 times for England, his only goal scored against West Germany prior to the triumphant 1966 World Cup. At the '66 World Cup, Alf Ramsey – a notorious 'team before the individual' man (the great Jimmy Greaves suffered at Ramsey's behest) – praised Stiles's man-marking of Eusébio in the semi-final against Portugal. Stiles played his part again against a talented West German team in the final, but it was his 'toothless dance' at the end of the final that remains one of 1966's most iconic images.

Stiles kept his England position in 1967, but Ramsey soon came to prefer Tottenham Hotspur's all-action Alan Mullery. The irony arose when Mullery was sent off in the 1968 European Championship semi-final; England beaten by a Dragan Dzajic inspired Yugoslavia. Stiles had been berated by other nations and portions of the media for his over-vigorous approach. Mullery was a more rounded player, but clearly no less aggressive!

Like the immaculate Bobby Charlton, Stiles attempted management with Preston North End, Vancouver Whitecaps and West Bromwich Albion without much joy. His coaching legacy is appreciated better by his return to United as a youth team coach helping forward the young careers of David Beckham, Nicky Butt, Paul Scholes and the Neville brothers Gary and Phil. In 2000 Stiles was awarded an MBE. The 'toothless wonder' of those halcyon days of '66 and '68 passed away in October 2020.

What to say about Bobby Charlton? He is simply one of the greatest players to ever grace an England shirt. Grace is an apt word to describe the manner in which Charlton played his football. The very best players make the game look easy, the way in which they glide across the pitch. I thought I was a half-decent, reasonably quick left-winger, but there was another young man playing for a nearby village team who effortlessly skimmed across the turf and was most certainly quicker than I. He went on to play for a local town team – I continued languishing in lower-level football. Charlton owned this effortless grace at the very highest level, a trait shared by the inimitable Jimmy Greaves.

Shortish at five feet seven inches, Bobby was referred to by elder brother Jackie as 'our kid'. Two years younger, but six inches shorter than Jackie, Bobby was the naturally talented one, an appraisal Jackie always graciously referred to himself. An attacking midfielder whose balletic style was allied to a truly explosive shot (that always seemed an injustice to me for whom power never came at all), Charlton began life in the professional game with United as a left-winger. I admired Bobby too greatly for his sportsmanship (only Gary Lineker equated to Charlton on this count in my eyes). Charlton was only booked twice in a top-level 20-year career, once for England against Argentina in the 1966 World Cup quarter-final (it's a wonder the whole team weren't booked in that game such was the provocation) and once for United.

The Charlton brothers' story is legendary. Born in Ashington, Northumberland, the Charltons were from mining stock, making them the classic 'rags to riches' tale, the classic instance of young working-class men rising above moderate beginnings. Charlton – acknowledged by Franz Beckenbauer as his most awkward opponent (they cancelled each other out in the 1966 World Cup Final) – was named in four World Cup squads – 1958, 1962, 1966 and 1970, although he did not play in the team in 1958. When he retired internationally in 1970, Charlton held the international caps record for England (106), although he has since been passed by six players. He was also England and Manchester United's record goalscorer for decades until surpassed on both counts by Wayne Rooney. Charlton's 49 goals for England were only five more than the 44 scored by Jimmy Greaves in 57 internationals (a ridiculous tally although many were scored in friendly internationals against nations whose standard was lower than it would be now). Charlton also held the Manchester United appearance record of 758 games in all competitions until Ryan Giggs passed that total in the 2008 Champions League Final.

The Charltons were not just from mining stock, but also from pure footballing stock, their mother's cousin Jackie Milburn being a legendary Newcastle United and England centre-forward in the 1940s and 1950s. The Charltons also had uncles who'd played for Leeds United, making the club an inevitable option for brother Jackie. Bobby's mother insisted upon him 'getting a trade' before he signed for United, the younger Charlton brother taking an apprenticeship as an electrical engineer.

Bobby scored regularly for youth and reserve teams at Old Trafford before making his first team debut against Charlton Athletic (a lovely irony) in October 1956. At the time he was doing national service with the Royal Army Ordnance Corps in Shrewsbury, a move suggested to him by Matt Busby, in order that he'd be able to play for United at the weekends. Also at Shrewsbury doing national service was Duncan Edwards, tragically lost in Munich in 1958. Charlton thought Edwards would have been the greatest ever England player. Edwards was a force of nature in midfield, a box-to-box player who might have been even better than United's later midfield powerhouse Bryan Robson of the 1990s. Edwards could also slot in at centre-back and play as if to the manor born. We will never know, but Bobby Charlton bestows Duncan Edwards with the highest praise.

Bobby played only 14 times in the 1956–57 season, but scored 12 goals, twice on his debut, and claimed his first hat-trick in February 1957 against... Charlton Athletic. Charlton became a regular first team player in the ill-fated 1957–58 season. As champions of England, United opted to play in the European Cup. It was Harry Gregg who found Bobby in the wreckage of the plane in Munich. He'd been thrown out of the cabin still strapped in his seat. Gregg – not an especially big man for a goalkeeper as I recall – hauled Bobby and Dennis Viollet away from a plane he feared was about to explode. Charlton and Viollet, astonishingly, had swapped seats with Tommy Taylor and David Pegg who'd decided it would be safer to sit at the back of the plane, such was the nervousness of the United players as the plane began its third attempt at take-off. This agreement between pals saved Charlton's life – Viollet also survived the crash – but can you imagine the guilt Charlton and Viollet then lived with? The heroic Gregg went back to the plane again to bring out Matt Busby and Jackie Blanchflower, the younger brother of Tottenham Hotspur captain and legend Danny. The pair also survived, aided by Gregg's utter selflessness. Bobby was hospitalised for a week, the Munich air crash ultimately claiming 23 lives. Bobby was the first survivor to leave hospital.

Upon returning to England Bobby received much media attention. It was hoped that he would be United's big hope for a resurrected team for the future – it was a huge burden for the quiet, private Bobby (Jackie was infinitely more extrovert in character) to saddle.

Bobby earned his first winner's medal in the 1963 FA Cup Final (at the third attempt). Although the 1965–66 season was a trophy-less one for United, Bobby's stock had risen so highly that he was awarded the Football Writer's Association Footballer of the Year Award. Even more impressively he won the Ballon d'Or – European Footballer of the Year – Bobby Charlton was now recognised as one of the greats of the game, joining the hallowed company of Puskás, Di Stéfano and Eusébio as one of Europe's finest. In this fondly remembered European Cup Final, Bobby scored two glorious goals, goals of great subtlety, testament to his unique talent. When he played his last game for United against Chelsea at Stamford Bridge in April 1973, coincidentally brother Jackie played his last game for Leeds United. Chelsea won the game 1-0. Two years earlier in an evening game at the Bridge I'd seen Charlton and Best tear Chelsea apart. United won 3-2, Charlton scoring two typical blockbuster goals, Best scoring the other before getting himself sent off. Thanks for the memory, Bobby.

Internationally, Charlton scored on his debut for England against Scotland in a 4-0 victory at Hampden Park with a thumping volley from a Tom Finney cross. Charlton then scored twice in his home debut at Wembley as England beat Portugal 2-1. Inexplicably, after such a great start to his international career, nerves got the better of him in his third game as England lost 5-0 to an emerging Yugoslavia side in Belgrade.

Although deemed not quite ready for regular starts at the 1958 World Cup, 1959 saw Charlton firmly establish himself in the England team. He scored hat-tricks against the United States in 1958 and 1961, going on to score in every

British Home Championship (what a shame this defunct England/Scotland/ Wales/ Northern Ireland tournament no longer exists) 1958–1970 except for 1963. In the tournament as a whole he scored 16 goals, claiming the trophy ten times (five times shared).

In the 1962 World Cup, Charlton scored against Argentina in the group games, but Brazil eliminated England in the quarter-finals, going on to win the tournament. Another hat-trick followed under new manager Alf Ramsey against Switzerland in 1963. By this juncture, Charlton, one-time left-winger, then an inside-forward, had been re-styled at United, and by Ramsey, as a central attacking midfield player, a role that suited his wonderful long-range passing ability, and even better suited his capacity for arriving at the perfect moment outside the penalty area to unleash those devilishly ferocious strikes. How fortunate it seemed to this youngster growing up in the 1960s to have not one, but two expert exponents of the piledriver shot, Bobby Charlton, and the equally explosive Scot Peter Lorimer at Leeds United.

1966 arrived, and England were now recognised as having three world-class players in Charlton, Bobby Moore and Gordon Banks. Ramsey himself thought left-back Ray Wilson was of a similar ilk, and I would add the ghost-like qualities of the 'Rolls-Royce' Martin Peters to the list. Charlton's goal against Mexico in the group games lives on in the memory, struck so ferociously that the ball hit the back of the net and ricocheted back on to the pitch. In the semi-final against Portugal two venomous strikes by Charlton were enough to take England into the World Cup Final. Charlton and Beckenbauer duly exorcised one another in the final, but England's one and only moment of senior international triumph resulted as West Germany failed to nullify an inspired Geoff Hurst revelling in the space that was denied Charlton.

Charlton struck a post in the 1968 European Championship semi-final, but England lost out to Yugoslavia and the expert dribbler Dragan Dzajic's 86th-minute solitary goal, having the scant consolation of finishing third after defeating Russia 2-0 in the play-off match, Charlton and Hurst the scorers. In the heat of Mexico in 1970 at the World Cup, Ramsey famously sacrificed Charlton for Colin Bell with England winning 2-0 against West Germany with 20 minutes remaining of the quarter-final in Leon. Ramsey genuinely thought the game was won, saving Charlton back for a potential semi-final. Never write off the Germans, who came back to win 3-2 in extra time. Bobby asked Ramsey not to consider him for the England team anymore on the flight home from Mexico. Now aged 32, he'd decided it was time for a new generation to have their day. At the top level it's apparent when you are past your best. Bobby continued with United for a further three seasons, but 1966 and 1968 remain the defining moments of a truly stellar career.

Bobby became manager of Preston North End in 1973, signing Nobby Stiles as his player-coach. The season ended with relegation, Charlton donned his boots to play as a player-manager, but management didn't seem to suit him. One of the greatest ever England footballers – he'd be in any best ever England team I could name, and I suspect many would agree – found management something altogether more complicated than the game of football that came so naturally to him. Bobby's stint at Preston was short-lived – until 1975. A caretaker manager's spell at Wigan Athletic occurred in 1983, but it's as a director of Manchester United since 1984 that his retirement days have been spent, the Charlton 'brand' irresistibly feeding into a club he served so gloriously.

Ironically, a 'United Trinity' statue stands outside Old Trafford of Charlton, Best and Law. Ironic, because the 'trinity' didn't always get on, despite their respect for each other as footballers. Best and Law represented the playboy side of the 1960s that Bobby did not associate with. Bobby's slicked back hair and appearance were more in common with Bill Foulkes than the off-field antics of Best and Law.

In 2008 brother Jackie presented the BBC Sports Personality of the Year Lifetime Achievement Award to his younger sibling Bobby, once again the older Charlton eulogising about 'our kid's god-given talent'. In January 2011 Bobby was voted fourth best player of all time by readers of *Inside United*, a club journal, behind Ryan Giggs, Eric Cantona and George Best. Personally I couldn't split Charlton and Best, but they would be above both Giggs and Cantona in my book. Does this suggest shorter memories on the part of *Inside United* readers or nostalgia on my part? Charlton was an inaugural inductee in the English Football Hall of Fame in 2002; he was given the freedom of the city of Manchester in 2009. Simply one of the greatest players I have ever witnessed, Bobby Charlton was a player full of grace, explosive power, supreme athleticism, and possessed an innate understanding of space on a football pitch – and he was an exemplary sportsman to boot.

Who could possibly match the peerless Charlton in this Manchester United team? Why, George Best, of course. Not only was Best a completely different character and personality to Charlton, but an altogether different, extravagantly gifted footballer. Nobody perfected the body swerve quite like Best. He was a veritable box of tricks, and when the box was empty he merely opened up another. Like Charlton, his appreciation of space on the football pitch was heightened like few others.

Like Charlton, Best became European Footballer of the Year (in this year of 1968). Best was ranked sixth in the FIFA Player of the Century vote at a gala in Rome in 2000 by *FIFA Magazine* readers and the FIFA Grand Jury. Pele was ranked first; Alfredo Di Stéfano (he looked like a magician when I saw footage of the 1960 European Cup Final, but this might be considered controversial) came second, ahead of Diego Maradona in third. Beckenbauer was fourth, and Best was ranked equal sixth with the Dutch genius Johan Cruyff. Behind Best were Roberto Baggio, the Brazilian wing wonder Garrincha (1958, 1962 World Cups, he was born with his right leg shorter than his left, a physical detriment that actually enhanced his free-kick taking and phenomenal dribbling skills), another Brazilian great in Zico, the French midfield playmaker par excellence Michel Platini, and West Germany's goal-machine Gerd Müller. I'd put Bobby Charlton ahead of Baggio given his overall contribution for England and Manchester United.

Like Garrincha, George Best was a maestro with a ball at his feet, an intuitive dribbler, a master of feinting and dummying an opponent. Best's individual talent was so great it could be easily forgotten that he was a committed team player. He was not afraid to track back, and despite his slight build he was never afraid to retrieve the ball in a tackle. The Irish Football Association has described Best as the greatest player to ever wear the green shirt of Northern Ireland – frankly he has no competitors on a pure skill level. What a contrast to Charlton though, as an individual. Charlton was the consummate professional, a committed family man. For Best the 60s and early 70s were about booze, 'birds' and the playboy lifestyle he revelled in. His dark hair and swarthy good looks made him a magnet to young women, more than one Miss World among them. I suspect from footage I've seen on television that before the demon drink changed his personality he was a decent human being too with a kind side to him, but drink ravages the body when imbibed to excess, and sadly Best drank too much to the detriment of his all-too short football career.

Best was around my height. I might be a shade taller than his five feet nine inches, but he was a million times more gifted with a football. United's scout Bob Bishop discovered the slight waif in Belfast when Best was 15. Bishop's words to Matt Busby were, "I think I've found you a genius." Northern Irish club Glentoran had rejected Best already as too small and light – how they would rue that decision, a decision surely on a par with Decca Records' telling Brian Epstein that "guitar records were on the way out" when The Beatles were famously passed over in 1962. Best trialled with United a year earlier than this famous moment in music – in 1961 (Best came to be tagged 'El Beatle' because of his black mop-top hairstyle) – returning home to Ireland after two days because he was homesick. Best was no 'mug' – he'd passed his 11-plus (something I was a borderline failure in) in 1957, so he was a smart cookie, but he missed his home and family inordinately during his teens. The astute Busby arranged for his return, setting up digs where he would be looked after well in a warm domestic setting.

Best debuted for United against West Bromwich Albion in September 1963 in a 1-0 home win. He didn't play again until December 1963, scoring in a 5-1 win over Burnley. Busby kept him in the side, the young genius scoring six goals in 26 games as United finished the season second behind Liverpool. Best captained United's youth team to victory in the 1964 Youth Cup under Jimmy Murphy, the man who'd trained the Busby Babes of the 50s.

In 1965 United fought a bitter battle with Yorkshire rivals Leeds United, pipping the Elland Road side to the title, but losing to them in the semi-finals of the FA Cup. Best ended the season with 14 goals from 59 competitive matches. In the European Cup quarter-finals in 1965–66 in the Estadio da Luz, Best gave one of the greatest individual performances of the decade, mesmerising the Portuguese greats Benfica, scoring twice in a 5-1 trouncing. After suffering a knee injury – his tantalising style made him a target for rough treatment from defenders – Best returned to score ten goals in 45 games in the 1966–67 season, United again winning the title.

United failed to retain their title in 1967–68, losing out to rivals Manchester City by a narrow two-point margin. What a consolation the European Cup would be. In the semi-finals Best scored the only goal at Old Trafford against Real

Madrid. In the return he was man-marked fiercely by Manuel Sanchis Martinez, eluding his adversary just once. Once was enough, his cross setting up Bill Foulkes for the goal that put United into the 1968 European Cup Final.

On a personal level, the 1967–68 season was arguably Best's greatest: European Footballer of the Year; European Cup winner; Best also equalled the 1st Division's top scorer with 28 goals, Ron Davies of Southampton – no mean feat as Best was a winger and Davies an out-and-out centre-forward. To win the European Footballer of the Year award Best received more votes than Charlton, Franz Beckenbauer and one of the unheralded stars of Europe in 1968, the brilliant Yugoslavian left-winger Dragan Dzajic (he came third).

In 1968–69 Best scored 22 goals in 55 games, but with Charlton and Law among a few of United's core players from previous years an ageing team looked to the younger players like Best for inspiration. Best felt he was carrying the team at times. In 1969–1970 United installed a new manager in Wilf McGuiness, promoted after Busby's retirement. Their league form improved a little, but it was the FA Cup game that United won 8-2 with Best scoring six goals against Northampton Town that was the highlight of this season for the Red Devils. The performance was voted No. 26 on Channel 4's list of the 100 Greatest Sporting Moments decades later.

Lack of discipline was beginning to bedevil Best. He was fined by the FA for receiving three bookings for misconduct in the 1970–71 season, and was suspended for two weeks for missing his train to Stamford Bridge for a league match. The reason: a lady. Best simply couldn't resist the charms of the fairer sex. With Frank O'Farrell in place as United manager in 1971–72 Best recorded hat-tricks against West Ham United and Southampton. He also missed a week's training, spending the time instead with a Miss World. Best could still turn it on football-wise, but did he have the desire? Sadly his drinking would begin to affect his performances to the point where it may have been kinder not to select him. Yet you were talking about a footballing genius here. The word genius is ludicrously over-used, but it definitely applied to George Best in his prime. Despite his 'wanderings' Best ended the 1971–72 season with 27 goals from 54 appearances, making him the club's top scorer for the sixth consecutive season. What might have he achieved if he'd been entirely sober? Best was such an appealing subject for TV programmes that he appeared not once, but twice as the subject of ITV's popular *This Is Your Life*, in 1971, and again in 2003. Best left Manchester United in 1974, having fallen foul of new manager Tommy Docherty, the fiery no-nonsense Scot. In total, Best scored 179 goals in 470 competitive games for United.

Best's professional career was essentially over, although he appeared briefly with old pals Bobby Moore and Rodney Marsh at Fulham in the 1976–77 season, exhibiting all his old skills at times, if none of the exhilarating pace of his early days. He continued playing, incredibly given his physical deterioration, until 1984, although many of his appearances were one-off games.

Internationally, Best played a meagre 37 times for Northern Ireland, scoring nine goals. It would have been many more but for his suspect fitness levels. Best also saw his international appearances as 'recreational' because he didn't have the calibre of player with him in a Northern Irish shirt that he luxuriated in at Manchester United. Evidence indeed that football is a team game – however good an individual is they cannot win a match on their own. Sensationally, Best scored one of the great 'non-goals' in a match against England at Windsor Park, Belfast in 1971. None other than Gordon Banks allowed the ball to leave his grasp as he attempted a drop-kick downfield. The outrageously alert Best nipped in, dinked the ball over Banks and raced past him to head the ball into the empty net. It was a piece of incredible opportunism on the part of Best, but the goal was disallowed by the referee Alistair Mackenzie. What a shame to be denied this moment of extravagant brilliance by the mercurial Best. It was Best's misfortune to be Northern Irish it seems (although he was a fiercely proud Irishman), as he never played in an international tournament on the big stage. He is regarded as one of the greatest international players never to have played in a World Cup or European Championship. If only he'd been born 20 years later.

Best's mesmeric dribbling skills made him one of the most feared opponents in world football in the 1960s and early 1970s. Defenders were terrified of him. I've never forgotten the comical episode at Stamford Bridge where Ron 'Chopper' Harris chased the elusive Best 70 yards down the pitch attempting to scythe him down, Best continually shrugging his shoulders, swerving this way and that, shaking off Harris's persistent 'Harrisment' and duly scoring for United. Best's balance was almost supernatural; defenders were often clueless as to the direction he would take. On top of this he was a scorer of great goals; he could pass, cross and head the ball equally well. His balance and dribbling were matched by Ryan Giggs later on, but only almost. Best in his pomp was like watching a ballet dancer slip past despairing defenders, a dazzling sight to behold. Alex Stepney has even related how Best would deliberately play the ball off a goalkeeper's shin (a 1-2) in order to score a goal. How does a player have that much time – especially in the rarefied atmosphere and express train speed of top-level professional football. Best's mastery of a football has rarely been matched – only by the true geniuses, Pele, Maradona and Cruyff.

Sadly, the drink got George in the end. In November 2005 he passed away, a victim of alcoholism, dying of a lung infection and multi-organ failure. It was not the way this greatest of players should be remembered, but Best was the essence of the term 'flawed genius'.

On 22 May 2006, Belfast City Airport was renamed George Best Belfast City Airport in memorial to one of Northern Ireland's greatest ever sportsmen. Not all politicians and public members agreed with the decision. As in life, in death George Best divided people.

With the dazzling talents of Charlton and Best prominent, the duo scorers of three superlative goals in this 1968 European Cup Final, you'd expect that one of them was Man of the Match. That honour fell to the other winger in United's team. With Best deployed on the right (I always preferred him on the left, a right-footer being so dangerous cutting in), John Aston on the left it was who won the accolade of the evening's best player. Aston came through United's youth ranks 1962–65. With the exotic, ridiculously talented Best outshining him, it is easy to forget what a wonderfully deft, balanced, excellent technician Aston was. Aston scored 27 goals in 187 appearances for United 1965–1972, later playing for Luton Town, Mansfield Town and Blackburn Rovers, retiring in 1979. Aston's father had also played for United post-World War 2. A fine player in his own right, John Aston junior.

The main striker in the United side at Wembley was Brian Kidd, only 19 years old on the night – it was his birthday, what a way to celebrate! Kidd joined United's academy in 1964. Kidd was a fine striker, exceptionally unfortunate to be around at the same time as Hurst, Chivers, Clarke, Osgood, Channon et al with regard to an England call-up. Brian Kidd guaranteed you goals, scoring 52 in 203 league appearances for United 1967–1974. Kidd transferred to Arsenal when United were relegated in 1973–74. He scored on his debut for Arsenal, going on to score 19 goals in 40 games in the 1974–75 season. Kidd scored 34 times in 90 appearances for the Gunners, but when the chance came to return to Manchester he did, but this time to United's rivals Manchester City in 1976. During the 1977–78 season Kidd scored three times in two games against United. He scored 44 goals in 98 matches for Manchester City.

Over the next four years Kidd played for Everton and Bolton Wanderers, adding a further 26 league goals to his tally before ending his playing days in the North American Soccer League where he continued to find the back of the net on a regular basis. Brian Kidd played just twice for England, predictably scoring on one occasion. A surprisingly mobile striker for a big man, Kidd came of age on this Wembley night in 1968. Kidd's post-playing days have largely been spent as a coach (with United 1988–1998, with City 2009 onwards, aiding the fledgling career of Ryan Giggs to name but one).

Manchester United's manager Matt Busby is regarded as one of the finest managers of his era, alongside Tottenham Hotspur's Bill Nicholson and Liverpool's Bill Shankly. Busby is indelibly linked with United, but the Scotsman's own playing days centred on Manchester City (204 league appearances) and Liverpool (115 league appearances). The Second World War interrupted Busby's playing career. After the war he was offered the position of assistant coach at Liverpool, but he had his eye on the manager's job. Instead he joined Manchester United. The rest is history as Busby went on to claim 13 trophies for United in a 25-year span at Old Trafford. Busby's father was a miner (it's ingrained in northern English football clubs) who died at the Battle of Arras on the French Western Front in 1917. Busby accompanied his father 'down't pit', but always cherished a football career.

Busby worked part-time as a collier while playing part-time football for Stirlingshire junior team Denny Hibernian in 1928. Manchester City soon came knocking, and Busby's top-level playing days as a right-half/inside forward took off. He won the FA Cup in 1933–34 with City before transferring to Liverpool for the 1935–36 season. Busby settled well at Anfield, eventually becoming club captain. In 1939 a certain Bob Paisley joined Liverpool, coming under the guidance of Busby. A lifelong friendship was formed.

Busby became a football coach to the Army Physical Training Corps during World War 2. It was during this period that Busby's football ethos was formed. Taking the reins in 1945, Busby soon imprinted his methodology on the Manchester

United set-up. United won the FA Cup in 1948, astonishingly finishing second in the league four times in five seasons, 1947, 1948, 1949 and 1951. They were being earmarked as 'nearly men', but finally won the title in 1952.

By 1952 a fine United side were ageing. The stage was set for the introduction of the Busby Babes. These included Bill Foulkes at right-back, centre-halves Jackie Blanchflower and Mark Jones, wingers Albert Scanlon and David Pegg (United have always been associated with wingers: Best and Aston, Best and Willie Morgan, Steve Coppell and Gordon Hill, Ryan Giggs and Andrei Kanchelskis), and forward Billy Whelan, not forgetting the incomparable Duncan Edwards, who was capped by England aged 17, Edwards being England's youngest international for 40 years thereafter. Busby managed the Great Britain football team at the 1948 Summer Olympics in London. In 1956, Santiago Bernabeu Yeste, the Real Madrid president, whose name is given to their iconic stadium, offered Busby the manager's role at Real. Busby remained in Manchester, his years of glory with the 'Babes' seemingly imminent, only to be tragically snatched away. Busby would then have to wait a decade to realise a long-cherished dream.

Busby had been appointed manager of the 1958 Scotland World Cup team prior to the Munich air crash. In the event he managed his country's national team just twice post-Munich, giving his future United star Denis Law his debut in one of them. What a loss to this final Law was, a 'jack-in-the-box', jack-knifing header of the ball, dynamic, athletic, a lethal goalscorer. United did supremely well to cover the loss of such a great player.

The emotion Busby, Bobby Charlton and Foulkes felt at the end of this evening in 1968 was there for all to see. Tears of joy and relief flooded from Charlton and Busby's faces. Matt Busby was awarded the CBE in 1958 and won the OBE post the glory of this 1968 European Cup triumph. After retiring, then briefly returning to his managerial duties at Old Trafford in 1970, Busby went on to be a club director for 11 years, being made president of the club in 1980.

Matt Busby gazumped his wing wonder Best by being the subject of *This Is Your Life* twice before his iconic player, in 1958 and 1971. As manager of United, Busby won the league title five times, 1951–52, 1955–56, 1956–57, 1964–65 and 1966–67; the FA Cup twice, 15 years apart in 1948 and 1963; but the crowning glory, the crème de la crème, was winning the European Cup in 1968. It was the end of a ten-year quest, a quest for retribution, a quest that not just Mancunians, but British football followers everywhere were willing him to realise in May 1968. Busby's legacy is one of instilling in Manchester United a footballing ethos built around a desire to attack, to take the game vigorously towards their opponents, to play on the front foot. It's a laudable and vivid legacy.

As an 11-year-old sitting watching this European Cup Final I was anxious that United should win. Not for me the tribal attachments, the blinkered views that said United are not my team. I wanted United to win for England. As a young boy, even as a young man, I always felt the nervousness of these occasions. I only played in two finals myself, and didn't do myself justice in either of them (one was lost, one was won). I desperately wanted to do well. They say a few nerves are a good thing, but I feel I wasn't relaxed enough. Even watching games, if I wanted a team, or my country, to win a game, I could feel my palms sweating, the tension rising in my body as a game progressed.

Could United become the first English club to win the European Cup, a trophy that belonged exclusively to a great Real Madrid team in its infancy, a trophy won twice earlier in the decade by this talented Benfica team – and the Lisbon club had the great Eusébio in their side. As a champion of attacking football in my younger days (I remain of that view, but time and greater wisdom give one a broader view of all the components required to make a good football team) I admired Busby's ethos, that attack was the best form of defence, a model he shared with the previous year's winning manager, Jock Stein.

Attacking being my reason for following football it was Benfica's midfield and attack that I was familiar with on this evening. I knew nothing of their defence. The scorer for Benfica on this night was Jaime Graca, wearing No. 6. Graca began his professional career with Vitoria Setubal 1961–66, scoring 32 goals in 103 league games. He transferred to Benfica in 1966, remaining with the club until 1975, scoring 29 goals in 229 games in all competitions. At Benfica he won seven league titles and three Portuguese Cups. Curiously, Benfica had a new hydro massage bath installed in December 1966. The bath short-circuited, killing Luciano Fernandes. Graca – an electrician before playing professional football – escaped with burns (Eusébio was also one of seven players in the bath lucky to escape with their lives), his past trade enabling him to help some of his teammates, but not the unfortunate Fernandes. Benfica wore black kit for the rest of the 1966–67 season as a mark of respect.

Graca played 36 times for Portugal 1965–1972, scoring four goals. He was part of the Portuguese midfield in the 1966 World Cup semi-final against England.

It was not black shirts, but black African origin players who shone in this Benfica team. Their captain for the night, Mário Coluna, like Eusébio, was Mozambican. Coluna was an outstanding player, a central midfield playmaker with wonderful control of a football. Coluna played 525 games in all competitions, scoring 127 goals in his 16 seasons with Benfica. Coluna's career in Lisbon began in 1954 – evidence of the passing of the years in this Benfica team. He was 32 on this Wembley evening. At Benfica, Coluna won 19 titles, including ten league titles and two European Cups.

An all-round sportsman, Coluna also excelled at basketball, and track and field athletics. He started football as an inside-forward, scoring 14 goals in 26 games in his first season in Lisbon. Coluna possessed a fine long-range shot, in addition to excellent technique. A strong player, stamina was also a major facet of his game. Coluna captained Benfica 1963–1970 over 328 games. Coluna scored in both of Benfica's European Cup victories, a long-range strike against Barcelona in 1961 in a 3-2 win, and the equaliser at 3-3 against Real Madrid in 1962, Benfica eventually winning 5-3.

Coluna, as a naturalised Portuguese, played 57 times for Portugal, captaining his adopted country. Upon retirement, Coluna became President of the Mozambique Football Federation, also serving later as the country's Minister of Sports 1994–99. Coluna's standing in European football was so great that he was chosen by the *World Soccer* magazine (that I read so avidly for around ten years) for their World X1 four years running 1963–66. Coluna was also selected by FIFA as one of the best 11 players at the 1966 World Cup in their FIFA World Cup All-Star team, and for their FIFA X1 Best World Players in 1967. Luckily for United, in Bobby Charlton they had (at least) Coluna's equal.

Another player in the Portugal World Cup team was left-winger António Simões, scorer of 72 goals in 449 games for Benfica. Simões became the youngest player to win the European Cup in 1962, aged 18 years and four months. Simões played for Benfica 1961–1975, winning ten league titles. His last title came in his very last season, 1974–75. He won 46 caps for Portugal, scoring three goals, one of which came as the Portuguese overcame a waning Brazil side, champions of the World Cup from 1958 and 1962, in the group stages of the 1966 World Cup.

The tall, rangy centre-forward for Benfica, José Torres, was unmistakable in stature at six feet three inches. Torres represented Benfica 1959–1971, winning 13 titles. Torres was also a prolific scorer, surpassed only in this team by the remarkable Eusébio. Initially used sparingly by Benfica (he still managed to score six goals in six games at one point), Torres came of age in the 1962–63 season, scoring 26 goals in the Portuguese Primeira Liga in 21 games. Benfica also won the Taca de Portugal (Portuguese Cup Final) in this season. Torres didn't retire from the top flight in Portugal until he was three months shy of his 42nd birthday. In 21 seasons he amassed 217 goals in 374 league games, ending his career at Estoril.

Torres played 33 times for Portugal, scoring 14 goals – it's surprising he didn't play more often as a hugely effective target man and regular goalscorer – 1963–1973. Torres scored three goals at the 1966 World Cup, including the winner against Russia in the third-place play-off with a header, Torres's main source of goals. Teammates Simões and Eusébio played their last international games against Bulgaria in a 1974 World Cup qualifying game alongside Torres. Along with José Augusto, this was a tight attacking unit for club and country.

Curiously, Torres played in only one World Cup. A chequered management career followed in Portugal, a low point being (through no particular fault of his own) when he managed the national team 1984–86. Torres guided his country to the 1986 World Cup finals in Mexico, but the notorious 'Saltillo Affair' damaged the team's prospects and reputation at that time. Hours before leaving to fly to Mexico for the tournament, defender Antonio Veloso tested positive for Primobolan, an anabolic steroid (a test later proved false). In addition to this doping suspicion, the players were threatening to strike unless their prize money for representing their country was increased. It was not Portugal's finest hour in football, and Torres's reign as manager ended shortly afterwards. Better to remember the towering Torres for his on-field performances, for his aerial presence, and for his gift for goals.

On the right wing for Benfica, José Augusto formally lined up in what we would now recognise as a midfield three with Coluna and Gracia. Augusto too appeared at the 1966 World Cup, while representing Portugal 1958–1968. Augusto spent four seasons at F.C. Barreirense, scoring 50 goals in 98 Primeira Liga games, a great return for a winger. He signed for Benfica in 1959. In his second season in Lisbon, Augusto scored 24 goals in 25 games. When he retired in 1970, Augusto was immediately named head coach. In 246 Primeira Liga games for Benfica,

Augusto scored 113 goals. For Portugal he scored nine goals in 45 internationals. He scored three goals at the 1966 World Cup – all with headers despite being five inches shorter than teammate Torres. Like Torres, Augusto had a brief stint as Portugal manager 1971–73, the team failing to qualify for the 1974 World Cup.

Far and away the player United feared most was the magnificent athlete Eusébio da Silva Ferreira. Born in Laurenco Marques, Mozambique, Eusébio was nicknamed the 'Black Panther' for a good reason. Eusébio had the remarkable multi-gifts of pace and power, stealth and athleticism. A fantastic striker of a football, he was the equal of Bobby Charlton for explosive shooting. Unsurprisingly, Eusébio is regarded as Portugal's best ever player, and in 1968 he was in his pomp, 26 years old, a strongly built player for another man a half inch shorter than myself at five feet nine inches.

Eusébio top-scored at the 1966 World Cup for Portugal with nine goals. Winner of the Ballon d'Or (European 'Footballer of the Year') in 1965, he was also runner-up in 1962 and 1966. Torres scored prolifically for Benfica, but Eusébio was Benfica's Pele or Jimmy Greaves, scoring 473 goals in 440 games in all competitions. With Benfica 1961–1975 he won 11 Primeira Liga titles, five Taca de Portugal Cups, a European Cup in 1962, plus he made three beaten finalists' appearances in the European Cup in 1963, 1965 and 1968. Eusébio is the eighth highest scorer in the history of the European Cup, and the second highest behind Alfredo Di Stéfano in the pre-Champions League era with 48 goals. Eusébio top-scored in the European Cup in 1964–64, 1965–66, and this season of 1967–68. He won the Bola de Prata (Portuguese league top scorer) a record seven times. *World Soccer* magazine awarded Eusébio tenth place in their poll of the 20th-century's greatest ever players. Like Pele, Eusébio became an ambassador for football beyond his playing days. Teammate Antonio Simões felt that Eusébio made the difference between Benfica winning competitions or not.

Eusébio was a typical product (as Maradona would be) of a very poor background. His Angolan father was a railroad worker who married a Mozambican woman. Eusébio used to skip school lessons to play barefoot football on pitches resembling wastelands with improvised footballs. When his father died from tetanus, Eusébio, aged eight, his mother's fourth child, would be raised by a single parent.

From early on Eusébio possessed explosive speed and power, being able to run 100 metres in 11 seconds, the capability of a world-class sprinter. Aged 20, Eusébio won the European Cup with Benfica, scoring twice in the 1962 final as his team beat the Spanish 'darlings' of the era, Real Madrid, 5-3. In October 1963, Eusébio was selected in the FIFA World team playing England in the Golden Anniversary match for the Football Association at Wembley, a match won by England 2-1 with Jimmy Greaves scoring the winner in the 90th minute. Interestingly, the only non-continental or South American player chosen for the Rest of the World team (captained by Alfredo Di Stéfano) was Scotland's Denis Law who scored their goal.

In 1968 and 1973 Eusébio won the Golden Boot as Europe's top scorer. He scored 317 goals in 301 Portuguese Primeira Liga matches; 59 goals in 78 UEFA club competition games (European Cup, European Cup Winners' Cup, UEFA

242

Cup). He top-scored for Portugal, his naturalised nation, with 41 goals in 64 matches, until Pauleta passed his total three decades later. Like so many of his 1970s peers, Eusébio dallied with the North American Soccer League after retiring from top-level European football, but he never stayed anywhere for any length of time. My own stand-out – and many others I'm sure – memory of Eusébio was his incredible virtuoso performance against North Korea at the 1966 World Cup in the quarter-finals. The North Koreans had already shocked Italy in the group stages to qualify for this game. The name of Pak Doo-ik still reverberates in my head. 3-0 down to surprise package North Korea after 25 minutes, Eusébio took it upon himself to single-handedly haul Portugal back into the match, netting four goals as Portugal recovered to win 5-3.

When the great man died of heart failure in 2014 aged 71, the Portuguese government declared three days of national mourning. One year after his death, the avenue in front of the Estadio da Luz (the Stadium of Light) was renamed Avenida Eusébio da Silva Ferreira. His remains are buried at the National Pantheon at the Church of Santa Engrácia in Lisbon, normally reserved for politicians and other notable Portuguese statesmen or personalities.

THE FINAL

What a memorable evening. A year ago I was proud to be British as Celtic won. This night I had my English hat firmly on.

Eusébio, marked tightly by the devilishly competitive Nobby Stiles, found space in the first half to hit United's crossbar. For United, George Best was double-marked, continually fouled – Benfica hadn't forgotten Lisbon 1965. Bobby Charlton's grace, movement and speed across the ground was ample consolation for Best's inability to throw off the shackles of Benfica's strong-arm tactics. The game was tense over the 90 minutes, a game that could have gone either way. Half-time saw a goalless scoreline.

Best, never one to be put off by close marking, displayed wonderful close control as he fought bravely to impact on the game in the second half. Torres headed over as Benfica showed they were not there to make up the numbers. Charlton then scored the first of two magnificent goals as he glided a beautiful header into the far corner of the goal from David Sadler's cross. Jaime Gracia responded with an equaliser, and soon afterwards Eusébio bore down on United's goal. It seemed the game was up for United, but Alex Stepney blocked Eusébio's piledriver shot. The great Eusébio stood over Stepney, praising his adversary in a show of true sportsmanship. The 90 minutes ended with the teams tied at 1-1. There was no hint of the drama to come.

In extra time, Best, manacled by tight marking all evening, wove his magic, slaloming through Benfica's defence to slide the ball into an empty net. The magician awoke at last. United had the bit between their teeth now and 19-year-old Brian Kidd celebrated his birthday scoring from his own rebounded header to make it 3-1. United now romped away with a game that looked precariously perched in the 90 minutes of normal time. The fourth goal was another example of Bobby Charlton's extraordinary skill. Kidd crossed from the right flank and Charlton wrapped his foot around the ball to angle a sublime shot into the far corner of the net. How did he do that? I've never seen another goal like it in the last 60 years.

The match ended with extraordinary scenes of grown men in floods of tears – Busby, Charlton – as the realisation hit them that United had won this trophy of trophies, the pinnacle of European club football, assuaging the horrors of Munich 1958. Busby and Charlton left television viewers in no doubt where their thoughts lay on that night. The loss of colleagues in that horrific disaster of 1958 would never be forgotten.

1969–1970 EUROPEAN CUP FINAL
Feyenoord 2 v 1 Celtic

Two years on from United's passionate triumph and three years on from their own memorable victory in 1967, the 'Lisbon Lions' attempted to roar again. This time the roar was muffled by a fine technical team, Feyenoord of Rotterdam, only Holland's second-best team in an emergent Dutch era inspired by Johan Cruyff's Ajax. Celtic showed only four changes from Lisbon, and one of them, David Hay, went on to have an illustrious career with Celtic and Chelsea, and might be considered a superior addition to the '67 side. The problem for Celtic lay in their opposition having outstanding upcoming members of the Dutch national side in Wim Jansen and Willem van Hanegem, classy experience in defence with their captain Rinus Israël, and skill aplenty in their Swedish international centre-forward Ove Kindvall. Even the Dutch strips seemed super-iconic in 1970: Feyenoord's red and white halved shirts and black shorts looked slick and classy like their team. Over in Amsterdam Ajax sported a classic white strip with a red vertical sash that suggested their swagger and verve.

Route to the Final
Celtic's route to the final seemed tougher than their Dutch opponents in 1970. After despatching the Swiss side Basel 2-0 in the first round, the Glaswegians found Benfica the sternest of opponents in round 2, winning 3-0 in Scotland, but losing 3-0 in Lisbon, only winning through on the toss of a coin as there were no penalty deciders in 1970. In the quarter-finals Celtic's home form ensured progress against Fiorentina, a 3-0 win followed by a 1-0 defeat in Florence. In the semi-finals an epic tussle with the great Leeds United side of this era ensued. George Connelly's first minute goal at Elland Road was sufficient for Celtic to take a slim lead to Glasgow. Billy Bremner swiftly restored parity for Leeds in Glasgow, but early goals from John Hughes and Bobby Murdoch in the second half turned the tide for Celtic.

Feyenoord won with ludicrous ease in their first-round tie, thrashing the Icelanders of Reykjavik 16-2 on aggregate, a 12-2 away victory secured with a hat-trick from Ove Kindvall and four goals by Ruud Geels. Leeds, incidentally, beat the Norwegians of Lyn 10-0 in the same round, Mick Jones feasting himself on a hat-trick. A brace each for Kindvall and Geels in Rotterdam completed Feyenoord's rout of Reykjavik.

Feyenoord's toughest tie followed as they lost 1-0 to Italian giants AC Milan in the San Siro, the Colombian international Néstor Combin the scorer. The great midfielders Wim Jansen and Willem van Hanegem turned the tables for the Dutch in Rotterdam, the latter's winner only arriving in the 82nd minute. The last eight tie was also tight, Feyenoord again losing 1-0 away to the East Germans Vorwärts Berlin, before resurrecting their trophy challenge in the return, Kindvall and Henk Wery scoring the goals. In the semi-finals Feyenoord secured a goalless draw in Poland against Legia Warsaw, winning 2-0 again in Rotterdam courtesy of goals from van Hanegem and Austrian midfielder Franz Hasil.

Goalkeeper for Celtic on this occasion was Evan Williams. He only played 82 league games 1969–1974 for the club, but such was Feyenoord's dominance of the play in this 1970 European Cup Final he was named the Man of the Match.

At right-back, David Hay played 230 games in all competitions for Celtic, scoring 12 goals, 1968–1974, being part of a group of players who eventually replaced the 1967 'Lisbon Lions'. These players were tagged "The Quality Street Gang", among them being Kenny Dalglish, Danny McGrain, Jimmy Quinn, and Lou Macari (later an impish player for Manchester United). Hay won five league titles, three Scottish Cups and one Scottish League Cup at Celtic. Hay played 27 times for Scotland 1970–74, featuring at the 1974 World Cup.

Following a dispute at the club, Hay signed for Chelsea, replacing the wonderful playmaker Alan Hudson when he moved to Stoke City. Hay eventually took on a more defensive midfield role at Chelsea, for whom he played 120 league games 1974–1980. Hay was influential in a young Chelsea team trying to revive itself after the halcyon King's Road days of Osgood, Cooke and Hudson. A serious knee injury forced Hay to retire while at Chelsea. More seriously, a detached retina caused him to lose full vision in his right eye.

Hay ventured into management, winning the Scottish 2nd Division title at the first time of asking with Motherwell in 1981–82. He then managed Celtic 1983–87, winning the Scottish Cup in 1985 and the Scottish Premier Division in 1986. After a season-long break, Hay managed Lillestrøm SK, immediately winning the Norwegian Premier League. Hay managed St Mirren – without success – in 1991–92, before moving back to Celtic to become chief scout. As a scout he was responsible for identifying Paolo di Canio and Pierre Van Hooijdonk for the club. Moving on to Livingston in West Lothian, he co-managed the club to the new Scottish 1st Division title in 2000–01 with Jim Leishman, the club's first promotion to the upper tier of Scottish football. As sole manager of Livingston, Hay won the Scottish League Cup in 2003–04, defeating strong favourites Hibernian. Only in his last management position at Dunfermline Athletic did Hay fail to win a title. Despite a lack of longevity in management positions, Hay's overall record is impressive. With Scotland as a player, Hay won (shared wins) the now defunct British Home Championship in1969–1970 and 1973–74.

Jim Brogan partnered the commanding Billy McNeill at centre-back on this evening. Brogan played 213 league games for Celtic, winning seven consecutive Scottish League titles 1967–68 to 1973–74, in addition to winning four Scottish Cups and three Scottish League Cups 1968–1975. Older brother Frank played for Ipswich Town. Jim Brogan won four Scottish caps in 1971.

John Hughes, deprived of his opportunity in 1967 by injury, featured this time as a striker. Hughes, muscular in build, revelled in the nickname Yogi, derived from the cartoon character 'Yogi Bear'. In 11 seasons with Celtic, Hughes scored 197 goals in 435 appearances. Hughes scored the first Celtic goal at Hampden Park in the semi-final against Leeds United, but like so many of his teammates here, was smothered by the smoothly competent Feyenoord team. Hughes – primarily as a left-winger, rather than a central striker – is eighth on the Celtic all-time scorers list. Hughes joined Crystal Palace in a joint deal with his Celtic teammate Willie Wallace in 1971. In 20 league games for the Selhurst Park club, Hughes scored four goals. Joining Sunderland in January 1973 – the season the Wearsiders shocked Leeds United in the famous 1973 Porterfield/Montgomery/Stokoe FA Cup Final – Hughes's fledgling career with Sunderland was shot down in flames. Fifteen minutes into his debut he suffered a career-ending injury. Between 1965 and 1970 Hughes played eight times for Scotland, scoring once. Ironically, John's younger brother Billy scored four goals en route to the 1973 Cup Final for Sunderland, and provided the corner-kick that led to Ian Porterfield's dramatic winner in the final.

Celtic's substitute in this 1970 European Cup Final, George Connelly, scored the solitary goal in the semi-final first leg victory over Leeds United at Elland Road. Connelly's fine technique and close control brought him many plaudits at the outset of his career, although his career was relatively short, 1968–1976 with Celtic, 136 league appearances, five goals and just one season at Falkirk 1976–77. Connelly played twice for Scotland in 1973. Connelly is regarded as a 'lost legend' at Celtic, many feeling he would go on to be of world-class status.

Captaining Feyenoord, Rinus Israël was tagged 'Iron Rinus' for his defensive solidity. With Feyenoord, Israël, the Amsterdam-born central defender, won three Dutch Eredivisie league titles, a KNVB Dutch Cup, this European Cup, and the 1973–74 UEFA Cup trophy (defeating Tottenham Hotspur). Highly regarded, Israël played 47 times for Holland 1964–1974, scoring three times. A player I know the esteemed Brian Glanville thought highly of, Israël, aged 32, was an unused substitute in the 1974 World Cup Final, having been usurped by the estimable Ruud Krol, a younger man, and by the players coach Rinus Michels relied upon to continually rotate within the team's 'total football' structure, Wim Rijsbergen and Arie Haan.

In 219 league games for Feyenoord 1966–1974, Israël scored 21 league goals. In a 20-year playing career exclusively in Holland, Israël completed 537 league games with DWS Amsterdam, Feyenoord, Excelsior and PEC Zwolle. Aged 40, the impressive Israël almost completed 220 league games for his last club, PEC Zwolle. A hugely respected man within Dutch football, Israël then enjoyed a 30-year management/technical director/scouting career up until 2012. Rinus Israël's playing ability was so influential he won Dutch Footballer of the Year twice, in 1970 and 1975 (the latter award coming a year after he'd been passed over for the 1974 World Cup Final).

I have spoken already of the physical strength and tactical astuteness of Wim Jansen and Willem van Hanegem (key players in the 1973–74 UEFA Cup victory over Tottenham Hotspur). The doughty van Hanegem was particularly effective for Feyenoord 1968–1976 with 88 league goals and countless crucial assists. There was something of Graeme Souness about van Hanegem, a silky touch allied to the love of a tackle. The Austrian midfielder in alliance with this pair on this evening, Franz Hasil, played 112 league games 1969–1973 for Feyenoord, scoring 33 goals. Hasil previously played six seasons at Rapid Vienna, and one in Germany with Schalke 04, but this European Cup win was the pinnacle of his career – although he did help Feyenoord win the Dutch Eredivisie the following year, thwarting their big rivals Ajax, who were absolutely in their pomp at the time as three-time European Cup winners 1971–73. Hasil was capped by Austria 21 times, scoring twice. Feyenoord played this final in 1970 with Hasil and van Hanegem pushed forward, Jansen behind them as the holding midfielder.

On the right of Feyenoord's front three, Henk Wery played 173 league games for the Rotterdam club 1968–1974, scoring 49 goals. Wery also scored three goals in 12 appearances for Holland 1967–1973. On the left side of the attack, Coenraadt 'Coen' Moulijn was considered by Johan Cruyff to be one of the best left-wingers ever to play in Dutch football. Moulijn's former teammate (1960–68) Hans Kraay thought the winger looked more like an accountant than a footballer, but Moulijn's swift and subtle forays down the left flank belied his appearance. Rinus Israël thought Moulijn was on a par with Cruyff. At 33 years of age in this final, Moulijn had already given Feyenoord exceptional service from 1955, playing on until 1972, completing 487 league games and scoring 84 goals. Moulijn played 38 times for Holland 1956–1969, scoring four goals.

Splitting the wide players, the Swedish international centre-forward Ove Kindvall was a prolific goalscorer for Feyenoord – and in his home country. Starting in Sweden with IFK Norrköping 1962–66, Kindvall racked up 70 goals in 84 league games. Moving to Feyenoord in 1966, staying until 1971, Kindvall scored 129 goals in 144 league games for the Rotterdam-based club.

Returning to Sweden for the 1971–72 season, Kindvall scored a further 60 league goals, 30 for each of two clubs, IFK Norrköping 1971–75, and IFK Göteborg 1975-77. Kindvall was the first non-Dutchman to top the Eredivisie scoring lists, in 1968, 1969 and 1971. Only the great Brazilian, Romario, has matched this feat in Dutch football. Kindvall won the Eredivise in 1968–69 and 1970–71, the KNVB Dutch Cup in 1968–69, as well as this European Cup in 1970. He was Swedish Footballer of the Year – '*Guldbollen*' – in the last year of his first stint at Norrköping in 1966. He played 43 times for Sweden, scoring 16 goals, playing in the 1970 and 1974 World Cup tournaments. Only five feet nine inches, Kindvall relied on his nimble skills and keen eye for goal over a lack of physical prowess. In 1969 he came fourth in the European Footballer of the Year award.

Feyenoord's manager was the highly regarded Vienna-born Ernst Happel. Happel played 14 seasons with Rapid Vienna as a defender, ultimately being chosen in Rapid's Team of the Century in 1999. Happel won 51 caps for Austria, helping the team to a creditable third place at the 1954 World Cup – winners Germany and beaten finalists Hungary were infinitely the best teams in the tournament.

As a manager, Happel's stock rose even higher as he won the league title in four different countries. Happel, a man of few words, managed Feyenoord 1969–1973, and then oversaw Holland's march to the 1978 World Cup Final, although

Argentina spoilt the party. Thirteen years after this European Cup final in 1970, Happel did it again as manager of Hamburger SV in 1983, the German club defeating Juventus in the final. Happel is one of five coaches to win the European Cup twice with different clubs: Ottmar Hitzfeld (Borussia Dortmund, Bayern Munich), José Mourinho (Porto, Inter Milan), Jupp Heynckes (Real Madrid, Bayern Munich), Carlo Ancelotti (AC Milan, Real Madrid) the others. At the end of his management career, Happel returned to Austria, winning the Austrian title twice (1989, 1990) with Swarovski Tyrol, the club named after the crystal manufacturer, evidence even then of the effect of business support for top-level football clubs.

THE FINAL

Dutch movement proved too hot for Celtic to handle in this final. From early in the game Celtic were chasing shadows. The game had moved on in the three years since their famous victory in Lisbon. Feyenoord were totally in control, if unable to score the goals to confirm the fact. Coen Moulijn's class was in evidence in the first half. Out of nowhere Celtic took the lead when Bobby Murdoch's cute back-heeled free-kick teed up Tommy Gemmell for a typically fierce drive to score against the run of play. Feyenoord equalised when a series of headers ricocheted around their penalty area, McNeill unable to clear the ball effectively. Rinus Israël got the final touch, his header evading Evan Williams and bouncing in off the post.

Celtic gamely absorbed Feyenoord's pressure in the second half – they would never lie down. Gemmell launched a hopeful cross into the penalty area, the ball narrowly creeping past the far post. Kindvall set up Franz Hasil who struck the post from 20 yards as Feyenoord begin to assert themselves. Henk Wery found himself in acres of space on the right, but screwed the ball badly wide of the goal.

Celtic hang on grimly in extra time, John Hughes breaking clear, shooting against the Feyenoord keeper, the ball spun back towards the goalline but the Dutch cleared the danger. Hasil almost scored at the end of the first period of extra time. The great servant McNeill found this was a game too far, reaching back to stop a long ball over his head with his hands. The referee played the advantage as Kindvall had broken clear, the deft striker hooking the ball over Williams's head. Williams had bravely defied everything thrown at him until this 117th-minute winner. Even then Feyenoord should have scored again, the unselfish Kindvall holding the ball up to allow Hasil to break to his left and strike the crossbar. Celtic were magnificent in 1967, but on this occasion were undone by Feyenoord's pace and movement, Willem van Hanegem every inch the player who bossed this game.

1974–75 EUROPEAN CUP FINAL
Bayern Munich 2 v 0 Leeds United

Bayern were the holders of the competition going into this final, having beaten Atlético Madrid 4-0 (after a 1-1 drawn first match) in 1973–74. This would be Leeds' only appearance in European club football's premier final. With Sepp

Maier in goal, but critically, with Franz Beckenbauer and Gerd Müller in their ranks, Bayern were favourites to win this game. Leeds, enormously proud of their achievements in the late 60s and early 70s actually dominated much of this game, only to lose in controversial circumstances. Curiously, Bayern had suffered a slump in the Bundesliga in the 1974–75 season, finishing only tenth – having won the title three years running 1971–72, 1972–73 and 1973–74. In tandem, Leeds United's team finished only ninth in the old English 1st Division after almost a decade of being there or thereabouts at the top of the league.

Route to the Final
The two teams had to play only three or four two-legged games to reach the final in Paris. Leeds beat FC Zürich of Switzerland 5-3 on aggregate in the first round. The first match at Elland Road sealed matters, Leeds winning 4-1 with two goals from Allan Clarke, a penalty from Peter Lorimer, and another from Joe Jordan. The 2-1 away defeat scarcely troubled Leeds' progress. Leeds effectively ended Hungarian resistance in the second round by beating Újpest Dosza 2-1 on their own patch, Lorimer and Gordon McQueen scoring the goals. McQueen scored again at Elland Road as Leeds ran out comfortable 3-0 winners. In the quarter-finals Leeds trounced the Belgians Anderlecht 4-0 on aggregate, 3-0 at Elland Road with goals from Jordan, McQueen and Lorimer; Billy Bremner scoring the only goal of the match in Belgium. In the semi-finals Leeds finally faced sterner resistance from a proud Barcelona team. Clarke scored a 78th-minute winner at Elland Road as Leeds came through 2-1. An early goal in the Nou Camp settled Leeds' nerves, and although Barcelona equalised in the 69th minute, Leeds had done enough to reach their first European Cup Final.

As holders of the European Cup, Bayern Munich were given a bye in the first round. They had to overcome East German rivalry in the second round in the shape of FC Magdeburg, two goals from Klaus Wunder overturning a 2-0 half-time deficit in Munich. Gerd Müller – who else – scored twice as Bayern won 2-1 in the away leg. A tricky quarter-final followed, Uli Hoeness and Jan 'Conny' Torstensson scoring in a 2-0 home win, Bayern losing 1-0 in Armenia to Ararat Yerevan. In the semi-finals Bayern held French club Saint-Étienne to a goalless draw in the Auvergne-Rhone-Alpes, winning 2-0 in Munich, the first goal scored in the 20th minute by Franz Beckenbauer. Gerd Müller was joint top scorer in the competition in 1974-75 with five goals. Clarke and Lorimer managed four each for Leeds.

Leeds named a very strong side indeed for this final. Welsh international goalkeeper Gary Sprake had been the club's regular goalkeeper in the late 1960s. David Harvey replacing him at times, but on this evening Scottish goalkeeper David Stewart wore the gloves. Leeds had been a massive force in English football for a decade, but their European record was none too tawdry either. Semi-finalists in the UEFA Cup's precursor, the Inter-Cities Fairs Cup in 1965–66 (beaten by Spanish club Real Zaragoza 3-1 in a play-off tie after drawing 2-2 on aggregate); beaten finalists in 1966–67, this time to then-Yugoslav, now Croatian club Dinamo Zagreb, 2-0 on aggregate; winners of the competition in 1967–68, 1-0 on aggregate against the Hungarians Ferencváros, thanks to Mick Jones's goal at

Elland Road; semi-finalists in the 1969–1970 European Cup, beaten by Celtic 3-1 on aggregate; winners of the last Inter Cities Fairs Cup competition in 1970–71 against the Italian giants Juventus, 3-3 on away goals; and beaten finalists in the 1972–73 European Cup Winners Cup, 1-0 against AC Milan. Leeds United were a team with serious domestic and European pedigree.

Stewart was signed to be David Harvey's understudy from Ayr United in 1973. A road accident kept Harvey out of the Leeds side late in this season of 1974–75. Stewart produced an inspired performance against a Barcelona team including the great Dutch players Johan Cruyff and Johan Neeskens in the semi-final of this European Cup competition, and didn't disgrace the team in this final against Bayern Munich, but Harvey resumed first team duties upon returning from injury. Stewart had been something of a hero at first club Ayr United, making 251 first team appearances, becoming the first goalkeeper to be introduced into the club's Hall of Fame. He won one cap for Scotland.

I have spoken of my (grudging!) admiration for this Leeds United outfit earlier in this book. Many of the fine players I have mentioned before: the lean, athletic Paul Reaney at right-back, the consummate professional. Another outstanding athlete in Paul Madeley, pairing with Norman 'bites yer legs' Hunter in the centre of defence after Jack Charlton's retirement. Leeds had the niggly, but supremely skilled Billy Bremner and Johnny Giles in midfield; the power shooting and athleticism of Peter Lorimer on the right flank; the gritty old school centre-forward play of Joe Jordan, paired in attack with Allan Clarke, the latter one of the greatest goalscorers of his generation.

Allan Clarke, nicknamed 'Sniffer' due to his innate ability to sniff out half-chances in the penalty area, stood six feet tall. He knew where the goal was, scoring 223 league goals in 514 league appearances with Walsall (1963–65), Fulham (1966–68), Leicester City (1968–69), Leeds United (1969–1978) and Barnsley (1978–1980). Clarke also had a hard side to his game, making him the perfect fit for Don Revie's ultra-committed Leeds United team. Clarke scored 110 of his league goals for Leeds in 273 appearances. A natural goalscorer, Clarke netted 41 goals for Walsall in 72 league games; 45 in 86 for Fulham; 12 in 36 for Leicester; and 15 in 47 for Barnsley at the tail end of his career.

Clarke was among the scorers as Leeds overcame Juventus in the 1971 Inter Cities Fairs Cup Final; his diving header in the 1972 FA Cup Final secured the trophy for Leeds against Arsenal. He left Leeds United in 1978 having scored 151 goals in 351 games in all competitions. Clarke's international career was a brief one – not because he lacked the talent, but because of the outstanding competition he faced in this era: Geoff Hurst, Francis Lee, Mick Channon, Martin Chivers, Peter Osgood, Kevin Hector. The ridiculously gifted Osgood, not a favourite of Alf Ramsey's due to his off-field activities, won only three England caps. Clarke debuted for England in the 1970 World Cup against Czechoslovakia. Pressure meant nothing to the ice-cool Clarke – he scored the only goal from the penalty spot. Less memorable for Clarke was his appearance for the England team that drew 1-1 with Poland in the 1973 World Cup qualifier at Wembley, a match that saw Ramsey pack his team with attacking talent, a match in which England rained in over 30 shots at goal and still failed to qualify for the 1974 World Cup.

Clarke's record for England mirrors his consistent club record: ten goals in only 19 games 1970–75. Clarke was the second of five brothers to play professional football, and infinitely the most successful.

At left-back on this evening, Frank Gray suffered by comparison to brother Eddie (one of the finest left-wingers I ever saw play in the flesh). Eddie was among the substitutes on this evening, coming on in the 80th minute when the game was all but lost. Frank, ironically, played 32 times for Scotland, where Eddie played 12 times. Eddie had to compete with the home-based favourites in Scottish football, Jimmy Johnstone and Willie Johnston. Frank's club career spanned 644 league games and 48 goals, beginning with Leeds United 1972–79 (17 goals). Frank could be deployed either as a left-back or as a left midfield player, taking Trevor Cherry's defensive berth in this final.

Having lost this European Cup Final, Frank Gray righted the wrong of defeat by being crowned champion in Brian Clough's Nottingham Forest Team in 1980, Forest beating Hamburger SV 1-0. He became the first British player to play in the European Cup Final for two different clubs, not bad for the less lauded of the two Gray brothers. After two seasons with Forest 1979–1981, Gray returned to Leeds, accepting an offer to return from then-manager and former teammate Allan Clarke. A further 139 league games were accrued to go with the 193 completed in his first stint at Leeds (he scored a further ten goals). Gray completed his professional career with stints at Sunderland (146 league appearances 1989–1992) and Darlington (85 league appearances). Gray managed one of my local semi-professional clubs, Woking, for a season 2007–08, but following the huge success enjoyed by former manager Geoff Chapple, he found lower-level football an unforgiving ride. The Gray legacy passed on to son Andrew who won two caps for Scotland in a 490-game league career, and via Andrew's cousin Stuart who won seven Scotland U-21 caps 1995–96.

Assisting the multi-talented Bremner and Giles in Leeds' midfield in Paris on this evening was Welsh international Terry Yorath, father of the millennium's widely acclaimed and eminently capable sports presenter Gabby Logan. Father Terry was an uncompromising player (another made for Revie's feared Leeds side) who won 59 caps for Wales 1969–1981, captaining his country 42 times. Yorath was a fine player in his own right, but like other equally talented Leeds players Mick Bates and Terry Hibbitt, struggled to break into this supremely talented Leeds team initially. Bates had to take a step down to play for Walsall, Bradford City, and Doncaster Rovers. Hibbitt, the brother of Wolves gifted Kenny, graced Newcastle United twice (1971–75 and 1978–1981), and Birmingham City between 1975 and 1978. Tragically, Terry Hibbitt died from cancer, aged just 46. Yorath toughed it out at Leeds, winning regular football in the 1972–73 season thanks to injuries and suspensions to teammates.

Yorath's career at Leeds spanned nearly ten years 1967–1976. His chances limited pre-1972, Yorath ended up with two final runners-up medals when he eventually broke into the team, a surprise 1-0 defeat against Sunderland in the 1973 FA Cup Final, followed by another 1-0 defeat against AC Milan in the 1973 European Cup Winners Cup Final. Yorath was a key member of the team in 1973–74 as Leeds won the English 1st Division title. When Don Revie departed to manage England in 1974, incoming manager Jimmy Armfield sold Yorath to Coventry City in 1976. Yorath stayed three seasons at Coventry, captaining the side for most of his 99 league games. He then moved to Tottenham Hotspur, where his experience helped the young Glenn Hoddle considerably. Yorath played 46 league games for Tottenham 1979–1981.

Yorath became player-coach at Bradford City in 1982. After helping supporters evacuate a bar during the horrors of the Bradford City stadium fire in May 1985, he jumped from a window, injuring himself in the process. Ending his playing time with a solitary league appearance with Swansea City in 1986, Yorath managed the club 1986–89, leading the 'sleeping giant' to promotion from Division 4 to Division 3 in the 1987–88 season. In 1989 Yorath was appointed part-time manager of Wales, but after accepting the role full time left Swansea to manage Bradford City. Manager of Wales 1989–1993, Yorath presided over victories against Brazil (1990) and Germany in a European Championship qualifier in 1991. When Wales narrowly failed to qualify for the 1994 World Cup, Yorath was replaced at the helm by John Toshack. Terry Yorath suffered his own personal tragedy when his 15-year-old son Daniel died from an undetected heart condition, prior to beginning a football career with his father's old club, Leeds United.

Among the substitutes for Leeds United at this European Cup Final was the cult hero Duncan McKenzie. Starting out with Nottingham Forest in 1969, McKenzie did not become a regular in the first team until the 1973–74 season, when he scored 26 goals. As a 2nd Division team at that time, Forest shocked 1st Division side Manchester City to the tune of 4-1 in a fourth round FA Cup tie, McKenzie scoring once and making the other three goals. This alerted Brian Clough (via Peter Taylor, his assistant and scout par excellence) who signed McKenzie for Leeds United during his brief 44-day spell as manager. Paired with Allan Clarke in the 1975–76 season, McKenzie scored 16 goals in 39 matches. McKenzie's sublime individual skills endeared him to supporters, but this talented player did not always fit into the structure of regimented team football. As a consequence, Leeds sold him to Belgian club Anderlecht at the end of the 1975–76 season. McKenzie soon returned, playing two seasons with Everton, scoring 14 goals in 48 league games 1976–78. Blackburn Rovers were his next port of call 1978–1981, McKenzie helping the club win promotion from Division 3 to Division 2 in 1980. He ended his career with a year at Tuba Roughnecks in the NASL in America. Duncan McKenzie delighted and frustrated in equal turns in the 1970s – what might he have achieved with a little more consistency?

Manager on this evening, Jimmy Armfield, established himself as a legend in English football in a one-club playing career with Blackpool 1954–1971. Starting with the club the season after the famous Matthews FA Cup Final of 1953 at Wembley, Armfield set about forging his own illustrious memories. Armfield, a right-back, played in Blackpool's highest ever finishing league team (second in Division 1) in 1955–56. He was voted Young Player of the Year in the English league in 1959 and was runner-up to the immaculate Bobby Charlton in the 1966 Footballer of the Year Award, the same year he was Blackpool's Player of the Year. He helped the club win promotion to the top flight in 1969–1970, but his loyalty was not rewarded by a cabinet full of trophies.

A stylish player, Armfield was acclaimed the best right back in the world at the 1962 World Cup, also being voted the best right back in Europe 1962–64. A groin injury in Blackpool's final game of the 1963–64 season opened the door for George Cohen, and although Armfield was selected for the 1966 World Cup squad, Cohen kept his place.

Jimmy Armfield won 43 caps for England 1959–1966, captaining the team on 15 occasions. Turning to management, Armfield won the 3rd Division title with Bolton Wanderers in 1972–74. After the debacle with Brian Clough, Leeds United turned to a 'safer' pair of hands in Armfield. Ably assisted by Don Howe – who would make his mark as a coach with Arsenal in the 1980s – Armfield kept Leeds in the top ten of the 1st Division 1974–78, but the golden era and glory days of Don Revie were over. Among many accolades for this distinguished man was Armfield's award of a CBE in 2010.

Bayern Munich's custodian for this final, the redoubtable Sepp Maier, earned the nickname '*Die Katze von Anzing*' (The Cat from Anzing) due to his lightning speed off his line and cat-like reflexes. I remember Maier had his detractors, and was not necessarily as highly regarded as our own Gordon Banks, but this one-club player had a stellar career. At Bayern from 1959 in youth football, he made his first team debut in 1962 and played at Bayern until 1980. With Bayern he won four West German league titles, three German Cups, three consecutive European Cups (1974, 1975, 1976), one European Cup Winners Cup, in the latter defeating Glasgow Rangers in 1967. In five European final matches (the 1974 European Cup Final going to a replay) Maier, incredibly, conceded only one goal. Mind you, it didn't hurt having Franz Beckenbauer policing the defence in front of him. Maier won German Footballer of the Year 1975, 1977 and 1978. He played 442 consecutive Bundesliga matches 1966–1979, a German national record to this day, and an enormous tribute to his fitness and conditioning.

Maier was selected for four consecutive World Cup squads, 1966, 1970, 1974 and 1978, although he was only stand-by for Borussia Dortmund's Hans Tilkowski in 1966. Maier represented West Germany 95 times. At the peak of his career in 1974 – as were fellow Bayern legends Beckenbauer, Gerd Müller and Paul Breitner – Maier won the World Cup on home soil, depriving the classic 'total football' of Holland a trophy their nation seemed destined to win. Maier was chosen in FIFA's World Cup All Star team for the tournament. The talented West German team of this era also won the 1972 European Championships, and were surprisingly beaten by Czechoslovakia in the 1976 final, the unfortunate Maier victim of the now much imitated Antonín Panenka chipped penalty kick.

Maier subsequently provided his goalkeeping expertise as goalkeeping coach for the German national team 1988–2004, and at his beloved Bayern Munich 1994–2008. Much admired at home, Maier received Bayern Munich's One Club Man Award in 2017; has been chosen in Bayern's All Time Best XI; and is a member of Germany's Sports Hall of Fame.

Franz Beckenbauer, '*Der Kaiser*' ('The Emperor') was aptly named. Was there ever a defender who so imperiously eluded attackers, skipping nonchalantly out of their reach? Beckenbauer exuded class, even if at times as a defender his former midfielder's habits could see him overrun the ball. As a libero – or sweeper – Beckenbauer set the template for those who followed. Only AC Milan's Franco Baresi comes anywhere near the class of the great Beckenbauer. Beckenbauer had the class player's stand-out ability to glide across a pitch, seemingly without exerting himself.

Twice European Footballer of the Year (1972, 1976), Beckenbauer also won West German Footballer of the Year 1966, 1968, 1974 and 1976. He won the FIFA World Cup Best Young Player Award at the 1966 World Cup in England where his foraging runs from midfield make it difficult to believe his talent could be sacrificed to play as a defender. It should come as no surprise that the young Beckenbauer started out as a centre-forward. Subsequently he simply became the greatest sweeper of his generation. He was named in the FIFA World Cup All-Star Team in three consecutive tournaments: 1966, 1970 and 1974. In 1994 FIFA selected him in their All-Time World Cup team. He was also selected in the UEFA Euro Team of the Tournament in 1972 and 1976. *World Soccer* magazine placed him fourth in their poll of the greatest players of the 20th century.

The International Federation of Football History & Statistics places Beckenbauer as the best European player from 1956–1990 – a decision it is difficult to disagree with for all Michel Platini's achievements with France in the 1980s or Johan Cruyff's magical displays in the 1970s.

Son of a postal worker, Franz Beckenbauer's playing career occurred almost exclusively with Bayern Munich 1964–1977. His debut came as a left-winger (further evincing his all-round skills) in a Bundesliga promotion play-off match in June 1964 – yes, Bayern Munich were in the second tier or Regionalliga Süd back in those days. Excelling as a fluid attacking midfielder at the 1966 World Cup in England, Beckenbauer switched roles after becoming Bayern captain in the 1968–69 season. His new libero, or sweeper position soon elevated this already outstanding player to superstar status. Bayern followed their 1967 European Cup Winners Cup success with their first Bundesliga title in in 1967–68. Bayern won three consecutive Bundesliga titles 1972–74 with Beckenbauer at the back, and upon winning their third consecutive European Cup in 1976 the trophy became theirs permanently.

Beckenbauer switched allegiances to the NASL in 1977, playing for the star-studded New York Cosmos for four seasons alongside Brazilian 1970 World Cup winners Pele and Carlos Alberto. In this time Cosmos won the NASL three times: 1977, 1977 and 1980. He returned to Germany in 1980, playing two seasons with Hamburger SV, winning the Bundesliga 1981–82. One more year back in New York provided Beckenbauer with an end to an illustrious career. In 427 Bundesliga games for Bayern, Beckenbauer scored 60 goals.

At international level Beckenbauer reigned supreme as one of the very best players in world football for a decade, winning 103 caps and scoring 14 goals. With Beckenbauer at his peak, West Germany finished second, third and first at the 1966, 1970 and 1974 World Cups. The team won the 1972 European Championships in 1972 and suffered a surprise defeat at the hands of a plucky Czechoslovakian team in the 1976 tournament final. He was joint third top scorer at the 1966 World Cup from an attacking midfield position. In the 1970 World

Cup quarter-final against England it was Beckenbauer's goal that rallied West Germany for that dramatic victory against England in Leon, Mexico. In the semi-final against Italy he dislocated his shoulder, but manfully played on as the Germans went down 4-3 in extra time. From 1971 Beckenbauer became his country's captain. He was named in the Team of the Tournament at all three of the 1966, 1970 and 1974 World Cups. He was also named in the 1972 and 1976 European Championship Teams of the Tournament – unsurprisingly.

As manager of West Germany Beckenbauer took his country to two consecutive World Cup Finals, losing in 1986 to Argentina, but gaining revenge in 1990 against the same country. Beckenbauer is one of only three men to win the World Cup as a player and a manager – the others being Brazil's Mario Zagallo, and France's Didier Deschamps. At club level Beckenbauer managed Marseille 1990–91, and Bayern Munich in two spells, 1993–94 and 1996. At Marseille the club won Ligue 1, after Beckenbauer left towards the end of the 1990–91 season. With Bayern he won the Bundesliga in 1993–94 and the UEFA Cup in 1995–96.

In 1994 Beckenbauer became Bayern's club president, and chairman of the advisory board in 2002. Uli Hoeness replaced him in 2009. In 1998 Beckenbauer became vice-president of the German Football Association. His latter career as a senior administrator has been mired in controversy over votes concerning the 2018 and 2022 World Cup allocations. What is beyond question is that Franz Beckenbauer is a legend in German football. The only defender to be twice named European Footballer of the Year, Beckenbauer's shimmering elegance on the football field was a sight to behold, an image that transfixed me in the 60s and 70s. He was unquestionably one of the greatest players to have ever played the game.

Completing Bayern's trio of world-class West German internationals, Gerd Müller is possibly the best goalscorer I have ever seen on a professional football field. Like Jimmy Greaves – his only peer in my eyes – Müller was relatively short, but stockier than Greaves, more dynamic, more explosive than England's finest goal-getter. Greaves glided around, where Müller's athleticism and power – witness the winning goal against England in the 1970 World Cup quarter-finals, a hooked volley – was allied to the same insatiable hunger for goals as Greaves. I admired Greaves enormously, but I think Müller edges him as the best finisher ever in European football.

Where the poised, composed Beckenbauer earned the title 'Der Kaiser', Gerd Müller was equally aptly coined 'Der Bomber'. Like Greaves with his national goals tally, Müller's international total (ridiculously) is even better than his English counterpart, 68 goals in 62 games compared to Greaves's 44 in 57, prolific beyond belief. The mark of Müller's prolific goal-rate is that, although only 19th on the list of all-time international goalscorers, Müller played fewer internationals than any of the first 48 players on that list. At the 1970 World Cup his ten goals won him the Golden Boot as top scorer. He was also top scorer at the 1972 European Championships with four goals, following this up with four in the 1974 World Cup, including the winner in the final against the mighty Holland as West Germany triumphed 2-1. Müller's 14 goals in World Cup matches stood as a record for 32 years. He was ranked ninth in the 1999 European Player of the Century poll held by the International Federation of Football History & Statistics, and 13th in the World Player of the Century poll. Pele thought he was one of the greatest players he played against. Müller's Bundesliga record stands at 365 goals in 427 games 1964–1979. *'Der Bomber'* scored goals for fun.

In the 1963–64 season Müller began playing professionally with his hometown club TSV 1861 Nördlingen. In 31 appearances he scored 51 goals. In transferring to Bayern Munich for the 1964–65 season, Müller immediately teamed up with Maier and Beckenbauer. In a total of 453 appearances for Bayern in all competitions Müller racked up 398 goals. He became German top scorer seven times, and European football's top scorer twice. His record of 40 goals in 1971–72 in the Bundesliga has only recently been broken by another goal machine, the Polish international Robert Lewandowski, with 41 in the 2020–21 season. Müller's record stood for 50 years in a league where fewer games are played at the top level as the Bundesliga comprises only 18 teams. Müller also held the record for most goals scored in a calendar year – 1972 (85 goals), a record held for 40 years until the peerless Lionel Messi surpassed it for Barcelona in 2012. Like Beckenbauer, Müller was lured by the 'quick buck' of the NASL at the end of his Bayern career, playing three seasons with Fort Lauderdale Strikers, scoring 38 goals in 71 matches. Unlike Beckenbauer, the leader on and off the football pitch, Müller found retirement from the game difficult, suffering from alcoholism. Müller's former teammates at Bayern (including Beckenbauer) encouraged him to join an alcoholic rehabilitation group, from which he emerged to take up a coaching post at his old club in Munich.

Gerd Müller didn't look like a footballer – off-field pictures reveal a bespectacled individual looking more like an academic or suited professional from the city. His physical stature wasn't textbook either. Short, stocky, not apparently quick at first glance, but utterly explosive over the crucial first few yards as a striker. Müller's penalty-box instincts were predatory in the extreme as he exploded into danger areas, and his agility in the air belied his appearance. Gerd Müller was a goal-scoring phenomenon who won four Bundesliga titles and four DFB Pokal Cups in a nine-year span 1965–1974. In 2003 he was voted the best player in 40 years of the Bundesliga 1963–2003 (despite the presence of the immaculate Beckenbauer). In the European Cup he was top scorer in seasons 1973, 1974, 1975 and 1977.

The player in this Bayern Munich team who lay only marginally below the 'super trio' of Maier, Beckenbauer and Müller, was Dieter Hoeness. Hoeness's career at the top was curtailed by a knee injury sustained in this 1975 European Cup Final against Leeds United. Playing amateur football with TSG Ulm 1846 in 1970, Hoeness signed professional forms for Bayern Munich's then-manager Udo Lattek that year. He remained with Bayern until 1979, even if his knee injury prevented him from reaching the iconic status of Maier, Beckenbauer and Müller.

Hoeness totalled 86 goals in 239 Bundesliga games. His most outstanding individual performance came in the 1973–74 European Cup Final replay as Bayern swept Atlético Madrid aside 4-0, Hoeness scoring twice. Loaned out to FC Nörnberg in 1978–79 with the view to the striker rehabilitating with an eye to returning to Bayern, Hoeness found himself instead retiring from professional football at the tender age of 27. In 35 games for Germany Hoeness scored five goals.

Immediately upon retirement, Hoeness was appointed commercial/general manager of Bayern Munich. In 2009 he was elected president of the club. Hoeness has overseen continued growth for Bayern Munich, the club winning 24 Bundesliga titles, 14 DFB Pokal Cups, two Champions League titles and one UEFA Cup. Hoeness's administrative acumen was also pivotal in the building of the Allianz Arena, the state-of-the-art stadium completed in 2005. As a player, Hoeness's long blonde flowing locks and relatively tall, rangy physique made him appear the epitome of the Germanic footballer circa 1975. A quick, probing, athletic player, Uli Hoeness would surely have reached even greater heights on the field of play but for injury.

On the opposite side to Hoeness, 'Conny' Torstensson was one of two Swedish internationals in this Bayern team, the other being the right-back Björn Andersson. Torstensson had the knack of playing well in European games, scoring ten goals overall in 21 European competition ties. In a similar vein, midfielder Franz Roth excelled in big game competition. Roth it was who scored the only goal of the 1967 European Cup Winners Cup Final against Glasgow Rangers. Roth then turned his big-game expertise upon Leeds United in this 1975 European Cup Final, opening the scoring, and ultimately winning the midfield battle against the indefatigable Billy Bremner. The following year, in 1976, Roth again scored the only goal of the 1976 European Cup Final against French club Saint-Étienne. With Bayern 1966–1978, Roth totalled 72 goals in 322 games in all competitions. He played only four times for West Germany – his competition as a midfielder coming from Wolfgang Overath, Günter Netzer, Helmut Haller, Rainer Bonhof and Paul Breitner.

At the back with Beckenbauer on this evening in Paris, Hans-Georg Schwarzenbeck was another player who didn't appear to be 'that good' – he suffered by comparison to the effortlessly brilliant Beckenbauer. Yet in a career spanning 1966–1981 Schwarzenbeck won six Bundesliga titles, three DFB Pokal Cups, three European Cups (1974–76) and the European Cup Winners Cup trophy of 1967. His goal against Atlético Madrid in the first, drawn game in the 1974 European Cup Final was utterly critical, his long-range effort in the last minute of extra time saving Bayern from defeat. Out of the ashes of near-defeat Bayern then overran Atlético in the replay.

In his senior career, Schwarzenbeck was a loyal one-club servant, playing 416 Bundesliga matches, scoring 21 goals. For his country, Schwarzenbeck earned 44 caps 1971–78, being part of the European Championship and World Cup-winning teams of 1972 and 1974.

THE FINAL

Leeds were certainly not cowed by their feted opponents, Bayern Munich. It was the Yorkshire club who took the game to the Germans in the first half. Typically, some of the Leeds player's tackles were, to put it diplomatically, 'tasty'. Goal chances in the game were half-chances, but they mostly fell to Leeds, Allan Clarke having a shot deflected past the post, Peter Lorimer blazing the ball over the crossbar. The imperious Beckenbauer got lucky, not once, but twice, falling on the ball in the penalty area, and looking like he handled the ball. The ever-dangerous Clarke appeared to be felled by Beckenbauer in the area on another occasion, but no penalty kick was given – the Leeds players were furious.

The second half continued in the same vein, Leeds' close passing the match of their much-vaunted German opponents. Bremner missed from three yards out as Maier closed him down quickly, Leeds continuing to dominate possession. Lorimer flashed another attempt narrowly over the bar. The game turned on a controversial moment as Leeds sought to make their possession count. A poor headed clearance allowed Lorimer to unleash a typically fearsome volley that beat the flailing Sepp Maier. Mysteriously the goal was disallowed. Maier coolly picked the ball out of the net, Bremner having been wrongly given offside. Terry Yorath, the perpetrator of some robust tackling, hounded the referee vigorously. Bremner and Maier were caught up in a pushing match – Bremner, a small man at five feet four inches, never ever backed down from an argument! For an hour Leeds were in total control until Franz Roth broke free on the left, eluded Paul Madeley and screwed a shot across David Stewart and into the net. Müller added to Leeds' woes with a typical near post goal, anticipating space where there seemed nothing on, putting a hugely unjust gloss on the final result.

Bayern spent the majority of the game keeping Leeds at arms' length. Lorimer felt with hindsight that although Beckenbauer was a great player he could unduly influence referees and did so on this occasion. This Leeds side should have won far more trophies than they did 1967–1975. This was yet another occasion when a trophy slipped through their grasp despite being the superior side – the 1970 FA Cup Final against Chelsea a classic example of them being unable to turn their possession into a victory. Bayern were fortunate here – come the 90s and 'noughties' the boot would be firmly on the other foot when they outplayed Manchester United and Chelsea in later Champions League finals. What goes around comes around?

1976–77 EUROPEAN CUP FINAL
Liverpool 3 v 1 Borussia Möenchengladbach

Liverpool have always been more than the sum of their parts, their team ethic admirable even when possessing so many great individuals down the years. Yet I will always remember this final as 'the Keegan final'. The human dynamo, nicknamed 'Mighty Mouse' in some quarters, ran the experienced no-nonsense man-marker Berti Vogts into the ground – and this was the man who'd nullified the great Johan Cruyff for West Germany against Holland in the 1974 World Cup Final.

Route to the Final
The two teams met in the Stadio Olimpico, Rome, in late May 1977. Some venues have a particular resonance when it comes to remembering football matches: Lisbon 1967, the sun shining in the Stadium of Light. So it was here. Perhaps it's the Mediterranean/sunshine evenings of European finals that stand out;

sometimes it's simply the atmosphere in the stadium; sometimes its controversial decisions as with Leeds in 1975.

Liverpool and Borussia Möenchengladbach's journeys to the final were completely contrasting experiences. Liverpool cruised to the final, beating Northern Irish club Crusaders 7-0 on aggregate in the first round. In the second round, Liverpool lost 1-0 in Turkey to Trabzonspor, overcoming their opponents 3-1 on aggregate with three first half goals at Anfield. The quarter-final was an altogether different 'ball game', literally. French club Saint-Étienne were finalists in 1976 (losing to the all-conquering Bayern Munich). Liverpool again lost 1-0 away. The home leg was an epic see-saw confrontation. Kevin Keegan scored in the second minute of the game, but the French club equalised early in the second half. At this stage Liverpool were going out by a 1-2 scoreline. Home advantage at Anfield for Liverpool has produced many a memorable European evening. The Merseysiders clawed their way back to a 2-1 home lead, 'supersub' David Fairclough working his magic 12 minutes from time to seal a 3-1 victory on the night. In the semi-finals Liverpool suffered no such drama, sweeping aside the Swiss team FC Zürich 6-1 on aggregate.

Borussia, by contrast, won all their ties narrowly. In the first round they lost 1-0 away to Austria Vienna, overturning their nearby opponents with three goals at home from Uli Stielike, Rainer Bonhof and Jupp Heynckes, class players all. Borussia won 2-1 in Italy against Torino in the second round, a 0-0 home draw securing their progress. With Belgian football on the rise in 1977, Club Brugge provided sterner opposition in the quarter-finals. Borussia soon found themselves 2-0 down at home in the first leg, but recovered to draw 2-2, although the Belgians appeared to hold the advantage with two away goals. Another tight affair ensued in Belgium, but Borussia held sway with an 80th minute solitary goal. In the semi-finals, Russian side Dynamo Kiev won their home match 1-0, but the Germans fought back to win the return leg 2-0 with another late 82nd-minute goal.

Liverpool's team comprised the large majority of those who'd played in their UEFA Cup victories of 1973 and 1976, hard-won matches against this night's opponents (3-2 on aggregate), and Club Brugge (4-3 on aggregate). The core of Liverpool's team were experienced players who knew how to win tight games in cup finals: Ray Clemence, Phil Neal, Tommy Smith, Ray Kennedy, Emlyn Hughes, Kevin Keegan, Steve Heighway. Incredibly, Ian Callaghan was still playing – and contributing greatly with his endless energy – after debuting for the club in 1959. His Liverpool career ended the following year in 1978.

There were only three players I have not mentioned before. The first is Joey Jones, a Welsh international left-back who made up with huge enthusiasm for what he may have lacked in finesse. Jones played 72 league games for Liverpool 1975–78, winning the European Cup twice during his short time at Anfield. Liverpool supporters in the Stadio Olimpico unfurled a banner that memorably stated that 'Joey Ate the Frogs Legs' (Saint-Étienne), 'Made the Swiss Roll' (FC Zürich), 'Now He's Munching Gladbach' – the latter tickles me particularly as my dear wife coined the German team on this night 'Munching Gladbags'. Jones left the club after totalling exactly 100 games in all competitions, finding the competition from Tommy Smith and the outstanding new Liverpool recruit Alan Hansen a little stiff.

Having started professionally with Welsh club Wrexham in 1973, Jones returned to North Wales 1978–1982. He then became a cult hero at Chelsea 1982–85, his never-say-die attitude and fist-pumping displays striking a chord with Stamford Bridge fans. Jones was part of the Chelsea side who were 2nd Division Champions in 1983–84. Despite his cult status Jones was sold to Huddersfield Town in 1985 where he became the club's Player of the Year 1985–86. Jones played 72 times for Wales 1975–1986. Wherever he played, Jones's colourful character endeared him to fans – if not all of his opponents!

Jimmy Case plied his trade as an electrician while training with Liverpool two mornings and two nights a week. Shortish at five feet nine inches, Cases' physical stature was slight in his teens, but Liverpool soon helped the determined scouser put on sufficient bulk to enable him to become a key player for the club 1973–1981. Case's moustachioed face gave him an apt 'cavalier' appearance as he often played the game with a buccaneering spirit. This was not to say he didn't adhere to the team structure, but there was a swagger to Cases' play that made him an enjoyable player to watch – and he had a dynamic shot when called upon.

At the end of his first full season as a regular starter (1975–76), Liverpool had won the League and the UEFA Cup, Case scoring in the first leg of the latter final against Club Brugge. Case was part of a Liverpool 'machine' (at the time they seemed insufferably mechanical to me, churning out results with great efficiency – hindsight is a wonderful thing, isn't it?). I now realise they were a great team, albeit well drilled, but possessing many fine players who won three further European Cups (1978, 1981, 1984). Manager Bob Paisley was concerned about the off-field friendship between Case and Ray Kennedy affecting the team, so when Sammy Lee emerged as another energetic midfield option, Case was offloaded to Brighton and Hove Albion in 1981. Paisley – wise old head who many thought could never follow the charismatic Bill Shankly – knew Case needed to be separated from the Liverpool drinking culture that he'd been embroiled in. Case, to his enormous credit, became a mainstay and an iconic player, both at Brighton (127 league appearances) and next club Southampton (216 league appearances). Case was a key player in the Brighton team that reached the 1983 FA Cup Final. Football being prone to serve up ironies, Case scored the winning goal in the fifth round tie at Anfield against Liverpool, scoring again in the quarter-finals and semi-finals. Brighton drew 2-2 with Manchester United in the final, only to lose 4-0 in the replay. In January 1984, Brighton, relegated from the top tier the previous season, beat Liverpool again in the FA Cup. Case it seemed, had made a point.

Moving to Southampton in March 1985, Case soon became club captain under new manager Chris Nicholl. Southampton reached the FA Cup semi-final in Cases' first full season (beating Brighton in the quarter-finals). This time Liverpool would not be denied, beating Case's Southampton in the semi-finals. Case lost pace as he aged at Southampton, but he compensated with tough tackling, improved passing, and greater awareness of the space on the pitch. I believe my best two seasons in village football were my last two seasons aged 36, 37. Gone were the days when

I might score goals in hot streaks, but my team awareness and ability to provide openings for my fellow strikers improved immeasurably. Experience helps, even if the legs begin to betray you. Case was voted Southampton Player of the Year in 1989–1990. Case seemed to relish playing former clubs. In October 1989, the Saints trounced Liverpool 4-1 with Case dominating the midfield. In 1991 another new manager decided to dispense with Case's services (Ian Branfoot), a decision Saints fans completely disagreed with. Case then played 40 league games for Harry Redknapp at AFC Bournemouth 1991–92. Stints at Halifax Town, Wrexham, among others, followed, before Case returned to Brighton as player/coach in 1993. In 1995 he took over the management of the Seagulls, but not before he'd played as a 41-year-old, the oldest registered outfield Premier League or Football League player at the time.

Jimmy Case won only one England U-21 cap in 1976, but his tigerish tackling, explosive shooting, and energetic performances at Liverpool are still fondly remembered. Case scored 23 goals in 186 league games for Liverpool, and for me he was a memorable figure at a time when Liverpool truly dominated English club football.

When I think of Terry McDermott, I think of Kevin Keegan. Different footballers with different skill sets, but I can't see them apart in my mind's eye. I just see two twin-permed, dark-haired, archetypal 1970s football players. McDermott wasn't the all-action type like Keegan but he was blessed with a lovely touch, and was a fine player in his own right.

Another scouser, Liverpool born and bred, McDermott began professionally with Bury in 1969, making 90 appearances and scoring eight goals. In 1973 he transferred to Newcastle United, where he played just one season 1973–74, playing in the 1974 FA Cup Final 3-0 defeat to Liverpool. 56 games and six goals with the Tynesiders encouraged Liverpool to make an offer. At Liverpool, McDermott really came of age. Like Jimmy Case, McDermott was an integral part of this excellent Liverpool team, his career at Liverpool lasting until 1982. In 232 appearances for Liverpool, McDermott scored 54 goals. Yet initially he struggled to break into the first team, unable to make sufficient starts to claim a medal from the 1975–76 league title-winning team. In this European Cup-winning 1976–77 season McDermott finally established himself. His turn and chip for the Goal of the Season in the semi-final of the FA Cup against Everton is one of the late 70s abiding football memories. The game was drawn 2-2, Liverpool winning the replay, but it was the FA Cup Final winner's medal that was to elude McDermott and his teammates, the club favourites to beat Manchester United, but losing 2-1, preventing Liverpool from winning a memorable treble of league, cup and European Cup. McDermott had the consolation of scoring the first goal on this famous night in Rome against Borussia Mönchengladbach.

In 1978 Liverpool reached their first League Cup Final, but uncannily McDermott had goals disallowed in the final and the final replay against eventual winners Nottingham Forest. Liverpool won the league five times while McDermott was at the club (although he didn't play enough games in 1975–76 to claim his medal); 1975–76, 1976–77, 1978–79, 1979–1980, 1981–82; they won the League Cup twice in 1981 and 1982; and most famously the European Cup three times in 1977, 1978 and 1981. In 1980 McDermott was voted PFA Player's Player of the Year, and won the Football Writer's Award, the first player to win both awards in the same season in England. A scorer of several spectacular goals for Liverpool, McDermott's first team place became less assured after 1982, bringing about a memorable return to Newcastle United. At St James's Park, McDermott reunited with Kevin Keegan in an exhilarating team that included Chris Waddle and Peter Beardsley, the team winning promotion back to the top flight in 1984. As usual it was the talismanic Keegan who won the hearts of Newcastle fans, but what a backup team of Waddle, Beardsley and McDermott, three of the most creative players of the era.

Terry McDermott represented England 25 times, scoring three goals. Curiously, his last days in club football came at a time when internationally England had lost their way a little. It took Bobby Robson to revive the country's fortunes in 1990. Joining Keegan again as first team coach to the former's manager, the pair took Newcastle back into the top flight – after a further relegation – and in 1995–96 Newcastle really should have won the Premier League title, being 12 points clear of Manchester United in the run-in. McDermott continued to coach under Kenny Dalglish, Graeme Souness at Liverpool, Glenn Roeder and Sam Allardyce at Newcastle, only leaving the latter when Keegan's second spell as a manager ended in 2008. Another player whose persona typified the era, McDermott's silky touch, movement, and eye for the spectacular goal made him a special player at Liverpool and Newcastle in those heady days of the late 1970s and early 1980s.

Among Liverpool's substitutes were the red-headed 'supersub' David Fairclough, and another excellent forward, David Johnson. Johnson signed for Everton in 1969, and despite constant interest from Bill Shankly, then-Everton manager Harry Catterick rebuffed the persistent Scotsman. Moving to Ipswich Town in 1972, Johnson forged an excellent partnership with Trevor Whymark in attack. Johnson's mobility and link-up play made him a difficult opponent for defenders. After 136 league appearances and 35 goals in four seasons at Ipswich, Tottenham Hotspur put in an offer for Johnson, but the player chose to return to Merseyside to play for Liverpool. At Liverpool Johnson's goal tally improved (55 goals in 148 league games). At first, Johnson partnered the incoming Kenny Dalglish, but despite two good years in 1979 and 1980, he soon lost his place to the prolific Ian Rush.

David Johnson did enough to win four league titles, two League Cups, and three European Cups in his time at Anfield. Internationally he played only eight times for England (1976–1980), but scored six goals, an excellent return. His best night came at Wembley against 1978 World Champions, England winning 3-1. Johnson scored twice against a team including Diego Maradona. He returned to Everton again 1982–84, but his career petered out as a player-manager at Barrow. When you look at Johnson's England record you wonder whether this fine striker could have contributed even more in his country's white shirt.

Bob Paisley was Liverpool's reluctant manager in 1977. Paisley spent nearly 50 years as player and manager at Anfield. A quiet, unassuming man, a man carved from another generation, Paisley was the antithesis of his charismatic predecessor Bill Shankly. Paisley was a surprise choice to take over from Shankly, but Liverpool in the 1970s had a clear policy of promoting from within the club. When Paisley eventually retired in 1983, another member of the club's back-up team, Joe Fagan, replaced him.

Born in Hutton-le-Hole, County Durham, Paisley came from a small mining community, his father Sam a miner. He played amateur football for Bishop Auckland 1937–39 as a left wing-half. In Paisley's second season the 'kings of Amateur Football' as Bishop Auckland were known, won the Northern League and the FA Amateur Cup (the latter now re-titled the FA Trophy competed for by semi-professional and professional non-league clubs). He signed for Liverpool in 1939, but the outbreak of World War 2 when he served in the British Army, meant his debut was postponed until 1946. Paisley served in Egypt and Sicily – while on active service he learnt that his 15-year-old son had died from scarlet fever and diphtheria. In his first full season of 1946–47 Liverpool won the 1st Division title for the first time in 24 years. Paisley was appointed club captain in 1951, remaining with Liverpool until he retired in 1954, having made 253 league appearances. If not for wartime Paisley would almost certainly have exceeded 500 appearances for the club.

Staying at Anfield, Paisley became reserve team coach and club physiotherapist. Shankly it was who promoted Paisley to assistant manager. In the 1960s Paisley's astute tactical acumen helped Shankly create the strong Liverpool Football Club that followers worldwide recognise today. After succeeding Shankly, despite his reluctance, Paisley oversaw a period of English club dominance that only Alex Ferguson has ever matched – or surpassed. Liverpool won 20 trophies in nine seasons: six league titles, three League Cups, six Charity Shields, three European Cups, one UEFA Cup, and one UEFA Super Cup. Bob Paisley remains the club's most successful manager to date. In January 2020 an eight-feet high sculpture of Paisley carrying an injured Emlyn Hughes from the field of play in 1968 was unveiled outside Anfield. For a man who stated that he'd "sweep the street" for Liverpool Football Club the statue seemed entirely apt.

The Möenchengladbach team consisted almost entirely of the players who had run Liverpool so close in the 1973 UEFA Cup Final: Vogts, Bonhof, Wimmer, Stielike, Heynckes. At this juncture in German football history they were almost on a par with the mighty Bayern Munich. If anything, it could be argued that this time around Möenchengladbach were even stronger than in 1973 with the quicksilver, elusive Dane Allan Simonsen at the top of his game in the German's attack. With Simonsen in full stride, Möenchengladbach won the 1975 and 1979 UEFA Cups. Moving to Barcelona, Simonsen then won the 1982 European Cup Winners Cup. The Dane is the only footballer to score in the finals of all three European club competitions, the European Cup, the European Cup Winners Cup, and the UEFA Cup.

Allan Simonsen didn't look imposing at five feet five inches, but this was a player who scored over 200 goals with Vejle BK in Denmark, Borussia Möenchengladbach, Barcelona and Charlton Athletic in England 1971–1989. He also played 55 times for Denmark, scoring 20 international goals. After a tough start at Möenchengladbach he eventually scored 76 goals in 178 Bundesliga matches. The 1976–77 season is regarded as Simonsen's greatest. His powerful shot equalised McDermott's opener for Liverpool on this evening in Rome. At the end of the 1976–77 season Simonsen was named European Footballer of the Year, the first Danish player to win the award, marginally winning the vote ahead of Kevin Keegan and Michel Platini.

In the 1978–79 season Möenchengladbach won the UEFA Cup, Simonsen scoring eight goals in eight games in the tournament, including the winning goal from the penalty spot against Red Star Belgrade in the second leg of the two-legged final. Transferring to Barcelona, Simonsen scored ten goals in each of his first two seasons in Spain. In his third and final season at the Nou Camp, Barcelona won the European Cup Winners Cup Final, Simonsen scoring the first goal in a 2-1 victory over Standard Liege of Belgium. When Barcelona signed Diego Maradona in 1982, foreign import restrictions (two players only) saw Simonsen move, unexpectedly, to Charlton Athletic in England's 2nd Division. He could have moved to Real Madrid or Tottenham Hotspur, but aged 32, he opted for a quieter life in London's south-east. Simonsen scored nine goals in 16 games for Charlton, but the Londoners couldn't really afford his transfer and wages, the Dane returning to Vejle BK in Denmark in 1983 where he finished his playing career in 1989.

THE FINAL

A sea of red and white flags and banners, red and white top hats, red polo shirts and t-shirts greeted Liverpool as they took to the pitch in Rome on this evening, a mark of Liverpool supporters' enduring affection and loyal support for their club. The Stadio Olimpico looked like the Maracana in Rio de Janeiro, Brazil, a huge bowl wrapping itself around the players. The captains for the two teams, Emlyn Hughes and Berti Vogts were both great competitors and great sportsmen. Borussia were the brighter side early on, moving the ball around freely. It was immediately evident that Vogts was shadowing the busy Keegan everywhere. It was almost first blood to Möenchengladbach when Rainer Bonhof ran swiftly from midfield to strike a post from 25 yards. Vogts did not shirk at bringing Keegan down at times in a valiant effort to restrain the 'buzzing bee' who refused to bend to his marker's will. The skilful Steve Heighway fed a lovely ball through to Terry McDermott who drifted a subtle shot wide of the Borussia keeper and into the net. Liverpool edged the first half, going in for the break leading 1-0.

Heighway's slippery skills caused Borussia problems as the second half commenced, but suddenly Alan Simonsen glided on to a ball on the left edge of the 18-yard box and lashed a powerful shot beyond Ray Clemence. Hughes, as always, led from the front, driving forward from defence to shoot wide. The irresistible tide of red shirts would not be denied however, Heighway's corner met by the darting Tommy Smith at the near post to restore the Reds lead. Astonishingly it was Smith's first goal of the season. It was ever thus in cup finals. The highlight of the evening came as Keegan scurried in from the right flank, Vogts' vain chase ending in a foul and a penalty kick. Vogts' desperation was so reminiscent of that pursuit of George Best by Ron Harris at Stamford Bridge earlier in the decade; a goal was only ever going to be the outcome. Phil

Neal, as sound a penalty taker as you could find, duly despatched the spot kick. Liverpool's 3-1 victory on this night was thoroughly deserved, the nagging Keegan a veritable thorn in the great Vogts' side. This was only the beginning of Liverpool's thirsty quest for European Cups.

1977–78 EUROPEAN CUP FINAL
Liverpool 1 v 0 Club Brugge

A year later Liverpool reached the final once more. Surely the 'home' venue of Wembley would see Liverpool reproduce the wonderful football seen 12 months previously against Borussia Möenchengladbach? Football has an uncanny habit of defying hope sometimes. Liverpool's awkward opponents from Belgium, Club Brugge, would see to it that there would be no goal feast this time. Never predict a football match.

Route to the Final
Liverpool cruised to the final. The club only played three ties to reach the final. Receiving a bye as holders in the first round, Liverpool entered the competition in the second round, playing their first game at Anfield against East German club Dynamo Dresden. Liverpool won the home leg convincingly by a 5-1 scoreline, Jimmy Case scoring twice. It mattered not that they lost 2-1 in Dresden. An early goal against them by Nene against Benfica in the quarter-finals proved only a temporary setback, Case and Emlyn Hughes righting the wrong in the second half. At 'Fortress Anfield' as it became known on European nights, Liverpool swept Benfica aside 4-1 to win 6-2 on aggregate. Curiously, Liverpool were matched against their final adversaries from the 1977 competition in this 1978 European Cup semi-final. The first leg in West Germany ended in defeat, Rainer Bonhof's last gasp free kick ensuring a 2-1 win for Borussia Möenchengladbach. Once again Liverpool prevailed in style at Anfield in the return, Ray Kennedy, Kenny Dalglish, and Case ensuring a 3-0 triumph.

The talismanic Keegan had moved on to Hamburger SV, being replaced by a player, who, miraculously, became even more of a 'folk hero' at Anfield in Dalglish. Dalglish didn't possess Keegan's dynamism, but his technique and subtlety (mixed with a steely resolve) made him arguably an even better striker in his playing days at Anfield than Keegan. Keegan had gone, but Liverpool had the Scots triumvirate of Dalglish, Graeme Souness and Alan Hansen in harness, making the next generation of Liverpool FC even greater and harder to beat than the early-mid 70s team of Keegan, Toshack et al.

Club Brugge defeated Finnish champions Kuopion Palloseura (KuPS) in the first round at a canter, winning 4-0 in Finland, and 5-2 at the Jan Breydel Stadium in Bruges in the return. Roger Davies, the gangly ex-striker from Derby County scored three goals in the two ties. Davies scored almost as many goals in one season for Club Brugge (21 in 34 games) as he did for Derby in five seasons (31 in 114 games). In the second round Panathinaikos ran the Belgians close, Brugge winning 2-0 at home, one of the goals a penalty from Davies, but losing 1-0 in Greece. Davies was voted Belgium Player of the Year in 1977, but didn't stay with Club Brugge long enough to take his place in the 1978 European Cup Final, returning to England to play for Leicester City in December 1977. An epic quarter-final followed against Spanish side Atlético Madrid, a 2-0 home win followed by a 3-2 reverse in Madrid, a 4-3 aggregate victory the result. Toughest of all for Brugge, the Belgians overcame the mighty Italians of Juventus in the semi-finals 2-1 on aggregate, losing 1-0 in Turin to a goal from the great Italian centre-forward Roberto Bettega. Brugge's home form just about held in the return, but it took an extra-time winner from Belgian international midfielder René Vandereycken to confirm their place in the final.

The 'new' players from 1977 appearing for Liverpool – apart from the sheer class supplied by Dalglish, Souness and Hansen – were Phil Thompson and David Fairclough. It was a rare start for the talented, if erratic, Fairclough. For Thompson, a virtual one-club man (he played 37 league games for Sheffield United at the end of his career), and a terrific servant to Liverpool FC, his appearance here was part of a 13-year tenure with the Anfield club. Thompson had been unlucky to miss the 1977 European Cup Final through injury – the veteran Tommy Smith stepping in and scoring that remarkable headed goal.

Thompson stood on the Kop watching his adored Liverpool as a boy, signing professional forms with the club as a 17-year-old in 1971. Thompson took a couple of seasons to 'bed in', but ultimately replaced Larry Lloyd as Emlyn Hughes's partner in the centre of defence. It was Thompson's eminent capability as the holding central player that enabled 'Crazy Horse' Hughes to rampage forward on those pulsating upfield surges of his. In 1974 Thompson marked Newcastle United talisman of the time, Malcolm Macdonald, out of the FA Cup Final after 'Macca' had unwisely spoken of his threat to Liverpool. Macdonald was one of the 1970s great characters. I happened to be at Wembley in 1975 when he scored all five goals as England beat Cyprus 5-0. I later played my only 'vets' football match against one of the Cypriot midfielders on that evening.

By 1979 Thompson was being paired with the classy Scot Alan Hansen in the centre of Liverpool's defence, the club regaining the league title at the end of the season. Hughes joined Wolverhampton Wanderers in 1979, Thompson replacing him as club captain. After Liverpool won the league title again in this 1979–1980 season, the club went on to win the European Cup again in 1980–81, Thompson lifting the trophy as captain. Bob Paisley gave Graeme Souness the captaincy in 1981–82, a decision Thompson wasn't happy about, but his performance levels remained high whatever Paisley's reasoning, Liverpool winning the league again in 1981–82 and 1982–83. Come 1984 Thompson found himself displaced by the younger Mark Lawrenson. In the 1983–84 season Liverpool again won the European Cup, although Thompson didn't play enough games to qualify for a medal. Liverpool also won the league title and the League Cup in 1983–84.

'Mr Liverpool', Phil Thompson, spent that short sojourn at Sheffield United, but returned within a season in 1985 as a coach recruited by new manager Kenny Dalglish. Thompson's affinity with Liverpool was so great that when rumoured to be seeking Graeme Souness's management position in 1992, he found himself dismissed from the club. When Gérard Houllier took over the helm in 1998, Thompson returned to replace the departing Roy Evans as a coach again. When

Houllier underwent emergency heart surgery in 2001, Thompson stepped into the breach while Houllier recovered. As assistant manager in the 2000–01 season, Thompson assisted the club to a treble of UEFA Cup, FA Cup and League Cup. When Houllier left Liverpool in 2004, Thompson followed him.

Phil Thompson played 42 times for England 1976–1982, being part of the team that left the 1982 World Cup undefeated. The defence conceded only one goal, but England needed to score a goal against West Germany and Spain and two 0-0 draws in addition to a convoluted second stage format ended Thompson and England's hopes of progress to the semi-finals. With Liverpool Thompson won an astonishing seven league titles: 1972–73, 1975–76, 1976–77, 1978–79, 1979–1980, 1981–82 and 1982–83. He won the FA Cup in 1974, the League Cup twice in 1981 and 1982, and most impressively, the European Cup three times, in 1977, 1978 and 1981, in addition to two UEFA Cup trophies in 1973 and 1976. Thompson was another player whose physical stature belied his resolve and commitment. Tall, but relatively spindly-legged, his covering play as a centre-back and his reading of the game were exceptional. This ability to read the game stood him in good stead as a senior coach at Liverpool.

The highest praise I can give Alan Hansen would be to say that he is the closest thing British football has produced to Franz Beckenbauer – and English football which has produced a conveyor belt of fine centre-halves/stoppers, has never really specialised in sweeper/centre-halves. This is a strange scenario to me as I played against a few players who perfected the sweeper role in village football. I loved playing off the shoulder of the last defender, anticipating the through ball that would elude a flat back four, but if a team played with a sweeper, the blighter would invariably pick me off!

Tall at six feet two inches, the rangy Hansen loved to emerge from defence, ball at feet, roam upfield and supplement the attack. Hansen was that rare specimen in British football defenders, technically accomplished, comfortable on the ball, in an age where continentals used the sweeper as a tactical ploy to help prevent shedding goals, the Brits continued with 'good old' 4-4-2 and 4-3-3 formations until forward-thinking managers like Ron Greenwood, Bobby Robson, Terry Venables and Glenn Hoddle began to tinker with formations, consider other possibilities. 3-5-2, 4-1-3-2, 5-3-2, all are possible in the modern British game, but it took the Brits decades to catch up with other increasingly progressive European football nations.

Hansen spent his formative professional days at 'home' in Scotland with Partick Thistle 1973–77. Hansen, a highly competent golfer, thought hard about a career with clubs on fairways and greens, turning down the offer of a contract with Hibernian as he weighed up his professional sporting options in his teenage years. An erudite man when appearing post-football as a pundit, Hansen also turned down the opportunity to study at the University of Aberdeen in order to join his older brother John at Partick Thistle.

In 1977 Hansen transferred to Liverpool for a fee of £100,000, a fortune in those days for a defender. He played 86 league games for Partick Thistle. Hansen's first goal for Liverpool came in the October 1977 European Cup drubbing of Dynamo Dresden at Anfield. Although selected for this European Cup Final,

Hansen's appearances in the 1977–78 season were sporadic. Establishing a regular place in the team in the 1978–79 season, Hansen and Liverpool won the league title, conceding only four goals at home in all their league fixtures, compiling a 68 points total, a record for the old two points for a win system. With Emlyn Hughes departed for Wolves, Hansen was now a regular first choice centre-back, Liverpool retaining the tile in 1979–1980 during a period of dominance in English club football – only Brian Clough's Nottingham Forest occasionally dented Liverpool's 'invincibility' and unquenchable thirst for trophies.

Although Liverpool won the European Cup again in 1981, and their first English League Cup in this 1980–81 season, a fine Aston Villa team overseen by Ron Saunders and inspired by Dennis Mortimer, Tony Morley, Gary Shaw and Peter Withe, denied the Reds a third consecutive title. The title returned to Anfield in 1982, but Liverpool surprisingly lost to the Bulgarians CSKA Sofia 2-1 on aggregate in the quarter-finals of the European Cup. Once again Liverpool retained the league title in 1982–83.

With Joe Fagan at the helm in 1983–84, Liverpool duly completed a hat-trick of league titles, in addition to winning the League Cup and European Cup again. As the titles continued to accumulate at Anfield, one can see why this Hansen-Souness-Dalglish combo can be considered even better than the wonderful Smith-Hughes-Heighway-Keegan team of the 70s. A rare trophy-less season ensued in 1984–85, a season culminating in the horrors of Heysel, the night of the 1985 European Cup Final when Juventus beat Liverpool 1-0, and more pertinently (football seems irrelevant on these occasions), 39 people died. Fagan retired after the events of Heysel, seemingly uncomfortable with the direction football took that night. The incoming player/manager was Kenny Dalglish, Hansen's great friend and fellow Scotsman. Dalglish appointed Hansen captain and Liverpool became only the third team in the 20th century after Tottenham Hotspur and Arsenal to achieve the double of league and FA Cup in 1985–86. In a period of sustained excellence for fellow Merseysiders Everton, the title was lost in 1986–87, but regained again in 1987–88. Another double was expected as Liverpool 'only' had to beat minnows Wimbledon in the 1988 FA Cup Final. In one of the great shocks in the history of the FA Cup, Liverpool, overwhelming favourites, lost to a team who had fought their way through the leagues from the semi-professional ranks.

A dislocated knee in a pre-season friendly against Atlético Madrid seriously curtailed Hansen's game time in the 1988–89 season. Although he recovered to play in Liverpool's FA Cup victory over Everton, the captaincy had been passed on to Ronnie Whelan. Returning to competitive football, but with only four games under his belt, Hansen was part of the team that narrowly failed again to complete the double, this time losing in ultra-dramatic fashion in the last game of the season. Inconceivably, Liverpool were beaten by an Arsenal team needing to win 2-0 to win the title themselves, Michael Thomas's 90th-minute goal one of those remembered forever in the pantheon of English football.

Hansen regained the captaincy the following season, Liverpool winning the title again (1989–1990). Another double loomed – Liverpool were becoming akin to the Leeds United team of the late 60s and early 70s, their dominance of English football at the time at least rewarded with more silverware than Don Revie's 'giants' could muster. Again surprisingly, the double was denied by defeat in an FA Cup semi-final against Crystal Palace. Come 1990–91, Hansen's knee problem was catching up with him. The club were trophy-less for only the third time in Hansen's 14 years at Anfield, and the talented Scotsman hung his boots up in March 1991, a month after Dalglish resigned as manager. The two of them had considerably affected Liverpool's trophy haul since the apparent 'disaster' of losing Kevin Keegan in 1978. Alan Hansen won eight league titles, three European Cups, two FA Cups and four League Cups with Liverpool. A serial winner and a seriously gifted footballer.

Hansen's international career began inauspiciously. His full debut came in the eviscerating 3-0 defeat against Wales in the now defunct British Home Championship. His nemesis that 1979 day – none other than John Toshack, Kevin Keegan's deadly co-striker from the early 1970s. The worldly-wise Toshack used all his experience against the largely untried Scottish team, claiming all three goals. Hansen's second game was a friendly against Argentina at Hampden Park, lost 3-1, one of the goals coming from an 18-year-old Diego Maradona, who Hansen described as "virtually unplayable". Welcome to international football, Alan! Ridiculously for such a sublimely talented player, Hansen played only 26 times for Scotland, then-national team manager Alex Ferguson preferring his tried and trusted combination of Aberdeen's Alex McLeish and Willie Miller.

Hansen eschewed the idea of football management, preferring instead to promote his considerable knowledge in media punditry. Initially he worked for Sky. BBC approached him to work for BBC Radio 5 Live. Over the next 22 years Hansen became one of the instantly recognisable faces of BBC football coverage on *Match of the Day*. Ironically, his name as a pundit was made (famously) when he observed that "you can't win anything with kids" of a Manchester United team that went on to win the double that season. Hansen's contract with the BBC expired after the 2014 World Cup.

Many images have lodged themselves in the minds of the 60-something follower. One of them is of a tall, gangly, dark-haired young Scotsman rampaging upfield from defence in the 1980s (of course, Emlyn Hughes had set the template before him). Like Beckenbauer, Hansen exuded composure on the football field. His confidence occasionally led to the odd lapse in defence – I suppose John Stones and Harry Maguire are the nearest equivalents in the modern British game, but what a player Alan Hansen was. I think you have to forgive the odd mishap when a player plays the game of football in such a positive fashion.

There were two distinctive sides to Graeme Souness. Never has the phrase 'silk and steel' been more appropriate for a footballer. For one whose temper was quick to rise, Souness was a remarkable technician. He had composure aplenty on the ball, yet could unleash a fierce shot, and, oh yes, he could be a fearsome tackler. Edinburgh-born, Souness was apprenticed to Tottenham Hotspur, signing professional forms as a 15-year-old in 1968. This was a very fine Spurs side indeed at that time, and Souness became frustrated at his lack of opportunities at the club. Considering the elevated standard he would reach ten years later, it's surprising that Souness appeared only once for Spurs 1970–72, as a substitute in a UEFA Cup tie. After summering in Canada with Montreal Olympique, Souness was sold to Middlesbrough in 1972. The Scotsman's tenacity at Ayresome Park over 176 games and 22 goals 1972–78 marked the player out for bigger things. Souness had great mentors at Middlesbrough: Jack Charlton as manager, ex-'Lisbon Lion' Bobby Murdoch as a midfielder Souness modelled himself upon. Souness helped himself to a hat-trick in the final game of the 1973–74 season as Boro reached the top flight with an 8-0 win over Sheffield Wednesday, finishing as 2nd Division champions.

Moving to Liverpool in January 1978 as a replacement for the evergreen Ian Callaghan, Souness's game went up several notches at Anfield where he won five league titles, three European Cups and four League Cups. It was Souness's delicate pass that set Kenny Dalglish up for the winning goal in this 1978 European Cup Final. In the 1980–81 European Cup campaign (Liverpool beat Real Madrid 1-0 in the final) Souness scored a hat-trick in the quarter-final against CSKA Sofia of Bulgaria. Paisley awarded Souness the captaincy for the 1981–82 season, causing something of a rift between the Scotsman and Phil Thompson. Under Souness's captaincy Liverpool continued to thrive. Titles kept arriving at Anfield. In the 1984 League Cup Final replay Souness scored the winner against Merseyside rivals Everton. Liverpool retained the league title for the third consecutive season in 1983–84. This was Souness's Liverpool swansong, completing 358 appearances and scoring 56 goals in his six years with the club.

Seeking pastures new, Souness and Trevor Francis added experience to upcoming Italian stars Gianluca Vialli and Roberto Mancini at Sampdoria in Serie A. In his first season (1984–85) Souness helped Sampdoria win the Coppa Italia. In 1986, now aged 33, Souness became player-manager of Glasgow Rangers. In his debut for the club he was sent off following a second yellow card after just 34 minutes. Disciplinary issues dogged his final playing days at Rangers. He retired aged 38 in 1991, doubtless frustrated by his body not allowing him to dominate games in the manner he'd adhered to so vigorously at Liverpool. At the Merseyside club Souness also had many great players around him. It's not easy to accept when your influence on a football match is waning, especially for the truly great players.

Graeme Souness played 54 matches for Scotland, scoring four goals, and competed in three World Cups, 1978, 1982 and 1986. Moving into player-management in April 1986, the 'Souness Revolution' began, the experienced Scot signing several players who, apparently past their best in England, boosted Ranger's fortunes instantly. Souness signed the heroic warrior of a centre-half Terry Butcher from Ipswich Town, and Chris Woods from Norwich City (England's second choice goalkeeper, understudying Peter Shilton in the 1980s). Further star signings followed: Trevor Francis and Ray Wilkins, England internationals who had been playing in Italy, plus two formidable professionals from Everton: wide midfielder Trevor Steven and right-back Gary Stevens.

In April 1991 with Souness about to complete a fourth Scottish title in five seasons, he upped and left, returning to Liverpool after being given the opportunity to succeed old teammate Kenny Dalglish as manager. Under Souness, several revered Liverpool youngsters forged places in the team: Steve

McManaman, Jamie Redknapp, Robbie Fowler. Unfortunately for Souness this was a transitional period for playing personnel at Anfield, and the club fell off the radar a little in trophy pursuits.

Souness has since managed Galatasaray, Southampton, coached Torino, managed Benfica, Blackburn Rovers and Newcastle United. His 'foreign' exploits proved difficult. Souness, a strong man with strong opinions, felt restricted by his chairmen on foreign shores. His understanding of the British game ensured considerably more success at Blackburn Rovers. In his first full season 2000–01, Souness oversaw Blackburn's return to the Premier League, young players Damien Duff, David Dunn and Matt Jansen thriving under the Scot's tutelage. In 2002 Blackburn beat Tottenham Hotspur 2-1 at Wembley to lift the League Cup. At Newcastle, Souness attempted to remedy Newcastle's ills by signing old Liverpool hero Michael Owen, but a broken metatarsal put paid to a promising start with Newcastle for Owen. Once again the abrasive Souness fell foul of a chairman, this time Freddy Shepherd, and was replaced in 2006 by Glenn Roeder.

Like so many great players before him, Graeme Souness found management a 'tough ask'. It's as a fiercely competitive player he is best remembered. Ferociously focused, his keen football brain giving him antennae on the football field that others lacked, his touch and explosive shooting masked an uncompromising attitude. A great footballer, Graeme Souness, for all his undeniably darker side, his influence on the Liverpool team 1978–1984 amply revealed by the amount of trophies won with him as the team's midfield fulcrum.

Is Kenny Dalglish the single greatest player to don the red jersey of Liverpool FC? It's a crowded field when you consider the merits of Steven Gerrard, and the recent crop of Anfield stars par excellence, Mo Salah, Sadio Mané and Virgil van Dijk. Yet Dalglish took on the mantle of Anfield folk hero from the irrepressible Kevin Keegan and scarcely put a foot wrong in his years at Liverpool 1977–1990. Dalglish had enormous shoes to fill in Keegan's, but his stylish, creative forward play elevated him to a higher plane than even Keegan. It's an argument that would rage for weeks over many a pint among supporters, but Dalglish gets my vote. Naturally we all have our own personal favourites; mine would be the greyhound winger Steve Heighway. I'm not alone though in saying Dalglish was THE best – in 2009 *Four Four Two* football magazine named the Scot the greatest striker in post-war British football, 1945–2009. Some accolade.

Dalglish was already a Glaswegian folk hero when he arrived at Anfield in 1977, having won four Scottish League titles, four Scottish Cups and one Scottish League Cup at Celtic. The conveyor belt of trophies kept rolling on at Liverpool: six League titles, one FA Cup, four League Cups and three European Cups. For Scotland, Dalglish received 102 caps, ending up joint top scorer for his country alongside the iconic Denis Law with 30 goals.

Incredibly, the super-talented striker with a football brain as sharp as a tack, started out as a goalkeeper at Secondary School. Before achieving greatness at Anfield, Dalglish, astonishingly, failed a trial at Liverpool, and another at West Ham United, in 1966 as a teenager. Despite his prodigious talent, the early years at Celtic were a testing time for Dalglish, first team football eluding him until the 1971–72 season. His football brain was sharpened by playing in midfield at times.

When chosen as a striker his goal return for Celtic's reserve team in 1969–70 and 1970–71 was 19 and 23 respectively. Finally established in the first team in 1971–72 he repaid Jock Stein's faith in him with 29 goals in 53 games. The following season, 1972–73, Dalglish trumped this total, scoring 39 goals in all competitions. Celtic were winning domestic titles for fun at this time, but further European success eluded them (after the glory of 'Lisbon 67'), coming close in 1973–74, but losing out in a physical battle in the semi-finals of the European Cup to Atlético Madrid (the Spanish side had three players sent off in Glasgow in the first leg).

Ironically, when Dalglish was appointed captain for the 1975–76 season, the club failed to win a trophy for the first time in 12 years. Celtic rectified the matter in 1976–77, winning the domestic double of league and Scottish cup, Dalglish scoring 27 goals in all competitions. Celtic fans adored Dalglish, and when he signed for Bob Paisley's Liverpool in August 1977 for a then-British transfer record fee of £440,000 (£2.75 million in today's money), they were deeply aggrieved, feeling Dalglish had turned his back on them. He made 320 appearances for the Glasgow club (another irony lay in the fact Dalglish supported Glasgow Rangers as a boy), scoring 167 goals in all competitions.

Kenny Dalglish, hero in Glasgow, was only just beginning to make his name. He scored on his Liverpool debut against Middlesbrough, following this with a home debut goal at Anfield against Newcastle United. At the end of his first season – this season of 1977–78 culminating with his European Cup-winning goal against Club Brugge at Wembley – Dalglish had amassed 32 goals in 61 games in all competitions. In 1978–79 Dalglish secured a personal best 1st Division goals tally of 21 and won the Football Writer's Association Footballer of the Year award. Dalglish's goal-scoring form receded for a couple of seasons, reviving significantly when asked to play 'in the hole' behind Ian Rush. The two formed a fabulously potent strike partnership. The melding of these two formidable footballing talents is akin to the one Bobby Robson discovered in playing Peter Beardsley in the space behind Gary Lineker for England. When you have players as intuitive as Beardsley and Dalglish 'floating' in the space between midfield and attack, their link play with the main striker becomes invaluable to the team. Having totalled only eight and 13 goals in 1980–81 and 1981–82, Dalglish revelled in the freedom of his new role, scoring 18 league goals in the 1982–83 title-winning season for Liverpool, winning the PFA Player's Player of the Year award to boot. The goals did dry up thereafter, although Dalglish is remembered vividly by Liverpool fans for scoring against Chelsea at Stamford Bridge in the last game of the 1985–86 season, a goal confirming Liverpool's 16th league title. Ironically it was the incoming Beardsley who struck up a new potent partnership with John Aldridge that led to Dalglish appearing less often in Liverpool's first team.

Dalglish tended to be the scourge of England internationally, nutmegging Ray Clemence to score the winning goal at Hampden Park in 1976; scoring again at Wembley in 1977 as Scotland beat England 2-1. Dalglish appeared in the 1978 and 1982 World Cups, scoring in Scotland's impressive 3-2 victory over Holland in 1978. Ultimately his 102 caps for Scotland became a national record.

Kenny Dalglish made a hugely impressive start to his management career with Liverpool 1985–1991. Initially he retained his boots for sporadic player-manager appearances, that 1986 title-winning goal followed by victory over Everton in the FA Cup Final to confirm Liverpool as the third team to win the double in the 20th century after Tottenham Hotspur and Arsenal. Dalglish acted swiftly and emphatically after a trophy-less 1986–87 season, signing John Aldridge and Ray Houghton from an emergent Oxford United club who'd won the 3rd Division title under the wise and astute management of Jim Smith.

Oxford United found life tough in the top flight in 1985–86, but won the 1986 League Cup Final 3-0 at Wembley, defeating Queens Park Rangers. It seems incredible to think now, but Oxford United would have played in the 1986–87 UEFA Cup tournament but for the Heysel ban.

Aldridge and Houghton proved smash hits at Anfield, an attacking unit par excellence supplemented by John Barnes playing more as a playmaker than as a wide left striker as he had done at Watford, and the ridiculously imaginative Peter Beardsley playing the old role Dalglish himself had perfected, this time behind Aldridge. The input of Dalglish on the creative explosion of the impish Houghton and Beardsley, the reincarnation of an even more potent Barnes, should not be underestimated. The 1987–88 season saw Liverpool top the league from almost start to finish, achieving a 37-game unbeaten run, playing a brand of attacking football that has only been matched in the 21st century in British football by Pep Guardiola's Manchester City and Jürgen Klopp's latter-day Liverpool. Ultimately Liverpool lost two games in 40 while winning the 1987–88 title. The quality of Liverpool's football had been as stratospheric as Dalglish's own playing career at the club, making it all the more surprising when the 1987 FA Cup Final was lost 1-0 to Wimbledon.

Despite coming close but missing out on further doubles in the 1988–89 and 1989–1990 seasons, Dalglish garnered three Manager of the Year awards during this period. It came as something of a surprise when Dalglish resigned as manager in February 1991 with Liverpool three points ahead of the field in the league and still in contention in the FA Cup. One wonders how badly he was affected by the deaths of the 96 at Hillsborough on 15 April 1989 at the ill-fated FA Cup semi-final between Liverpool and Nottingham Forest. Dalglish's reaction to and the support he proffered to the Hillsborough families received wide acclaim.

Dalglish returned to management after a short break in October 1991, taking the helm at 2nd Division Blackburn Rovers. His impact on his new club was instant, although the team's form faltered towards the end of the 1991–92 season. They squeaked into the play-offs, eventually beating Leicester City in the play-off final. Back in the Premier League, Dalglish achieved a coup by signing Alan Shearer from Southampton for a record £3.5 million fee. An injury put paid to Shearer's first season at Blackburn, but the team still finished fourth in their first season back in the top flight. The following season with Shearer back in the team, Blackburn finished second. The ambitious Dalglish wanted to sign Roy Keane, but failed. In 1994–95 with Chris Sutton, Tim Flowers and David Batty on board, Blackburn won the Premier League, making Dalglish only the fourth manager after Tom Watson, Herbert Chapman and Brian Clough to win the top-tier title with two different clubs.

Moving to Newcastle United in January 1997 he oversaw the talented Beardsley-Les Ferdinand-David Ginola team to a second successive second place finish at the end of the 1996–97 season. His short-term fix of replacing some of the incumbent stars at St James's Park with John Barnes (34), Ian Rush (36) and Stuart Pearce seemed less prescient. Ultimately he lost his job to Ruud Gullit as chairman Freddie Shepherd became frustrated.

A short spell back at Celtic followed, the club winning the Scottish League Cup, beating Aberdeen 2-0 in his one and only season back in Glasgow. Ten years later, Dalglish was invited by Rafael Benitez to oversee Liverpool's youth academy. When Roy Hodgson failed to impact in the senior manager's role at Anfield in 2010–11, Dalglish took over again as Liverpool's first team manager. In early 2011 Dalglish signed Luis Suarez from Ajax. The Argentinian signing proved to be a short-term masterstroke. In the 2011–12 season Liverpool won the League Cup, losing the FA Cup Final to Chelsea, but failed to qualify for the Champions League for the third consecutive season. In a modern era of must-win trophies in double-quick time, Dalglish lost his job in May 2012. A year later he returned to Liverpool as a non-executive director.

In October 2017, Anfield's Centenary Stand was renamed the Sir Kenny Dalglish Stand in honour of the Scot's fulsome contribution to Liverpool Football Club. Kenny Dalglish, a hero in Glasgow with first club Celtic, underwent a stratospheric elevation of his football career at Liverpool. Rarely in British football does such a clever, artful player with a consummate tactical football brain allied to an exquisite touch reveal himself. Dalglish was almost continental in his touch, awareness and appreciation of space on a football pitch. After making himself, arguably, Liverpool's greatest ever football player, he applied his sharp football brain to management with a reasonable degree of success. Apart from the aforementioned stack of trophies won at Celtic and Liverpool, Dalglish was also the FWA Footballer of the Year 1978–79 and 1982–83, the PFA Player's Player of the Year in 1982–83 and came second in the prestigious Ballon d'Or (European Footballer of the Year) behind Michel Platini in 1983. As a manager Dalglish won three 1st Division titles with Liverpool, 1985–86, 1987–88, and 1989–1990; the FA Cup in 1985–86, 1988–89; and the Football League Cup in 2011–12. He also took Blackburn Rovers to that shock Premiership title in 1994–95, the year the famous 'SAS' Shearer and Sutton combination came up trumps. At Celtic, Dalglish oversaw the Scottish League Cup victory in 1999–2000. Kenny Dalglish received an OBE in 1985. Quite a player, quite a manager.

The Club Brugge team in opposition to Liverpool on this evening contained two Danish internationals, goalkeeper Birger Jensen (winner of five Belgian titles 1976–1988 and two Belgian Cups 1976–77 and 1985–86), and striker Jan Sorensen (Belgian league winner 1977–78, 1979–1980). Austrian defender/midfielder Eduard Krieger won three league titles with Club Brugge and the Belgian Cup in 1976–77. Otherwise the team comprised Belgian internationals and non-internationals, the two best known being Julien Cools and René Vandereycken in midfield. On the face of it, they shouldn't have troubled a Liverpool team packed with quality and creativity, but as stated before, Belgian football was firmly on the rise in the late 70s and early 80s, if lacking the refined skills of a modern-day Kevin De Bruyne or Eden Hazard. What the Belgians had in spades was professionalism, organisation and a strong team ethic.

THE FINAL

The game proved a hard-fought contest for Liverpool, won by one moment of sheer quality provided by the classy Scots pair Graeme Souness and Kenny Dalglish. David Fairclough threatened early on for Liverpool with his pace, heading down Ray Kennedy's long ball, but he couldn't quite get beyond the last Brugge defender. Jimmy Case found space on the right-hand side as Liverpool attempt to exert pressure, but again the Belgians cleared the danger. It's all Liverpool, but clear-cut chances are few and far between. Fairclough's pace got him in behind the defence again but his cross was slightly behind his onrushing teammates. Kennedy almost scored at the far post but sliced his shot wildly. Case and Souness struck ferocious long-range shots that came near to opening the score. The inconsistent Fairlcough caused all manner of problems with his pace, but half-time saw the game goalless.

In the early phases of the second half Dalglish was to the fore, his clever brain allowing the ball to run and set up Terry McDermott for a chance, but the latter's shot was too close to the keeper. Dalglish then struck wildly wide from the left-hand side. The breakthrough came in the 64th minute. Souness, not for the first time, freed Dalglish with the cutest of chipped passes, and Dalglish matched his fellow Scot's touch with a sublime clipped shot that drifted into the far corner of the goal. Dalglish skied another chance as Liverpool continued to dominate possession. At last a rare momentary lapse of Liverpool concentration allowed the Belgians to break clear. The covering Ray Clemence blocked the first shot, the ball rebounded to Jan Simoen who shot for goal. Luckily for Liverpool, Phil Thompson spotted the danger and cleared the ball off the line. In a match of missed half-chances for a dominant Liverpool, Club Brugge were resilient to the last, almost defying the odds to equalise. Liverpool were worthy winners, but Club Brugge were not here simply to make up the numbers.

1978–79 EUROPEAN CUP FINAL
Nottingham Forest 1 v 0 Malmö FF

What a period this was for English club football. At a time when England's national team were struggling to qualify for World Cups – they failed in 1974 and 1978 – English football teams were dominant in the European Cup. Nottingham Forest's win in the Olympiastadion, Munich, in May 1979 was the third of six (yes, six) consecutive wins by English football clubs.

Brian Clough's achievement in winning English football's top-tier league with two provincial clubs, Forest and Derby County in the 1970s, was little short of astonishing. This was in part due to seriously talented Scottish players Archie Gemmill and John Robertson (it wasn't just Dalglish, Souness and Hansen at Liverpool). Secondly, Clough's specialism seemed to be taking players who were marginal successes for other clubs and transforming them into champions. Clough only resorted to an expensive transfer with the signing of Trevor Francis from Birmingham City in February 1979. Francis became Britain's first £1-million footballer when signing for Forest. Banned from playing for three months due to UEFA rules, Francis's first ever European football match was this 1979 European Cup Final. He scored the only goal of the game. Malmö, for their part, were unfortunate that key players Bo Larsson and Roy Andersson were injured. On the eve of the final their captain and midfielder Staffan Tapper broke his toe in training. All this conspired to see Malmö set up with an even more defensive formation than Club Brugge implemented against Liverpool in the 1978 final.

Route to the Final

Of all the teams for Forest to have to face in the first round they were drawn to play holders and fierce English club rivals Liverpool. Forest won the home leg 2-0 with goals from Garry Birtles and Colin Barrett, grinding out a hard-fought 0-0 draw at Anfield. Forest made short work of the Greeks AEK Athens in the second round, winning 2-1 in Athens with goals from Birtles and John McGovern, easing through to the quarter-finals with a resounding 5-1 win at the City Ground, Birtles again on the scoresheet (twice). Forest eased through the last eight too, courtesy of another thumping home victory against Grasshoppers of Zürich, to the tune of 4-1 at the City Ground, Birtles again among the scorers. Martin O'Neill's goal was enough to secure aggregate victory in a 1-1 draw in Switzerland.

The game appeared to be up for Forest in the last four when they failed to overcome the Germans 1. FC Köln in Nottingham. A 3-3 draw was not in Brian Clough's game plan as Forest had to recover a 0-2 deficit in the game. Three away goals against his team, the stage was set for one of Clough's defensive master plans in the return in Cologne. A solitary goal from Ian Bowyer and a typically resolute rearguard action by the Forest defence overcame the odds stacked against the Midlands club.

The Swedish side Malmö FF were a surprise finalist in 1979, especially with perennially successful giants such as Real Madrid and Juventus in the competition, but the draw fell more kindly for Malmö than Forest. In the first round the Swedes defeated French club Monaco 1-0 on aggregate, albeit by winning the tie in France having been held to a goalless draw in Sweden. I may be harsh on Malmö as they had to defeat top Ukrainian side Dynamo Kiev 2-0 on aggregate in the second round, drawing in the Ukraine never an easy task. Swedish teams are not renowned for their goal-scoring prowess, more their team spirit and organisation. A subsequent 5-3 aggregate victory over Polish side Wisław Kraków in the last eight came as another surprise as the goals flowed. The 4-1 home win all but secured Malmö's progress, a hat-trick from Anders Ljungberg (including two penalties) ensuring victory. Ljungberg (no relation to Arsenal's Freddie) did revel in the nickname 'Puskás' after the great Real Madrid and Hungary star.

Forest had the tougher semi-final with German opposition 1. FC Köln, Malmö coming through two tight semi-final ties with Austria Wien, winning 1-0 in Sweden after a 0-0 draw in Vienna in the first leg. Garry Birtles was the second top scorer in the 1978–79 European Cup competition with six, a total surpassed by the Swiss striker Claudio Sulser of Grasshoppers who scored in both quarter-final ties with Nottingham Forest. Sulser ended up with a competition total of 11, massively aided by five in one game against Maltese minnows Valetta in the first round, although he also scored three times against Real Madrid in the second round.

Forest were a team apparently cobbled together by master-manager Brian Clough and his inseparable assistant manager and master scouter of players, Peter Taylor. Look back at their line-up now and you see a team of international players. What is beyond doubt is that there were players here in Munich on this evening (as there had been at the Baseball Ground when Derby County won the 1971–72 league title) who played their best football under Clough and Taylor.

In goal for Forest was England's second best-ever keeper (after the incomparable Gordon Banks), Peter Shilton. Before even wearing the red of Nottingham Forest, Shilton had already played 396 league games for Leicester City and Stoke City 1966–1977. Shilton holds the England international caps record of 125, and the all-time record for the most competitive appearances in world football, 1,390. Even the great Pele couldn't quite match that tally (despite a slew of friendly games for Santos around the world). On the international stage Shilton did not play for England until he was 32, but played 17 tournament finals games thereafter, his record of ten clean sheets in those games equalled only by Frenchman Fabien Barthez.

Shilton's early career is intertwined with his England predecessor Gordon Banks. Banks noticed Shilton as a 13-year-old pupil at King Richard 111 School, Leicester. Such was Shilton's promise that after making his debut for Leicester City against Everton, Banks was sold on to Stoke City. In October 1967 Shilton replicated the feat of Tottenham Hotspur's custodian Pat Jennings by scoring a goal at Southampton's The Dell Stadium with a hefty clearance. In 1969 Leicester were relegated from the 1st Division, but the 19-year-old Shilton played in an FA Cup Final defeat at Wembley to Manchester City.

When Banks departed Stoke City for a swansong spell in the North American Soccer League, there could be only one replacement for the master. In came the junior master Shilton for a world record transfer fee (for a goalkeeper at that time) of £325.000. Shilton played in a Stoke City side in 1974–75 that narrowly missed out on the league title. It was a Stoke City team containing stalwarts Mike Pejic, Denis Smith and Jimmy Greenhoff, also including Geoff Hurst in the twilight of his career, and a personal favourite of mine, Alan Hudson, who'd attempted to escape the excesses of the King's Road in London. The club eventually finished fifth behind Brian Clough's champions, Derby County, but only four points adrift. A severe storm at Stoke's Victoria Ground meant the club were struggling to keep up player's financial demands, and after being relegated to the 2nd Division, Shilton was sold on to Nottingham Forest in September 1977.

England's incumbent international goalkeeper, Shilton would now enjoy the most successful period of his club career under Clough and Taylor. In 1977–78 Forest won the League Cup (without the cup-tied Shilton), and went on to win the 1st Division title in their first season back in the top flight. Shilton conceded just 18 goals in 37 matches, his performances earning him the PFA Player's Player of the Year award. The League Cup was retained in 1979 with Shilton in goal, but lost in 1980 when Shilton and David Needham allowed Andy Gray a tap-in for Wolves' winning goal. It was ever thus with goalkeepers. Shilton's overall performances at the highest level were consistency personified, but he is remembered for the occasional blip. It's the curse of the player at either end of the field, the goalkeeper who lets in the 'soft' goal, or the striker who misses the open goal.

Shilton's career at Forest peaked in 1979 and 1980 with the winning of two European Cups. These were the pinnacles of Peter Shilton and Brian Clough's careers. Shilton joined ex-international teammates Kevin Keegan and Alan Ball at Southampton in 1982. In 1983–84 the team reached the FA Cup semi-final, only to lose to eventual winners Everton. An addiction to gambling notwithstanding, Shilton was surprised by Eamonn Andrews at London's Waterloo Station in March 1986 when he was chosen as the subject of the popular ITV institution *This Is Your Life.*

Moving again to Derby County in 1987, Shilton helped the Midlands side to a fifth-placed finish in the 1st Division which would have led to UEFA Cup football but for the Heysel ban. When Derby were relegated in 1991, Shilton decided (February 1992) to accept a player-manager's role at Plymouth Argyle at the age of 42. He'd played 202 league games for Nottingham Forest, a further 188 and 175 respectively for Southampton and Derby County. Shilton couldn't prevent relegation for Argyle although he helped the club reach the Division 2 play-off semi-finals in 1995. His later career consisted of one appearance for Bolton Wanderers and nine for Leyton Orient, matches he undertook simply to overtake the 1,000 league appearance record.

Internationally, although Shilton went on to win a record number of caps for England 1970–1990, he spent the 70s sharing the goalkeeper's position with Ray Clemence. A succession of managers seemed unsure which of the two excellent custodians was England's premier goalkeeper. Under Bobby Robson, Shilton captained the England side when Bryan Robson and Ray Wilkins were unavailable. In 1973 Shilton bore the brunt of media criticism when allowing Jan Domarski's shot to beat his flailing dive – though had Norman Hunter not lost possession near the halfway line the goal for Poland that ensured England failed to qualify for the 1974 World Cup would not have occurred. Latterly, it was Shilton's misfortune to be undone by Diego Maradona's brace for Argentina in the 1986 World Cup quarter-final – he could do nothing about either the 'Hand of God' goal or Maradona's scintillating second, legitimate or otherwise.

When Shilton called time on his international career after the 1990 World Cup he was 40 years old. An imposing, barrel-chested man, Shilton was a commanding presence in goal and a fine shot-stopper, agile, with excellent reflexes. He was renowned for his perfectionism, work-rate, and discipline.

Viv Anderson at right-back for Forest became the first black footballer to represent England at international level in 1978 – against Czechoslovakia at Wembley (1-0 England, I was there). Anderson, at six feet, was a tall man for a full-back; his natural pace allied to an athletic disposition made him the perfect modern defender. He played for Forest 1974–1984 (328 league appearances) and although he'd debuted for the club pre-Brian Clough, he was a prime example of a player whose level soared under the maestro Clough's management.

Largely neglected as England's right-back in favour of Liverpool's Phil Neal initially, Anderson subsequently found himself playing second fiddle to Everton's Gary Stevens in the mid-80s, despite reviving his club career at Arsenal 1984–87 (120 league appearances). His time in North London culminated with a 2-1 League Cup Final win over Liverpool in 1987.

Anderson became Alex Ferguson's first signing for Manchester United in 1987. After making a good impression initially, Anderson gave way to one of the 1990s' most iconic defenders in Irishman Denis Irwin. Far from being finished, Anderson moved to Sheffield Wednesday, where he not only helped Wednesday win promotion from Division 2 to Division 1, but aided the club's run to Wembley, where, cup-tied, he was unable to take part in Wednesday's League Cup Final win over Manchester United in 1991. Back in the top tier, Wednesday reached the FA Cup Final and the League Cup Final in 1993, losing out in both matches to Arsenal.

A disciplined player, Anderson's on-pitch behaviour marked him out as a potential manager. At Barnsley as a player-manager the club narrowly avoided relegation from Division 1 to Division 2 in 1993–94. Joining Middlesbrough as Bryan Robson's assistant manager, he helped Robbo's Boro team to both domestic cup finals in 1996–97, although both were lost. A relegation followed, and then another League Cup Final defeat after regaining promotion. The duo stabilised Boro's fortunes while failing to win silverware.

Admired for his lung-busting capacity to supplement his attack, equally admired for his tackling and intuitive reading of the game, Viv Anderson was voted into Nottingham Forest's greatest XI in 1997. He was awarded an MBE in January 2020, and in a British football game – and on a wider World/European stage beset by damaging racial prejudice – is remarkable for being England's first-ever black footballer selection.

At left-back, Frank Clark established himself as a dependable defender with Newcastle United 1962–1975, completing 389 league matches on Tyneside. Born in Rowlands Gill, County Durham, the redoubtable Clark began as a semi-professional player with Crook Town, a local team for Clark, and winners of the FA Amateur Cup no less than five times – Clark won it with Crook Town 1961–62. Clark's finest moment with Newcastle United came with the club's 6-2 aggregate drubbing of the Hungarians Újpest Dosza in the 1969 Inter-Cities Fairs Cup Final. Clark became an ever-present for Brian Clough upon signing for Nottingham Forest in 1975 on a free transfer (a nod to Peter Taylor's wise summarisation of players), helping Forest up into the top tier from Division 2. Frank Clark's last game for Forest would be this 1979 European Cup Final.

Clark completed 117 league games for Forest 1975–79. Astonishingly, he scored only one goal in 506 league matches for Newcastle and Nottingham Forest. This clearly indicates where Clark's priorities lay – to perfect the art of defending, a skill-set Clough and Taylor recognised at once with the Geordie. Lank-haired, moustachioed, Clark was an instantly recognisable face at St James's Park and the City Ground. Clark became assistant manager at Sunderland 1979–1982, then manager of Leyton Orient in 1983. Relegation from Division 3 to Division 4 followed in 1985, but Clark revived the 'Os', guiding the club to promotion in 1989. He ultimately became managing director at Leyton Orient before returning to Nottingham Forest as replacement manager for the retiring Clough. Having brought unprecedented success to the City Ground, Clough's final act was to oversee relegation from the Premier League in 1993. Clark had to deal with the departure of Roy Keane and Nigel Clough, two key players, but with the lion-hearted Stuart Pearce in the side, helped Forest back to the Premiership immediately as runners-up in Division 1.

Forest began life back in the Premiership 1994–95 impressively, the team eventually finishing third, qualifying for European football for the first time in 11 years. In the 1995–96 season Forest reached the UEFA Cup quarter-finals, but the sale of striker Stan Collymore to Liverpool derailed Clark's plans at the club. Clark found life tougher thereafter, being discarded by Forest in 1996. A short spell as boss of Manchester City followed, 1996–98, but City were in a period of transition and success eluded Clark.

Clough's two centre-backs in the Olympiastadion, Munich, on this evening were as colossal as the nearby Bavarian Alps. Larry Lloyd's career had been reinvigorated by Clough and Taylor after his time with Liverpool; Kenny Burns was a fearsome competitor, a good player at Birmingham City, but a great player under Clough and Taylor. Lloyd's career I have chronicled from his time with Liverpool, so I'll turn to the passionate Scots competitor Burns. Released by his local team, Glasgow Rangers, aged 17, Burns signed for Birmingham City in 1971. He was signed as a centre-back, but like Chris Sutton at Blackburn Rovers, was converted to centre-forward, in his case because of the sale of Bob Latchford to Everton. In that season of 1974–75 Burns won Birmingham's Player of the Year award.

The astute Clough and Taylor re-converted Burns back to centre-back upon signing him for Forest in 1977. Forest had won promotion back to the top flight in 1977. The conversion of Burns to central defence, in addition to the top signings of Peter Shilton and Archie Gemmill, saw Forest win the 1977–78 1st Division title. Forest also beat Liverpool 1-0 in a replayed match to win the 1978 League Cup. Burns won the FWA Footballer of the Year award. Burns and Lloyd formed a mountainous presence at the heart of Forest's defence as the club won two successive European Cups in 1979 and 1980.

In his last season at the City Ground, 1980–81, Burns won the club's Player of the Year award. Seen in some quarters as a 'wild man', Burns's aggressive style disguised a smart tactical brain. Leaving Forest for Leeds United in 1981, Burns promptly became their club Player of the Year in the 1982–83 season. After spells at Derby County and Barnsley, Burns represented numerous non-league clubs as a player-coach. Burns played 20 times for Scotland 1974–1981. Burns's blond, bearded 'Viking' image reinforced his 'wild man' image, but the Scot was far more than an aggressive beast of a player.

In a team full of Clough and Taylor disciples, captain John McGovern stood out as the player who seemed to benefit most from his mentors' support and encouragement. McGovern worked through professional football the hard way, playing in all four divisions of the Football League. John McGovern was one of those players who go under the radar a little, hard-working, unfussy, yet his Forest teammate John Robertson summed up McGovern perfectly as the kind of player every team needs. McGovern was the cog that enabled the midfield machines at Derby County and Nottingham Forest to run smoothly.

McGovern wanted to be a striker like his heroes Denis Law and Jimmy Greaves, but unsuited to the role, he began as a winger before converting to midfield. He debuted for Hartlepool United as a 16-year-old in 1965, under the auspices of Clough and Taylor in their first management roles. When Clough and Taylor moved in tandem (they were inseparable for a decade and a half) to Derby County in May 1967, McGovern was on their radar. Eighteen years old, McGovern signed for Derby in September 1968. Witnessing the total dedication to being the model professional that Dave Mackay, fellow Scotsman, embodied, Mc Govern realised he needed to work harder in order to achieve his goals. McGovern possessed a rare ability to play off either foot (most players are heavily oriented towards either right or left foot). Seeing this, Clough and Taylor, switched McGovern to central midfield. Aged 19, John McGovern won promotion with Derby County to the 1st Division. Having been promoted from 4 to 3 with Hartlepool United, McGovern had played in all four divisions of the Football League before the age of 20.

In a four-way title fight for the old 1st Division in 1971–72, Derby County won their first league title at the expense of Liverpool, Leeds United and Manchester City. McGovern scored the only goal of the game as Derby beat Liverpool 1-0 in the penultimate game at the notoriously muddy Baseball Ground. How on earth did the talented Derby team with skilful players like Kevin Hector and Alan Hinton play such a great brand of attacking football on that quagmire? As a bit of a lightweight myself, heavy pitches during the winter were always my undoing in village football. I'd usually start a season well before winter pitches got the better of me. Aged 22, John McGovern lifted his first league title, although a disallowed John Toshack goal at Highbury against Arsenal, and a surprise 2-1 defeat for Leeds at Wolves, made it a hairs-breadth success.

In the 1972–73 season Derby were controversially defeated in the European Cup semi-final by Juventus of Italy, the match in Turin seeing Juve's over-robust tackling go unpunished, while any similar Derby tackles were penalised heavily. It would be the closest Brian Clough came to European glory prior to this night of 1979. When Clough resigned as manager of Derby in October 1973, Derby's fans were outraged. Dave Mackay took over as manager – McGovern supported the new manager's emplacement, and then found his starting position taken by the more attack-minded Bruce Rioch.

Taken on as manager of Nottingham Forest in January 1975 after his abortive 44-day tenure at Leeds United, one of Brian Clough's first acts was to sign John McGovern and John O'Hare from Leeds United where they'd briefly joined him. Clough had these trusted players at Derby County in their successful early 70s team. Neglected at Leeds with Billy Bremner and Johnny Giles selected ahead of him, McGovern (and O'Hare) were suspected by Leeds players of being part of a Clough regime.

In McGovern's second season (1975–76) reunited with Clough at Forest, he became Clough's club captain and trusted 'lieutenant'. Forest finished eighth in that season in Division 2, but scraped promotion with a third-placed finish in 1976–77. In the top flight in 1977–78 Forest conceded only 24 goals in 42 league games (thanks in no small part to Peter Shilton's arrival) in winning Division 1 at the first time of asking. In the 1978–79 season Forest lost an impressive 42-match unbeaten run – defeated by Liverpool in December 1978, a run only surpassed by the Arsenal 'Invincibles' side of 2004. McGovern went on to captain Forest in this first European Cup triumph of 1979.

Clough's successful team broke up in 1982, Peter Taylor decided to resign, and McGovern transferred to Bolton Wanderers in the 1982 close season. With hindsight Taylor thought the ageing team broke up too soon. McGovern played 324 competitive games for Forest. He then joined Bolton as a player-manager, but played only 16 times for them. He won two Scottish U-23 caps, but never represented the full international team.

John McGovern managed one of my local semi-professional teams, Woking, in the 1997–98 season, but was unable to transfer his former boss and mentor Brian Clough's success to the club. I remember he was criticised in some quarters for the club's playing style. I believe he wanted to instil in Woking some of the traits that he'd learned from Clough, but Clough's man-management style was utterly unique. John McGovern was one of those players whose selflessness on a football pitch allowed more talented individuals to shine. A fine man-marker, he was deceptively gifted himself with energy to burn.

Like McGovern, Ian Bowyer alongside him in midfield in central midfield was a player for whom the 'journeyman' tag might have been coined, yet possessed talent and a shrewd football brain. Used as a fringe player by first club Manchester City (50 league appearances, 13 goals), Bowyer picked up useful European experience 1968–1971 with City in the successful 1969–1970 Cup Winners Cup campaign. Out of favour when Malcolm Allison took over the management reins from Joe Mercer, Bowyer transferred to 2nd Division Leyton Orient in 1971–72. Bowyer – who seemed like a typical product of Brian Clough's ability to improve a player – was actually signed for Forest by then-incumbent manager Allan Brown. In 1975 Clough took over as Forest manager, Peter Taylor joining him as his assistant manager in 1976. Clough and Taylor valued Bowyer's all-round game, his consistency and tenacity. Bowyer scored the vital solitary goal against 1. FC Köln in this 1979 semi-final victory, playing in both the 1979 and 1980 European Cup Finals.

Ian Bowyer left Forest for Sunderland in 1981, but re-joined Forest in 1982, adding a further 200 league starts to an overall tally of 564 competitive matches for the club, scoring a highly respectable 96 goals in all competitions 1973–1989. Like McGovern, Bowyer tried his hand at management and coaching, notably as Peter Shilton's assistant manager 1994–96 at Plymouth Argyle.

This Nottingham Forest team were renowned for the obdurate manner of their football, their team ethic instilled in them by Clough and Taylor. You couldn't watch Forest circa 1977–1982 without grudgingly admiring their sheer will to win and competitive spirit. Yet Clough harnessed two exceptional forwards in the wide positions in this 1979 final with something of a maverick approach to the game. Trevor Francis only played 70 league games for Forest 1979–1981, but proved pivotal here in the Munich Olympiastadion. At five feet ten inches Francis was relatively slight, but agile and quick. Born in Plymouth, south Devon, Francis was a prodigy in the professional game, debuting for Birmingham City in 1970, aged 16. In a match shortly before his 17th birthday, Francis scored four goals against Bolton Wanderers.

An astute man off-field, Francis secured a secondment to play in the North American Soccer League for Detroit Express in 1978. For Birmingham City he'd amassed 118 goals in 280 league appearances. For Detroit Express he scored 22 goals in 19 games, being selected in the NASL First XI alongside Franz Beckenbauer, and ace goalscorer in the NASL, Giorgio Chinaglia (formerly of Lazio, who began his professional career with Swansea City in 1964). True to form, when Brian Clough signed Francis for that record £1-million transfer fee he was photographed impatiently waiting to play a squash match in a Forest red gym kit, racquet in hand. Reputedly, Clough set the fee at £999, 999 in order that the fee didn't go to Francis's head!

After this match-winning performance (Clough wouldn't have described it as such, it's a team game after all!), Francis was allowed to return close season to play in the NASL once more, once again being named in the League's best XI – this time Johan Cruyff was among his peers. Francis's record of 36 goals and 18 assists in the NASL surpasses the great Pele by a margin of one! Francis's pinnacle at Forest had already been achieved here in Munich in 1979. Clough's insistence on him playing on the right side of the pitch instead of his preferred central striking role hampered him somewhat; in addition, a ruptured Achilles tendon prevented his appearance in the 1980 European Cup Final against Hamburger SV. At the end of his time at Forest, Francis had scored 28 goals in 70 league games. He never quite made the impact his obvious talent promised, although an England international regular during this time. He played 52 times for England, scoring 12 goals.

Transferring to Manchester City in 1981 for £1.2 million, Francis played 26 league games in the north-west, scoring 12 goals. Francis was signed by John Bond despite a disagreement on the fee and the payment of bonuses to Francis. As a consequence Francis was swiftly sold on to Italian club Sampdoria. In the 1984–85 season Francis helped Sampdoria win the Coppa Italia, defeating AC Milan in a two-legged final 3-1 on aggregate. He played alongside Graeme Souness (scorer of the only goal in the first leg in the San Siro), Gianluca Vialli, and Roberto Mancini (manager of Italy at the triumphant Euro 2020 tournament). It wasn't a bad team to be in. Francis then joined Atalanta, the Bergamo, Lombardy-based Northern Italian team, but scored only once in 21 games in the 1986–87 season. He returned to Britain the following season to play under new Glasgow Rangers manager Graeme Souness, ending the season with a Scottish League Cup trophy after a penalty shoot-out with Aberdeen. Francis's club career was almost at an end, but not before spells with Queen's Park Rangers and Sheffield Wednesday, enduring relegation from the top flight with the latter, although Wednesday won the 1991 League Cup (Francis was a non-playing substitute). In 1991–92 Francis helped the club regain their top-flight status immediately.

Trevor Francis, eight seasons at his first club Birmingham City, became an inveterate traveller, playing across the world in his later career. As an international 1977–1986 he was selected for the 1982 England World Cup squad in Spain, scoring in group games against Czechoslovakia and Kuwait. Between 1988 and 2003 Francis managed Queens Park Rangers, Sheffield Wednesday, Birmingham City and Crystal Palace. At Wednesday after replacing the popular Ron Atkinson, Francis guided the club to a third place finish in the 1st Division in 1992. In 1993 the club lost both the FA Cup Final and the League Cup Final to Arsenal, a 13th-place finish not enough for Francis to keep his job. In 1992 Francis gave Eric Cantona a trial at Sheffield Wednesday. Snowy conditions in Yorkshire meant Cantona could only be trialled on AstroTurf. Francis wanted to see how Cantona performed on grass. Offended, Cantona signed for Leeds United instead – the rest is history, Cantona helping Leeds to the 1st Division title in 1991–92 before becoming a legend at Old Trafford with Manchester United. Not Francis's finest decision! At Birmingham City – his spiritual home – Francis helped the club to the Division 2 play-offs on more than one occasion, but could not take the final step to promotion. He also took Birmingham to the 2001 League Cup Final where they were beaten only on penalties by Liverpool.

A highly skilled player, one feels Trevor Francis could have achieved even more in his career. An especially articulate man for a footballer, a smartly dressed man of fashionable appearance in decades (the 70s and 80s) when money in football first became easily obtainable, Trevor Francis almost seemed out of step with the traditional image of a professional footballer, yet he encapsulated the persona of the modern player. A man of his own mind, he agreed to disagree with the eminently knowledgeable Brian Clough when asked not to attend the 1980 European Cup Final when injured. He didn't attend, but the feeling persists that Francis felt the decision was wrong.

What a player John Robertson was. Not tall, slightly rotund, not apparently quick, but a devastating dribbler, and almost impossible to tackle or knock off the ball. He made his mark too in the successive European Cup triumphs of Nottingham Forest in 1979 and 1980, crossing for Francis's headed goal here in 1979, and scoring the solitary winning goal in the 1980 final. Once again Robertson was a player who improved immeasurably under Clough and Taylor. Used sporadically as a midfielder until Clough's arrival at Forest, the wily old fox Clough and his trusted aide Taylor converted him into an orthodox left-winger who was at times unplayable.

John Robertson played for Scotland at Schoolboy and Youth levels before joining Forest in May 1970, but his career was stuck in neutral before Clough and Taylor arrived. Clough thought Robertson was scruffy and disinterested initially but saw something in the Scot worth persevering with. Ultimately, Clough described Robertson as a 'Picasso' in the game of football, an artist among artisans, while coach Jimmy Gordon thought Robertson possessed more of a football brain than either Stanley Matthews or Tom Finney. John McGovern claimed that the two-footed Robertson was a better player than Ryan Giggs.

Upon leaving Forest for Derby County in 1983 (Taylor had become manager there in 1982 – the move broke a seemingly unbreakable bond between the two men), Robertson injured himself shortly after signing, his form subsequently never hitting the heights he'd revealed at the City Ground. The Scot played in non-league football for a while, but his halcyon days of 1976–1980, when he played 243 consecutive games for Clough and Taylor, could never be recaptured. Robertson played 28 times for Scotland, scoring eight goals.

Upon retirement, John Robertson followed former teammate Martin O'Neill as chief scout or assistant manager at Wycombe Wanderers, Norwich City, Leicester City, Glasgow Celtic and Aston Villa. The measure of his standing in Nottingham came in 2015 when he was voted top of the *Nottingham Post's* list of all-time Forest players.

Forest were fortunate to possess two very fine strikers in Garry Birtles and Tony Woodcock in Clough's fairly traditional (even for 1979) 4-4-2 formation (the majority of European clubs were experimenting with 3-5-2, 5-3-2, and 4-1-3-2 formations, and sweepers were de rigeur on the continent).

Garry Birtles was Nottingham-born, but spent his teenage years playing for non-league Long Eaton United, not signing professionally for Forest until he was 20. Birtles played his first game for Forest as a winger in March 1977, but then waited 18 months for further first-team game time while Clough relied upon the wily, experienced Peter Withe as his centre-forward. Birtles first goal for Forest came in his third match, the first round European Cup win over Liverpool. Birtles didn't look back, retaining his place, scoring 14 league goals in 1978–79, and scoring twice as Forest overcame Southampton 3-2 in the 1979 League Cup Final. In the following season at Forest, Birtles played every game and scored 12 league goals. 1980–81 began well for Birtles as he scored six goals in the first nine games of the season. He'd scored 32 goals in 87 league games 1978–1980, alerting other big clubs to his unorthodox striking skills.

Gangly, slightly awkward, but persistent, Birtles took these attributes to Manchester United in 1980, but 11 goals in 58 league games later, returned to Forest where he felt more at home. Birtles had a couple of useful seasons on the goal front, scoring 15 in 1983–84 and 14 in 1986–87 when he joint-top scored with Neil Webb and Brian Clough's son Nigel.

Garry Birtles spent the last four seasons of his professional career at Notts County and Grimsby Town, winning successive promotions with the latter. He eventually accumulated over 400 Football League games. Birtles slightly awkward style made him an unconventional striker, yet he was good enough to win three caps for England in 1980. He was voted Forest's Player of the Year in 1978–79, and the Supporters' Player of the Year in 1989–1990 at Grimsby where he won the Lincolnshire Senior Cup ten years after winning his second successive European Cup with Forest!

Tony Woodcock was a player I admired greatly (probably because I was the same height with about 100th of Woodcock's delightful ball control and dribbling skill). Woodcock signed a professional contract with Forest in 1974. Loaned out in his early years at Forest to Lincoln City and Doncaster Rovers, Woodcock was particularly impressed with the leadership skills of Graham Taylor (Watford, England) at Lincoln. Woodcock returned better for the experiences and helped Forest win promotion to Division 1 in 1976–77. When Forest won the 1st Division title and the Football League Cup in 1977–78, Woodcock won the PFA Young Player of the Year award. In addition to winning this 1979 European Cup, Woodcock scored in the 1979 League Cup Final win over Southampton.

Impressed with his dribbling skills, mobility, vision and eye for goal, FC Köln signed Woodcock for the 1979–1980 season. In three seasons in Germany Woodcock scored 28 goals in 81 Bundesliga matches. Woodcock then returned to England, signing for Terry Neill's Arsenal in 1982. Woodcock continued to shine at Highbury, being Arsenal's top scorer for three successive seasons. His best tally in 1983–84 was 21, including five in one game against Aston Villa, a post-war record for individual goals in a single match for the club. A serious injury in March 1985 brought Woodcock's career to an abrupt halt, incoming manager George Graham deeming him surplus to requirements in 1986. Woodcock scored 68 goals in 169 competitive matches for Arsenal.

Woodcock wasn't finished, despite his career-threatening injury. Returning to FC Köln in 1986 he played a further 49 Bundesliga games, scoring 11 goals. Five goals in 37 games for second tier Fortuna Köln brought Woodcock's professional career to a close.

Appearing twice for England U-21s, the swift and elusive Woodcock scored five goals. Progressing to the senior side Woodcock went on to win 42 full England caps, scoring 16 goals. Woodcock was part of the 1982 World Cup squad that returned home after the second group stage round robin undefeated. Woodcock was voted Nottingham Forest Player of the Year in 1977, and Arsenal Player of the Year in 1983. Swift, mobile, hungry for the ball, hungry for goals, a fluid striker who was always a handful for defences, Tony Woodcock graced top clubs in England and Germany with his pace and purpose.

What a team, what a unit, Nottingham Forest were. Not as overtly entertaining as Liverpool or Manchester United, but no one could deny their unity, their team spirit. Epitomising this togetherness were Brian Clough and Peter Taylor. Previously only Bill Shankly seemed to possess charisma as a manager. Brian Clough came along and the modern charismatic manager, as important as players, was born. Clough's man-management style could be brusque, yet you always felt that he knew when to put his arm around the shoulder of a young player. As a manager he was at times abrupt, volatile, opinionated, yet endlessly interesting, informed and informative. Documentary footage of Clough talking of an interview with a player who gave his opinion, Clough gave his, and they decided Clough was right, is legendary, as was the occasion he chastised a player for missing the goal from a few yards out.

As a player himself, Brian Clough was one of the greatest finishers the Football League has ever seen – hence his strong opinions about finishing. In 274 league starts with Middlesbrough and Sunderland, Clough scored an incredible 251 goals, making him the third highest-ever scorer in the Football League. He just happened to be around at the same time as Jimmy Greaves, hence the awarding of only two England caps to Clough. An anterior cruciate ligament knee injury cut short Clough's playing career at the age of 29. It's my feeling that Clough's insatiable hunger for success as a manager came from a feeling of unfinished business as a player.

Clough was the sixth of nine children born to a local sweet-shop worker – then manager – in Middlesbrough. He never forgot how hard his mam worked in raising nine children. He failed his 11-plus, going on instead to secondary school (I can relate to this as one of four 'borderline' failures at primary school). Clough did his national service with the RAF 1953–55, though he was never selected for the RAF National team (I was never selected for the school team, although I'd like to think I made amends later).

Clough scored 204 goals in 222 league matches for Middlesbrough. Irked by his team's leaky defence at times, his teammates were equally upset by Clough's annoyance with them. After a series of transfer requests, Clough finally moved to Sunderland, where he scored 63 goals in 74 matches. It was the notoriously harsh winter of 1962–63 (in December 1962, before the country went into a winter lockdown January–March 1963). In December 1962 Clough challenged for a ball with Bury goalkeeper Chris Harker and tore the medial and crucial ligaments in his knee. The match was played on a frozen pitch in torrential rain. I only played a couple of matches on frozen pitches, but the playing of them was a mistake. The game becomes simply a question of who can keep their feet, rather than a contest of skill – and more pertinently, as Clough discovered, frozen pitches are distinctly dangerous.

Although only 41st on the list of all-time league goalscorers along with Steve Bull and Ivor Allchurch, Clough's goals per game ratio puts him top of all English strikers. Greaves, incidentally, is third on a list topped by Arthur Rowley (1946–1965) with 434 goals, with his tally of 357. Clough scored all of his goals in the English 2nd Division – another reason he was largely overlooked at international level. But his scoring record from 1956–57 for seven successive seasons with Middlesbrough is phenomenal in anybody's book: 40, 42, 43, 40, 36, 34 and 28 (the latter in his injury-curtailed season). He was the 2nd Division's top scorer in 1958–59 and 1959–1960.

Space disallows me the opportunity to extol the full virtues of his management career. Suffice to say that with Derby County the club were 2nd Division Champions in 1968–69, and 1st Division Champions in 1971–72 (the club going on to win the 1st Division again in 1974–75 under Dave Mackay). With Nottingham Forest the club won the 1st Division title in 1977–78; four League Cups 1977–78, 1978–79, 1988–89, and 1989–1990, and most significantly, two European Cups in 1979 and 1980.

Individually Clough was awarded Manager of the Year 1977–78, the European Coach of the Year, the Sepp Herberger Award in 1979 (awarded for the top European coach in a calendar year), and European Coach of the Season for 1979–1980. Brian Clough was awarded the OBE for services to football in June 1991. In August 2005, a stretch of the A52 linking Nottingham with Derby was renamed Brian Clough Way. On 28 August 2010, a statue of Clough and Peter Taylor was unveiled at Pride Park, Derby County. Pertinently, these old comrades were sculpted with arms around each other's shoulders, shared hands gripping the Football League trophy. An extraordinary man, an extraordinarily controversial and opinionated player and manager, but a highly skilled man-manager, Brian Clough remains one of football's most cherished characters to this day. I'll never forget his punditry during the 1974 World Cup either, his forthright opinions, deliberate mispronunciation, but above all his effusive energy and enthusiasm. Brian Clough in full verbal flow was a joy to hear and behold, redefining charisma and magnetism in a football manager.

How did Brian Clough link up with, and become so close to Peter Taylor? Taylor spent the years 1942–45 with Nottingham Forest as a goalkeeper, appearing for the youth team, but never the senior team. After the Second World War, Taylor spent ten years at Coventry City, until the1953–54 season. Sold to Middlesbrough in 1955, he kept goal for the first team for four seasons in the 2nd Division. Staying in the Midlands and the north, Taylor joined Port Vale in the 1961–62 season, but played only one game. He ended his playing days 1962–65 with non-league Burton Albion, a club Brian Clough's son Nigel went on to manage. Taylor forged a close relationship with Brian Clough while the pair played for Middlesbrough in the late 1950s, the friends coaching schoolboys to supplement their wages.

Taylor became manager of Burton Albion in 1962, leading the club to the Southern League Cup in 1964. My hometown club, Guildford City (it's not a city), played in the Southern League until their extinction in the early 1970s. Brian Clough asked Taylor to become his assistant manager at Hartlepool United in 1965. A legendary team was born. Taylor always supported Clough senior, telling him he should be a 1st Division player and an international when the two of them played in the 2nd Division for Middlesbrough.

As a management duo Clough and Taylor helped Hartlepool United to 18th place and eighth place finishes in 1965–66 and 1966–67. Conflict with chairmen would be a constant thread running through the pair's management of all the clubs they oversaw. Moving to Derby County in May 1967, the pair began to rebuild the 3rd Division team, Taylor coming into his own by earmarking Dave Mackay and Roy McFarland for the club. Mackay was a tremendous player, a consummate professional, and had been a part of Bill Nicholson's early 1960s Tottenham Hotspur team, missing the 1963 winning European Cup Winners Cup match against Atlético Madrid with a stomach injury. McFarland, a cultured centre-half, signed from Tranmere Rovers, would go on to play 434 league games for Derby County and represent England 28 times 1971–76. McFarland became Clough and Taylor's first signing for Derby and began a trend for Taylor of spotting talented players either playing in lower leagues or players who would fit the Clough and Taylor template for the successful provincial – and historic, because these clubs had no previous history to speak of – Derby County and Nottingham Forest teams. John McGovern and Archie Gemmill were notable signings for Derby on the strength of Taylor's scouting nous.

Taylor and Clough's unprecedented success with Derby and Forest came to an end when Taylor became manager of Derby County in 1982, souring what seemed an indestructible relationship with Clough. Taylor oversaw Derby's 2-0 defeat of Forest in the 1983 FA Cup, further marring their relationship. Derby went on to be relegated from Division 2 to Division 3 in 1983–84 – Taylor resigned a month before the team went down. When John Robertson transferred to Derby in 1983, the pair never communicated again. It was a bitter divorce after a long, happy marriage of footballing ideals.

Forest's five substitutes for this 1979 European Cup Final were all outstanding players in their own right, players either on the cusp of being better still, in the case of reserve keeper Chris Woods, or players who had been great servants to Clough and Taylor, like Martin O'Neill, Archie Gemmill and John O'Hare who were at the end of their careers. O'Neill was a mainstay at Forest 1971–1981, a Northern Ireland international, and a man who became an astute manager post-playing days, and subsequently an unusually erudite and insightful pundit for both the BBC and ITV. Gemmill was a superb player at his peak (with Derby County) and for a time with Nottingham Forest. Scorer of a quite wonderful goal for Scotland against Holland in the Scots' famous 3-2 victory at the 1982 World Cup, Gemmill was slippery, quick, skilful, feisty and a great competitor (he played 43 times for Scotland, scoring eight goals). His goals ratio for his country was higher than it was for Derby and Forest – four in 58 for Forest, 17 in 261 league appearances for Derby. John O'Hare was part of the fabric of Clough and Taylor's professional career, following them from Derby to Forest via a fleeting cameo with the pair at Leeds United in 1974, a player Clough and Taylor trusted implicitly. An excellent team player, O'Hare scored 65 goals in 248 league games for Derby, 14 in 101 for Forest. Seen as slightly cumbersome by some, O'Hare proved the perfect foil for the quicksilver Kevin Hector at Derby County.

Chris Woods was with Nottingham Forest 1976–79 without ever playing a senior game due to the sustained excellence of Peter Shilton. From 1979 to 1996, Woods established himself as one of the country's leading goalkeepers at Queens Park Rangers, Norwich City, Glasgow Rangers and Sheffield Wednesday, winning the League Cup with Norwich City in 1984–85, and four Scottish league titles and four Scottish League Cups with Glasgow Rangers. Woods played 43 times for England 1985–1993, initially playing second fiddle to Shilton, but usurping the great man after the 1990 World Cup. Woods was first choice at the 1992 European Championships, but later lost his place to Arsenal's David Seaman. Central defender/utility player David Needham signed from Queens Park Rangers in 1977, playing 86 league games for Forest until 1982. Needham played six times for the England 'B' team, remaining an unused substitute in the 1979 and 1980 European Cup Finals.

British football followers knew nothing of the Malmö FF team in opposition to Forest on this evening in Munich. Goalkeeper Jan Moller tended to be understudy to Ronnie Hellström at international level, winning 17 caps. He went on to play for Bristol City in England's 2nd Division 1980–82. Left-back Ingemar Erlandsson won 69 caps for Sweden. Midfielder Robert Prytz was a useful goalscorer, netting 27 goals in 80 league games 1977–1982 for Malmö FF, ending with a career total of 121 in 576 league games. It was a career that included a stint with Glasgow Rangers 1982–85. He played 56 times for Sweden. Captain Staffan Tapper represented Sweden at the 1974 and 1978 World Cups, winning 36 caps. There were no outstanding individuals in this Malmö FF team. There was no mobile, swift striker in the mould of Ove Kindvall who'd terrorised Celtic for Feyenoord in 1970; there was no Tomas Brolin who would be England's nemesis in 1992. Malmö FF epitomised all that we know now of Swedish football teams. They were organised, disciplined, with great team spirit. As such, Nottingham Forest with international stalwart Peter Shilton, gifted individuals Trevor Francis and John Robertson, and Garry Birtles and Tony Woodcock in attack, were marginal favourites, despite this being their first appearance in a major European final.

THE FINAL
Clough's team rose to their 'favourites' tag. Taking the game to the resolute Swedes from the off, Robertson showed all his technical mastery as he jinked inside a defender on the halfway line and spotted Birtles breaking free. Birtles latched on to Robertson's ball but lifted the ball on to the top of the net. Robertson was clearly Forest's main threat for providing a goal, and so it proved as he attacked two defenders on the left flank and crossed to the far post where Trevor Francis arrived ahead of the ball – usually a sign of a missed chance – and somehow contrived to arch his head underneath the ball and score from a difficult angle. 1-0 at half-time.

Forest should have scored more in the second half as their ascendancy continued. Francis used his speed to reach the bye-line on the right beating two defenders, cutting the ball back to the opposite side of the penalty area. Robertson, strolling in from the left, hit the post when it looked easier to score. Woodcock slalomed in from the left flank, showing great persistence after running into traffic in the penalty area, and drifted the ball towards the far post. Birtles was just unable to connect with his head. Forest run out worthy winners of a final that was anti-climactic in content – but just try telling that to Clough and company after winning European football's top trophy against this resolute, if uninspiring Malmö FF side.

1980 EUROPEAN CUP FINAL
NOTTINGHAM FOREST 1 V 0 HAMBURGER SV

The inimitable Clough led Forest back to the European Cup Final one year later. This time they were not favourites, German club Hamburger SV having beaten Real Madrid in the semi-finals, and possessing in Kevin Keegan, Liverpool's old talisman, and a recent two-time European Footballer of the Year (1978, 1979).

Route to the Final
Ironically, Forest had to overcome another Swedish side, Oster, in the round of 32. Two goals from Ian Bowyer at the City Ground and a single goal from Tony Woodcock in Sweden saw Forest through comfortably, 3-1 on aggregate. Forest's winning margin in the last 16 was even greater, this time the Romanians of Arges Pitesti their victims. A 2-0 home win with goals from Woodcock and Birtles was followed by a 2-1 away win, goals coming from Bowyer and Birtles. In the quarter-finals Forest faced East German club Dynamo Berlin who would win ten successive league championships 1979–1988. A shock was in store in the first leg at the City Ground. Pacy striker Hans-Jürgen Riediger scored the only goal of the game, one of ten the striker scored in European Cup matches 1973–1984. Fortunately for Forest, Trevor Francis was in inspired form in the return leg in Berlin, scoring twice in the first 35 minutes. A Robertson penalty meant one of

their own for the Berliners was not enough to prevent a 3-2 aggregate victory for Clough's men. It was a repeat prescription in the semi-final against Ajax, Francis scoring, Robertson converting a penalty kick as they ran out 2-0 winners at the City Ground. A single goal from the talented Dane, Soren Lerby, was insufficient for Ajax to overturn Forest's lead in the second leg in Amsterdam. Lerby topped the scoring list in the 1979–1980 European Cup campaign with ten goals. Hamburger SV's Horst Hrubesch netted seven, but was only a substitute in this final against Forest, an ankle injury preventing him from playing any more than the second 45 minutes. This was fortunate for Forest as Hrubesch scored twice in the 1980 European Championship Final for West Germany against Belgium, the Germans winning 2-1 in the Stadio Olimpico, Rome. Hrubesch also captained Hamburger SV to a 1-0 victory in the 1983 European Cup Final. The gods smiled on Forest.

Hamburger SV thumped the Icelanders of Valur 5-1 on aggregate in the round of 32, 3-0 in Iceland (Hrubesch scoring twice) and 2-1 in Northern Germany, Hrubesch again scoring. The Germans steamrollered Georgian club Dinamo Tbilisi 6-3 on aggregate in the last 16, 3-1 at home, 3-2 away, Keegan scoring in both ties. The quarter-final was a much bigger ask for the German club, their opponents Hadjuk Split of Croatia pushing them all the way in a 3-3 drawn set of games, Hamburg winning 1-0 at home, two early goals in Split enough to forestall a buoyant Hadjuk side who scored three goals on the night to win the second leg 3-2. Away goals saw Hamburg through. Hamburger SV saved their best performance of the competition for the semi-final against Real Madrid. Two goals from striker Carlos Santillana gave the Spaniards a two-goal cushion going into the second leg at the Volksparkstadion, Hamburg. English winger Laurie Cunningham scored for Real, but the Germans exploded back into the tie with five goals, two coming from Hrubesch.

Frank Gray replaced Frank Clark at left-back for the 1980 European Cup Final. Clark may have been a better defender, but Gray gave Forest a more attack-minded left sided player – not that Clough would have encouraged Gray to push up too much, preferring Gray to stay in position, maintaining the team's shape, and allow the magician Robertson ahead of him the space to unpick the Hamburger SV defence.

The surprise selection of this evening was that of the 17-year-old Gary Mills on the left side of midfield – Clough was not one to allow others (with the exception of his trusty ally Peter Taylor) to influence his thinking on team selection. Mills became the youngest player in history to play in a European Cup Final, replacing the injured Trevor Francis. Mills played 58 league games for Forest 1978–1982, going on to complete a massive 727 senior games in the NASL with Seattle Sounders, in the Football League with Derby County, Forest again 1983–87, Notts County twice, 200 games for Leicester City, and over 200 games in non-league football by the end of his career. A lengthy career highlighted by Clough's inspired handling of a precocious talent.

Martin O'Neill's senior career began in his native Northern Ireland, appearing in seven Irish League games for Distillery, scoring three goals. A former Derry City youth player, O'Neill helped Distillery win the 1971 Irish Cup, scoring twice in a 3-0 win over his former club Derry. Playing for Derry in the 1971–72 European Cup, O'Neill scored against Barcelona in a 3-1 home reverse in September 1971. Spotted by a Nottingham Forest scout, O'Neill signed for Forest in October 1971, cutting short his university studies.

In November 1971, 0'Neill scored on his league debut for Forest in a 4-1 win over West Bromwich Albion. Forest, pre-Clough, were relegated at the end of the 1971–72 season. An injury prevented O'Neill's appearance in the 1979 European Cup Final, but the doughty Northern Irishman would not be denied, returning in this 1980 final to win back his place on the right side of Forest's attack, essentially replacing Francis's attacking role. O'Neill played 285 league games for Forest 1971–1981, scoring 48 goals. A feisty, committed player, an excellent dribbler, a great team player, O'Neill exemplified the spirit engendered by Clough and Taylor at Nottingham Forest. He went on to play for Norwich City, Manchester City and Notts County, but a knee injury ensured his retirement in 1985. Capped 64 times for Northern Ireland, O'Neill scored eight international goals, winning the now defunct British Home Championship twice in 1980 and 1984.

A sharply intelligent man, O'Neill was an obvious candidate among the Forest players of 1980 to become a manager. Taking up the reins at non-league Wycombe Wanderers in 1990, O'Neill led the club into the Football League in 1992–93. The following season, 1993–94, he guided Wycombe up another tier into Division 3. Another promotion followed. O'Neill became manager of Norwich City in June 1995, but left in December 1995 after a dispute with his chairman over a transfer. Joining Leicester City, O'Neill helped the club win promotion to the Premier League in his first season as boss (1995–96). Under O'Neill, Leicester reached the League Cup Final three times, winning in 1997 and 2000, losing in 1999. Leaving Leicester City to take the manager's position at Glasgow Celtic in June 2000, O'Neill oversaw the first domestic treble for Celtic since 1968–69 in 2000–01. They retained the league title in 2001–02, the first time the feat had been achieved since 1982. O'Neill took Celtic to the 2003 UEFA Cup Final in Seville, the club beaten 3-2 in extra time by José Mourinho's Porto. O'Neill only resigned at Celtic in May 2005 after his wife contracted lymphoma. He'd been the most successful Celtic manager since Jock Stein.

Where did it all go wrong for Martin O'Neill the manager? Returning to management with Aston Villa in August 2006, the Villains started life under O'Neill with a nine-game unbeaten run in the 2006–07 season. A mid-season slump was bookended with another nine-game unbeaten run at the end of the season. At the end of the 2009–2010 season Villa finished sixth for the third consecutive season. O'Neill took the club to the 2009–2010 League Cup Final, but Manchester United beat them 2-1. O'Neill resigned in August 2010. He'd moved Aston Villa forward, but the reality in the 21st-century Premiership is that (with the notable exception of Leicester City in 2015–16) all the other clubs are unable to compete with the monied Top 6 of Manchester United, Manchester City, Liverpool, Chelsea, Tottenham Hotspur and Arsenal.

The livewire Tony Woodcock had moved on, leaving Garry Birtles as a lone spearhead with two extremely able wide players in Martin O'Neill and John Robertson in support. Among the substitutes were Clough/Taylor stalwart

John O'Hare, David Needham once more, and a stand-by goalkeeper in Jim Montgomery who pulled off a save to match Gordon Banks's 1970 Pele effort with a double block in Sunderland's shock 1973 FA Cup Final win over Leeds United.

With Forest set up in a 4-3-3 formation, Hamburger SV opted for their own continental shape with captain Peter Nogly operating as a sweeper behind wide defenders Croatian Ivan Buljan (Yugoslavian Footballer of the Year 1975), and Ditmar Jakobs, the latter interchanging with Nogly when matters dictated it. The unfortunate Jakobs (323 Bundesliga games for Hamburg) retired from football in 1989 when he cleared a ball off the line and fell on to the hooks fixing the goal-net to the ground. The hooks had to be cut from his scalpel, missing his spinal cord by two inches.

Manfred Kaltz was ostensibly Hamburg's right-back with a licence to roam upfield. Kaltz played in this game therefore as more of a wing-back as we know them now. Kaltz's forte, the *'bananenflaken'* (banana crosses) predated the curve on a ball that David Beckham wickedly imparted for Manchester United and England. Kaltz scored 76 goals in 568 Bundesliga appearances, 53 of them penalties. Kaltz is not remembered in England like Berti Vogts, yet played 69 times for West Germany, scoring eight goals. Kaltz won the German Bundesliga three times, the DFB Pokal Cup twice, the DFB-Ligapokal (German League Cup) once, the European Cup in 1982–83, and the European Cup Winner's Cup in 1976–77, defeating the Belgians Anderlecht in the latter.

Thanks to the *'Kaiser'* Franz Beckenbauer, the role of sweeper was endemic in German football. Alongside Felix Magath was one of three sweepers in this Hamburg team (Nogly, Jakobs), Holger Hieronymus. Like Jakobs, Hieronymus's career ended in sad circumstances, a cruciate ligament rupture, menisci and knee cartilage injury the cause. He was just 26. Along with the human whirlwind Keegan, Felix Magath was Hamburg's most threatening player on the night. Magath scored in both the 1977 European Cup Winners' Cup Final victory and the solitary winning goal in the 1983 European Cup Final win over Juventus. Again in a 70s/80s era of wonderful German midfielders (Overath, Breitner, Netzer, Bonhof), Magath is less well remembered, but an absolute mainstay for Hamburger SV 1976–1986 (306 Bundesliga appearances, 46 goals). Magath played in the 1982 and 1986 World Cups, West Germany beaten finalists on each occasion, Magath playing in the latter final. He played 43 times for his country, scoring three goals.

A chequered start to his management career followed at Hamburger SV, IFC Nurmberg, Werder Bremen, Eintracht Frankfurt, and VFB Stuttgart. Impressing at Stuttgart, Bayern Munich gave Magath their manager's job in 2004. Two seasons running Bayern won the League and Cup double, 2004–05 and 2005–06, but failure to qualify for the Champions League in 2006–07 cost Magath his job. Moving to VfL Wolfsburg for the 2007–08 season, Magath managed the club to the Bundesliga title for the first time in the club's history. Moving again to Schalke 04, his new club finished runners-up in the 2009–2010 season. Returning to VfL Wolfsburg he helped the club stave off relegation before leaving in October 2012 by mutual consent. A brief sojourn in England followed in 2014. Magath was unable to save Fulham from relegation, and following four successive defeats – among a winless run of 11 games from the Premiership down to the Championship – the German was sacked. Magath tried his luck in China with Shandong Luneng 2016–17 before calling time on his management career.

Felix Magath's management methods were not always popular, his emphasis on discipline, fitness and conditioning, at times at odds with professional players. Perhaps he wanted players under his tutelage to play in the typically Germanic disciplined way he'd experienced in his own playing days. Being organised, solid, team-oriented hasn't harmed German national prospects over the decades – but a little flair and creativity always help. Magath won three Bundesliga titles as a player, one European Cup and one European Cup Winners' Cup. He also won the European Championships in Italy with West Germany in 1980, although he did not feature in the final.

Willi Reimann and Jürgen Milewski were useful goalscorers for Hamburger SV, but it was the man splitting them in the middle as a 'false 9', Kevin Keegan, who posed the biggest threat to Nottingham Forest – and the shrewd Clough had a plan in place to stifle the ex-Liverpool legend. Keegan assisted Hamburger SV's revival in West German football. It seemed surprising at the time that the explosive Keegan joined a team who had not finished higher than sixth in the Bundesliga in two decades, but after a difficult first season where he was adapting to learning a new language – and new teammates who resented the new 'superstar' arrival – matters improved. Real Madrid and Juventus wanted to sign Keegan after he'd been awarded a second consecutive Ballon d'Or (European Footballer of the Year) in 1979, but Keegan opted to try and win the European Cup with Hamburg. His inability to achieve this goal helped his decision to move back to England and Southampton in 1980. He may also have been exhausted by manager Branislav Zebec's training methods (Magath was absorbing these). Keegan claimed he'd never run so much in training.

THE FINAL

Brian Clough – as usual – had done his homework before this match. Hamburger SV felt that Forest simply put 11 men back behind the ball after taking an early lead – and it was difficult to disagree with that supposition. Prior to Forest's goal, Magath's piledriver free kick was athletically saved by Peter Shilton. When an opportunity arose for Forest, how John Robertson took it. Sweeping in from the left flank, Robertson attempted to play a 1-2 with Garry Birtles. Birtles appeared to have lost the ball, but somehow squeezed the ball back to Robertson while straddled on the ground. It was typically ungainly, but hugely effective link-play by Birtles. Robertson took the ball in his stride and drove it into the far corner of the net. The rest of the match produced a litany of goal chances for Hamburger SV, Magath and Keegan heavily involved. Shilton was magnificent in repelling everything the Germans threw at him. Keegan chested the ball down into Jürgen Milewski's path, the latter's shot again parried by an inspired Shilton. The master scout Peter Taylor correctly asserted upon Shilton's signing that "he wins you matches".

294

In the second half Magath drove the ball across goal from the left, but the ball was blocked. Manfred Kaltz erupted a 20-yarder against the outside of an upright as Hamburger SV cranked up the pressure. Shilton's save from another 20-yarder from Milewski was exceptional. The 17year-old Gary Mills cleared the ball away from danger in another dangerous Hamburg attack. It was a lucky escape for Forest. Totally against the run of play, Birtles evaded the German defence, raced towards goal, but exhausted, trod on the ball as he was about to shoot. It didn't matter, Forest, under the cosh all evening, held on, and Clough and Taylor had their second consecutive European Cup trophy. Kevin Keegan had dropped deep, attempting to defy Clough and Taylor's 'handcuffing' of him, but wherever Keegan went he was shackled. Forest rode their luck, but the wily Clough won the day.

1981 EUROPEAN CUP FINAL
Liverpool 1 v 0 Real Madrid

A third appearance in the final for Liverpool; a ninth for their feted Spanish opponents, but Liverpool were in their pomp, and a Real team containing the streetwise German Uli Stielike and England's own Laurie Cunningham couldn't prevent a third trophy win for the Merseysiders in five years.

Route to the Final
The early rounds of the 1980–81 European Cup were something of a procession for Liverpool. Playing against the Finnish side Oulun Palloseura at the multi-purpose sports stadium on Oulu, Koskikeskus, Liverpool scored first through Terry McDermott, but were pegged back to 1-1. At Anfield Liverpool ran riot, thrashing the Finns 10-1 with hat-tricks from McDermott and Graeme Souness, and a brace from David Fairclough. Drawn to play Alex Ferguson's Aberdeen in the second round, the Scots restricted Liverpool to a solitary McDermott goal in Scotland, but had nothing in reply. At Anfield, Liverpool romped home, Kenny Dalglish and Alan Hansen among the scorers in a 4-0 victory. In the quarter-finals Liverpool trounced CSKA Sofia of Bulgaria 5-1 at Anfield, Souness again scoring a hat-trick (not bad for a midfield player). I once top-scored for a local club with 22 goals, only to be gazumped for Player of the Season by a very deserving midfielder who scored 20. I never got that close again. A solitary David Johnson goal gave Liverpool a second leg victory in Bulgaria, cementing a 6-1 aggregate win.

Only when Liverpool reached the semi-finals did they face the might of European football in the shape of Bayern Munich. Liverpool were unable to breach the German's defence for all their Anfield support, the home game ending 0-0. Faced with adversity, Ray Kennedy scored seven minutes from time in Munich, only for Karl-Heinz Rummenigge to equalise with two minutes remaining. Liverpool held on for an away goals victory.

Similarly, Real Madrid cruised through the first two rounds, first defeating Irish club Limerick 2-1 away, crushing them 5-1 at the Bernabeu Stadium, Cunningham among the scorers. Surprisingly, Real managed only a single goal victory against Hungarian champions Honved at the Bernabeu in the second round. In Budapest, Honved were beaten 2-0, Cunningham scoring again. A tighter contest ensued in the last eight, Real held 0-0 in Russia by Spartak Moscow. Two goals from Isidro in Madrid secured a semi-final place for Real. Another stern contest awaited. Goals from Santillana and Juanito won the day for Real in the semi-final first leg in Spain. Opponents Inter Milan pulled a goal back through defender Bini in the San Siro in Milan, but a second goal was not forthcoming.

Going into the final, Kenny Dalglish had not trained for weeks. Alan Kennedy – soon-to-be-hero – had missed match play for six weeks with a broken wrist. The jet-heeled Cunningham, pacy and tricky, had not played for Real since November 1980. Cunningham played in this final, but his lack of match fitness betrayed him. I played in only two cup finals, the first on the morning of the birth of my first son after three hours sleep; for the second I suffered a silly, self-induced Achilles heel injury through wearing screw-in studded boots on a hard pitch instead of the required moulded studded boots I opted not to use. I didn't do myself justice in either final. One was lost. The other won. The point being if you miss six games, as I did, your match fitness suffers. Cunningham hadn't played competitive football for nearly six months!

Much of this Liverpool 1981 European Cup-winning team were familiar from 1978: the ever-reliable Ray Clemence in goal, Phil Neal, Phil Thompson and Alan Hansen in defence; the fiery, yet silkily skilful Graeme Souness in midfield with Ray Kennedy, and the hard-running, deft-touched Terry McDermott; Kenny Dalglish in attack, this time with the tireless, mobile David Johnson in support. Newcomers to the team were few: Alan Kennedy at left-back, Sammy Lee on the right side of midfield.

Alan Kennedy began his professional career with Newcastle United, aged 18, in 1972. Kennedy played 158 league matches for the Tynesiders, his nine goals evidence of a full-back who liked to join the attack. Joining Liverpool in 1978, Kennedy's night here proved to be the high-point of his career, his goal breaking the deadlock in another tight final match for the Reds. Kennedy amassed 359 league games for Liverpool 1978–1986, a permanent fixture in this hugely successful team of the late 70s, early 80s, chipping in with 20 useful league goals. The cup competitions saw Kennedy adding to his goal tally. In 1981 he scored in the first League Cup Final match against West Ham United that ended in a 1-1 draw, Liverpool winning the replay 2-1. In the 1983 League Cup Final against Manchester United, Kennedy scored the equaliser with 15 minutes remaining, Liverpool winning the match 2-1 after extra time.

Post-Newcastle United and Liverpool, Sunderland-born Kennedy played for the Tyne and Wear home-town club of his birth in 1986–87, eventually completing 506 matches in the Football League, ending his playing days at Wrexham. Kennedy – in competition with the likes of Ipswich Town's Mick Mills and Arsenal's Kenny Sansom for the left-back berth – played just twice for England in 1984. He won five league titles with Liverpool, four League Cups and two European Cups.

Sammy Lee, stockier than Jimmy Case, but still energetic, had a relatively short playing career, completing 261 league matches. One hundred and ninety-seven of these were for his home-city club, Liverpool. His Anfield career spanned ten years 1976–1986, although he only debuted for the club in 1978, scoring after coming on as a substitute against Leicester City in a 3-2 victory. Short in stature at five feet seven inches, but a sharp passer with a fine shot and a good 'engine', Lee became a regular in the side from 1980. Asked to man-mark Real Madrid's legendary midfielder Paul Breitner in the semi-final of this 1981 European Cup competition, Lee performed the task admirably. Lee would again shine in the 1984 European Cup semi-final, scoring the decisive goal at Anfield against Romania's Dinamo Bucharest. Lee also scored on his England debut (one of 14 appearances) against Greece in 1984. Injuries began to impact on Lee, and he lost his place after 1985 to the skilful Danish playmaker Jan Mølby.

Sammy Lee has almost made a bigger impact in football with his coaching career. Graeme Souness took him on in 1993, subsequent managers Roy Evans and Gerard Houllier retaining his services at Liverpool. Lee became a part-time coach for England under Sven-Göran Eriksson in 2001, going full time in the role in 2004. An unsettled period with Bolton Wanderers followed before Lee returned to Anfield as Rafael Benitez's assistant manager in 2008. His third stint at Anfield ended by mutual consent in 2011. Lee has tended to follow Sam Allardyce since, coaching with him for England (one game!), Crystal Palace, Everton and West Bromwich Albion. Lee won four league titles, four League Cups and two European Cups in his time with Liverpool. Passionate, enthusiastic, hard-working, Lee suffered a little in comparison to the previous right-sided midfielder Jimmy Case, who seemed more dynamic, but there was no doubting Sammy Lee's work ethic and commitment to the team, and his game knowledge has made him a sought-after football coach.

This would be manager Bob Paisley's final European hurrah. The introverted Paisley had long since quelled doubts of his suitability to manage this proud north-western football giant, banishing cherished memories of the 'irreplaceable' Bill Shankly.

Liverpool's opponents Real Madrid were not the modern 21st-century *Galacticos* of Cristiano Ronaldo, Roberto Carlos, Karim Benzema, Gareth Bale et al, nor the first great incarnation of world stars (in my memory) of Ferenc Puskás and Alfredo Di Stéfano, but in the German Uli Stielike they possessed a nemesis to the England national team. In the lightning quick English player Laurie Cunningham they had a potential threat to Liverpool's defence. Sadly for Cunningham, lack of match-play prevented him impacting on this final. Otherwise Real's team comprised nine Spanish nationals.

Among Liverpool's substitutes on this evening, Howard Gayle became the first black player to play for Liverpool in 1977. In the years up until 1983, Gayle played in only four league games, being loaned out to Fulham and Newcastle United during this period. Gayle's performance against Bayern Munich in the semi-final of this competition won him a place on the bench for the final, covering the absence of Kenny Dalglish without blemish. Only at Blackburn Rovers 1987–1992 did Gayle play regularly, scoring 29 goals in 116 league matches.

The stand-out defender in Real's team was the left-back José Antonio

Camacho. Like Liverpool's Alan Kennedy, Camacho loved to forage down the flanks in support of his strikers. After playing youth football with Albacete and Castilla, Camacho signed for Real Madrid in 1974, aged 18. He went on to play nearly 600 matches in all competitions for Real, even overcoming a serious injury in 1978. An absence of nearly two years didn't deter the determined Camacho who returned to feature in a Real team that won two consecutive UEFA Cups. The tough-tackling Camacho played 81 times for Spain 1975–1988, playing in the 1982 and 1986 World Cups, and the 1984 and 1988 Euros, retiring from international football, aged 33.

Camacho went on to manage the Spanish national team 1998–2002, overseeing two quarter-final defeats in the 1998 and 2002 World Cups, the first to France, the second, unexpectedly, to South Korea in 2002, after which he resigned.

As a player, José Camacho won no less than nine La Liga titles with Real Madrid, in addition to five Copa del Reys (Spanish Cups), and the UEFA Cup twice at the end of his playing days in 1984–85 and 1985–86. For his country, Camacho was on the losing side to a France side at the 1984 European Championships that contained the best midfield unit I have ever seen in European football: Luis Fernandez, Jean Tigana, Alain Giresse and the super-talented Michel Platini. Despite being at the helm of many of Spain and Portugal's leading clubs, as a manager Camacho has only the Taca de Portugal with Benfica (the Portuguese Cup) in 2003–04 (beating José Mourinho's Porto in the final – no mean feat) to show for a long career in football management.

On the right side of the Real Madrid midfield, Vicente del Bosque has become better known eventually for his management achievements. He played 445 La Liga matches for Real 1964–1984, scoring 30 goals. He won five La Liga titles and four Copa del Reys with Real 1974–1982. His only tournament as player for Spain came in 1980 at the Euros in Italy, among 18 caps he won for his country.

As a manager Del Bosque reached unparalleled heights. He was a caretaker manager for Real Madrid in 1994 and 1996, before becoming full-time manager 1999–2003. In this period Real won La Liga twice in 2000–01 and 2002–03, and the European Cup twice in 2000 and 2002. The idea of *Los Galacticos*, some of the world's best overseas players representing Real Madrid, began under Del Bosque's tenure, beginning with Portuguese superstar Luis Figo, and continuing thereafter with Zinedine Zidane, the Brazilian centre-forward Ronaldo,and David Beckham. Calm, dispassionate, Del Bosque removed himself from confrontations and let his teams 'do the talking'. He resigned as manager of Real Madrid in 2003, but tellingly it took the club a further ten years to win what became the Champions League (the modern European Cup) under Carlo Ancelotti.

An unsuccessful spell with Besiktas in Turkey followed 2004–05. A four-year hiatus ensued before Del Bosque became Spain's national team manager in 2008. He would oversee a renaissance in Spain's tournament fortunes – although he was blessed with a golden generation of fabulous players including Barcelona's midfield maestros Xavi and Iniesta, and an inspirational defensive leader in Real Madrid's Sergio Ramos. The 2010 World Cup in South Africa began inauspiciously with a 1-0 defeat at the hands of Switzerland. Spain rallied, winning their next two group games to qualify for the knockout stages. Three consecutive 1-0 victories against Portugal, Paraguay and Germany saw them reach the final in Johannesburg. An extra-time goal from Andrés Iniesta won Spain their first World Cup, Del Bosque becoming the oldest manager of a World Cup-winning country at the age of 59. Spain, in their absolute pomp, demolished Italy 4-0 to win the European Championship Final in Kiev in 2012. Del Bosque's success didn't last, as in the 2014 World Cup Spain suffered defeats against Holland (1-5) and Chile (0-2). Del Bosque consequently retired as Spanish national team manager in 2016. To date Del Bosque is the only manager to have won the Champions League, the European Championship, the World Cup and the Intercontinental Cup, competed for by the winners of the European Cup/Champions League and the South American Libertadores Cup, the latter competition ceasing in 2004.

On the left flank in attack for Real, it was Laurie Cunningham's misfortune to have suffered serious injury earlier in the season, considerably lessening his impact on this 1981 European Cup Final – a black and white photographic still of Cunningham being sandwiched between Phil Neal and Graeme Souness reveals the threat Liverpool felt Cunningham could still impose. Cunningham's professional career began in more low-key fashion. Rejected by Arsenal, Cunningham began in the lower leagues with Leyton Orient in 1974. Seventy-five appearances, 15 league goals and three seasons later he signed for Ron Atkinson's West Bromwich Albion, forming only the second trio of black English players to play in any one team at the time (1977) in the top tier. Along with defender Brendan Batson and cavalier centre-forward Cyrille Regis, Cunningham gave West Brom serious impetus 1977–79. Cunningham impressed sufficiently for Real Madrid to sign him in 1979. In five seasons at the Bernabeu, Cunningham made only 44 La Liga appearances, his playing time cruelly curtailed by injuries – but he won La Liga once and the Copa del Rey twice before being loaned (briefly) to Manchester United and Sporting Gijon. A permanent move to Marseille in France in 1984–85 was more successful, six goals scored in 30 Ligue 1 games. During 1979–1980 Cunningham won six England caps.

A broken toe early in the 1980–81 season diminished his appearance in this 1981 European Cup Final. The following season a thigh injury meant scarcely any first team action for Real. Cunningham moved back to England to join Leicester City in 1985–86, but further injury saw his game time reduced to 15 league matches. Moving back to Spain to play for Rayo Vallecano in Spain's Segunda Division, he scored the goal that secured the club's promotion to the Primera Division. Tragically, Cunningham died in a car crash on 15 July 1989, aged 33. In November 2004, Cunningham was voted one of West Bromwich Albion's 16 greatest players in a poll organised to celebrate the club's 125th year since being founded in 1879. A statue by Graham Ibbeson commemorates Cunningham in Coronation Gardens, Leyton, near Leyton Orient's Brisbane Road ground. The genial Ron Atkinson culled the term (after the US soul singing trio) 'The Three Degrees' in reverence to Cunningham, Cyrille Regis and Brendan Batson. Batson became an influential administrator and vocal champion for black English footballers; Regis was a charismatic, powerful, bustling centre-forward with an explosive shot, but by degrees Laurie Cunningham was the most skilful of the trio, his playing career severely hampered by costly injuries.

Real manager Vujadin Boskov, a former Yugoslavian international player, had the misfortune to manage Real here, and Sampdoria in 1992 as the losing manager of two European Cup Finals. Compensation came in the form of a La Liga title and a Copa del Rey triumph in the 1979–1980 season, and an impressive spell with Sampdoria in Italy, the club winning the European Cup Winner's Cup in 1989–1990, Serie A in Italy 1990–91, and two Coppa Italias in 1987–88 and 1988–89.

THE FINAL

A second tight final for Liverpool after their 1-0 win over Club Brugge in 1978. Belief coursed through Liverpool teams at this time – they took the game to Real in the first half, Phil Neal spreading play from right to left where Alan Kennedy flashed a low drive that was saved at the near post. Kenny Dalglish's ability to weave magic in tight spaces was evident as he conjured up an opportunity for himself only to shoot straight at the goalkeeper. Liverpool had a let-off when a lobbed shot drifted wide of the far post after a lovely set-up by Juanito. Graeme Souness tried to drive Liverpool on, but unusually shot tamely at goal after taking up a good position on the edge of the penalty area.

Real almost took first blood in the second half when the ever-dangerous José Camacho broke free of Liverpool's defence, chipped Ray Clemence and saw the ball sail narrowly over the bar. Alan Hansen was caught napping here, revealing a chink in his defensive armour that occasionally came about through his adventurous sorties upfield. At last the breakthrough came from that unlikely left-back source. When I first watched this game I thought it was Alan Kennedy's sheer determination that brought him his goal. Watching TV footage again as Kennedy broke into space to accept Ray Kennedy's throw-in, I see an appalling error by the usually flawless Uli Stielike, fly-hacking at the ball, helping Alan Kennedy's cause immeasurably. Undeterred, Kennedy surged forward and drove the ball into the far corner of the net. Liverpool sought another goal to calm their jangling nerves, but despite Dalglish's purposefulness and resolve in shielding the ball and shrugging off a defender, McDermott and Souness were unable to contrive a goal from his pass. Real were not out of the contest, but Liverpool generally bossed affairs with their slick passing style.

Cunningham, sadly, was largely anonymous, lack of fitness telling on him. The star man for Liverpool was the ingenious Dalglish, his ability to link play, bring players into the game around him, reminiscent of the great Pele. I could pay Dalglish no higher compliment – here was a player in a British team with a seriously clever football brain.

1982 EUROPEAN CUP FINAL
Aston Villa 1 v 0 Bayern Munich

Here was a scoreline to make anybody other than a die-hard Aston Villa fan shake their heads in disbelief. Aston Villa, a perennially under-achieving English

Midlands club with a wonderful old ground at Villa Park (I've been there twice, once extremely fortuitously for the memorable 1999 FA Cup semi-final when Manchester United beat Arsenal 2-1 in extra time with ten men, Roy Keane having been sent off – it was the night of a shirtless Ryan Giggs celebrating an incredible solo goal; of Dennis Bergkamp missing a last gasp penalty kick in normal time). The coloured balloons of both teams illuminating the Birmingham night sky is something I have never forgotten. What an atmosphere! What a game!

This Aston Villa side – largely prepared and established by Ron Saunders, but led in the De Kuip Stadium, Rotterdam, by the quieter Tony Barton – shouldn't have had a prayer against a hugely experienced Bayern Munich side containing Paul Breitner, Dieter Hoeness and Karl-Heinz Rummenigge, should they? Villa, a highly organised team with no little flair, had other ideas. Driven on by the tireless Dennis Mortimer, and inspired from the left flank by Tony Morley, Aston Villa duly upset the odds as distinct underdogs.

Route to the Final
Apart from a 7-0 aggregate humbling of the Icelanders Valur in the first round, Villa's progress to the final was a tense series of games, hard-fought. In contrast, Bayern swept all before them, scoring 20 goals in four ties to reach the final.

In the first round at Villa Park, centre-forward Peter Withe scored twice as Valur were dismissed 5-0. The talented Gary Shaw sealed the 7-0 aggregate won with two goals in Iceland. Villa scored a notable victory over the East Germans Dynamo Berlin away in the first leg by a 2-1 margin, this time the rapid left-winger Tony Morley the scorer of both goals. Having done the hard bit, Villa lost the home leg 1-0 to a Frank Terletzki goal, scraping through to the next round on away goals. A better outcome occurred in the last eight, Villa drawing 0-0 in the Ukraine with Dynamo Kiev, Shaw and Ken McNaught confirming their semi-final place with goals at Villa Park. Another tense pair of ties secured Villa's final place in the last four. Morley's goal was enough to give Villa a slender advantage travelling to Belgium to play the second leg against Anderlecht. A goalless draw saw Villa narrowly through to their first – and only European final. With Belgian football in the ascendancy, Villa's performances were meritorious indeed.

A Karl-Heinz Rummenigge penalty ensured a 1-0 victory for Bayern Munich in their first round, first leg tie in Sweden against Osters IF. Two goals apiece for Rummenigge and Dieter Hoeness in a 5-0 rout in Munich confirmed Bayern's superiority. In the second round Bayern held Portuguese champions Benfica to a goalless draw in Lisbon, running out comfortable winners courtesy of a Hoeness hat-trick and a Paul Breitner goal in a 4-1 home victory. Romanian side Universitatea Craiova were beaten 2-0 away in the last eight, goals coming from Breitner and Rummenigge. Although held to a 1-1 draw in Munich by the plucky Romanians, Hoeness's goal ensured Bayern's progress to the last four. Bayern were involved in two unusually high scoring games in their semi-final against Bulgaria's CSKA Sofia. Beaten 4-3 in Sofia, Hoeness and Breitner among their scorers, Bayern's home form was simply too much for the gallant Bulgarians, Breitner and Rummenigge scoring twice apiece as Bayern ran out conclusive 4-0 winners. Bayern possessed the 1981–82 European Cup's three leading scorers in

Hoeness (seven), Rummenigge (six) and Breitner (shared with Anderlecht's Willy Geurts (five). Villa's Tony Morley totalled four in the competition.

Villa's starting goalkeeper Jimmy Rimmer began his playing days at Old Trafford. The *Birmingham Mail* described Rimmer as "perhaps the greatest goalkeeper in Aston Villa's history" – sadly for Rimmer his game time here in Rotterdam totalled just nine minutes before he came off injured. Ironically, Rimmer won two European Cup medals, having played only nine minutes in total. His first medal came in 1968 as Alex Stepney's stand-by in the epic 4-1 win over Benfica. Rimmer spent 11 seasons at Old Trafford with Manchester United 1963–1974 as Stepney's understudy before being signed by Arsenal in 1974. Rimmer won Arsenal's Player of the Year award in 1975, but the incoming manager Terry Neill brought Pat Jennings with him from Tottenham Hotspur, Rimmer moving to Aston Villa after 124 league games for Arsenal. Nigel Spink's performance in this 1982 European Cup Final was a portent of things to come for Rimmer, his six-season stint as Villa's No. 1 goalkeeper ending with a permanent move to Swansea in 1983.

Right-back Kenny Swain moved from college football to Wycombe Wanderers as a non-contract player in 1973. After six non-league games Swain was signed by 2nd Division Chelsea. As a striker Swain partnered Steve Finnieston in Chelsea's promotion-winning side of 1976–77. After 119 league games and 26 goals, and a further relegation from the top flight for Chelsea, Swain signed for Aston Villa in 1978. Redeployed as a full-back by Ron Saunders, Swain helped Villa win the 1st Division title in 1980–81, followed by this famous European Cup Final victory. Later career moves saw Swain win a 2nd Division runners-up medal with Portsmouth and a 4th Division promotion with Crewe Alexandra. Swain ultimately turned his talents to management and coaching, spells with England U-16 and U-17 included.

Centre-back Ken McNaught, Kirkcaldy-born, came from Scottish footballing stock, his father having held Raith Rovers' club appearance record (657 games –1941–1962) and appearing five times for Scotland. Son Ken was a rugged, resilient defender who formed a fine defensive partnership with Allan Evans. McNaught junior signed for Everton in 1974, playing against Villa in the 1977 League Cup Final – a final that went to three games (in the days of replays) and was decided by Gary Shaw's equally talented predecessor Brian Little in the 119th minute of the third match. McNaught had played 66 league games for Everton when signing for Aston Villa in 1977.

McNaught went on to play 207 league games for Villa, chipping in with eight goals, and scoring in the European Super Cup win over Barcelona that resulted from Villa's European Cup victory (a match between the winners of the European Cup and the European Cup Winners' Cup). McNaught didn't win a full cap for Scotland, but shares the honour of being one of two Scotsmen to win the European Cup without being an international (the other being Nottingham Forest's John McGovern).

Allan Evans, McNaught's central defensive partner, was the more offensive-minded of the pair, scoring 51 goals in his 380 league games for Villa 1977–1989. Evans's capacity for goals came from starting out as a centre-forward with hometown club Dunfermline Athletic in 1973 (14 goals in 98 league games). Although Evans appeared 14 times for Leicester City 1989–1990, his best days were behind him. Capped four times by Scotland, Evans is remembered fondly by Villa fans as a skilful defender, happy venturing forward, with McNaught an able anchor man behind him.

A third Scotsman, Des Bremner, filled the left midfield berth in Villa's 4-3-3 formation. The moustachioed Bremner played 199 league games for Hibernian in Scotland (scoring 18 goals) 1972–79, thereafter featuring at Villa Park until 1984. Like midfield teammates, Dennis Mortimer and Gordon Cowans, Bremner was a hard-working player. Compared to the hard-running Mortimer and the slighter built, but gifted Cowans, Bremner's efforts went under the radar a little – but were not lost on his teammates. Bremner played 174 league games with Villa, scoring nine goals. He moved to Birmingham City in 1984, playing a further 168 games under his former Villa manager Ron Saunders. With Saunders, Bremner helped Birmingham back into the 1st Division, only to endure two relegations with the club – Bremner was now in his mid-30s. Des Bremner won a solitary Scotland cap while playing for Hibernian in 1976.

Liverpool-born Dennis Mortimer was an inspirational player and captain for Aston Villa. Competition fierce for international honours, the unfortunate Mortimer was capped by England at Youth, U-23 and England B level, but never received a full England cap. He can count himself incredibly unlucky, such was his influence upon the two Midlands clubs he played for, Coventry City (1969–1975, 193 league appearances, nine goals) and Aston Villa (1975–1985, 403 appearances in all competitions, 36 goals). A player of promise at Coventry City, Mortimer flourished fully at Aston Villa, his relentless running, committed team ethic and occasional spectacular goals, made him one of the most influential players in this Villa team. Mortimer's football knowledge post-playing days extended to being the PFA Football in the Community Officer at West Bromwich Albion (1991); regional director of coaching in the Midlands 1996–2005; and part of the Football Association's Education Coaching Department 2008–2015. A great team player, Dennis Mortimer's football knowledge has benefited hundreds of aspiring players.

The five feet eight inches Gordon Cowans belied his slight build with tenacious tackling. Two-footed – centre-back and teammate Derek Mountfield rated him the best two-footed player he played with – Cowans played 286 league games for Villa 1976–1985, scoring 42 goals and supplying countless assists. In his youth career Cowans won the FA Youth Cup with Aston Villa, playing also for England Youth. Cowans debuted for Villa in 1976, aged 17, while still an apprentice at the club. Established in Villa's first team, Cowans was voted the PFA Young Player of the Year in 1980–81 as Villa won the 1st Division title.

Things turned sour for Cowans when he broke a leg in a pre-season friendly in Spain, resulting in him missing the entire 1983–84 season. He recovered, but was sold to Italian club Bari in 1985. In three seasons with Bari in Italy's deep south, Cowans played 94 league games, faring well in a notoriously tough environment for overseas players. Villa retained the option of re-signing Cowans, an option Graham Taylor took up in 1988. Cowans' second spell at Villa was not without success: Villa finished runners-up in the 1st Division to Liverpool – who else in the 1980s? Taylor left Villa to manage England, but the home-coming Cowans completed another 117 league games for Villa (three goals) 1988–1991.

Ron Atkinson sold Cowans to Blackburn Rovers in November 1991. Cowans was not finished though, helping Rovers win promotion to the newly formed FA Premier League in 1992. Rovers, of course, went on to be the surprise winners of the Premier League in 1994–95. Cowans had moved on by this time, a third stint with Villa in 1993–94 suggesting his love for the club. By the time Cowans had turned out for Derby County, Wolverhampton Wanderers, Sheffield United, Bradford City, Stockport County and Burnley, it was time for him to hang up his boots. Gordon Cowans had completed 690 league matches, scoring 54 goals. In total for his beloved Aston Villa, Cowans scored 49 goals in all competitions. He returned to Villa one fourth time in 1998. From 1998–2016, Cowans's roles at Villa Park included First Team Academy Coach and assistant manager to the first team in 2014. Gordon Cowans received ten England caps, scoring twice, 1983–1990.

The blond-locked Tony Morley epitomised the 1980s footballer. Long-haired – when it was still fashionable – Morley, like Cowans, five feet eight inches and slight, skipped across the turf like the proverbial greyhound. Ormskirk, Lancashire-born, Morley played youth football with Preston North End, signing professional terms in 1972. Morley was regarded as skilful, but inconsistent – the savvy Ron Saunders rectified this matter at Aston Villa, moulding Morley into one of the most dangerous forwards in English football.

With Preston, Morley played 84 league games (15 goals), and at Burnley he played 91 league games (five goals). Joining Villa in June 1979, Saunders put the pace of Morley to great effect as he built his formidable late 70s/early 80s Aston Villa team. In the shape of Morley, Cowans and Gary Shaw, Villa possessed gifted individuals, but Saunders' essence was for a team to play as a team, akin to the mode Brian Clough was achieving at Nottingham Forest at this time.

Morley's pace and eye for the spectacular shot was now gaining him new respect. A typical dribble and long-range shot won Morley the 1980–81 Goal of the Season. It was Morley's solo dribble and cross that set up Peter Withe for the solitary winning goal in this 1982 European Cup Final. Morley's inconsistency led to his being transferred to West Bromwich Albion in 1983, where he played 33 league games over two seasons. Thereafter Morley's career petered out somewhat, playing for Seiko in Hong Kong (1985–86); Den Haag in Holland (1986–87 – a successful 31 game spell in which he scored 13 Eredivisie goals and scored in a losing Dutch Cup Final appearance); Tampa Bay Rowdies in the NASL (briefly in 1989); and Hamrun Spartans in Malta (1990). In between times Morley returned to West Brom in 1987, completing 28 league games, scoring a respectable seven goals to go with his four in 33 games in his first spell at the Hawthorns.

Tony Morley won six caps for England (all in the 1981–82 season), yet did not find favour with attack-minded national manager Ron Greenwood in selection for the 1982 World Cup squad, Arsenal's Graham Rix being preferred ahead of Villa's gifted winger. Enigmatic, ridiculously talented, it seems Tony Morley's career reached the heights under the stern Ron Saunders, one of football's great intangibles. Saunders appeared dour at times, yet got the best out of English football's most wayward players. It's a funny old game, isn't it?

At six feet two inches, Peter Withe was an archetypal English centre-forward, big, strong, powerful in the air, an excellent target man who shielded the ball superbly. Withe was extremely adept at bringing teammates into play, and formed two outstanding little and large á la Toshack and Keegan relationships, firstly with Tony Woodcock at Nottingham Forest, then with Gary Shaw at Aston Villa.

Liverpool-born Withe started at Merseyside club Southport, but left after only three games. One game at Barrow, and Withe began a nomadic professional career, playing in South Africa in 1972–73, two seasons at Wolverhampton Wanderers, where he played second fiddle to the terrific Derek Dougan-John Richards pairing. Withe then played in the NASL with Portland Timbers before returning to the Midlands. In the 1975–76 season Withe played for Birmingham City, scoring nine goals in 35 league appearances. Curiously, Withe had yet to establish himself anywhere at the age of 25, but the maestro management pairing of Brian Clough and Peter Taylor took a chance on him in 1976 and the imposing striker's career undertook a serious upswing. The pairing of Withe and Tony Woodcock was an immediate success, Withe scoring 19 and Woodcock 17 goals by the end of the 1976–77 season. Withe, despite only playing from November 1976, was voted the club's Player of the Year. Forest won the long defunct Anglo-Scottish Cup in December 1976, defeating Leyton Orient over two legs. It may seem like winning a 'tin pot trophy' to many, but Clough maintained that winning the cup was the beginning of Forest's successful period until 1981, the simple act of winning a trophy instilling in his players a thirst for more success.

Withe found himself surplus to Clough and Taylor's requirements soon afterwards, the more mobile Garry Birtles taking his place. Withe moved on, joining Newcastle United 1978–1980, where he scored 25 goals in 76 league games. Withe's next move gave the imposing striker his best trophy return during his entire career.

Staying longer at Aston Villa than he'd previously done at any professional club, Withe, by then 29 years old, was at the peak of his powers. Aston Villa were surprise winners of the English 1st Division in 1980–81, pipping the perennially strong Liverpool and Bobby Robson's excellent Ipswich Town team to the title. In his first season with Villa, Withe scored 20 goals, finishing joint top scorer in Division 1 with Tottenham Hotspur's Steve Archibald. The two strikers could scarcely have been more different, Withe a central defender's nightmare with his height and imposing physique, Archibald a quicksilver, predatory player. Withe played over 200 games for Villa, scoring 90 goals, his partnership with another quicksilver forward, Gary Shaw, the perfect pairing. A reasonably successful stint with Sheffield United followed, 1985–89 (18 goals in 74 league appearances), Withe ending his career at Huddersfield Town 1989–1990.

Peter Withe played 11 times for England 1981–84, scoring once, being part of the 1982 World Cup squad. Withe's partnership with Gary Shaw was a thing of physical and graceful wonder. Withe the towering, bruising, battering ram centre-forward; Shaw the slighter specimen with a blond mane that could have stepped off the pages of a modelling magazine, a player who relied on touch.

The boyish-looking Gary Shaw had his career effectively ended in 1983 after suffering a hefty challenge against Nottingham Forest. Birmingham-born Shaw, the local lad made good, continued playing – or attempting to play – until he was 30 years old, but the quick-footed striker couldn't regain his former peak post-1983.

Starting professionally with Aston Villa in 1978, Shaw completed 165 league games with the club 1978–1988, scoring 59 goals. The only Brummie in Ron Saunders' 1980–81 and 1981–82 Villa teams, Shaw was voted the PFA Young Player of the Year in 1980–81, and won the prestigious Bravo award in 1981–82 as the best European player in all European competitions. What a sad outcome for Shaw the tackle against Forest turned out to be. Shaw was capped seven times for the England U-21 team, scoring twice. He was also picked in the provisional 40 for the England 1982 World Cup squad, not making the final 22. A player of massively untapped potential, Gary Shaw, his touch and footwork a joy to behold in his early 80s glory days with Aston Villa, faded into memory. There was so much more to come.

Imagine being reserve goalkeeper for your club, having played only once for the first team. The regular keeper, Jimmy Rimmer, is injured after only nine minutes of the biggest club game in European football, the crème de la crème, the European Cup Final. You enter the field of play totally inexperienced at this rarefied level, perform magnificently, and become your club's first-choice goalkeeper for nearly two decades. This was the extraordinary tale of Nigel Spink's entry on to the pitch in Rotterdam in May 1992.

Spink spent a short time with West Ham United as a schoolboy, swiftly reverting to non-league football to play for Chelmsford City in the 1976–77 season. Aston Villa signed Spink in 1977, but it was almost five years before he established himself – in the biggest European club game of them all. He went on to play 361 league games for Villa until moving across the Midlands to play 19 times for West Bromwich Albion in the 1996–97 season. Spink ended his professional playing days at Millwall 1997–2000, retiring shortly before his 42nd birthday. His performance in Rotterdam on this evening was sensational.

Among the other substitutes for Villa on this evening, Colin Gibson enjoyed a fine career, totalling 364 Football League games chiefly with Villa (185 appearances, ten goals), Manchester United (79, nine goals) and Leicester City (59, four goals) 1978–1995. An excellent left-back or left-sided midfielder, Gibson provided dependable cover as a utility player. Attacking substitute David Geddis appeared in the 1978 FA Cup Final for Ipswich Town, providing the cross for Roger Osborne to score the only goal of the game, the Tractor Boys defying the odds to beat Arsenal at Wembley. Geddis had an impossible task separating Tony Barton's first-choice strike pairing of Peter Withe and Gary Shaw, consequently playing for Barnsley and Birmingham City – the latter under departed boss Ron Saunders. He helped Birmingham win promotion to the 1st Division in 1984–85.

Tony Barton inadvertently became Aston Villa's manager in February 1982. Quieter than the stern disciplinarian Ron Saunders, Barton's promotion from assistant manager ensured his 15 minutes of fame. Barton won England

Schoolboy (one) and Youth (five) caps as a player, going on to play professionally with Fulham, Nottingham Forest and Portsmouth. A right-winger in old football parlance, Barton scored 43 goals in 201 league games. This tells us that Barton was a seasoned player himself, and as Saunders's right-hand man he moved seamlessly into the Villa hot seat. Yet the feeling persisted that this Aston Villa team had been built by Saunders during his tenure at the club 1974–1982. Barton took over in February 1982, overseeing the club for the last three months of this historic season for this historic old club. When Villa's league form dipped in 1982–83 and 1983–84 (sixth and tenth respectively – actually quite respectable) Barton was dismissed. His managerial career ended at one of his former clubs, Portsmouth, as caretaker manager in 1991. It was the culmination of a short managerial career; very short indeed in the spotlight with Aston Villa 1982–84. Barton's life was sadly curtailed when he died from a heart attack in 1993. Villa's feat in winning the 1982 European Cup won Barton the European Coach of the Season award for 1981–82.

Bayern Munich, one of European football's giant clubs – along with Real Madrid, Barcelona, Inter Milan, AC Milan and Juventus – were overwhelming favourites to win the 1982 European Cup Final. Centre-back Klaus Augenthaler was a Bayern Munich club legend, playing 23 times for West Germany 1983–1990. A one-club man, Augenthaler took the traditional (late 60s onwards due to the success of Franz Beckenbauer's switch from midfield to sweeper) German route of moving from central defence to the last-man libero role in the Bayern team. Augenthaler played 404 Bundesliga games for Bayern, scoring 52 goals – a great return for a defender. He won seven Bundesliga titles and three DFB Pokal Cups. He was twice runner-up in this European Cup competition, again in 1987 when the team lost 2-1 to Porto. In all, Augenthaler made 89 appearances in the European Cup 1976–1991. An utterly dependable player, Augenthaler played centre-back for West Germany in the 1990 World Cup Final team that defeated Argentina 1-0. He was a squad member of the team that reached the 1986 World Cup Final – a 3-2 defeat against Diego Maradona's 'Hand of God' Argentina.

Captain and midfield maestro Paul Breitner was simply one of the world's best players in the 1970s and early 1980s. At a FIFA Awards ceremony in 2004, Pele named Breitner one of the Top 125 Greatest Living Footballers. Breitner scored for West Germany in the 1974 and 1982 World Cup Finals (2-1 v Holland, 1-3 v Italy), becoming one of only four players to score in two finals on the biggest international stage, the others being the Brazilians Pele and Vava (1958 and 1970), (1958 and 1962) and France's Zinedine Zidane (1998 and 2006). Breitner was named in the FIFA World Cup All-Time Team in 1994 – the English supplied two of that team, players I greatly admired for their class on the field and off it, Bobby Charlton and Bobby Moore.

Paul Breitner book-ended his professional career with Bayern Munich 1970–74 and 1978–1983. In between he enjoyed three seasons at Real Madrid, and lesser known, one season at Eintracht Braunschweig in 1977–78. It's almost forgotten that Breitner began his playing days as a left-back who roamed all over the pitch, supplanting his attacking teammates. Astonishingly, Breitner, something of a rebel, played only 48 times for his country. Ridiculous for such an outrageously talented player. This was due to Breitner, whose long dark hair in the 70s typecast him as a player given to rebellion, withdrawing from the West German national team until invited back by Jupp Derwall in 1981, following his transfer to Real Madrid in 1974. That's seven lost years of international football, years when he was at his peak.

Paul Breitner won five Bundesliga titles. 1971–72, 1972–73, 1973–74, 1979–1980 and 1980–81. It was only the devastating Ajax team of the early 70s that surpassed Bayern Munich in his early years at the club. He also won the DFB Pokal Cup twice, in 1970–71 and 1981–82. Breitner won the European Cup just once thanks to Nigel Spink's obstinacy and Aston Villa's terrific team pride, the replayed 1973–74 4-0 triumph over Atlético Madrid. At Real Madrid, Breitner won La Liga twice, in 1974–75 and 1975–76, also winning the Spanish Copa del Rey in 1974–75.

Internationally Breitner won the 1972 European Championship, and the 1974 World Cup, being a losing World Cup finalist against Italy in 1982. Breitner was chosen in the UEFA European Championship Team of the Tournament in 1972 and the FIFA World Cup All-Star Team in 1974. He was Footballer of the Year in Germany in 1981, and the Ballon d'Or (European Footballer of the Year) runner-up in the same season, ironically behind his Bayern teammate Karl-Heinz Rummenigge. In a year dominated by West German players, Barcelona's West German international midfielder Bernd Schuster finished third in the Ballon d'Or poll.

An extraordinary player whose political beliefs overtook his footballing exploits for a while, Breitner enjoyed great success either as a left-back (in the 1972 European Championships) or as a rampaging midfielder from 1974 onwards. Quick, mobile, occasionally volatile, an excellent all-round team player, Paul Breitner lit up international football in the 1970s and early 1980s with his explosive energy.

Dieter Hoeness was the younger, and arguably less talented brother of the career-shortened Uli. Dieter came to Bayern Munich in the latter stages of his career, quickly repaying the club with a surfeit of goals (102 in 224 Bundesliga matches). Dieter scored 90 goals in 208 matches with VfR Aalen and VfB Stuttgart 1973–79, helping Stuttgart win promotion to the Bundesliga with 16 goals in the 1978–79 season. At Bayern, Hoeness junior hit double figures five times 1979–1987, winning the Bundesliga five times, and the DFB Pokal three times. He was twice runner-up in the European Cup Final, here against Aston Villa, and against Porto in 1986–87. Dieter played six times for West Germany, scoring four goals. He was selected for the 1986 World Cup squad, appearing after an hour in the final defeat against Argentina, at 33 years old, the oldest player on the field that day. Less obviously talented on the ground than his older brother Uli, Dieter Hoeness made his mark as a tall (six feet two inches) striker whose main threat was his aerial prowess.

Bayern's star striker of this era, Karl-Heinz Rummenigge, had the thankless task at international level of following the irreplaceable Gerd Müller, his country's foremost goalscorer. Rummenigge figured as an outstanding dribbler upon signing for Bayern Munich in 1974 from Westphalian amateur side Borussia

Lippstadt. Only in later seasons did Rummenigge develop into an outstanding central striker on the bigger stage. Any stage fright dissipated as Rummenigge became one of Europe's top strikers post-1976. He'd already won two European Cups by this juncture, 1974–75 and 1975–76, although not appearing in the former final. In the latter final he wore the number 7 shirt, while Gerd Müller retained the number 9 shirt.

Rummenigge's trophy haul seems slight for such a remarkably talented player: two Bundesliga titles with Bayern 1979–1980 and 1980–81, two DFB Pokal Cups in 1981–82 and 1983–84. At international level Rummenigge posed a serious threat to defences with his pace, dribbling skills and penalty area presence. Again titles largely eluded him, only the 1980 European Championship trophy coming his way as he finished a runner-up in two consecutive World Cup finals versus Italy in 1982 and Argentina in 1986.

Rummenigge was the Bundesliga's top scorer in 1979–1980, 1980–81 and 1983–84 with 26, 29 and 26 goals respectively. Sadly, his latter career was hampered by injury, a move to Inter Milan in Italy 1984–87 bringing him 24 Serie A goals in 64 appearances, but he was unable to play regularly enough to show his true worth. He ended his professional playing days at Servette in Switzerland where he scored 34 goals in 50 league games, top scoring in Switzerland with 24 goals in his last season 1988–89.

Personal accolades were plentiful for Rummenigge: Footballer of the Year in Germany in 1980; twice European Footballer of the Year (Ballon d'Or) 1980, 1981; chosen as part of the UEFA European Championship Team of the Tournament 1980; European Cup top scorer (jointly with Terry McDermott and Graeme Souness) with six goals in 1980–81; Swiss Foreign Footballer of the Year 1988–89; chosen by Pele as one of the Top Greatest Living Footballers in March 2004.

In the autumn of 1991 Bayern Munich invited Rummenigge and Franz Beckenbauer to return to the club as vice-presidents, a position Rummenigge held until 2002. He then became chairman, relinquishing his CEO role in 2021 to Oliver Khan. During his tenure at Bayern as CEO the club moved to the state-of-the-art Allianz Arena, the world's first full-colour changing exterior stadium, opened in 2005. A wonderful player, Karl-Heinz Rummenigge, another German with Bayern Munich steeped in his veins.

THE FINAL

Peter Withe recalled how relaxed Villa were going into this game – surprising given the quality of the opposition. Villa's team bond was obviously strong. Was their optimism misplaced? You might have thought so in the early stages of this game as Bayern dominated. Rummenigge first was denied by the newly-on-the-field Nigel Spink's extended palm. A spectacular goal was avoided fortunately for Villa as Rummenigge's overhead kick narrowly evaded the far post from Breitner's right-wing cross. Half-time arrived and Villa were clinging on, 0-0.

As in the previous year's final when Hamburger SV dominated possession against Nottingham Forest, Bayern continued to have the lion's share of the ball in the second half. Rummenigge featured prominently, setting up teammates with his mobility and awareness of the right pass. A great break from defence by Klaus Augenthaler saw the defender's shot glide past a post. Breitner was everywhere, a positive menace to Villa, setting up another chance for Augenthaler who had crept beyond Villa's defence from deep. The recovering Allan Evans spotted the danger and headed Augenthaler's header off the line.

Out of nowhere Villa contrived the only goal of the game. Withe competed fiercely for the ball near the halfway line, fed Gary Shaw who in turn fed Tony Morley. Morley twisted one way, then the other, disorienting Bayern's defence and sending the perfect ball across goal to the lurking Withe who could not miss from two yards out, the ball entering the net via a post. Two years running English clubs had beaten German teams who'd dominated the play. It seems inconceivable now, knowing what we know about England's fortunes against the German national team 1990–2021, until 'the monkey' finally fell from England's backs at the delayed 2020 European Championships. An offside goal by Dieter Hoeness gave Villa a late scare, but Villa held on. It was a night of glory for Nigel Spink, and a tribute to the Saunders/Barton team ethic instilled in a stubborn Aston Villa side.

1983–84 EUROPEAN CUP FINAL
Liverpool 1 v A.S. Roma 1
(Liverpool win 4-2 on penalties)

Curiously, the remarkable Liverpool team of the late 1970s and early 1980s won the majority of their European Cups in this period by very close margins. The excitement produced by the Kevin Keegan-inspired 1977 team was followed by several victories won by a technically more accomplished team grinding out wins in challenging circumstances. This final was a case in point, Roma having home advantage (this can be a curse, especially for Italian teams whose fans expect nothing but victory), making them slight favourites, despite Liverpool's obvious prowess at this time.

Route to the Final
Liverpool's progress to the final fluctuated, some ties tight, others won comfortably. Roma, by contrast, had a series of tough contests before reaching the final in their own Stadio Olimpico in Rome. A solitary goal from Kenny Dalglish was enough to seal a 1-0 victory for Liverpool over Denmark's Odense in the first round, first leg. At Anfield Liverpool made short work of the Danes, Michael Robinson adding two goals to a double from Dalglish in a 5-0 win.

Spanish opponents Athletic Bilbao were made of altogether sterner stuff in the second round, holding Liverpool to a goalless draw at Anfield. The pressure was on, but Liverpool's team spirit and resilience held sway in the return leg in the Bay of Biscay region, super-striker Ian Rush scoring the only goal of the tie. Rush again took the plaudits in a 1-0 home victory over Benfica of Portugal in the quarter-finals. Surprisingly, Liverpool overwhelmed their opponents 4-1 in the return match, Rush again scoring, while Ronnie Whelan notched a brace. Two tight matches with the Romanians of Dinamo Bucharest ensued in the semi-finals, Liverpool securing a marginal lead at Anfield with a Sammy Lee goal. In the second leg Rush did the business again, scoring twice as Liverpool won 2-1.

Roma sealed their first-round success with a 3-0 home win against the Swedes of IFK Göteborg, Bruno Conti among the scorers. Although Roma could score only through Roberto Pruzzo in Gothenburg, two goals against were insufficient to halt their progress. Two 1-0 wins in the second round ensured Roma's further progress against Bulgarian side CSKA Sofia, the great Brazilian midfielder Falcão netting in Sofia, while striker Francesco Graziani scored in Rome. Graziani and Pruzzo netted in a 3-0 home quarter-final win against East German side Dynamo Berlin. A 2-1 defeat in Berlin only came courtesy of two late goals, Roma winning through 4-2 on aggregate.

Scottish side Dundee United were surprise semi-final opponents for Roma, running their feted Italian foes very close, the might of Rome winning through 3-2 on aggregate. Dundee United would reach the 1986–87 UEFA Cup Final during a period of sustained Scottish success for the lesser lights north of the border – Alex Ferguson's Aberdeen having won the European Cup Winners' Cup in 1982–83. Dundee United even had the temerity to win the semi-final first leg of this 1983–84 semi-final at Tannadice 2-0, with goals from David Dodds and Derek Stark. Sadly, they could not prevent Roma from overturning the deficit by 3-0 in Rome, Pruzzo scoring twice for the Italians. Pruzzo and Ian Rush totalled five goals apiece for the 1983–84 European Cup finalists.

In goal for Liverpool on this night, Zimbabwean Bruce Grobbelaar may have lacked predecessor Ray Clemence's solidity, but compensated copiously with charisma and a devil-may-care approach to the game of football. Athletic, gymnastic, super-confident, Grobbelaar had his critics, but completed 440 league games for Liverpool 1981–1994, not a bad return for one who clowned his way through games at times. As is often the case with players of Grobbelaar's flamboyance, a thoroughly professional player lay underneath the veneer of outrageousness. You don't win six league titles, three FA Cups, three League Cups and this 1983–84 European Cup by being a clown.

A talented cricketer, Grobbelaar was also offered a baseball scholarship in the United States, but chose football as his preferred sporting career. A handful of appearances in Zimbabwe 1973–76 led to a contract at Durban City FC in South Africa for the 1977–78 season, before he transferred to Vancouver Whitecaps in the NASL in 1979. A loan spell with Crewe Alexandra in England led to his Liverpool period. Only work permit difficulties prevented Grobbelaar signing for Ron Atkinson's West Bromwich Albion – the one that got away. Grobbelaar's early Liverpool career was beset by inconsistency, but he overcame his wobble to become Liverpool's No. 1 goalkeeper for 13 seasons. In fact the only wobble in later years was Grobbelaar's off-putting leg-shake, faking loss of control in his legs as penalty-takers were about to attempt to beat the charismatic Zimbabwean from 12 yards. Grobbelaar only lost his position ultimately to David James because of his insistence on playing internationally for Zimbabwe during the league season (he won 32 caps).

Moving to Southampton in 1994, Grobbelaar was caught up in match-fixing allegations in November of that year, eventually being cleared in 1997. The aftermath of the allegations and court costs led to him being declared bankrupt. Since retiring from the professional game Grobbelaar has coached in South Africa, Zimbabwe (player-managing the national team 1997–98), and in the UK. Liverpool fans loved 'Brucie', recognising a character they saw in their own scouse image. Bruce Grobbelaar lived in a village four miles from my hometown, my youngest son attending a party for his daughter as they were school friends back in the late 1990s/early 2000s.

The ever-reliable Phil Thompson no longer a Liverpool regular, the incoming Mark Lawrenson proved a stylish alternative in the middle of Liverpool's defence. Before wearing the red shirt of Liverpool with some distinction, Lawrenson made his name with first Preston North End, then Brighton and Hove Albion 1974–1981. After 73 appearances with Preston, Lawrenson signed as a 19-year-old for a Brighton side then managed by Alan Mullery. Liverpool expressed interest in Lawrenson at this juncture, but were outbid by Brighton. Lawrenson left Brighton with the club in financial difficulties, signing for Bob Paisley's Liverpool in the summer of 1981.

Lawrenson went on to complete 241 league matches for Liverpool, scoring 11 times. It was his defensive partnership with Alan Hansen that he was best known for, although the skilful, versatile player could also play at left-back or in midfield. Phil Thompson's career curtailed by injury, Lawrenson stepped up to the plate to make the Hansen-Lawrenson central defence for Liverpool a formidable combination of pace, skill, and athleticism. Eventually Lawrenson too would suffer an injury – a damaged Achilles tendon – that cost him his career and place in the Liverpool team to Gary Gillespie.

Lawrenson flirted with management at Oxford United (1988) and Peterborough United (1989–1990), but is better remembered as a forthright and erudite football pundit. Internationally he played 39 times for the Republic of Ireland 1977–1987, scoring five goals.

Two of Liverpool's midfield four in 1984 had changed from their last European Cup triumph in 1981. Only the silky, steely Graeme Souness and the effervescent Sammy Lee retained their places on this night. The wide midfield players in the Olimpico Stadium, Rome on this evening were excellent replacements. South African-born Craig Johnston filled the wide right berth with flair and vitality. Yet Johnston could easily have failed to reach a football field of any description. Born in Johannesburg to Australian parents, Johnston returned to Australia as a small boy, contracting osteomyelitis age six, almost losing his leg to the debilitating bone infection. An American specialist visiting Australia at the time applied his expertise to Johnston's condition, allowing the South African-Australian Johnston the chance to live a normal life and later become a sporting champion.

Aged 14, Johnston wrote to four English clubs, Manchester United and Chelsea included. They did not reply, but Middlesbrough, managed by Jack Charlton, gave Johnston a chance. Struggling to make a mark initially, Johnston wasn't too proud to take on cleaning jobs and washing player's cars to ensure Charlton hadn't made a mistake, despite being homesick. In 64 league games for Boro 1977–1981, Johnston scored 16 goals, rewarding Charlton with his persistence.

Johnston's Australian heritage earned him the nickname 'Skippy' with reference to the much-loved TV kangaroo. Moving to Liverpool in 1981 for £650,000 – the largest transfer fee in English football at that time – Johnston ultimately played 271 league games for the club, scoring 40 goals. Critically, he was part of Liverpool's 1985–86 double-winning team, only the third team to achieve the feat in English football in the 20th century.

Johnston declined an offer from Jock Stein to play for Scotland due to his father's ancestry. He also declined to play for Australia, opting instead to chance his arm with England. His reward: two England U-21 caps. An inventive player, and an inventive man with an entrepreneurial spirit, Johnston's biggest claim to fame post-playing days came in designing the prototype for the famous Adidas Predator football boot, a boot worn at professional level by Zinedine Zidane, David Beckham, Steven Gerrard and Barcelona's midfield maestro Xavi. Possessing an analytical mind with regard to football, Johnston also believed that football studs were too big, causing boots to stick in the ground and increase injuries to knees, ankles, and in particular, metatarsals. He also co-wrote Liverpool's 1988 FA Cup Final song (it didn't bring them luck), 'Anfield Rap'. A man of many talents, Craig Johnston.

On the other flank, Republic of Ireland international Ronnie Whelan supplied finesse and consistency. A poll of 110,000 Liverpool fans in 2006 to establish 100 Players Who Shook The Kop ranked Whelan in 30th place. Whelan was born into a footballing family, his father an Irish international; his brother played for Bohemians FC and Shamrock Rovers in Ireland. Ronnie trialled unsuccessfully for Manchester United (despite scoring against Liverpool's B team), making his League of Ireland debut for Home Farm on his 16th birthday in 1977.

In September 1979 Bob Paisley signed Whelan for £35,000, the fee becoming a veritable bargain as Whelan went on to complete 362 league games for Liverpool, scoring 46 goals, many of them important strikes. He also netted crucial cup goals in his time at the club 1979–1994. Among these were a late equaliser, and subsequent winner in extra time of the 1981–82 League Cup Final against Tottenham Hotspur. In 1982–83 Liverpool retained the cup, Whelan scoring the winner in extra time again, this time against Manchester United.

Initially a wide left midfield player, Whelan switched to central midfield with his customary minimal fuss when John Barnes arrived at Liverpool to play as a left-sided midfielder. From 1989 onwards Whelan suffered too many injuries to retain a regular place in Liverpool's first team. Despite this, Whelan took on the role of club captain in 1988–89 when Alan Hansen was injured early on in the campaign. In all competitions Whelan played 493 times for Liverpool, scoring 73 goals, winning six league titles, three FA Cups, three League Cups and this European Cup.

By the time he was 20, the consummate footballer Whelan had played schoolboy, youth, amateur, U-21 and senior level football for the Republic of Ireland. Whelan gained 53 full international caps, scoring three goals, but his precise style didn't fit comfortably with Jack Charlton's preferred midfield methods. It was at Liverpool where Whelan's technical prowess shone brightly.

Partnering Kenny Dalglish in attack was one of British football's greatest strikers in recent memory, Ian Rush. Rush deserves to be mentioned in the same breath as the very best British strikers of the last 60 years: Jimmy Greaves, Alan Shearer, Gary Lineker. Rush served Liverpool in two spells, the first 1980–86, the second including a loan back from Italian club Juventus for the 1986–87 season, continuing on from 1988 to 1996. Rush is Liverpool's all-time leading goalscorer, surpassing Roger Hunt, Michael Owen, Robbie Fowler, great strikers all. In all competitions for Liverpool, Rush totalled 346 goals. Rush was the kind of player who upon seeing the whites of a goalkeeper's eyes you would back him to score every time. In the same poll of 100 Players Who Shook The Kop that teammate Whelan finished 30th in, Rush, an unflappable finisher, finished third.

Rush began his professional career as a 16-year-old at Chester City, scoring 14 goals in 34 league appearances as a teenager. Manchester City expressed interest in signing him, but Rush, a boyhood Everton fan, became a Liverpool staple of the next decade and a half when signing for the Anfield club in 1980. In his first full season as a first-teamer in 1981–82, Rush became the club's top scorer, netting 30 goals in 49 appearances in all competitions. He scored a crucial goal in the 119th minute as Liverpool won the 1982 League Cup Final against Tottenham Hotspur.

Rush was voted PFA Young Player of the Year in 1983 after Liverpool won the league and League Cup 1982–83 for a second successive season. He ended the 1982–83 season with 24 league goals including four in a Merseyside derby with Everton, the most in a single game in the derby post-war. In 1984 Rush was awarded the PFA Player of the Year, as well as being BBC Wales Sports Personality of the Year. In this European Cup-winning season Liverpool also won the league and League Cup again. At this point the 'red machine' was virtually unstoppable, domestically and in Europe. He also won the Football Writer's Footballer of the Year Award, matching co-striker Kenny Dalglish's feat of 1983. In total Rush scored 47 goals in 65 games in 1983–84, an astonishing achievement. Incredibly, the Anfield machine ground to a (near) halt in 1984–85 as they lost the fateful Heysel European Cup Final to Juventus 1-0, lost their league title to Merseyside rivals Everton, and failed in their quest to win a domestic cup trophy. It seemed inconceivable that Liverpool remained trophy-less in 1984–85. In the 1985–86 Liverpool gained a semblance of revenge over Everton in the FA Cup Final, the ravenous Rush gorging himself on two goals in a 3-1 victory, adding the Man of the Match award to a growing list of personal and team titles.

Rush agreed a transfer to Italian giants and 1985 European Cup conquerors Juventus at the end of the 1985–86 season. He remained on loan to Liverpool for the 1986–87 campaign, the club failing to win a trophy again despite the striker's 30 1st Division goals. Rush also opened the scoring in the League Cup Final, but Liverpool lost out to winners Arsenal. In the previous 144 games that Rush had scored in for Liverpool the team had not lost. Ian Rush played 29 Serie A games in 1987–88 for Juventus, but like so many before him from British shores he found the ultra-defensive Italian top flight a serious nut to crack. He managed seven goals, but the style of Italian football did not suit him.

Rush returned to Anfield for the 1988–89 season, a year after Liverpool's extraordinary attacking combination of John Barnes, Ray Houghton, Peter Beardsley and John Aldridge had set – impossibly – ever higher standards at the club. Rush was immediately partnered with Aldridge and Beardsley in a 4-3-3 formation, although the arch-supplier Beardsley tended to drift into the 'hole', threading balls through for the lookalike deadly duo directly in front of him.

At times Rush was relegated to the bench as new scoring supremo Aldridge won selection ahead of him, yet the 1989 FA Cup Final arrived and with Rush replacing Aldridge for extra time, the Welshman delivered two goals in a 3-2 thriller over Everton again. The final was a terrific advert for English football, yet was overshadowed by the horrific deaths of 96 fans at Sheffield Wednesday's Hillsborough ground in the semi-final against Nottingham Forest. Rush's last act of the 1988–89 season came in the famous 0-2 home defeat against Arsenal. With both teams potential title winners – Liverpool only needed to draw, Arsenal, incredibly needed to win by two clear goals – Rush came off injured in the first half of a game Liverpool had enough chances to win, and Michael Thomas achieved the unlikely with an injury-time winner for the Gunners.

Rush did manage to win his fifth and final league title in 1989–1990, but the club were knocked out of the FA Cup in the semi-finals 4-3 by Crystal Palace, having demolished the South Londoners 9-0 in a league game earlier in the season. After serving a six-year suspension following the horrors of Heysel Liverpool were finally re-admitted to the UEFA Cup in the 1991–92 season. European glory eluded Liverpool, but consolation came with a third FA Cup win for Rush, the Welshman again scoring in a 2-0 victory over Sunderland. Season 1992–93 saw Rush relegated to the bench at times, Ronnie Rosenthal and Paul Stewart picked in front of the prolific striker, a selection that would have been unthinkable when Rush was at his peak.

Rush rallied late in the season with 11 goals, taking his tally to 14 and finishing top-scorer at Anfield once more. In the 1995–96 season Rush began up front alongside Stan Collymore, only to be replaced by a new young Anfield favourite in Robbie Fowler.

Short spells at Leeds United and Newcastle United followed in 1996–97 and 1997–98, but the ageing Rush's goal exploits were now behind him. He finally retired in 2000, aged 38, after a brief flirtation in Australia with Sydney Olympic. Rush's international career with Wales spanned the years 1980–1996. He scored 28 goals in 73 internationals, his finest moment coming when scoring the winner against Germany in a 1992 European Championship qualifier. His record as Wales's top scorer was only surpassed by Gareth Bale in 2018, another player who has been expected to carry the mantle of one of the few world class players playing for his country – think George Best and Northern Ireland.

Rush dallied with management at Chester City in 2004–05, but has found greater success as a pundit with ESPN, the American cable sports company, and Sky Sports. Ian Rush was inducted into the English Football Hall of Fame in 2006, and was asked to be the ambassador for the 2017 Champions League Final that took place in Cardiff between Juventus and Real Madrid, a final won handsomely by four goals to one by Real, with Cristiano Ronaldo in his prime, scoring twice. It was a privilege to witness Ian Rush at his regal best for Liverpool. The great strikers make the art of goal-scoring look effortless. Ian Rush is certainly in the top five strikers in British football in my memory.

Managing Liverpool on this evening, Joe Fagan was part of the Liverpool coaching dynasty, a man who had been associated with the club since 1958, two years after I was born – that seems a lifetime ago! As a young coach Fagan helped develop the careers of Liverpool legends Roger Hunt, Ian Callaghan and Tommy Smith.

Fagan played mainly for Manchester City as a wing-half 1938–1951, but his coaching/managerial career is inextricably linked with Liverpool. Like his predecessor Bob Paisley, Fagan believed in the simple basics of football, and like Paisley, shunned the media spotlight. Liverpool-born, Fagan was initially offered a professional contract with Liverpool in 1938, but opted to play for Manchester City instead as he thought his first team opportunities would be restricted at Anfield. Popular at City due to his loyal nature and strong team ethic, Fagan would take these qualities to Liverpool in 1958, moving his family to a house near Anfield, and remain at Anfield for the rest of his career.

Joe Fagan was instilled as reserve team coach at Anfield in 1958, a role he held until 1971. He is credited with creating the Anfield Boot Room, a room designated for coaches convening with Bill Shankly to discuss team matters. Fagan was promoted to first team coach 1971–79, then assistant manager 1979–1983, finally succeeding Bob Paisley on 1 July 1983. Shankly, Paisley, Fagan, latterly the likes of Kenny Dalglish and Graeme Souness, Liverpool always sought continuity from within until recent times, when first Brendan Rogers, then the effervescent, excellent man-manager Jürgen Klopp took the reins, In his first season as Liverpool manager, Fagan became the first manager of an English club to win the treble of European Cup, League Championship, and League Cup, consequently winning the English Manager of the Year Award. In his second season, 1984–85, despite signing great players in Jan Mølby and John Wark, the club failed to win a trophy. Purportedly, Fagan never recovered from witnessing the deaths of Juventus supporters during the Heysel disaster in Brussels, He retired as Liverpool manager on 29 May 1985, Kenny Dalglish succeeding him.

Playing the final in their own Stadio Olimpico ground, A.S. Roma were marginal favourites for this 1984 European Cup Final. The passion of Italian football fans may actually have proved counter-productive to Roma. In essence the team looked very strong. In goal, Franco Tancredi played 12 times for the Italian national team, winning the Serie A Scudetto league title in 1983, plus four Coppa Italia trophies. He completed 288 Serie A matches for Roma. The defence in front of Tancredi were not well known to English football fans, but one never dismisses Italian defenders, defence being an art form in Italy.

It was in midfield and attack that Roma appeared most threatening to Liverpool's hopes of a fourth European Cup success, their fourth in only seven years. Captain of Roma, Agostino Di Bartolemei, was capped at U-21 level eight times, scoring seven goals, yet never won a full international cap. Regardless of this, Di Bartolemei is regarded as one of Roma's greatest-ever players. On this evening he sat in front of the back four, acting as playmaker for Roma, his passing used to create chances for his attacking midfielders and forwards. In Roma's 1982–83 Scudetto-winning season Di Bartolemei was used as a sweeper, a ploy to maximise his vision and technical skills. Tragically, Di Bartolemei committed suicide ten years to the day Roma lost this final after suffering from clinical depression.

In front of captain and playmaker Di Bartolemei in Roma's 4-1-2-1-2 formation were two contrasting Brazilian superstars of their generation. The more defensive-minded Toninho Cerezo began his professional career with Atlético Mineiro in the city of Belo Horizonte, playing 111 league games 1972–1983. Joining Roma in 1983, Cerezo completed only 70 Serie A games for the club until 1986, scoring 13 goals. Moving on to Sampdoria, Cerezo played a further 145 Serie A games, scoring 14 times 1986–1992. While in Italy, Cerezo won the Coppa Italia four times, twice with Roma, twice with Sampdoria, also winning Serie A with Sampdoria in 1990–91. At Sampdoria he won the Cup Winners' Cup in 1989, being a runner-up in 1990; he was also a runner-up to Barcelona in the 1992 European Cup Final.

Cerezo returned to Brazil in 1992. He appeared 72 times for Sao Paulo over two seasons, playing ten times with Cruzeiro in 1994. Cerezo played 57 times for Brazil, scoring five goals. Cerezo was happy to be the anchor man in midfield, supplying passes to others while scoring the occasional goal himself. He was part of the 'nearly' national team of 1982, who many pundits thought would win that year's World Cup. Italy's Paolo Rossi had other ideas, his hat-trick ending Brazil's hopes in the second stage/quarter-finals.

The more obviously charismatic Paulo Roberto Falcão with his fair, wavy locks and elegant ball-playing skills was arguably the star of this Roma team. Roma fans dubbed him the 'eighth King of Rome' so enamoured were they of his performances in the deep maroon shirts of the club. Falcão began professionally at Internacional Porto Alegre in Brazil, playing 158 matches there 1972–1980. With Internacional, Falcão won three Brazilian national championships, 1975, 1976 and 1979.

In Falcão's first season with Roma 1980–81 the club finished second to Juventus in Serie A. Consolation came as Roma beat Torino on penalties in the Coppa Italia Final, Falcão scoring the decisive winning penalty kick. Roma finished third in Serie A in 1981–82, but Falcão was called up for the Brazil squad for the 1982 World Cup, playing in one of the country's most celebrated midfields alongside Zico, Socrates, and Eder. In 1982–83 Falcão finally helped Roma lift the Serie A title. In 1983–84 Roma finished second, again behind Juventus. Unfortunately for Falcão a knee injury sustained in a Serie A game prior to the semi-finals of the 1984 European Cup limited his appearance against Dundee United to the triumphant 3-0 second leg victory in Rome, and impacted greatly upon him in the final against Liverpool.

Falcão's time in Rome came to an unhappy end when he flew to New York for an unauthorised knee operation. Roma subsequently terminated his contract after five successful seasons with the club. He scored 22 goals for Roma 1980–85, the same total he achieved at Internacional. He returned to Brazil to play for Sao Paulo for the 1985–86 season, winning the Brazilian league title, the Campeonato Paulista. His performances at Roma were sufficient to see him inducted into the club's Hall of Fame.

Surprisingly for such a talented player, Falcão played only 34 times for

Brazil, scoring six goals, 1976–1986. The feted Brazilian 1982 midfield of Zico, Socrates, Eder and Falcão scored some spectacular goals in that tournament – but for consistency and flair they didn't quite match the 1970 World Cup-winning quartet of Jairzinho, Clodoaldo, Gerson and Rivelino.

Nominally a winger, Bruno Conti played in front of the two Brazilians on this evening in Rome. A Roma stalwart, Conti completed 304 Serie A matches for his native club (he was born in the Rome commune of Nettuno, a coastal town 60 kilometres from Rome City), scoring 37 goals. Conti's service with Roma 1973–1991 was broken only by two loan seasons with Genoa, 1975–76 and 1978–79, the first of which saw him win the Serie B title. The grand master of Italian football in the 1960s, Helenio Herrera, thought Conti too slight in physique to succeed at the very top level when he was Roma manager in the late 60s. The five feet seven inches Conti defied the odds, going on to win Serie A with Roma in the season preceding this European Cup Final, also winning the Coppa Italia with the club in 1980, 1981, 1984, 1986 and 1991. Roma also reached the 1991 UEFA Cup Final, only to lose 2-1 to Italian rivals Inter Milan over two legs. Sadly for Conti he missed his penalty kick in the shoot-out at the end of this 1984 European Cup Final. Roma fans coined the nickname 'The Mayor of Rome' for their popular winger-cum-midfield player.

Conti played 47 times for Italy 1980–86, scoring five goals. His crowning glory for his country came in the 1982 World Cup Final in Spain, contributing to the second goal (scored famously by a joyfully celebrating Marco Tardelli), and breaking free down the right to provide the cross for Alessandro Altobelli to net the third, decisive goal as Italy defeated West Germany 3-1. Pele thought Conti was the Player of the Tournament in 1982. Conti played every game in the 1982 competition, and again at the 1986 World Cup, earning a second nickname at these tournaments of Mara-Zico a reference to the highly revered Diego Maradona and Brazilian legend Zico. Conti, left-footed, preferred to play on the right and cut in (a favourite ploy of mine in local football from the left-wing – I was hopeless on the right wing). Conti's connection with his beloved Roma continues to this day, his current role being head of the Youth Sector at Roma (2021).

Roma possessed two excellent strikers in Roberto Pruzzo and Francesco Graziani. Pruzzo, like Conti, also played at Genoa 1973–78, scoring 57 times in 143 appearances. He spent ten seasons with Roma from 1978. Pruzzo it was who scored Roma's goal on this evening. A highly regarded striker, he played only six times for Italy, without scoring, but his record at club level is impressive, top-scoring in Serie A in 1980–81, 1981–82 and 1985–86. Pruzzo is the only player to score five goals in a single Serie A match, Roma versus Avellino (1986). Between 1978 and 1988 Pruzzo scored 106 goals for Roma in 240 Serie A matches.

Co-striker Graziani fared better with Italy, scoring 23 goals in 64 internationals. He was not as prolific in Rome as Pruzzo, scoring 12 goals for Roma in 57 Serie A matches 1983–86. After playing for Arezzo 1970–73, Graziani signed for Torino in 1973, staying until 1981 and enjoying his best goals return at club level, 97 goals in 221 appearances, winning the Serie A Scudetto in 1975–76. In 1976–77, Graziani top-scored in Serie A with 21 goals. Like Conti, Graziani missed a penalty kick in this 1984 European Cup Final shoot-out. Leaving Roma in 1986, Graziani ended his Italian playing days with Udinese. A fine player who improved markedly with experience, Graziani certainly impacted in an Italian national shirt, even if he tended to be second choice striker when Paolo Rossi was at his peak.

THE FINAL
Roma lost the toss, playing in an unfamiliar white strip instead of their customary blood-red maroon shirts. It was Liverpool who wore red on this evening. Liverpool started strongly, taking the lead when Craig Johnston's right-wing cross was dropped by Tancredi under challenge from Kenny Dalglish. Phil Neal was on hand to stab the loose ball home. Roma responded with Graziani's attempt at the near post denied by Bruce Grobbelaar. Rush's left-foot shot at the other end was similarly thwarted by Tancredi. Three minutes from the end of the first half Bruno Conti's left-wing cross was met by a fine angled header by Roberto Pruzzo and Roma were level. 1-1 at half-time.

Roma started the second half strongly, willed on by their passionate home supporters. Credit to Liverpool, whose game plan was clearly to pacify the hostile home support, content as they were to suffocate and stifle the Italians. Dalglish had a volley comfortably saved by Tancredi, and then fed Steve Nicol through smartly for another blocked shot. Extra time came and went without too much incident, the only notable save coming from the extrovert Grobbelaar from Conti after the Italian cut in from the flank to unleash a 25-yard shot.

Penalties: Nicol skies Liverpool's first effort – luckily for the Scotsman Roma felt the pressure of the shoot-out in front of their own fans, Conti and Graziani skying penalties badly. By contrast, Souness, Rush (49 goals in this 1983–84 season), Neal, and Alan Kennedy were calmness personified with their kicks. Grobbelaar's famous jelly legs were enough to break Graziani's concentration, and it was left to Alan Kennedy to score the winning kick after his solitary goal had won the 1981 European Cup for Liverpool.

After the glorious triumph in 1977 against Borussia Möenchengladbach, Liverpool seemed to do just enough in winning their subsequent European Cup Finals in 1978, 1981 and 1984. At the time I mistakenly thought Liverpool a little machine-like. Retrospectively I recognise the machine to be an extremely well-oiled one, and no one could deny their unquenchable team spirit, nor the influence and technical skills of the likes of Hansen, Lawrenson, Dalglish, Souness, Rush et al.

1984–85 EUROPEAN CUP FINAL
Juventus 1 v 0 Liverpool

The less said about this final the better really. The final is remembered sadly for the horrors of Heysel, Liverpool supporters being allocated space at the Heysel Stadium in Brussels adjacent to Juventus supporters. Missiles were thrown between rival fans. A group of Liverpool fans charged a perimeter wall which crumbled, resulting in 39 deaths and 600 injured spectators. Rioting fans from Juventus at the other end of the ground marched towards Liverpool fans. Only the Belgian police on the pitch prevented a further catastrophe. The match took place an hour later – for 'public policy doctrine' reasons – Belgian law essentially deeming abandoning the match would cause further violence. In my opinion the match should not have taken place, but I understand the reasons and ramifications of the decision to go ahead.

Route to the Final

Liverpool glided through qualification to the final fairly serenely, only the Portuguese champions Benfica troubling them in the second round. Polish champions Lech Poznán were summarily dismissed in the first round, John Wark scoring the only goal in Poland, the same player scoring a hat-trick in a 4-0 win at Anfield to confirm a 5-0 aggregate victory. Ian Rush's hat-trick at Anfield secured a 3-1 victory over Benfica in the second round, and although Maniche's early penalty goal in Lisbon made the holders sweat, they held on for a 3-2 aggregate victory. A 1-1 draw in Austria against Austria Wien in the last eight was handsomely negated by a 4-1 home victory, Paul Walsh scoring twice, as Liverpool triumphed 5-2 on aggregate. Liverpool swiftly crushed Greek resistance at Anfield in the semi-finals, Rush scoring twice in a 4-0 victory. Mark Lawrenson's solitary goal in Athens against Panathinaikos confirmed Liverpool's place in the 1985 European Cup Final.

Juventus's first opponents in the first round were Ilves from Tampere, south-west of Helsinki in Finland. Finnish football not being of the highest standards in those days, the legendary centre-forward Paolo Rossi helped himself to a hat-trick in Finland in a 4-0 romp. The Finns, a proud nation, rallied in Turin, opening the scoring through Raimo Kuuluvainen. Another legend on the world stage, Michel Platini, replied twice for Juventus, the Italians cruising through 6-1 on aggregate. Similarly, Swiss football was not in 1985 of the standard the country has elevated itself to in 2021. Grasshoppers of Zürich were beaten 6-2 on aggregate by Juve in the second round, Rossi on the mark again in a 2-0 win in Turin, Platini netting twice in a 4-2 away victory. The Czech club Sparta Prague were beaten 3-1 on aggregate in the last eight, Juve's 3-0 win in Turin making the return leg a formality, Rossi again netting, along with 1982 World Cup hero Marco Tardelli. The French club Bordeaux at last offered some resistance to Juventus in the semi-finals, although another 3-0 win in Turin for Juve made Bordeaux's task a tough one in the south-west of France, Platini among the scorers in Turin, and the man who would be match-winner in the final, Zbigniew Boniek, also scoring. The German centre-forward Dieter Müller, reduced the arrears for Bordeaux in the 20th minute in the second leg, but the French side were only able to add one further goal through international defender Patrick Battiston.

The final contest should have been a memorable affair – supposedly the football played was of a high standard, but after the pre-match horrors football seemed irrelevant. Liverpool's line-up contained players who'd won the European Cup at will in the previous decade – Hansen, Dalglish, Phil Neal and others who'd featured in 1984 in Rome: Steve Nicol, Bruce Grobbelaar, Ian Rush. Jim Beglin, the Republic of Ireland international (15 caps) featured at left-back. It was Beglin's misfortune to badly break his leg in 1986–87 in a tackle with Everton's

Gary Stevens in a fifth round League Cup tie. A further cartilage injury to a knee in 1988 while playing for Liverpool reserves meant Beglin's career was savagely curtailed.

In attack, the five feet eight inches Paul Walsh had an interesting career. Looking at times too small to be a success on the higher stages, Walsh belied a lack of physique with supreme talent. Walsh's father was an electrician, his mother worked for the famous sugar company Tate & Lyle. Walsh played as if shot through with electricity and a heavy dose of sugar, he was such a livewire striker. Signing for Charlton Athletic in 1979 (after being overlooked by football scouts because of his small stature), Walsh was paired with Derek Hales as a striker in the 1980–81 season after starting professional life as a right midfielder. Walsh responded with 18 league goals, among them a hat-trick at The Valley against Brentford, making him the youngest hat-trick scorer in Charlton Athletic's history. Hales – aided and abetted by Walsh's wizardry – was named in the 3rd Division's PFA Team of the Year.

Walsh began to make a name for himself at his next club, Luton Town. Playing for the first time in the old 1st Division, Walsh repaid manager David Pleat's attacking philosophy with a hat-trick against Notts County. Pleat's celebration when Luton staved off relegation in the last game of the season with a 1-0 win over Manchester City has gone down in football lore (racing down the touchline manically, his cream suit jacket flapping wildly). The next season brought another hat-trick for Walsh (against Stoke City). Luton ended in 16th place, but Walsh won the PFA Young Player of the Year award, pipping Ian Rush and John Barnes. These players were soon to be his teammates.

Walsh scored 13 goals in 39 games in all competitions in his first season at Anfield (1984–85), but largely played second fiddle to Ian Rush as a regular starter. The following season saw Kenny Dalglish restricting Walsh's appearances, but he still scored 18 goals in 32 appearances in all competitions. The signing of the mercurial Peter Beardsley from Newcastle United signalled the end of Walsh's time at Anfield.

Walsh became embroiled in a drinking culture at next club, Tottenham Hotspur, hampering his fitness considerably. With Paul Stewart and Gary Lineker chosen ahead of him, Walsh became disenchanted at Tottenham, a contretemps with reserve team manager Ray Clemence leading to a suspension.

Moving to Portsmouth in 1992, manager Jim Smith even assisted Walsh in selling his London home in an attempt to get Walsh back on the rails again. Walsh established a potent strike partnership with Guy Whittingham at Portsmouth in 1992–93, the latter scoring 47 league and cup goals, but it was Walsh who won the fan's hearts, winning their vote as club Player of the Year. Walsh moved again in March 1994 to Manchester City before returning to Portsmouth in September 1995. A serious cruciate ligament injury eventually ended his career. Walsh played five times for England 1983–84, scoring once, general opinion being that he remained a little too individualistic – but on his day what a joy Paul Walsh was to watch.

This final should have provided the mother of all match-ups – best defender Juventus's Gaetano Scirea (the best Italian libero/sweeper other than the incomparable Franco Baresi) or Liverpool's highly talented pair of Alan Hansen and Mark Lawrenson. Best attacking link player – 1984 World Cup-winning Frenchman and three-time Ballon d'Or winner (1983, 1984, 1985) Michel Platini or Liverpool's master magician Kenny Dalglish? Best centre-forward – Italian genius Paolo Rossi or Liverpool's prolific goal machine Ian Rush? Best source of goals outside the conventional number 9 – Polish international superstar for Juve Zbigniew Boniek or Liverpool's John Wark? In the event of 39 people dying none of this mattered.

Juve's left-back – ostensibly Juve liked him to push up in a nod to the legendary Giacinto Facchetti of Inter Milan in the 1960s – Antonio Cabrini was a fine footballer. Cabrini was part of a great Italian national team unit of the time – goalkeeper Dino Zoff, defender Scirea, and the leech-like man-marker Claudio Gentile. Cabrini was voted the Best Young Player at the 1978 World Cup. He is among the handful of players to win all three European club competitions: the European Cup, the European Cup Winners' Cup and the UEFA Cup. Cabrini's tally of nine goals in 73 international games is an Italian national record for a defender. A progressive, athletic footballer, Antonio Cabrini also scored 33 goals in 297 Serie A games for Juventus 1976–1989.

Captain for the night, Gaetano Scirea, amassed 377 Serie A games for Juventus, scoring 24 goals. Scirea also won all three European club trophies with Juventus in a career in Turin spanning nearly 15 seasons. Scirea's consummate ability actually stalled the elegant Franco Baresi's international career for four years. Scirea earned 78 caps for Italy 1975–1986, scoring twice. A classy player on the ball, Scirea's class extended to never being red-carded in his career, like our own Bobby Charlton. Scirea liked to join the attack, creating many chances for teammates, the libero role behind a back four giving him license to roam. Scirea won 7 Serie A titles with Juventus, plus two Coppa Italias, the European Cup Winners' Cup in 1983–84, the UEFA Cup in 1976–77 and this 1985 European Cup Final.

The levels of energy Marco Tardelli possessed were evinced to the full in his excitable celebration of his 69th-minute goal in the 1982 World Cup Final against West Germany. Energetic, athletic, comfortable offensively and defensively, Tardelli was the complete midfield player. With Juventus Tardelli won 5 Serie A titles, two Coppa Italias and each of the three European club competitions, scoring the decisive goal in the first leg of the 1979 UEFA Cup Final against Spain's Athletic Bilbao, securing the Turin club's first-ever European title. In 259 Serie A games for Juve he scored 35 goals. In 81 internationals Tardelli scored six times. He was named in the Team of the Tournament at the 1980 European Championships. Tardellis' goal celebration in the 1982 World Cup Final was voted fourth greatest moment in World Cup history by the BBC – who needs a spectacular goal when you can have a celebration like that?

Michel Platini, along with Zinedine Zidane, is regarded as the greatest French footballer of all time. His high regard in France is shown by the award of the Legion d'honneur, the highest French Order of Merit award given to high-achieving military and civilian persons. Along with his three Ballon d'Or awards, Platini was voted the seventh best player in the FIFA Player of the Century poll of the 20th century. His part as the fulcrum of that great early 1980s midfield of Giresse, Tigana and Fernandez is permanently etched in my mind. It would have been interesting to see a Manchester United midfield of Beckham, Keane, Scholes and Giggs in direct confrontation with them. Platini was his country's record goalscorer until 2007; he holds the record for the most goals in a European Championship Finals (1984 – nine goals).

Born to parents of Italian ancestry in Joeuf, Lorraine, north-eastern France, Platini began his professional career in 1972 at AS Nancy where father Aldo played and was a director at the start of his son's playing days. Platini's early playing time was interrupted by French national military service, but an early friendship with Nancy goalkeeper Jean-Michel Moutier saw him practise free kicks continually with a row of dummies placed in front of Moutier. Platini won his first player's trophy in the 1978 French Cup Final against Nice, scoring the only goal of the match.

It was clear at the 1978 World Cup that in players like Platini, Saint-Étienne's Dominique Rocheteau, and Lens' Didier Six, that France were a 'coming' team, but two 2-1 defeats against the powerful Italian and Argentinian teams halted their progress in the competition. Ironically, Platini's influence in the Italy game was diminished by future teammate Marco Tardelli. In 1982, France qualified from the group stages behind England, but after winning the second phase Group D they were pitted against West Germany in the semi-finals. The stage was set for an epic confrontation where Platini's French team were denied by the resilient West Germans after extra time and the near-inevitable penalty shoot-out victory – not forgetting 'Toni' Schumacher's awful head-high challenge on Patrick Battiston. No penalty was awarded, the French having to wait until 1984 for their first international title. Enough had been seen in '82 to see the potential of the Platini-led midfield – Giresse and Tigana appeared in the epic semi-final – Fernandez did not.

Platini scored 98 goals in 181 appearances for AS Nancy, before transferring to Saint-Étienne in 1979 where he scored 58 goals in 104 appearances. Only one piece of silverware came his way with Saint-Étienne, the 1981 French Ligue 1 title. Moving to Italy, Platini replaced the great Irishman and Arsenal legend Liam Brady in the number 10 shirt at Juventus. He was not an instant hit in the demanding Serie A, but along with Zbigniew Boniek he called for a change in the team's tactics, Juve reaching the 1982–83 European Cup Final, only to lose to Hamburger SV (Kevin Keegan had moved back to England to join Southampton, missing out on another European trophy), but winning the Coppa Italia 3-2 on aggregate against Verona after overturning a 2-0 deficit from the first leg, Platini equalising in normal time, then scoring the winner in the 119th minute in extra time.

Platini had made his point, subsequently making his mark as Juventus won Serie A in 1984 and 1986, won the 1984 European Cup Winners' Cup (2-1 against Porto, Platini assisting the first goal). Platini was absolutely in his magisterial pomp during this period. My old love, *World Soccer* magazine, named him World Player of the Year in 1984 and 1985. Platini scored the only goal of this climactic 1985 European Cup Final from the penalty spot. Aged

32, Platini retired while still a Juventus player, having scored 68 goals in 147 appearances for the Turin club.

Internationally, Platini's goal return of 41 in 72 games for France is testimony of his influence on the French international team, his desire to attack, his belief in football being a game played with the feet and the head, in contrast to those who believed the modern game had become more about organisation and fitness. Platini was also a great on-field orchestrator, a master of tactics, switching of play, his football brain working overtime to unlock resolute defences. Another player never sent off in his career, a master playmaker, Platini earned the moniker in France of 'Le Roi' ('The King'). His performances for France in the early 1980s lit up the international stage.

Platini managed France 1988–1992. In qualifying for the 1992 European Championships, France won all eight of their group matched under Platini, but after a record 19-match unbeaten run, first round elimination saw him stand down as manager. Platini, a man full of ideas, took over from Sweden's Lennart Johansson as President of UEFA in 2007, a role lasting just over eight years, but decided against standing beyond 2016. Like another great world-class footballer, Franz Beckenbauer, Platini has been accused of undue influence in voting and allocation of major football tournaments. Football at the highest levels has always been susceptible to this. It was ever thus – and the International Olympic Committee is the same.

The other great player on the international stage in the Juventus line-up in Brussels was the Polish international forward Zbigniew Boniek. Pele considered him to be one of the 100 Best Living Footballers in the 2004 poll. Boniek played at three World Cups for Poland, helping his country finish in third place at the 1982 World Cup. He scored 24 times in 80 internationals for Poland 1976–1988.

Boniek came to Juve's attention in 1982 after scoring 50 goals in 172 league games for Widzew Lodz in Poland. Boniek's first season (1982–83) in Italy coincided with Platini's – the two dovetailed together telepathically at times. Boniek, along with Platini, won the Coppa Italia in 1982–83; but the 1982–83 European Cup Final was lost to Hamburger SV. The 1983–84 season brought Boniek greater personal success. Serie A was won in Italy; Boniek scored the winner in the 1984 European Cup Winners' Cup Final. The Pole came to be the scourge of Liverpool, scoring both goals in Juve's 2-0 victory over the Merseysiders in the 1984 European Super Cup, and then making the run that brought about the foul and subsequent penalty converted by Platini in this 1985 European Cup Final.

Boniek scored 14 Serie A goals for Juventus in 81 matches. Leaving the club to play for A.S. Roma in 1985, he scored a further 17 goals in 76 Serie A games, winning the Coppa Italia again in 1985–86, Roma defeating a Sampdoria team containing Roberto Mancini – and in the second leg, our own Trevor Francis – 3-2 on aggregate.

Boniek's finest hour in a Poland shirt came when scoring a hat-trick against Belgium in Spain at the 1982 World Cup. Unfortunately, the four-goal Boniek's place in the losing semi-final against Italy was lost due to suspension. He was chosen in the FIFA 1982 World Cup All-Star Team. A great dribbler, a fine finisher, an athletic and powerful player, Boniek. Juventus president of the time, Gianni Agnelli, dubbed Boniek 'Bello di Notte' ('Beauty at Night') due to his outstanding night-time performances in European games.

Paolo Rossi's slight stature and physique – he stood five feet nine inches – made him something of an enigma on the world stage – but no football follower can ever forget his sensational impact at the 1982 World Cup where his six goals earned him the Golden Boot as the tournament's top-scorer. He also won the Golden Ball for the Player of the Tournament at the 1982 World Cup. As a trophy winner at the tournament he won three awards – a feat matched only by Garrincha of Brazil in 1962 and Mario Kempes of Argentina in 1978.

Rossi scored prolifically for Vicenza 1976–79 (60 goals in 94 appearances), plus 13 goals in a 28-game loan spell at Perugia during this period. Persistent problems with knee injuries had seen Rossi, originally a Juventus player in 1973, loaned to Como in 1975 where he debuted in Serie A. Initially a right-winger, upon moving to Vicenza, coach Giovan Fabbri moved Rossi to centre-forward. Rossi scored 21 Serie B goals in his first season (1976–77) at Vicenza. He followed this with 24 Serie A goals in 1977–78, making him the first player to top the Serie B/Serie A goal-lists in consecutive seasons, Vicenza finishing second in Serie A behind only Rossi's co-owners, Juventus.

Selected by Enzo Bearzot for the 1978 World Cup, Rossi interchanged attacking positions in the tournament with Franco Causio on the right flank and co-striker Roberto Bettega to great effect. Italy finished fourth in the tournament, Rossi scoring three goals and providing four assists. Rossi was named in the Team of the Tournament, winning the Silver Ball as the tournament's second-best player behind Mario Kempes.

1978–79 brought mixed fortunes for Rossi. He netted 15 Serie A goals, debuted in European football in the UEFA Cup, suffered a series of injuries, and Vicenza were relegated to Serie B, instigating his loan to Perugia in Serie A for the 1979–1980 season. 13 goals followed for Perugia, but the Italian betting scandal 'Totonero' of 1980 – players accused of placing bets on matches – saw Rossi banned for three years. Rossi protested his innocence, the ban being reduced to two years. This meant Rossi missed the 1980 European Championships where Italy again finished fourth.

Rossi's moment in the world spotlight came at the 1982 World Cup in Spain. You could be forgiven for thinking highly of him as a football player during Italy's dire struggle to qualify from the group stages. Three draws from three games is not always sufficient to put a country through to the next stage of a world tournament. This was Italy's lot: 0-0 versus Poland; 1-1 versus Peru (an opponent they definitely would have been favoured to beat); and 1-1 with Cameroon, a doughty, if less talented adversary. Drawn against world giants in the shape of South Americans Brazil and Argentina in the next phase, Italy fared better, defeating the latter 2-1, the experience of Scirea and Gentile negating the new wonderkid Diego Maradona. Then in an epic contest against fancied Brazil with their midfield maestros Zico, Falcão and Socrates, a hitherto less than match-fit Rossi exploded into life with a classic striker's hat-trick, enabling a 3-2 victory. A 2-0 semi-final victory over Boniek-less Poland, Rossi netting twice more, saw

Italy into the final. Rossi again shone in the final, opening the scoring early in the second half, Tardelli subsequently shutting the trapdoor on the redoubtable West Germans.

Major social unrest in Italy, allied to the fitness doubts over Rossi pre-tournament were brushed aside in a wave of euphoric Italian fervour after the country won the 1982 World Cup. Italian fans proclaimed Rossi Man of the Match in the final, perhaps blinded by his exploits in the previous two matches. The pundits loved him, the world sports media, football experts bestowed overwhelming praise upon him, and awards for European Player of the Year and World Player of the Year for 1982 followed.

Despite defeat to Hamburger SV in the 1982–83 European Cup Final, Rossi emerged as the competition's top scorer with six goals. In the 1983–84 European Cup Winners' Cup-winning season Rossi netted 13 times in Serie A, winning his second Scudetto with Juve. The following season, his last with Juventus, Rossi scored five goals in the European Cup tournament, finishing only behind teammate Platini and IFK Göteborg's Swedish international striker Torbjörn Nilsson who scored seven apiece.

Selected for the Italian 1986 World Cup squad, injury prevented Rossi's selection in Mexico, the high altitude hampering his recovery. Rossi totalled 20 goals in 48 internationals; his nine goals over two World Cups in 1978 and 1982 ensuring his parity with Roberto Baggio and Christian Vieri as Italy's all-time World Cup goalscorer. Rossi's athleticism, keen eye for goal, speed, technique and agility enabled him to defy a slight physique. Anticipating passes and crosses into the penalty area marked Rossi out as a goal-poacher extraordinaire at his peak.

Juve's manager/coach Giovanni Trapattoni was a wily old fox, a centre-back-cum defensive midfielder who played 274 Serie A games for AC Milan 1959–1971, winning two Serie A titles and two European Cups in 1963 and 1969. He played for the Italian national team 17 times, 1960–64. Management is what Trapattoni is now better known for. In Italy alone he has managed AC Milan, Juventus (twice), Inter Milan, Cagiliari and Fiorentina. His vast experience has also been called upon in foreign countries with Bayern Munich and VfB Stuttgart; with Benfica in Portugal; and with Red Bull Salzburg in Austria. He has also managed the Italian national team 2002–04 and the Republic of Ireland 2008–2013.

Trapattoni is one of five coaches to have won league titles in four different countries: Carlo Ancelotti, Ernst Happel, Tomoslav Ivic – and the 'marmite', love him or hate him José Mourinho. Trapattoni garnered six Serie A titles and two Coppa Italias 1976–1986, winning all three European club competitions during this period. Moving to Inter Milan, he won Serie A in 1988–89, and the UEFA Cup in the 1990–91 season. Returning to Juventus in 1991, he helped the club win the 1992–93 UEFA Cup. In Munich the 1996–97 Bundesliga and the 1997–98 DFB Pokal were secured; in Lisbon the Portuguese Primeira Liga was won in 2004–05; in Austria he won the Austrian Bundesliga with Red Bull Salzburg in 2006–07. The press recognised his talent, making him the European Football Coach of the Year in 1985 and 1991.

Trapattoni's teams were renowned for their organisation and mental strength.

He was an early disciple of Italian defensive nous, yet able to make his teams fluid, particularly through the deployment of a libero or sweeper to organise play from the back. He tinkered with many different formations, and while labelled defensive – it's merely an Italian trait – he benefited from great playmakers in between the lines at his clubs. He was lucky to have a second brain on the pitch in Brussels in this 1985 European Cup Final in the shape of the intuitive Michel Platini.

THE FINAL
The series of flares set off on the terraces pre-match set an unfortunate tone for the evening, antagonised supporters distracted from the potential classic final awaiting them. It was Liverpool's misfortune to lose Mark Lawrenson within the first ten minutes of the match, a recurring shoulder injury ending his evening prematurely. The first half was one of intense Juventus pressure, Platini being earmarked for some rough treatment by the ever-committed Liverpool defenders. The two great international stars Paolo Rossi (Italy) and Zbigniew Boniek (Poland) took advantage of Liverpool's decision to tight-mark Platini. Rossi was full of energy; Boniek revelled in the space allowed him by the over-zealous attention paid to Platini. Sadly for Liverpool, the inventive Platini refused to be fazed by Liverpool's close attention to him, still managing to make things happen for Juve despite the tight marking. Boniek found the space that Liverpool tried to deny Platini, having a long-range shot saved well by Bruce Grobbelaar, then being fouled in ungainly fashion by John Wark following a mazy run. Full-back Antonio Cabrini tested Grobbelaar with another long-range strike as Juventus piled on the pressure. Kenny Dalglish sent two efforts wildly wide in response; Wark was just unable to latch onto Steve Nicol's cutely clipped through ball.

In the second half Paul Walsh ducked inside a challenge and drove the ball towards the near post, but Juve keeper Stefano Tacconi was equal to the shot. It was a rare sortie for Liverpool as Juventus regained the upper hand. Platini's long ball from inside his own half freed Boniek who was unceremoniously bundled to the ground in the 18-yard box. Platini sent Grobbelaar the wrong way from the penalty spot and Juve had a deserved lead. In retaliation Ronnie Whelan flashed a long-range shot wide, but Liverpool had little left in the locker. It was a sad, unfortunate end to a period of Liverpool dominance in Europe, although footage from the game reveals a gap between the Reds fading team and opponents Platini and Boniek who were at the top of their game. Boniek's pace and persistence troubled Liverpool all through the game. One also wonders whether Liverpool's players' hearts were in this match after the appalling pre-match incidents.

It would be another 14 years before a British team reached a European Cup Final – and the indefinite ban placed on English clubs, which became a five-year absence from European competition, was entirely justified. It would take Liverpool until a sixth season following the ban to re-enter European football in the 1991–92 UEFA Cup. Astonishingly for a club with such a proud tradition – and wealthy backing – this was Juventus's first-ever European trophy.

1998–99 CHAMPIONS LEAGUE FINAL
Manchester United 2 v 1 Bayern Munich

Arguably the most iconic British European Cup triumph ever – with apologies to Celtic, Liverpool and Chelsea. I was fortunate to be present at the 1999 FA Cup semi-final victory for United over Arsenal, part of United's historic treble, a match of high emotion, high-level technique and remarkable atmosphere, the best of any football match I've ever attended (superseded in my mind only for volume by my wife and I being even luckier to receive tickets in the raffle for Super Saturday in the London Olympic Stadium when Mo Farah, Jessica Ennis,and Greg Rutherford won three Gold medals in 45 minutes for Team GB at the 2012 Summer Olympics – the decibel levels were several notches higher). These two different sporting occasions will stay with me forever.

Route to the Final
The last European Cup was held at Wembley Stadium in the 1991–1992 season, the game won by Ronald Koeman's free kick for Johan Cruyff's Barcelona against Sampdoria, 1-0. Re-christened, heavily marketed and re-branded, the Champions League came into being in the 1992–93 season, UEFA deeming the revised league format a) more profitable through television rights, and b) by expanding the competition it gave a greater number of clubs an increased opportunity to be included in European football's greatest club event. Whether the heightened format has achieved greater parity and success for lesser European clubs is highly debatable as the major clubs from Italy, Spain, Germany and England continued to dominate the competition: Juventus, AC Milan, Real Madrid, Bayern Munich, Liverpool, Manchester United and Chelsea.

The 1992–93 Champions League season did throw up a surprise winner in Marseille (French national manager Didier Descamps captaining the side); José Mourinho's Porto providing the only other break in the super-club's dominance of the competition in 2003–04 – but that was almost 20 years ago now.

Manchester United's achievement in 1999 is rightly regarded as special, it being part of that incredible treble won in this 1998–99 season of the Champions League, Premiership and FA Cup – a treble that may never be repeated in English football. United secured 2-0 aggregate victory over LKS Lodz of Poland in the second qualifying round (2-0 at home, 0-0 away). This took the club through to the main group stage of the competition where they faced formidable opposition in the shape of the team they would eventually meet in the final, Bayern Munich, and Spanish giants Barcelona. Poor Brondby of Denmark were the fourth team in Group D, mere cannon fodder for the super-clubs. Credit to the Danes, their first match in Copenhagen brought their only success, a 2-1 victory over the mighty Bayern Munich.

United's first game in Group D was a dramatic 3-3 home draw with Barcelona, The Class of 92 coming up trumps, Ryan Giggs and Paul Scholes giving United a two-goal cushion. Barcelona fought back early in the second half with goals from Brazilian striker Anderson da Silva and a penalty from Brazilian midfielder Giorami. David Beckham restored United's lead in the 63rd minute, but a further penalty kick from international manager of Spain at the 2020 Euros, Luis Enrique, levelled the scores for a final time.

Unsurprisingly, given the quality of the three super-clubs in this group, United's second game also ended in a draw, 2-2 in the Olympiastadion, Munich, Brazilian striker Elber opening the scoring for Bayern. United replied through Dwight Yorke and Scholes, but Elber had the last word with an 89th-minute equaliser. United subsequently put Brondby to the sword in Copenhagen to the tune of 6-2, two goals from Giggs, in addition to strikes from Yorke, Andy Cole, Roy Keane and recent manager Ole Gunnar Solsjkaer. In the return match at Old Trafford, United again pulverised the Danes, winning 5-0 with efforts from Beckham, Cole, Yorke, Scholes and Phil Neville.

Incredibly, United's trip to the Nou Camp brought another exciting 3-3 draw against Barcelona. Anderson da Silva scored in the first minute for Barca. Unbowed, United replied through Yorke, ending the first half tied at 1-1. Andy Cole gave United the lead, Yorke added another, his second goal sandwiched between two strikes from the great Brazilian midfielder Rivaldo. United's final group match also ended in a home draw with Bayern Munich, Keane's first half goal matched by a second half strike from Bosnian midfielder Hasan Salihamidzic. United had not lost to their Spanish and German superstar rivals, nor had they beaten them over four drawn games. Fortunately for United, Barcelona narrowly lost both their games with Bayern Munich, home and away, leaving United grateful for a second-place qualifying spot in Group D, their ten points tally two more than Barcelona's eight. Bayern Munich topped the group with 11 points.

Bayern's jittery start when losing to Brondby 2-1 in Copenhagen (their only goal coming from future Liverpool full-back Ryan Babbel) was soon forgotten. The 2-2 draw with Manchester United seemed to leave the Germans a mountain to climb, but successive wins against Barcelona restored Bayern's claims to win this tightest of groups. Midfielder Stefan Effenberg scored the only goal of the game for Bayern in Munich; striker Alexander Zickler and Salihamidzic scored second half goals to overturn Giorami's penalty goal for Barcelona in the Nou Camp. Bayern left it until the second half to see off plucky Brondby in Munich, goals from striker Carsten Jancker and wide man Mario Basler enough for victory. Salihamidzic's goal at Old Trafford secured Bayern's place at the top of Group D.

United were paired with Italian greats Inter Milan in the quarter-finals, two goals from Dwight Yorke earning them a 2-0 win at Old Trafford. Striker Nicola Ventola gave Inter hope at the San Siro, but the mercurial Paul Scholes levelled matters in the 88th minute, earning United a 3-1 aggregate victory. Italian giants again stood in United's way in the semi-finals. Ex-Chelsea and current Tottenham Hotspur manager (July 2022) Antonio Conte opened the scoring for Juventus at Old Trafford. It took until the 92nd minute for the resilient Red Devils to equalise through Ryan Giggs. A dramatic second leg in Turin saw United fall 2-0 down in 11 minutes to two goals by livewire striker Filipo Inzaghi. This was a season when United (who should really have lost that incredible FA Cup semi-final against Arsenal that I attended if Dennis Bergkamp had netted his injury-time penalty kick) refused to be beaten. Goals from Keane and Yorke gave United half-time parity, Cole then scored an 84th-minute winner for the defiant reds.

Bayern had German rivals Kaiserslautern in the last eight, giving them a comfortable passage to the semi-finals. Elber and Effenberg ensured a 2-0 cushion going into the away leg. Bayern brushed aside Kaiserslautern in the Fritz Walter Stadion, winning 4-0 with goals from Effenberg, Jancker, an Uwe Rosler own goal (Rosler scored 50 Premiership goals for Manchester City 1994–98), and Basler. In the semi-finals Bayern were taken all the way by Ukrainian champions Dynamo Kiev. Two goals from one of the great European strikers of the last 50 years, Andriy Schevchenko, gave Kiev a two-goal lead in the Olmpiyskiy Stadium. Michael Tarnat replied for Bayern, but Kiev's two goal lead was restored by midfielder Vitaliy Kosovskyi in the 50th minute. Bayern, as resilient as Manchester United, fought back to cling on to a 3-3 draw courtesy of goals from Effenberg and Jancker. A hard-fought return leg saw Bayern triumph through a solitary goal from Basler. Both United and Bayern lived by the sword in their semi-final contests.

It's not very often that a goalkeeper captains a football team, but when that goalkeeper was Peter Schmeichel it becomes understandable. Schmeichel, whose son Kasper hasn't fared badly either at Leicester City, is rightly regarded as the best goalkeeper to ever grace the English Premier League. Physically imposing at six feet three inches, a fierce competitor, Schmeichel was never afraid to bawl out defenders he felt weren't doing their job properly. Astonishingly – for a goalkeeper – Schmeichel scored 11 goals in his professional career, including one for his country, Denmark. The IFHHSC (International Federation of Football History & Statistics) voted Peter Schmeichel the world's best goalkeeper in 1992, 1993 and 2003, also including him among the best ten goalkeepers of the 20th century. A public poll held by the famous Reuters international news organisation in 2001 even voted him ahead of our own Gordon Banks and the great Russian goalkeeper of the late 1950s and early 1960s Lev Yashin as the greatest keeper of all time.

Curiously, Schmeichel, among the most famous of Danes, was born to Inger, a Danish nurse, and Antoni, a Polish jazz musician father. It seems hard work and creativity were bywords for the Schmeichel family. Born in 1963, Peter Schmeichel held Polish citizenship until 1970 until his father and his three sisters became Danish citizens. Before becoming a professional footballer, Schmeichel worked in the dyeing department of a textile factory, as a cleaner in an old people's home, and as a manager/administrator for the World Wildlife Fund. His last jobs before becoming the Great Dane goalkeeper admired worldwide were with his father's flooring company (this job did not suit the goalkeeper's heavy 15-stone frame), and for first football club Hvidovre's chairman's advertising company. Clearly instilled with an ultra-strong work ethic, Schmeichel swapped his 'have hands will travel' work mantra to 'have hands will travel' football career.

Schmeichel's professional football life truly took off with Brondby in Denmark, winning the Danish League in his first season with the club, 1987–88. Schmeichel helped a strong Brondby team reach new heights, the team winning the league in four of the five seasons he spent there. Schmeichel also significantly aided the teams' progress through to the semi-finals of the 1990–91 UEFA Cup semi-finals, the Danes only beaten by a last-minute winner by A.S. Roma's outstanding German striker Rudi Völler. Schmeichel ensured Brondby kept seven clean sheets in that year's UEFA Cup competition.

Schmeichel's international feats for Brondby and Denmark saw Alex Ferguson swoop for his signature in August 1991. Schmeichel cost £505,000 – Ferguson described the fee as "the bargain of the century". The 1999 Champions League Final would be Schmeichel's United swansong. In his eight seasons with Manchester United, Schmeichel won the Premier League five times, 1992–93, 1993–94, 1995–96, 1996–97 and 1998–99; the FA Cup three times in 1994, 1996 and 1999; the League Cup in 1991–92; and this astonishing Champions League victory in 1999. When Schmeichel left United at the end of the 1998–99 season, Ferguson had awful problems finding a suitable replacement. French international Fabian Barthez came close to solving Ferguson's dilemma, but not until Dutchman Edwin van der Sar took his place 'between the sticks' at Old Trafford in 2005 did Ferguson ever feel he'd found a true successor to the irrepressible Schmeichel.

Aged 36, feeling that the gruelling 60-game season in English football would curtail his longevity in the professional game, Schmeichel signed for Sporting Lisbon in Portugal, winning the 1999–2000 Portuguese Primeira Liga at the first attempt. Returning to Aston Villa for the 2001–02 season, Schmeichel became the first goalkeeper to score in the Premier League (he loved to venture upfield for corner-kicks). Five keepers have since matched the feat: Brad Friedel (Blackburn Rovers), Paul Robinson (Tottenham Hotspur), Tim Howard (Everton), Asmir Begovic (Stoke City) and Alisson Becker (Liverpool). Joining Manchester City for just one further season, 2002–03, Schmeichel maintained his exceptional record of never losing a Manchester derby, this time in the sky blue of United's fiercest city rivals.

Peter Schmeichel played 129 times for Denmark, scoring a penalty against Belgium in a 2000 European Championship warm-up match that ended in a 2-2 draw. His coup de grace came in 1992, eight years earlier, as Denmark became one of international football's great shock winners of the European Championships. Denmark opened the tournament by drawing 0-0 with England, Schmeichel defying his week-in, week-out English opponents. Hotly fancied France were beaten 2-1 in the last eight, Schmeichel deterring French legends Eric Cantona and Jean-Pierre Papin. In the semi-finals a 2-2 draw with Holland ended with an extra-time penalty shoot-out. Only one penalty was missed, the great Marco Van Basten denied by Schmeichel. In the final, Germany – again hot favourites – were beaten 2-0 thanks to Denmark's unquenchable team spirit, and Schmeichel's eternal defiance. He even caught one cross one-handed.

Peter Schmeichel was an extremely imposing figure to opposing strikers, regularly intimidating them with his physical presence. He was unusually athletic for such a big man, his star jump saves attributed to playing handball as a young man at home in Denmark. A great shot-stopper, largely unflappable – despite a tendency to temper at times – his organisational ability as last man of his defence was second to none.

United's full-backs on this legendary evening were of the highest calibre. At right-back, Gary Neville played his entire career at Old Trafford 1992–2011, completing 400 Premier League matches, scoring five goals. He lies only behind Ryan Giggs as the longest serving player in Manchester United's history. Neville won 20 trophies during his 19 seasons with the club, including eight Premier League titles, three FA Cups, two League Cups and two Champions League titles. Neville captained United for five seasons.

Bury-born Neville comes from a strong sporting family: father Neville Neville played league cricket, mother Jill played local league netball, sister Tracey (twin of brother Phil who also played successfully for United) is a former netball player and manager/coach.

In his first season as a youth player for United upon leaving school, Gary Neville captained the club's youth team to FA Cup Youth victory. Making his senior debut for United in September 1992, Neville became an integral part of the side in addition to the other members of the Class of 92, Ryan Giggs, David Beckham, Paul Scoles and Nicky Butt. Neville had to be patient to claim the right-back spot at first, England incumbent Paul Parker preventing regular appearances initially, Alex Ferguson also deploying Denis Irwin (the best and most versatile Premier League full-back ever?) at right-back with Lee Sharpe at left-back in the 1992–93 season. In 1994–95 Neville gained a regular right-back berth, the ultra-dependable Irwin shifting across to left-back. From this point on, Neville formed a formidable right-back/right midfield axis with Beckham, the two totally supportive of each other – if Neville wanted to join the attack, the team-focused Beckham simply dropped back to cover him. If one had to be critical of these two outstanding club and country competitors, one might say they lacked explosive pace for wide players. That aside (I think it stops Beckham especially as being regarded in quite the same breath as Pele, Maradona, Cruyff, Zidane, Messi and Cristiano Ronaldo), Ferguson thought Gary Neville was the best right-back of his generation. Certainly his commitment to the team and Manchester United football club in general is beyond question. When celebrating Rio Ferdinand's 90th-minute headed winner against fierce north-west rivals Liverpool in 2006, Neville's actions were enough to see him charged with improper conduct by the Football Association. Neville – Manchester red through and through – protested that footballers were emotional, not robots. His passion for the club was intense in the extreme.

When Roy Keane departed United in 2005, Neville became United's club captain, a cherished honour for this one-club servant. In total in all competitions, Gary Neville played over 600 times for Manchester United.

Internationally, Gary Neville played 85 times for England, 1995–2007. When Phil Neville joined him in the England team versus Chile in 1996 it was the first time since 1966 (the Charltons) that two brothers had played together for England. The Nevilles hold the record as most-capped brothers with 142 appearances for England in total, superseding the previous record held by Bobby and Jack Charlton. Gary Neville was the youngest first choice player for England at Euro 1996, missing the semi-final defeat against Germany after being yellow-carded twice earlier in the tournament. Might this commitment-plus player have made the difference had he played? A calf injury saw Neville's international career end before the player would have liked.

Tough-tackling, tenacious, committed, totally team-oriented, aggressive, positionally astute, Gary Neville was every attacker's worst nightmare. He became part of England's coaching team post-playing, being assistant manager at the 2014 World Cup and during the 2016 Euro qualifying campaign. A subsequent venture with Spanish club Valencia, which the dynamic, motivated, intelligent Neville took on as a massive challenge, ended ignominiously.

A more successful venture for Neville has been the purchase of Salford City in time for the 2014–15 season along with brother Phil, Ryan Giggs, Paul Scholes and Nicky Butt with the view to taking the club into the Football League from the Northern Premier League, a feat achieved in May 2019 when Salford beat Eastleigh in a penalty shoot-out in the National League play-off semi-final, followed by a 3-0 victory at Wembley in the final over Fylde. Scholes and Phil Neville have acted as caretaker managers as bosses have come and gone. David Beckham even took a 10% ownership – the other members of the Class of 92 having bought their own 10% cut – from Singapore businessman Peter Lim, giving the ex-Manchester United core a 60% share in Salford City. Thus far, for all Gary Neville's passion for Manchester and Salford City as a Greater Manchester team, the club have been unable to make the further step from Division 2 to Division 1 of the Football League.

Gary Neville has other property business interests, in addition to having forged a media career since 2011–12 with Sky Sports. A man of many ideas and opinions, Neville's latest tirade came against plans for a European Super League that would have included Manchester United. He is as forthright off-field as he was on-field.

What a superlative defender Denis Irwin was. Right-back or left-back (although he became firmly established in the latter role) it didn't matter. Irwin was simply a supreme defender, the consummate professional whose level never seemed to drop, yet he spent 1983–1990 playing for Leeds United and Oldham Athletic, seemingly condemned not to reach his full potential. Alex Ferguson has been quoted as saying that Irwin was his best value signing at any of his clubs – Aberdeen, Manchester United in particular. High praise indeed. Irwin shares the title of most successful Irish footballer ever, along with Roy Keane, his teammate at Old Trafford. The duo each won 19 career trophies.

An all-round sportsman, Irwin excelled in his early teens at Gaelic football and hurling. It was football that Irwin turned to, a major plus for the professional game. Beginning with Leeds United in 1983, Irwin made 72 appearances in the 2nd Division. He moved to Oldham Athletic, helping the club reach the semi-finals of the FA Cup and the final of the League Cup in 1990 as a 2nd Division outfit, the latter final lost to Nottingham Forest. Irwin played 167 league games for Oldham.

Alex Ferguson had seen enough of the committed, ultra-competent Irwin to sign him in 1990. Between 1990 and 2002 Irwin played 368 times for Manchester United, contributing 22 goals with his attacking forays, including two against former club Oldham Athletic in a 6-3 league win in 1991 after the Boundary

Park team had finally reached the top flight. An expert free-kick taker, Irwin won seven Premier League titles, two FA Cups (1994, 1996), a League Cup winner's medal, a European Cup Winners' Cup in 1991 and this Champions League trophy in 1999 with United.

Moving to Wolverhampton Wanderers in 2002, Irwin instantly aided the Black Country's elevation to the Premiership in 2003, but aged 38 he decided to retire when the team were relegated the following season. Denis Irwin played 56 times for the Republic of Ireland 1990–1999, scoring four goals, playing at the 1994 World Cup. Mr Reliable, Denis Irwin, a player who exuded professionalism.

United were equally blessed on this evening with two classy foreign international centre-backs, Ronny Johnsen and Jaap Stam. Johnsen went under the radar a little due to the commanding presence of Stam, but centre-backs should complement each other and Johnsen and Stam dovetailed beautifully.

Johnsen could happily slip into a defensive midfield role, but it's at centre-back that he's best remembered. He actually started senior football in the Norwegian 2nd Division with Eik Tønsberg as a striker, a position he would have liked to continue in – this gives us a picture of Johnsen's comfort on the ball, his all-round skills. Following almost a decade in Norwegian football, Johnsen signed for Turkish club Besiktas in 1995. He only played half a season in Turkey when Alex Ferguson came knocking, Johnsen signing for £1.2 million for Manchester United in the 1996 pre-season, a record fee at the time for a Norwegian defender. With United, Johnsen won four league titles, 1997, 1999, 2000 and 2001, the FA Cup in 1999, and the Champions League in that same historic treble-winning season. English teams have been desperately attempting to emulate United's feat ever since, the strength of Pep Guardiola's Manchester City team of recent years sees them constantly associated with a quadruple of Premier League, FA Cup, League Cup and Champions League. Liverpool too fell marginally short in 2022. It's virtually unattainable. The flurry of games in close proximity in English football, and a small matter of competing with Real Madrid, Barcelona, Atlético Madrid, Juventus, Bayern Munich, Paris Saint-Germain, and our own Chelsea, Liverpool and Manchester United make a quadruple unrealistic. The hardest of them all to win is the Champions League, the crème de la crème of European football.

Johnsen played two seasons at Aston Villa upon leaving Manchester United, completing 49 Premier League appearances (alongside the 99 with seven goals he played in Manchester). A brief dalliance with Newcastle United followed in the 2004–05 season, but Johnsen's lack of fitness saw him released swiftly. He returned to Valerenga in Norway for three seasons, retiring in 2008. Internationally, Johnsen played 62 times for Norway, scoring three goals. His lack of a regular position for his country – winger, striker, midfielder – cost him his chance to represent Norway at the 1994 World Cup, but established as a centre-back par excellence he played all four matches for his country at the 1998 World Cup. When he ceased playing international football, aged 38, he was Norway's second oldest international player in Norwegian football history. An underrated player, Ronnie Johnsen.

Jaap Stam's power, commitment and enormous drive, marked him out as a candidate for one of the best-ever centre-backs to play in the Premier League. The 67-times capped Stam (three goals for Holland) courted controversy later in his United career when falling out with Alex Ferguson. A typically forthright Dutchman, Stam's personal disagreement with Ferguson does not disguise the supreme quality of his performances as a Manchester United player.

Surprisingly, Stam played only 79 Premier League games for United, scoring only once, but no pundit or football fan was ever in doubt as to his status as one of the club's greatest ever defenders. Before joining United in 1998, Stam played six seasons in Holland, culminating in the winning of the Dutch Eredivisie title and the KNVB Dutch Cup with PSV Eindhoven. When signing for United in 1998 Stam became the world's most expensive defender at £10.6 million. The price tag certainly didn't weigh Stam down. Three league titles in England followed, along with this Champions League, and the FA Cup in 1999. Stam eventually left under a cloud, having made comments about United in his biography Head to Head. Some thought Ferguson took umbrage, others that the dispassionate Ferguson simply moved Stam on when in slight decline, replacing him with French World Cup winner Laurent Blanc. Ferguson later admitted selling Stam – then 29 – prematurely. Over the next six seasons Stam won the Coppa Italia with Lazio, reached the final of the Champions League with AC Milan in 2005, losing an epic final against Liverpool, and won the Dutch KNVB Cup with Ajax in Holland.

Internationally Stam reached three major competition semi-finals with Holland, the 1998 World Cup, the Euros in 2000 and again in 2004, Holland unable to take the final step on each occasion. A powerhouse of a player, Stam also possessed excellent technical ability. Despite his discord with Ferguson, Stam returned to Manchester United in 2008 as a scout with responsibility for unearthing new talent in South America.

Best known as a left-winger, Ryan Giggs wore the number 11 shirt, but played wide right in the 1999 Champions League Final. I was present when he scored THAT extraordinary goal against Arsenal at Villa Park in extra time of the 1999 FA Cup semi-final. The goal epitomised Giggs's close control and dribbling skills – the showboating, shirt-twirling celebration that followed matched the astonishing moments before it.

Welsh-born to international Rugby League player Danny Wilson, Giggs moved to Manchester aged six, and has forever been associated with Manchester United. Giggs signed for United as a 14-year-old schoolboy, making his full debut in 1991. From that time on he was an integral part of the club's first team squad, retiring aged 39 after 18 season's involvement. He is one of 28 players to have completed 1,000 career performances in English football. Only two football clubs, United and Liverpool, have won more league championships than Ryan Giggs's 13. Giggs also won the FA Cup four times, the League Cup three times and the Champions League twice (again in 2007–08 versus Chelsea).

Renowned for his electric pace and dribbling skills, Giggs was no one-trick pony. He holds the record (162) for the most assists in Premier League history, proving his commitment to the team ethic. He won the PFA Young Player of the Year Award in 1992, 1993, the first player to win in two consecutive seasons; the PFA Player of the Year Award in 2009. He was the only player to play in each of the first 22 Premier League seasons; the only player to score in each of the first 21 Premier League seasons. He was selected in the Premier League Team of the Decade in 2003 to mark the league's tenth anniversary, and selected in the PFA Team of the Century in 2007. Giggs also received the OBE in the Queen's Birthday Honours List in 2007 for services to football.

Fittingly, given his current association with Salford City, Giggs captained Salford Boys to victory over a Blackburn team in the final of the Granada Schools Cup held at Anfield in 1987. He received the trophy from former Liverpool legend Ron Yeats. Giggs could have followed father Danny Wilson into Rugby League, but Old Trafford steward Harry Wood recommended Giggs to Alex Ferguson. Giggs scored a hat-trick for Salford Boys against a United U-15 side. It was enough for Ferguson to offer Giggs two-year associate schoolboy forms. Under his paternal name of Ryan Wilson, Giggs went on to captain England Schoolboys against Germany in 1989. When his parents separated Ryan changed his name to his mother's name of Giggs.

As a 17-year-old, Giggs had competition for the left-wing spot initially from 19-year-old Lee Sharpe. Sharpe looked set for a fabulous career of his own at this point, but Giggs's career soon stratospherically superseded Sharpe's. Ferguson was looking to fill the left-wing berth held down with some success by the Dane Jesper Olsen. Although he became a first team regular in the 1991–92 season, Giggs remained captain of United's youth team, leading them to FA Youth Cup glory in 1992. For the first team Giggs played in a team finishing second to an Eric Cantona-inspired Leeds United in the last season of the old 1st Division. 1992–93 saw Giggs – and the other members of the Class of 92 – inspire United to a Premier League title, a top-flight win of their own, the first of the Premier League era, a title they retained in 1993–94, and won again in 1995–96, 1996–97, 1998–99, 2000–01 and 2002–03. It was an era of utter dominance under Ferguson – and from season 2006–07 the club won the title in four out of the next five seasons.

In 1996–97 United reached the semi-finals of the Champions League, Giggs and other young pretenders to the crowns of Bobby Charlton and George Best like David Beckham to the fore. Alessandro Del Piero, the great Italian player, claimed he'd only "cried" watching two players – Roberto Baggio – and Ryan Giggs. 1998–99 was actually a mixed bag of a season for Giggs who missed many games through injury. He was still able to take Tony Adams, Lee Dixon and Martin Keown – incredible defenders all – to the cleaners in THAT FA Cup semi-final against Arsenal, and score a 90th-minute equaliser in the home semi-final of the Champions League against Juventus. In the final Giggs set up Teddy Sheringham for United's equaliser in the 90th minute.

His form apparently dipping, Giggs came alive as an early substitute for Diego Forlan, scoring twice against Juventus in a 2002–03 Champions League tie. Speculation was rife that Giggs would transfer to Italy – possibly to Inter Milan. Giggs stayed, took up yoga to combat persistent hamstring injuries and his form picked up again. Latterly Giggs began to drift inside in games, his capacity to impact on games unhindered.

In the 2007–08 season Giggs had to accept a rotation system implemented by

Ferguson (to protect the player's fitness) whereby the Portuguese Nani alternated at times with him in first team selection. On 21 May 2008, Giggs equalled Bobby Charlton's appearance record for Manchester United of 758 appearances, celebrating in style by scoring and helping United win a tenth Premier League title. The record was broken by Giggs's appearance as a substitute for Paul Scholes in the Champions League Final against Chelsea, the Welshman converting the decisive strike in the penalty shoot-out. Giggs only played a dozen matches in the Premier League in 2008, but aided by stout support from Ferguson with regard to his longevity, service and sheer quality of performance at Old Trafford and beyond, he was awarded the PFA Player of the Year for 2009. He went on to receive the BBC Sports Personality of the Year Award in December 2009. Later in the month he was named United's Player of the Decade.

In April 2012 Giggs scored against Schalke 04 of Germany, making him the oldest player to date to score in the Champions League, aged 37. He also appeared in the Champions League Final of 2011 against Barcelona, although the Spanish super-team at their peak showed United no mercy, winning 3-1. The scoreline did not fully reflect Barcelona's superiority on the night. In the 2011–12 Champions League campaign Giggs's goal in the 1-1 draw with Benfica in the Estadio da Luz (the famous Stadium of Light where British success in the European Cup/Champions League all began with Glasgow Celtic in 1967) meant he'd scored in 16 different Champions League campaigns. In February 2012 Giggs marked his 900th appearance for United at Carrow Road against Norwich City by scoring the winner in the 90th minute in a 2-1 victory. In March 2014 Giggs made his 1,000th appearance for United, his presence insufficient to deter Real Madrid from beating his team 2-1 at Old Trafford.

Turning to coaching, Giggs was appointed player-coach by then United manager David Moyes in July 2013, becoming interim manager at Old Trafford when Moyes was dismissed in April 2014. Remaining signed as a player, Giggs overhauled Real Madrid's Raul as the leading appearance holder in the Champions League when coming on as a substitute against Shakhtar Donetsk in October 2013.

Ryan Giggs appeared 64 times for Wales 1991–2007 (Ferguson's decision to refuse some international call-ups because of Giggs's suspect hamstring prevented further caps), scoring 12 goals. Debuting against Germany in 1991 as a 17-year-old, he became Wales's youngest international, a record he held until 1998. Giggs also managed Wales briefly, helping his country qualify for Euro 2020, not leading them in the competition due to an off-field matter.

Initially Giggs did not seem the best crosser of the ball for all his lightning pace, athleticism and trickery (I suffered the same problem in local football, I couldn't cross to save my life, yet could facilitate decent enough passes through the lines), but he was able to redefine his game to become a champion assist-maker for United. Like one of his Old Trafford mentors, Bobby Charlton, Giggs was never sent off in his time at Manchester United, although he suffered the fate playing for Wales against Norway and suffered a delayed two-match suspension following an incident against Russia in the Euro 2004 play-offs. Giggs's whippet-like quality, his capacity to score great goals, made him United's biggest poster boy since George Best – although he had a serious rival in those stakes in David Beckham. In 672 Premier League games, Giggs scored 114 goals.

On the other flank, Jesper Blomqvist was chosen ahead of outstanding strikers in the shape of Ole Gunnar Solskjaer and Teddy Sheringham to give the team balance. A football team must have balance – Ferguson recognised this in selecting Blomqvist, who only played 25 Premier League games for United 1998–2001. Blomqvist came to prominence with IFK Göteborg in his home country of Sweden, scoring 18 goals in 73 Swedish League appearances, 1993–96. Spells in Italy with AC Milan and Parma followed before he moved to Old Trafford, but goals eluded him thereafter. Voted Göteborg Player of the Year in 1996, it was Blomqvist's performance against United in a Champions League tie that caught Ferguson's eye. Ferguson signed the Swede as back-up to Giggs primarily. Substituted by Sheringham in this 1999 Champions League Final, it was Blomqvist's misfortune to suffer a serious knee injury shortly afterwards, making his United career a short one.

Moving to Everton in 2001–02, Blomqvist's injury woes persisted. A dalliance with Alan Curbishley's Charlton Athletic followed in 2002–03. Even returning home to Sweden didn't help the unfortunate Blomqvist who was only able to complete 25 league matches for Djurgårdens, Enköping and Hammarby IF across seven seasons. At international level Blomqvist partook in the successful bronze medal-winning Swedish team at the 1994 World Cup. In all, he won 30 caps for Sweden 1994–2002, but the noughties were clearly a write-off for a player unable to fulfil his true potential.

Could any other player match the new poster boy Ryan Giggs? Well. Yes, United had another within their ranks in David Beckham. Not blessed with Giggs's electric pace and dribbling skills, but for sheer personality, charisma and unstinting team ethic, Beckham was more than equal to Giggs. While not possessing Giggs's speed and hip-swivelling elusiveness, Beckham possessed his own unerring weapons: deadly free kicks, an outstanding eye for long-range shooting and a right foot that bent inch-perfect crosses into the penalty area better than any player in English football during the last 50 years. Liverpool's current right-back Trent Alexander-Arnold threatens to equal the masterful Beckham.

From his early beginnings as an exceptional youth player with Tottenham Hotspur's academy, Leytonstone-born Beckham's star burned so brightly that he became the first English footballer to win the league title in four different countries: England, Spain, the United States and France. With United, Beckham won six league titles, two FA Cups and this 1999 Champions League trophy. Beckham was the first British player to play 100 Champions League games.

Married to the former Spice Girl Victoria Adams (Beckham), signed to the Simon XIX Fuller Entertainment Agency, David Beckham's off-field financial security has been firmly secured – he was the highest paid footballer in the world at one point – if not the best, that sobriquet would have to be shared by Lionel Messi and Cristiano Ronaldo. His parents, fanatical Manchester United supporters, travelled nearly 200 miles to watch the club regularly. Young David attended one of Bobby Charlton's Soccer Schools in Manchester, winning the chance to partake in a Barcelona training session. Despite being part of Tottenham

Hotspur's youth set-up, and playing for Enfield-based Brimsdown Rovers (his father was co-coach) David signed for Manchester United on his 14th birthday. He did not represent England Schoolboys, his slight frame at the time working against him. Part of the 1992 FA Youth Cup-winning team, Beckham's first team debut followed swiftly afterwards, his first appearance as a substitute for the whip-fast Russian Andrei Kanchelskis in a League Cup tie against Brighton & Hove Albion in September 1992. United lost the 1993 FA Youth Cup Final to Leeds United, compensation for Beckham coming in the form of a Reserve League trophy. His Champions League debut came in December 1994, scoring in a 4-0 victory over Turkish side Galatasaray, although United finished third in their group.

Loaned to Preston North End for five games – a policy Alex Ferguson encouraged, players being 'farmed' out to lower league clubs to experience playing men's football, to cope with the physicality – Beckham scored twice, once direct from a corner-kick. Returning to United for the 1995–96 season, Beckham made his Premier League debut against Leeds in a goalless draw. Linked with England international Darren Anderton and superstar Dutch and Italian internationals Marc Overmars and Roberto Baggio, Ferguson instead gave the Class of 92 their heads. Beckham took the place of the flying Kanchelskis, redefining the right-side forward role in United's team as a wide right midfield player rather than a winger. This 1995–96 season, Beckham's first as a regular first-teamer, saw United win the double of League and FA Cup.

Beckham was not selected for the Euro '96 tournament in England, vastly more experienced players chosen in front of him. In August 1996, at the beginning of the 1996–97 season, he gave the England hierarchy a taste of what might have been. Spotting the Wimbledon goalkeeper off his line, he drifted a 57-yard shot from inside his own half to score United's third goal of the game. A 2016 Sky Sports poll voted it the best opening day goal in Premier League history. The following season, 1997–98, Beckham's 13 assists were the most in the Premier League, but United finished second in the league behind Arsenal.

Following criticism of Beckham after his sending off against Argentina in the 1998 World Cup, it was speculated he would leave Old Trafford. Needing to beat Tottenham Hotspur at Old Trafford to win the 1998–99 Premier League, Beckham's curler equalised an early goal for the North Londoners. United went on to win 2-1. Suspensions to key midfielders Roy Keane and Paul Scholes (another reason for Blomqvist's selection?) meant Beckham switched inside in this Champions League Final against Bayern Munich. Beckham's excellent technique and close control allowed the switch, even if the dynamic Keane and deft Scholes were sorely missed. Beckham's dead-ball accuracy did prove crucial, his two corner-kicks converted in the final by Teddy Sheringham and Ole Gunnar Solsjkaer. His outstanding contributions in the 1998–99 season saw him finish runner-up to the great Brazilian and Barcelona midfielder Rivaldo in both the European Footballer of the Year and the FIFA World Player of the Year awards.

Linked with Juventus in the 1999–2000 season, Beckham remained at Old Trafford, helping United retain the Premier League by an 18-point margin, scoring five goals in an 11-match winning streak in the season's denouement. United won the title for a third consecutive season in 2000–01, Beckham excelling, but the celebrity hoo-hah surrounding him began to fracture his relationship with manager Ferguson. A fracture of a different kind occurred when Beckham broke a metatarsal bone in his left foot in a Champions League match against Deportivo La Coruna. Despite missing many games in the 2000–01 season as a result, Beckham scored 16 goals in all competitions, his best goal return at Old Trafford. The next season proved to be his last at Old Trafford, Solskjaer often replacing him on the right side of midfield. There was also the matter of the Alex Ferguson boot-kicking incident that left Beckham with a cut eye. Despite the friction in the dressing room – the boot incident came after United lost to Arsenal in an FA Cup match, Ferguson hating losing to his arch-rivals of that time – Beckham helped United win the Premier League. Ultimately David Beckham totalled 265 Premier League appearances and 61 goals for United, chipping in with 15 Champions League goals in 81 appearances. After 12 senior seasons at Manchester United, Beckham left the club in the 2003 summer transfer window as United's second-longest serving player behind Ryan Giggs.

Seemingly set to join Barcelona, Beckham instead moved to Real Madrid, part of Real president Florentino Perez's 'Galactico' foreign superstar signing programme. Beckham joined a team containing Zinedine Zidane, the Brazilian centre-forward Ronaldo, Portuguese star Luis Figo, Brazilian left-back Roberto Carlos, and Spanish international legends striker Raul and goalkeeper Iker Casillas.

Beckham settled in quickly, scoring five goals in his first 16 matches, partnering Zidane and Figo in a three-man midfield. It was some midfield – but Real didn't win major silverware in the 2003–04 season. A curious season followed in 2004–05 – Real again failing to win La Liga. Beckham was sent off three times in the season, but led the list of assists in La Liga. Second in 2005–06, Real, despite their superstar contingent, could not usurp a formidable Barcelona team. Beckham's lack of lightning pace cost him as the speedier José Antonio Reyes started ahead of him in the 2006–07 season.

Beckham signed for the American team LA Galaxy in January 2007, Real's then-coach Fabio Capello (Real changed coaches rapidly at this time) feeling the player had been swayed by Hollywood overtures. Capello rescinded his comments, brought Beckham back into the fold, David repaying his faith with improved performances. In his last Champions League appearance for Real, the Bernabeu side were beaten on away goals, but not before Beckham assisted in all three goals in the home tie, a performance Bayern Munich goalkeeper Oliver Khan called 'world class'. Remarkably Beckham ended the season at the Bernabeu before moving to America by finally winning La Liga – although he went off injured in Real's title-clinching 3-1 win over Real Mallorca, Reyes replacing him and scoring twice.

Beckham's move to LA Galaxy enabled him to gain experience of another country's culture, even if the standard of football surely didn't tax a player of his considerable talent. In May 2008, Beckham scored from 70 yards against Kansas City Wizards, perhaps vindicating my judgement of American football compared with the European game – but clearly he had a penchant for the long-range goal, and one cannot deny his vision on a football pitch.

Beckham then went on loan to AC Milan, intent on returning to the NASL in March 2009. Carlo Ancelotti, Milan's boss, felt Beckham's awareness on a football pitch compensated greatly for a lack of speed. He also felt Beckham was stronger and more tactically astute as a 33-year-old in Italian football. In Italy Beckham played with Brazilian superstars Kaka and Ronaldinho, as well as Dutch legend Clarence Seedorf, and the peerless Italian midfield playmaker Andrea Pirlo, then 29 years old. Beckham's loan to Milan was extended through to July. When he returned three months later to LA Galaxy, American fans accused him of being a 'part-time player'.

Beckham returned again to Milan for a second loan period. In this spell he returned to Old Trafford in a Champions League tie for Milan, coming on as a substitute. He impressed, making chances for his teammates, but United won the match conclusively 4-0. In Milan's next match against Chievo he tore his left Achilles tendon, causing him to miss the 2010 World Cup. His intention in playing for Milan had been to ensure his fitness and match-playing standard enabled him to be called up for England.

In September 2010, Beckham returned to LA Galaxy from Italy. He eventually signed off in America winning two successive Major League Soccer Finals in 2011 and 2012. In January 2013 Beckham signed a five-month deal with Paris Saint-Germain, so ending an illustrious career in France by winning another league title, Ligue 1, as PSG defeated Lyon 1-0 in their penultimate league fixture. A very wealthy man by this stage, he donated all his PSG wages to a children's charity.

On the international scene, Beckham's sending off for retaliation against Argentina in the last 16 at the 1998 World Cup will forever live with him. There is no doubt that the cunning Diego Simeone taunted Beckham into the act, but with England down to ten men after Michael Owen's stunning strike, the Argentines were able to turn the tables on Glenn Hoddle's team, albeit via a penalty shoot-out after extra time. Fan abuse aimed at Beckham after the incident continued for a couple of seasons, but the resilient East Londoner won England supporters over eventually, becoming captain of his country under caretaker manager Peter Taylor in 2000, retaining the armband under permanent manager Sven-Göran Eriksson.

Beckham starred as England famously beat Germany 5-1 in Munich in the 2002 World Cup qualifying group. Better still, his 90th-minute 30-yard free-kick equaliser against Greece at Wembley in England's final group game in the qualifiers was the difference between England going or not going to the 2002 World Cup. The magical moment ensured Beckham won the BBC Sports Personality of the Year Award in December 2001. At the 2002 World Cup, Beckham avenged the Argentinian fiasco from 1998, scoring the winning goal from a penalty kick, but England lost to Brazil in the last eight, courtesy of Ronaldinho's long range shot and David Seaman's misjudgement. Ironically, Beckham then missed crucial penalties at Euro 2004, one in a 2-1 defeat to France, another in the quarter-final shoot-out against Portugal. In October 2005 Beckham was sent off against Austria, becoming the first player to be sent off twice playing for England – it was never all roses for David Beckham.

At the 2006 World Cup Beckham's free kick was turned into his own net by Paraguay's Carlos Gamarra, England winning 1-0. Two late assists for goals by Peter Crouch and Steven Gerrard enabled struggling England to beat Trinidad and Tobago in their next match. In the second round, Beckham's 59th-minute free-kick goal made him the first English player to score at three different World Cups. Illness and dehydration saw him substituted in the last eight against Portugal, England again losing to the Iberian nation on penalties after extra time. An emotional Beckham asked to be relieved of the captaincy directly after the tournament, John Terry taking the armband. He then lost favour under Steve McLaren and Fabio Capello. Capello reprieved him, Beckham ending up with 115 caps and 17 goals for England.

Beckham's desire for self-improvement as a footballer (constant repetition of his fabled free kicks in training) enabled him, like Kevin Keegan, to perform significantly on the World and European stages. His work ethic and discipline in training, and his great team ethic was occasionally belied by a tendency to be riled by lesser talented players than himself. He possessed great humility, and his dedication to his profession was of the highest order. His crossing ability, the ability to bend and shape the ball to his will was his outstanding trait – if only he had genuine pace!

David Beckham's off-field activities have ensured his profile remains higher than any other British sportsman of the modern age. He has been a Goodwill Ambassador for UNICEF since 2005, and played an integral part in Great Britain being awarded the 2012 Olympic Games. He was awarded an OBE in the Queen's 2003 Birthday Honours. For good or for bad, David Beckham has never been out of the news over the last 25 years – or it seems off the small screen in the corner of our living rooms, his presence noticeable at events such as Wimbledon or the delayed 2020 European Football Championships.

The Class of 92 contained several outstanding technical footballers; Ryan Giggs, David Beckham, Paul Scholes. The least fashionable of the group, the player who was employed on a football pitch as a nuts and bolts player, the player to do the dirty business, was Nicky Butt. Butt played 270 Premier League games for United, scoring 21 goals, but by necessity his role in the team ensured a considerably lesser profile than his more glamorous teammates. Butt spent 12 seasons at Old Trafford, winning six league titles, three FA Cups,and this Champions League trophy. Like Blomqvist, he may not have played on this night had Keane and Scholes not been suspended, but Alex Ferguson knew he would get grit, determination and a tireless team ethic with Nicky Butt.

After early season success with United in the 1990s as a direct replacement for Paul Ince, Butt's selection for the first team became more sporadic – he was named in the 1997–98 PFA Team of the Year. Butt moved to Newcastle United in 2004, completing 134 Premier League games on Tyneside, scoring five goals. The signing of Scott Parker and Turkish international Emre Belözoglu limited Butt's game time again, Butt riding the storm to continue his career at St James's Park, regaining regular football when Parker moved to West Ham United in 2007.

An injury to Steven Gerrard gave Butt the chance to play alongside teammates Beckham and Scholes – in the midfield holding role – at the 2004 Euros. In all, Nicky Butt played 39 times for England. In October 2012 Butt returned to Old Trafford as Reserve Team Coach, being appointed Head of the Academy in February 2016. In July 2019 Butt was appointed Head of First Team Development, reporting directly to manager Ole Gunner Solsjkaer. In March 2021 Butt left United once more after nine years in various coaching positions.

When you think of strikers – perhaps less so in the modern game as 4-5-1 or flexible takes on that system became de rigeur – you think of them in pairs. Manchester United on this evening had a devastating pair in Dwight Eversley Yorke and Andrew Cole. Except that in this remarkable treble-winning season United possessed four great strikers. Yorke and Cole were largely Alex Ferguson's preferred striking partnership, but he could also call on two outstanding forwards in Teddy Sheringham and Ole Gunnar Solsjkaer. Both players came on as substitutes in this final – both scored to etch United's name upon the 1999 Champions League trophy.

Trinidad and Tobago international Yorke (72 caps, 19 goals) made his name at Aston Villa 1990–98, scoring 73 goals in 231 top-flight appearances. Yorke won the League Cup with Villa in 1996. A hat-trick against Newcastle United in a 4-3 defeat, with Villa down to ten men (he had a fourth equalising goal disallowed for offside) stirred Manchester United's interest in him. Villa wanted Andy Cole in exchange for Yorke when Ferguson made enquiries – the Scot would have none of it.

Instead Yorke and Cole formed a fearsome strike pair in the 1998–99 season, Yorke scoring in the Champions League against Bayern Munich, Barcelona, Inter Milan and Juventus. He also topped the Premier League scoring list with 18 goals and won the Premier League Player of the Season award. Essentially Yorke played two great seasons with United, scoring 23 goals in all competitions in 1999–2000. Despite scoring a hat-trick in a top of the table clash with Arsenal in 2000–01, Yorke failed to win a regular place in that season.

In July 2002, Yorke reunited with Andy Cole at Blackburn Rovers, the pair helping the Lancashire club to UEFA Cup qualification, but it was Yorke's 65 goals in 152 matches in all competitions for Manchester United that caught the eye.

Andy Cole was the more prolific goalscorer, scoring goals for fun at Bristol City (12 in 29 league games), Newcastle United (55 in 70 Premier League games), 93 in 195 Premier League games for Manchester United 1995–2001, Blackburn Rovers (27 in 83 Premier League games), Fulham (12 in 31 Premier League games), and Manchester City (nine in 22 Premier League games).

Andy Coles' goal-scoring record in particular for Newcastle, then Manchester United for six seasons, made him one of the most feared strikers in British football for a little under a decade. Yet he began life as a youth player in London with Arsenal, playing only one league game for the Gunners as a substitute against Sheffield United.

At Newcastle Cole scored 12 goals at the end of the 1993–94 season including two hat-tricks. The following 1994–95 season Cole scored 34 Premier League goals in 40 games, a lethal partnership formed with Peter Beardsley. Beardsley was an arch creator of chances for fellow forwards – Gary Lineker for England, John Aldridge at Liverpool benefited from the artful, incisive play of Beardsley.

Cole, for his part, won the 1994–95 PFA Young Player of the Year Award, netting 41 goals in all competitions.

Cole left Newcastle in January 1995, becoming the first player to score five goals in a Premier League match versus Ipswich Town in a 9-0 drubbing of the Tractor Boys for new club Manchester United. The 1995–96 season was problematic for Cole as the forward play centred around the charismatic Frenchman Eric Cantona. Cole came good towards the end of the season, scoring crucial goals as United became the first team to win the English domestic league and cup double twice. The following season was even more traumatic for Cole initially, two broken legs suffered in a reserve match against Liverpool, in addition to the signing of Norwegian Striker Ole Gunnar Solskjaer restricting his game time. Again Cole came back strongly, scoring the Best European Goal of the Season against Porto in the Champions League, and contributing a Premier League title-clinching goal in 1996–97, ironically against Liverpool, to secure a third Premier League trophy in four seasons for United.

Cantona's retirement in 1997 gave Cole the opportunity to claim regular football again at Old Trafford. He repaid Ferguson's faith in him with his first European hat-trick against Feyenoord of Holland; won the fans' vote for Goal of the Season with a chip against Everton; and finished runner-up in the 1997–98 PFA Player's Player of the Year to Arsenal's Dennis Bergkamp. Cole's near-telepathic relationship with Dwight Yorke saw the pair record 53 goals between them in all competitions in 1998–99. Andy Cole finally departed United in December 2001 after Ferguson signed the Dutchman Ruud van Nistelrooy from PSV Eindhoven. Cole won 15 caps for England 1995–2001, surprisingly scoring only one goal against Albania. The speed and shoot-on-sight attitude of Cole, allied to the trickery of the elusive Yorke made the pair feared throughout Europe in the last two seasons of the 20th century.

Reputedly, Teddy Sheringham and Andy Cole were not always on the same page, but any differences were cast aside in the common cause of winning football matches at Manchester United. I must confess I did not always find the same in the clique-ridden life of local village football. There were always times when those that selected teams chose their friends or drinking pals above players who should rightfully have been in the team; always players who would not pass the ball to you if they chose not to. I have always believed firmly in team spirit being the overriding factor at a football club – even if I only played for one team (in my early 20s) where everybody definitely pulled together without favouritism, animosity or envy.

A very clever footballer, Teddy Sheringham's tactical awareness and technique compensated greatly for his lack of pace. He also scored a large amount of goals for a player not blessed with speed. With Sheringham it was always the classic case of speed of thought. He began his professional career with Millwall, scoring 111 goals 1983–1991, being the club's second highest scorer of all time. Sheringham played one season with Nottingham Forest, scoring the club's first ever Premiership goal in 1992, a feat he repeated for Portsmouth later in his career in the 2003–04 season. The shrewd Sheringham also scored a hat-trick against Bolton Wanderers in that season of 2003–04, becoming the oldest player

(38) in Premier League history to do so.

Sheringham enjoyed two spells with Tottenham Hotspur, 1992–97 (75 goals in 166 Premier League games) and 2001–03 (22 goals in 70 Premier League games). He won the PFA Player's Player of the Year and the FWA Footballer of the Year awards at Manchester United, but endured a difficult spell at United despite these accolades. His overall contribution to England, Tottenham, and Manchester United – 31 goals in the Premier League at Old Trafford 1997–2001 – won Sheringham the respect of fellow player and football writers, but he was never a regular starter with Manchester United. Redemption for Sheringham came in this 1999 Champions League Final, as he first scored the equaliser in injury time, and then flicked the ball on for Solskjaer to score the winner.

A late developer whose keen football brain won him admirers such as Terry Venables for England, Sheringham's first international cap came as a 27-year-old in 1993. Sheringham won favour with Venables during the 1996 European Championships despite competition from Andy Cole, Ian Wright, Les Ferdinand and Robbie Fowler to partner Alan Shearer in attack. The two formed a second famous 'SAS', Shearer and Sheringham partnership after Shearer's former pairing with Chris Sutton at Blackburn Rovers. Sheringham dropped in the whole, laying important balls off to Shearer, the out-and-out striker who loved nothing but scoring goals. Sheringham continued to be chosen for England until the emergence of the jet-heeled Michael Owen at the 1998 World Cup. Sheringham, obdurate, obstinate, as well as tactically and technically adept, hung around until 2002, scoring a crucial, largely forgotten goal in the 2-2 draw with Greece (thanks to David Beckham's dramatic last minute free-kick equaliser) that ensured World Cup qualification for England.

Recognised now as a great provider of assists for others – the cute lay-off to Shearer for his goal in the 4-1 defeat of Holland at the 1996 Euros is fondly remembered, Sheringham lies 11th on the list of all-time goalscorers in the Premier League with 146 goals (February 2022). A surprise package, Teddy Sheringham.

Manager at Manchester United 2018–2021, Ole Gunnar Solskjaer was the other exceptional substitute creating history for Manchester United here in the Nou Camp, Barcelona, in 1999. Solsjkaer was an incredibly prolific goalscorer in his home country of Norway, scoring 115 goals in only 109 league games for the Kristiansund club (his birthplace) Clausenengen in the Norwegian 3rd and 2nd divisions. Joining top-tier club Molde in 1994, Solsjkaer promptly netted 31 times in 45 league games. Molde's then-manager Age Hareide offered Solsjkaer to Everton and Manchester City, but neither club were prepared to gamble on the slight, will o' the wisp Solsjkaer.

Solskjaer instead joined Alex Ferguson's Manchester United in 1996–97, was given the number 20 shirt in anticipation of being a squad member, but ended up as the club's leading Premier League scorer with 18 goals. Solsjkaer scored important Champions League goals against Rapid Vienna of Austria in 1996–97, and Monaco in 1997–98, but United's moment had not yet arrived in Europe. Being used in the David Fairclough (Liverpool) supersub role in much of the 1998–99 season, Solsjkaer could have transferred to Tottenham Hotspur at the start of the campaign, but remained loyal to United despite the form of Yorke and Cole ahead of him in the pecking order. Coming off the bench in the 71st minute against Nottingham Forest in the Premier League, Solskjaer showed his worth with lightning pace and reflexes enabling him to score four goals in 19 minutes as United triumphed 8-1. Solskjaer won his second Premier League title in three seasons this season, played the whole of the FA Cup Final victory over Newcastle United, and had the last laugh with the winning goal in the 92nd minute of this Champions League Final.

In the 1999–2000 season Solsjkaer repeated his four-goal scoring feat, this time against Everton in a 5-1 win at Old Trafford. The quarter-finals stage saw United relinquish their Champions League trophy at the hands of the great Real Madrid, 3-2 on aggregate. In the 2001–02 season Yorke and Cole found themselves relegated to the bench, the persistent Solskjaer partnering Ruud van Nistelrooy in attack – the Norwegian repaid Ferguson with 17 goals in 30 Premier League games, including a hat-trick in a 4-0 win over Bolton Wanderers. In 2002–03 Ferguson reverted to playing van Nistelrooy as a lone striker with Paul Scholes in support – or the Uruguayan Diego Forlan. Solsjkaer again persisted at United, playing as a wide right midfielder when David Beckham picked up an injury.

A persistent knee injury of his own finally brought down the curtain on the determined Solsjkaer's United career in 2007, the Norwegian ending up with 91 Premier League goals in 235 appearances. The 'David Fairclough supersub' impact is reflected in Solsjkaer's 28 goals for United as a substitute in all competitions. The livewire Norwegian also scored 23 international goals for his country in 67 appearances. If you picked Ole Gunnar Solsjkaer in your first team you were guaranteed goals – in all competitions in Norway and England he scored 237 goals in 386 games, an outstanding record.

On paper this Bayern Munich team didn't appear to be of the standard of other Bayern teams containing greats like Maier, Beckenbauer, Gerd Müller, Karl-Heinz Rummenigge, Paul Breitner et al, yet they dominated this 1999 Champions League Final without winning it.

In Oliver Kahn they had a splendid goalkeeper who played 429 Bundesliga games for Bayern 1994–2008, plus 86 times capped by Germany. Known as 'Der Titan' due to his aggressive style, Kahn is the only goalkeeper in World Cup history to win the Golden Ball for best player in the tournament. Individually he won four consecutive UEFA Best European Goalkeeper awards, three IFFHS World's Best Goalkeeper awards, and two German Footballer of the Year awards. With Bayern he won eight Bundesliga titles, six DFB Pokal Cups, the 1998 UEFA Cup and the 2001 Champions League. It could be argued that Kahn was better than Sepp Maier in the great 1970s Bayern team. He captained the team on this evening.

Playing at sweeper – he'd been transposed there in the great modern traditional methodology from midfield – was Lothar Matthäus, one of the greatest players of his generation. A dynamic, irresistible force as a midfield player, Matthäus switched roles to become an astute reader of the game from the back, able to intercept passes with his sharp reading of the game; able to play long balls to his attackers due to his foresight and vision.

Matthäus won the Ballon d'Or for World's Best Player when Germany won the World Cup in 1990. It was one of five World Cups he played in: 1982, 1986, 1990, 1994, 1998, a feat only matched by Mexico's Rafael Márquez in 2018. Matthäus also won the 1980 Euros with Germany. He is the most capped player of all time in Germany with 150 caps, scoring 23 goals.

Matthäus began his professional career in 1979 with Borussia Möenchengladbach, scoring 36 goals in 162 appearances. Transferring to Bayern Munich in 1984, he stayed until 1988, scoring 57 goals in 113 games as an inspirational driving force in midfield. Italy called next, Matthäus's goal return of 40 goals in 115 Serie A games with Inter Milan extremely impressive in a league notorious for defensive football. Returning to Bayern in 1992, Matthäus clocked up another 189 games in Munich, scoring 28 further goals. Like so many players post-1970 he ended his playing days in the North American Soccer League in 2008 with Metrostars (now known as New York Red Bull).

A box-to-box player with an insatiable desire to win, and seemingly endless stamina, Matthäus could also launch unstoppable long-range drives, scoring some spectacular goals. A great athlete, Matthäus, and as England players will attest, an annoying opponent, whose self-motivation soared above the average player. Diego Maradona thought Matthäus was his toughest opponent.

The rest of the Bayern team was stuffed with German internationals: right-back Marcus Babbel (51 caps), offensive midfielder Steffen Effenberg (35 caps), defensive midfielder Jens Jeremies (55 caps), winger Mario Basler (30 caps), centre-forward Carsten Jancker (33 caps) to mention a few, and the Ghanaian international centre-back Samuel Kuffour, who played 175 Bundesliga games for Bayern 1993–2005. A Manchester United side containing the energy and drive of Roy Keane and the clever artistry of Paul Scholes might have been favourites for this final, but the experienced Bayern side took advantage of their absence to overwhelm United's midfield at times.

THE FINAL

United started the final with a slightly lopsided look. Ryan Giggs was less influential on the right side of midfield; David Beckham played in the centre of the park instead of his customary right flank station; Nicky Butt, a fierce competitor in the centre with Beckham, and the Swede Jesper Blomqvist on the left of midfield. Even though Bayern only played the final, ostensibly, with two midfield players –Effenberg and Jeremies – Bayern dominated possession throughout the match.

Ronnie Johnsen brought down Carsten Jancker on the edge of the penalty area after six minutes. Mario Basler curled a quite brilliant free kick into the corner of the net, giving Peter Schmeichel no chance. 1-0 Bayern. United's only response in the first half was a messy missed opportunity by Andy Cole in a goalmouth melee.

United vainly tried to get a foothold in the game in the second half. Blomqvist edged ahead of the last defender on the left but skied the ball over the crossbar as the intimidating Oliver Kahn advanced on him. Bayern responded by regaining the midfield. Basler spotted Schmeichel straying off his goalline and attempted an audacious shot from the halfway line. Luckily for United Schmeichel's momentary lapse was not punished. Effenberg attempted to loft the ball over Schmeichel, this time the big Dane tipped the ball over the bar. Bayern then hit the woodwork twice as the game threatened to drift away from United. First substitute Mehmet Scholl chipped the ball delightfully over Schmeichel, the ball rebounding flush from the far post. Then Jancker's overhead kick struck the crossbar. United were living very dangerously indeed.

Never one afraid of throwing caution to the wind, Alex Ferguson brought Sheringham and Solsjkaer into the fray. A very cute back-heel by Solsjkaer set Sheringham up, but the latter's shot lacked power. The 90th minute – Bayern were almost celebrating a deserved win. Beckham swung a corner-kick into the penalty area, Giggs miss-hit a shot goalwards, and the ever-alert Sheringham swept the ball into the net, Bayern vainly calling for an offside that would not be given – correctly. The 92nd minute – Sheringham flicked on another Beckham corner-kick and Solsjkaer instinctively stuck his right foot out and jabbed the ball over the line from a yard out. The game had been utterly transformed in the space of less than two minutes.

This was the most exciting, dramatic finale to a European Cup/Champions League Final in the competition's entire history. Bayern couldn't believe their misfortune, having had considerably more chances than United – their disbelief at the final whistle was tangible, even to those of us simply watching the game on television. United simply refused to accept defeat – a feat they'd already achieved weeks before in that incredible FA Cup semi-final with Arsenal.

The influential Matthäus went off exhausted after 80 minutes – the game suddenly turned. Solskjaer flashed a couple of headers towards goal that Kahn was equal to. United's sheer self-belief meant glory ultimately. When you've got the pace and creativity of Giggs, Cole, Yorke, Beckham, Sheringham and Solsjkaer in the 13 players on the pitch in those 93 minutes you've always got a chance of winning the match. Matthäus claimed it was like watching a "horror film" when he came off, after Bayern dominated the match for 89 minutes. It just seemed to be fate – Schmeichel obviously thought so, claiming he knew the game had changed when Scholl's chip rebounded safely back into his arms.

2004–05 CHAMPIONS LEAGUE FINAL
Liverpool 3 v 3 AC Milan (Liverpool win 3-1 on penalties)

The drama of the Nou Camp in Barcelona in 1999 was almost matched by Liverpool's epic recovery in Istanbul in 2005 after a six-year English hiatus in reaching the final. Steven Gerrard never had the satisfaction of winning a Premier League title in his 17 seasons at Liverpool, but my goodness he produced a captain's performance here, the performance of a lifetime in the biggest European club game of them all. I think that's a massive consolation for not winning your own country's domestic league title.

Route to the Final
The enlarged format of the newly designed Champions League meant each

club played 12 matches in total. Initially there were three qualifying rounds. Liverpool entered the competition in the third qualifying round as they finished only fourth in the 2003–04 Premier League, only the top three teams qualifying automatically for the group stages of the 2004–05 Champions League. The route to the final was a long and arduous one for Liverpool. The third qualifying round saw the Reds matched with Austrian side Grazer AK. Steven Gerrard scored twice in the Liebenauer Stadium, Graz, Liverpool winning 2-0. The home tie was surprisingly lost 1-0, but the result proved irrelevant. The major relevance of the tie was the beginnings of an outstanding tournament for the irrepressible Gerrard.

Liverpool progressed to Group A in the group stage matches, finishing second behind AS Monaco. Liverpool defeated the eventual group winners from France 2-0 in their first game at Anfield with goals from French striker Djibril Cissé (fast, but inconsistent) and Czech striker Milan Baros (quick, more consistent, but injury prone). Liverpool promptly lost their second game in Piraeus, Greece, to Olympiakos, 1-0. A goalless draw at Anfield against tricky Spanish opponents Deportivo La Coruna from the Spanish north-western region of Galicia placed Liverpool's future in the competition in extreme jeopardy. Fortunately a subsequent 1-0 victory in Spain courtesy of a 14th-minute own goal by the Portuguese central defender Jorge Andrade put Liverpool's progress back on track.

Even then Liverpool made life extremely difficult for themselves in their first group match, losing 1-0 to Monaco, the only goal in the French principality coming from the diminutive, but hugely talented Argentine forward Javier Saviola. Everything hinged on the last game. Liverpool had to win and hope for a Greek loss. Both events occurred fortuitously, and it was that man Gerrard who unleashed a spectacular 25-yard half-volley to confirm Liverpool's good fortune, the third goal four minutes from time in a 3-1 victory against their closest rivals for the second spot Olympiakos. The great Brazilian, Rivaldo, still an immensely impressive force in midfield for the Greeks despite being in the latter stages of his career, opened the scoring in the 26th minute. Better known for his Barcelona career 1997–2002 (86 goals in 157 games), Rivaldo still garnered 36 goals in 70 appearances for Olympiakos 2004–07. In all, the Brazilian colossus scored 293 career goals in 553 matches, an incredible goal return for a midfield player. Florent Sinama Pongolle, the Reunion-born forward (anyone remember him?) equalised in the 47th minute, but it took until the 81st minute until the 'Anfield Roar', legendary on European nights, almost willed the second goal from striker Ian Mellor, another fringe player at Anfield. Gerrard put the icing on the cake four minutes later in a dramatic finale. Liverpool and Olympiakos both finished Group A on ten points, the Merseysiders progressing to the knock-out stages by dint of a superior goal difference to the Greeks.

AC Milan suffered no such traumas in qualifying for the knock-out stages, topping a Group F including the mighty Barcelona with 13 points. Their first game in the Ukraine resulted in a 1-0 over Shakhtar Donetsk, the goal scored by the fine Dutch midfielder Clarence Seedorf. Celtic were next to feel the force of Milan's firepower, goals from Ukrainian maestro Andriy Shevchenko and

Italian national striker Filippo Inzaghi supplemented by an injury time goal from the wily midfield master Andrea Pirlo. Slovakian centre-back Stanislav Varga equalised Shevchenko's early strike in the 74th minute, only for Milan to leave it late before triumphing 3-1. Shevchenko was again on the mark in a second consecutive home game for Milan, his goal the only difference between 'I Rossoneri'('The Red and Blacks') and Barcelona.

Barcelona reversed matters in Milan's fourth group game. Shevchenko opened the scoring in the 17th minute, but Cameroon striker Samuel Eto'o (four times African Footballer of the Year, UEFA Club Forward of the Year the following year, 2006) equalised before half-time. Ronaldinho, the great Brazilian forward, Ballon d'Or winner 2005, scored the winner as Barcelona came through 2-1. No disgrace for Milan to lose a game where the scorers netted a combined total of 178 goals between them for Barcelona. It was Barcelona's curse to be surprisingly held at home in their next match by Celtic – courageous striker John Hartson scoring in a 1-1 draw – and subsequently to lose 2-0 in the Ukraine to Shakhtar Donetsk, another exciting African player, the Nigerian Julius Aghahowa scoring both goals.

Milan went about their business in their usual slick, professional style, despatching Shakhtar 4-0 at the San Siro, two goals apiece from exciting foreign forwards, the Brazilian Kaka and the Argentine Hernán Crespo. A last-game defeat for Barcelona in the Ukraine merely confirmed Milan's place at the top of Group F, Milan drawing 0-0 in Glasgow against Celtic.

In the round of 16 in what seemed an eternally long competition 2004–05, Liverpool were paired with German club Bayer Leverkusen. Liverpool promptly won both ties by a 3-1 scoreline, goals at Anfield from Spaniard Luis Garcia, Norwegian left-back John Arne Riise, and German midfielder Dietmar 'Didi' Hamann (evidence of the multinational nature of the modern Premier League). Two goals from the wide midfielder-cum-winger Garcia, and a further strike from Milan Baros repeated the scoreline in the north-Rhine Westphalia region of Germany, concluding a 6-2 aggregate victory.

The last eight was a completely different story as Liverpool faced the mighty Italians Juventus. Early goals from Finnish centre-back Sami Hyypiä and Garcia (he was having quite a tournament too) gave Liverpool a cushion, but a second-half response from Italian defensive legend Fabio Cannavaro, the captain of Italy's World-Cup winning team the following year of 2006, put the tie on a knife-edge. Liverpool subsequently used all their European experience and know-how to defy Juve in Turin, somehow contriving a goalless draw to progress with a 2-1 aggregate victory.

The semi-final against Chelsea, an all-English affair (with scarcely an English player on the pitch!), proved to be a tight, feisty affair that is remembered by both sets of fans for vastly differing reasons. Liverpool won the home tie 1-0, Garcia scoring the only goal. Baros appeared to be felled by the onrushing Petr Cech, Garcia followed up forcing the ball goalwards. The goal was given – but in pre-VAR days – Chelsea vigorously contested that the ball had not crossed the line. Jerzy Dudek saved from Frank Lampard's free kick in the first half. Eider Gudjohnsen's second-half drive cleared the far post as Liverpool held on.

Liverpool fought tooth and nail to protect their lead in the second leg at Stamford Bridge. The Blues laid siege to Liverpool's goal, but the Merseysiders defended heroically to reach the final in Istanbul. It had been a coruscating journey at times.

AC Milan were pitted against our own Manchester United in the last 16, winning both ties 1-0. Crespo scored a 78th-minute winner at Old Trafford, repeating the feat in the San Siro, Milan winning two close encounters by a 2-0 aggregate score. Somewhat surprisingly Milan won a derby contest in the quarter-finals by a huge 5-0 aggregate margin. Facing Inter Milan in the first leg, goals from Dutch defender and ex-Manchester United star Jaap Stam and Shevchenko clinched a 2-0 win. With AC winning the second leg 1-0 flares were thrown on to the pitch by Internazionale fans. One struck AC's Brazilian goalkeeper Dida. AC Milan were awarded an abandoned match by a 3-0 margin. Equally controversial to Liverpool's 'ghost goal', as embittered Chelsea manager José Mourinho called it, Milan went through to the last four in unfortunate circumstances; although at 3-0 the tie was virtually over anyway. Shevchenko had given AC a 30th-minute lead. The flares were thrown after Esteban Cambiasso's 72nd-minute equaliser for Inter was disallowed for a push. Cambiasso, the Argentinian midfielder, enjoyed a brief spell with Leicester City in 2014–15, his class obvious even if his fitness betrayed him. Controversy mired this 2004–05 Champions League tournament.

A 2-0 home victory in the first leg of the semi-finals against Dutch club PSV Eindhoven, goals coming from, inevitably, Shevchenko, and skilful Danish second striker Jon Dahl Tomasson, suggested a serene passage to the final for 'I Rossoneri' – although Tomasson's second goal only came in the 90th minute. PSV had other ideas. A ninth-minute goal from livewire South Korean midfielder Park Ji Sung gave PSV hope – Park would sign for Manchester United the following season, completing 135 games for Alex Ferguson's side in a lively seven-season stay. Two further goals by Dutch international midfielder Phillip Cocu arrived in the 65th and 92nd minutes. Fortunately for Milan, midfielder Massimo Ambrosini's 91st-minute strike that sandwiched Cocu's goals just about saved the day for Milan, who won through to Istanbul on away goals. It had been quite a ride for Liverpool and AC Milan – the final would provide even greater drama.

The kingpins of Liverpool's defence on this dramatic evening were the centre-backs Jamie Carragher and Finnish international Sami Hyypiä, These titanic central defenders were flanked by able full-backs in the Republic of Ireland's Steve Finnan and the Malian international Djimi Traoré. Traoré won only six caps for Mali, where Finnan represented his country 53 times, scoring twice. Polish goalkeeper Jerzy Dudek (60 international caps) was a fine athletic presence between the posts for Liverpool.

In his formative years as a young Polish professional with 3rd Division Concordia Knurow, Jerzy Dudek set a record of 416 minutes without conceding a goal. After four seasons with Concordia and one with Sokol Tychy, Dudek joined Feyenoord in Holland in 1996. Made to wait a whole season before debuting for Feyenoord, he made up for lost time, playing in every Eredivisie game for four seasons beginning 1997–98. Feyenoord won the 1998–99 Eredivisie. Dudek won the Dutch Golden Shoe – Dutch Footballer of the Year – in 2000, the first non-Dutch player to achieve the feat.

Dudek joined Liverpool – along with Chris Kirkland (signed from Coventry City, ostensibly to replace Sander Westerveld, but Dudek supplanted him in the race for new first-team goalkeeper) – in August 2001. Settling in well at Anfield, Dudek was nominated at the season's end alongside Bayern Munich's Oliver Kahn and Juventus's Gianluigi Buffon for the 2001–02 UEFA Goalkeeper of the Year award – Kahn won it. In 2002–03 Dudek suffered a few lapses (the great Peter Shilton endured the odd mishap) but recovered to win the Man of the Match award as Liverpool beat Manchester United in the League Cup Final 2-0. Dudek cemented his place in the hearts of Anfield fans with a double save from Andriy Shevchenko late in extra time of this 2004–05 Champions League Final, in addition to saving spot-kicks in the penalty shoot-out from Andrea Pirlo and Shevchenko as Liverpool triumphed. Dudek thought the second save in extra time from the great Shevchenko was his best-ever save – it was certainly the most crucial.

In 2005–06 Dudek lost his place to the Spaniard Pepe Reina following an injury. Dudek's 'Shevchenko double' has been voted the greatest Champions League moment of all time in a poll conducted by UEFA.com.

Moving to Real Madrid in 2007–08, Dudek played only two La Liga games in four seasons due to the presence of the iconic goalkeeper Iker Casillas. Dudek's calmness when called upon, and his loyalty to the team, earned him great admiration from his peers, even though his appearances for Real were rare in the extreme. Liverpool fans felt a debt of gratitude for this fine shot-stopper at the end of this Miracle of Istanbul.

Steve Finnan had been round the block a bit by the time he joined Liverpool in 2003. Part of Wimbledon's youth set-up, Limerick-born Finnan first played semi-professionally for Welling United 1993–95. Finnan's professional debut came with Birmingham City in 1995–96. A loan spell with Notts County culminated in a permanent transfer for the 1996–97 season. Sadly for Finnan, County were relegated to the 3rd Division. Finnan subsequently helped County win the 3rd Division title in 1997–98 with a record points total, a season in which the club won ten consecutive matches, a record still standing in 2021.

Signed by Liverpool hero Kevin Keegan for 2nd Division Fulham in November 1998, the Cottagers promptly won that division in the spring of 1999. In 2000–01 Fulham won the 1st Division Championship under French midfield legend Jean Tigana. Playing for Fulham in the Premier League 2001–02, Finnan was voted into the PFA Team of the Year in addition to winning Fulham's Player of the Year. The next incoming manager, Welshman Chris Coleman, presided over a flirtation with relegation in 2002–03, but Premiership clubs were queuing for Finnan's signature.

Liverpool won the race to sign Finnan in August 2003. Injury disrupted his first term at Anfield, but the Irishman returned strongly in 2004–05. He scored his one and only Liverpool league goal against West Bromwich Albion, played in the League Cup Final, and only a thigh injury at half-time of this Champions League Final prevented him completing the match. An ever-present in 2005-

06, Liverpool broke their previous highest points total in the Premier League (although finishing third, nine points behind winners Chelsea), securing 82 points. 2006–07 saw Liverpool reach the Champions League Final again, this time losing to AC Milan, Finnan resisting the challenge of Spaniard Alvaro Arbeloa to hold on to the right-back berth. Losing out to Arbeloa in the main in the following season, Finnan decided on pastures new.

Moving to Spain, further injuries restricted Finnan's appearances with Espanyol to a meagre four games. A better season followed, after mutually terminating his contract in Spain, at Portsmouth on England's south coast. Finnan appeared 21 times for the Fratton Park club, his last game coming in the 2010 FA Cup Final, a 1-0 defeat against Chelsea, a match decided by a Didier Drogba goal. Finnan's finest international moments occurred at the 2002 World Cup, the Republic of Ireland making the second round of the tournament for only the third time in their history. Sadly, the Irish lost a penalty shoot-out 3-2 to Spain after extra time.

How different were the Liverpool centre-backs on this wonderful evening in Istanbul. Jamie Carragher, Bootle-born, a proud scouser, an Everton supporter as a boy, and beside him the stylish, classical centre-half, the Finn Sami Hyypiä. I have never forgotten the sound of Carragher's voice floating noisily in the air at Crystal Palace's Selhurst Park ground, a day on which I took my sons to see Liverpool play in South London. Carragher was clearly the organiser-in-chief, his high voice chirruping orders to fellow defenders. It was my abiding memory of the day.

Despite his allegiance to the blue half of Merseyside as a youngster, Carragher cemented his place in Liverpool's history 1996–2013, completing 508 Premier League games, not playing professionally for any other club. Carragher was vice-captain; the club's second longest serving player; he appeared the most times for Liverpool in European competition (149 games); and completed a total of 737 games for the club.

Marked out as a player with a big future from a young age, Carragher attended the FA's School of Excellence at Lilleshall in his youth. Carragher did indeed attend Everton's School of Excellence aged 11, only switching to Liverpool due to the superiority of their School of Excellence, then supervised by Steve Heighway. No surprise there, given the classy, cultured manner of Heighway's own football. Liverpool defeated West Ham United 4-1 on aggregate in the 1996 FA Youth Cup Final – Frank Lampard and Rio Ferdinand featured in opposition to Carragher for the Hammers. Carragher admits that Liverpool were not the best team technically in the competition, but won out by virtue of sheer team spirit – and the goals of Michael Owen.

Carragher alternated between midfield and defence early in his Liverpool career – scoring for the first team against Aston Villa with a header, but it's as a defender he became best regarded. In the 1998–99 season (his third in the first team set-up) Carragher was named the club's Player of the Year. For all Carragher's motivational and organisational skills Gérard Houllier preferred Hyypiä and the Swiss player Stephane Henchoz as centre-backs, Carragher switching to full-back in this scenario. In the 2000–01 season Carragher played at left-back as Liverpool won the FA Cup, the League Cup and the UEFA Cup.

A knee injury put Carragher out of the 2002 World Cup; a broken leg continued an ill-fated run in 2003. The emergence of Finnan and the Norwegian John Arne Riise threatened Carragher's Liverpool future, but his positivity saw him return in 2004–05. Then-manager Rafael Benitez moved him to centre-back, Carragher remaining there for the rest of his career. Carragher forged a commanding partnership with Hyypiä – the rest is history. Carragher won Liverpool Player of the Year at the end of the 2004–05 season, even being nominated for the prestigious Ballon d'Or – he finished joint 20th in the poll – Steven Gerrard's Champions League exploits earned him a third placing behind Frank Lampard and winner Ronaldinho of Barcelona.

This 2004–05 Champions League Final was undoubtedly a career highlight for Carragher and Gerrard. Carragher continued his cup successes with Liverpool in 2006, the club defeating West Ham United 3-1 on penalties after drawing the match in the 120 minutes 3-3. Carragher had the misfortune to score an own goal to put West Ham 1-0 up. Reaching the Champions League Final again in 2007 was a massive achievement – winning the Premier League continued to elude the Merseysiders. Liverpool again defeated Chelsea at the semi-final stage – but Milan gained revenge for their 2005 defeat in the final. Carragher's personal consolation came in winning Liverpool Player of the Year for a third time – the Anfield fans loved his total commitment. The level of Carragher's commitment was shown in 2009, when he clashed on-field with teammate Arbeloa, his desire to keep a clean sheet against West Bromwich Albion the reason.

Having joined Liverpool aged nine, Carragher finally retired on 7 February 2013. Jamie Carragher holds the record for the most England U-21 caps (27), largely playing as a defensive midfielder. He played 38 times for England seniors. Controversially he opted to withdraw from England duties in 2007, feeling Steve McLaren was overlooking him. Fabio Capello recalled him in 2010 as England were suffering injuries to key defenders before the South Africa World Cup. He was selected by Capello for the first two games of the tournament, but a booking kept him out of the third match. Capello then selected West Ham United's Matthew Upson – a mistake in my view – for the knockout stage match against Germany. England lost 4-1.

As a full-back Carragher was sometimes criticised for lacking pace and technique, but his renaissance came under Benitez, the central defenders position suiting his organisational skills, motivation and reading of situations to a tee. Carragher's tackling could be ferocious, his team ethic and club loyalty seeing him retrieve many a last-gasp situation in front of his own goal. Didier Drogba named Carragher as his toughest opponent in football – some reckoning from the monster-like competitor of Chelsea folklore. As a pundit and football writer, Carragher's formerly aggressive approach has been replaced by an eloquent, erudite commentator on the game he made such an impact on as a player for 17 seasons at Anfield.

Sami Hyypiä was a player blessed with similar organisational skills to Carragher, though arguably, blessed with superior technique. The Finn also stood three inches taller than Carragher at six feet four inches, his height guaranteeing him aerial supremacy in defence, and making him a serious threat at set-pieces for Liverpool. Hyypiä was born in the medieval city of Porvoo in southern Finland, 50 kilometres from Helsinki. He played one season as a professional with Kumu 1990–91, then four with MyPa in Kourda, 134 kilometres north-east of Helsinki. With MyPa, Hyypiä swiftly became team captain, winning the Finnish Cup in 1992 and 1995. Moving to Willem II IN Tilburg, southern Holland in 1995, Hyypiä's leadership qualities saw him become captain again in Holland, winning the Player of the Year Award in his last season at Willem II, 1998–99, as the club qualified for the Champions League.

Hyypiä, who trialled under Kevin Keegan at Newcastle in 1995, did not partake in Willem II's 1999–2000 Champions League adventure, instead belatedly moving to England (surely Keegan and Newcastle missed a trick), signing for Liverpool and Gérard Houllier. A Liverpool supporter as a boy, Hyypiä had been recommended to Liverpool former chief executive Peter Robinson by a TV cameraman. Unknown in England, Hyypiä was expected to be used as cover, but instantly formed an exceptional partnership with Stéphane Henchoz. Ten years later Liverpool man mountain and legendary captain from the 1960s, Ron Yeats, described the deal as one of Liverpool's best-ever signings.

In 2000–01 Hyypiä became joint captain with Robbie Fowler and Jamie Redknapp – Redknapp's injury-plagued season deeming Hyypiä and Fowler as shared captains at the end of a triple trophy-winning season. Hyypiä's impact was so great at Liverpool he won three consecutive FAF Finnish Footballer of the Year awards 2001–03. He became overall captain of Liverpool in 2002 when Fowler and Redknapp left the club, but an upsurge in his performances resulted when Steven Gerrard relieved him of captaincy duties in 2003. After this astonishing Champions League triumph in 2005, Hyypiä found himself third in the captaincy pecking order behind Gerrard and Carragher.

Permanently linked with other Premier League clubs – he had plenty of admirers among his peers – Hyypiä remained with Liverpool until May 2009, Benitez feeling he was an excellent mentor to upcoming central defenders Martin Skrtel and Daniel Agger. Liverpool offered Hyypiä a coaching role at Anfield after he'd completed ten seasons with the club, but Hyypiä decided to continue playing instead, joining German club Bayer Leverkusen in the summer of 2009. Hyypiä came 19th in a Sky Sports Poll of the Top 50 Premier League Foreign Players, and 45th in Four Four Two magazine's 100 Greatest Foreign Players.

Hyypiä's form didn't dip in the Bundesliga, despite being aged 36. He stayed two seasons, being included in the Bundesliga Team of the Year for 2009–10, while German sports magazine Kicker voted him Bundesliga Defender of the Season. Like his scouse teammate Carragher at the heart of this Liverpool side, Hyypiä received 27 Finnish U-21 caps. He succeeded his great friend Jari Litmanen as Finnish national team captain in 2008, going on to play 105 times for the senior Finnish national team, a record only surpassed by the gifted Litmanen.

Upon retirement, Hyypiä's outstanding football brain was put to immediate use with both the coaching staff of the Finland national team and at Bayer Leverkusen. Hyypiä aided Leverkusen's assault on the Bundesliga title 2012–14, but usurping Bayern Munich and Borussia Dortmund was always a tall order.

Third and fourth placed finishes were achieved in 2012–13 and 2013–14. Hyypiä tried his hand with Brighton and Hove Albion in management the following season without success. The same fate occurred with FC Zürich in Switzerland in 2015–16. In 2020 he returned to coaching, assisting with FC Haka from the Tampere region, north of Helsinki. In the same year my youngest son Daniel, a Liverpool supporter with a poster of the 2005 Champions League-winning team adorning his bedroom wall as a boy, met Sami Hyypiä, a hero of his, at an ice hockey match in Helsinki city centre. Dan's wife Heidi hails from Helsinki.

AC Milan would target Djimi Traoré's flank as the least experienced of Liverpool's defenders on this momentous evening. Thankfully, Liverpool could call upon a vast array of experience and attacking talent in the midfield and forward positions. Playing immediately in front of the back four as a playmaker par excellence was the Spanish international Xabi Alonso. Born in Tolosa in the Basque region of northern Spain, Alonso personified the steady hand at the tiller in this Liverpool team. His first success in the professional game came under former Liverpool striking legend John Toshack at Real Sociedad. Toshack named him captain, Alonso leading the San Sebastian-based club to the runners-up position in La Liga 2002–03, just two points behind the mighty Real Madrid. It was the closest Real Sociedad had come to winning La Liga in 20 years – they'd won the title two years running 1980–81, 1981–82. Alonso was voted Best Spanish Player of the Season by Spanish sports magazine Don Balon. He scored 12 crucial goals in this 2002–03 season. Toshack centred training round Alonso to ensure his touch and control became pivotal to the team.

This 2004–05 season was Alonso's first with Liverpool after five years with Real Sociedad – his impact on the team was instant. Real Madrid were seriously vetting Alonso, but the Basque decided to join the Spanish contingent of players at Anfield instead. Alonso it was who scored the third equalising goal in the 60th minute of this Champions League Final as Liverpool astonishingly netted three times in 15 minutes after the half-time interval to recover a 3-0 deficit.

In the 2005–06 season Liverpool won the FA Cup. A broken ankle in a tackle with Frank Lampard kept Alonso out of the team for three months, but his return was timely, aiding the Merseysiders in a 0-0 draw against Juventus in the Stadio delle Alpi in the Champions League quarter-finals, his astute football brain compensating for his lack of match fitness and the absence of Steven Gerrard through injury. A yellow card received in the 0-0 semi-final draw at Stamford Bridge against Chelsea consequently kept Alonso out of the return leg at Anfield, much to the Spaniard's chagrin. His recompense would come in the final.

This was a season exemplifying the new standards Alonso and Gerrard were setting with their passing ability. In a third-round FA Cup tie with Luton Town, Alonso's vision was evinced with one goal from 45 yards; another from a staggering 65 yards in a 5-3 victory after Liverpool had trailed 3-1. The signing of the Argentine Javier Mascherano and the Brazilian Lucas left Alonso undaunted, Benitez continuing to regard him as his anchor man in midfield, a player of the highest class. In the 2008–09 season Alonso reinforced his importance to Liverpool despite persistent transfer talk, scoring the goal at Stamford Bridge in a 1-0 victory that brought Chelsea's first home defeat in four years.

When Alonso did move to Real Madrid for the 2009–10 season, Gerrard cited his move as the reason Liverpool's form dipped. Again an instant success at the Bernabeu, Alonso helped Real secure a club record 96 points in La Liga in his first season in Spain – it wasn't enough to overcome Barcelona's 99 point haul. This was the third time in Alonso's career this occurred: Real Sociedad 2002–03, Liverpool 2008–09 and now Real Madrid in 2009–10. The Marca daily national sports newspaper voted him into their La Liga Team of the Year as the defensive midfielder.

José Mourinho replacing Manuel Pellegrini at the helm, Real Madrid won the Copa del Rey in season 2010–11; the following season Alonso finally won La Liga with 'Los Blancos' (2011–12). In 2013–14 he won the Champions League again as Real defeated Madrid city rivals Atlético 4-1 after extra time. Sergio Ramos had deprived Atlético of the trophy with a dramatic 93rd-minute equaliser. In extra time Real ran away with it, with further goals from Gareth Bale, Marcelo and a Cristiano Ronaldo penalty.

Alonso ended a career including playing for three of the greatest European football clubs of all time by signing for Bayern Munich for the 2014–15 season. Alonso's metronomic passing style saw him break the record for most completed passes in the Bundesliga in a single game in his first season in Munich (196). Alonso won the Bundesliga three seasons running with Bayern, retiring at the end of the 2016–17 season, along with Bayern captain and highly respected German international full-back Philipp Lahm. Not a prolific goalscorer, but when he did score they were invariably goals of the highest quality, Alonso's 15 Premier League goals with Liverpool were his highest league tally at any professional club (2004–09).

In the era of Barcelona's Xavi, Iniesta and Busquets, Alonso could not always find a place in Spain's midfield, for all his estimable passing quality. Ex-Manchester City legend David Silva and the ex-Arsenal starlet Cesc Fàbregas also came into the Spanish international midfield equation at this time. Alonso did feature in four of Spain's six matches at the Euro 2008 tournament, Spain wining the final 1-0 against Germany, Alonso appearing as a 63rd-minute substitute. At the 2010 World Cup, Alonso started every game as Spain won the tournament for the first time, a chest injury endured in the final meant Alonso was replaced near the end of the 90 minutes, Spain winning 1-0 in extra time through Iniesta's goal. Alonso played in a second European Championship Final in 2012 as Spain swept Italy aside 4-0 to win the trophy again. A disappointing 2014 World Cup followed, defeats suffered against Holland and Chile, Spain exiting in the first round. Alonso announced his international retirement in August 2014. A proud Basque, Alonso also represented the Basque Country national team whenever his other commitments allowed.

As a deep-lying playmaker Alonso was able to display his full range of passing skills. Adept at playing long or short, Alonso's supreme technique and awareness made him the perfect midfield player. Gerrard believes Alonso was the best midfield player he ever played alongside. This wonderful player began managing Real Sociedad's B team in 2019.

On the right side of midfield Luis Garcia's goals were crucial in this 2004–

05 Champions League campaign – three in the first knockout stage games against Bayer Leverkusen; one at Anfield against Juventus in the last eight; the winner against Chelsea in the semi-finals – five in all. Garcia didn't control a game like fellow Spaniard Alonso, but he brought a lively attacking verve to the Merseysiders. Garcia enjoyed a long, varied career 1997–2018, largely in Spain, spending three seasons at Anfield after spending the previous two seasons with Atlético Madrid and Barcelona. At Atlético, Garcia played 30 games, scoring nine goals 2002–03. Moving to Barcelona he netted four times in 25 games as his new team finished second in La Liga behind Valencia – a season in which Real Madrid could only finish fourth. Garcia joined Alonso and fellow Spaniards Josemi and Antonio Nunez (substitutes on this evening) in a four-man contingent at Anfield. Others like goalkeeper Pepe Reina would also join Benitez's procession of Spanish players at Anfield.

In season 2005–06 Garcia's impact diminished, although his clever goal put Chelsea out of the FA Cup semi-finals. Booked in a league game against West Ham United, Garcia duly missed the FA Cup Final against the same opponents. Garcia amassed 30 goals in 121 appearances in all competitions for Liverpool – ten of them coming in the Champions League, proving Garcia's big-game ethos. He returned to Atlético Madrid in 2007–08, playing a further 48 La Liga games, but only a successful season with Puebla in Mexico 2011–12 lit up the later stages of his career (12 goals in 32 games).

Garcia appeared at the 2006 World Cup in Germany. In the qualification period he scored a hat-trick in the 5-1 drubbing of Slovakia in November 2005. In the finals proper he played against Ukraine and Tunisia, appearing as a substitute as Spain lost 3-1 to France in the last 16. In all he played 20 times for Spain, scoring four goals 2005–08.

The left-sided midfielder John Arne Riise, lacked consistency, but at times he could be a powerful force aiding his attack. A stocky presence, Riise played most of his senior football at Anfield 2001–08, completing 234 Premier League games, scoring 21 goals. Starting with Aalesund in Norway in 1996–97, Riise soon joined French side Monaco in 1998. He was a regular in Monaco's Ligue 1 title-winning team of 1999–2000, falling out with then-manager Claude Puel (later of Southampton and Leicester City) when he asked to leave. Fulham and Leeds United expressed interest, but Riise chose Liverpool as his next destination in the summer of 2001, scoring on his debut in a 2001 UEFA Super Cup Final game, won 3-2 by Liverpool against Bayern Munich. In his first full season, 2001–02, Riise chipped in with important Premier League goals, scoring ten in all by the season's end.

Having pipped Chelsea twice in the Champions League semi-finals in 2005 and 2007, Liverpool's jinx on the Blues ended at the same stage in 2008, 4-3 on aggregate. It was Riise's misfortune to score an own goal at Anfield in the first leg in the 95th minute. His place in the team less secure in this season due to the signing of the Brazilian Fábio Aurélio, Riise joined Roma in June 2008. Riise instantly won favour with Roma fans, scoring vital goals against the Milan clubs, Internazionale and AC. Riise also netted against Juventus in January 2010, sealing a dramatic 2-1 victory. There was clearly little wrong with Riise's big match temperament.

Returning to Britain in July 2011, Riise finally joined Fulham, his suitors in 2001 while at Monaco. He played 87 games for the Cottagers, but his best days are remembered in the red shirt of Liverpool. He won the Cypriot Cup with APOEL (Nicosia) in 2015, scoring the fourth goal in a 4-2 win over AEL. APOEL also won the league that season. Internationally, Riise was an unused substitute for Norway at the 2000 Euros co-hosted by Belgium and Holland. Ultimately he played 110 internationals for Norway, scoring 16 goals. He is the most capped Norwegian footballer. One wonders whether fluctuating between left back, left midfield, left-wing hampered Riise's consistency, because when on song he produced many a barnstorming performance.

My youngest son Daniel and I watched a 19-year-old Steven Gerrard raking 70 yard cross-field balls all over the Anfield pitch on a 1999 day as Liverpool defeated Leeds United 3-0. It was evident then that Gerrard was to become one of England's greatest ever players – although his performance in this Champions League Final, along with that in the following year's FA Cup Final, are remembered more vividly than any he produced in the white shirt of England. There is little doubt that Gerrard remains one of the country's best ever midfielders – successive national coaches simply couldn't get the best out of the golden generation of Gerrard, Frank Lampard, Paul Scholes, David Beckham et al.

Gerrard, unsurprisingly, was named Man of the Match in both this 2004–05 Champions League Final and the 2006 FA Cup Final. Liverpool did win the League Cup in 2011–12, beating Cardiff City 3-2 on penalties after extra time, but it was the Premier League Gerrard, as one of the country's top players, craved. It was not to be. Istanbul 2005 was his crowning glory – and what a mighty consolation (in my book it surpasses winning a domestic league title) it turned out to be. The 2018 documentary film about Gerrard, Make Us Dream, reveals pertinently how the boy footballer used to rampage through opponents, single-handedly winning football matches. However good an individual is, football is – and always will be – a team game. Great players sometimes struggle in indifferent teams – but how Gerrard influenced this Istanbul night.

Steven Gerrard had to settle for this glorious Champions League victory, two FA Cups, three League Cups and the 2001 UEFA Cup. He never played in professional football for any other British club in a career spanning 1998–2015 – although Chelsea would have taken him in the blink of an eye had Liverpool relented in the noughties. That might have been interesting given that the problem in the national team at that time was how to accommodate both Gerrard and Frank Lampard. Only after leaving Liverpool in 2015 did Gerrard enjoy an Indian summer playing with LA Galaxy in the NASL.

Gerrard, not a Catholic, was assigned to a Catholic High School upon leaving primary school because the football standard was the best in his locality. Amazingly, Gerrard did not represent England Schoolboys. He trialled with Manchester United, but his heart was set on Anfield, signing for Liverpool professionally in 1997. His nervousness got the better of him initially as a first-team player, games as a right-winger ensuring a stuttering start to his Anfield career. Accelerated growth and persistent playing in his teens were also giving him back problems. Yet in 2000–01, Gerrard played 50 games in all competitions for Liverpool, scoring ten goals, and contributing massively to Liverpool's epic treble trophy-winning season. Scoring in the UEFA Cup Final, Gerrard won the PFA Young Player of the Year award, voted for by his peers.

In the Champions League-winning season o0f 2004–05, Gerrard was awarded the UEFA accolade Club Footballer of the Year. A toe fracture – an ailment I am suffering with as I write, though some 40 years older than the young Gerrard, but still football-related – kept Gerrard out for two months in the 2007 season. Come December, Gerrard had become the first Liverpool player since John Aldridge in 1989 to score in seven consecutive games in all competitions. At the end of the season he was selected in the PFA Team of the Year, marking his 100th European club competition game in 2009 with two goals in a 4-0 victory over Real Madrid in a Champions League tie. Zinedine Zidane remarked that Gerrard's all-round game, while lacking the individuality of a Messi or Ronaldo, made him one of the best players in the world, praising too his inspirational qualities to his teammates. Gerrard also won the 2009 Football Writer's Association Footballer of the Year award.

Gerrard could have moved to Bayern Munich in 2011 but resisted, professing his loyalty to Liverpool, and claiming that to win the league title at Anfield was a greater challenge than winning the Bundesliga with Bayern. How his words would ring true. In 2012, Liverpool were able to overcome the upcoming Manchester City – their rivalry would intensify tenfold in the next decade – 3-2 on aggregate in the League Cup semi-finals, Gerrard scoring in both ties. Cardiff were beaten, not without a scare, in the final. Gerrard celebrated his 400th Premier League match by scoring a hat-trick as Liverpool beat Everton 3-0 in the Merseyside derby. In the 2013–14 season, Gerrard broke Billy Liddell's long-standing record by scoring in 15 successive league campaigns. Sadly for Gerrard, he slipped on the Anfield pitch where he was idolised by Liverpool fans, allowing Demba Ba to skate away and score as Chelsea and José Mourinho deprived him of his long-cherished Premier League title in April 2014. This Suarez-Sturridge-Gerrard team under Brendan Rogers lit up that season with some wonderful attacking football. Sometimes that's not enough in the professional stratosphere of the Premier League. Gerrard, for his part, should be remembered anyway for shouldering the responsibility of Liverpool's vain attempts to win the title over 17 seasons of unswerving commitment to the club's cause.

A player of tremendous drive and passion, Steven Gerrard's range of passing, long-range shooting, tactical intelligence and above all his motivational powers, mark him out as one of Liverpool's greatest ever players. In 114 internationals for England, Gerrard scored 21 goals, a scant return for this exceptional player, and evidence perhaps that his best form was invariably found in the Liverpool shirt he wore with such pride.

Playing in the hole behind the Czech international Milan Baros, it could be argued that Harry Kewell is one of the greatest Australian footballers to grace the Premier League. Indeed, in 2012 Australian fans, players and the Australian media named him Australia's greatest footballer. Kewell's career was blighted by injury. This may be linked to his inconsistent performances at the highest level. No one doubted Kewell's technical gifts and ability.

Born in Sydney to an English father and an Anglo-Australian mother of English descent, Kewell, aged 14, travelled to Thailand, Italy and England with the Marconi Fairfield Australian U-14 side that had won state titles. Leeds United invited him back when he was 15 for a successful trial. He played for Leeds' youth team for three seasons, graduating to the first team, aged 17, in 1996. Come 1999 he played alongside fellow Australian striker Mark Viduka for a talented Leeds side. At the end of the 1999–2000 season Kewell had won the PFA Young Player of the Year award and been selected in the PFA Team of the Year. Inter Milan bid £25 million for him, Leeds rejecting the offer. With Leeds suffering financial difficulties, Kewell left for Liverpool for the 2003–04 season having scored 45 goals in 180 matches for Leeds in eight seasons.

AC Milan, Chelsea, Barcelona, Manchester United, Arsenal – Kewell had no shortage of admirers. Kewell only ended up at Anfield to assuage the desires of his agent. An out of court settlement followed. Despite the controversy, Kewell stayed with Liverpool until 2008, scoring his first goal for the club in the Merseyside derby against Everton. He ended his first season at Anfield level with Emile Heskey on seven goals, the pair trailing Michel Owen as Liverpool's top scorer. Kewell's tally of ten goals overall included three in the UEFA Cup, suggesting that international/European football suited his technical skills. Ironically, the 2004–05 season of this Champions League Final was not his best as he suffered a succession of niggles. His injury plight affected his performance in this Istanbul final.

The following season, a better one for the injury-plagued Australian, saw him start the FA Cup Final against West Ham United, only to be withdrawn with an abdominal/groin strain. In the 2007 Champions League Final against AC Milan, Kewell came on as a substitute for the Dutchman Boudewijn Zenden as Liverpool lost 2-1. Persistent groin strains saw Liverpool cancel his contract in May 2008. Kewell scored just 12 goals in 93 Premier League matches, an unfair reflection of a highly skilled player.

Moving to Turkish club Galatasaray – Leeds supporters resented the decision following clashes that resulted in the deaths of two Leeds supporters in the 1999–2000 UEFA Cup semi-final – Kewell found a new lease of life despite a hernia operation in December 2008. This surely explained Kewell's previous inconsistency. In the 2009–10 season Kewell scored 14 goals in 28 matches in all competitions, a fairer reflection of the talented forward's game. He scored nine goals in 17 League games, playing as the main striker due to his ex-Liverpool and then-current Galatasaray teammate Milan Baros's injury. Curiously, Kewell, an obviously attack-minded player, had twice been asked to fill in at centre-back earlier in the season. Seeking a longer-term contract in 2010, Galatasaray refused that option and Kewell returned to play in Australia. Kewell scored 22 goals in 63 league games for Galatasaray.

Kewell became the youngest player to debut for Australia, aged 17 years and 7 months in April 1996. Australia lost out to Iran in a 1998 World Cup qualifying decider, despite Kewell scoring in both of the two-legged ties. At the 1997 Confederation Cup, Kewell scored the golden goal decider against Uruguay in extra time of the semi-final, only for the Australian upstarts to lose 6-0 in the final against Brazil. Uruguay exacted their revenge, beating Australia in a 2002 World Cup qualification tie. In February 2003 Australia beat England 3-1 in a friendly international, Kewell scoring his country's second goal. At the 2006 World Cup, Kewell scored Australia's second goal as Croatia were held 2-2, securing last-16 qualification for the first time. Septic arthritis – initially diagnosed as gout – put Kewell out of the last 16 game, a 1-0 defeat against Italy. Harry Kewell scored a highly respectable 17 international goals in 58 games,

Since retiring from playing, Kewell has tried his hand at management in English football's lower tiers at Watford, Crawley Town, Notts County, Oldham Athletic and Barnet. Success has eluded him in the cut-throat world of football management.

The Czech striker Milan Baros spearheaded Liverpool's attack in Istanbul. Baros was not a prolific scorer for Liverpool – 19 goals in 68 Premier League matches, but his international record of 41 goals in 93 matches is impressive. Sadly, Baros's time at Liverpool was also marred by injuries.

Starting out with Banik Ostrava in his homeland, Baros scored 22 times in 76 games 1998–2001, winning the Talent of the Year award at the Czech Footballer of the Year Awards. Joining Liverpool in 2002, Baros scored twice on his Premier League debut away to Bolton Wanderers in a 3-2 victory. A broken ankle in September 2003 incurred against Blackburn Rovers was a portent of things to come for Baros at Liverpool. In season 2004–05 he joint top-scored for the club with 13 goals, yet Fernando Morientes was preferred to the Czech in the 2005 League Cup Final, a defeat against Chelsea. Baros started the Istanbul Champions League Final, being substituted after 85 minutes by Frenchman Djibril Cissé after 85 minutes.

Baros's best goals return with any professional club came at Turkish club Galatasaray 2008–13, 48 goals in 93 games. He tried his hand at Aston Villa 2005–07, and Lyon in France 2007–08, and played 12 games on loan with Portsmouth in 2008 without scoring. The Galatasaray move revitalised his career as he became Turkish Super Lig top scorer in 2008–09 with 20 goals. Clearly a Banik Ostrava man at heart, Baros enjoyed four spells with his first club, 1998–2001, 2013, 2014–15 and 2017–2020, totalling 45 league goals in all, an impressive 16 in 58 games in the latter spell as his career petered out at the age of 38 in 2020.

Internationally, Baros impressed at the 2004 Euros, scoring in victories over Latvia (2-1) and Holland (3-2). In the third match he appeared only as a substitute against Germany, but scored the winning goal in a 2-1 victory. In the quarter-finals, Baros netted twice as the Czechs defeated Denmark 3-0, finishing with the Golden Boot as the tournament's five-goal top-scorer. Having beaten giants Holland and Germany, the Czech Republic fell at the semi-final stage, beaten 1-0 by surprise eventual winners Greece in extra time. A further five goals followed in 2006 World Cup qualification, but a foot injury kept Baros out of the team until the Czech's final group game with Italy, a 2-0 defeat condemning his country to non-qualification to the knockout stages. Baros eventually lost his centre-forward's position to the more traditional No. 9 in the shape of Jan Koller, who ultimately passed Baros's total of 41, reaching 55 international goals. Koller had his merits as a conventional aerial presence, but couldn't match Baros's mobility and dribbling skills.

The substitutes who entered the field of play for Liverpool in Istanbul all offered the team considerable quality: the German midfielder Dieter Hamann gave the side poise and control; Cissé gave the Reds pace and goal threat if lacking consistency; Baros's Czech international teammate Vladimir Smicer offered consistency, all-round skills and excellent technique.

What a daunting prospect AC Milan were in opposition to Liverpool in Istanbul. The final lives on in memory as the Miracle of Istanbul, and miraculous it was as Liverpool overcame an Italian team with four outstanding Italian internationals and seven overseas superstars. By rights Liverpool should have been beaten, but never doubt the Liverpool team spirit.

In goal, Brazilian keeper Dida was a giant of a man at six feet five inches. In the 2003 Champions League Final 0-0 draw with Juventus, Dida's three penalty saves enabled AC Milan's victory in the penalty-shoot-out – a scary prospect for the Liverpool players at the end of 120 minutes here in Istanbul. Dida spent the years 1992–2000 plying his trade in Brazil, primarily with the Belo Horizonte club Cruzeiro (120 games 1994–98). Transferring from Corinthians in 2000, Dida completed 206 games for AC Milan 2000–10. Initially behind Christian Abbiati as Milan's first choice keeper, Dida came good in the 2003–04 season, winning the Serie A Goalkeeper of the Year award, the first non-Italian to do so. In this 2004–05 season, Dida conceded only three goals in Milan's first ten Champions League ties, including a run of five consecutive clean sheets (it helped having Paolo Maldini and Alessandro Nesta in front of him, not forgetting Cafu and Jaap Stam). Dida extended his clean sheet run to seven by the semi-final stage of this 2004–05 season before PSV Eindhoven and future Manchester United star Park Ji-Sung finally scored against him. At the end of this season he came a career second-best in the 2005 IFFHS World's Best Goalkeeper award behind Chelsea's Petr Cech. Milan lost in the semi-final to Barcelona the following season (2005–06), Dida's seven-match goalless streak in the tournament surpassed by Arsenal's German international Jens Lehmann (ten clean sheets). Despite a personal dip in form, Dida helped Milan win the trophy in 2007, avenging their 2005 defeat against Liverpool.

Capped 91 times for Brazil 1995–2006, Dida was sometimes guilty of errors – lapses of concentration being the goalkeeper's lot. He was part of Brazil's triumphant 2002 World Cup squad, although only as backup to Marcos in goal. A commanding presence, an outstanding penalty-kick saver, perhaps at six feet five inches Dida found it difficult to get down quick enough to low shots? He belied his physique with a degree of athleticism, but question marks hang over his placing in the very top tier of world goalkeepers.

At right-back, Brazilian international captain Cafu offered exceptional energy and reliability. He is the most capped Brazilian player of all time (142 caps), representing his country at four consecutive World Cups 1994–2006, and the only player to have ever appeared in three consecutive World Cup Finals, 1994, 1998, 2002. Cafu may have lacked the charisma and galloping runs of the classic 1970 World Cup-winning team's Carlos Alberto, but was arguably a better defender. In 1994 Cafu was named South American Footballer of the Year, a mark of the regard with which he was held in that continent.

Cafu spent eight seasons in Brazil, mainly with Sao Paulo, before signing for Roma in 1997, staying until 2003, completing 163 Serie A games in the Italian capital. Nicknamed 'Il Pendolino' ('The Express Train') at Roma, Cafu won his first Serie A title with the club in 2001. Moving to AC Milan for the 2003–04 season, Cafu promptly won the Scudetto in his first season at the San Siro.

Cafu held the record for winning the most World Cup matches (15) until surpassed by Germany's Miroslav Klose in 2014. Brazil were unable to repeat their previous successes at a World Cup – winners 1994, beaten finalists 1998, winners 2002, in 2006, the 36-year-old Cafu retiring from international football two years later. A rapid, energetic, team-oriented player, Cafu represented the best of modern-day Brazilian players.

With Stam losing favour with Alex Ferguson at Manchester United, here forming an exceptional centre-back pairing with Alessandro Nesta, Paolo Maldini played at left-back in Istanbul. I consider Maldini possibly the best defender I have ever seen in world football. Franz Beckenbauer may be the best footballing defender I've seen, but Maldini had everything. A better defender than Beckenbauer, Maldini possessed great technical skills and positional awareness also. The complete defender then, raised and versed in the Italian art of defending, and part of a famous footballing family, father Cesare played nearly 350 games for AC Milan 1954–1966, winning Serie A four times, and the European Cup in 1963. Paolo's son Daniel now plays as an attacking midfielder for AC, scoring his first senior goal in 2021.

Paolo Maldini played for AC Milan for 25 seasons, winning 25 trophies, including five Champions League titles (the mark of a top, top player), seven Serie A titles and one Coppa Italia. Paolo held the record Serie A appearance record with 647 appearances until surpassed by long-time international teammate goalkeeper Gianluigi Buffon of Juventus in 2020. Buffon and Fabio Cannavaro are the only two players to have beaten Maldini's 126 international caps. Amazingly, Maldini didn't win an international tournament, reaching the final of the 1994 World Cup and the Euros 2000 (defeat to Brazil on penalties, followed by defeat against France). Beaten in the semi-finals of the Euros 1988 and World Cup 2000, Maldini's consolation came in being named in the Team of the Tournament at all four of these competitions.

Maldini's stock as one of the greatest defenders of all time came in being selected in the FIFA World Cup Dream Team in 2003 alongside the likes of Beckenbauer, Zidane, Platini, Maradona, Cruyff and Pele, a poll conducted among 1 million and a half fans worldwide. Second to George Weah in the FIFA World Player of the Year poll in 1995, a travesty given Maldini's consistency and longevity compared to Weah, Maldini also came third in the Ballon d'Or in 1994 and 2003. Aged 39, Maldini won the UEFA Club Football Award for Best Defender, as well as Serie A Defender of the Year in 2004. Incredible! Most outfield players nearly 40 would have seriously lost pace, be retired, or thinking about old age!

Paolo Maldini – his hypnotic eyes suggested total concentration – was the archetypal disciplined, composed defender who read the game superbly. He led by example, his precision tackling compensating for a (slight) lack of pace as he neared 40. An additional attacking threat as a left-back, Maldini's positional sense enabled him to pay his final seasons as a centre-back or libero (sweeper). A great organiser, Maldini could be vocal, but scarcely needed to be, all those playing with him were well aware they were in the presence of greatness.

Alongside Stam, Alessandro Nesta was virtually the young pretender to King Paolo. Nesta also possessed superb man-marking ability, combined with speed, artistry, elegance and excellent ball distribution. Nesta made his name with Lazio in Rome 1993–2002, captaining the team to victory over AC Milan in the 1998 Coppa Italia (3-2 on aggregate, Nesta even scoring the winning goal in the second leg in Rome). In this same season Nesta won Serie A Young Footballer of the Year. In the 1998–99 season Lazio won the European Cup Winners Cup in its final season, 2-1 against Real Majorca of Spain, Nesta captaining the side. Such was Nesta's consistency during this period he was named Serie A Defender of the Year for three seasons running, 2000–2002.

Financial problems forced Lazio to sell the immaculate Nesta to AC Milan for the 2002–03 season. Nesta went on to play 204 Serie A games for AC 2002–2012, winning Serie A twice (2003–04, 2010–11), the Coppa Italia again in 2002–03 – he'd won it again with Lazio in 1999–2000 – and the Champions League twice (2003, 2007). Nesta was one of three successful penalty takers in the penalty shoot-out victory over Juventus in the 2003 Champions League Final.

Like Maldini, Nesta could play anywhere across the back line due to his technical proficiency, balance and ball skills, although centre-back was his best position. Adept at slide-tackling, this skill cost him dearly internationally, as he missed the knockout stages of three World Cups in which he took part through injury. A classy player possessing pace, athleticism, great positional sense, Nesta was only marginally behind the great Maldini in the pantheon of top Italian defenders, receiving 78 caps for his country, winning a World Cup winner's medal in 2006, despite being unable to play in the final because of injury.

AC Milan's midfield was packed with experience and creativity on this night. Playing at the base of a midfield four, the gifted playmaker Andrea Pirlo made up for lack of pace with guile, precision passing, and a Xabi Alonso propensity for building play from the back. Pirlo's standing in world football grew the older he became as he led his team's style of play at will, yet he began life with Brescia as an attacking midfielder, rather than one who imposed a team's style from the back. Pirlo signed for Inter Milan in 1998, but gained little game time. Transferring to city rivals AC Milan, Pirlo became a world-class performer, winning two Serie A titles and two Champions League trophies. AC's technical style suited Pirlo better than Inter's more disciplined approach. He played 284 Serie A games for AC, scoring 32 goals. Trophy-wise, Pirlo fared even better upon moving to Juventus, winning Serie A four times, plus a Coppa Italia trophy. Pirlo is the fifth most capped player for Italia (2022) at international level with 116 caps, being selected in the 2006 World Cup Team of the Tournament. Pirlo was named Serie A Footballer of the Year three times in three consecutive seasons 2012–14. Renowned for his composure, technique, awareness and close control, Pirlo was a fine purveyor of the long ball, and a free-kick specialist to boot.

Ahead of Pirlo on the pitch to his right, fellow Italian international Gennaro

Gattuso was a completely contrasting type of midfield player. A defensive midfielder, but lacking Pirlo's finesse, Gattuso's role relied on his aggression, tackling ability and fearsome work-rate. Beginning with Perugia in 1995, the battling Gattuso spent a season in Glasgow with Rangers in 1997–98. Dutch coach Dick Advocaat curiously played Gattuso as a full-back, making a return to Italy to play for newly promoted Salernitana a formality in Gattuso's mind. AC bought him from the Campania, southern Italy club for the 1999–2000 season.

Gattuso spent the large majority of his career in Milan 1999–2012, becoming captain of the team when Paolo Maldini retired in 2009. He completed 335 Serie A games for AC, scoring nine goals, but it was his competitiveness and capacity to break up opposing attacks that marked Gattuso out as one of the most uncompromising defensive midfielders of his generation. A player opponents disliked playing against, the ultra-competitive Gattuso played 73 times for Italy, competing at three World Cups (2002, 2006, 2010) and two European Championships (2004, 2008).

The left side of AC Milan's midfield was occupied by Dutchman Clarence Seedorf, winner of the Champions League as early as 1995 when, aged only 19, he won the trophy with Ajax of Amsterdam. Seedorf was part of a great second generation (the first being the hallowed Cruyff/Neeskens/Krol group) of Dutch players that included Ruud Gullit, Marco Van Basten and Frank Rijkaard. Seedorf's stock is high enough to make him a four-time Champions League winner (twice with AC Milan, 2003 and 2007, previously also with Real Madrid in 1998).

Surinam-born, Seedorf moved to Flevoland in central Holland as a two-year-old with his family. His father Johan was a former player and talent agent. A talent agency set up by the other Johan – Cruyff – recruited Seedorf to the Ajax Youth Academy. The same agency also scouted Frank and Ronald de Boer, Edgar Davids and Patrick Kluivert. Seedorf debuted for Ajax aged 16 years and 242 days, the youngest ever debutant for the club at the time. In his second full season he helped Ajax win a Dutch treble of Eredivisie, KNVB (Dutch) Cup and Dutch Super Cup (held between the league winner and the KNVB winner), the latter the equivalent of the English Charity Shield, otherwise known as the Johan Cruyff Shield.

A season with Sampdoria led to his transfer to Real Madrid in 1996, the club immediately winning the 1997–98 Champions League Final against Juventus 1-0. A season at Inter Milan followed, Seedorf scoring Inter's first goal in a 2-1 aggregate Coppa Italia win over Lazio. Seedorf moved to AC Milan in 2002 in an exchange deal with Franco Causio. It seems AC got the better deal, Seedorf helping Inter's rivals win the Coppa Italia in the 2002–03 season 6-2 on aggregate against Roma. Seedorf played an important role in this AC Milan team, dropping a little deeper to enable the more attack-minded Kaka to push on. The 2003 Champions League was won, the 2007 trophy followed, Seedorf being voted the best midfielder in the competition. Passing 395 appearances, Seedorf overtook legendary Swedish player Nils Liedholm as Milan's most appearing foreign player. Seedorf won Serie A twice with AC, 2003–04, 2010–11. Upon leaving after a hugely successful decade, AC'S Chief Executive Adriano Galliani praised Seedorf's "world class" contribution to the club.

On the international scene, Seedorf appeared in three tournament semi-finals with Holland: the 1998 World Cup, and the 2000 and 2004 Euros. His country were unable to take the final step. Fit, creative, athletic, tactically astute – he earned the nickname 'Il Professore' in Italy – Seedorf was another complete all-round midfield player. He played 87 times for Holland, scoring 11 goals, scoring on his debut, a 5-0 rout of Luxembourg, in 1994. His last match for Holland came in 2008.

The Brazilian Kaka revelled in his license to break forward and support Hernán Crespo and Andriy Shevchenko thanks to the discipline of Pirlo, Gattuso and Seedorf behind him. The latter's presence allowed Kaka to play in the hole as a supplementary striker. Kaka is one of eight players to have won the World Cup, the Champions League, and the Ballon D'or (2022) – the latter won in 2007, acquiring twice as many votes as Cristiano Ronaldo and Lionel Messi in second and third, the players who would dominate the voting in the coming decade. Aged 18, Kaka suffered a serious spinal injury in a swimming pool accident. The spiritual Kaka attributed his recovery to God.

Twenty-three goals in 59 games for first professional club Sao Paulo in Brazil alerted top European clubs. AC Milan paid £8.5 million for Kaka in 2003, then-chairman Silvio Berlusconi feeling the talented Brazilian was a snip in the world football transfer market. Joining a team that had just won the 2003 Champions League, Kaka instantly replaced the impressive Portuguese midfielder Rui Costa in Milan's starting line-up. In this 2004–05 Champions League Final, Kaka's positioning in the hole, his linking play, made him unplayable in the first half, winning the free kick leading to the first goal, starting the move for the second, and supplying the assist for the third as AC seemed out of sight at 3-0 at half-time. In the 2007 final he won the free kick for AC's first goal, and supplied the assist for the second as the 'Rossoneri' (the red and blacks) exacted their revenge upon Liverpool 2-1.

When Shevchenko departed for Chelsea at the beginning of the 2006–07 season, Kaka pushed forward to support Filippo Inzaghi, scoring his first Champions League hat-trick against the Belgians Anderlecht in the group stages. Kaka was voted Top Forward in this 2006–07 Champions League campaign, and UEFA Club Footballer of the Year, also being voted into the UEFA Team of the Year, and in addition being voted the 2007 IFFHS World's Best Playmaker. He also won the Ballon D'or and Serie A Footballer of the Year for 2007 in January 2008. Quite a season for Kaka.

The BBC reported an offer for Kaka from Manchester City in January 2009, Kaka professing he would be happy to stay with AC Milan indefinitely. At the end of the season Kaka was named in the UEFA Team of the Year for the third time. Money always talks, and after scoring 70 goals in 193 Serie A games for Milan, Kaka left for Real Madrid in time for the 2009–10 season.

Kaka's first season was the record points total season in which Real Madrid could still only finish second behind Pep Guardiola's Barcelona. In August 2010 Kaka underwent knee surgery. A further knee injury in March 2011 didn't stop Real and a resurgent Kaka winning the Copa del Rey in 2011. 2011–12 brought the elusive (in this Barca-dominated era) La Liga title for Real and Kaka, this time Barca having the consolation of the Copa del Rey. After 120 appearances for Real in all competitions, scoring 29 goals and providing 32 assists, Kaka opted to return to AC Milan.

Kaka was immediately made vice-captain with AC, completing over 300 appearances during his second spell at the club. A further seven goals in Serie A followed in 2013–14, but the player opted to spend the last stages of his playing career in the Major Soccer League in America with Orlando City, thereafter returning to his parent club in Sao Paulo in Brazil.

Kaka was part of a Brazilian international team that promised much and delivered little. Their problem? An imbalanced side with outstanding attacking players in Ronaldinho, Ronaldo, Adriano and Kaka that mirrored England's own problems in accommodating Gerrard, Lampard, Beckham and Scholes in the same team. However good individuals are, a team needs balance. Kaka appeared only as a substitute against Costa Rica in the 2002 World Cup, Brazil winning 5-2, in the first round of games. He did not reappear on the World Cup stage until 2006, the Brazilians losing at the quarter-final stage to Thierry Henry's solitary goal for France. Brazil lost out at the same stage 2-1 to Holland in 2010, the usually disciplined Kaka surprisingly sent off against the Ivory Coast for allegedly elbowing an opponent.

Kaka would not win a World Cup with Brazil other than the 2002 tournament in which he briefly appeared. He did not win the FIFA Confederations Cup for the holders of each continent's championship in 2005 and 2009 while at the peak of his powers. Kaka was an unusually athletic and mobile player for a tall man (six feet one inch), his ability to turn exceptional, a trait more witnessed in a player with a lower centre of gravity. Kaka also scored goals aplenty and provided copious assists. As a 'false nine' or player 'in the hole' Kaka is almost without parallel.

At his peak, Ukrainian centre-forward Andrei Shevchenko was regarded as arguably the best striker in Europe. A competitive boxer as a youth, Shevchenko chose football in preference, making a strong impact in his teens at Dynamo Kiev. Debuting at 16, Shevchenko won five consecutive domestic league titles with Dynamo. In his early 20s he alerted top European clubs with his Champions League performances. Incredibly, Shevchenko scored a hat-trick at the Nou Camp in the 1997–98 season, Dynamo astonishingly routing Barcelona 4-0. Shevchenko then scored three times against Real Madrid over two legs. In 23 league matches in 1997–98 Shevchenko scored 19 goals, adding six in ten Champions League matches. In season 1998–99 Shevchenko scored 28 goals in all competitions. The whole of European football was on red alert.

Shevchenko joined AC Milan for the 1999–2000 season. He won Serie A at the first attempt, scoring 24 goals in 32 matches. In 2000–01 he scored 24 goals in 34 matches, including nine in 14 Champions league games. Injury blighted 2002–03, his impact diminished, but he still won the Champions League. In 2004–05 he scored 17 goals in another injury-marred season, scoring all four goals in a 4-0 defeat of Fenerbahce in the Champions League. In doing so he joined an elite group of players: Messi, Van Basten, Inzaghi, Croatian Dado Prso, Ruud van Nistelrooy and Robert Lewandowski. He was the only player to achieve the feat in an away game until Chelsea's Olivier Giroud emulated him at Seville in the 2020–21 season. Shevchenko became Milan's second highest ever goalscorer in 2006, behind the Swede Gunnar Nordahl (1949–1956 at the San Siro, 210 goals), scoring 175 goals in 296 games.

Russian owner of Chelsea, Roman Abramovich, was desperate to sign Shevchenko. The move happened in 2006 after a protracted two-year pursuit, but the Ukrainian, while obviously a class player still, never settled at Stamford Bridge, scoring nine goals in 48 games. When Luiz Felipe Scolari took over at Chelsea, Shevchenko was loaned back to AC Milan. No goals in 18 matches in Serie A in 2008–09 reflected the great Ukrainian's decline. Only a return to Dynamo Kiev revitalised Shevchenko, playing often as a left-winger rather than as a recognised striker. In three seasons Shevchenko netted 23 goals in 55 games, ending with an impressive career total of 235 goals in 497 games.

Shevchenko netted 14 times in Milan derbies – the best return of any forward of any nationality. For Ukraine he scored 48 goals in 111 internationals, helping his country to the quarter-finals of his first World Cup in 2006. Shevchenko won the Ballon d'Or in 2004, the third Ukrainian to achieve the feat after Oleg Blokhin and Igor Belanov, both former Dynamo Kiev stars. Shevchenko quit football for politics in 2012, but has since returned to the game as first assistant manager, then manager of the Ukraine national team. As a player he was fast, mobile, composed in front of goal, a deadly striker in his pomp.

The Argentine Hernán Crespo partnered Shevchenko in attack in Istanbul. Another fine goalscorer, Crespo's time at AC Milan was short-lived, appearing only as a loan player in this 2004–05 season, scoring ten goals in 28 Serie A games. Crespo carried the epithet of the world's most expensive player when transferred from Roma to Lazio in 2000 (£35.5 million). With 35 international goals he lies behind only Sergio Agüero, Gabriel Batistuta and Lionel Messi as Argentina's top scorer.

Crespo has scored goals everywhere he has played: River Plate, 1993–96 (24), Parma 1996–2000 (116), Lazio 2000–02 (39), Inter Milan in three spells 2002–03, 2006–08, 2008–09 (19 in total), Chelsea 2003–08 (20), Genoa 2009–10 (5), and Parma again 2010–12 (10), a total of 197 league goals. Crespo top-scored in Serie A with Lazio in 2000–01 with 26 goals. Considered something of a misfire in his spell in England at Chelsea, he still netted 20 goals in 49 games, often being used only as a backup to the Mourinho favourite (with good reason) Didier Drogba. Winning the Premiership in 2005–06 was Crespo's first league title in European football, amazingly.

Crespo scored six goals in six games for the Argentina U-23s, before graduating to the full national side in 1995. At the 1998 and 2002 World Cups, Crespo was considered backup to Batistuta (a wonderful player my sons and I saw score the only goal for Fiorentina against Arsenal in a Champions League tie at Wembley) At the 2006 World Cup Crespo scored against the Ivory Coast and Serbia and Montenegro before Argentina were knocked out in the quarter-finals by Germany.

With Parma Crespo won the Coppa Italia and the UEFA Cup in 1998–99 (voted Man of the Match in the latter); with Inter Milan he won three Serie A titles in three consecutive seasons 2007–09. Crespo was named in the FIFA World Cup All-Star Team in 2006. Fast, intelligent, positionally aware, two-footed, good in the air, Hernán Crespo was a top striker whose spell at Chelsea, like much of his career, was blighted by injury.

Substitutes for AC Milan in Istanbul included the aforementioned Portuguese midfielder Rui Costa, the highly accomplished centre-back Alessandro Costacurta (59 caps for Italy, 458 appearances for AC Milan), Brazilian left-sided player Serginho (185 Serie A games for AC), and the ex-Newcastle United misfire Dane Jon Dahl Tomasson – he fared better with Feyenoord in Holland and at AC Milan 2002–05.

Liverpool's opponents offered eye-watering opposition, a team of masterful worldwide opponents and highly skilled Italian adversaries versed in the ways of obdurate, organised Italian methodology. In all, the perfect combination of flair and discipline. AC Milan were hot favourites going into this final.

Managers Rafael Benitez and Carlo Ancelotti would match up many times more over the next decade and a half. Benitez's prior experience to this epic final came exclusively in Spain with lesser Spanish clubs. He has since managed Valencia and Real Madrid in Spain; Inter Milan and Napoli in Italy; Newcastle United and Everton in England. Many Everton fans resented his appointment as an ex-Liverpool manager. I have never understood this tribal nonsense. Benitez is a top manager. If he had won something while at Everton 2021–22 the fans would have thought differently. Now he has gone, replaced by Frank Lampard, but I'm sure if Everton had won a cup in his time at Goodison Park resentment would have waned, although tribalism never goes away.

Carlo Ancelotti played 26 times for his country, something Benitez did not (five appearances for the Spanish Universities XI); Ancelotti's club prior to managing AC Milan was Juventus. This appeared to give the Reggiolo-born Emilio Romagna Ancelotti an advantage in experience at the highest level. Ancelotti too would go on to manage Chelsea, Paris Saint-Germain, Real Madrid, Bayern Munich, Napoli, and precede Benitez, ironically, at Everton 2019–2021. A top manager, Ancelotti, in charge of a top team in Istanbul, May 2005.

THE FINAL

How to compete with this ridiculously multi-talented AC Milan team? Liverpool must have wondered as they were rocked in the very first minute of the game. Pirlo's free kick from the right was rifled into the net by Paolo Maldini, a rare scorer. Liverpool battled back, Sami Hyypiä's header saved by Dida. Dudek saved a near-post header at the other end, then breathed a sigh of relief as Kaka's run and feed to Shevchenko saw the latter's goal disallowed for offside. Luis Garcia headed off his own goalline as Liverpool fought off crushing Milan pressure, and then drove a shot over the bar at the opposite end. The pressure showed when Kaka and Shevchenko linked up to enable Crespo to fire a slick second goal. A third, terrific goal was set up by Kaka's wonderful 30-yard ball that bisected Liverpool's usually tight defence, Crespo dinking a delightful shot over the onrushing Dudek. Liverpool could scarcely believe the way they had been overrun as the half-time break arrived with a 0-3 scoreline.

Liverpool came out in the second half with a nothing-to-lose approach. Xabi Alonso drove one shot wide, and then Gerrard's leaping header from a free kick brought one goal back for Liverpool. Gerrard raced back to the halfway line rallying his teammates vociferously. Vladimir Smicer, on as a substitute, fired a cross-shot into goal that deceived Dida in AC's goal thanks to Milan Baros allowing the ball to pass across his stomach. It was enough to put the Brazilian custodian off and Liverpool suddenly had a foothold in the match. The insatiable Gerrard was driving Liverpool on now. When he burst onto Baros's neat back-heel, Gattuso hauled him down in the penalty area. Alonso's penalty kick was saved by Dida, but the Spaniard's swift reaction enabled him to drive the rebound left-footed into the roof of the net. In 16 second-half minutes Liverpool had improbably recovered to 3-3, but it was still AC Milan who looked the more likely to score again in the remaining half an hour of the 90 minutes. Djimi Traoré earnt his corn, clearing off the line from Shevchenko, Jaap Stam glancing a header off the outside of a post.

The first half of extra time saw AC substitute Jon Dahl Tomasson narrowly missing a deep left-wing cross at the far post. In the second period of extra time Dudek saved incredibly from Shevchenko, first from the Ukrainian's bullet header, then with an astonishing reflex save right on the line from the forwards' follow-up, mercifully, the ball cleared the crossbar. The passionate Jamie Carragher then proved his worth as a centre-back with a marvellous recovering tackle after Crespo broke clear. Carragher shone again as he deflected another cross away from lurking Milan forwards. Dudek's heroic double save took the game to penalties.

The immense Dida stood before Liverpool's quest to win the trophy, but the Italian sides' penalties gave Liverpool the edge. Serginho's lofted kick cleared the bar by some distance; Andrea Pirlo's kick was too soft. Liverpool players remained calm with their penalty kicks, and when the hitherto impressive Shevchenko's final penalty kick for Milan was as weak as Pirlo's, Dudek trumped the penalty-save 'King,' Dida, with a save that clinched the cup for Liverpool. Liverpool simply refused to be beaten. AC had the lion's share of the play, but Liverpool's fighting spirit and greater composure in the penalty shoot-out won the night. The game almost equalled the drama of 1999 and Manchester United. These were the two greatest Champions League Finals in English minds in living memory.

2006 CHAMPIONS LEAGUE FINAL
Barcelona 2 v 1 Arsenal

If ever Arsenal were going to win the premier European trophy, this was their time. Blessed with the immaculate Thierry Henry and fellow Frenchman Robert Pires; blessed also with wonderful midfield players in Spain's Cesc Fàbregas and Sweden's Freddie Ljungberg; a rock-like defence starring England's Sol Campbell and Ashley Cole; a reliable anchor man in midfield in the Brazilian Gilberto Silva. Unfortunately for Arsenal they faced a Barcelona side preceding Pep Guardiola's great 'tika-taka' team. Not the team from who you could not retrieve the ball that revolved around Xavi, Iniesta and Messi, but a team who still boasted world-class stars in Portugal's Deco, Brazil's Ronaldinho, and Cameroon's Samuel Eto'o. Winners of the European Cup Winners' Cup in 1994, defeated finalists against Real Zaragoza in 1995, Arsenal had decent recent pedigree themselves in European football – and they possessed better players here in 2006. It wasn't to be enough to overcome a classy Barcelona team.

Route to the Final
Arsenal were confronted by a mediocre set of opponents in Group A at the beginning of the campaign, topping the table comfortably with five wins and a draw. They didn't commence group hostilities in convincing style, edging out Swiss 'minnows' Thun 2-1 at Highbury only by dint of Dennis Bergkamp's injury-time winner. A sterner test faced them in Amsterdam in their next game, Ajax beaten by the same score of 2-1 thanks to a Freddie Ljungberg goal and a Robert Pires penalty. Sparta Prague were beaten comfortably enough in the next match, 2-0, both goals coming from the irrepressible Thierry Henry. Henry and Robin van Persie's double sealed an even more emphatic 3-0 win over Sparta in the return match in London. Another Pires penalty clinched a 1-0 victory over Thun in Switzerland, their final match ending 0-0 against Ajax at Highbury, sealing progression for both teams to the knockout stages.

The Gunners certainly didn't have it easy from here on in. Paired with Real Madrid in the last 16, Henry's 47th-minute goal at the Bernabeu Stadium proved to be the only goal of two ties. Next up: another European giant in Juventus. Cesc Fàbregas and Henry gave Arsenal a 2-0 home win, the Arsenal rearguard again standing firm in a 0-0 draw in Turin. Kolo Touré gave Arsenal a 1-0 advantage at Highbury in the semi-final. Guess what? Arsenal again stood firm in the return match against Villareal in Spain. No goals conceded against three of Europe's top teams in the knockout stages; only two conceded in their group. Sadly, the attacking attributes of Barcelona in the final represented an altogether stiffer test for Arsenal's resolute defence. Anyway, George Graham would have been proud of Arsene Wenger's defensive cohorts.

Barcelona replicated Arsenal's won five, drawn one group stage achievement in Group C, but scored goals for fun. Deco and a Ronaldinho penalty secured their first win, 2-0 over Werder Bremen in Germany. A hat-trick for Ronaldinho (including a penalty kick) and another Deco goal saw Barcelona trounce the Italians Udinese 4-1 in the Nou Camp. Away to Panathinaikos, Barca drew 0-0, subsequently putting the Greeks to the sword 5-0 at the Nou Camp, Samuel Eto'o netting a hat-trick this time, Lionel Messi and Dutch midfielder Mark van Bommel adding the others. A 3-1 win at home to Werder Bremen including goals by Ronaldinho and ex-Glasgow Celtic hero Henrik Larsson was followed by a final 2-0 victory against Udinese, Andres Iniesta, the skilful playmaker, scoring the second goal.

The route forwards was not easy for Barcelona either. Up first, José Mourinho's obdurate Chelsea team. A Thiago Motta own goal gave the Blues the lead shortly before the hour, but John Terry suffered the same fate 12 minutes later, and the livewire Eto'o won the game for Barca in the 89th minute at Stamford Bridge. Ronaldinho netted in the Nou Camp in the 78th minute, Frank Lampard's penalty goal insufficient to stall Barca's progress in the second leg. Barcelona's 0-0 draw in Lisbon against Benfica in the last eight set them up for a 2-0 home win, goals coming from Ronaldinho and Eto'o. Two tight, tense matches followed in the last four, French winger Ludovic Giuly's goal at the San Siro the only goal in two ties with AC Milan. Both Arsenal and Barcelona achieved the hard yards in 2005–06, thoroughly deserving their places in the final.

The German international Jens Lehmann (61 caps 1998–2008) in goal for Arsenal at the Stade de France, Saint-Denis, Paris, didn't always convince with Arsenal – yet his statistics are mightily impressive, especially in the Champions League. Lehmann kept a clean sheet in eight consecutive Champions League matches, going 853 minutes without conceding a goal, eventually completing ten Champions League games without conceding in this 2005–06 season.

Between 1987–1998 Lehmann played 274 Bundesliga games for Schalke 04, even scoring two goals. Schalke won the 1997 UEFA Cup against Inter Milan, both legs won 1-0 by the home teams, Schalke winning 4-1 on penalties, Lehmann saving two spot kicks. This glorious night for Lehmann earned him a prestigious transfer to AC Milan in 1998. Sadly for Lehmann the move quickly backfired, a Gabriel Batistuta hat-trick for Fiorentina against him one of the reasons he lasted only five matches with AC. Returning to Germany, Lehmann continued to suffer inconsistent performances, but he revived sufficiently to win the Bundesliga 2001–02 with Borussia Dortmund. The club also reached the 2001–02 UEFA Cup Final, but lost 3-2 to Feyenoord in the De Kuip Stadium, Rotterdam.

With David Seaman departing Arsenal after 405 Premier League games, Lehmann moved to Arsenal in July 2003. Lehmann could scarcely believe his luck, being part of the 'Invincibles' unbeaten team that won the 2003–04 Premier League with 26 wins and 12 draws, conceding just 26 goals. It didn't hurt having Lauren, Kolo Touré, Sol Campbell and Ashley Cole as a barrier to Lehmann's goal, the tenacious and committed Campbell and Keown applying Italian-style ferocity to the art of defending. Again suffering lapses of concentration, Lehmann lost his place during the 2004–05 season, but fought back to play in the 2005 FA Cup Final, won on penalties after a 0-0 draw with Manchester United, saving Paul Scholes's kick to win the trophy for Arsenal.

Outstanding in 2005–06, better than adequate in 2006–07, Lehmann again lost his place to Manuel Almunia in 2007–08, slipping to third choice at times behind the Pole, Lukacz Fabianski. Lehmann moved to VFB Stuttgart in 2008, returning to Arsenal in 2011 as cover for Almunia, Fabianski and Vito Mannone as the Gunners endured a goalkeeping injury crisis, but played only once more in the Premier League. Lehmann also broke a German international record of not conceding a goal for 681 minutes in March 2006, although his 61 caps included 32 friendly internationals as he was used primarily as back-up to Oliver Kahn. Lehmann clearly peaked 2005–08, notable especially for his prowess as a penalty-kick saver. Adept at intercepting crosses, Lehmann's career was marked by occasional bouts of indifferent form.

The Ivorian Emmanuel Eboué played at right-back on this evening in Paris. An energetic presence, Eboué, like Lehmann, could be prone to inconsistency, making his deployment by Arsenal that of a replacement when the more reliable

Cameroonian Lauren was injured. Eboué played 132 Premier League games for Arsenal 2004–2011, contributing nine goals. Eboué moved to Turkish club Galatasaray in 2011, winning the Turkish League 2011–12, 2012–13 and 2014–15, and the Turkish Cup in the interim season of 2013–14, but along with teammate Didier Drogba suffered abuse from home fans. It seems racist chants were as abundant in Europe then as they have been in recent times. The world is an often intolerant place and football, sadly, attracts its share of xenophobes.

Arsenal had a succession of very decent left-backs from the 1970s onwards: Sammy Nelson, Nigel Winterburn, but Ashley Cole was the best of the lot. A success with Arsenal, he became even better when moving to Chelsea in 2006, many of his peers and the sports media considering him the best left-back in the world. Stepney, East London-born Cole began professionally with Arsenal in 1999, completing 156 Premier League games at Arsenal, scoring eight goals. As adept as an auxiliary attacker as a defender who was able to save countless goals, Cole's pace, athleticism and sheer verve lit up Highbury in the first half of the new decade post-Millennium. With Arsenal Cole won the Premier League twice 2001–02 (a double-winning season) and 2003–04, and the FA Cup three times, 2001–02, 2002–03 and 2004–05. He was voted in to the PFA Team of the Year in 2002–03, 2003–04, 2004–05 and in 2010–11, and into the UEFA Team of the Year in 2004 and 2010.

When Cole moved to Chelsea the transfer saga aroused an almighty rumpus. Arsenal had offered the player a new contract and £55,000 a week. At Chelsea, come 2009 he would be earning £120,000 a week. The Arsenal fans subsequently dubbed him 'Cashley', thinking he'd moved solely for money. Vying with Wayne Bridge for the left-back slot at Stamford Bridge, Cole eventually made the position firmly his own. Chelsea's Player's Player of the Year in 2008–09 and 2010–11, England Player of the Year in 2010, Cole's performances screamed quality when fit, although knee and ankle injuries hampered him during his time at Chelsea. Cole helped the Blues win the Champions League in 2011–12, the following season aiding the club's Europa League triumph (2012–13). He won the FA Cup with Chelsea 2006–07, 2008–09, 2009–10 and 2011–12 during a period when Chelsea seemed to dominate the historic competition. Cole also won the Premier League with Chelsea in 2009–10.

Cole signed for A.S. Roma in Italy's Serie A in 2014, but played only 11 games in two seasons. He tried his luck with LA Galaxy in America's Major Soccer League before returning for a nine-game swansong with Derby County in England's Championship under ex-teammate Frank Lampard. Cole played 107 times for England, debuting under Sven-Göran Eriksson in 2001. He played in three World Cups – 2002, 2006 and 2010, being named in the Team of the Tournament at the 2004 Euros. Considering his attacking qualities, Cole, surprisingly, never scored for England. Cole linked especially well with Thierry Henry and Robert Pires in his time at Arsenal. Cole has been labelled an over-zealous player in some quarters, but his occasional bursts of temper spoke only of a highly committed player whose defensive qualities improved greatly over time. He simply wanted to be the best at what he did, and he probably was for nearly 15 seasons in the Premier League.

Equally tenacious and committed, Sol Campbell possessed a similar streak to Cole. A tough competitor, but also a fine footballer, Campbell immensely strengthened Arsenal's core after achieving the same contribution for North London rivals Tottenham Hotspur. Born Sulzeer Jeremiah Campbell in Plaistow, East London, not far from Cole's upbringing, Campbell enjoyed a 20-year career at the highest level. Born to Jamaican parents, a railway-working father and a Ford factory-working mother, Campbell claims he expressed himself through football as a means of escaping his crowded, claustrophobic childhood. An outstanding youth player, Campbell was part of the FA's School of Excellence at Lilleshall.

Joining Tottenham Hotspur's youth team set-up, Campbell was earmarked as much for his physical presence as his pure ability. With Gerry Francis at the helm, Campbell became club captain in the 1996–97 season. Christian Gross and George Graham followed Francis as Tottenham managers, the strong-minded Campbell not always seeing eye to eye with his bosses. Despite this, Campbell led Tottenham to League Cup success in 1998–99, 1-0 over Leicester City, the injury-time winner coming from long forgotten Danish midfielder Allan Nielsen.

In the summer of 2001 several of the continent's top clubs were eyeing Campbell. He chose to move across London to join Arsene Wenger's Arsenal, Wenger admiring Campbell's powerful presence on a football field. Tottenham fans were less enamoured of Campbell, labelling him 'Judas' – football tribalism again. Campbell felt strongly supported by both Wenger and vice-Chairman David Dein, feeling wanted and protected from homophobic abuse. The move elevated Campbell's career, instant success coming with double success in league and FA Cup in 2001–02, the cup final won 2-0 against Chelsea with goals from Ray Parlour and Freddie Ljungberg. The 2002–03 season saw Campbell selected for the PFA Team of the Year alongside teammates Lauren, Cole, Patrick Vieira, Henry and Pires, half the Arsenal team. The same six players were selected again at the end of the 'Invincibles' season in 2003–04. It was Campbell's third selection in the team.

Campbell's form began to dip post-2004 as he suffered a series of injuries. He recovered sufficiently to be Arsenal's scorer in Paris in this 2006 Champions League Final, but sought pastures new in the summer of 2006. Joining Harry Redknapp's Portsmouth, Campbell captained the team to a surprise 2008 FA Cup Final triumph, 1-0 against Cardiff City, the ex-Arsenal Nigerian striker Nwankwo Kanu scoring the goal. Campbell returned to Arsenal after an abortive one-game spell with Notts County in 2010. A further transfer to Newcastle United saw Campbell become only the second player after Ryan Giggs to play in the Premier league for 19 seasons. Sadly the mind was willing, but the body began to betray Campbell, and he retired in May 2012.

Campbell's early excellence saw him win the 1993 UEFA European U-19 Championships with England, a final triumph coming with a 1-0 win against Turkey. He wasn't able to replicate this success in the senior side, but there were some close moments. Campbell was used as defensive back-up by Terry Venables in the 1996 Euros, the never-to-be-forgotten semi-final penalty shoot-out defeat to Germany. In 1998, Campbell captained England, becoming the second youngest ever captain after Bobby Moore. Campbell's header from a corner-kick in the last

16 of the World Cup appeared to condemn Argentina to defeat, despite David Beckham's sending-off, but the wily Argentines recovered and went on to win on penalties.

At the 2000 Euros, Campbell played in all three group games under Kevin Keegan, but England exited after defeat by Romania. Campbell next partnered Rio Ferdinand at the 2002 World Cup, being the only player from England's team to be selected for the Team of the Tournament. In the quarter-finals of the 2004 Euros, Campbell had a header disallowed against Portugal, another penalty shoot-out defeat resulting. Coming on as a substitute in the 2006 World Cup for the injured Ferdinand, Campbell became the first player to represent England in six consecutive international tournaments. Comfortable in possession, Campbell's distribution was less effective, but his strength, power, pace, and serious threat at set-pieces made him an extremely intimidating opponent. Campbell played 73 times for England, always proud to wear the shirt – not always evident in the past, although the present incumbents seem patriotic.

Alongside Campbell, the Ivorian Kolo Touré exemplified many of his teammates' attributes, pace and power in particular. Touré perhaps lacked Campbell's consistency, but for a while his impact was as great, partnering Campbell in that 'Invincibles' team of 2003–04. Touré signed for Arsenal from Ivory Coast club ASEC Mimosas, going on to play 326 times for the Gunners in all competitions 2002–09. He is to date (2022) the player with the most Premier League appearances from the African continent. As an international player, Touré immediately received a British work permit upon signing for Arsenal. He began his career in England as a defensive midfielder or right-back, only later becoming a stellar centre-back with Arsenal, Manchester City and Liverpool. Touré also struggled for form after succeeding initially, losing his place at Arsenal to either Philippe Senderos or Pascal Cygan. With Campbell moved on after 2006, Touré formed a central defensive pairing with Senderos and went on to captain Arsenal at times from 2007.

In July 2009 Touré joined Manchester City, helping his new club secure a top-four place in his first season. Then-manager Mark Hughes made Touré club captain. In July 2010, younger brother Yaya joined City, the start of a period when, along with David Silva, Yaya was City's most influential midfielder. In and out of the team over the next two seasons, Kolo's 14 Premier League appearances in 2011–12 were enough to secure him his second Premier League title alongside brother Yaya. Touré senior then signed for Liverpool in 2013, playing three seasons at Anfield, but hampered by injuries his performances became increasingly erratic. No one doubted Kolo's powerful impact when fit, and Brendan Rogers signed him to Glasgow Celtic after moving there himself from Liverpool. Touré's season in Glasgow was a successful one, winning the treble of league, Scottish Cup and Scottish League Cup. After not receiving a new contract offer, Touré took on a coaching role at Celtic, subsequently rejoining Rogers' coaching staff at Leicester City in 2019. Touré has been capped 120 times by the Ivory Coast.

Arsenal's midfield on this evening was an extraordinary melange of talents. The guile and trickery of Robert Pires and Cesc Fàbregas; the solidity provided by Gilberto Silva, extra unpredictability supplied by the Belarussian Alexander

Hleb. Pires was a wonderful player, occasionally looking lightweight despite his six feet one inch stature, but a deft ball-player with a supreme touch. His class is borne out by selection into the PFA Team of the Year in 2001–02, 2002–03 and 2003–04. He was also voted the FWA Player of the Year in 2001–02. Arsenal fans voted him the sixth greatest player in the club's history.

I think of Pires as an attacking midfielder, although he liked to come in off the left flank. Ironically, he wore the number 7 shirt on this evening. Born in Reims to a Portuguese father and Spanish mother, Pires was attached to Reims and Metz in his youth career while beginning a two-year sports degree aged 15. Graduating from the Metz youth academy to the first team, Pires won the Coupe de Ligue (the French League Cup) in 1996, Metz finishing runners-up in Ligue 1 on goal difference behind Lens in the 1997–98 season. Pires was also voted Ligue 1 Young Player of the Year in the 1995–96 season. Pires scored 43 goals in 162 matches at Metz.

Joining Marseille for the 1998–99 season, the club were runners-up in Ligue 1 that season, a point adrift of Bordeaux. Marseille also lost the UEFA Cup Final 3-0 to Parma, Hernán Crespo and Enrico Chiesa (father of 2020 Euro-winners Italy's Federico) among the scorers.

Arsenal signed Pires for £6 million in 2000, fending off interest from Real Madrid and Juventus. Pires had big shoes to fill, Arsenal having sold the electric Dutch winger Marc Overmars to Barcelona. Pires struggled initially, commenting on the sheer physicality of English football. Pires began to cast aside his reservations, scoring twice against North London rivals Tottenham Hotspur in the FA Cup semi-final. Pires loved playing against Tottenham, scoring eight times against them in all. Unfortunately for Arsenal they lost the FA Cup Final 2-1 to Liverpool, both goals scored by Michael Owen, although Pires assisted Freddie Ljungberg's goal for Arsenal.

In the 2001–02 season Pires led the assists chart and was voted FWA Footballer of the Year – football writers clearly appreciated Pires's class, even if doubts persisted about the Frenchman's adaptability to the robust Premier League. Arsenal were happy with him as he was voted the club's Player of the Year, the Premier League won to boot. Sadly a cruciate ligament injury kept Pires out of the 2002 FA Cup Final (2-0 versus Chelsea to complete the double) and the subsequent 2002 World Cup. Playing only 20 Premier league games in 2002–03 thanks to his serious injury, Pires, remarkably, scored 14 goals. In addition he scored the solitary winning goal in the FA Cup Final against Southampton.

In the feted 'Invincibles' season that followed, Pires started slowly, but contributed a combined total of 57 goals with Thierry Henry eventually. He contributed the joint best tally of seven assists alongside Dennis Bergkamp as Arsenal remained unbeaten in the league all season. A Pires goal in the first leg of the Champions League quarter-final against Chelsea was insufficient to send Arsenal through, Chelsea winning 3-2 on aggregate. In the 2004–05 season Pires scored another 14 goals, Arsenal beating Manchester United on penalties in the FA Cup Final. Pires's Arsenal career ended here in Paris on a sad note: Arsenal goalkeeper Jens Lehmann sent off in the 18th minute, Arsene Wenger sacrificed him for substitute keeper Manuel Almunia. The decision remains a bone of contention between Pires and Wenger to this day.

Suffering a back-up role with the signings of Ljungberg, Hleb and Antonio Reyes, Pires moved to Villareal after this Champions League Final. Pires, scorer of 62 goals in 189 Premier League games for Arsenal, netted 13 in 103 for Villareal, but a further cruciate ligament knee injury marred his time in Spain. Surprisingly, Pires returned to England in 2010, signing for Aston Villa, but aged 37, his time at Villa amounted to a brief nine league games and one FA Cup goal against Blackburn Rovers.

Pires received 79 caps for France, scoring 14 goals, his most significant contribution on the world stage the pass for David Trezeguet's Golden Goal winner at the 2002 Euros. Pires's record is impressive – doubts lingered about his desire in the Premier League. But two Premier League titles, two FA Cups, a FIFA World Cup (1998) and a European Championship (2002) is not a bad return for a player who had his doubters. In reality, Pires's silky skills showed he was a class act – and when Harry Redknapp took a team of old retired pros to France for the ITV documentary Harry's Heroes in 2021, Pires in opposition to the ex-England players was far and away the best player on the pitch! You don't lose class.

Alexander Hleb was born in Minsk, Belorussia. His father volunteered to help demolish houses made uninhabitable by the Chernobyl nuclear disaster in 1986. Hleb believes the radiation caused his father's ill health. Hleb was still playing for Minsk-based club Isloch Minsk Raion in 2019, the culmination of a 21-season career in professional football. Never a prolific scorer, Hleb's dribbling skills saw him dubbed 'Zauberlehrling' or 'Sorceror's Apprentice' during his time in Germany with VFB Stuttgart.

VFB Stuttgart signed Hleb from BATE Borisov in 2000. In his first full season of 2001–02 in the Bundesliga, Hleb was voted Belorussian Footballer of the Year. In 2002–03 VFB Stuttgart were runners-up in the Bundesliga, though a long way behind predictable winners Bayern Munich. Hleb became VFB's playmaker, helping his team to a victory over Manchester United in the Champions league. In his last season, 2004–05, Hleb topped the assists chart in the Bundesliga.

Arsenal signed Hleb in June 2005. Arsene Wenger deployed Hleb right across his midfield, but usually on the right flank. Hleb was the first Belorussian to play in a Champions League Final in 2006. Arsenal fans appreciate Hleb's skill and commitment. Hleb's finesse led to a move to Barcelona in July 2008. He featured briefly for Barcelona in the Copa del Rey Final won 4-1 against Athletic Bilbao, but was not chosen for the club's Champions League victory over Manchester United in 2009.

Unable to break into Barcelona's star-studded midfield, Hleb was linked with Bayern Munich and Inter Milan, but chose to return to VFB Stuttgart on loan. In 2010 he returned to England to play for Birmingham City, but injury kept him out of the club's surprise 2011 League Cup Final victory over former club Arsenal, 2-1. Not enjoying his football at Birmingham, Hleb returned to Germany on loan to VfL Wolfsburg. Hleb has since played out his final years of football in Belorussia. He played 80 times for his country, scoring six goals, occasionally captaining the team.

Arsenal were fortunate to have the Brazilian central midfielder Gilberto Silva in their side as an enforcer. Silva slipped into the Patrick Vieira role comfortably in the noughties. Since Silva left the club in 2008, Arsenal have been totally bereft of an adequate ball-winner in midfield. Raised in poverty in Lagoa da Prata, Minas Gerais, in south-eastern Brazil, hard work was ingrained in Silva. Starting out as a centre-back, Athletico Mineiro head coach Carlos Alberto Perreira converted him to defensive midfielder, a positional change that supercharged Silva's career. Silva adopted the role with ease as Brazil won the 2002 World Cup, beating Germany 2-0 in the final. On the back of his performances in South Korea and Japan, Arsenal signed Silva in August 2002. In September 2002, Silva scored the fastest ever Champions League goal in 20.7 seconds against PSV Eindhoven in a group stage game. Silva played in the 'Invincibles' season of 2003–04. In 2004–05 he suffered a career-threatening back fracture. Rehabilitation at home in Brazil worked for Silva, the player returning to Arsenal for the 2005–06 season. Patrick Vieira's departure from Highbury increased Silva's importance to the team, although the club suffered indifferent form in this season. Silva was appointed vice-captain for the 2006–07 season, even finishing up as Arsenal's second highest scorer with ten goals. The emergence of young Frenchman Mathieu Flamini began to impact on Silva's regular starting place, and it was Flamini who moved to AC Milan in May 2008.

Silva eventually moved himself soon afterwards to Panathinaikos in Greece, winning league and cup in the 2009–10 season. In 2011 Silva returned to Brazil, playing out his last years with Gremio and Athetico Mineiro in southern Brazil. It was Silva's good fortune that captain and defensive midfielder Emerson injured himself in training just before the 2002 World Cup. Silva stepped in and played every game of Brazil's trophy-winning tournament, setting up chances for Ronaldo and Rivaldo, crucially the former's goal that defeated Turkey 1-0 in the semi-final. Beaten 1-0 by France in the quarter-finals in 2006, Silva's next big international game came when captaining Brazil against England in the inaugural match at the new Wembley Stadium in 2007. Silva had a header disallowed, then set up Brazil's goal in the 1-1 draw. An unfussy player, Silva's forte came in shadowing players, forcing them into errors, rather than through tough tackling. Arsene Wenger greatly admired Silva's ability to keep things simple. Silva's adroit positioning between defence and attack earned him 93 caps for Brazil, scoring three goals. He netted 17 times in 170 Premier League games for Arsenal 2002–08.

What a football brain Cesc Fàbregas possessed. No player in recent memory in the Premier League has been able to see the next pass before even receiving the ball quite like Fàbregas. A product of Barcelona's famous La Masia youth academy (he signed as a ten-year-old), Fàbregas was used initially as a defensive midfielder in a youth team including Lionel Messi and Gerard Piqué. Fàbregas's propensity for forward play was evident even then as he scored over 30 goals a season as a youth player. Despite this he did not start a first team game at Barcelona.

Barcelona's loss was Arsenal's gain as Fàbregas joined Arsenal's youth academy as a 16-year-old in September 2003. Fàbregas sensed he would have trouble breaking into the Xavi-Iniesta-Busquets midfield at the Nou Camp. Fàbregas lost no time making an impression at Highbury, debuting in October 2003 against Rotherham United in the League Cup, becoming the club's youngest ever first team player aged 16 years and 177 days. He then became the club's youngest goalscorer, netting in a 5-1 League Cup victory over Wolves. Wenger kept him under wraps league-wise, meaning the young Spaniard did not win a league medal at the end of the 2003–04 'Invincibles' season.

Fàbregas signed a full professional contract with Arsenal in September 2004. In scoring against Norwegian side Rosenborg in the Champions League in 2004 he became the team's youngest Champions league scorer. Fàbregas started in the successful FA Cup-winning team of 2005, Arsenal beating fierce rivals Manchester United on penalties.

Fàbregas began to implement his own slick passing style into Arsenal's game. Real Madrid wanted to take him back to Spain, but Fàbregas committed to Arsenal and Arsene Wenger. The 2006–07 and 2007–08 seasons were successful personally for Fàbregas as he won the Golden Boy award for the best young European footballer, and the Arsenal Player of the Year Award in 2007. He was also voted into the 2006 UEFA Team of the Year. Fàbregas was selected in the PFA Team of the Year in the 2007–08 season, also winning the PFA Young Player of the Year Award. Unfortunately for Fàbregas the great Arsenal teams of Vieira, Petit, Overmars et al were disintegrating, and trophies became scarcer at Arsenal.

Mixed fortunes followed Fàbregas. Astonishingly, he fractured his leg in a Champions League game against Barcelona, then scored to earn Arsenal a 2-2 draw. Eliminated in the return leg, Fàbregas was later named in the PFA Team of the Year for 2009–10. On 15 August 2011, Fàbregas finally got his wish to play for Barcelona. At Arsenal Fàbregas had made an incredible 466 chances for his teammates, provided 86 assists for goals, and scored 48 himself. Joining Barcelona, the club had won three consecutive La Liga titles, and two Champions League trophies in three seasons. Fàbregas ended his first season at the Nou Camp by winning the Copa del Rey, 3-0 against Athletic Bilbao, even though he only appeared as a substitute. In a team containing Xavi, Iniesta, Messi and David Villa, Fàbregas was still struggling to stake a place in the first team at Barcelona. When he did play, his contribution was massive: 15 goals, 20 assists in 48 games. Fourteen goals and 12 assists followed in 2012–13. Barca won La Liga with a record total of 100 points. Eight goals in 36 matches in 2013–14 were not enough to confirm in Fàbregas's mind that he truly belonged at Barcelona.

Arsenal were captained on this night by their talismanic striker, Thierry Henry. Henry was regarded as one of the very best players in the world in the noughties: runner-up in the FIFA World Player of the Year Award in 2003 and 2004, behind Zinedine Zidane and Ronaldinho respectively. PFA Player's Player of the Year twice in 2002–03 and 2003–04; he was named in the PFA Team of the Year for six consecutive seasons 2000–01 to 2005–06; and named in the UEFA Team of the Year five times between 2001 and 2006, missing out only in 2005. I have touched on Henry's epic contribution to Arsenal previously (175 goals in 254 Premier League games). He was no slouch at Barcelona either: 35 goals in 80 La Liga games. His career goals total of 290 in 600 senior games speaks volumes.

Extremely fast, direct, tricky, a lethal goalscorer, Thierry Henry seemed to be everybody's favourite striker at the time.

Playing just behind the immaculate Henry in this final, Sweden's Freddie Ljungberg carried plenty of his own goal threat. Ljungberg's skilful contribution to senior football, curiously, packed in only 46 goals in 216 Premier League games. Ljungberg was as adept at assisting goals as scoring them. He had a happy knack of scoring crucial goals, netting in two FA Cup Finals. An all-round sportsman, he excelled at ice hockey and handball, playing for the Swedish U-15 national team in the latter sport. At Halmstad in his native Sweden, Ljungberg first won the Svenska Cup (Swedish Cup) in 1995, going on to win the top tier league, the 'Allsvenskan' in 1997. Barcelona, Chelsea, Aston Villa, Arsenal and Parma all had Ljungberg on their radar.

Arsenal won the race to sign the talented Swede in 1998. Arsene Wenger was sufficiently impressed by Ljungberg's performance against England on television to rubber-stamp the player's signature. Ljungberg impressed immediately with his verve and vitality. In the 2001 FA Cup Final, Ljungberg gave Arsenal a 22nd-minute lead, only for Michael Owen to spoil the party with two goals in the last seven minutes. Ljungberg scored Arsenal's second goal as Chelsea were beaten 2-0 in the 2002 FA Cup Final. With Robert Pires injured, Ljungberg was highly influential in this season as Arsenal won the double. 2001–02 proved to be Ljungberg's best season as he scored 17 goals in all competitions. The FA Cup seemed to inspire Ljungberg. In the semi-final of the 2002–03 competition he scored the winner against Sheffield United. Pires won the final for Arsenal against Southampton with the only goal of the match.

Ljungberg played 30 times in Arsenal's 2003–04 'Invincibles' season. In 2004–05 he came on as a substitute in his fourth FA Cup Final, scoring a penalty kick in the winning shoot-out against Manchester United. Persistent hip and ankle injuries put an end to the Swede's time at Arsenal. Highly thought of, Ljungberg was placed 11th in Arsenal.com's poll in 2008 of Gunners' Greatest Players.

Ljungberg moved to West Ham United for the 2007–08 season, playing 25 Premier League games for the Hammers. A serious rib injury after Newcastle United's Steven Taylor landed on top of him brought Ljungberg's contract with West Ham to a premature end. Thereafter Ljungberg dallied with football in America, Glasgow (at Celtic), Japan and India, but to all intents and purposes his career was over.

Ljungberg's record with Sweden is highly creditable – 14 goals in 75 games. Sweden's head coach Lars Lagerbäck thought Ljungberg too small as a young player, but Ljungberg's speed across the ground and speed of thought persuaded him otherwise. At the 2002 World Cup Sweden held England to a 1-1 draw, defeated Nigeria 2-1, and drew 1-1 with Argentina, Ljungberg playing in the first two games. His hip problem prevented him playing against Argentina, and in the 2-1 defeat against Senegal in the last 16. At the Euros in 2004, Ljungberg opened the scoring as the Swedes routed Bulgaria 5-0. Two drawn matches against Italy and Denmark put Sweden through to the next round. A 0-0 draw with Holland ended with a 4-5 penalty shoot-out defeat in the quarter-finals. Ljungberg then headed an 89th-minute winner against Paraguay to put Sweden through to the last 16 at the 2006 World Cup, where they lost to Germany.

Ljungberg captained Sweden in the 2008 Euro qualifiers, but his rib injury meant playing in the tournament with a specially protected brace, not an ideal scenario. Despite this impediment the Swedish media thought Ljungberg was Sweden's best player in the competition, although defeat against Spain and Russia saw Sweden crash out in the first round. Ljungberg's love for Arsenal saw him take on various coaching roles at the Emirates 2016–19. Here was another player whose impact could have been greater but for repeated injuries.

One look at Arsenal's substitute's bench suggests their team could have taken on a different dimension, especially in the forward positions. Dennis Bergkamp and Robin van Persie were outstanding options – at their peak. Sadly this was Bergkamp's last season and he was 37 years old. The unfortunate van Persie suffered a broken toe earlier in the season, Arsene Wenger deeming him not fully fit for this final. More's the pity as van Persie scored 96 goals in his 194 Premier League games for Arsenal 2004–2012, going on to impress at Manchester United 2012–15 (48 goals in 86 matches). The Dutchman if fully fit would surely have been an excellent addition to the Arsenal team. He also scored 50 times in 102 appearances for Holland. A proven goalscorer, van Persie. José Antonio Reyes and Mathieu Flamini were the players to enter the field of play in Paris as substitutes, considerable attacking players themselves. It was to no avail.

Barcelona were approaching their peak years. No Messi, Xavi or Iniesta here in 2006, but the team was packed with splendid international stars, and captained by Carlos Puyol, a player whose attachment to Barcelona matched that of Sergio Ramos's allegiance to Real Madrid, his commitment to Barcelona matching that of English football club stalwarts down the years: Billy Bonds at West Ham, Bryan Robson at Manchester United, Steven Gerrard at Liverpool.

Carlos Puyol was instantly recognisable due to his shock of permed hair, a throwback to the English game's Keegan and McDermott era at Liverpool. A one-club man, Puyol was also a magnificent defender, willing to throw himself into any situation to prevent a goal. Born in the small Catalonian town of La Pobla de Sogur, Puyol joined Barcelona's famed La Masia youth set-up, playing as a defensive midfielder – he'd even played in goal for Pobla de Sogur as a teenager. Progressing to Barca's 'B' team, Puyol became a right-back, switching to centre-back in the first team. Manchester United showed interest in Puyol as Barcelona suffered financial straits in 2005, but Puyol committed to a further five-season contract at the Nou Camp. Puyol eventually played 481 La Liga games for Barca, chipping in with 18 goals.

In 2002 Puyol was voted European Football's best right-back. In season 2003–04 Puyol became club captain after Luis Enrique (Spain's national coach at the 2020 Euros) retired. Countless trophies followed in the coming years, but injuries too prevented Puyol breaking the 500 La Liga game mark, knee problems ultimately bringing about his retirement in 2014. Carlos Puyol won six La Liga titles, two Copa del Reys and three Champions League trophies in 2006, 2009 and 2011. In all Puyol won 21 trophies with Barcelona, spending ten seasons as captain.

Individually, Puyol was voted into the UEFA Team of the Year in 2002, 2005,

2006, 2008, 2009 and 2010, and declared the Best Club Defender in Europe in this season of 2005–06. He was also selected into the FIFA/FIFPRO World XI in 2007, 2008 and 2010. On the international stage this committed defender played in the winning 2008 Euro team with Spain, and again in the triumphant Spanish World Cup-winning team in South Africa in 2010. Puyol was selected into the 2008 Euros Team of the Tournament. In the semi-final of the 2010 World Cup he scored the only goal against Germany with a powerful header. Spain conceded only two goals in this tournament, including five clean sheets, a World Cup record shared with 1998's French team, and the Italian winning team of 2006. Puyol was again named in the 2010 World Cup Team of the Tournament.

Teammate Xavi praises Puyol's never-say-die spirit. These players (Gerrard at Liverpool) are always invaluable to a football team and much admired by teammates. Strong, quick, a great leader and inspiration, aggressive, vocally loud like Liverpool's Carragher, Puyol tended to be the defensive-minded one of a pair playing in central defence, allowing the likes of Gerard Piqué to be the ball-playing centre-back. The kind of player opponents dislike playing against, Carlos Puyol.

Partnering Puyol in the centre of Barcelona's defence, Rafael Márquez (third-most capped player in Mexican football history with 147 caps) joined the club after winning Ligue 1 in France with Monaco. He became the first Mexican player to win the Champions League in this final. Márquez won Ligue 1 with Monaco in his first season after signing from Guadalajara-based club Atlas in 1999, going on to win the Coupe de la Ligue (League Cup) 4-1 against Sochaux in his last season in France, 2002–03.

In 12 seasons in European football, Márquez played 46 Champions League games, the most by a Mexican or CONCACAF (North/Central American/ Caribbean) player until Javier Hernández (known to Manchester United and West Ham fans) broke the record in 2017. The only other CONCACAF player to play in a Champions League Final previously was Manchester United's Trinidad and Tobagian Dwight Yorke in 1999. Márquez played 163 La Liga games for Barca, scoring nine goals.

Internationally Márquez debuted for Mexico in 1997, although he was not chosen for the 1998 World Cup squad. Aged 23 he captained his country at the 2002 World Cup in South Korea and Japan. In the 2006 World Cup round of 16, Márquez gave Mexico an early lead against Argentina, but his country eventually lost 2-1 after extra time. The same opponents defeated Mexico again at the same stage in 2010, Márquez captaining the side in a 3-1 defeat. Márquez had scored Mexico's goal in the opening 1-1 draw with hosts South Africa on the tournament's opening night.

Márquez achieved two notable feats at the 2014 World Cup, captaining the team at a fourth World Cup, and scoring in a third World Cup in the 3-1 victory over Croatia that took Mexico through to the last 16 again. This time Holland defeated Mexico 2-1. Appearing in his fifth World Cup at the age of 38 in 2018, Márquez equalled Lothar Matthäus's and fellow countryman Antonio Carbajal's record (Carbajal was Mexico's goalkeeper in his last tournament in England in 1966). Márquez has been labelled the 'Kaiser of Michoachan' in reference to 'Der

Kaiser' Franz Beckenbauer, for his comfort on the ball, his capacity to play out from the back.

At left-back, the Dutchman Giovanni van Bronckhorst had transferred to Barcelona from Arsenal in 2003 after two seasons at Highbury. At Highbury I did not think he matched the quality of Ashley Cole or even the dependability of Nigel Winterburn, yet the stats suggest he settled in better with Barcelona. He was also capped 106 times by Holland, scoring six goals, suggesting his national team benefited from his attacking qualities better than Arsenal.

Giovanni van Bronckhorst played 105 La Liga games for Barcelona, scoring five times. He also scored 22 goals in his 103 games at first club Feyenoord. He left Feyenoord, the club unable to break the PSV/Ajax stranglehold on the Dutch Eredivisie, in 1998, joining up with ex-Dutch U-16 and U-18 manager Dick Advocaat at Glasgow Rangers. He scored 22 goals in all competitions for Rangers 1998–2001 in a playmaker midfield role. Arsenal signed him as a nominal replacement for Emmanuel Petit in June 2001 (in my mind Petit and Vieira have never been adequately replaced at Arsenal). Unfortunately for van Bronckhorst a cruciate knee ligament injury sidelined him, although he was part of Arsenal's double-winning and FA Cup-winning teams of 2000–01 and 2001–02.

The Dutchman opted to take a loan deal with Barcelona in 2003–04 when fellow countryman Frank Rijkaard managed the team. Rijkaard converted him to left back. Permanently transferred in 2004–05, van Bronckhorst won La Liga, settling in well in his new role within the team. He was the only player to play every Champions League game in this 2005–06 Champions League campaign.

Returning to Feyenoord on a free transfer in 2007, coach Bert van Marwijk made him captain of the team. In the 2008 Dutch KNVB Cup Final, van Bronckhorst led the club to a 2-0 victory over Roda JC. He took a while to settle in the Dutch international team, but eventually played in three World Cups (1998, 2006 and 2010) and three European Championships (2000, 2004 and 2008). He was the regular left-back under Advocaat in the 2004 Euros, Holland losing 2-1 to Portugal in the semi-finals (two goals against them, inevitably from Cristiano Ronaldo). At the 2006 World Cup Portugal again eliminated Holland in the last 16 'Battle of Nurnberg' match, 1-0. The match was so called because of the four players sent off – two from each team. The apparently mild-mannered van Bronckhorst was the last of the four sent off late in the game.

At the 2008 Euros, van Bronckhorst scored against the defending champions Italy in a stunning 3-0 victory. With Ruud van Nistelrooy and Robin van Persie in their attacking ranks, Holland promised much in this tournament. 4-1 and 2-0 victories over France and Romania respectively augured well, but typical of recent Dutch inconsistency they fell at the first knockout hurdle 3-1 after extra time against an Andrey Arshavin-inspired Russia. A long-range blockbuster goal against Uruguay in the semi-final of the 2010 World Cup took Holland into the final where he captained the team, Spain's Andres Iniesta scoring the only goal in extra time. Inconsistent at Arsenal, van Bronckhorst almost led his country to the ultimate football triumph.

Going into management after retiring in 2010, van Bronckhorst led Feyenoord to 2015–16 KNVB Cup Final success, defeating Utrecht 2-1. In 2016–17 he led

Feyenoord to the Dutch Eredivisie title, their first in 18 years. Not bad for a player remembered largely at Arsenal as one who didn't quite fill the shoes of Ashley Cole or Manu Petit.

Barcelona's midfield appeared in this final in the form of a tall, but somewhat ungainly defensive midfielder in the Brazilian Edmilson; a robust, but technically adept Dutchman in Mark van Bommel; the immensely gifted and previously praised Brazilian-Portuguese Deco; and the diminutive, pacy Frenchman Ludovic Giuly.

Giuly's record in French football won him his contract with Barcelona in 2004. A sprightly character and a sprightly player, Giuly's five feet five inches stature won him the nickname 'the magic elf' at first professional club Lyon. His most successful season at Lyon came in 1996–97 as he scored 16 times in 37 matches. Leaving for Monaco in 1998 he impressed even more in the principality, scoring 47 times in 184 matches. Giuly was a key player as Monaco won Ligue 1 in 1999–2000. The following season he was not as successful. 2001–02 promised better before Giuly ruptured knee ligaments, wrecking hopes of a place in the French 2002 World Cup squad.

Recovering from injury, Giuly captained Monaco to their 2003 Coupe de la Ligue victory, scoring twice in the 4-1 final triumph. In the 2003–04 season Giuly scored crucial goals in Champions League matches against AEK Athens and Deportivo La Coruna. In the knockout stages, Giuly again impressed as Lokomotiv Moscow and Real Madrid were eliminated, Giuly scoring twice against 'Los Blancos'. In the final, lost to Porto 3-0, Giuly left the field with a groin injury in the 23rd minute, devastated.

Barcelona had seen enough of Giuly's talent to sign him in June 2004. He scored on his Barcelona debut against Racing de Santander in a 2-0 win. He made a good start to life in Spain, scoring 11 goals as Barcelona won La Liga in the 2004–05 season, their first title win for six years. The title was won again in this famous 2005–06 Champions League-winning season. Giuly scored the only goal against AC Milan in the semi-final of the tournament. In the final he netted in the moment Jens Lehmann committed the foul that led to his sending off, the goal being disallowed. Giuly's time at Barcelona came to an end due to an emerging world football superstar – one Lionel Messi.

Dutchman van Bommel played only one season with Barca, this 2005–06 Champions League-winning season. At six feet two inches, van Bommel, a tall man for a midfielder, provided plenty of steel and strength, combined with typical Dutch technique. At PSV Eindhoven 1999–2005 he won four Eredivisie Dutch League titles, the team reaching the 2004–05 Champions League semi-finals, only to be beaten by AC Milan on away goals. Linked with Borussia Dortmund in 2004, van Bommel went to Barcelona and Frank Rijkaard on a free transfer at the end of the 2004–05 season. He'd scored 46 goals in 169 games for PSV.

Barcelona, possessing so many other creative players, rotated van Bommel in his one season at the club with Xavi, Iniesta, Edmilson, Thiago Motta and Deco. As a result van Bommel played in only 24 La Liga games and a further 12 cup games. Seeking regular first team football, he moved to Bayern Munich the following season. In his first season at Bayern, van Bommel won the double of Bundesliga and DFB Pokal Cup, and was voted Bayern's Player of the Year. When Oliver Khan retired in 2008, van Bommel became the club's first non-German captain, a mark of the respect in which he was held. Louis van Gaal replaced Uli Hoeness as team manager – van Bommel simply continued his strong vein of form, captaining Bayern to another double in 2009–10. Bayern reached the 2010 Champions League Final, a treble being denied by Inter Milan and their canny manager, José Mourinho, who was happy to let Bayern have the ball and punish them on the counter-attack, his team triumphing 2-0 with two goals from Argentine international striker Diego Milito. The strength of van Bommel solidified an already powerful Bayern side, his 123 games comprising 11 goals in the Bundesliga.

Moving to AC Milan in January 2011, again for just one season, van Bommel integrated well into Massimiliano Allegri's team, winning the Italian Scudetto (Serie A) at the first attempt. Offered a new contract in April 2012, van Bommel opted to return to PSV. He couldn't quite replicate his previous impact at the club, PSV finishing the 2012–13 season second behind Ajax in the Eredivisie and losing the KNVB Cup Final to AZ Alkmaar 2-1.

He debuted for Holland in October 2000 against Cyprus, the first of 79 internationals (ten goals). He may have won more caps but for disagreement over his role in the side under Marco van Basten. He played in the 2006 World Cup, but was substituted twice by van Basten. When Bert van Marwijk (van Bommel's father-in-law) replaced van Basten, he was used more regularly, the team losing the 2010 World Cup Final 1-0 to Spain. After a two-year international absence, van Bommel reluctantly took the captain's armband from van Bronckhorst in his latter years representing Holland. A strong, athletic, tough-tackling player, van Bommel represented a different type of Dutch player in the modern game.

In attack Barcelona possessed two extraordinary talents in Ronaldinho and Samuel Eto'o. Ronaldinho played more as a wide player or auxiliary striker rather than as an out-and-out striker, but he was blessed with spectacular individual skill, always capable of providing the unexpected.

The Porto Alegre southern Brazilian born Ronaldinho began his senior career with Gremio in Brazil, scoring 47 goals in 89 games 1998–2001. He won the FIFA World Player of the Year Award twice (2004, 2005) and the Ballon d'Or in 2005. Aged 20, he signed for Paris Saint-Germain, scoring 17 times in 55 Ligue 1 games 2001–03. Ronaldinho is a typical product of Brazilian football, honing his skills in futsal and in beach football. Tragically, as an eight-year-old, he lost his father who hit his head and drowned in the family's swimming pool. Astonishingly, as a 13-year-old he scored all 23 goals in a 23-0 local match. Unusually, Ronaldinho came from a more affluent family than the average Brazilian player. Before signing for Paris Saint-Germain, Arsenal sought to sign Ronaldinho in 2001, the move collapsing as the player could not obtain a work permit due to his lack of international status at that time. Imagine Ronaldinho playing with Petit, Vieira and Overmars. What a loss to English football that was! In Paris, manager Luis Fernandez, part of the great 2004 European Championship-winning team for France, felt Ronaldinho was influenced too much by Parisian nightlife.

Ronaldinho joined Barcelona, making a far stronger impact in Catalonia than he had in Paris. The years spent at the Nou Camp 2003–08 were his peak years. Barcelona benefited to the tune of 70 goals in 145 La Liga games, a one-goal-in-every-two-games ratio. Ronaldinho was one of three players coveted by the extrovert Barcelona president of the time, Jean Laporta – the others were David Beckham and Thierry Henry. Henry eventually ended up at the Nou Camp in 2007; Beckham did not, plying his silky skills instead at rivals Real Madrid, who outbid Barca for his services.

Ronaldinho's first Barca coach Rijkaard felt he excited every time he received the ball. His first goal against Sevilla in September 2003 came with a dribble past two players and a 30-yard shot cannoning in off the crossbar. This was a player specialising in the spectacular. Injury marred his first season, Barca only finishing second in La Liga behind surprise champions Valencia. Xavi thought that this was the season Barcelona began to rise again. La Liga was finally won in 2004–05 after a six-season wait. Carlos Puyol felt the club was playing with a smile on its face, in no small part thanks to Ronaldinho's contribution.

In winning the Champions League in this 2005–06 season, Barcelona claimed the trophy for the first time in 14 years. The season is regarded as Ronaldinho's finest. He finished the season with a career best 26 goals, providing countless assists for Eto'o, including the pass in this final that resulted in Jens Lehmann being sent off. He'd been instrumental in the team reaching the final, ghosting past three Chelsea players to score in the last 16 scoring against Benfica in the last eight; and assisted Giuly's goal in the semi-final. He was chosen in the UEFA Team of the Year for the third consecutive season, and also named 2005–06 UEFA Club Footballer of the Year and selected in the FIFA World XI.

In 2006–07 Barcelona were eliminated in the last 16 of the Champions League by Liverpool. Ronaldinho scored a career best 21 La Liga goals, but Barca lost the title to Real Madrid on an inferior head-to-head record after the teams totalled the same points. A muscle tear in April 2008, and an increasingly nocturnal lifestyle meant Ronaldinho left Barca at the end of the season. His biggest regret: not playing for long enough with the emergent maestro Lionel Messi.

Ronaldinho rejected the chance to join Manchester City's renaissance in July 2008, opting to sign for AC Milan on a three-year contract. Ronaldinho scored ten goals in 32 Serie A games in the 2008–09 season, manager Carlo Ancelotti never doubting his supreme talent, although partying in Milan mirrored that of his time in Barcelona and Paris. Under new manager Leonardo in 2009–10, Ronaldinho revived, performing near the top of his form after shifting to the left side of midfield from the centre. During this season, David Beckham joined AC on loan from LA Galaxy, forming an impressive triumvirate with Ronaldinho and Kaka. Ronaldinho ended the season at the top of the assists table in Serie A. He claimed the 2010–11 Serie A with Milan although he played only 16 games, leaving for Flamengo in Brazil in January 2011. He terminated his contract at Flamengo after a season in which he scored 23 goals in 56 games, moving again to Atlético Mineiro, where he scored a further 20 goals in 58 games. Although past his prime, Ronaldinho helped Atlético Mineiro win the Copa Libertadores, the club competition for all South American nations, beating Paraguay's Olimpia in the final. Ronaldinho, now 33, was voted 2013 South American Footballer of the Year.

At the 1999 Confederations Cup, Brazil lost the final 4-3 to Mexico in the Estadio Azteca in Mexico City, but Ronaldinho was both Golden Ball winner (Best Player in the Tournament) and Golden Shoe winner (top scorer in the tournament). Ronaldinho's World Cup impact is well documented in England. English fans remember only too well Ronaldinho's influence on the 2002 World Cup. In the five games he played, Ronaldinho first scored against China, then memorably, regrettably for David Seaman, his 40-yard free kick caught Seaman unawares to seal a 2-1 win for Brazil over England in the quarter-finals. He'd also set up Rivaldo's equaliser to Michael Owen's early goal for England. He was then sent off for fouling England full-back Danny Mills. Suspended for the semi-final, he returned to help Brazil beat Germany 2-0 in the final and claim the trophy. Ronaldinho also provided three assists in the tournament.

The 2006 World Cup tournament was a disappointment, the feted quartet of Ronaldinho, Adriano, Ronaldo and Kaka unable to help Brazil beat France in the quarter-finals. Brazilian fans felt the players lacked application; ex-Brazil forward and legend from 1970, Tostão (a superb, guileful player), felt Ronaldinho lacked the aggression to put him on a par with the true greats, Pele and Maradona.

Ronaldinho was subsequently omitted from the 2010 and 2014 World Cup squads under Dunga and Luiz Felipe Scolari. In the interim period between tournaments, he'd captained his country occasionally, but was particularly disfavoured by Dunga who preferred players with total commitment in his own hard-working image in an era when Brazil's style changed from their previous all-out attacking instincts. Despite losing favour latterly, Ronaldinho played 97 times for Brazil, scoring 33 goals. He surely would have been among Brazil's most-capped players with better fitness in the latter stages of his career.

Ronaldinho's individual skills were on a par with the very greatest players: Pele, Maradona, Cruyff – if only he'd applied himself at the level of these players. His speed, athleticism, dribbling skills, feinting, overhead kicks, 'no-look' passes, were of the very highest order. He was also a deadly free-kick taker – as David Seaman found to his embarrassment in 2002. His biggest legacy is that he wanted to play football with a smile. In my own infinitesimal way that was how I tried to play local football. I always wanted to score the perfect goal. With hindsight I wish I'd just put the ball in the net in the manner of two of my teammates over the years who each scored 50 plus goals in a season. We're all temperamentally different aren't we?

Ahead of Ronaldinho, receiving the balls which he promptly fired into the net, Cameroon's Samuel Eto'o was a prolific goalscorer. Eto'o's pace, power and unerring eye for goal earned him the African Player of the Year Award a record four times: 2003, 2004, 2005 and 2010.

The precocious Eto'o signed for Real Madrid aged 16 in 1997. Restricted with first team opportunities as a teenager, he was loaned out to Real Mallorca in 2000. In four seasons Eto'o scored 70 goals in all competitions for the Balearics team. Moving to Barcelona in 2004 he scored 130 goals in five seasons in all competitions during his peak years. Eto'o scored in this 2006 Champions League Final, repeating the feat in a three-pronged attack with Messi and Thierry Henry in 2009 in the 2-0 victory over Manchester United. Eto'o was selected in the FIFA FIFPRO World XI in 2005 and 2006. Joining Inter Milan in 2009–10, Eto'o became the first player to win back-to-back continental trebles (league, cup, Champions League) with Barcelona and Inter Milan. He is the fourth player to win the Champions League two years in succession with different teams after Marcel Desailly (Marseille 1993, AC Milan 1994). Paulo Sousa (Juventus 1996, Borussia Dortmund 1997), and Gerard Piqué (Manchester United 2008, Barcelona 2009).

Eto'o won the Pichichi Trophy, named after the Athletic Bilbao striker Rafael 'Pichichi' Moreno, the trophy for La Liga top scorer awarded since 1952–53, scoring 26 goals in this 2005–06 season. He also scored six goals during the 2005–06 Champions League campaign, winning the UEFA Best Forward of the Year Award for his efforts in Europe. Thirty goals in the 2008–09 La Liga season left him only in second place on the scorer's list, Atlético Madrid's Diego Forlan gazumping him with 32. Forlan never hit that kind of form in his two seasons with Manchester United 2002–04! The 2008–09 season was an extraordinary one for Eto'o, along with Messi and Henry the famous trio scored a total of 100 goals in all competitions as Barcelona won the treble of La Liga, Copa del Rey and the Champions League: Messi (38), Eto'o (36) and Henry (26).

In July 2009 Eto'o moved to Inter Milan in exchange for Zlatan Ibrahimovic and £46 million. The Champions League Final win over Bayern Munich in 2010 was Eto'o's third Champions League trophy. Scoring two goals in the Coppa Italia Final 3-1 victory over Parma gave Eto'o a seasons' total of 37 goals in all competitions, a personal record.

Why, with the plaudits of Inter chairman Massimo Moratti ringing in his ear, did Eto'o in his pomp, sign for Russian club Anzhi Makhachkala in the Dagastan region on the Caspian Sea? The fact that he became the world's highest paid player didn't deter him, naturally. After two years in Russia, Eto'o, aged 32, decided to try his hand in England, playing 21 Premier League games for Chelsea 2013–14 (nine goals) and Everton 2014–15 (14 games, three goals). It was a token contribution to English football as he moved to Sampdoria for the 2015–16 season, playing only one season before spending the last significant years of his playing career at Antalyaspor in Turkey 2015–18, scoring 44 goals in 76 games, filling in as player-manager for a month until the Portuguese José Morais took over as permanent manager in January 2016.

For Cameroon, Eto'o scored 56 goals in 118 internationals, making him the country's all-time leading scorer. Many African footballers possess great power, but few have been able to match Eto'o's technique and reliable scoring ability. Normally a striker, Eto'o could play wide if required. Predictably, under José Mourinho at Inter Milan, Eto'o played wherever he was required. Fast, with great close control, Eto'o's timing to anticipate passes and crosses was excellent. He is rated the best African striker of all time alongside Didier Drogba and George Weah.

Torn knee ligaments earlier in the season meant the great Xavi was only an unused substitute here in Paris in 2006. Given the impact he and Xavi made on the national team in the coming years, it was a surprise too to see Andrés Iniesta only come on as a substitute in this final for Edmilson in the 46th minute. The Swede Henrik Larsson was a massive success in Glasgow with Celtic. At Barcelona he had to contend with Ronaldinho and Eto'o for striking positions, but his impact as a substitute shortly after the hour in this 2006 Champions League Final proved significant, assisting both goals. Ex-Arsenal and Brazilian left-back Sylvinho was among the unused defensive substitutes.

The managers were hugely respected figures, Arsene Wenger for all he'd brought to English football in terms of diet, better preparation and (in his early years) astute signings; and Dutchman Frank Rijkaard for Barcelona, as much for his stellar playing career with Ajax, AC Milan, and Holland, as part of a truly great triumvirate of Dutch players: Ruud Gullit, Marco van Basten the others, as for his fledgling managerial career at this point.

THE FINAL

Arsenal's hopes were hampered by Lauren being declared unfit at right-back, Emmanuel Eboué replacing him. Ashley Cole at left-back was playing only his third game of the Champions League campaign due to injury. The inexperienced Eboué started strongly, playing in a cross that Thierry Henry could have done better with as he was completely in the clear, but he only shot straight at keeper Victor Valdés. Henry attempted to rectify the matter with a fierce long-range shot. Ludovic Giuly replied with a rasping right-foot shot that went close. Jens Lehmann was sent off for felling Samuel Eto'o, the Cameroonian international seeking to take advantage of Ronaldinho's cleverly weighted ball. The incident changed the complexion of the game at a stroke. Ronaldinho's crossfield ball almost set up Giuly, but Ashley Cole diverted the danger. Eboué's strong run down the right was halted by the ever-competitive Carlos Puyol, but Eboué was lucky to win a free kick. The free kick from Henry was headed into goal powerfully by Sol Campbell. Against the odds Arsenal were ahead. Eto'o then turned Campbell to shoot left-footed against the post. Ronaldinho now began to exploit the space offered him by Lehmann's sending-off, a sharply worked free kick almost bringing Barcelona back into the game.

In the second half, Alexander Hleb shot wide for Arsenal. Freddie Ljungberg had a left-foot shot parried over by Valdés. Henry had another shot saved. A typical Eto'o goal followed as Arsenal's brave resistance faltered. A flicked pass from Andrés Iniesta, on as a second half substitute, was followed by another substitute, Henrik Larsson's fine through ball, leaving Eto'o to shoot Barcelona level. Larsson subsequently turned Arsenal inside out on the right flank, and a third substitute Italian defender Juliano Belletti supplemented the attack to drive the ball through Manuel Almunia's legs. Ronaldinho had been a constant menace throughout the match, bringing all his inventiveness to bear. Arsene Wenger's face at the end seemed prescient. It was almost as if he knew that this was Arsenal's time. The sending off of Lehmann was just too big a hurdle against such a potent attacking team as Barcelona.

2006–07 CHAMPIONS LEAGUE FINAL
AC Milan 2 v 1 Liverpool

A repeat of the 2005 final, but no repeat success for Liverpool. On this occasion, despite being minus the great international forwards Ronaldinho and Eto'o, AC Milan were good value for their victory, both goals coming from another prolific striker, the Italian international striker Filippo Inzaghi.

Route to the Final

Liverpool topped Group C ahead of PSV Eindhoven, Bordeaux and Galatasaray. The group stage was not without its difficulties. Indeed, their first game resulted in a 0-0 draw in Holland. 'The Reds' first home tie produced a 3-2 win over Galatasaray, two goals coming from Peter Crouch and the other from Luis Garcia. I liked Crouch, who at six feet seven inches could appear ungainly, but one always felt his touch for such a tall man belied his spidery frame – and his goals return for Liverpool wasn't bad (22 in 85 Premier League games). Never a popular choice in an England shirt, Crouch's 22 goals in 42 internationals were even more respectable. A far better player than he was ever given credit for, Peter Crouch. Crouch it was again who scored the only goal on France's west coast against Bordeaux in Liverpool's third game. A fortnight later it was Steven Gerrard's turn to score twice, Garcia netting the final goal as Liverpool beat Bordeaux 3-0 in the return tie.

Gerrard and Crouch were on the scoresheet as PSV were beaten 2-0 at Anfield in November 2006. The two qualifying teams in Group C then lost their last games, Liverpool losing 3-2 in the hostile atmosphere of Galatasaray's Sana Yen stadium, Robbie Fowler scoring both Liverpool's goals. PSV lost 3-1 at home to Bordeaux, but still qualified for the last 16.

AC Milan topped Group H but made extremely heavy weather of their task. There were no hints of trouble in their first game, won in the San Siro 3-0 against AEK Athens of Greece, Inzaghi scoring the first goal. A goalless draw followed in France against Lille. In their third game in Belgium, Kaka's goal secured a 1-0 victory against Anderlecht. A hat-trick from Kaka in the return against the Belgians ensured a comfortable 4-1 victory. With qualification all but secured, the Italians then took their feet off the gas, losing 1-0 to AEK in Greece, courtesy of Brazilian Júlio César's goal, and shockingly, lost 2-0 at home to Lille.

Liverpool had the almighty task of defeating Barcelona in the last 16 and somehow achieved it. The feisty and explosive Welshman Craig Bellamy and the sturdily powerful Norwegian John Arne Riise replied to an early goal from Deco in the Nou Camp, giving Liverpool an unlikely goal advantage 2 to 1 returning to Anfield. Although Liverpool lost 1-0 at Anfield thanks to a goal from the former Chelsea striker, the Icelander Eider Gudjohnsen, away goals took the Merseysiders through to the last eight. Playing PSV Eindhoven again in the quarter-finals, Liverpool swept the Dutchmen aside at the Philips Stadion 3-0 with goals from Gerrard, Riise and Crouch, the latter then scoring the only goal at Anfield as Liverpool ran out comfortable 4-0 aggregate winners. A repeat of their 2005 semi-final against Chelsea followed. Again the two ties were too close to call, full of tension and drama. Joe Cole scored the only goal of the game at Stamford Bridge. Liverpool's Danish centre-back Daniel Agger replied in kind at Anfield. Liverpool won the penalty shoot-out conclusively at the end of the tie, 4-1, the otherwise wonderful winger Arjen Robben, and the Cameroonian Geremi missing penalties for Chelsea. A repeat semi-final victory from 2005 would not be matched by a repeat final victory over AC Milan.

AC Milan struggled against Glasgow Celtic in the last 16, drawing 0-0 at Celtic Park, just doing enough (it's the Italian way) in the San Siro, winning 1-0 with an extra-time goal from Kaka. A Celtic team featuring future manager Neil Lennon in midfield ran 'I Rossoneri' really close. Surprisingly, AC Milan made a better fist of beating the mighty Germans of Bayern Munich in the last eight, drawing 2-2 in the San Siro, Andrea Pirlo and a Kaka penalty, but won 2-0 impressively in Munich with goals from Clarence Seedorf and Inzaghi. In the last four AC met a Cristiano Ronaldo and Wayne Rooney-inspired Manchester United, losing 3-2 at Old Trafford, Ronaldo one and Rooney twice (including an injury-time winner) scoring the home goals, while Kaka netted twice for AC. Sadly for United, Milan were imperious in the return, Kaka, Seedorf and Alberto Gilardini netting in a 3-0 victory.

Liverpool's team showed six changes from 2005. The five players to play again here were Steve Finnan, Xabi Alonso, Steven Gerrard, John Arne Riise and Jamie Carragher. In goal, Pepe Reina, Spanish international (36 caps) replaced Jerzy Dudek. Son of former Barcelona keeper Miguel Reina, Pepe played for Barca's reserves 1999–2000, debuting for the first team in December 2000. Upon signing German keeper Robert Enke, Barcelona released him.

Reina subsequently spent three seasons at Villareal before signing for Rafael Benitez and Liverpool in July 2005. Benitez hailed Reina as Spain's premier goalkeeper. Reina went on to play 285 Premier League games for Liverpool 2005–2014, the most appearances at any one club during his career. In December 2005, Reina kept a sixth consecutive clean sheet against Wigan Athletic in the Premier League, creating a new club record. Reina's record of 29 goals conceded in his first 50 matches broke the club record set by Ray Clemence in 1970–71. Reina saved three of the four penalties he faced in the 2006 FA Cup Final against West Ham United. After making a few errors during the game he atoned for his misdemeanours in the penalty shoot-out. He saved two of the three penalty kicks he faced against Chelsea in the 2006–07 Champions League semi-final. Nineteen clean sheets were kept in the 2006–07 Premier League season, earning Reina the Golden Glove Award for Best Goalkeeper for the second consecutive season. His exploits earned him a new five-year contract at Anfield.

In the 2007–08 season Reina became the quickest goalkeeper in Liverpool's club history to reach 50 clean sheets. The Golden Glove was won for the third consecutive season, this time with 18 clean sheets. A six-year contract was his reward, signed in April 2010. The contract was broken when Reina reunited with Benitez on loan to Napoli in July 2013. In May 2014 Reina won the Coppa Italia with Napoli, 3-1 over Fiorentina. Reina then joined Bayern Munich in August 2014, playing second fiddle to Manuel Neuer, Germany's national goalkeeper. He returned to Napoli 2015–18, playing 111 Serie A games, the second highest amount at any of his clubs; he played 109 times for Villareal. Reina was still playing in Serie A with Napoli in 2020 after interim deals with AC Milan and Aston Villa in England.

At international level Reina was usually understudy to Real Madrid's Iker Casillas, although he competed and won with Spain the 2008 and 2012 Euros, and the 2010 World Cup. Pepe Reina was a fine shot-stopper, and may well have influenced the trend in English football for 'sweeper-keepers', goalkeepers who can distribute the ball, play out from the back. This is a tendency in the modern game I am not at all sure about. It very often does not come naturally to a goalkeeper to play like a ball-playing centre-back. Many mistakes occur as a result – Danny Ward as I speak for Wales against the Czech Republic in a World Cup qualifying match, attempted to flick a ball up and allowed the ball to roll under his foot, conceding a goal. Goalkeepers are under the magnifying glass enough without asking them to be Franz Beckenbauer. I am all for goalkeepers assessing play and throwing or kicking the ball out swiftly in order to take advantage of positional lapses, but realistically goalkeepers are not outfield technicians.

The Danish centre-back Daniel Agger enjoyed a 175 Premier League game stint with Liverpool 2006–2014. Agger had the thankless task of following Liverpool legends Ron Yeats, Alan Hansen and Sami Hyypiä. At times I wasn't sure that Agger had the presence to replicate these iconic defenders, but he came good after an uncertain start with the club.

Agger made an impressive start to his professional career with Brondby in Denmark, winning the Danish Superliga and the Danish Cup in his first season, 2004–05. Agger was awarded the Talent of the Year, the Danish equivalent of the English PFA award. He would go on to win the Danish Footballer of the Year Award in 2007 and 2012.

Agger's £6 million transfer to Liverpool in January 2006 made him Denmark's most expensive football export at that time. Injuries prevented his appearance in the 2006 FA Cup Final, continuing to hold him back at the start of the 2006–07 season. He also had to compete with Carragher and Hyypiä for a centre-back position. He began to make inroads at the club when scoring from 35 yards against West Ham United, the goal voted Liverpool's Premiership Goal of the Season. In the first leg of this 2006–07 Champions League semi-final, the 'monster' Didier Drogba (such a powerful player for Chelsea) dribbled easily past Agger to set up Joe Cole's goal, drawing widespread criticism of the Dane. Agger's response came in the second leg at Anfield, scoring another delightful goal to set up extra time and Liverpool's eventual penalty shoot-out victory. He ultimately played every minute of the final. A metatarsal injury in 2007–08 saw Agger lose his place again to the redoubtable Hyypiä. Surgery for a recurring back injury followed in August 2009. Martin Skrtel was preferred in 2010–11 as Agger continued to suffer injury problems. Injuries dogged Agger constantly in the next few seasons, the player deciding to return to Brondby in August 2014.

Agger's goal return – for a defender – with Denmark is impressive: 11 goals in 75 internationals. He took over his country's armband as captain from Christian Poulsen in 2012 and led his country to successful 2012 Euro qualification. In a tough group the Danes finished third behind Germany and Portugal in a tournament held in Poland and the Ukraine. He retired from international football in 2016.

Alongside Xabi Alonso this time in midfield was another outstanding foreign international, the Argentine Javier Mascherano. My only reservation here was that the two players both preferred to sit in midfield rather than get forward to supplement the attack. This was Gerrard's role immediately in front of them. In addition, wide player Jermaine Pennant and Boudewijn Zenden were positioned to support Dirk Kuyt, the lone striker,

Javier Mascherano was one of the best defensive midfielders of his generation. Mascherano began professionally with River Plate, winning the Argentine Primera Division in his first full season, 2003–04. After two seasons he transferred to Corinthians, the Sao Paulo-based Brazilian club, winning the Brazilian Serie A in his first and only season there. In 2006–07 he signed for West Ham United, playing only five times due to contractual difficulties.

Loaned out to Liverpool at the beginning of 2007, the move became permanent, a fee of £18.6 million paid for Mascherano's services. Alonso immediately praised the Argentinian's cool mind and tactical intelligence on a football pitch – the Argentine was then only 22 years of age. In this 2006 Champions League Final, Mascherano and Alonso were able to stifle the creativity of Kaka and Seedorf – but at a price. Bobby Charlton found out in the 1966 World Cup Final when nullifying Franz Beckenbauer – the same thing happened in reverse, that you fail to create yourself. Liverpool fans appreciated Mascherano's endeavours in this game, voting him their Man of the Match.

Mascherano swiftly became a regular fixture in the Liverpool team, even if his disciplinary record left something to be desired. In the 2009–10 season the Argentine had the worst disciplinary record in the Premier League with five yellow cards and two red cards.

Returning from the 2010 World Cup unsettled (players talk at tournaments), Mascherano put in a transfer request. In August 2010 he signed for Barcelona. Barca remodelled him into a centre-back. At a team including Messi, Xavi and Iniesta, a team under Pep Guardiola regarded as the greatest club team of all time, Mascherano won five La Liga titles, two Champions League titles and two FIFA Club World Cups 2010–18. He played 203 La Liga games, only scoring once after being converted into a central defender. Initially only appearing from the bench in this multi-talented team, Mascherano cemented his place in the team in his second season, 2011–12. The 2015 Champions League was won, Barca defeating Juventus 3-1 in Berlin. Mascherano played the whole match, other match-winners Luis Suarez (Uruguay) and Neymar (Brazil) now in the team, both scoring on the night.

At the end of his first full professional season, Mascherano played in the 2004 Copa America (the South American International Championship, their continent's equivalent of the Euros) in Peru against Brazil. The match ended 2-2 after extra time, Brazil winning on penalties. Mascherano's performances earned him the Argentine Player of the Tournament tag from his teammates. The 2007 Copa America Final was lost to Brazil again, this time emphatically, 3-0, despite the Argentines fielding Messi, Carlos Tevez, Juan Riquelme, Gabriel Milito, Javier

Zanetti, Sebastian Veron. Mascherano was again named Argentina's Player of the Tournament.

At the 2006 and 2010 World Cup tournaments, Argentina lost at the quarter-final stage, on both occasions to Germany, Mascherano having succeeded Zanetti as captain of his country. In 2014 Argentina reached the World Cup Final. In a freak accident, Mascherano tore his anus making a slide tackle on Holland's elusive Arjen Robben in the semi-final. Argentina prevailed on penalties after 120 minutes failed to produce a goal. With Mascherano leading from the front Argentina had not conceded a goal in 330 minutes of tournament football. That changed in the final as Germany once more proved their nemesis, Mario Götze scoring the only goal of the game in extra time. Mascherano made more tackles than any other player at the 2014 World Cup and played the third most passes in the tournament with an 89% success rate. Mascherano finally retired from international football after the 2018 World Cup last 16 defeat to France, having played 147 times for his country, scoring three goals. Nicknamed 'El Jefecito' ('The Chief') for his superb organisational skills and reading of the game, Mascherano's tough tackling and sure distribution made him an invaluable teammate and a safe pair of hands.

Jermaine Pennant's career stuttered somewhat over 20 seasons of professional football. Born and raised in The Meadows area of Nottingham, Pennant escaped a crime and drug-ridden youth, but never seemed to fully shake off his upbringing, his chequered playing time not a full reflection of an unfulfilled talent.

A precocious talent, Pennant was signed by Arsenal for £2 million from Notts County in 1999, a record fee for a trainee at that time. Arsenal must have seen something in Pennant, but despite being at the club for six seasons, Pennant could not break into what was an exceptional Arsenal team at that time. His skill did not go unnoticed by England, as he won 24 U-21 caps during this period. At Arsenal, Pennant was continually loaned out: to Watford, Leeds United, Portsmouth. Loaned again to Birmingham City for the last half of the 2004–05 season, Pennant was convicted for drink-driving and sentenced to three months imprisonment. The sentence was reduced to 30 days. Pennant suffered the ignominy of being electrically tagged in a match against Tottenham Hotspur. Relegated in 2005–06 with Birmingham, Liverpool made a surprise bid for Pennant.

Finding some consistent form at last in the 2007–08 season playing on both wings, Rafael Benitez backed Pennant for England inclusion, but then-England manager Steve McLaren ignored the player's form. Loaned out by Liverpool to Portsmouth in the 2008–09 season, Pennant never returned to Anfield. Real Zaragoza 2009–10, Stoke City in August 2010, were his next loan moves. Pennant settled briefly at Stoke, completing 52 games 2011–14, scoring four goals. Tony Pulis, and subsequently Mark Hughes, persevered with the talented Pennant, but a propensity to miss training and break club curfews was not helping his cause. A player of considerable talent, the troubled Pennant simply could not settle anywhere. He played 353 senior games 1999–2017, his 25 goals a ludicrously scant return for such a talent. In recent years he has appeared on ITV's Jeremy Kyle Show and Celebrity Big Brother. It's one of the curses of the modern age, the adoration of celebrity.

What a contrast the left-sided wide player in Liverpool's team on this night was. Dutch international Boudewijn Zenden was a prodigiously hard-working player who played in the highest leagues in Holland, Spain, England and France. His father Pierre was an expert judo practitioner, and sports broadcaster for NOS, the public sports broadcasting company based in Hilversum, northern Holland, for whom he worked from 1968 to 2005. Zenden junior was also competitive in judo, earning a black belt, aged 14, and being a three-time champion of his province of Limburg.

Beginning his professional career with PSV Eindhoven, Zenden developed the left-wing position gradually, eventually displacing Peter Hoekstra from his regular starting role. In his fourth season at PSV, Zenden helped the club win the Dutch Eredivisie. He also won the 1997 Dutch Talent of the Year Award. Scoring 12 goals in 23 games in the 1997–98 season, Zenden was snapped up by Barcelona. Although signed by compatriot Louis van Gaal, another fellow Dutchman, the quicksilver Marc Overmars kept Zenden out of the Barcelona starting 11. Having to rethink his role at Barcelona, the persistent Zenden replaced local favourite Sergi as a left-back, Barcelona going on to win La Liga in 1998–99. When van Gaal left, Zenden lost favour.

Zenden moved to Chelsea in 2001, playing in the 2002 FA Cup Final defeat to Arsenal, but injuries plagued him. He was loaned out to Middlesbrough for the 2003–04 season. At The Riverside Stadium Zenden found success, scoring the winning goal from the penalty spot as Boro won their first trophy in the club's history, the 2004 League Cup. Zenden was deployed as a central midfielder in the 2004–05 season, winning the fans' vote as Player of the Year.

Moving to Liverpool in July 2005, Zenden's luck ran out again in December 2005 as he suffered a serious cruciate ligament injury to his right knee. Further knee surgery was required in November 2006. He played in both legs of the Champions League semi-final in April 2006, scoring Liverpool's first goal in the victorious penalty shoot-out against Chelsea. Zenden started the final, only to be replaced by Harry Kewell just before the hour mark.

An abortive move to Marseille followed in July 2007. He was unable to attain regular football in the south of France. Expressing a desire to return to England, Blackburn Rovers and Portsmouth showed interest. In October 2009, Zenden trialled for Steve Bruce's Sunderland, subsequently earning a permanent contract. He stayed for two seasons, ending his playing days in the north-east.

Zenden played 54 times for Holland 1997–2004, scoring seven goals. He represented Holland at the 1998 World Cup, and the 2000 and 2004 Euros, his best displays coming at the 2000 Euros when Holland thrashed Yugoslavia 6-1 in the quarter-finals. He started the semi-final against Italy, Holland ultimately being eliminated on penalties after a goalless 120 minutes.

Fellow Dutchman Dirk Kuyt forged a fine relationship with Anfield fans, his work ethic even greater than Zenden's. At Utrecht, Kuyt played 160 Eredivisie games, scoring 51 goals, winning the KNVB Cup in his final season with the club, 2002–03, scoring the first goal as his team beat the club he would join next, Feyenoord, 4-1. Moving to Feyenoord for the following 2003–04 season, Kuyt surpassed his previous goals total in style, 71 in 101 Eredivisie games. He also became club captain in 2005. He top-scored in the Eredivisie in the 2004–05 season, top scoring at Feyenoord for three consecutive seasons. Kuyt formed an excellent partnership with the Ivorian Salomon Kalou who would later join Chelsea in 2006.

Kuyt joined Liverpool for £10 million in August 2006, making 233 appearances in all competitions 2006–2012, making 179 consecutive appearances between 2001 and 2006, a rare case of a player free of injuries it seemed. At Liverpool, Kuyt's goal return was slightly less prolific, a roughly 1-in-4 ratio, 51 goals in 208 Premier League games. What was never in doubt was the Dutchman's prodigious work rate. Kuyt endeared himself to the Anfield faithful by walking to every corner of the ground after a game and applauding them. It was Kuyt's winning penalty kick against Chelsea in the last four that took Liverpool through to this 2007 Champions League Final. With Fernando Torres introduced to the team and instantly becoming a new cult hero as Liverpool's centre-forward, Kuyt switched to the wings in order to preserve his place in the first team in the 2007–08 season.

In the semi-finals of the Champions League, Kuyt opened the scoring at Anfield in the first leg. This time Chelsea exacted revenge on the Reds, winning 4-3 on aggregate over the two legs. A remarkable four years for Liverpool in the Champions League – winners 2005, finalists 2007, semi-finalists 2008, would not be repeated for another decade or so. The 2010–11 season saw Kuyt top-score for Liverpool with 13 Premier League goals, 15 in all competitions, including his first Premier League hat-trick against fierce rivals Manchester United in a 3-1 win at Anfield. Only used as a substitute in the 2010–11 League Cup Final against Cardiff City, Kuyt came on for Andy Carroll and scored in the extra-time period. He subsequently scored a penalty in Liverpool's successful shoot-out win.

Kuyt then spent three seasons in Turkey with Fenerbahce 2012–15, before returning to Feyenoord for the 2015–16 season. Twenty-six goals for Fenerbahce over three seasons were followed by 31 in 63 Eredivisie games 2015–17, Feyenoord also winning the KNVB Cup, beating Utrecht 2-1 in the final in Kuyt's first season back at the club. Kuyt ended his playing days in rare fairy-tale style (something the deserving Steven Gerrard was unable to do in that desperately unfortunate 2013–14 Premier League season) by helping Feyenoord win their first Eredivisie title since 1999, scoring a hat-trick on the final day of the season. Three days later, in 2017, he retired from playing football. What a way to go out! Kuyt played 636 senior games, scoring 284 goals, a proper goalscorer – yet it's his insatiable drive and energy that's best remembered at Anfield.

Kuyt played 104 times for Holland, scoring 24 goals. He played in the notorious 'Battle of Nuremburg' last 16 defeat in the 2006 World Cup against Portugal, but has better memories of the 2008 Euros, assisting two goals in the 3-0 defeat of Italy in the group stages, and scoring the second goal in the impressive 4-1 win over 2006 World Cup finalists France. Holland then lost to the Andrey Arshavin-inspired Russians in the last 16. Runners-up to Spain in the 2010 World Cup, Kuyt scored against Denmark in the group stages, assisted Wesley Schneider's winning goal against Brazil in the last eight, and Arjen Robben's goal against Uruguay in the last four. At the 2014 World Cup, Kuyt, under Louis van Gaal, played in unfamiliar full-back positions, right and left, as Holland reached the semi-finals only to lose on penalties to old foes Argentina.

Kuyt's efforts in the red shirt of Liverpool and the orange shirt of Holland were there for all to see, and his commitment to Feyenoord was absolute. All football fans love a trier, and Dirk Kuyt always seemed to be giving 110% effort. He wasn't a bad goalscorer either.

Liverpool's substitutes in Athens included Dudek, Hyypiä and Kewell, all from the 2005 final. Only Kewell entered the fray. Other substitutes included strikers Peter Crouch and Craig Bellamy. Manager Rafael Benitez did not call on the nippy Bellamy, preferring to use Crouch as an attacking replacement for Mascherano in the 78th minute with the game slipping away.

AC Milan's full-backs changed from 2005, Massimo Oddo (34 caps for Italy) and Czech international Marek Jankulovski (78 caps) in place of Cafu and the great Paolo Maldini. Liverpool still had to bypass two internationals in the full-back berths. Maldini switched to centre-back here in the Olympic Stadium, Athens alongside Alessandro Nesta. AC Milan were arguably stronger in the centre of defence in 2007 with these two masters of the art of defending.

AC opted to play with a 4-4-1-1 formation on this occasion, Andrea Pirlo still the playmaker, but with Gennaro Gattuso to his right, Clarence Seedorf on the left side of midfield, and another tireless worker, Massimo Ambrosini alongside Pirlo in the centre of midfield. Ambrosini, unusually for an Italian footballer, blond-haired, played 344 Serie A games for AC Milan, scoring 29 goals. In his 18-year career at the San Siro, Ambrosini won much respect for his stamina and aggressive style of play, his capability as a six-footer at set-pieces, and his ball-winning capacity. Ambrosini captained the team 2009–2013 after Maldini retired. Recurring injuries prevented a greater impact and a lengthier appearance record for Milan. Ambrosini represented Italy on 35 occasions without scoring due to his deployment as a defensive midfielder.

With Kaka in his favoured role of second striker, in the hole, Filippo Inzaghi led the line for AC Milan in Athens. One could easily confuse the Piacenza, Emilia Romagna-born Inzaghi with Liverpool's 2005 striker Milan Baros, both players adorned with long, dark shocks of hair. Inzaghi scored more goals than Baros, 197 career Serie A goals in 466 games.

Starting with hometown club Piacenza, Inzaghi helped the team win Serie B in 1994–95, scoring 15 goals in 39 games. A muted season at Parma 1995–96 followed, two goals in 15 Serie A games, but he exploded into life at Atalanta in 1996–97, topping Serie A's scoring list with 24 goals, scoring against every team in the league that season, a remarkable feat. Unsurprisingly, he won the 1996–97 Serie A Young Footballer of the Year Award.

Moving to Juventus, Inzaghi formed a formidable attacking triumvirate with Alessandro Del Piero and Zibeline Inane. In the seasons 1997–2001 Inzaghi scored 57 times in 120 Series A games for Juve. He became the first Juventus player to score two Champions League hat-tricks, against Dynamo Kiev and Hamburger SV. In the 1997–98 season Juventus won the Scudetto, Inzaghi scoring 18 goals, adding a further six in the Champions League, although Juve lost the final to Real Madrid 1-0 in Amsterdam. His teammate on this 2007 occasion, Clarence Seedorf, was in the opposition line-up. In the 1998–99 Champions league semi-final Inzaghi score twice against Manchester United, United's refusal to be beaten surfacing as they overturned Inzaghi's early goals in Turin to win 3-2. With 16 goals in all competitions in 1999–2000, Inzaghi was Juve's top scorer for the third consecutive season. The copybook was being blotted by a change in his relationship and on-field partnership with Del Piero. Individualists both, the pair no longer combined in harmony for the sake of the team.

The arrival of Frenchman David Trezeguet in Turin compromised Inzaghi's position in the Juventus team. As a consequence, Inzaghi moved to AC Milan in 2001. Inzaghi's goal return at AC Milan tells you everything you need to know about the move: 73 goals in 202 Serie A games. In the 2002–03 Champions League Final, Inzaghi, having formed a positive new strike partnership with the great Ukrainian Andriy Shevchenko, helped AC Milan beat his former club Juventus 3-2 in a penalty shoot-out after a goalless 120 minutes. The 2002–03 Coppa Italia followed, a 6-3 aggregate victory over A.S. Roma, Inzaghi scoring in the home leg at the San Siro. Inzaghi notched a third Champions League hat-trick in this season against Deportivo de la Coruna, totalling 12 goals in all in Europe in the 2002–03 season. AC Milan won the 2003–04 Scudetto, but knee injuries began to restrict Inzaghi's appearances. Still he notched four goals in five Champions League games in the 2005–06 season, recovering sufficiently to be the match-winner in this 2007 Champions League Final.

In all, Filippo Inzaghi scored ten hat-tricks in Serie A, the most in the 25 years that preceded his time with AC Milan, surpassing Hernán Crespo's eight and Roberto Baggio, Marco van Basten and Gabriel Batistuta's seven. Inzaghi became the all-time top scorer in all European club competitions with a Champions League goal in 2010 against Real Madrid in a 2-2 draw, the goal being his 70th. The record has since been surpassed by Cristiano Ronaldo, Lionel Messi, Robert Lewandowski and Real Madrid's Raul and Karim Benzema.

A member of Italy's 1994 European U-21 Championship-winning team, Inzaghi went on to attain 57 full caps, scoring 25 goals. His opportunities in tournaments were largely restricted by injuries and the competition he faced from Del Piero and Francesco Totti. A rangy, not especially physical player, Inzaghi relied more on anticipation than strength, earning a reputation as a goal poacher in the mould of our own Jimmy Greaves and Gary Lineker. Johan Cruyff felt he wasn't that great a player, but always managed to be in the right position (a skill in itself), while Alex Ferguson thought Inzaghi "was always offside!" I liked to play off the shoulder of the last defender myself, relying on the ability of my midfielders to thread the ball through the defence at the right moment. At least Inzaghi had top international players to put that into practice! Inzaghi relied on intelligence over physicality to time his runs correctly, no bad thing for a striker.

THE FINAL

There was to be no miracle in 2007. On this occasion, AC Milan proved worthy winners, and Liverpool had no response. Two teams who'd competed for the trophy only two years before, two managers whose stock was rising, and would grow substantially in the coming years, Rafael Benitez and Carlo Ancelotti.

It was immediately evident that Kaka was on top of his game, the Brazilian exhibiting wonderful footwork during the first half. Jermaine Pennant had the first chance for Liverpool, but Dida in AC's goal denied him. Xabi Alonso drove another chance wide. The irrepressible Kaka caused Liverpool endless problems. After he was fouled, Andrea Pirlo's free kick deflected off the lurking Inzaghi and into the net. There was an element of luck about the goal, but the manner of it was Inzaghi's forte. Inzaghi joked afterwards he'd scored four goals in Serie A that season in a similar vein. Liverpool battled away, Steven Gerrard skied a volley over the crossbar, John Arne Riise rifled a 25-yard shot high also. Dirk Kuyt had a shot blocked, but it was Kaka who was the stand-out player of the first half.

In the second half a rare loss of possession for Milan saw Gerrard break away on the left but Dida remained defiant, saving his shot. Riise again tried his luck from distance, this time the ball sailing wide. Kaka then fed the ball through for Inzaghi, Liverpool's defence stepping up in an attempt to play the poacher offside, but Inzaghi had read the line correctly and rounded Pepe Reina to score the decisive goal into an empty net. Liverpool refused to go quietly, Pennant's corner-kick headed on by Daniel Agger and Kuyt diverted his own header past Dida. Peter Crouch, on as a substitute, blasted narrowly over the bar as Liverpool grasped at straws against a superior Milan outfit. Ironically, Milan were not as good as 2005, but neither were Liverpool. Pennant's skill and pace was a reminder of a lost talent; Gerrard was as combative as ever, but this was not his night for shooting. In the end it was Kaka and Inzaghi's night. Paolo Maldini underwent knee surgery two days after the final.

2007–08 CHAMPIONS LEAGUE FINAL
Manchester United 1 v 1 Chelsea (United win 6-5 on penalties)

This was the first all-English final in the history of the Champions League or European Cup. Extraordinarily, the match marked United's 100th anniversary of their English League triumph in 1907–08; the 50th anniversary of the tragic Munich air disaster of 1958; and the 40th anniversary of the club's first European Cup victory of 1968. In winning there was much to celebrate for United. The game was played by two teams revelling in great years after barren spells in the 1970s and 1980s. United came good when Alex Ferguson became manager in 1986, although it took Fergie until the 1990s to begin a United domination of English league football. Chelsea's upsurge happened after José Mourinho took over at the club (although the small matter of Roman Abramovich's money contributed greatly) in 2004, although it was Avram Grant who managed Chelsea on this night. United had outstanding forwards in Paul Scholes, Cristiano Ronaldo, Wayne Rooney and Carlos Tevez. Chelsea were enjoying their own dominant John Terry, Frank Lampard, Didier Drogba era.

Route to the Final
United topped Group F in the group stages comfortably with a 16-point haul. Their first match against Sporting CP in Lisbon was won 1-0 with a goal by who else… Cristiano Ronaldo. The second match, a home tie with A.S. Roma,

followed suit, the 1-0 victory this time coming courtesy of a Wayne Rooney goal. Goals flowed in their third game, a decisive 4-2 victory in the Ukraine over Dynamo Kiev, Rio Ferdinand, Rooney and Ronaldo (twice) the scorers. The Ukrainians were dismissed even more comprehensively at Old Trafford, to the tune of 4-0, a rare start and rare goal for Gerard Piqué, pre-Barcelona fame days, Tevez, Rooney and Ronaldo adding the others. United only beat Sporting CP at the death at Old Trafford, right-back Abel Ferreira giving Sporting an early lead. Tevez equalised shortly after the hour mark, the winner in a 2-1 victory coming in the 92nd minute from... Cristiano Ronaldo. Ronaldo had a habit of scoring against his countrymen in European games. Strangely, Piqué scored again in United's last match of the group stage in Roma in a 1-1 draw, giving United the lead. The scorer for Roma was Mancini, a Brazilian winger, not the better known Roberto who managed Italy to Euro 2020 success against England.

Chelsea topped Group B equally comfortably, four points clear of German club Schalke 04. Their opening game didn't suggest comfortable at all, a surprise 1-1 home draw with Norwegian team Rosenborg of Trondheim who opened the scoring at Stamford Bridge through Finnish central defender Miika Koppinen in the first half. Andriy Shevchenko's goal in the second half spared Chelsea's blushes. An anticipated harder second game brought Chelsea a better scoreline, a fine 2-1 victory against Valencia in Spain. David Villa opened the scoring for the Spaniards, Joe Cole equalising soon after. Didier Drogba sealed victory with a 71st-minute winner. Florent Malouda and Drogba scored as Schalke 04 were beaten 2-0 in Chelsea's first encounter with the Germans, the return game resulting in a 0-0 draw. Chelsea made a better fist of their trip to Trondheim on Norway's western coast, winning 4-0 with two goals from Drogba and additional strikes from Brazilian centre-back Alex and Joe Cole. Rosenborg previously proved their worth by beating Valencia home and away by the same 2-0 scoreline. Chelsea's last game fizzled out into another goalless draw at Stamford Bridge against Valencia.

The passionate Greeks of Olympiakos held Chelsea to a goalless draw in the last 16 first leg. At The Bridge, Chelsea ran out 3-0 winners with goals from the great German international midfielder Michael Ballack, Frank Lampard and Salomon Kalou. Against Fenerbahce in Istanbul in the last eight, Brazilian Deivid de Souza put through his own net to give Chelsea the lead. Colin Kazim-Richards, an itinerant forward who has played variously in England for Bury, Brighton & Hove Albion, Sheffield United, Blackburn Rovers and latterly Derby County, equalised. Deivid then scored an 81st-minute winner for the Turkish club as they ran out 2-1 winners. Ballack and Lampard were able to turn the tables on the Turks in the return game.

Once again Chelsea faced Liverpool in the semi-final for the third time in four years, Liverpool's 'Indian sign' on The Blues finally broken. John Arne Riise's 94th-minute own goal saved a 1-1 draw for Liverpool at Anfield. The return was the same torrid, tense affair of 2005 and 2007, but with more goals. Drogba and Fernando Torres exchanged goals in normal time. Lampard's penalty goal gave Chelsea the lead in extra time, Drogba adding his second, Ryan Babbel pulled one back, but Chelsea held on to win 3-2. Drogba's performances in Europe were exceptional, his presence often giving Chelsea a match-winner. In the Premier League his physical strength and power was brutal as he often bullied teams into submission.

United too were held in their first game in the last 16, a 1-1 draw with Lyon, the prolific striker Karim Benzema giving Lyon the lead. Benzema has since forged an impressive career with Real Madrid. He scored 43 goals in 112 Ligue 1 games with Lyon. At Real his goal return in La Liga is an astonishing 219 in 451 La Liga games as I write (July 2022)). Carlos Tevez scored an 87th-minute equaliser to salvage a draw in Lyon. At Old Trafford, a player who would surpass even Benzema's goal return, scored the only goal for United – Cristiano Ronaldo. A Roma team containing Francesco Totti were dismissed 2-0 at the Stadio Olimpico in the last eight first leg, Tevez scoring the only goal in the return leg as United secured a 3-0 aggregate victory. United edged out the great Barcelona in the semi-finals, the only goal of the ties scored by Paul Scholes at Old Trafford. Barcelona would exact their revenge on United stylishly in the finals of 2009 and 2011.

In goal for United, the Dutchman Edwin van der Sar was the first keeper to properly replace the 'irreplaceable' Peter Schmeichel when he arrived at Old Trafford in 2005. Schmeichel is indubitably the best goalkeeper the Premiership has ever seen – with apologies to Petr Cech – but van der Sar is not far behind them. He was considered to be part of Ajax's second golden generation (after the Cruyff/Neeskens/Krol era). In his career, van der Sar secured 26 trophies, most of them with Ajax or Manchester United. In the 2008–09 season with United, van der Sar set a world record of not conceding a league goal for 1,311 minutes. He is the oldest player to win a Premier League when United won the title in 2010–11. On a personal level he was voted Best European Goalkeeper of the Year in 2009.

Ajax won the 1994–95 Champions League Final against a considerably more experienced AC Milan team containing Maldini, Baresi, Costacurta and Marcel Desailly. The young Ajax team were captained by Danny Blind, father of the future Manchester United player Daley, and featured Rijkaard, Seedorf, the Doer brothers Frank and Ronald, Edgar Davids, Marc Overmars and the fine Finnish striker Jari Litmanen. Ajax were not expected to win, but Patrick Kluivert's goal gave them the trophy. Edwin van de Sar made the goalkeeper's jersey his own by this time. He completed 226 games for Ajax 1990–99, winning the Dutch Goalkeeper of the Year Award in his first four seasons at Ajax. Moving to Juventus, van der Sar's reputation grew in his time in Turin 1999–2001, but he was ultimately ousted by Gianluigi Buffon, who also went on to be one of the world's greatest goalkeepers.

Unhappy about losing his place, van der Sar moved to newly promoted Fulham, spending four seasons at Craven Cottage. In a game in his last season with Fulham, van der Sar saved two penalty kicks from Aston Villa's Colombian striker Juan Pablo Angel. Alex Ferguson took note, signing the Dutchman in June 2005. Totalling 21 clean sheets in the 2008–09 season that followed this Champions League victory, van der Sar won the 2008–09 Barclays Golden Glove as a result. He also won Best European Goalkeeper in 2008–09, 14 years after winning as an Ajax goalkeeper. The Premier League recognised him by making him part of their 2008–09 PFA Team of the Year. His appearance in the 2011

Champions League Final against Barcelona made him the oldest player to play in a final in the Champions League era at 40 years, 211 days – only Juventus's Dino Zoff surpassed the feat back in the European Cup era, playing in goal for Juve in the 1-0 defeat to Hamburger SV in 1983, aged 41 years, 86 days.

Edwin van der Sar's misfortune in international tournaments for Holland could have seen him cast as an 'English player' – being knocked out on penalties at the 1996 and 2000 Euros, and at the 1998 World Cup. He was Holland's most capped player with 130 caps until Wesley Schneider exceeded the total in 2017.

At right-back for United, Wes Brown was a product of the club's youth academy. Born in Longsight, three miles south of Manchester city centre, Brown joined the academy aged 12. He was part of Lilleshall's FA School of Excellence, signing professional forms for United aged 17. Alex Ferguson believed Brown was the club's most natural defender, but injuries marred Brown's progress after being a valuable squad member of the 1998–99 treble-winning team. With Nemanja Vidic partnering Rio Ferdinand in one of the club's best ever centre-back pairings, Brown switched successfully to right-back, assisting Cristiano Ronaldo's goal in this 2008 Champions League Final.

Brown completed 232 Premier League games for United before moving to Sunderland in 2011, playing 76 times for the north-eastern club until 2016. In the 2014–15 season he was sent off against Manchester United incorrectly after another former United defender John O'Shea committed a foul. The red card was later rescinded. He played 8 U-21 games for England, and received 23 full caps 1999–2010.

The Senegalese-born French internationalised left-back Patrice Evra was quick across the ground, and occasionally quick of temper. At his peak, Evra was one of the best left-backs in Europe. Evra was rejected by Toulouse and Paris Saint-Germain as a teenager due to his small stature. How PSG in particular would come to rue that decision. Serie C team Marsala in western Sicily approached Evra, and it was in the southern Mediterranean that the player started his professional career. A move to Serie B side Monza proved a further frustration for Evra.

Evra's family moved to France when he was one year old, his father a diplomat. Evra decided to return to France from Monza, when he finally began to make headway in the game with first Nice, and then AS Monaco. Initially Evra played for Nice as a left-winger, even as a centre-forward, only dropping to left-back due to injuries suffered by teammates. At the end of the 2001–02 season, Evra was named in the Ligue 2 Team of the Year in the left-back position.

Moving to Monaco for the 2002–03 season, Evra wanted to play left-wing, but manager Didier Deschamps insisted he play left-back. Evra later declared that Deschamps made him a better player. Evra played alongside the cultured Mexican centre-back Rafael Márquez and the future Arsenal centre-back Sébastien Squillaci in Monaco's defence. Monaco finished second to Lyon in Ligue 1 that season, winning the Coupe de la Ligue (League Cup). In the 2004–05 season Evra was in the team that defeated Chelsea 5-3 on aggregate in the Champions League semi-finals. The final was lost 3-0 to José Mourinho's Porto, but Evra was voted the UNFP (National Union of Professional Footballers) Young Player of the Year, and also named in the French Ligue 1 Team of the Year. The 2005–06 season would be Evra's last with Monaco after playing 120 Ligue 1 games.

Injuries and disaffection with lack of playing time when fit caused Gabriel Heinze, the Argentinian full-back and central defender, to be sidelined at Old Trafford. The stubborn Ferguson refused to sell Heinze to Liverpool and moved for Evra as a replacement, with Heinze eventually sold to Real Madrid. Heinze had been United's Player of the Year in 2004–05. Evra would soon win equal affection among the regular crowd at Old Trafford. His first season was a difficult one, his transition to the Premier League tougher than he'd imagined it would be. Evra was only used as a substitute as United beat Wigan Athletic 4-0 in the 2006 League Cup Final. A confrontation with Liverpool's Steve Finnan led to allegations of racism that were never substantiated. Ferguson also favoured Mikael Silvestre over Evra in his first season with the club. Evra only played 24 Premier League games in 2006–07, but he was still named in the PFA Team of the Year, despite his irregular starts. In 2007–08 Evra finally held down the left-back position permanently, playing 48 games in all competitions, United winning a second successive Premier League title, and reaching this Champions League Final.

Evra, an opinionated player, suffered further problems at Chelsea with a groundsman in 2008–09, causing more friction when United defeated Arsenal 4-1 on aggregate in this season's Champions League semi-final by stating it had been "men against boys". The PFA liked him anyway, selecting him for their Team of the Year for a second time. The 2009–10 season was a mixed one for Evra and United. The Senegalese-Frenchman's increased competitiveness saw him captain United to a 2010 League Cup victory, 2-1 over Aston Villa. United lost out in the Premier League to Chelsea, and were beaten in the Champions League quarter-finals by Bayern Munich. Evra's personal consolation came in being named in the FIFPRO World XI for the 2009 calendar year. In 2011–12 Evra's confrontation with Luis Suarez of Liverpool led to a third allegation of racial abuse since he joined United. The feisty Evra was also building up a threat as an attacking full-back, remarkably scoring three headers in 13 Premier League games in the 2012–13 season against Newcastle United, Arsenal and Swansea City. Another Premier League goal against Newcastle and an FA Cup goal against Stoke City made this his best scoring season with United. Evra completed 273 Premier League games with United, scoring seven times.

Evra moved to Juventus in Italy in July 2014, playing in the 2015 Champions League defeat against Barcelona. The defeat meant Evra became the first player to lose four Champions league Finals – thank heavens for the fortuitous penalty shoot-out victory over Chelsea here in 2008! His consolation at Juve came with two successive Serie A titles in 2014–15 and 2015–16. Returning to France with Marseille in January 2017, Evra became embroiled in an incident with a fan who ridiculed him in November 2017 while warming up for a Europa League match. It seems controversy was never far away from Evra, but his commitment while playing made him one of Manchester United's best ever left-backs.

Evra played 81 times for France 2004–2016. He used the perceived snub of missing out on the 2006 World Cup as motivation to be recalled after injury. In his early international years, Evra was often cast as reserve to Eric Abidal of Lyon, then Barcelona. Abidal's move to centre-back before the 2010 World Cup opened the door for Evra's inclusion at left-back. Evra went on to captain France. Evra, in supporting a dispute involving Nicolas Anelka, led the players in a strike action at the World Cup when they refused to train. He was stripped of the captaincy soon afterwards. In and out of the team under Laurent Blanc, he was eventually selected for the 2012 Euros when France were eliminated 2-0 in the quarter-finals by Spain. He played in four of France's five 2014 World Cup games, again the last eight the last stage for France as they were beaten 1-0 by Germany. Evra's excellent technique made him especially effective in both defence and attack. He was a wonderful technician, even if his aggression sometimes spilled over in his career into off-field altercations. At his peak he was among the best left-backs in the world.

Rio Ferdinand – England's best ever footballing centre-half? United's current England incumbent Harry Maguire valiantly attempted to be Ferdinand's successor, although he may not be as good defensively. Back in Ferdinand's day it was great to see England playing football from the back through Ferdinand, and the Camberwell, Southwark-born Londoner also made the perfect foil for the more traditional stopper John Terry.

The son of an Irish mother and an Afro-Saint Lucian father, Ferdinand was never your typical working-class footballer, despite his mother being one of six children and his father bringing ten children with him from St Lucia. His parents never married, separating when he was 14. A childhood evolved where his mother worked as a child carer, and his father as a tailor. In his second year at Blackheath Bluecoat School in the borough of Greenwich, fellow pupil Stephen Lawrence was killed while waiting for a bus in Eltham in April 1993. The infamous case revealed to Ferdinand the ever-presence of street violence in London. Ferdinand expressed himself through sport, but general exercise too, competing in the London Youth games at gymnastics for Southwark. He also won a scholarship to attend the Central School of Ballet, classes he attended aged 11–15. Two of my own sons represented Woking Gymnastics Club, competing for Surrey in the national championships at Lilleshall. It never harmed their performance in football, where one was exceptional in the air, while they were both athletic and disciplined due to their time in gymnastics aged 6–16. It didn't harm Rio Ferdinand's balance and aerial prowess either. Ferdinand played as an attacking midfielder for Eltham Town, but scouts saw him as a centre-back because of his physique. He trained with Chelsea, Charlton Athletic, Millwall and Queens Park Rangers before joining West Ham United's youth system in 1992, playing alongside Frank Lampard (junior) in the youth academy. At 16 he joined the England youth team squad to compete in the UEFA European Championship.

Scouted by Frank Lampard (senior), Ferdinand earned a senior contract, coming on for Tony Cottee in his first senior game, a 1-1 draw with Sheffield Wednesday in May 1996. Manchester United enquired about him in the summer of 1997, West Ham rebuffing them. Loaned to AFC Bournemouth for ten games in 1996, Rio returned to West Ham to win the 1997–98 Hammer of the Year, aged 19.

Leeds United paid an £18 million transfer fee for Ferdinand in November 2000, a British record at the time, as well as being the world's costliest fee for a defender. After a faltering start at Elland Road, Ferdinand excelled, scoring a header in the 2000–01 Champions League quarter-final against Deportivo de la Coruna, won 3-2 on aggregate. The semi-final proved a step too far, a Gaizka Mendieta-inspired Valencia putting Leeds out 3-0 on aggregate. After the 2002 World Cup, Ferdinand forced the belated move to Manchester United through against Leeds' will. The £30 milllion fee paid by Alex Ferguson's United in July 2002 meant for a second time Ferdinand was Britain's costliest player, and the world's most expensive defender.

Ferdinand went on to play 312 Premier League games for United (seven goals), winning the Premier League title in his first season. Ferdinand was selected for the PFA Team of the Year four times in five seasons 2004–05 to 2008–09, missing out only in 2005–06. Ferdinand captained United in this Champions League Final. In a portent of the appalling racial abuse happening across central and Eastern Europe a decade and more later, Ferdinand criticised FIFA's inertia after Emile Heskey was abused after England beat Croatia 4-1 in Zagreb.

Back and knee injuries spoiled the 2009–10 season for Ferdinand, the knee ailment causing him to miss the 2010 World Cup. How England missed him in that fateful 4-1 thrashing against old foes Germany in the last 16. On 12 May 12 2013 Ferdinand scored the final goal of the Alex Ferguson era (the club are still trying to bring back the good old days) in a 2-1 win over Swansea City. A new contract for the 2014–15 season not forthcoming, Ferdinand moved to Queens Park Rangers, but played only 12 times as QPR were relegated from the Premiership in May 2015.

Rio Ferdinand's 81 caps for England make him the second highest-capped black player behind Ashley Cole (107). A missed drugs test and England's failure to qualify for Euro 2008 meant Ferdinand never played in a European Championship. He earned his first cap for England against Cameroon in 1997, aged 19, the youngest defender to play for England until Manchester City's Micah Richards broke the record in 2006. First choice centre-back under Sven-Göran Eriksson at the 2002 and 2006 World Cups, it was Ferdinand's misfortune to be beaten by the mischief of Ronaldinho of Brazil in the former, and the lottery of a penalty shoot-out against Portugal in the latter, both times in quarter-finals. In seven of the ten World Cup finals matches played with Ferdinand in the centre of England's defence clean sheets were kept, confirming the magnitude of his absence when England lost to Germany in 2010.

Ferdinand was left out of the 2012 World Cup squad chosen by Roy Hodgson following an incident between his brother Anton and John Terry in a Queens Park Rangers versus Chelsea match in which England teammate Terry was accused of abuse. When Gary Cahill withdrew injured from the squad, Hodgson even called up untried 22-year-old Martin Kelly from Crystal Palace. The decision caused quite a stir. With Terry retiring from international football, Hodgson recalled Ferdinand in March 2013, but he withdrew with fitness concerns, retiring from international football himself in May 2013.

Confident on the ball, composed, Ferdinand was an atypical English defender.

He was especially elegant for a player standing six feet two inches. Ideal with Vidic or Terry as the aggressor of the pair of centre-backs, Ferdinand's excellent technique and spatial awareness enabled him to play equally well as a sweeper in a back three with the other two defenders slightly in front, and supported by wing-backs on the flanks. A good leader who overcame inconsistencies in his early days, only his waning pace in later years detracted from his reputation of being one of the very best centre-backs in world football.

The Yugoslav Nemanja Vidic made an excellent partner for Ferdinand in this final. Vidic is one of only three (and the only defender) players to win the Premier League Player of the Season twice, the others being Thierry Henry and Cristiano Ronaldo. Vidic's first years in professional football were spent at Red Star Belgrade where he won the 2001–02 Yugoslav Cup, by now renamed the Serbia and Montenegro Cup. Vidic became captain, scoring 12 goals in 67 matches and ending his tenure in Belgrade by winning the domestic double of league and cup in 2003–04. Signing for Sparta Moscow in Russia in July 2004, Vidic became the most expensive defender in the Russian Premier League, although no fee was disclosed.

Manchester United had Vidic on their radar, but only signed him in January 2006 after a protracted wrangle over a work permit and competition from Serie A's Fiorentina in Italy. Vidic came on as a substitute for Wes Brown in the 2006 League Cup Final win over Wigan Athletic, sportingly donating his medal to teammate Guiseppe Rossi for his contribution in earlier rounds of the competition. Vidic won the Premier League title in 2006–07, forming a formidable partnership with Ferdinand. The club repeated the feat in 2007–08, Vidic winning his first European medal in this Champions League Final. In the 2008–09 season United kept 14 consecutive clean sheets in the Premier League with Vidic and Ferdinand supreme. Vidic was named United's Player's Player of the Year and Fans' Player of the Year for 2008–09. The 2010–11 Premier League title was Manchester United's 19th winning of England's top tier. A twisted knee put Vidic out of the second half of the 2011–12 season. Another knee injury curtailed Vidic's appearances in the 2012–13 season, but United won their 20th Premier League title, 11 points ahead of holders Manchester City. That must have been sweet. In his last home match for United in May 2014 against Hull City, Vidic received a standing ovation from the fans during a pre-match presentation made to him by director Bobby Charlton.

Vidic moved to Inter Milan in Italy, but injuries meant he only played 23 games in Serie A 2014–16. Vidic played 367 senior games 2000–2016, scoring 38 goals, 15 of them at United in the Premier League. During the 2006 World Cup qualification period, Serbia and Montenegro conceded only one goal with Vidic in their back four, a new record for the fewest goals conceded. Injured knee ligaments, sadly, put him out of the 2006 World Cup proper where his country finished bottom of a 'group of death' featuring Argentina, Holland and the Ivory Coast. Again Serbia and Montenegro had the best defensive record in qualification for the 2010 World Cup (in a group containing France and Romania); again they finished bottom in their group at the 2010 World Cup. Physically strong at six feet three inches, strong in the air, aggressive in the tackle, Nemanja Vidic was the perfect centre-back. His positioning and decisive play compensated for a slight lack of pace.

The deeper players in United's midfield were Michael Carrick and Paul Scholes. Carrick, a six feet two inches Geordie born in Wallsend, Newcastle-upon-Tyne, started out as a centre-forward, his height a natural indicator of this decision. Carrick's forte was technique, not power, despite his size. He became a pivotal playmaker for both West Ham United and Manchester United thanks to his control and passing ability.

Only upon becoming a member of West Ham's youth squad did Carrick convert to midfield, winning the FA Youth Cup Final in 1998–99 with a record 9-0 aggregate victory over Coventry City. At the end of his first senior season, 1999–2000, Carrick was voted West Ham's Young Player of the Year. His breakthrough season came in 2000–01, playing 41 games in the first team in all competitions. Previously manager Harry Redknapp had been concerned with Carrick's growth spurts, and his inability to cope with the physical demands of senior football. At the end of this 2000–01 season he was voted West Ham's Young Player of the Year for the second successive year. A recurring groin injury kept him out of England's 2002 World Cup squad. When West Ham were relegated at the end of the 2002–03 season, Carrick stayed put for another year after star players Frederic Kanoute, Joe Cole and Jermain Defoe moved on. In the 2003–04 season West Ham reached the 1st Division Play-Off Final, only to lose 1-0 to Crystal Palace. Carrick was selected in the PFA Team of the Year for the 1st Division.

Portsmouth, Arsenal, Everton and West Bromwich Albion clamoured for his signature, but Carrick opted to move to Tottenham Hotspur. Carrick couldn't win a place in the first team under Jacques Santini, but when Martin Jol took over the Dutchman utilised Carrick's poise and passing proficiency. Carrick ended a relatively disappointing season for Tottenham making more passes and crosses than any of his teammates, sharing top assists with Egyptian striker Mido.

Jol didn't want Carrick to leave, rejecting an initial offer from Manchester United, but the Tynesider moved to Old Trafford in July 2006 as a replacement for Roy Keane. Carrick was never going to replace a midfield powerhouse like Keane. Instead he gave United another dimension, that of a metronomic playmaker in the Andrea Pirlo mode. Carrick liked to sit at the base of the midfield where he could influence the game with his passing, unlike the box-to-box Keane.

Carrick scored his first Champions League goals (two) in April 2007 in an astonishing 7-1 routing of Roma in the last eight in a second leg tie at Old Trafford. Unfortunately for United, AC Milan would prevent an all-English final with Liverpool. The Premier League title served as a sizeable consolation. Carrick's luck was not so good in October 2007 against Roma in the Champions League, an elbow break putting him out of action for six weeks. The title came to Old Trafford again in 2008. This Champions League success of 2008 in which Carrick converted a penalty kick in the shoot-out would be the player's first European success. The title was won for a third consecutive season in 2009, but European success eluded United, beaten 2-0 by a Barcelona team at the peak of their powers in the Champions League Final. Carrick stated that the game just passed him by, so superior were Barca.

Worse was to come in 2011 at the hands of the same opponents. The 2009–10 season saw Carrick playing as a utility centre-back when United suffered an injury crisis. In February 2010 Carrick – who always appeared mild-mannered compared to many of his peers – was sent off for the first time in his career against AC Milan at the San Siro. United won the 2010 League Cup Final against Aston Villa, but conceded the title to Chelsea by a single point, the first season at United that Carrick had failed to win the Premier League.

Responding to another injury crisis in the 2012–13 season, Carrick filled in at centre-back again for United, earning selection to the PFA Team of the Year. Carrick hung on to his place (at times) in the United team as David Moyes came and went. Louis van Gaal made Carrick vice-captain when taking over the management reigns in 2014. When José Mourinho stepped in, Carrick's passing and control impressed the Portuguese, Mourinho rueing the fact that the playmaker was now 35 years old. When Wayne Rooney departed in July 2017, Carrick became club captain. Retiring at the end of the 2017–18 season, Carrick became an important member of United's coaching staff. He had completed 316 Premier League games in 12 seasons, scoring 17 goals.

Between 2001 and 2015 Carrick played 34 times for England, having been capped at U-18 and U-21 level. As a central midfield player, Carrick's opportunities were scarce as he was overlooked in favour of the more forceful Steven Gerrard and Frank Lampard – both of whom also scored considerably more goals. It was Carrick's ability to dictate the tempo of games that made him almost continental in style. He may have suited AC Milan or Barcelona better than the English game. Carrick's unassuming nature seemed to hold him back a little, his quieter approach to the game disguising a deep-thinking, intelligent purveyor of football skills.

Carrick had the sharpest of football brains beside him in Paul Scholes. The Salford-born Scholes possessed the typical shorter man's facility of being able to turn sharply (he stood five feet six inches in his boots). Scholes's instincts took him into great attacking positions, his linking play admirable. He rarely lost possession, his strength and awareness enabling him to keep the ball, his inbuilt antennae telling him when danger was imminent. Thierry Henry thought he was the best player he played against in English football.

In his final term at Cardinal Langley Roman Catholic High School, Scholes was selected to represent Great Britain National Schools at football. Although a member of Manchester United's famous 1992 FA Youth Cup-winning team (and a member of the 'Class of 92'), Scholes did not play regular first team football until the 1994–95 season. The 1992 FA Youth Cup was won 6-3 on aggregate against Crystal Palace, Ryan Giggs named United's Young Player of the Year. Scholes was named the 1992–93 Young Player of the Year, although United lost the FA Youth Cup Final to Leeds United 4-1 over two legs.

In his breakthrough season Scholes came on in the losing 1995 FA Cup Final against Everton (0-1). When Mark Hughes moved to Chelsea for the 1995–96 season, Scholes received more game time, sometimes playing up front alongside Andy Cole. He scored 14 goals in all competitions as United retained the Premier League in 1996–97. Scholes only made the positional switch to central midfield when Roy Keane suffered a knee injury in September 1997. In this famous 1998–99 season Scholes was instrumental in the team's treble achievement. He scored one of United's two goals in the FA Cup Final victory over Newcastle United; he scored a crucial late equaliser against Inter Milan in the quarter-finals of the Champions League; then picked up a yellow card coming on as a substitute for Jesper Blomqvist in the semi-final against Juventus, putting him out of the final against Bayern Munich. Manager Alex Ferguson had been opting for Nicky Butt in certain games, rather than Scholes.

The signing of the Argentine Juan Sebastian Veron in the summer of 2001 saw Scholes's role altered again as he pushed up in the hole behind Ruud van Nistelrooy. In European away games Scholes and Veron played alongside each other with Keane behind anchoring. Scholes scored a career-best 20 goals in all competitions in the 2002–03 season. In the 2005 FA Cup Final, Scholes was one of those whose penalty kick was saved by Jens Lehmann as Arsenal snatched the cup from United's grasp. In 2006–07 Scholes's fine season was rewarded by selection in the PFA Team of the Year. In the semi-final of this 2007–08 Champions League, Scholes scored the only goal of two titanic games against Barcelona to take United through to the final. In September 2008, Paul Scholes was inducted into the English Football Hall of Fame.

Scoring against AC Milan in February 2010 in the Champions League, Scholes became the first player to score against both AC and Inter Milan in the San Siro. The goal was Scholes's 25th in Champions League football, the highest total of any central midfielder in the history of the competition. On 31 May 2011, Scholes announced his retirement, joining the club's coaching staff immediately. After training with the reserves, Scholes declared himself available again for first team duty, returning in January 2012 when United suffered an injury crisis – he then played on until May 2013. In his final match against West Bromwich Albion he was yellow-carded for the 97th time in the Premier League, a record leaving him third behind Lee Bowyer (102) and Kevin Davies (101)! He also amassed 32 yellow cards in the Champions League – only Real Madrid's Sergio Ramos has been booked more times. Better to remember Scholes's sharp tactical brain and explosive shooting.

Scholes played 66 times for England 1997–2004, scoring 14 goals. The difficulty of integrating this class player, admired so much abroad for his technical and tactical acumen, always came about as a result of the presence of two top central midfielders in Steven Gerrard and Frank Lampard. The idea of playing Scholes as a left-sided midfielder never worked. A midfield of Beckham, Gerrard, Lampard and Scholes should have been world-beating. The idea was good, in practice these four wonderful players never fully gelled in England shirts, too often they were playing in unfamiliar roles or positions.

Scholes scored against Tunisia in a 2-0 victory at the 1998 World Cup; in March 1999 he scored a hat-trick against Poland; he scored both goals at Hampden Park as England beat Scotland 2-0 in a Euro 2000 play-off first leg. He also became the first and last player to be sent off at the old Wembley Stadium. He seemed to be a key player going into the 2002 World Cup, but shunted out to the left to accommodate Gerrard and Lampard, his impact was diminished and England lost to Brazil in the last 16. In 2004 Scholes decided to retire from international football, citing family and club commitments with United as his reason. Surely being asked to be a square peg in a round hole also influenced his decision. Future managers Sven-Göran Eriksson and Fabio Capello wanted him to return to the fold. Scholes resisted, later stating he wished he'd at least gone to the 2010 World Cup in South Africa.

Scholes's capacity as a midfield player, although he could play as a second striker, was highly regarded. His range of passing, short and long, was consummate, his shooting exceptional, his timing of a tackle not always so finely tuned! Scholes's tenacity was at odds with calmness on the ball, and an outstanding football brain that allowed him to see situations swiftly, much like Cesc Fàbregas. Many of his peers admired Scholes's slant on the professional game. He was not particularly media-friendly, unlike teammate David Beckham. Scholes preferred to keep a low profile off the pitch, letting his football do the talking. Asthmatic, suffering with the Osgood-Schlatter inflammation of the knee disease, the gutsy Scholes wasn't going to let minor ailments prevent him having a long career with his beloved Manchester United. A one-club man, Scholes played 466 Premier League games, scoring 102 goals, His commitment to his locality was borne out in being part of the Manchester United cartel that purchased Salford City in 2014, along with Gary Neville, Ryan Giggs, Nicky Butt and Phil Neville.

On the right side of midfield, the hard-working and luckless Owen Hargreaves played his football in Germany long before it became an outlet for young English players to gain experience in the Bundesliga (Jadon Sancho, Jude Bellingham). Born in Calgary, Alberta, Canada, to an English father and a Welsh mother, Hargreaves's work ethic was much admired by Bayern Munich, and later Manchester United after moving to Old Trafford in 2007. He just couldn't stay fit.

Hargreaves didn't start playing football seriously until he was 15. Aged 16 he moved to Germany, playing for Bayern Munich's U-19 team for two and a half years. In his first full season (2000–01) with Bayern the team won the Bundesliga and were crowned European Champions beating Valencia in a penalty shoot-out after a 1-1 draw (both goals in the match proper were also penalties). Hargreaves is one of only two players to have won the Champions League with a non-British club, Steve McManaman achieving the feat twice with Real Madrid 1999–2000 and 2001–02 after leaving Liverpool. The Bundesliga was lost to Borussia Dortmund in 2001–02, but won again by Bayern in 2002–03, one of four Bundesliga titles won in Hargreaves's time in Munich. In 2004–05 Bayern won the double of Bundesliga and DFB Pokal Cup. In this season, Hargreaves scored the very first goal in the newly-designed Allianz Arena stadium against Borussia Möenchengladbach. A broken leg in 2006–07 started the beginning of Hargeaves's injury woes. In total, Hargreaves played 145 games in all competitions for Bayern.

In May 2007 Hargreaves joined Manchester United. Incredibly, Hargreaves would play only 27 Premier League games 2007–2011 due to injury. There was little hint of the troubles to come in his first season, Hargreaves playing all 120 minutes of this Champions League Final, United also winning the Premier League. The 2008–09 season saw Hargreaves suffer a recurring knee injury.

Specialists in London and Sweden were unable to help him. He finally went under the knife with notable knee surgeon Richard Steadman in Colorado, USA, in November 2008 and January 2009, both knees operated on in an attempt to cure patellar tendinitis. In May 2011, having stood by Hargreaves in 2009 and 2010, Alex Ferguson decided to deny him a new contract. Hargreaves signed for local rivals Manchester City for the 2011–12 season, but played only one Premier League match.

A tireless worker in midfield, Hargreaves, astonishingly, played more times for England than he did for Manchester United over four seasons. He is the only player to have played for England (while with Bayern Munich) without having lived in the United Kingdom. Capped at U-19 level by Wales, Hargreaves opted for England instead when approached by England U-21 manager Howard Wilkinson in August 2000. Hargreaves's second cap came in the famous 5-1 victory over Germany in the Olympiastadion, Munich, as a substitute, the night of Michael Owen's hat-trick. Hargreaves generally received a negative press in England, but was widely regarded as one of England's better performers at the 2006 World Cup. Rarely can a player have been so cruelly hit by injuries. English football never saw the best of him.

On the left of Manchester United's midfield, ostensibly as a wide midfield player, but the team's third attacker along with Wayne Rooney and Carlos Tevez, Cristiano Ronaldo went on to become one of the best players in the world. Not as naturally gifted as Lionel Messi, Ronaldo compensated with prodigious dedication to his fitness. The Ronaldo-Messi argument as to who has been the best player in the world over the last two decades trundles on in the third decade of the century.

Ronaldo has won five Ballon d'Or Awards: 2008, 2013, 2014, 2016, 2017) – Messi has won six 2009, 2010, 2011, 2012, 2015, 2019. Ronaldo has won four Golden Shoe Awards (European top scorer) – Messi has won six. Ronaldo's goal record is phenomenal: 84 for Manchester United in 196 Premier League games 2003–09; a ridiculous 311 in 292 La Liga games for Real Madrid 2009–2018; 81 in 98 Serie A games for Juventus 2018–2021. He has won 32 career trophies to date (July 2022). He is Real Madrid's all-time top goalscorer. The American business magazine Forbes declared Ronaldo the world's highest-paid sports athlete in 2016 and 2017. He is the first footballer to earn beyond $1 billion in his career.

Madeira-born Ronaldo played youth football for Andorinha in Portugal 1992–95 where his father was a kit man. Aged 15 Ronaldo was diagnosed with a 'racing heart', a condition that required laser surgery cauterising multiple cardiac pathways into one. Thereafter the only thing that was racing was Ronaldo himself as defenders vainly tried to prevent this goal machine scoring for fun. In November 2002, Ronaldo met Arsene Wenger at Arsenal's training grounds. Not for the first time in the coming decade or so, Alex Ferguson gazumped Wenger, encouraging the Madeiran to go to Old Trafford. Even then it was the will of United's players (they thought him ready for first-team action) who won the day as Ferguson sought to loan him back to Sporting Lisbon for a year. Ronaldo signed permanently to United for the 2003–04 season. The first season for the 18-year-old Ronaldo was a question of trials and errors. The Madeiran's dribbling skills were mesmeric, his step-over terrorising opponents, but he needed to learn when to play the final telling pass.

Ferguson thought Ronaldo was one of the most exciting players he'd ever seen. In turn Ronaldo saw Ferguson as a father figure, one of the most influential people in his career. Appearing as a substitute against Bolton Wanderers in August 2003, George Best thought Ronaldo's debut minutes were unparalleled in a United shirt. The 2004–05 FA Cup Final was won, the 2006 League Cup followed. Greater controversy followed in the 2006 World Cup when Ronaldo, a Portuguese international first and foremost, was involved in the sending off of his United club-mate Wayne Rooney as Portugal defeated England. Booed by fans across England throughout the 2006–07 Premier League season, Rooney graciously put aside any differences in the common pursuit of silverware with United. Ironically, Ronaldo scored more than 20 goals in the Premier League for the first time, and the title was won. Ronaldo was beginning to see the bigger picture on the field of play, making himself harder to mark with his acute positional sense. The showboating of his teenage years was on the backburner, Ronaldo won the PFA Player's Player, Fans Player and Young Player of the Year awards, and the Football Writer's Association Footballer of the Year award, the first player to win all four awards in a season. His 31 goals in the Premier League earned him the Golden Boot, as well as the European Golden Shoe. Ronaldo scored United's goal in this 2008 Champions League Final, but failed with his spot-kick in the penalty shoot-out. It proved irrelevant. As Champions League top scorer, Ronaldo also received the UEFA Club Footballer of the Year Award.

The 2007–08 season was prolific for Ronaldo, 42 goals scored in all competitions. Ankle surgery kept him out for ten weeks at the beginning of the 2008–09 season. Winning the 2008 Ballon d'Or and the 2008 FIFA World Player of the Year, Ronaldo became the first player from United to win the former since George Best in 1968, and the first Premier League player to be awarded the latter. Scoring against Porto from 40 yards in the quarter-finals of the Champions League earned Ronaldo the inaugural FIFA Puskás Award for best goal of the year.

Following a long pursuit of the player, Real Madrid signed Ronaldo before the 2009–10 season for a world record transfer fee at the time of £80 million. Eighty-thousand supporters turned up at the Santiago Bernabeu stadium to welcome him to Spain. He scored 33 goals in all competitions in his first season in Madrid, but 'Los Blancos' remained trophy-less. Goals were raining in for Ronaldo in the 2010–11 season. He scored four in a match for the first time against Racing Santander in a 6-1 drubbing, part of a run of 11 goals in six matches including internationals. He equalled his 42 goals in all competitions record scored at United in 2007–08. His first trophy at Madrid, the Copa del Rey in 2011, saw him score an extra-time winner against fierce rivals Barcelona. He became the first player to score 40 goals in La Liga in a season, and won the Golden Shoe again, the first player to win the award playing in different leagues.

Astonishingly, Ronaldo scored 60 goals in all competitions in 2011–12. I played with two players at local level who exceeded 50, but you don't normally see that amount of goals in top-tier football – 40 is exceptional. Real wrenched the La Liga title from Barcelona's grasp, achieving a record 100 points total. His 100th goal (in 92 matches) for Real against Real Sociedad in March 2012 broke the previous record held by the great Ferenc Puskás, the first (along with Alfredo Di Stéfano) truly genius player I witnessed as a boy. Unbelievably, Ronaldo's 46 goals in La Liga were four short of a new record set by... Lionel Messi. Ronaldo, at least, became the first player to score against all 19 La Liga teams in a single season. On 30 January 2013, Ronaldo became the first non-Spanish player in 60 years to captain Real Madrid on the occasion of his 500th club appearance against Barcelona.

Incredibly, the 2013–14 season resulted in 69 goals for Ronaldo in all competitions as he formed a 'BBC' attacking triumvirate with Gareth Bale and Karim Benzema. He automatically won the 2013 FIFA Ballon d'Or, an amalgamation of the Ballon d'Or and the FIFA World Player of the Year. Real won La Decima, their tenth European Cup/Champions League. In defeating Atlético Madrid 4-1 in the 2014 Champions League Final, Ronaldo scored twice, becoming the first player to score in a European Cup Final/Champions League for two different clubs (Manchester United/Real Madrid), yet he played the 2014 final with patellar tendinitis (the same ailment plaguing Owen Hargreaves) and hamstring problems. He was the Champions League's top scorer with 17 goals, a record, and was subsequently named the Best UEFA Player in Europe. He was also named Best Player in La Liga, an audacious back-heeled volley against Valencia in May 2014 not harming his selection.

In 2014–15 Ronaldo scored 61 goals in all competitions. His 23rd La Liga hat-trick helped him reach 200 goals in 178 matches, the fastest the total was reached in. Ronaldo won the 2014 Ballon d'Or, equalling the record of Johan Cruyff, Michel Platini and Marco van Basten as a three-time winner. On 15 April 2015, Ronaldo scored five goals in a match against Granada in a 9-1 victory. Upon scoring his 31st hat-trick for Real against Getafe, Ronaldo passed 30 hat-tricks for the club. The previous highest club record lay with the wonderful Alfredo Di Stéfano on 28. Forty-eight LA Liga goals earned him a second consecutive Pichichi Trophy as Spain's top scorer, and a fourth European Golden Shoe.

Another five-goal haul against Espanyol in September 2015 took Ronaldo to 230 goals in 203 La Liga games, surpassing Raul's previous record. Also in September 2015, Ronaldo set another best first, scoring 11 goals in the Champions League Group stages. A hat-trick followed against VfL Wolfsburg in the quarter-finals. Suffering injuries in the final against Atlético Madrid he still managed to score the conclusive penalty shoot-out winner. For six seasons running Ronaldo had scored over 50 goals in all competitions. He was named UEFA Best Player in Europe in 2015–16 for the second time.

Ronaldo scored both goals in a quarter-final first leg Champions League match against Bayern Munich in the 2016–17 competition, becoming the first player to score 100 goals in the Champions League. He overtook the player I regard as the best British goalscorer of all time, Jimmy Greaves, on 17 May 2017 as he became the all-time top scorer in the top five European Leagues: England, Spain, Italy, Germany and France. He ended the season with 42 goals in all competitions, Real winning their first La Liga since 2012. Scoring two goals in the 4-1 Champions

League victory over Juventus he became the competition's top scorer for the fifth consecutive season, and the first player to score in three Champions League Finals in the modern era. He also won the 2016–17 Ballon d'Or and the 2016 Best FIFA Men's Player (formerly the FIFA World Player of the Year).

On 6 December 2017 Ronaldo became the first player to score in all six Champions League group games. The next day he won the 2017 Ballon d'Or. A bicycle kick goal against Juventus in a 3-0 win in Turin in the 2017–18 season was persuasion enough for Ronaldo's next destination post-Madrid. He finished the competition as top scorer for the sixth consecutive season with 15 goals, Real Madrid beating Liverpool 3-1 in the final.

In his first season in Turin having moved to Italy, Juventus secured an eighth successive Scudetto title, Ronaldo becoming the first player to win titles in England, Spain and Italy. He ended the season with 21 goals, winning the inaugural Serie A award for Most Valuable Player. At the end of the 2019–20 season Ronaldo became the oldest player since Ronnie Rooke at Arsenal in 1948 to score over 30 league goals, aged 35 years and 166 days. Serie A was won for the ninth consecutive season, Ronaldo scoring in the final game of the season in the 2-0 victory over Sampdoria. In November 2020 Ronaldo took three weeks to recover from Covid-19 as the debilitating virus swept the world. By the season's end he'd surpassed all previous Serie A records, top-scoring with 29 goals, an Italian league all-time best. He became the first player to be the top scorer in the English, Spanish and Italian leagues.

Returning to Manchester United, Ronaldo scored three goals in his first five Premier League games, and a dramatic 95th-minute winner against Villareal in the Champions League group game in October 2021. The jury is out on whether this phenomenal goalscorer will be United's saviour at the age of 36, or whether he will imbalance a United team desperately searching for a new identity after a slew of managers followed Alex Ferguson.

Ronaldo made his international debut for Portugal aged 18, coming on as a substitute for the great Luis Figo in August 2013. A 1-0 win over Kazakhstan. Called up for Euro 2004, Ronaldo assisted Portugal's passage to the final, scoring in the semi-final against Holland, before the Portuguese came unstuck against shock winners Greece. Ronaldo was selected to the Team of the Tournament. His wink to the Portuguese bench after Wayne Rooney's dismissal in the 2006 World Cup quarter-final probably lost him the Best Young Player Award, which went to Germany's Lukas Podolski.

A golden generation of players were bringing Portugal closer and closer to winning a major tournament. Deco and Figo couldn't quite manage it – Ronaldo eventually did, but only played 25 minutes of the final at the 2016 Euros. During the tournament he became the first player to score in all the four Euros he'd played in, making a record 17 appearances in all since 2004. Extraordinarily, Portugal finished third in their Euro 2016 group, behind Hungary and Iceland, qualifying for the knockout stages only due to a protracted new format granting best goal difference teams progress. Wales having defied all the odds to reach the semi-finals (in no small part due to the excellence of Gareth Bale and Aaron Ramsey), Portugal then denied them a dream final 2-0, the first goal inevitably coming from Ronaldo. Despite Ronaldo going off injured, Eder's 109th-minute goal extra-time winner over France finally claimed a major trophy for Portugal with a team arguably less talented than some that had gone before it. Their team spirit proved inexhaustible, Ronaldo kicking every ball from the touchline after leaving the field through injury.

In the 2018 World Cup, Ronaldo became the oldest player to score a hat-trick in a remarkable group match against Spain, Portugal recovering to draw 3-3 thanks to an 88th-minute trademark free kick from the Madeiran. Uruguay's 2-1 win in the last 16 condemned Portugal to an early trip home. Two goals against Hungary in the delayed first game of Euro 2021 took Ronaldo's tally in the competition to 11, surpassing Michel Platini's previous best of nine.

In his early days at Manchester United, and with Real Madrid, Ronaldo was something of a free-kick specialist, his 'knuckle-ball' style of getting under the ball and bending it ferociously his trademark. A swift player with immense dribbling capacity early on, Ronaldo became a devastating goalscorer – the best of all time probably – with his increasingly astute penalty-box positioning. He likes to roam freely out on to the flanks to find space, but in later years used his brain to be in the right place at the right time in the penalty area. He clearly hates losing, his passion to be the best and his dedication to personal fitness outside of normal training hours, has taken him to levels beyond most players.

Wayne Rooney exploded into English football consciousness on 19 October 2002, aged 16, five days short of his 17th birthday. Rooney's blockbuster shot in the last minute at Goodison Park ended a 30-match unbeaten run for Arsenal and made the Croxteth, Liverpool-born teenager an instant folk hero. Staff at Goodison knew it was coming – Rooney held the record for goals scored for Liverpool Schoolboys (72) until it was broken in 2010. He scored 99 goals in his last season with Copplehouse Boys Club in the Walton and Kirkdale junior league. Attaching himself to Everton, he scored 114 goals in 29 games for Everton's U-10 and U-11 teams. At 15 he was playing for Everton's U-19 side.

Debuting for the senior side in August 2002, Rooney assisted a goal for Mark Pembridge. He was the club's second youngest first team player behind club legend Joe Royle. In scoring as a 16-year-old against an Arsenal side who were exceptionally strong at the time he became the youngest scorer in Premier League history, a record since surpassed by James Milner and Everton's own James Vaughan. In December 2002 Rooney was named BBC Young Sports Personality of the Year. Rooney's first, significant, spell with Everton ended at the end of the 2003–04 season. He'd scored 15 goals in 67 Premier League games.

Still only 18, he joined Manchester United (having claimed lifelong allegiance to Everton) in the summer of 2004. In September 2004 he scored his first hat-trick in the Champions League against Fenerbahce of Turkey, the youngest player to achieve the feat. Semi-final defeat to Chelsea in the League Cup was followed by a penalty shoot-out defeat in the FA Cup Final against Arsenal, but Rooney received the PFA Young Player of the Year Award. Rooney scored 16 goals in 26 Premier League games in the 2005–06 season, but a broken metatarsal incurred in a tackle with Chelsea's Paulo Ferreira was a portent of things to come. Fourteen goals to his name, Rooney won his first Premier League title in 2006–07.

In the opening day 0-0 draw with Reading in August 2007 Rooney broke the same metatarsal in his left foot. Many aficionados of the game were blaming the new lightweight football boots favoured by modern players. Somehow Rooney ended the season with 20 goals in all competitions, despite also suffering a hamstring injury in January 2008. In the 2009–10 season Rooney scored all four goals as United beat Hull City 4-0. In April 2010 Rooney was named the PFA Player's Player of the Year. Rooney regarded a bicycle kick he scored against Manchester City in the 2010–11 season as his best ever goal, a little poignant no doubt since the goal was scored against their city rivals. It is one of the Premier League's most fondly remembered goals. Rooney scored crucial goals against Chelsea in the last eight of the Champions League, and against Schalke 04 in the last four. Beating Barcelona in the final proved too tough an obstacle. United's consolation was their 19th Premier League title, Rooney's fourth.

In October 2011, Rooney's two goals against Romanian club Otelul Galati surpassed former teammate Paul Scholes as the highest scoring Englishman in Champions League history. United lost the Premier League in the 2011–12 season to rivals Manchester City, thanks to Sergio Agüero's 94th-minute winner against Queens Park Rangers. Alex Ferguson left at the end of the 2012–13 season. Rooney appeared set to go too, but staying on he ended the season with 17 goals and ten assists, claiming the most assists also in the Champions League (eight).

Louis van Gal named Rooney club captain for the 2014–15 seasons when Nemanja Vidic left. Rooney's 14 goals for this season made him top scorer, but with the lowest total of any United strikers since 1982. In November 2016 Rooney overtook Ruud van Nistelrooy as United's top scorer in European competitions with 39 after scoring in a 4-0 Europa League win at Old Trafford. United won the 2016–17 Europa League Final 2-0 against Ajax of Amsterdam, Rooney appearing as a substitute. The match was Rooney's last in the famous red shirt. He'd scored 253 goals for the club, making him their top all-time goalscorer, surpassing Bobby Charlton. His 183 Premier League goals leave him just behind Sergio Agüero (184) as the league's all-time top scorer.

Rooney returned to Everton for the 2017–18 season, eventually scoring ten goals in 31 Premier League games. The highlight of his season was a hat-trick against West Ham United, including a strike from 60 yards.

Wayne Rooney became England's youngest ever debutant, aged 17 years and 111 days, when playing against Australia in February 2003. His goal in a 2004 Euro qualifier in a 2-1 win over Macedonia made him his country's youngest ever scorer. Injury in the quarter-finals of the 2004 Euros against Portugal arguably cost England qualification. Rooney had been magnificent in the opening games, scoring twice against Switzerland (3-0), and twice more against Croatia (4-2). He'd swiftly become his country's talisman. Sadly this was as good as it got for Rooney at international level.

The 2006 World Cup came, Portugal again England's conquerors, this time Rooney sent off – he was clearly fouled by Chelsea's Ricardo Carvalho first, but retaliated. In the 2010 World Cup qualifiers, Rooney scored nine goals, yet with England as a team failing to gel, he did not score in the 2010 World Cup competition. Knocked out in the Euro 2012 quarter-finals by Italy, Fabio Capello,

417

England's incumbent manager, claimed that Rooney played well for his club, but not for his country. This was a harsh appraisal, 2004 and 2006 revealed a player who might turn games for his country. I feel that successive injuries prevented him from making the impact he'd so richly promised. Like Michael Owen, Rooney's explosiveness dissipated through his 20s, injuries a major factor.

Rooney top-scored again with seven goals in the 2014 World Cup qualifiers. Astonishingly for such a talented player, Rooney's first World Cup tournament goal came against Uruguay in a 2-1 defeat. Rooney's best days at international level were firmly behind him. His stubbornness, doggedness and pride, kept him playing for England until 2018, finishing his international career with 53 goals, an England record.

Wayne Rooney managed a Derby County club in administration 2020–2022. Since taking on the role in 2020 Rooney has at times been able to inspire a team lacking in quality to unlikely victories – but managing such clubs (with a famous past thanks to Brian Clough and Peter Taylor) is a poisoned chalice.

Wayne Rooney combined power and athleticism in a way no other English player has in the modern game. The owner of an explosive shot, he also possessed a sharp eye for a chance and explosive pace, until injuries blighted his career. Rooney's work rate was exceptional, like his former teammate David Beckham, tracking back was an accepted part of his game. Like Beckham he could be accused of trying too hard at times. Weight issues may have also affected his speed over time. 'If only' is the phrase one thinks of in relation to his injury in that 2004 Euro quarter-final. Rooney's peak seemed to be as a younger player, in contrast to the accepted norm of a professional player peaking around the age of 28.

The hard-working, dynamic Carlos Tevez gave United a fiery strike partnership indeed alongside Rooney. Being accidentally burned with boiling water as a child, the ensuing scar earned the Ciudadelda, Buenos Aires-born Tevez the nickname 'El Apache'. Tevez debuted for Boca Juniors in his home city in 2002–03 (ten goals in 32 games). The 2003 Copa Libertadores was won, Boca beating Pele's old club Santos 5-1 on aggregate, Tevez scoring in the Sao Paulo city of Santos. Tevez was championed as the heir to Diego Maradona at Boca, ending his first spell at the club with 26 goals in 75 games. When Tevez transferred to Corinthians of Sao Paulo in Brazil in January 2005, his transfer (£22 million) was the biggest in South American football at that time. Twenty-five goals in 38 Brazilian Serie A games saw him voted the best player in the league by the Brazilian Football Confederation in 2005–06, the first non-Brazilian to win the award since 1976.

Controversially, Tevez and Javier Mascherano switched allegiances from Corinthians to West Ham United for the 2006–07 season. A player's rights issue meant other bigger Premier League teams fought shy of signing the in-demand Argentinians. Ultimately West Ham were fined a record £5.5 million for breaching Premier League rules. Most fans don't care about financial implications if their team are successful. Tevez was subsequently voted Hammer of the Year, scoring the only goal of the final league game of the season in a 1-0 victory over Manchester United, helping the Hammers stave off relegation. Relegated

Sheffield United were furious, deeming Tevez's part in West Ham's safety illegal. The clubs reached an out of court financial settlement. Tevez scored seven goals in 26 Premier League games for the Upton Park club.

Financial ramifications still prevalent, Manchester United took Tevez on loan 2007–09. Alex Ferguson thought Tevez would guarantee him 15 goals – a slightly optimistic projection as it transpired, but Tevez did score five goals in the 2007–08 Champions League campaign. Tevez totalled 19 goals in 63 Premier League games for United. He was offered a permanent contract, but opted to move again.

His next move was his most successful – to United's chagrin it was across the city with rivals Manchester City. In the 2009–10 League Cup semi-finals, City played United, Tevez scoring in both legs, but United triumphing 4-3 on aggregate. At the season's end Tevez won both Etihad Player of the Year and the Player's Player of the Year awards. Unsettled for family reasons, Tevez persevered at City, captaining the team to a 1-0 League Cup Final win over Stoke City.

Tevez's next move occurred in June 2013, signing for Italian giants Juventus. In the ultra-defensive minded Serie A, the combative Tevez scored an impressive 39 goals in 66 games. In his first season in Turin, Juve won the Scudetto and Tevez was the club's top scorer with 21 goals in all competitions. He was promptly named Juve's Player of the Season. Another 20 goals came in the 2014–15 season, but Juve were unable to defeat Barcelona in the 2015 Champions League Final. On 14 December Tevez was named the 2014–15 Serie A Footballer of the Year. The domestic double was won, Juventus winning the Coppa Italia 2-0 over Lazio.

Tevez returned to his first love, Boca Juniors, in June 2015. He scored 14 goals in 34 games as Boca won the double of Argentine Primera Divisi and Copa Argentina, Tevez becoming the first footballer to win a domestic double in two different leagues in the same calendar year.

Tevez received 76 caps for Argentina, scoring 13 goals. He played at two World Cups, 2006 and 2010, and was awarded South American Footballer of the Year three times: 2003, 2004, 2005, and Argentinian Footballer of the Year twice: 2003, 2004. Five feet seven inches, Tevez's stocky physique made him difficult to shrug off the ball. He was quick, powerful, an excellent dribbler and a hard worker for his team with his immense stamina.

United had great options on the bench in Ryan Giggs and the Portuguese international winger Nani (112 caps, 24 goals). Anderson, the Brazilian midfielder and Scotland's Darren Fletcher constituted midfield options; Irishman John O'Shea and Frenchman Mikael Silvestre offered defensive cover.

In opposition Chelsea possessed the second best goalkeeper in Premier League history in the Czech international Petr Cech, 333 games in the Premier League for the Blues. Moving to Arsenal in 2015 after 11 seasons with Chelsea, Cech won a fourth Premier League Golden Glove at the Emirates, having won three with Chelsea. This award for the most clean sheets in a season is shared, surprisingly, with Joe Hart, or not so surprisingly, since Hart's record came as goalkeeper for the 2010's most successful English team, Manchester City. Incredibly, Cech has been voted Czech Footballer of the Year eight times 2008–2016, only failing to win the award in 2014. The safest pair of hands in Premier League football outside of Peter Schmeichel, Cech had two English defenders in front of him in the commanding John Terry and the dynamic left-back Ashley Cole.

Chelsea's other defenders in the Luzhniki Stadium, Moscow, were the Ghanaian full-back-cum midfield player Michael Essien, and the stylish Portuguese centre-back Ricardo Carvalho. Essien was a powerful player who played more often as a midfielder than as a full-back. With the holding role in midfield taken by Frenchman Claude Makélélé, manager Avram Grant utilised Essien's strength and power here at right-back. Essien joined Bastia in France in 2000 from Accra-based Liberty Professionals in Ghana. Joining Lyon in 2003, he won consecutive Ligue 1 titles, winning Ligue 1 Player of the Year in 2005.

Signing for Chelsea in August 2005, Essien became the most expensive African-transferred player at that time. His contributions to Chelsea were recognised by the fans when he won Chelsea Player of the Year for 2006–07, the first African player to win such award. He scored Chelsea's Goal of the Season in 2006–07 and 2008–09. Essien lost favour when the Portuguese Andre Villas-Boas took over as manager for the 2011–12 season, being only an unused substitute in the 2012 Champions League Final, a match Chelsea won on penalties against Bayern Munich. Essien played his best football at Chelsea, scoring 17 times in 168 Premier League games, as well as scoring crucial cup goals.

Essien was loaned to Real Madrid under former boss José Mourinho for the 2012–13 season, before transferring to AC Milan for the 2014–15 season, then to Panathinaikos in Greece. A formidable Chelsea career behind him, the Ghanaian's last seasons were less memorable. Essien was capped 59 times by Ghana (nine goals) 2002–2014. Nicknamed 'The Bison' due to his tough tackling, Michael Essien belied his physique with fine technique and struck a powerful shot.

Ricardo Carvalho was one of José Mourinho's best signings for Chelsea. In some ways Carvalho reminded me of John Dempsey in the 1970–71 successful Chelsea side, a tall, lean player with a deft touch for a defender. Carvalho's form for·Porto brought about the departure of club captain Jorge Costa to Charlton Athletic in 2001. Third-choice at that juncture, Carvalho ousted Costa to form a splendid centre-back partnership with Jorge Andrade. José Mourinho came to Porto and Carvalho slipped to third choice again, but swiftly persuaded Mourinho of his worth, cementing a place in Porto's 2003 UEFA Cup-winning team. Carvalho was named Portuguese League Footballer of the Year for 2002–03. In 2003–04 Porto won the Champions League, Carvalho a fixture in their defence. In this season he was named UEFA Club Best Defender of the Year and voted into the UEFA Team of the Year.

Inter Milan, Barcelona, Real Madrid, and Manchester United clamoured for his signature, but Chelsea outbid them all. Success was instant at Chelsea, the Premier League won in both his first two seasons at the club, 2004–05 and 2005–06. Chelsea also won the 2005 League Cup Final, beating Liverpool 3-2.

In 2007–08 Carvalho was voted by his peers Club Player's Player of the Year. Chelsea won the 2009–10 Premier League title, Carvalho's third, the double being secured with Didier Drogba's solitary goal winning the FA Cup Final against Portsmouth.

Incoming Chelsea manager Carlo Ancelotti (2009–2011) favoured Carvalho's inclusion in the team, but Carvalho chose to follow mentor Mourinho to Real Madrid in the 2010–11 season. Carvalho's composure helped Real have the best defence in the 2010–11 Champions League campaign, conceding only five goals. It didn't stop Barcelona claiming the trophy, knocking Real out 3-1 on aggregate in the semi-finals. Carvalho ended his time in Europe with Monaco 2013–16.

Carvalho played 89 times for Portugal (five goals) 2003–2016. Despite losing the final to Greece, Carvalho was named in the Euro 2004 Team of the Tournament. Clever on the ball, Carvalho was also clever in game manipulation, playing his part in Wayne Rooney's sending off at the 2006 World Cup. Stamped on by Rooney, Carvalho initiated Rooney's retort with the first foul. Carvalho also played in the 2008 Euros and the 2010 World Cup. Aged 38 he became the oldest outfield player at the 2016 Euros in France, although he was not part of the trophy-winning team in the final. Carvalho's intelligence and technical prowess made him an ideal partner for a traditional-style centre half like John Terry or Jorge Andrade. I always admired Carvalho's technical capacity while feeling, like the previous generation's Uli Stielike that some of his tackles were knowing in his team's hour of need.

At the base of the midfield for Chelsea, Claude Makélélé was the N'Golo Kanté of his time, arguably the best defensive midfielder around in 2008. Born in Kinshasa, Zaire, Makélélé became a nationalised Frenchman, his family moving to Savigny-le-Temple, Paris in 1977 when Claude was four years old. Makélélé played senior football first with Nantes, winning Ligue 1 in the 1994–95 season, the club reaching the 1995–96 Champions League semi-final, Makélélé scored the most goals of his career at Nantes – nine in 169 Ligue 1 games 1991–97. The next season was spent in Marseille 1997–98, and then he moved to Celta Vigo in Spain 1998–2000.

In 2000 Real Madrid signed him for a reputed £14 million, a fee Celta thought was too low. Makélélé played 94 La Liga games for Real, but in a team of 'Galacticos': Zinedine Zidane, Luis Figo, Ronaldo (the Brazilian forward), Roberto Carlos, Steve McManaman, he felt undervalued. Pushing for an improved contract, Real refused, and Makélélé moved instead to Chelsea in the summer of 2003.

Unappreciated as a lower-key member of a superstar Real Madrid team (by the board, not his teammates), Makélélé became integral to Chelsea's successes 2003–08. Presaging the relentless Kanté a decade later, Makélélé was regarded as the 'battery' of the Chelsea team, charging and recharging Chelsea's forward play with his pressing from the back, and instigating attacks with his neat ball distribution.

His first season at Stamford Bridge brought a runners-up medal in the Premier League, and elimination in the semi-finals of the 2003–04 Champions League semi-finals, disappointingly, 5-3 on aggregate against AS Monaco. 2004–05 brought massive consolation as Chelsea won the Premier League and League Cup, defeating Liverpool 3-2 after extra time in the latter. Described by then manager José Mourinho as the team's best player, Makélélé was named in the FIFPRO World XI for 2004–05. Although aged 35, Makélélé was selected ahead of Michael Essien as Chelsea's defensive midfielder-cum deep-lying playmaker for this 2007–08 Champions League Final, forcing Essien's switch to full-back.

Returning to France with Paris Saint-Germain in July 2008, Makélélé won the Coupe de France (French Cup) at the end of his last season, 2009–10, PSG defeating AS Monaco 1-0 after extra time. Makélélé first appeared in a tournament for France at the 2002 World Cup, becoming a regular by the time of the 2004 Euros. At the 2006 World Cup, France knocked out Spain, Brazil and Portugal, only to come unstuck against Italy in the final. France's defensive record with Makélélé and Patrick Vieira providing cover was three goals conceded, four clean sheets, bettered only by the masters of the art, Italy.

Claude Makélélé's style of play became the template for the archetypal defensive midfielder. An excellent reader of the game, Makélélé broke up play and promptly released the ball swiftly to the creative players in his teams. It was an energy-sapping role, one since resurrected and magnified at Chelsea by N'Golo Kanté.

The German midfielder Michael Ballack gave excellent service in European Football to Bayern Munich and Chelsea – and to Germany. Ballack's worth in Germany came with recognition as German Footballer of the Year three times, 2002, 2003 and 2005. Best known for his time at Bayern and Chelsea, Ballack was no slouch prior to arrival at Bayern in 2002. In his first full season with the unfashionable FC Kaiserslautern in the German Rhineland Palatinate, Ballack won the Bundesliga at the first attempt (1997–98), the last time the club won the title – the first ever newly promoted team to win the Bundesliga, having won Bundesliga 2 the previous year.

Joining Bayer Leverkusen for the 1999–2000 season, Ballack had the misfortune of scoring an own goal in a match against SpVgg Unterhaching, helping send his team to a shock 0-2 defeat. A draw would have given Leverkusen the title – Bayern Munich were the team to take advantage of the slip. In 2001–02, incredibly, Ballack ended up with four runners-up medals – second to Borussia Dortmund in the league; a 2-4 defeat in the DFB Pokal Final against Schalke 04; a Champions League defeat against Real Madrid; and rubbing salt in the wounds, a World Cup Final defeat for Germany, 0-2 against Brazil.

Real Madrid were keen on Ballack, but the Gorlitz, Saxony-born midfielder opted to stay in Germany, signing for Bayern Munich in 2002. Bayern won the 2002–03 domestic double in his first season, Ballack scoring twice against old club FC Kaiserslautern in the DFB Pokal Final 3-1 victory. Trophy-less in 2003–04, Bayern won the double again in 2004–05. In his four seasons with Bayern Munich the double was won three times, Ballack scoring 44 goals in 107 Bundesliga matches. Critics suggested Ballack was not playing at the same level in important European games.

Moving to Chelsea, Ballack won the League Cup and FA Cup in his first season, although again critics thought that for a player of his stature, his performances were underwhelming. Left out of the 2007–08 Champions League group games – Steve Sidwell was preferred; Ballack's summer ankle operation had not helped his cause. Regaining his place for the knockout stages, Ballack scored against Olympiakos in the last 16, going on to score the winning goal in the last eight against Fenerbahce. The season ended sourly for Chelsea, beaten here by Manchester United in the Champions League, they finished second to United in the Premier League, and lost the League Cup Final to Tottenham Hotspur 2-1 after extra -time – the last trophy won by the North London team. Mirroring Ballack's treble losses of 2000–01 at Bayern Leverkusen, Ballack went on to play in the Euro 2008 Final 1-0 defeat for Germany against Spain. Any reservations about Ballack's commitment can surely be dismissed by his lowest loss record of any player with more than 100 Premier League matches under their belt – ten in his 105 appearances.

Michael Ballack returned to Bayer Leverkusen in June 2010, having scored 17 goals in 105 Premier League games. His return was unremarkable, a shin injury marring future performances. He announced his retirement in October 2012. A fleeting appearance at the Euros in 2000 was followed by goals in matches against the United States and South Korea at the 2002 World Cup. Booked in the semi-final against hosts South Korea, Ballack promptly missed the final against Brazil. Despite his absence he was named in the 2002 World Cup All Star Team. Beaten 2-0 after extra time by eventual winners Italy in the semi-finals of the 2006 World Cup, Ballack was again named in the World Cup All Star Team for 2006. Ballack's header helped Germany defeat Portugal in the last eight of the 2008 Euros. A calf strain meant he played the losing final (0-1) to Spain at less than 100% fitness. An ankle injury prevented Ballack's appearance at the 2010 World Cup. Lothar Matthäus felt his absence helped Sami Khedira and Mesut Ozil blossom in the tournament.

Ballack ended his international career with an impressive 42 goals in 98 games. Joachim Low, Germany's national manager, praised Ballack's calm and authority on the pitch. The six feet two inches Ballack was an archetypal German footballer, technically proficient, strong in the tackle, with the additional bonuses of powerful shooting and a strong aerial presence in his armoury.

The fourth Englishman after Terry, Ashley Cole and Lampard in this Chelsea team took the right side of midfield in this final. Joe Cole, Paddington, London-born, promised a great deal at times in his career. As it transpired, his longest, most successful stint at any club came with Chelsea.

Touted as a child prodigy, Cole was reputedly the subject of a £10-million offer from Manchester United while still a 16-year-old with West Ham United Youth. Cole was part of the West Ham Youth team that humbled Coventry City 9-0 in the 1998–99 FA Youth Cup Final – along with an opponent on this night, Michael Carrick. Cole played 126 Premier League games for West Ham 1998–2003, scoring ten goals. He played his last game for the club in a 2-2 draw against Birmingham City in May 2003, relegation resulting. Cole, by consolation, won Hammer of the Year.

In August 2003, Cole was signed by Claudio Ranieri as a replacement for the departing cult hero Gianfranco Zola. At first he was used as a replacement when others were unfit, but injuries to both wingers, Damien Duff and Arjen Robben in 2004–05 opened the door for Cole. He scored ten goals in the season, winning his first Premier league title medal. He repelled the claims of Duff and Shaun Wright-Phillips in the 2005–06 season, being named in the PFA Team of the Year. A stress fracture to a foot in late 2006 blighted the 2006–07 season, although he started the 2007 FA Cup Final against Manchester United, won by Didier Drogba's extra-time goal. Cole started in this 2008 Champions League Final, being substituted by Nicolas Anelka, but was awarded Chelsea's Player of the Year for 2008. Cole's ability to produce the unexpected always endeared him to fans. He appeared as a substitute in the 2010 FA Cup Final, a 1-0 victory over Portsmouth that enabled the double for Chelsea for the first time in their history. Cole ended his Chelsea career with three Premier league titles, two FA Cups and one League Cup.

Cole moved to Liverpool in July 2010, but it was an ill-fated stay including a loan spell with Lille in France. He couldn't match his 28 goals in 182 games for Chelsea. Steven Gerrard likened him to the almost incomparable Lionel Messi (Maradona and Mo Salah circa 2022 could enter the equation), but Cole never settled at Anfield. While loaned out to Lille he played with a new emerging star, Eden Hazard. Lille manager Rudi Garcia wanted to retain Cole, but incoming Liverpool manager Brendan Rogers requested Cole's return for the 2012–13 season. Tweaked hamstrings saw Cole lose his place to another emerging star, Raheem Sterling. It was not to be for Cole at Anfield.

Cole came full circle by returning to West Ham on a free transfer in January 2013. Thirty-seven games and five goals later, Cole's hamstrings betrayed him again. Stints with Aston Villa and Coventry followed, but Cole was essentially finished as a force at top level. With England, Cole occasionally excelled. Capped at U-16, U-18 and U-21 level, Cole scored seven goals in an 8-1 drubbing of Spain in an England Schoolboys game. A squad member at the 2002 World Cup and the 2004 Euros tournament, Cole scored a spectacular volley against Sweden in Group B at the 2006 World Cup, earning the Man of the Match Award. It was to be his shining moment as an England player. Sadly his exceptional individual skills, his balance and dribbling were undermined by a string of injuries.

French Guianan, French nationalised left-winger Florent Malouda completed Chelsea's five man midfield. Born in Cayenne, French Guiana, Malouda combined early on in his career with Didier Drogba at Guingamp, Brittany. Malouda moved to Lyon in 2003, linking up with another future Chelsea star, Michael Essien. In the 2006–07 season, Malouda's ten goals helped Lyon win their sixth consecutive Ligue 1 title. Malouda won 2006–07 French Ligue 1 Player of the Year.

Malouda moved to Chelsea in July 2007. His first significant contribution came in scoring Chelsea's second goal in a 3-2 victory over Birmingham City, the club overtaking Liverpool's previous 63 straight home games unbeaten record. Regular game time at Chelsea was not guaranteed. Malouda scored twice against Bordeaux in a 2008 Champions League game. In the 2008–09 FA Cup Final Malouda assisted Didier Drogba's equaliser, but was denied a goal himself when his 35-yarder cannoned off the crossbar, crossing the line as it ricocheted. The goal was not given – oh for VAR. A better goal return resulted in 2009–10, 12 scored, eight assisted in the Premier League, 15 goals and 15 goals assisted in all competitions. In 2010–11 Malouda even outscored Drogba and Anelka, the official strikers in the team, with 13 Premier League goals.

In season 2011–12 Malouda scored as Chelsea demolished Tottenham Hotspur 5-1 in the FA Cup semi-finals, coming on as a substitute as the Blues won the final 2-1 against Liverpool, Drogba scoring the winner. After his Chelsea career, Malouda's playing days petered out rather in Turkey, France, Italy, Egypt and Luxembourg.

Internationally, Malouda played 80 times for France, scoring nine goals. He was part of the team beaten on penalties by Italy at the 2006 World Cup. A swift player with a decent shot, Florent Malouda's time at Chelsea was his most productive in senior football as he scored 35 goals in 149 Premier League games.

The spearhead of Chelsea, Didier Drogba, was simply a force of nature. The six feet two inches powerhouse centre-forward won many a big game for Chelsea 2004–2015. At Chelsea he scored more goals than any other foreign player to wear the shirt (104 Premier League goals). Drogba was twice African Footballer of the Year, 2006 and 2009. I'm only surprised it was not more.

Born in Abidjan, Ivory Coast, Drogba and his family fluctuated between Africa and France in his formative years. Finishing school, Drogba moved to Le Mans to study accountancy at university, apprenticing himself to French Ligue 2 club Le Mans concurrently. He struggled to establish himself at Le Mans, but Guingamp saw something in him. He went up a league to his new employers, initially failing to convince. In his second season with Guingamp he forged a relationship with Florent Malouda, crediting the winger with his transformation as he netted 17 goals in 34 games in 2002–03.

It seemed a light had switched on as Drogba moved to Olympique Marseille. He scored 19 goals in the 2003–04 season, including five in the Champions League and six in the UEFA Cup (the latter final lost 2-0 to Valencia). Drogba, predictably, won the National Union of Professional Footballers (UFNP) Player of the Year for 2003–04.

Drogba won the Premier League with Chelsea in his first season in London in 2004–05, the last time Chelsea had won the title being back in 1954–55 when Ted Drake managed the club and Roy Bentley top-scored with 21 goals. Drogba could only total 16 in all competitions in 40 games in 2004–05, but his goal in the 3-2 League Cup Final win over Liverpool was the first of many big game contributions. Drogba again finished with a total of 16 goals in 2005–06. 2006–07 marked an upturn, this time the Ivorian scoring 33 goals, including 20 in the Premier League, earning the Golden Boot for league top scorer. The 2006–07 League Cup Final saw Drogba scoring both goals in a 2-1 victory over Arsenal. Unsurprisingly he then scored the winner in the FA Cup Final against Manchester United, becoming the only player to score in and win both domestic cup finals in the same season. He was named in the 2006–07 Premier League Team of the Year, finishing second to Cristiano Ronaldo in the individual PFA Player of the Year award.

Saddened by José Mourinho's departure in 2007 – Drogba felt Mourinho created a family at Chelsea – his future seemed uncertain for a while. A knee operation kept him out of key games in 2007–08, but he returned to score in the 2008 League Cup Final (the 1-2 defeat to Tottenham Hotspur), the goal giving him four in League Cup Finals, the best in the competition. Accused of diving by Rafael Benitez in the 2008 Champions League semi-final, Drogba struck back in the right manner, scoring two of the goals in the second leg that brought Chelsea through to the final, 3-2 on aggregate. Drogba also became Chelsea's top scorer in European competition with 17, surpassing Peter Osgood's 16. Drogba was sent off in the 117th minute of this 2008 Champions League Final for slapping Nemanja Vidic – the pair were old adversaries – but Chelsea held on for the final three minutes, only to lose the penalty shoot-out. Drogba would have taken the fifth penalty that John Terry missed.

Injuries and Luiz Felipe Scolari's preference for a one-man attack led by Nicolas Anelka kept Drogba out of the team for a while in 2009–10. He revived under temporary manager Guus Hiddink, scoring four goals in five games upon returning. The cup games once again brought the best out in Drogba. In the FA Cup semi-final against Arsenal he netted an 84th-minute winner as Chelsea triumphed 2-1. In the final he equalised as Chelsea saw off Everton 2-1. Chelsea went on to win the 2009–10 Premier League, Drogba back in fine form with 29 league goals, winning the Golden Boot for the second time. In the 2010 FA Cup Final Chelsea beat Portsmouth 1-0, the only goal of the game coming from… Didier Drogba.

The problems with players serving international duty during the season were exemplified by Drogba's absence for a period in 2010–11 having contracted malaria. 2011–12 brought Drogba's importance to Chelsea back to notice, a vital goal scored as Chelsea beat Barcelona 1-0 in the first leg of the Champions League semi-finals, followed by the entirely predictable winner as Chelsea beat Liverpool 2-1 in the FA Cup Final. In scoring the latter he became the first player to score in four FA Cup Finals – some feat. Alex Ferguson felt Drogba's presence was paramount when Chelsea beat Bayern Munich on penalties in the 2012 Champions League Final. In November 2012, a poll of 20,000 fans voted Drogba Chelsea's greatest ever player for Chelsea Magazine – quite a testimony to him given the likes of Zola, Osgood, Cooke, Tambling and Bentley before him, and Lampard alongside him.

Leaving Chelsea having scored over 100 goals in 266 Premier League games, Drogba spent the next two seasons in China and Turkey, winning the Turkish league title with Galatasaray in 2013–14 (15 goals in 37 games). True to form he also scored the only goal of the 2013 Turkish Super Cup (League winners versus Cup winners) against Fenerbahce, the club's Istanbul rivals.

José Mourinho having returned to Chelsea, Drogba returned too in July 2014. The 2014–15 season brought limited success for Drogba (four goals in 28 league games). Time moves on and the club now started most games with Diego Costa as their main spearhead. Ironically, Costa was the closest Chelsea came to replacing Drogba's power and aggression. Thirty-five goals in 55 games for Montreal Impact and Phoenix Rising in the MSL and the USL leagues in America brought Drogba's senior career tally to 210 goals in 497 games.

Drogba's 65 goals in 105 internationals reflect his importance to the Ivory Coast. Drawn in a 'group of death' at the 2006 World Cup, Drogba scored against Argentina, but his team lost 2-1. The same scoreline against Holland put the Ivory Coast out at the first stage, although they beat Serbia and Montenegro 3-2 in the last game. In 2010 at the World Cup in South Africa, Portugal were held 0-0, Drogba scored as the Ivory Coast lost 3-1 to Brazil, and North Korea were beaten 3-0. Drogba was unable to repeat his Chelsea finals heroics for the Ivory Coast, the country losing the 2006 and 2012 African Nations Cup Finals, 4-2 on penalties after a 0-0 draw with Egypt, and 8-7 on penalties against Zambia after a 0-0 draw respectively. To outsiders, knowledgeable of the Ivory Coast's exceptional players that included the Touré brothers Kolo and Yaya, Emmanuel Eboué and Didier Zakora, it seemed inconceivable that the Ivory Coast failed to win the African Nations Cup during this era.

I am not a great fan of 5-4-1 or any formation that isolates a single forward in attack on his own, but if you're going to have a lone striker it might as well be Didier Drogba. A powerful focal point in a team, Drogba's physicality intimidated many a defence. He possessed a great shot, was dominant in the air, robust in the tackle, and had the physical prowess to shield the ball and hold off defenders, making him the perfect target man. His 71 assists at Chelsea prove he wasn't just a goal-hogging centre-forward. Peers such as Nemanja Vidic, Laurent Koscielny at Arsenal, and Carlos Puyol and Gerard Piqué at Barcelona rate him their toughest ever opponent. Add in his big game temperament in semi-finals and finals, for Chelsea in particular, and you have arguably the greatest, most effective number 9 in the modern era of the Premier League.

Chelsea, like United, possessed great strength in depth on the substitutes' bench: Brazilians Alex and Juliano Belletti in defence; the Nigerian midfield enforcer John Mikel Obi in midfield; and outstanding attacking replacements in the great Andriy Shevchenko and Nicolas Anelka, and the less great, but still lively Ivorian Salomon Kalou.

Manager Avram Grant, an Israeli, managed Chelsea for this 2007–08 season. He was a surprise appointment until you knew that he was a personal friend of club owner Roman Abramovich. Not holding the top flight UEFA 'A' or 'B' level licences made Grant a controversial appointment, and after the first Mourinho era of sustained success the fans were not happy. Yet Grant took Chelsea to this Champions League Final. Grant's contract was terminated three days after this final, showing Abramovich's ruthlessness, friend or not.

THE FINAL

United started strongly, Cristiano Ronaldo's trademark stepover taking him past Michael Essien, his deep cross eluding Owen Hargreaves. Another Ronaldo cross was met by a flying header from Carlos Tevez to no avail. Another Tevez header was saved, Michael Carrick's follow-up suffering the same fate. A neat 1-2 between Paul Scholes and Wes Brown saw the latter's cross headed into goal at the far post by Ronaldo. 1-0 United. Tevez couldn't quite reach another pinpoint cross from Wayne Rooney. Chelsea responded strongly, Essien's shot deflected fortuitously off of both Nemanja Vidic and Rio Ferdinand into the path of the ever-alert Frank Lampard. Lampard, always following up in these situations, clipped home left-footed. 1-1, but the first half belonged to United.

The second half was all Chelsea, the game changing complexion, but Drogba's shot hit the post, and Michael Ballack fired a long-range shot over the bar. Extra time was called for. In the added 30 minutes Lampard struck the crossbar from inside the penalty area. Then Drogba was sent off following a 22-man fracas as

Tevez was accused of taking advantage of a break to assuage the players' cramp. Ryan Giggs stabbed the ball towards the Chelsea goal, but the defiant John Terry deflected the ball to safety.

The rain poured down on this Moscow evening as the penalty shoot-out ended in dramatic fashion. Ronaldo stuttered before striking his kick, Petr Cech saved easily. The much-maligned Hargreaves struck United's strongest penalty into the roof of the net. If it rained like this, surely Mancunians were used to it? Not sure about the non-English and three non-Mancunians though. The unfortunate Terry slipped as he prepared to hit the ball and his shot hit the outside of a post. Anelka's penalty was not strong enough and Edwin van der Sar saved – United win 6-5 on penalties. Chelsea, the stronger side in the second half and extra time, would have to wait to claim the trophy in 2012.

2009 CHAMPIONS LEAGUE FINAL
Barcelona 2 v 0 Manchester United

With Alex Ferguson at the helm, Cristiano Ronaldo and Wayne Rooney at the top of their game, and van der Sar, Ferdinand, Vidic and Patrice Evra shoring up their defence, Manchester United reached three Champions League Finals in four years: 2008, 2009 and 2011. They were unable to win the last two due to the supreme quality of the same opponent: Barcelona. Barcelona's peak proved too high a mountain to climb in 2009 and 2011. 2009 was the fifth consecutive year an English team or teams reached the final, a strong indicator of the impact of foreign players playing in the Premier League.

Route to the Final
Manchester United, as holders from 2008, did not enter the competition until the group stages. Barcelona entered in the third qualifying round, dismissing Wislaw Krakaw of Poland 4-1 on aggregate. The home leg for Barcelona was a procession, won 4-0 with two goals from Samuel Eto'o, one apiece from Xavi and Thierry Henry.

United topped their group by a point from the Spanish team Villareal. The two clubs shared an initial goalless draw at Old Trafford. United won their second game in Denmark comfortably, beating Aalborg BK 3-0 with goals from Dimitar Berbatov (two) and Wayne Rooney. A second successive 3-0 win followed, this time at home to Glasgow Celtic, Berbatov (two) and Rooney again the scorers. Scott McDonald gave Celtic a 13th-minute lead in Glasgow, Ryan Giggs only equalising six minutes from the end. Another goalless draw between two well matched sides, United and Villareal, followed in Spain. United might have failed to top Group E but for Villareal being beaten 2-0 in Glasgow against Celtic, while United could only draw 2-2 with Aalborg BK at Old Trafford, Carlos Tevez and Rooney scoring for the home team.

Barcelona topped Group C by a point from Portuguese club Sporting CP. Barcelona beat the Lisbon-based club 3-1 in the first game at the Nou Camp, Rafael Márquez, an Eto'o penalty and Xavi the scorers. Shakhtar Donetsk of the Ukraine looked to have beaten Barcelona at the RSC Olimpiskiy, Donetsk with a first-half goal from Brazilian midfielder Ilsinho, but the little genius Lionel Messi turned the game on its head with two late goals in the 87th and 94th minutes. The Swiss side Basel suffered the ignominy of a 0-5 home defeat at the hands of this irrepressible Barcelona team, Messi, Xavi, Sergio Busquets and Bojan (two) scoring at St. Jakob-Park. Curiously, Basel held Barca to a 1-1 draw in the return at the Nou Camp, Messi again on the scoresheet. Barcelona handed out another thumping to Sporting CP in Lisbon, 5-2, Henry, Gerard Piqué, Messi, an own goal and a Bojan penalty the Spanish goalscorers. Qualification ensured, Barcelona lost their last home game against Shakhtar Donetsk 3-2, Sylvinho and Busquets scoring for Barca.

In the last 16, Manchester United were paired with Inter Milan, drawing the first leg in the San Siro 0-0. A tough ask, but United proved equal to the task, Nemanja Vidic and Cristiano Ronaldo netting in a 2-0 home win at Old Trafford. Porto in the last eight proved awkward opposition, opening the scoring at Old Trafford through Uruguyan winger Cristia Rodriguez. Rooney swiftly equalised; Tevez gave United an 85th-minute lead, but Argentinian midfielder Mariano González equalised with a minute remaining. Two away goals to the good, Porto were unable to capitalise, Ronaldo scoring the only goal of the return leg in Portugal in the sixth minute. United crushed Arsenal 4-1 in the semi-finals; John O'Shea scoring the only goal at Old Trafford. South Korean international Park Ji-sung and Ronaldo (two) confirmed United's progress to the final at Arsenal.

Barcelona were pitted against French champions Lyon in the last 16. The first game in France saw Brazilian midfielder Juninho give Lyon a seventh-minute lead. Henry replied in the second half for Barca. The home tie was less of a struggle, Barcelona sweeping Lyon aside 5-2, Henry (two), Messi, Eto'o and Malian midfielder Seydou Keita the scorers. Bayern Munich would be considerably stiffer opposition for Barca in the last eight, wouldn't they? Not for this peaking Barcelona team who ran out 4-0 winners at the Nou Camp, Messi (two), Eto'o and Henry unstoppable in attack. Bayern applied heavy pressure in Munich, but had only a 47th-minute Franck Ribéry goal to show for it. A 17-pass move from this exquisite possession-based Barca team resulted in a Keita equaliser. The only team to pose any sort of threat to Barcelona's seemingly unassailable conquest of the 2008–09 Champions League competition were the Chelsea team of great fortitude, now managed by Guus Hiddink. A resolute Chelsea held Barca to a goalless draw in the Nou Camp in the last four. All they had to do was score at Stamford Bridge and keep a clean sheet against a Barca team with the best attack in the world at this point. Michael Essien volleyed Chelsea into a ninth-minute lead. Barca, predictably, dominated possession, but Chelsea looked the likelier scorers as the game progressed. When Eric Abidal was sent off for fouling Nicolas Anelka, the game was there for the taking for Chelsea. Incredibly, Andres Iniesta equalised in the 93rd minute to put the Spaniards through on away goals. Chelsea had several penalty claims waved away by Norwegian referee Tom Henning Ovrebo who the media thought too inexperienced for a match of this magnitude.

The incoming players for this 2009 Champions League Final (from 2008) for Manchester United were O'Shea, Anderson, Ryan Giggs (captain for the night) and Park Ji-sung. John O'Shea had a lengthy career with United (1999–2011) playing largely as a defender, sometimes as a defensive midfielder. Here he played at right-back. Born in Waterford, Ireland, O'Shea joined United, aged 17, going on to play 393 games in all competitions (15 goals). Only United stalwarts Denis Irwin and Roy Keane, and Liverpool stalwarts Steve Heighway and Ronnie Whelan have won more honours at club level than O'Shea (14 trophies in all).

Initially O'Shea was loaned out to AFC Bournemouth and Belgian team Royal Antwerp from 1999–2002 to gain experience of the physicality of senior men's football. At six feet three inches O'Shea had the physical stature, he just needed regular experience at first team level. A versatile player, O'Shea played right and left-back, centre-back and defensive midfield in his first full season at United of 2002–03. In 2003–04 Rio Ferdinand was injured, O'Shea taking over in central defence, but when United won the 2003–04 FA Cup Final he found himself playing left-back. O'Shea suffered indifferent form over the next two seasons. In the 2007–08 season O'Shea even played as an emergency striker, completing the feat of playing in every single outfield position for the club since 2002. I've stated this before, but I feel a player needs to play regularly in one position to bring consistency to a team. In the 2008–09 season injuries to Gary Neville and Wes Brown gave O'Shea the right-back berth on a regular basis. It brings consistency.

O'Shea moved from United in July 2011 to play under former United captain Steve Bruce at Sunderland. A hamstring injury subsequently ended his interest in the 2011–12 season. Sadly, two relegations occurred with Sunderland – this grand old club now a Football League Division 1 team – in O'Shea's time at the Stadium of Light. He played nine games for Reading 2018–19, retiring in April 2019 aged 38.

John O'Shea received 118 caps for Ireland (three goals) 2001–2018. Again, O'Shea's versatility and reliability saw him utilised by the Republic of Ireland at full-back, or at centre-back where he often partnered Manchester City's Richard Dunne. O'Shea was part of the team that controversially lost to France in a 2010 World Cup play-off game, France winning 2-1 thanks to a handball incident involving Thierry Henry. It was not Henry's – a magnificent player – finest moment, but was probably an instinctive action. O'Shea also appeared in the 2012 and 2016 Euros.

Considering his United career spanned 2007–2015, Brazilian Anderson Oliveira was something of a misfire. He played 105 Premier League games (five goals), but was never consistently in the first 11 at Old Trafford. Born in Porto Alegre, southern Brazil, Anderson earned iconic status in November 2005 by scoring the goal that earned his home city club Gremio promotion to Brazilian Serie A from Serie B against Nautico from Recife in Brazil's north-east – when the team were down to seven players!

Anderson moved to Porto in Portugal in January 2006, helping the team win the 2005–06 Primeira Liga title within months. A broken leg against Benfica cost Anderson five months of the 2006–07 season, but the title was won again. He moved to United in July 2007, joining the club's other Brazilian midfielder Kleberson. Neither player was a raging success at Old Trafford – imagine coming from sunny Brazil to the incessant rain of Manchester!

In his first season of 2007–08 in Manchester, Anderson came on as a substitute for Wes Brown in the Champions League Final in Moscow and converted the sixth, conclusive penalty kick in the penalty shoot-out. On 6 December 2008 Anderson won the Golden Boy award given to the Best Young Player in Europe by sports journalists. It was a very promising start to Anderson's United career. Again he scored the winning penalty kick in the 2009 League Cup Final against Tottenham Hotspur, after the game finished goalless. A cruciate knee ligament injury then ruled Anderson out of the second half of the 2009–10 seasons and the 2010 World Cup.

Anderson's best goal return in the Champions League came in the 2010–11 season, scoring in the group match against Valencia, bettered by two rare goals in the semi-final against Schalke 04, won 4-1 on aggregate by United. A series of injuries kept Anderson's performances in the first team to a minimum over the next four seasons, even being loaned out to Fiorentina in Italy for the end of the 2013–14 season. He played 50 games for International in Brazil 2015–18, ending his career in the Turkish 2nd Division with Adana Demirspor. Anderson's career at Manchester United promised much early on, but injuries, and the relentless pace of top-level English football, cost him dearly.

As a teenager Anderson won the Golden Ball (most valuable player) in the 2005 FIFA U-17 World Championships as Brazil lost the final to Mexico 3-0. Anderson was stretchered off injured in the final after 15 minutes. A portent perhaps? Highly rated as a young player, Anderson's surprising strength (he stood only five feet nine inches), speed, technique and all-round passing game made him a much-touted player. Injuries and a questionable work-rate worked against him. He played only eight times for Brazil 2007–08.

The same height as Anderson, Park Ji-Sung was a far more energetic, productive player for United. Playing in front of the Anderson-Carrick-Giggs three-man midfield, Park was essentially a midfield player, but his great energy allowed him to supplement Rooney and Cristiano Ronaldo in attack.

Slight in stature, Park first played for Myongi University and the South Korean Olympic team, but South Korea failed to advance to the knockout stages of the 2000 Summer Olympics in Australia. Having coached the South Korean international team, Guus Hiddink took Park to PSV Eindhoven in Holland along with Park's teammate Lee Young-pyo. It was left-back Lee who made the bigger impression initially. Park had an operation to remove his meniscus from a knee. Still struggling upon returning from injury, his fortunes changed when Arjen Robben joined Chelsea. Park's pace and trickery complemented the height of fellow midfielders Mark van Bommel and Philip Cocu. The highlight of Park's PSV career came when scoring against AC Milan in the Champions League semi-final in 2004–05, PSV narrowly losing out on away goals.

When Park Ji-Sung signed for Alex Ferguson and Manchester United in July 2005 he became the second Asian player to sign for the club after the Chinese forward Dong Fangzhou. Dong played just one Premier League game for United. Park's regularity was considerably greater, playing 134 Premier League games, scoring 19 goals. Park's United career, like Anderson's , began brightly. Like Anderson, injuries soon curtailed his appearances. Park's bane was recurring knee injuries. Ferguson left Park out of the squad facing Chelsea in the 2008 Champions League Final, a decision Ferguson said was the hardest he'd ever taken.

Park's compensation came in the season of 2008–09. In playing in the semi-finals against Porto, Park became the only Asian player to take part in four Champions League semi-finals. He subsequently became the first Asian player in football history to play in a Champions League Final. Alex Ferguson clearly trusted Park's ability – only his fitness was questioned.

Park Ji-Sung moved to south-west London to join Queens Park Rangers for the 2012–13 season, being made club captain, but injuries meant he played only 20 Premier League games, and QPR were relegated. After returning to PSV Eindhoven on loan for the 2013–14 season, Park's persistent knee injuries won the day and he retired on 14 May 2014.

Park played 100 times for South Korea, scoring 13 goals. Park's brilliant goal put Portugal out of the 2002 World Cup, South Korea advancing to the knockout stages. The South Korean hosts then beat heavily fancied Italy (2-1 after extra time) and Spain (0-0, 5-3 on penalties) to reach the semi-finals where they were beaten by Michael Ballack's solitary goal for Germany. South Korea did not advance to the knockout stages of the 2006 World Cup. They did not lose a single game in qualifying for the 2010 World Cup. At the tournament proper, Park scored in his third consecutive World Cup in the 2-0 victory over Greece, the feat also the first of any Asian player in three successive World Cups. He is also the only Asian player to be awarded four Man of the Match awards at World Cups.

I was greatly enamoured of Park's effervescent displays in a Manchester United shirt. A lively presence, he made and scored crucial goals for United. Alex Ferguson also praised his defensive work for the team, and his elevated displays in important games. Andrea Pirlo, the great Italian playmaker, found Park's livewire displays among the hardest he faced in European football. Wayne Rooney admired Park's self-sacrifice to the team. This is Park Ji-Sung's legacy: the team was always more important than the individual.

Substitutes for United on this evening in Rome included Brazilian full-back Rafael, and Northern Irish centre-back Jonny Evans for defensive cover; the Portuguese winger Nani, Paul Scholes, Carlos Tevez and Dimitar Berbatov for midfield/attacking replacements. Berbatov, a Bulgarian international, was a splendid, technical centre-forward with a respectable goals track record with Bayer Leverkusen (69 goals in 154 Bundesliga games), Tottenham Hotspur (27 goals in 70 Premier League games) and with United 2008–2012 he would net 48 goals in 108 Premier League games. For Bulgaria, Berbatov scored a further 48 goals in 78 internationals 1999–2010. He was named Bulgarian Footballer of the Year seven times; surpassing the great Hristo Stoichkov's five.

In goal for Barcelona, Victor Valdés was a brilliant keeper in one-on-one situations. Valdés played 93 games for Barcelona's 'C' and 'B' teams, then 387 La Liga games for the first team. Valdés won the Spanish Zamora trophy, awarded for the lowest goal ratio per games conceded. After 13 seasons at the Nou Camp, Valdés joined Manchester United for the 2015–16 season. He played only twice for United, playing second fiddle to David de Gea. He played 20 times for Spain 2010–14, but similarly was used as backup to de Gea or Iker Casillas. Valdés ended his playing days between the sticks at Middlesbrough 2016–17, playing 28 times as the north-eastern club returned to the Premiership from the Championship under fellow countryman Aitor Karanka. Valdés was encouraged to play out from the back for Barcelona in the now commonplace mode of modern goalkeepers.

Full-backs were Carlos Puyol, the club captain, and the Brazilian ex-Arsenal left-back Sylvinho. Patrolling the central defensive area were two very fine technical footballers, the Ivorian Yaya Touré (better known as a midfield giant at Manchester City), and the elegant Spanish international Gerard Piqué. Yaya, younger brother of Kolo, was a dominant player, wherever he played on the pitch. He would win African Footballer of the Year four times in succession 2011–2014. Before being recognised as a player of top stature, Touré junior travelled the European circuit a little, playing for Beveren in Belgium, Metalurk Donetsk in the Ukraine, Olympiakos in Greece, and AS Monaco in France for six seasons 2001–07. It was in Greece that Touré became known as the 'new Patrick Vieira', Olympiakos winning the domestic double of league and cup in 2005–06.

Touré joined Barcelona in August 2007, playing and scoring in his first Champions League match, the quarter-final home leg against the Germans of Schalke 04. With Sergio Busquets preferred by manager Pep Guardiola as the holding player in midfield, Touré found himself deployed as a centre-back in this 2009 Champions League Final due to injuries. Touré stayed three seasons with Barcelona (74 La Liga games, four goals), but chose to move to Manchester City in July 2010 with regular occupancy in midfield foremost in his mind.

Yaya Touré became a sensation at City, his powerhouse performances from his favoured central midfield position an integral part of Manchester City's successes in the early part of the decade of the 2010s. Touré's power and drive perfectly complemented the silky skills of the pocket genius David Silva in City's new look team of the new decade. Touré's industry for City was phenomenal, covering 90 yards of the pitch to score for his team in a 4-3 win over Wolves. In the semi-final of the 2011 FA Cup, Touré scored the winner against Manchester United, then enabled City's first major trophy in 35 years, scoring the winner in the final against Stoke City. The last trophy won by City came in the days of the great Bell-Summerbee-Lee-Doyle Manchester City team I remember so well from my teens in the late 1960s.

Interestingly, Touré claimed in February 2012 after being racially abused in a Europa League tie against Porto in Portugal that the reason he loved playing in England was that similar abuse did not occur in England. Fast-forward to Euro 2020 and the appalling abuse hurled at Jadon Sancho, Bakary Saka and Marcus Rashford for missing penalty kicks against Italy in the final beggars belief. Have the English football supporters become less tolerant in the last decade? It would appear so. I feel in the tribal world of English football that if these players were playing well for their clubs, reaction would be different. Have we lost the facility to be tolerant of people of any colour other than white? There is nothing more interesting when travelling than absorbing the cultures of other countries. People should open their minds and open their hearts more.

That incredible 2011–12 season followed, Manchester City winning their first league title in 44 years on the last day of the season. Six games remaining, City trailed rivals Manchester United by a seemingly insurmountable eight points. United stuttered, lost to City and a Vincent Kompany header in a crucial game. Touré, magnificent in that game, then scored both goals as City beat Newcastle United 2-0. Every football follower knows what happened next as Sergio Agüero's injury-time winner secured a 3-2 victory over Queens Park Rangers, the club's first league title since 1968.

City's quest for the holy grail of the Champions League began in 2012–13 – the quest goes on. Touré was again magnificent as City lost 3-2 at the Bernabeu Stadium to Real Madrid, Cristiano Ronaldo, predictably, scoring the winner. Touré was Man of the Match as Chelsea were beaten 2-1 in the FA Cup semi-final, but in one of the great cup upsets City lost the final 1-0 to Wigan Athletic and a 91st-minute Ben Watson goal.

In March 2014 Touré equalised in the League Cup Final against Sunderland, City going on to win 3-1. In April 2014 Touré was named in the PFA Team of the Year. The season ended with a second successive Premier League title for City, Touré becoming only the second Premier League midfielder to score 20 Premier League goals after Chelsea's Frank Lampard. Touré's passing accuracy rate of 90.76% for the season equalled his goals output.

Touré's last four seasons never quite matched his amazing impact 2011–14 and the Ivorian returned to Olympiakos in Greece in 2018, without further success. Internationally, Touré was named captain of the Ivory Coast after Didier Drogba retired. Touré played 101 times for his country, scoring 19 goals. He appeared at the 2006, 2010 and 2014 World Cups, scoring against North Korea in 2010. In February 2015, Touré managed what Drogba could not, in captaining the Ivory Coast to their first African Cup of Nations victory since 1992, won with a penalty shoot-out victory over Ghana after a goalless match in Equatorial Guinea, the competition having been moved from Morocco due to concerns over the ebola outbreak in West Africa. The penalty shoot-out went to a 9-8 scoreline, both Touré brothers Yaya and Kolo converting their kicks.

Yaya Touré's initial spell at Manchester City helped transform the club's fortunes in the modern era. Formerly a striker, capable of playing as a centre-back, Yaya was never happier than when being allowed to join his team's attack. His surging runs from midfield at City defied human belief, his stamina and strength matched by great technique, and at six feet two inches, he proffered a massive aerial threat. Touré scored 59 goals in his 230 Premier League games, an impressive return by any standards.

Curiously, for a player now strongly associated with Barcelona's peak years of the late noughties and early 2010s, Gerard Piqué left Barcelona for Manchester United in 2004, spending four seasons at Old Trafford. A promising product of Barca's famed La Masia academy, Piqué enrolled with United's academy. He played only 12 Premier League games for United, always down the pecking order behind Ferdinand and Vidic, for all his promise.

Returning to Barcelona in 2008, Piqué's fortunes looked up. At United he'd struggled to find his feet; at Barcelona for nearly a decade Piqué looked like

Ferdinand's successor, one of the best footballing centre-backs in Europe. Along with Xavi, Iniesta, Busquets, Messi, Dani Alves and Pedro, Piqué became among the only players to have been part of both Barcelona's treble-winning teams, the Champions League, La Liga, the Copa del Rey, of 2009 and 2015. Detrimentally, Piqué's pace deteriorated towards the end of the 2010s. His last-minute header against Seville in the 2021 Copa del Rey semi-final saved Barcelona from a 2-1 defeat, the Catalonians going on to win 3-2 in extra time. Barca then went on to slam Athletic Bilbao 4-0 in the final with goals from Antoine Griezmann, Frenkie de Jong and a brace from the immaculate Messi.

Capped 102 times by Spain, Piqué has scored five international goals. Partnered with Carlos Puyol as centre-backs in the 2010 World Cup finals, the pair scarcely put a foot wrong as Spain won the tournament in the final against Holland 1-0. At the 2012 Euros similar central defensive dominance was achieved for Spain with Piqué alongside Sergio Ramos. By beating Italy 4-0 in the final, Spain completed a fifth consecutive clean sheet. One goal conceded in the whole of the tournament, Piqué was one of seven of the Spanish team included in the Team of the Tournament. Reaching the final of the 2013 FIFA Confederations Cup Spain lost 3-0 to Brazil, ending their world record run of 29 undefeated matches. Piqué retired from international football in August 2018. An imposing presence at six feet four inches, Piqué belied any thoughts of him being a lumbering centre-back with typically precise Spanish technique. Criticised in some quarters for inconsistency and a lack of pace, Puyol preferred to think of Piqué as the best centre-back of his kind due to his positioning and football intelligence.

The combination of Xavi and Iniesta in Barcelona's midfield in the noughties and 2010s gave the Catalonian team almost complete control of a football in their games. The pair were relentless in terms of short passing and retaining the ball, a rare occasion if they did not. Xavi, the stockier of the two, stood five feet seven inches, the same height as Iniesta. I remember well how Alan Ball was frowned upon by professional football experts when I was a boy, being told he was too small to make the grade. It didn't stop Ball winning a World Cup, and it didn't deter these two marvellous Spanish midfield players repeating the feat.

Xavi joined the La Masia academy, aged 11, learning the Barcelona team ethos from these early beginnings. He progressed through the Barcelona youth team, Barcelona 'B', making his full debut late in the season of 1997–98. His La Liga debut came in October 1998, integrating himself into Louis van Gaal's 1997–98 title-winning team, initially modelling himself on Pep Guardiola, Barca's incumbent playmaker. Xavi was named the 1999 La Liga Breakthrough Player of the Year, ultimately replacing Guardiola in the Barcelona first team line-up when Pep was injured. In the seasons 2001–02 and 2002–03 Xavi became the chief supplier of assists for goals for Barcelona. Xavi was named vice-captain in 2004–05, another La Liga-winning season for Barca. He was named 2005 La Liga Spanish Player of the Year. His appearance on the substitute's bench at the 2006 Champions League Final was purely down to torn knee ligaments earlier in the season.

Named Player of the Tournament at Euro 2008, Xavi was targeted by Bayern Munich, but Guardiola, now head coach at Barcelona, persuaded him to stay.

It was a good call. In 2008–09, Xavi scored in the Copa del Rey Final, a 4-1 drubbing of Athletic Bilbao. In 'El Clasico', the classic Barcelona versus Real Madrid annual matches, Xavi assisted four of Barca's goals in a 6-2 thrashing of 'Los Blancos'. Xavi crossed the ball for Messi to head one of Barcelona's goals in this 2009 Champions League Final. Beaten manager Alex Ferguson praised Xavi and Iniesta's ball retention in this final. Xavi won the award for UEFA Champions League Best Midfielder for 2008–09. In this same season he made 20 assists in La Liga, 29 in all competitions. Not only did Xavi seemingly never give the ball away, he also always spied the final ball threaded through precisely to his forwards. In the 2009–10 La Liga season, Xavi topped the assists table again. World Soccer magazine voted him World Player of the Year, even if he did finish third in the Ballon d'Or poll behind teammates Messi and Iniesta. If Ferguson thought Xavi immaculate in this 2009 Champions League Final, Xavi and his teammates gazumped this performance in the repeat final of 2011, widely regarded as the best performance by a team in the final in the modern Champions League era.

In the 2012–13 season Barcelona virtually won La Liga by January (Manchester City and Liverpool had similarly dominant seasons in the 2010s in England). Xavi, Iniesta, Messi and Dani Alves were named in the FIFA World XI for the 2012–2013 season. 2013–14 was less successful, Barca beaten by Real Madrid 2-1 in the Copa del Rey Final – Gareth Bale scoring an 88th-minute winner. Atlético Madrid, so difficult to beat under Argentine manager Diego Simeone, pipped Barca to the La Liga title. In the 2014–15 season, Barcelona won the Champions League again, defeating Juventus in the final. In his last season with Barca as a player, Xavi came on as a substitute for Iniesta as Barcelona won 3-1. The victory gave Barcelona a fifth European Cup.

Curiously, Xavi turned to Qatar to end his club playing days in Doha with Al Sadd, his mission as much to be an ambassador for Spain with the upcoming 2022 Qatar World Cup in mind. Xavi completed 767 games in all competitions for Barcelona, winning eight La Liga titles and four Champions Leagues.

One can scarcely divide or distinguish the abilities of Xavi and Andres Iniesta, the impact of the pair immense upon Spanish football as a whole, whether in service to Barcelona or to their country's standing in world football. A winner of a total of 35 trophies with Barcelona (including the same four Champions Leagues as Xavi) and nine La Liga titles, Iniesta is the most decorated Spanish footballer of all time. Iniesta has been selected for the FIFA FIFPRO World XI nine times, and the UEFA Team of the Year six times. He was also chosen as UEFA Best Player in Europe in 2012 and named the IFFHS World's Best Playmaker in 2012 and 2013.

Schooled in La Masia's pass and move tradition, Pep Guardiola thought that Xavi would retire him personally (true), and Iniesta was so good that all previous midfielders would pale by comparison. Iniesta played 49 times for Barcelona 'B' 2001–03, transitioning to the first team during the 2002–03 season, going on to play 442 La Liga games, scoring 35 goals, compared to Xavi's 58 in 505 La Liga games. Neither player was a prolific scorer from midfield. It was more about keeping the ball at all costs, playing the final ball through to the likes of Messi, Henry, Eto'o et al. When the French winger Ludovic Giuly moved to A.S. Roma in 2007, Iniesta became a permanent fixture in Barcelona's midfield. Iniesta's curling strike from 25 yards in injury time at Stamford Bridge in the 2009 semi-final prevented Chelsea matching up with Manchester United for a second successive Champions League Final. It was heart-breaking for the Blues, but indicative of a master technician.

Iniesta's forte was to make his team tick. Less flamboyant than some of his greater lauded striking teammates, no Barcelona player or football observer doubted Iniesta's importance to the team. He tended to be behind the Messis and Ronaldos for the top individual awards, but his worth to his team was immeasurable. Iniesta it was who scored Spain's winning 2010 World Cup goal, despite a fractured season in La Liga after returning from injuries. In the 2011–12 Champions League he scored important goals against AC Milan in the last eight, and again versus Chelsea in the last four – this time Chelsea prevailed 3-2 on aggregate. When Carlos Puyol retired, and Xavi departed, Iniesta became Barcelona's club captain. The 2015 Champions League Final saw Iniesta win the Man of the Match award as Juventus were defeated 3-1. Having spent his life with Barcelona 1996–2018, Iniesta decided to play out his final days with Vissel Kobe in Japan where he remained in 2022, aged 38.

Iniesta was part of Spain's winning UEFA European U-16 team in England in 2001, and again at U-19 level in Norway in 2002 – Fernando Torres scoring each time in 1-0 victories over France and Germany respectively. Iniesta's first goal for Spain at senior level came against England in February 2007, literally a warning shot to English players in coming years. Man of the Match in the 2008 Euro semi-final against Russia, Iniesta was named in the Team of the Tournament after Spain beat Germany 1-0 in the final. When Spain won their first World Cup in South Africa in 2010, Iniesta scored the decisive goal and won the Man of the Match award. At the 2012 Euros, Iniesta won the Man of the Match award three times, including the final won 4-0 against Italy. He was chosen as the UEFA Euro 2012 Player of the Tournament. Italy exacted revenge upon Spain in the last 16 of the 2016 Euros. Iniesta's last World Cup came in 2018. His 131 caps for Spain see him lie fourth-highest capped player behind Iker Casillas, Xavi and Sergio Ramos. He scored 14 times for his country.

Starting as a defensive midfielder, Iniesta progressed to become an inventive passing midfielder with greater attacking intent, even playing as a winger under Frank Rikjaard. Pep Guardiola sees Iniesta as a master of spatial awareness and time on the ball. His understanding with Xavi was purely intuitive – each always seeming to know where the other was. They must have been an absolute nightmare to play against. Iniesta's ability to play the game either slowly or quickly at the right moment is an object lesson to English footballers who are brought up to play the game at a ludicrously high tempo in the English Football Leagues.

Lionel Messi – the best player in the world 2004–2021? – Cristiano Ronaldo has every right to dispute this, but individually Messi is surely the most gifted footballer of the last two decades, his balance and finesse not seen since the 'marmite' love him or hate him days of Diego Maradona. The same height as Xavi and Iniesta – five feet seven inches, Messi's ability to twist and turn out of tight situations, the ball permanently glued to his magical left foot, has been a mesmeric presence in club and international football in the 21st century.

Messi matches, and occasionally surpasses Cristiano Ronaldo with his goals return for Barcelona. He surpassed Ronaldo individually in European recognition, having won the Ballon d'Or six times 2009–2012, and again in 2015 and 2019. Where Ronaldo specialised in goal-scoring (although his early individualism gave way to the broader picture eventually), Messi has always been considered not only a goalscorer, but a playmaker. Like Iniesta, Messi won 35 career trophies with Barcelona, including ten La Liga titles, seven Copa del Reys and four Champions Leagues. Messi holds the record for the most La Liga hat-tricks (eight) and the most La Liga assists (192). He is the scorer of over 750 career goals for club and country, his 474 La Liga goals in 520 games the most by a player for a single club.

Born in Rosario, Santa Fe, Argentina to a steel factory manager father and a magnet manufacturing mother, it was Messi's magnetic football skills that marked him out as the most skilful player of his generation. Messi joined the local team, Newell's Old Boys (named after Isaac Newell of Kent, England, one of the pioneers of Argentine football – we were once great, but as is the English way, held on to the mantle too long without learning from others as they improved while we stood still) as a six-year-old, scoring nearly 500 goals in six seasons for Newell's youth sides. The juvenile Messi entertained crowds at half-time with his ball juggling skills at Newell's senior home games. A hormone growth deficiency diagnosed when he was ten threatened his development. Ironically, as a boy Messi idolised Ronaldo – not his fierce Portuguese rival, but the great Brazilian striker of the 1990s and noughties.

Messi never played senior football for his local Newell's Old Boys team, moving instead to Barcelona, the Messi family having Catalonian relatives (his father and mother have Spanish and Italian ancestry). Assimilating into La Masia, Messi's growth hormone programme was completed when he was 14. Friends at La Masia included Cesc Fàbregas and Gerard Piqué, the trio becoming part of Barcelona's greatest ever youth side, the 'Baby Dream Team'. Thirty-six goals in 30 games for the Cadetes A team helped secure a treble of league, and Spanish and Catalan cups. Fàbregas moved to Arsenal, Piqué to Manchester United. Arsenal wanted Messi too, but the magician stayed at Barcelona. What a loss for Arsenal!

Messi played 32 games for Barcelona's 'C' and 'B' teams (11 goals), swiftly being elevated to the first team squad in 2004. If he was chopped down by rough-house defenders he simply got up, dribbled past four or five players and scored. Marked by Sergio Ramos (then Seville in 2004, soon-to-be defensive talisman and leader of Barca's great rivals Real Madrid) in a Barcelona 'C' game, Messi scored a hat-trick, aged 17, in eight minutes. In season 2004–05 Barcelona won La Liga for the first time in six years, the goal scored by Messi against Albacete in May 2005 making him the club's youngest ever goalscorer at that time. In a pre-season game against Juventus in August 2005, Messi's talents brought an offer from Inter Milan that would have trebled his wages.

Acquiring Spanish citizenship in September 2005, Messi stayed to form an exquisite attacking triumvirate with Ronaldinho and Samuel Eto'o. A hamstring injury incurred against Chelsea put Messi out of the 2006 Champions League Final. A metatarsal fracture in November 2006 stalled the young starlet's stellar progression. In 2007 Messi scored a Copa del Rey semi-final goal against Getafe similar to Maradona's outrageous individual goal against England at the 1986 World Cup. Collecting the ball near the halfway line he waltzed past five defenders and scored from a tight angle. 5-2 up from the first leg at the Nou Camp, Messi was ludicrously rested from the return leg and Barcelona lost 4-0! Ronaldinho's form dipped and Messi earned the sobriquet from the Spanish press of 'Mess-iah' as he became the team's main protagonist, aged 20 in 2007. A torn hamstring in December 2007 led Puyol to claim that Messi was being unfairly loaded physically.

Assigning the genius a personal physiotherapist, Messi recovered so well he scarcely missed a game in the next four seasons. In season 2008–09 Messi scored 38 of the 100 goals amassed by himself, Thierry Henry and Eto'o. He was the Champions League top scorer with nine goals, and the youngest player to achieve the feat in the competition's history. In 2009 Messi won both the Ballon d'Or and the FIFA World Player of the Year awards, both won by the greatest margin in each awards' history. After losing the 2011 Copa del Rey to Cristiano Ronaldo's extra-time winner for Real Madrid, Messi evened matters up with a typically slaloming effort as Barcelona won the first leg of the Champions League semi-final four days later against the same opponents in the Bernabeu Stadium, Barca winning 2-0. The 1-1 draw at the Nou Camp in the second leg was enough to take Barcelona through to a second confrontation with Manchester United in three seasons. Topping the Champions League scoring charts again, this time with 12 goals, Messi scored against United in the final during a Man of the Match performance. Fifty-three goals and 24 assists made him Barcelona's all-time single season top scorer, and the first player to pass 50 goals in Spanish football. The following season, his 73 goals and 29 assists in all competitions obliterated the previous season's totals.

In March 2012, a fortnight after netting four goals against Valencia, Messi scored five times against Bayer Leverkusen in a last 16 Champions League tie. These goals helped Messi to a Champions League total of 14, matching José Altafini's 1962–63 tally with AC Milan in a European Cup campaign, also equalling Gerd Müller's record of being top scorer in four European Cups. Another fortnight on and Messi became Barca's top scorer in the club's history, aged 24, overtaking a 57-year-old record held by César Rodriguez. His individual form didn't enable Barca to beat Chelsea in the 2011–12 Champions League, the little genius proving fallible as he struck the bar with a penalty kick, Chelsea eventually triumphing 3-2 on aggregate thanks to Fernando Torres's 92nd-minute equaliser at the Nou Camp. Messi had to settle for surpassing Gerd Müller's 67 goals in the 1972–73 Bundesliga season with his 73 goals in all competitions. He also broke Müller's record of 85 goals in a calendar year in 2012 with 91. Four goals against Espanyol in Barca's final La Liga match in May 2012 didn't harm his cause.

2-0 down from the first leg of their last 16 Champions League game of 2012–

13 against AC Milan, Barcelona swiftly turned the tie around, winning 4-0 in the Nou Camp, Messi scoring twice. An astounding 7-0 aggregate reversal at the hands of Bayern Munich, 0-4 in the Allianz Arena, Munich, and 0-3 at home in the Nou Camp, ended Barca's hopes of European success in this season at the semi-final stage. Struggling for the first time in four years with a hamstring injury, Messi played ineffectively in the first leg, and not at all in the home tie. He still managed to score in 21 consecutive league games, scoring 33 goals in this run, becoming the first player to win the European Golden Shoe (top scorer in all European leagues) three times. In the 2013–14 season, Messi registered his lowest goals output in five seasons – and still managed to score 41 goals in all competitions!

In 2014–15 Messi surpassed the 59-year-old record of 251 La Liga goals, previously held by Athletic Bilbao's Telmo Zarra. A new super triumvirate of Messi, the Brazilian Neymar and Uruguayan Luis Suarez smashed the 100 goals 2008–09 season of Messi, Henry and Eto'o, the trio amassing 122 goals in all competitions, a record in Spanish football, Messi scoring 58. Not bad for a player seemingly blighted by injury and slight decline. He also surpassed Luis Figo's previous best La Liga assists total with 18 in 2014–2015. Messi struck twice in the 2015 Copa del Rey Final defeat of Athletic Bilbao, the 3-1 victory securing Barcelona's sixth double in the club's history. In the Champions League semi-final 3-0 victory over Bayern Munich, Messi again score twice, a dribble and chip over Manuel Neuer earning him the UEFA Goal of the Season award. Messi didn't score in the 3-1 final success over Juventus, but assisted all three goals. His ten Champions League goals helped him become the first player to top-score in five Champions League seasons. He subsequently won the UEFA Best Player in Europe Award for the second time.

In September 2015–16, Messi became the youngest player to make 100 Champions League appearances in the 1-1 draw with Roma at the Stadio Olimpico. English club Arsenal suffered at his hands (and magical feet) in the last 16 first leg Champions League tie at the Emirates Stadium, both goals conjured by the magician in a 2-0 victory. Once again, Messi, Neymar and Suarez smashed the previous combined goals record of Barca's front three, this time amassing 131 goals, Messi's contribution 41 – and 23 assists.

Scoring his sixth hat-trick in the Champions League in September 2016 in a group stage 7-0 thrashing of Celtic, Messi's tally of hat-tricks surpassed any previous player in European Cup history. A groin injury ruled him out for three weeks. When he returned, he scored another hat-trick against Manchester City in the Champions League, his 37th hat-trick in all for Barcelona. His 54th Champions League goal in the return group match in Manchester (a 3-1 defeat), took him beyond Real Madrid's Raul as the competition's highest scorer.

Messi ended 2016–17 with 51 goals, one ahead of Zlatan Ibrahimovic. In February 2017, Messi's 27th free-kick goal for Barca against Athletic Bilbao in a 3-0 win surpassed the 26 previously scored for Barcelona by Ronald Koeman. The 2017 Copa del Rey Final saw Barca defeat Alaves 3-1, Messi voted Man of the Match. His 37 La Liga goals earned him the Pichichi (Spanish top scorer) and European Golden Boot for the fourth time.

Messi's 100th goal in all UEFA European competitions arrived in October 2017 against Olympiakos, coming in 21 fewer games than Cristiano Ronaldo's 100. A fifth Golden Shoe arrived with his 34 La Liga goals in 2017–18. Barcelona devoured Sevilla 5-0 in the 2018 Copa del Rey Final, Messi among the scorers. A 25th Barcelona La Liga title was secured in May 2018, Barcelona's 5-1 defeat of Villareal earning the longest unbeaten streak (43 games) in La Liga history.

With Iniesta departing in May 2018, Messi became Barca's new club captain for 2018–19. His eighth Champions league hat-trick in Barca's opening group game in September 2018 helped his team to a 4-0 win over PSV Eindhoven, setting a new hat-trick record for the competition. His two free-kick goals in a 4-0 'Derbi Barceloni' victory over Espanyol took him to double figures in December 2018, the first player to achieve the feat in La Liga for 13 consecutive seasons. In February 2019 his 50th penalty goal in La Liga in a 2-2 draw with Valencia made him only the third player in the league's history to achieve this feat. The others: Cristiano Ronaldo (predictably) and Hugo Sanchez, the Mexican striker who played for both Atlético Madrid and Real Madrid in the 1980s and 1990s. Two goals against Manchester United in the Champions League quarter-finals helped Barca to a comfortable 4-0 aggregate victory. He repeated the feat at the Nou Camp in a 3-0 semi-final victory over Liverpool, only for the super-resilient Merseysiders to rally with recent top-level football's most dramatic turnaround victory, the amazing 4-0 victory at Anfield in the second leg. Messi had to settle for a sixth Pichichi and Golden Shoe awards. His goal in the 2019 Copa del Rey Final was insufficient to avert a 2-1 defeat to Valencia.

A calf injury sidelined Messi at the beginning of the 2019–20 season. His earlier heroics in 2019 ensured his selection as 2019 FIFA Best Men's Player. The persistent rivalry with Cristiano Ronaldo continued – a rivalry both players revelled in – as Messi's 420th La Liga goal in a 4-0 win over Sevilla surpassed Ronaldo's previous best 419 in Europe's top five leagues. Messi's 25 La Liga goals earned him a seventh Pichichi trophy, but Real Madrid pipped Barca to the 2019–20 La Liga title. However good a player or team are, a rude awakening lurks around the corner. With Covid-19 dictating venues for European games, a delayed last eight one-off tie with Bayern Munich brought Barcelona's biggest European humiliation, an 8-2 defeat at the Stadium of Light, Lisbon. I remember witnessing the score on screen on the red button of my television in utter disbelief. Teams of this standard are not supposed to suffer such catastrophic losses.

In December 2020 Messi was selected for the FIFA FIFPRO World XI for the fourteenth consecutive year. His 644th Barcelona goal against Real Valladolid in December 2020 took him past Pele's tally with Santos for goals scored with a single club. Messi continued to score goals for Barcelona at a rapid rate, but the loss of Xavi and Iniesta to the team's midfield was too hefty a blow to endure; Barcelona's invincibility eroded. Paris Saint-Germain's 5-2 dismissal of Barca in the last 16 of the 2020–21 Champions League was the club's first elimination at this stage for 14 years. Compensation came with two Messi goals as Barca defeated Athletic Bilbao in the 2021 Copa del Rey Final. His second goal broke Gerd Müller's record of 30 plus goals in 12 consecutive club seasons, this being Messi's 13th. I remain steadfast in my assertion that Gerd Müller is the best pure penalty box striker I have ever seen. It's simply that Messi's all-round skills put him individually in another sphere altogether. This Copa del Rey, Messi's 35th trophy with Barcelona, saw him supersede Ryan Giggs as the most decorated player with any single European club.

Fittingly, Messi scored in his final match with Barcelona. Even more tellingly, the match ended in a 2-1 defeat against Celta Vigo. Barca's reign as Europe's top team seemed over. Messi settled again for his eighth Pichichi trophy as La Liga top scorer. His fifth La Liga title surpassed Alfredo Di Stéfano and Hugo Sanchez's previous best of four. It seemed inconceivable that Messi could be associated with any other European clubs, but leave he did, La Liga regulations and Barcelona's individual financial straits cited as the reasons.

Messi moved to Paris Saint-Germain in June 2021 on a two-year deal with an option for a further year. Unlike Cristiano Ronaldo, who scored in his first three games upon returning to Manchester United in 2021, Messi failed to score in his first three Ligue 1 games in France. Instead, Messi reserved his untouchable skills for Manchester City in the 2020–21 Champions League group match on 28 September 2021, playing a 1-2 with the new world superstar Kylian Mbappé before unleashing a typical left foot 20-yarder beyond a helpless Ederson in City's goal. Now 34, perhaps Messi will not yet go quietly on the grandest of European stages.

Why then could Lionel Messi not replicate his phenomenal club form at international level? The simple answer is, firstly, that even the best players need quality players around them, and while Argentina were still a team to be reckoned with at World Cups, they were not quite the force of the Mario Kempes or Diego Maradona years 1978 to 2000. Secondly, there has been far too great an emphasis on Messi carrying the international team, the over-reliance on him constantly producing moments of magic. There are many great teams on the world stage, as there are many great clubs in European football. Messi's Argentinian teams have rarely fielded an all-round solid 11 that have given him the platform to be a regular match-winner, as he has been with Barcelona.

It all started well enough in the sky blue and white vertical striped shirt for Messi in the 2005 FIFA World Youth Championship, goals against Colombia, favourites Spain, and Brazil, followed by two penalty goals against Nigeria as Argentina won the championship, Messi winning the Golden Ball as Player of the Tournament, the little magician being compared to Diego Maradona, who'd won the tournament with Argentina in 1979.

His first full international against Hungary in August 2005 at the Ferenc Puskás Stadium in Budapest ended disastrously. Appearing as a 63rd-minute substitute, he fended off a shirt-grab from full-back Vilmar Vanczok and was sent off within two minutes of entering the field. He was a marked man already. At the 2006 World Cup he came on as a substitute in the 6-0 drubbing of Serbia and Montenegro in the 74th minute, assisting and scoring in a 16-minute cameo. In scoring he became the youngest player to score at the 2006 World Cup. Manager José Pékerman described Messi as a jewel, but was reluctant to start him with other experienced players placed ahead of him. Knocked out 4-2 on penalties against Germany in the quarter-finals, the Argentine media reacted with incredulity at the young Messi's non-selection as a starter in the team.

The 2008 Copa America Final saw a 3-0 defeat to a Brazil side lacking many star players. Despite the reversal, Messi was named the Best Young Player of the Tournament by CONMEBOL (The South American Football Confederation). Unfortunately, Argentina fell at the last eight stage against Germany once more at the 2010 World Cup, this time conclusively, 4-0. The old chestnut of a team requiring balance surfaced as Messi struggled to gel in the same side as Carlos Tevez. Not an outwardly sociable individual in the manner of Cristiano Ronaldo, the reserved Messi became Argentina's captain, aged 24, under Alejandro Sabella. Messi's tendency has always been to lead by example, rather than vocally. This has arguably heaped even greater pressure on him to produce personally. Messi's goal-rate at least exploded, 25 in 32 games in three years after becoming captain – 17 in 61 under previous managers. His 12 goals in nine matches in 2012 for Argentina equalled a record held by the great Gabriel Batistuta for a calendar year. He scored ten goals in 14 matches during qualification for the 2014 World Cup. A corner appeared to have been turned.

Injuries incurred with Barcelona during the 2013–14 season hampered Messi going into the 2014 World Cup. Putting his misfortune behind him, he won the Man of the Match Award in Argentina's first four games, scoring in group matches against Bosnia and Herzegovina, Iran and Nigeria. Switzerland and Belgium were beaten 1-0 in the last 16 and the last eight, Holland were narrowly defeated on penalties after a goalless draw in the semi-final, Argentina reaching their first final since 1990. Who should await them in the final but Germany, and despite Messi's individual talent, it was the Germans' team ethic that won the day, Mario Götze scoring an extra-time winner. Messi again won the Golden Ball as the Player of the Tournament, but the arguments against him being billed on the same page as Pele and Maradona rumbled on. Messi provided the most assists at the 2014 World Cup, suggesting he was more than a one-man show, but as a man with the weight of his country on his shoulders, the expectation proved too great.

Argentina, hosts, were knocked out of the 2011 Copa America. In 2015 they were beaten 4-1 on penalties in the final after a 0-0 draw with Chile. In 2016 the same result occurred, 0-0 with Chile, a 4-2 penalty shoot-out defeat. Chilean manager Juan Antonio insisted that the world's "best ever" player had partaken in the final – Messi. Messi decided to retire from international football after four final defeats with Argentina. A campaign in Argentina started in Buenos Aires; even Argentina's President Mauricio Macri pleaded with Messi not to quit. The Mayor of Buenos Aires unveiled a statue of 'the world's greatest Player' of the last two decades in the city. Weeks later, Messi retracted his decision.

A 3-0 group stage defeat by Croatia at the 2018 World Cup brought into focus the problem of Messi being asked to produce magic, the Croatians, led by magnificent midfield players in Luka Modric and Ivan Rakitic, played as a team to deny Messi the ball. The last 16 match reproduced the same problems: Messi assisting two of Argentina's goals in a disjointed display as France ran out 4-3 winners.

Destined it seemed to never win a trophy with Argentina. Messi's moment finally arrived at the 2021 Copa America Final in Brazil. Argentina beat the hosts Brazil 1-0 in the final, the first time his country had won the Copa America since 1993 – astonishing given the perception of Argentine football outside of South America. Europeans always regard Brazil and Argentina as the leading exponents of South American football. In this 2021 Copa America tournament Messi was directly involved in nine of Argentina's 12 goals, scoring four, assisting five. He jointly won Player of the Tournament. Having promised retirement on more than one occasion, Messi produced a hat-trick in September 2021 as Argentina beat Bolivia 3-0 in a 2022 World Cup qualifier, taking him beyond Pele as South America's top all-time scorer with 79 goals.

Dubbed 'La Pulge Atomica' ('the Atomic Flea') in Spain, Messi's low centre of gravity, short, stocky stature and astonishing acceleration make him virtually impossible to subdue on a football field. Players who think they have got tight to him watch in astonishment as he skips lightly between them and away from them. Pep Guardiola says Messi is the only player in his experience to run faster with the ball than without. The ball seems glued to his hypnotic feet. Messi's immaculate balance and touch enable him to act as the perfect link player with his midfield and defence, as well as allowing him the capacity to score the most spectacular goals. Rarely, if ever, has such a sublimely talented player been such a fine team player.

The best player in world football ever? You have to say Pele and Maradona remain above him as World Cup winners. What I would say is Messi has been the best player in club football at world level – ever. Pele's 1,000-plus goals for Santos included numerous goals scored on world tours – such was Pele's popularity – and in close-season friendlies. Messi's 750 senior goals (474 in 520 La Liga games, 80 in 156 internationals, November 2021) have largely been scored at the very highest level of club and international football. Experiencing two players of the phenomenal consistency of Lionel Messi and Cristiano Ronaldo in the first two decades of the 21st century has been extraordinary.

Barcelona used two substitutes in this 2009 Champions League Final, the versatile Malian midfielder Seydou Keita, and the excellent winger-cum midfielder Pedro. Pedro's 99 goals in 321 appearances in all competitions for Barcelona reflect his importance to the club. Progressing through Barca's 'C' and 'B' teams, Pedro was integral to the club's successes 2008–2015. Upon joining Chelsea in 2015 he scored a further 43 goals in 206 games, helping the South Londoners win the Premier League in 2017, the FA Cup in 2018, and the Europa League in 2019. Santa Cruz de Tenerife-born, Pedro was a typical product of the Barcelona style 2008–2015, a fine passer of the ball, an excellent finisher, and a supreme technician.

THE FINAL

Cristiano Ronaldo did his utmost to carry the night for United in the early exchanges, seeing a free kick parried by Victor Valdés, then chesting the ball down and volleying wide of the far post. The lively Park Ji-Sung exuded energy, but Barcelona responded with Samuel Eto'o evading the attentions of three defenders to poke a shot past Edwin van der Sar at his near post. 1-0. The irrepressible Messi drifted in from his favoured right flank and exploded a shot narrowly over the bar. Ronaldo replied with another shot fizzing wide from the left flank. Ryan Giggs fired another shot over the bar as United desperately attempted to gain a foothold in a match slipping away from them. Anderson and Park offered plenty of energy in midfield for United, but Barcelona's tika-taka football kicked in, their keep-ball frustrating United. Rio Ferdinand excelled defensively in preventing Messi's through ball from creeping through with the deftest of touches. Half-time, 1-0 Barcelona.

In the second half Thierry Henry turned Ferdinand beautifully, but van der Sar saved his tame shot. Barcelona began to exert severe pressure upon United's goal. The immaculate Xavi bent a beautiful free kick against United's left-hand post, van der Sar beaten by Xavi's speed of thought and pace of shot. Soon after it was 2-0 as Messi met Xavi's deceptively simple angled ball with an outstanding guided header. United vainly tried to respond, Giggs missing a ball that the alert Ronaldo seized on, only to have his close range shot blocked by Valdés. Carlos Puyol broke free at the other end as Barca threatened to overwhelm United, but the stubborn van der Sar again blocked the effort. Dimitar Berbatov, on as a substitute, headed over the bar as United fought valiantly. Barca manager Pep Guardiola sported dark hair on the touchline here in 2009 – what a difference a decade makes! Xavi won the Man of the Match Award – but it could easily have been Messi or Iniesta – these three players all bore the hallmark of genius.

2011 CHAMPIONS LEAGUE FINAL
Barcelona 3 v 1 Manchester United

This match is remembered for being one of the greatest expositions of modern football. If United found it difficult to dispossess Barcelona in 2009, in 2011 it was virtually impossible. English football followers were able to enjoy an exhibition of perfect football, anti-United fans positively wallowing in the team's total humbling by a Barcelona team at the absolute peak of their powers.

Route to the Final
In the group stages, Manchester United headed Group C from Valencia. An all-British affair between United and Glasgow Rangers ended 0-0. It's never a good thing in my eyes to be paired with a Scottish team in Europe – or another English team. The contest invariably disintegrates into a club-style derby game, with neither side willing to give quarter, and neither team playing their natural game. Inter-British or Inter-English European games tend to dissolve into wars of attrition. Better to be competing against a team of contrasting style. Better still for a club's learning process to be competing against foreign players with different skill sets.

United squeaked through their second game in Valencia, Mexican striker Javier Hernández coming on as an 85th-minute substitute, scoring instantly to seal a 1-0 win. The Turkish team Bursaspor suffered two heavy defeats against Valencia, 0-4 and 1-6. United beat the Turks without conceding a goal, albeit less comprehensively. First United won 1-0 at Old Trafford with a goal from

Portuguese winger Nani in Turkey, winning the home tie 3-0 with goals from Darren Fletcher and sometime players, French winger Gabriel Oberton and Portuguese midfielder Bebe. Oberton flirted briefly with United 2009–11, playing only 14 Premier League games, without scoring. Bebe appeared even less, playing only twice in the Premier League 2010–14. Both players' careers stuttered after leaving Old Trafford, only Oberton making minor impact in Bulgaria and Turkey with Levski Sofia (2017–19) and BB Erzurumspor (2019–21) respectively.

United saw the group stage phase through with another all-British stalemate averted thanks to Wayne Rooney's 87th-minute penalty goal in Glasgow against Rangers, and a 1-1 draw at home to Valencia, Brazilian midfielder Anderson scoring United's goal.

Barcelona finished with the same 14 points total in winning Group D, starting with an emphatic 5-1 win against the Greek side Panathinaikos, two goals from Lionel Messi followed a David Villa strike, further strikes following from Pedro and Dani Alves. A trip to Russia to play Rubin Kazan ended in a 1-1 draw for Barca with Villa scoring a 60th-minute penalty for the Spaniards. Long flights and awkward delays in airport security are not conducive to good performances in the Soviet bloc countries, cold weather being an additional detrimental factor. Two goals from the irrepressible Messi gave Barcelona a 2-0 win at home against Copenhagen; the return game in Denmark a tighter affair, Messi's 31st-minute goal equalised within a minute by the Danes' Brazilian midfielder Claudemin.

Barcelona swept Panathinaikos aside again in the Olympic Stadium, Athens, winning 3-0 with Pedro scoring twice, Messi once. Qualification secured, Barcelona rang the changes in their last group game, still beating Rubin Kazan 2-0 with goals from squad players centre-back Andreu Fontàs and midfielder Victor Vasquez.

In the last 16 Manchester United drew with Marseille 0-0 in France. United defeated the French team 2-1 at Old Trafford, both goals scored by Javier 'Chicarito' Hernández. United's competition with Chelsea during these years matched that of Chelsea's intense European rivalry with Liverpool. Paired with Chelsea in the quarter-finals, two tight games went United's way, Rooney scoring the only goal of the game at Stamford Bridge. United's 2-1 win at Old Trafford secured a 3-1 aggregate victory, goals from Hernández and Park Ji-Sung coming either side of a Didier Drogba goal for Chelsea. This time Drogba couldn't reproduce his big game magic. A surprisingly comfortable semi-final victory ensued, United beating Schalke 04 2-0 in Germany with goals from Ryan Giggs and Rooney, following this with a 4-1 win at Old Trafford (Antonio Valencia, Irish midfielder Darron Gibson, and two goals from Anderson – it seems he scored more often in Europe than in the Premier League), completing a 6-1 aggregate victory.

Barcelona's march to the final came with a tidal wave of goals, although Arsenal in the last 16, and Real Madrid in the semi-finals, were worthy opponents. Arsenal achieved the feat of scoring three times in their two ties with Barca, but you can't keep that man Messi down. Goals from Robin van Persie and Andrey Arshavin overcame Villa's early goal for Barca at the Emirates Stadium in London, but Messi's brace at the Nou Camp, and a further Xavi goal were enough to give Barcelona a 3-1 home win and a 4-3 aggregate victory. Arsenal could only reply through a Sergio Busquets own goal.

Shakhtar Donetsk of the Ukraine lost the quarter-final at the Nou Camp in the first leg, Barcelona easing to victory 5-1, Andres Iniesta, Dani Alves, Gerard Piqué, Seydou Keita and Xavi scoring. Five goals, and not a single one for Messi or Villa, their recognised goalscorers in 2011. Messi's first half goal secured a 1-0 win in the Ukraine, Barcelona sweeping through to the last four 6-1 on aggregate. Once again the home team were helpless to avoid the Barcelona surge in the semi-finals. Bitter rivals Real Madrid failed to stop the Messi tide, the mercurial Argentinian scoring twice in Madrid in the last 14 minutes to give Barca a crucial two-goal cushion for the return. Real fought tooth and nail to retrieve the deficit, but it was Barca scoring again through Pedro to give his team a 3-0 aggregate lead at the Nou Camp that killed the tie off. Brazilian full-back Marcelo replied with one goal, but Barcelona would not be denied.

Manchester United showed only three changes to the starting 11 of this 2011 Champions League Final from their last encounter with Barcelona in 2009: Brazilian right-back Fabio, Antonio Valencia, the marvellously athletic and competitive Ecuadorian international in the right midfield slot ahead of Fabio, and Javier Hernández as the main striker. Hernández was an excellent finisher, but he was not Cristiano Ronaldo.

Fabio da Silva, twin brother of Rafael, only played 22 Premier League games 2008–2014 for United. Brother Rafael made the bigger impact at Old Trafford, completing 109 Premier League games 2008–2015. The brothers were signed together by Alex Ferguson from Brazilian club Fluminense after being spotted playing in the 2005 Nike Premier Cup in Hong Kong by United scout Les Kershaw. Kershaw described the brothers as "whippets". The twins joined United in January 2008 without ever partaking in a Fluminense first team game. It was a huge gamble, one that didn't quite come off for Ferguson.

Fabio's debut for United was delayed by shoulder surgery, preventing him from debuting for United until the January 2009 2-1 FA Cup victory over Tottenham Hotspur. He seemed fated not to succeed. In the second half of this match he sustained a calf injury. He would not debut in the Premier League until August 2009 against Birmingham City. Unable to hold down a starting place, Fabio was eventually loaned out to Queens Park Rangers for the 2012–13 season. He has since completed two seasons each with Cardiff City and Middlesbrough. Fabio then moved to Nantes in France, where he was employed in the autumn of 2021. Alex Ferguson probably saw the da Silva brothers as excellent replacements for the Neville brothers Gary and Phil, but it didn't work out for Fabio.

Javier 'Chicarito' Hernández established himself with home city team Guadalajara in Mexico 2006–10. Interestingly, Hernández's minutes per goals ratio is among the best ever in the Premier League. An out-and-out goalscorer, it was Hernández's misfortune to follow Cristiano Ronaldo at Manchester United. Hernández scored 26 goals in 64 games for Guadalajara. United signed the Mexican in April 2010. Hernández's competitive debut came in the 2010 FA Community Shield game against Chelsea. United won 3-1, Hernández scoring soon after coming on as a second half substitute. Hernández repeated the feat off the bench on his Champions League debut away to Valencia in September 2010.

Two goals from the Mexican against Marseille sent United through to the last eight of the 2010–11 Champions League. He also netted as Chelsea were beaten in the quarter-finals. In scoring after 36 seconds against Chelsea on 8 May 2011, Hernández became the first player since 2001–02 to score 20 goals for United in his debut season. He ended the season clutching the Sir Matt Busby Player of the Year Award at the club, the fan's award. The IFFFHS named Hernández the World Goalgetter 2011 with 13 goals, ahead of Cristiano Ronaldo, Lionel Messi and Guiseppe Rossi, the Italian striker who'd played a mere five Premier League games for United 2004–07 but struck 54 goals in 136 La Liga games for Spanish club Villareal 2007–13.

The 2012–13 season brought mixed fortunes for Hernández and United. Returning from the 2011 CONCACAF Gold Cup with Mexico – he top-scored with seven goals as Mexico won the tournament – Hernández suffered a minor concussion when hit on the head with the ball in a training session, a worrying incident for the Mexican as he'd suffered migraines as a teenager. United were unable to repeat their 2009 and 2011 Champions league heroics, losing to Athletic Bilbao in the last 16 of the Europa League, although Hernández had scored in each of the of the two last 32 ties against Ajax.

Ferguson tended to use Hernández often in the 'David Fairclough' role of supersub, utilising the Mexican's explosive energy around the penalty area as an impact substitute. It fell to Hernández to score the opening goal of Ferguson's last game as manager at Old Trafford against Swansea City; and to score the last goal of the Ferguson era on the final day of the 2012–13 Premier League season in an astonishing 5-5 draw away to West Bromwich Albion.

Hernández continued in the same vein when David Moyes replaced the great Sir Alex as manager, scoring the first goal of the new manager's reign to knock Liverpool out of the 2013–14 League Cup in September. Out of favour under Moyes, and his replacement, Louis van Gaal, Hernández took a season-long loan with Real Madrid in 2014–15. The problem for Hernández at Real was the scale of the players ahead of him in the pecking order for striking roles: Cristiano Ronaldo, Karim Benzema, Gareth Bale. Even with a meagre 23 La Liga starts, Hernández scored seven goals.

Moving to Bayer Leverkusen for the 2015–16 season, Hernández netted 28 goals in 54 Bundesliga games in two seasons, three times winning Bundesliga Player of the Month in his first season in Germany. In January 2017, Hernández surpassed Rafael Márquez's 46 appearances in the Champions League when playing his 47th game in the competition against Atlético Madrid. He then returned to England to play for West Ham United under Slavan Bilic. When Bilic was sacked, David Moyes replacing him, a question mark arose for Hernández, despite Moyes referring to him as an outstanding finisher. Again Hernández suffered the ignominy of being used as a substitute too often for his liking. Hernández scored 16 goals in 55 Premier League games with the Hammers. He moved again, to Sevilla in Spain, in September 2019, but played only nine games (one goal) in La Liga before transferring to LA Galaxy in the American Major Soccer League in January 2020 – becoming the league's highest paid player. No more mercenary than any other professional footballer, money does talk, particularly when a player is seeking financial security at the end of his career.

Javier Hernández is Mexico's all-time top scorer with 52 goals in 109 internationals. Even for Mexico he has worked the oracle as a substitute, scoring in the 2010 World Cup against France in a 2-0 victory. It was a poignant moment for the young Hernández, then 21, as his grandfather Tomas Balcazar also scored against France at the 1954 World Cup. Hernández was elected Man of the Match. Selected to start the match against Argentina in the last 16, he repaid the faith shown in him by scoring, but Mexico lost 3-1. Statistics revealed Hernández to be the quickest player at the 2010 World Cup. He scored again in the 3-1 victory over Croatia at the 2014 World Cup, but Mexico lost 2-1 to Holland in the last 16 after leading with two minutes remaining – Hernández was again used only as a substitute. At the 2018 World Cup, Hernández assisted Hirving Lozano's solitary match-winning goal against Germany. In the second group game Hernández scored the winner as Mexico beat South Korea 2-1, winning the Man of the Match award. The goal made him equal top Mexican scorer at World Cups with 90s and noughties striker Luis Hernández.

A goal-poacher extraordinaire, Javier Hernández's capacity to strike from nothing bears comparison with the great Gerd Müller. Hernández lacked the all-round skills of Cristiano Ronaldo at United; he didn't quite possess the metronomic goal-scoring capacity of the incomparable Bayern Munich legend Müller. What Hernández possessed in abundance was the ability to know where the ball will land in the penalty area. The great German striker Rudi Völler, his sporting director at Bayer Leverkusen, Mexican national coach Juan Carlos Osario, and Alex Ferguson, were all massively aware of Hernández's goal potential in these moments. Quick, potent in front of goal, I wonder whether Hernández's coaches simply didn't trust him enough.

It seemed strange to see a player associated indelibly with Liverpool among United's substitutes that night in 2011. Michael Owen, explosive pace severely diminished, scored 118 goals in the Premier League for Liverpool; 13 La Liga goals for Real Madrid, 26 for Newcastle United 2005–09. He managed just five in 31 Premier League appearances for Manchester United 2009–12. A hamstring injury curtailed his first season at Old Trafford; a thigh injury in November 2011 incurred against Romanian team Otelal Gulati hampered him further. Owen still possessed a natural goalscorer's instinct, but the ability to escape defenders seeking to block him come what may had long deserted him. Paul Scholes did enter the field of play in the 77th minute as a substitute for Michael Carrick, but he could not influence a game that had long passed United by. Scholes, a master passer himself, could not dispossess a Barcelona team toying with United any more than his teammates. Brazilian midfielder Anderson and Portuguese winger Nani offered Alex Ferguson other midfield/attacking options, the latter entering play before Scholes to no avail. Chris Smalling was there as defensive cover, the versatile Darren Fletcher another option that Ferguson disavowed.

Take a look at Manchester City circa 2021/22 and one can see a team without a recognised centre-forward – unless you count Brazilian forward Gabriel Jesus. There has been much furore over City's failure to sign Harry Kane from Tottenham Hotspur throughout 2021 – they opted for the younger model when signing Norwegian international Erling Haaland in 2022. Look back at Barcelona circa 2011 under the same manager Pep Guardiola and the same scenario existed. The only recognised forward, David Villa, was not a traditional centre-forward – and Villa's role in Barca's team came as a wide player with licence to roam into the box, while Guardiola used Lionel Messi as a false nine, a ploy he's still utilising at Manchester City in 2022 with Phil Foden or Bernardo Silva.

Barcelona's defence showed three changes from 2009, Dani Alves, under Guardiola arguably the world's most potent attacking full-back; Eric Abidal at left-back, and Javier Mascherano as a centre-back. Mascherano's presence in a role he played latterly – I thought him more influential as a defensive midfielder – was entirely due to injuries suffered by the Barcelona club legend Carlos Puyol.

Eric Abidal has to be seen as a defender first and foremost – in 328 senior games in France, Spain and Greece he didn't score a single goal. He played with Monaco, Lille and Lyon before joining Barcelona in 2007, playing 125 La Liga games for Barca until 2013. Abidal inhabits the typical defender's mantra of 'they shall not pass', seeing his duty to the team as that of needling his opponent by his constant presence. Deprived of a place in the 2009 Champions League Final after a disputed foul on Nicolas Anelka in the 2009 semi-final led to a red card, 2011 was Abidal's moment of retribution. After a tumour on his liver was revealed in March 2011, Puyol graciously handed the captain's armband to Abidal in this 2011 final, allowing Abidal to be the first to hold the European Cup aloft in front of the 85,000 fans at Wembley – although Xavi captained the side on the pitch, Puyol remained club captain. In March 2012, Abidal underwent a liver transplant (his cousin the donor). A mark of the team spirit at Barcelona came with Dani Alves offering part of his liver for the transplant. Abidal refused, knowing Alves's own career could be affected.

Abidal won 67 caps for France, playing in the losing finalists' team against Italy at the 2006 World Cup. At the 2008 Euros and 2010 World Cup, Abidal was deployed as a centre-back by French manager Raymond Domenech, his six feet one inch stature making him an ideal candidate to switch into the middle of the defence. Abidal won Ligue 1 three times with Lyon; La Liga four times with Barcelona, in addition to winning the Copa del Rey twice. He also won two Champions League winners' medals, thanks to sufficient game time in the 2008–09 competition, despite his non-appearance in the final.

Javier Mascherano won his first senior trophy with River Plate in his home country of Argentina in 2003–04, the Argentine Primera Division. Moving to Corinthians in Brazil he promptly won the Brazilian Serie A in his one and only season there in 2005–06. The controversial move to West Ham United in 2006 only amounted to five Premier League games, the influence of his and Carlos Tevez's agent questioned. Liverpool took Mascherano on loan, his debut coming in February 2007. It was at Liverpool where Mascherano revived his career, he and Xabi Alonso stifling Kaka and Clarence Seedorf in the 2007 Champions League Final, but unable to prevent a 2-1 defeat to AC Milan.

Converting to centre-back upon joining Barcelona, the tenacious Mascherano won five La Laga titles, five Copa del Reys and two Champions League trophies 2010–18. The second most capped player for Argentina (147) behind Lionel Messi,

Mascherano has had the misfortune to be a four-time runner-up in the Copa America with his country, and he was a beaten finalist at the 2014 World Cup. At least in winning two Olympic Gold medals at the 2004 and 2008 Olympics, Mascherano earned the accolade of being the first player to achieve the feat since Hungarian defender Deszo Novak (1964, 1968).

Sergio Busquets, born in Sabadell, Barcelona, has been synonymous with Barcelona Futbol Club throughout the 21st century. A defensive midfielder or central defender par excellence, Busquets joined Barcelona's youth ranks in 2005. Johan Cruyff remarked in 2008 how easy Busquets makes the game look with his innate positional sense. Busquets never played three touches where one or two would suffice – in essence he is the epitome of Barcelona and Spanish football in general. Winning the ball and distributing it efficiently, Busquets was the perfect foil in the best Barcelona teams to Xavi, Iniesta and Messi.

Busquets didn't always win a place in Barcelona's first 11 initially, with the similar Seydou Keita holding down the team's defensive midfield place, but once established Busquets became an immovable force in the team's midfield. Busquets overcame the challenges of Keita and Yaya Touré to win a place in midfield for the 2009 Champions League Final against Manchester United. In winning the match Busquets became part of the third father and son combo to claim the trophy after Cesare and Paolo Maldini (AC Milan) and Manuel and Manolo Sanchis (Real Madrid). Busquets' father Carlos, a goalkeeper, won the trophy in 1991–92 in the Guardiola/Hristo Stoichkov/Ronald Koeman/Michael Laudrup team that defeated Sampdoria of Italy 1-0 courtesy of Koeman's extra-time goal. In January 2021 Busquets made his 600th appearance for Barcelona – only Xavi, Iniesta and Messi have played more times for the club. In August 2021, Busquets became club captain after Messi moved to Paris Saint-Germain. Busquets remained at Barcelona in the latter stages of 2022, a true servant to the club.

Busquets had to fight equally hard to stake his place in Spain's national team, with Xavi, Iniesta, Cesc Fàbregas and David Silva for competition. Busquet's forte as the perfect holding player eventually allowed him to become as integral to Spain as he was to Barcelona. At the 2010 World Cup his pass accuracy rate was the third highest, alongside teammate Carlos Puyol. At the 2012 Euros, again won by a Spanish side at their peak, Busquets was named in the Team of the Tournament. Busquets remained in the hub of the Spanish midfield as his country reached the final of the newly formed UEFA Nations League in October 2021, the team losing the final 2-1 to France. Busquets won the Player of the Finals Award. A career of great longevity, Busquets is reluctant to leave the grand stage just yet.

Legendary Spanish manager Vicente del Bosque relates how Busquets is the kind of player you don't 'see' in a football match. Unfussy, but relentlessly efficient, every midfield needs a player like Sergio Busquets.

David Villa forged an impressive professional career in Spain, his status established at Real Zaragoza and Valencia before joining Barcelona in 2010. Aged four, Villa fractured the femur in his right leg. Being young, Villa recovered well, but in the interim his father worked on strengthening his left leg. As a consequence, Villa became ambidextrous, capable of using both feet to a high standard, a skill lacking even in many a professional footballer whose reliance on one foot is tangible. Being able to use both feet, Villa's balance and decision-making were higher than the average player.

Joining Sporting Gijon, Villa scored 38 goals in 80 La Liga games 2001–03. His form earned him a transfer to the top flight with Real Zaragoza. At Zaragoza he netted 32 times in 73 La Liga games, helping his new club lift the Copa del Rey, a 3-2 win over Real Madrid in which Villa scored the second goal. His next move, to Valencia, saw Villa's stock soar, his scoring powers improving (108 goals in 166 La Liga games). Villa's goals tally in 2005–06 was the best at the club since Edmundo Suárez over 60 years previously. In his first season with Valencia, Villa's 25 goals in 35 La Liga games left him only one behind Barcelona's Samuel Eto'o as top scorer. Combining well with Fernando Morientes, the pair netted a combined total of 43 goals in 2006–07 in all competitions. The Copa del Rey was won again in 2007–8, Getafe beaten 3-1 in the final. Better still came in 2008–09, Villa's 28 goals in 33 games his best season with Valencia. The 28 goals also equalled the previous season's best total of the great Argentinian Mario Kempes in 1978, and the Montenegrin Predrag Mijatovic in 1996 at the club. Only Eto'o surpassed him in this La Liga season in a Barcelona team scoring an incredible 129 goals more than Valencia. Villa's tally was a tribute to his personal impact on the Valencia team. 2009 was a great year for Villa, 43 goals coming in 54 games for Valencia and Spain.

Villa signed for Barcelona for £40 million in May 2010. Villa's first season with Barca ended with him scoring from 25 yards against Manchester United in this 2011 Champions League Final. A broken tibia in a Club World Cup match in Yokohama against Qatari team Al Sadd caused Villa to miss the entire 2011–12 season and the 2012 Euros with Spain. A mixed season was endured in 2012–13, Villa's injury seeing him used primarily from the bench. The tibia injury cost Villa dearly at Barcelona. He scored 33 goals in 77 La Liga appearances, but moved again to Atlético Madrid after failing to be selected regularly after the injury. In one season (2013–14) at Atlético, Villa scored 13 goals in 36 La Liga games, helping the team win their first La Liga since 1996. Atlético also reached the 2014 Champions League Final, only to be beaten 4-1 after extra time against city rivals Real.

Villa finished his professional career, in essence, with New York City FC in the Major Soccer League, scoring 80 goals in 124 games – at an admittedly lower level. Villa's senior career total of 333 goals in 624 games mark him out as a seriously impressive goalscorer.

On the international stage, the period 2008–10 when Spain were virtually unbeatable at world level was also Villa's international career highlight. At the 2006 World Cup, Villa and Fernando Torres were Spain's top scorers with three apiece. In qualification for the 2008 Euros Villa scored six times. At the 2008 Euros, Villa scored a hat-trick against Russia, and the winner against Sweden (2-1) in the 92nd minute. A thigh injury sustained against Russia once more in the semi-final prevented Villa's appearance in the final. Despite this, his four goals earned him the tournament's Golden Boot as top scorer and a place in the Euro 2008 Team of the Tournament alongside Torres in attack. Villa attributes much of his goals return at this time with Spain to Torres's work ethic and unselfishness.

Spain suffered a shock defeat in their first 2010 World Cup game at the hands of Switzerland with Villa as their lone striker. Villa scored both goals in a subsequent 2-0 win over Honduras, scoring again as Spain beat Chile 2-1. Villa again scored in the last 16 as Portugal were beaten 1-0. Paraguay came next, beaten 1-0 again with another Villa goal. 1-0 it was again against Germany in the last four. Starting in the final against Holland – another 1-0, Villa was replaced in extra time by his ever-reliable teammate and good friend Fernando Torres. Villa's five goals in eight World Cup games earned him the Silver Shoe. He scored the same amount of goals as Germany's Thomas Müller, but with fewer assists – Müller won the Golden Boot consequently. Villa was named in FIFA'S 2012 World Cup All-Star Team.

David Villa scored his final, 59th goal for Spain, and his ninth in World Cups – a Spanish record – against Australia at the 2014 World Cup in a 3-0 win. Villa's mobility and intuition in the penalty area make him one of Spain's greatest ever strikers. His movement and selflessness, his passing ability and eye for goal made him a perfect player for Spain. Villa's additional importance to Spain – and the clubs he played for – came with his capacity to play across the front line in any position. Villa's 59 goals in 98 internationals make him Spain's all-time top scorer.

THE FINAL

Manchester United started strongly enough, Ryan Giggs sliding through and almost setting up a chance, only for Gerard Piqué to intercept. It soon became apparent that Xavi was pulling the strings in midfield, setting up first Busquets, then Villa for a shot speared past the post. A sharp diagonal ball from Xavi with the outside of his boot set up Pedro on the right, the stubborn Edwin van der Sar this time beaten unequivocally. One moment of class saw United equalise, Wayne Rooney playing a marvellous 1-2 with Giggs and shooting firmly past Victor Valdés.

In the second half Barcelona's relentless pressure and impeccable ball retention took the game away from United. Dani Alves and Iniesta had shots saved. Shortly afterwards, Messi's quick feet inflicted a second goal upon United (his 53rd of the season!), cutting in and unleashing a 20-yarder that van der Sar could only blink at. Xavi had a fierce 25-yarder saved – if ever a player deserved to score it was him. Messi then fed Villa who curled a delightful 25-yarder past van der Sar. Messi was declared Man of the Match – but it could easily have been Xavi again, as in 2009.

The tidal wave of Barcelona's red and blue shirts simply overwhelmed United eventually. The match is remembered as an exhibition of Barcelona's phenomenal passing game, but it was an exhibition too of great attacking football and sublime footwork from Xavi, Messi, Iniesta, Pedro and Villa. United simply couldn't live with Barcelona on the night – especially in the second half. Wembley hadn't seen the like, probably since 1953 when the 'Galloping Major' Ferenc Puskás inspired Hungary to a 6-3 win that shook English football to the core. Once again English football was forced to look at itself in a rigorous manner – Barcelona set the bar here for the peak of European club football.

Chelsea: finalists in 2008, champions in 2012. Liverpool: champions in 2005, finalists in 2007. Manchester United: champions in 2008, finalists in 2009 and 2011. This seven-year period was a purple patch for English football clubs. Why? Not because of an especially good core of English players, but because of a huge influx of quality foreign players into English football. The three clubs mentioned had the core of the golden generation of English football in the noughties in their ranks: Steven Gerrard, John Terry, Ashley Cole, Frank Lampard, Wayne Rooney, Rio Ferdinand, Paul Scholes, but these players failed to gel with England on the international stage sufficiently. Not until Gareth Southgate's England would my home country produce a new younger generation of players gelling as a team and reaching the latter stages of a World Cup (2018) and a Euros (the delayed 2020 tournament, held in 2021).

Route to the Final
Chelsea topped Group E by a point from the German team Bayer Leverkusen. Valencia, Juan Mata's old team, finished third. Mata scored the second goal in Chelsea's first victory, 2-0 over Bayer Leverkusen at Stamford Bridge, Brazilian defender-cum-midfielder David Luiz netting the first. Chelsea then drew 1-1 against Mata's old club Valencia in Spain, Frank Lampard scoring for the Blues. The Belgian side Genk held no worries for Chelsea at the Bridge, a conclusive 5-0 home win resulting with goals from Portuguese midfielder Raul Meireles, two from Fernando Torres, one from muscular Serbian defender Branislav Ivanovic, and a fifth from Salomon Kalou. Didier Drogba's opener for Chelsea in Germany was not enough to stave off a 2-1 defeat in the return match with Bayer Leverkusen. The Brazilian midfielder Ramires's solitary goal in Belgium in the return game with Genk brought Chelsea a 1-1 draw. In their last match Chelsea produced the goods in style, Drogba twice, and Ramires sealing a 3-0 home win against Valencia.

Bayern Munich were a seeded team in the third qualifying play-off round, an unseemly route for a proud club who'd won three European Cups in a row in the mid-1970s. Paired with FC Zürich, the Swiss side were beaten by Bastian Schweinsteiger and Arjen Robben goals (2-0) in Germany, and by a Mario Gómez goal (1-0) in Zürich. Bayern subsequently won Group A by two points from Napoli, and three from Manchester City, whose Champions League quest was in its infancy.

Bayern won their first two games 2-0, Tony Kroos and Brazilian right-back Rafinha scoring away to Villareal; City the next to feel the Germanic force in Munich, Gómez scoring twice. Kroos gave Bayern a second-minute lead in Naples, but a Holger Badstuber goal equalled the tie for Napoli. Gómez was on fire in the return game, his hat-trick earning Bayern a 3-2 victory over Napoli. Bayern defeated Villareal again, 3-1, in Munich, Frenchman Franck Ribéry scoring twice, Gómez, inevitably, scoring the third. Qualification secured, Bayern lost 2-0 to Manchester City at the City of Manchester stadium, David Silva and Yaya

Touré scoring. Drawing at home 1-1 to Napoli cost City qualification as they lost 2-0 in Naples. The scorer of all three goals for Napoli was the excellent Uruguyan striker Edinson Cavani who shone brightly periodically for Manchester United in 2021 when fit. In the round of 16 Chelsea were exposed to Cavani and Naples' threat, winning through to the quarter-finals by the narrowest of margins, 5-4 after extra time. Beaten 3-1 in Naples thanks to a Cavani goal and two from Argentine forward Ezequiel Lavezzi, Juan Mata with the consolation for Chelsea, the Blues turned the tie around 4-1 at Stamford Bridge. The scores were level 3-1 to each team at 90 minutes after Drogba, Terry and a Lampard penalty took the match into extra time. The Serbian Branislav Ivanovic, so often the scorer of crucial goals for Chelsea, found a winner for his team in the 105th minute.

Salomon Kalou scored the only goal in Lisbon as Chelsea beat Benfica 1-0 in the quarter-final first leg. Lampard and Mereiles netted in the 2-1 home win to put Chelsea through 3-1 on aggregate. In the semi-finals, Chelsea achieved the impossible by defeating holders Barcelona (who'd produced the performance of the Champions League era in beating Manchester United in 2011).

Drogba's goal gave Chelsea a slender 1-0 lead to take to the Nou Camp. Gritty to the last, Chelsea, 2-0 down to Busquets and Iniesta goals, retrieved one on the stroke of half-time through Ramirez. Typically, Spanish striker Fernando Torres sealed their passage to the final with a breakaway second goal in the 92nd minute. All was never quite lost with the Chelsea side of José Mourinho and the post-Mourinho years, in no small part due to the money ploughed into the club by Roman Abramovich.

Having beaten one Swiss side (FC Zürich) to emerge into the group stages, Bayern Munich were even more dismissive of a second Swiss side in the last 16. Basel shocked Bayern in Switzerland, winning 1-0 with a goal from midfielder Valentin Stocker. How Bayern exacted their revenge in Munich. Two goals from the elusive Arjen Robben, a goal from attacking midfielder Thomas Müller, and four from striker Mario Gómez brushed Basel aside 7-0. Olympique Marseille were equally helpless in the quarter-finals, Bayern winning both ties 2-0, home and away, Croatian striker Ivica Olic scoring both goals in Munich.

Four outstanding teams competed in the semi-finals. Chelsea's dramatic recovery in Spain had seen them edge out the outstanding Barcelona team 3-2 on aggregate. Bayern's task was equally difficult in the last four. Pitted against a Real Madrid side scoring goals for fun, the Germans came through 3-1 on penalties after the two ties ended in identical 2-1 home victories for each team. In Munich, Ribéry opened the scoring, the mercurial Mesut Ozil, in his prime, equalising for Real. Gómez had the last laugh, winning the match for Bayern in the 90th minute. Cristiano Ronaldo (who else?) scored twice in the first 14 minutes in Madrid. Robben replied with a penalty goal for Bayern, and the resolute Germans held on, taking the game to extra time and penalties. The Germans were always going to win the penalty shoot-out, weren't they? Ronaldo, Kaka and Ramos missed their spot kicks, only the reliable Xabi Alonso scoring for Real. Bayern won the match 3-1 on penalties.

Chelsea lined up in this 2012 final with a notable defence including Petr Cech, the Premiership's second best ever goalkeeper (behind Peter Schmeichel). Right-back José Boswinga won the Champions League with José Mourinho's Porto in 2004, repeating the feat here with Chelsea. Zaire-born, Portuguese-nationalised (he won 27 Portugal caps 2007–15), Boswinga won four Primeira Liga titles, and one Taca de Portugal (equivalent to the FA Cup), as well as the 2004 Champions League with Porto.

Boswinga transferred to Chelsea along with the attacking midfield maestro Deco when Brazilian-born, Portugal manager of the time Luiz Felipe Scolari switched to Stamford Bridge in the summer of 2008. Boswinga completed 89 Premier League games for Chelsea 2008–12. An athletic player, Boswinga gained more notoriety for his remarks about the referee of the 2009 Champions League semi-final against Barcelona at Stamford Bridge, receiving a three-game European match ban that was reduced to two on appeal. During his four years at Stamford Bridge Boswinga was in competition for the right-back spot with Portuguese compatriot Paulo Ferreira and the sturdy Serb Branislav Ivanovic. Boswinga's finest moment in a Chelsea shirt came in the semi-finals of this 2011–12 Champions League, covering expertly at centre-back after John Terry was sent off at the Nou Camp against Barcelona, Chelsea triumphing 3-2 on aggregate. A lack of consistency and occasional indiscipline cost Boswinga more game time with Chelsea.

The players making up the rest of Chelsea's back four in the Allianz Arena, Munich, were the excellent Ashley Cole, the enigmatic Brazilian David Luiz and the English centre-back Gary Cahill. Cahill's form with Bolton Wanderers 2008–12 led to his transfer to Chelsea in January 2012. Cahill subsequently excelled in the semi-final of the Champions League against Barcelona after David Luiz picked up an injury. Terry and Ivanovic's injuries paved the way for the six feet four inches Cahill to play in this 2012 Champions League Final, just months after arriving in top flight football after eight years of football played with lesser clubs Aston Villa, Burnley, Sheffield United and Bolton Wanderers.

On paper this Chelsea side didn't look quite as strong as that of earlier Chelsea teams from the 2005 José Mourinho era onwards. The midfield comprised strength and power with Mikel John Obi, finesse and power provided by Frank Lampard, pace and width through Salomon Kalou and Ryan Bertrand, and guile and trickery in the guise of Juan Mata. Aged 12, Obi (91 Nigerian caps) showed rich early promise, chosen from 3,000 potential footballers to play in the Pepsi Football Academy that travelled across Nigeria with the idea of playing professionally. Obi stood out for Nigeria at the FIFA U-17 World Championships in Finland in 2003, scoring against Australia, although Nigeria did not qualify for the knockout stages. The Player of the Tournament, incidentally, was the super-talented Cesc Fàbregas for Spain.

Obi joined Lyn in Norway soon after the U-17 tournament. Manchester United thought they'd signed him in April 2005, but furore persisted concerning the presence (or lack of) agents involved in the deal. United made an official complaint to FIFA, but ultimately Chelsea mediated with United and Lyn, the consequence being Obi became a Chelsea player for the 2006–07 season. Chelsea – and United – identified Obi as a defensive midfielder par excellence. Mikel went on to play 249 Premier League games for Chelsea 2006–17. Mikel suffered discipline problems initially, but once installed in the team in front of the back four he started to use his height, power, and passing range in an influential manner for Chelsea. Obi replaced Claude Makele as Chelsea's midfield enforcer, and resisted the challenge of Michael Essien for his position, Essien switching to right-back.

After announcing himself in Finland at the 2003 FIFA World U-17 World Championships, Obi Mikel reinforced his stature at the 2005 FIFA World Youth Championships, winning the Silver Ball for second-best player (Lionel Messi won the Golden Ball after scoring twice in Argentina's 2-1 Final victory over Nigeria). Injuries and indiscipline blighted his early international career until Obi came good with a vengeance at the 2013 African Cup of Nations, Nigeria winning their third African Nations title, beating Burkina Faso 1-0 in the final. Obi was named in the Team of the Tournament by the Confederation of African Football. He appeared at the 2014 World Cup, helping Nigeria qualify for the last 16 for the first time since 1998, where they lost 2-0 to France. Obi Mikel was appointed captain of the 2016 summer Olympics Nigerian football team, his country losing 2-0 to Germany in the semi-finals. Nigeria beat Honduras 3-2 to win the bronze medal, becoming the first country to win all three medal colours: gold (1996), silver (2008) and bronze (2016).

A powerful presence in Chelsea's midfield for over a decade, Mikel's promise didn't quite reach fruition – he was projected to be a world great in his teens. I'm sure he found solace in two Premier League titles, three FA Cup winners' medals, one League Cup win, this Champions League triumph of 2012, and the Europa League Final victory in 2012–13.

Ryan Bertrand was affiliated to Chelsea over a decade 2006–15, yet only played 28 Premier League games for the first team due to his role as understudy to Ashley Cole. Nominally a left-back, Bertrand started this 2012 Champions League Final as a wide left midfielder. Astonishingly, this final, the premier game in European club football, was Bertrand's debut, his presence making him the first player to debut in a Champions League Final.

Bertrand promised much, being capped for England at U-17, U-18, U-19, U-20 and U-21 levels. He has received 19 caps for England's senior team, but has long since languished behind Kieran Trippier, Ben Chilwell and Luke Shaw in the running for the England left-back berth. Although a Chelsea player in name, Bertrand spent his decade as a Blue on loan to Bournemouth, Charlton Athletic, Norwich City, Reading, Nottingham Forest, Aston Villa and Southampton. Only at Southampton did Bertrand finally settle into regular first team football, playing 192 Premier League games 2015–2021 after 22 loan games at the club in the 2014–15 season.

Bertrand was employed by Leicester City in 2021, but hadn't established himself at the King Power Stadium club. In his first loan season at Southampton, Bertrand was named in the PFA Team of the Year. A swift, tenacious player, Bertrand was unfortunate to be behind the immaculate Ashley Cole at Chelsea.

Salomon Kalou shone for Feyenoord in the Dutch Eredivisie 2003–06, scoring 35 goals in 69 appearances. Kalou won the Johan Cruyff Award in 2005 for the most promising Young Player of the Year. In his first season at Chelsea, Kalou came on as a substitute in both the League Cup Final against Arsenal (won 2-1 with two goals from his fellow Ivorian Didier Drogba) and the FA Cup Final (won 1-0 against Manchester United, with a goal in extra time by, who else, Didier Drogba). Kalou it was who crossed the ball that John Arne Riise diverted into his own net in the 2008 Champions League semi-final. Kalou converted his penalty kick in the shoot-out at the end of extra time in the final against Manchester United, but Chelsea lost 6-5 on penalties. Kalou started both the 2012 FA Cup Final and this Champions League Final. The FA Cup brought Chelsea further success, a 2-1 victory, the magnificent Drogba again scoring the winner. At Chelsea from 2006 to 2012, Kalou scored 60 goals in 254 appearances in all competitions, a respectable one goal in every four games ratio.

Moving to Hertha Berlin in 2014, Kalou scored 48 Bundesliga goals for Hertha in 151 games. Kalou's time in Berlin came to an unfortunate end when he broke Covid-19 protocols by shaking hands with players and coaches. He was subsequently released, joining Rio de Janeiro club Botafogo in July 2020. Holidaying in Brazil in 2007 brought one of the sporting highlights of my life. Staying in Rio, two blocks from the famous Copacabana beach, our hotel offered tickets to watch Botafogo versus Sao Paulo's Corinthians for £30 per person including coach travel to the game. My wife and I visited the Maracana Stadium, a ground I'd read so much about in my boyhood, a ground that purportedly housed 200,000 spectators (official figures state it was actually 173,850) for the 1950 World Cup Final that Brazil lost 2-1 to Uruguay. The Maracana in 2007 when I visited was nothing special architecturally, just a massive bowl of an arena. What made the match memorable was a bright attacking display from both teams, Corinthians winning 3-2. Even my non-football-following wife enjoyed the atmosphere, the constant hum of the fans beating their club's drums accompanying the game. What an experience for a life-long football advocate like myself. The season was not a successful one for Kalou (2020–21) as he scored only once in 27 Brazilian Serie A games. Salomon Kalou, an energetic presence in attack, scored 27 goals in 93 internationals for the Ivory Coast.

Paulo Ferreira was manager Roberto Di Matteo's full-back cover, along with Michael Essien. Florent Malouda came on for Bertrand in the 73rd minute. Fernando Torres took the field in the 84th minute, replacing Kalou. Daniel Sturridge, prior to an impressive stint at Liverpool, was an unused forward substitute.

Chelsea's opponents on the night, German giants Bayern Munich, could count themselves unlucky to lose this match as I recall, having the lion's share of possession. This was a Bayern Munich team packed with outstanding German internationals at the peak of their powers. In addition the team contained three excellent overseas players, the Ukrainian midfielder Anatoliy Tymoschuk, the French wide midfielder Franck Ribéry and the twinkle-toed Dutch winger Arjen Robben.

Goalkeeper Manuel Neuer set the prototype for the modern keeper-sweeper with his swift advances from his goalline. IFFHS (The International Football Federation of History and Statistics) rate him the best European Goalkeeper of the 2010s. Between 2006 and 2011 Neuer played 156 Bundesliga games for

Schalke 04. In the 2010–11 season Neuer became club captain, leading Schalke to its first Champions League semi-final against Manchester United, although Neuer couldn't prevent a landslide 6-1 aggregate defeat to United. He did win the DFB Pokal German Cup in this last season with Schalke 04, Spanish legend Raul's solitary goal enough to defeat Bayern Munich 1-0 in the semi-final, before MSV Duisburg were trounced 5-0 in the final.

Signing for Bayern Munich in June 2011, Neuer has since won 26 trophies with Germany's leading club with a further Bundesliga title all but assured as I write. Bayern supporters were unhappy about buying a goalkeeper from Schalke, but Neuer won them over swiftly, breaking Oliver Kahn's previous clean sheets record within weeks of signing for the club. Neuer saved penalties from Cristiano Ronaldo and Kaka as Bayern Munich defeated Real Madrid in the semi-finals of this 2011–12 Champions League. He took and scored a penalty kick in this final against Chelsea, but couldn't prevent a 3-4 reverse in the shoot-out.

Neuer excelled in the 2013 Champions League Final as Bayern beat Borussia Dortmund 2-1 with an 89th-minute winning goal from Arjen Robben. Robben was awarded the UEFA Man of the Match Award – but Neuer won the fan's vote. In the knockout stages of the 2012–13 Champions League, Neuer, incredibly, kept four consecutive clean sheets against European giants Juventus and Barcelona. On 7 January 2014 Neuer was announced as the World Goalkeeper of the Year for 2013.

In the 2013–14 season Neuer won the German Footballer of the Year Award and was voted into the FIFA Team of the Year. In January 2017 Neuer was voted into the FIFA Team of the Year for 2016. In July 2017, Neuer replaced the retiring Philipp Lahm as Bayern Munich's club captain. Injuries to a foot, and then his left calf, deterred Neuer, but he returned stronger than ever, winning his seventh consecutive Bundesliga title in May 2019, completing the domestic double with DFB Pokal victory over RB Leipzig 3-0. In May 2020 Neuer won his second Champions League as Bayern defeated Paris Saint-Germain 1-0. PSG were much fancied with the thrilling Kylian Mbappé and Brazilian virtuoso Neymar in attack, but you discount German teams at your peril. Ironically, French international forward Kingsley Coman scored the only goal of the game for Bayern. In October 2020 Neuer kept his 200th clean sheet in 394 Bayern matches, surpassing Sepp Maier's previous record of 199 in 651 games.

Manuel Neuer has thus far received 107 caps for Germany (November 2021). In the group stages of the 2010 World Cup in South Africa he conceded only one goal, against Serbia. Germany eventually lost to Spain 1-0 in the semi-finals. After three undefeated group games at Euro 2012, the Germans lost 2-1 to Italy in the semi-finals. The 2014 World Cup brought success for Germany, a 1-0 quarter-final victory over France followed by the incredible 7-1 demolition of Brazil in the semi-finals. Germany won the trophy, beating Argentina 1-0 in the final with an extra time Mario Götze goal. Neuer won the Golden Glove as the tournament's best goalkeeper. Beaten by Italy at the 2016 Euros in the quarter-finals, Neuer replaced Bastian Schweinsteiger as national team captain at the 2018 World Cup. The tournament was not Germany's finest hour, defeats to Mexico and South Korea seeing them eliminated in the group stages. In June 2019 Neuer kept a 37th clean sheet internationally, beating Sepp Maier's previous record. In June 2021 Neuer's 100th cap against Latvia made him the first German goalkeeper to reach a century of international caps.

Neuer's speed off his line, his athleticism, his penchant for playing out from the back, and his imposing six feet four inches frame have made him the leading exponent of his specialised position in the 2010s. An outfield player in youth football, Neuer is the perfect modern goalkeeper.

Philipp Lahm, Bayer's captain for the evening, was one of European football's very best full-backs for the first decade and a half of the 21st century. Lahm is almost entirely associated with Bayern Munich, joining Bayern's Junior Team aged 11. Highly thought of from a young age, Lahm only broke his Bayern association with a two-year loan period with VfB Stuttgart 2003–05 while gaining experience and biding his time to replace Bayern's talented full-backs of the time, Frenchmen Willy Sagnol and Bixente Lizarazu. A cruciate ligament injury in his second season at Stuttgart threatened his progress, the injury meaning it was November 2005 before he began playing semi-regularly for Bayern, even then sharing the left-back berth with Lizarazu. Manchester United and Barcelona were eyeing Lahm, but the player remained loyal to Bayern, at last playing in his preferred right-back position under Louis van Gaal in the 2009–10 season. Bayern won the domestic double, but that man Mourinho trumped their Champions League hopes in the final, 2-0, this time with Inter Milan – no wonder he arrived at Real Madrid the following season with the self-endowed sobriquet 'the special one'.

When Mark van Bommel left Bayern for AC Milan in 2011, Lahm was appointed new club captain. Although Lahm struck a successful penalty kick in this 2012 Champions League Final shoot-out, Chelsea held firm. The 2012–13 season was a triumph for Lahm and Bayern, the club winning the treble – league, cup and Champions League – defeating Borussia Dortmund in the latter. It was their third final appearance in four years, but their first victory in this period, for all their obvious class. It's just very, very difficult to be the best team in Europe. Pep Guardiola took over as manager of Bayern for the 2013–14 season, Guardiola instantly praising Lahm's game intelligence. Guardiola chose to deploy Lahm as a defensive midfielder, Lahm captaining the team to a record 24th Bundesliga title. When the Chilean midfielder Arturo Vidal and German midfielder Joshua Kimmich joined the club for the 2015–16 season, the versatile Lahm reverted to full-back. When Lahm retired in the final game of the 2016–17 season – at the same time as Xabi Alonso – he'd captained Bayern to a fifth successful Bundesliga title (eight titles in all, three as non-captain). In 332 senior Bundesliga appearances Lahm scored 12 goals.

The relatively slight and short Lahm compensated for lack of height (five feet seven inches) and physique with an astute football brain. His intelligence on the pitch earned him a place in the 2006, 2010 and 2014 World Cup Teams of the Tournament; a place in the Euros Teams of the Tournament in 2008 and 2012; and in UEFA's Team of the Year in 2006, 2008, 2012, 2013 and 2014. At the 2010 World Cup in South Africa Lahm became the youngest player to captain Germany at this elevated stage, after Michael Ballack's withdrawal through injury. Under Lahm's on-field auspices Germany waltzed through ten Euro 2012 qualification games unbeaten. At the tournament proper they failed to overcome Italy in the semi-finals, losing 2-1. Lahm started the 2014 World Cup as a central midfielder, but reverted to full-back from the quarter-finals onwards, eventually leading Germany to World Cup victory in the final, 1-0 versus Argentina. Lahm retired internationally after the 2014 World Cup – he was only 30. He'd received 113 caps for Germany, scoring five goals.

Centre-back Jérôme Boateng spent most of his senior career in Germany (in 2021–22 he was employed by Lyon in France). An early spell with Hertha Berlin was followed by a successful stint with Hamburger SV, the team reaching the Europa League semi-finals in both of his full seasons with the club. He broke into the German national squad for the 2012 World Cup as a result of his form. Moving to Manchester City, Boateng played 24 times in 2010–11, but failed to hold down a regular starting place.

Boateng felt his international prospects were being harmed at City, consequently returning to Germany, signing for Bayern Munich in July 2011. His first season at Munich was the fateful 2011–12 term when the team were runners-up in league, cup, and the Champions League. In 2012–13 Bayern won all three competitions, Boateng a regular starter. Come 2022, Boateng had won eight consecutive Bundesliga titles with Bayern – not a bad decision to leave City, even if one could argue the Premier League has become harder to win than the Bundesliga.

Since 2009, Boateng has played 76 times for Germany (November 2021), playing against his half-brother Kevin-Prince Boateng (Ghana) at the 2010 and 2014 World Cups. Considered inconsistent early in his career, his move to Bayern Munich clearly settled Boateng down, his performances making him a starter during most of his career in Germany, playing 229 Bundesliga games, 2011–2021, scoring five goals.

The Ukrainian centre-back-cum midfielder Anatoliy Tymoschuk always stood out on the football field due to his long, lank, fair hair. More than a poster boy player, Tymoschuk made sure it was his footballing skills that did the talking. Comfortable on the ball, this fine technician was destined for success early on. At Shakhtar Donetsk, Tymoschuk won three Ukrainian Premier League titles and three Ukrainian Cups. Captain for Shakhtar, Tymoschuk was alerting Italian giants Juventus and Roma; also Feyenoord in Holland and Celtic in Scotland.

Tymoschuk completed 227 games for Shakhtar, scoring 32 goals. He moved to Zenit St Petersburg in Russia for two seasons (2007–09), manager Dick Advocaat swiftly naming him captain. His first season – 2007–08 – saw Zenit win the Russian Premier League for the first time in their history. The Russian daily sports newspaper Sport-Express named him League Player of the Year for 2007–08. Zenit also won the UEFA Cup in this season, beating Glasgow Rangers 2-0 in the final, the team including the skilful future Arsenal star Andrey Arshavin.

Tymoschuk moved again to Bayern Munich in February 2009. His first season was mixed, often appearing primarily as a substitute. He didn't find favour under Louis van Gaal (many Manchester United players would find the same), but when Jupp Heynckes took over in 2011, Tymoschuk regained favour, Heynckes praising the Ukrainian's team ethic and ability to play in different positions. After winning the 2013 Champions League with Bayern, Tymoschuk returned to Zenit St Petersburg for a further two seasons.

Tymoschuk's long fair hair and aggressive demeanour belied an intelligence and team-first attitude. A powerful striker of the ball also, he scored 64 career goals in 533 senior games, four in 86 Bundesliga games with Bayern. With 144 caps, Tymoschuk is the Ukraine's most capped player. His impact is attributed to his country's appearance at the 2006 World Cup. In December 2011 he was named the Ukraine's best ever player – not quite sure how he exceeded Andriy Shevchenko in the poll, but Tymoschuk was an excellent team player.

In Bayern's 4-2-3-1 line-up, the two deep-lying midfielders were players of high intelligence. Excellent ball-players both, Bastian Schweinsteiger and Tony Kroos were the platform for Bayern's attacking play. In 17 seasons with Bayern, Schweinsteiger played 500 matches in all competitions, scoring 68 goals. He won eight Bundesliga titles, seven DFB Pokal Cups and the 2013 Champions League.

Schweinsteiger joined Bayern's youth team on 1 July 1998. He had the option of taking up professional skiing – his stocky physique and six feet height would have been perfect, but he chose football. Initially rebellious, Schweinsteiger settled down to become one of Bayern and Germany's most important players 2002–16. Unfortunately for Schweinsteiger it was his penalty kick that Petr Cech saved in this 2012 Champions league Final, allowing Didier Drogba to win the trophy for Chelsea. Schweinsteiger and Bayern didn't look back, the treble-winning 2012–13 season seeing the player voted German Player of the Year.

After 17 years at Bayern – and scoring against his future employers in the 2013–14 Champions League quarter-final, first leg at Old Trafford, (Bayern won 4-2 on aggregate, but were trounced 5-0 by Real Madrid in the semi-finals) – Schweinsteiger joined Manchester United in July 2015. The move didn't work out for the German, who played only 18 Premier League games for United 2015–17. He fell foul of José Mourinho during the Portuguese manager's tenure at Old Trafford. Several United players felt the German international had been mis-treated. It was a curious misfire for Schweinsteiger, one of the previous decade's top world midfielders. Had he lost pace? You could see his quality in the few games he played for United. Curious indeed.

At the 2006 World Cup in Germany, Schweinsteiger struck two outstanding long-range goals against Portugal in the third place play-off game as Germany won 2-1. Against the same opponents in the 2008 Euros quarter-finals, Schweinsteiger scored one and set up two as Germany won 3-2. He also scored in the 3-2 semi-final victory over Turkey. Schweinsteiger couldn't prevent Germany losing the final 1-0 to Spain. His performances were those of a leader with his sweeping passes from midfield as Germany won the 2014 World Cup. When Philipp Lahm retired from international football, Schweinsteiger was appointed captain of Germany. After losing 2-0 to France in the 2016 Euros semi-finals, Schweinsteiger retired from international football after winning 121 caps for his country (the fourth highest capped player) and scoring 24 goals.

Powerful, physical, yet elegant on the ball, Schweinsteiger could play as a holding midfield player, or as the team's main playmaker. He read the game superbly, and like the Spanish players he possessed excellent technique. Until his ill-fated Manchester United 'misadventure' Schweinsteiger had proven himself to be one of world football's most complete midfielders.

Similarly, Tony Kroos, alongside Schweinsteiger, was as technically proficient a player as the Spanish players of the last two decades – he ended up at Real Madrid. Kroos, a precise passer and a free-kick specialist, debuted for Bayern Munich aged 17, in 2007. He was the youngest player to debut for Bayern at that time. At Bayern, Kroos won the Bundesliga three times, the DFB Pokal Cup two times, and the 2013 Champions League. He was voted the IFFHS World's Best Playmaker in 2014 and German Footballer of the Year in 2018. Kroos's European football debut came in October 2007, away to Red Star Belgrade in the UEFA Cup. Only appearing as an 81st-minute substitute, Kroos assisted a goal for Miroslav Klose, then scored the winner in injury time. Deemed inexperienced at this level despite this dramatic introduction, Kroos was loaned out to Bayer Leverkusen for part of the 2008–09 season and the subsequent 2009–10 season. At Leverkusen he played 43 Bundesliga games, scoring ten goals.

Kroos returned to Bayern Munich for the 2010–11 season. In the next two seasons he became indispensable to Bayern's midfield along with Schweinsteiger. Injured in the Champions League quarter-final against Juventus in the 2012–13 season, Kroos missed the triumphant finale to Bayern's treble-winning season.

Kroos joined Real Madrid for the 2014–15 season, but only after Manchester United's bid faltered at the last minute. David Moyes agreed terms with Kroos, but when Moyes was sacked, Louis van Gaal pulled the plug on the deal. It was certainly United's loss as Kroos went on to win 13 trophies with Real 2014–21. Forming a midfield initially with the sublime Croatian Luka Modric and the talented, if inconsistent Colombian James Rodriguez (he flattered to deceive at Everton in 23 Premier League games 2020–21 after an impressive start at Goodison Park), Kroos helped Real achieve a 22-match unbeaten run in the latter part of the 2014–15 season. Kroos was named in the FIFA World XI and UEFA Team of the Year for 2014.

Managers came and went at Real Madrid: Carlo Ancelotti, Rafael Benitez, Zinedine Zidane, but Kroos remained a constant in Real's midfield. In 2016, Kroos was again selected in the FIFPRO World XI and UEFA Team of the Year. When Real won the 2017 Champions League Kroos became the first German player to win the trophy three times.

Kroos impressed instantly as a teenager for his country. At the 2007 FIFA U-17 World Cup, Kroos was named the tournament's Best Player, although Germany lost the semi-final 3-1 to Nigeria. The strength in depth of German football was evinced when Horst Hrubesch left Kroos out of the German U-21 squad for the 2009 U-21 Championships in Sweden, and Germany won the tournament without him, a side containing Manuel Neuer, Jérôme Boateng, Mats Hummels, Sami Khedira and Mesut Ozil – they beat England 4-0 in the final. Kroos was knocking hard on the senior international door, finally winning game time in the 2010 World Cup quarter-finals, semi-finals, and third place play-off. Joachim Low's decision to use Kroos to man-mark Andrea Pirlo in the semi-final of Euro 2012 against Italy did not meet with approval in the German media. Shades of Bobby Charlton and Franz Beckenbauer cancelling each other out in the 1966 World Cup Final, it was felt Kroos's playmaking skills had been sacrificed. Germany lost 2-1.

In the famous 7-1 humiliation of Brazil at the 2014 World Cup, Kroos scored twice in the semi-final. Kroos was named Man of the Match, but such was Germany's dominance against a surprisingly shambolic Brazil any of the German 11 might have won the award. Kroos is the only East German player to win a World Cup with Germany (2014). Kroos's retirement from international football followed Germany's 2-0 defeat to England at Wembley in the delayed Euro 2020 last 16 game.

Tall, athletic, a fine passer, an expert free-kick taker, Kroos dictated the tempo of Bayern Munich and Real Madrid's midfield in a similar manner to Bastian Schweinsteiger. Kroos, the archetypal all-round midfielder, reads the game superbly. He scored 13 goals in 130 Bundesliga games for Bayern Munich 2007–14, 19 in 243 La Liga games for Real Madrid (July 2022) for whom he still played in 2022, and 17 goals in 106 internationals for Germany 2010–2021.

Arjen Robben is my kind of player. Sometimes criticised for inviting tackles that cause him to fall, Robben's ability to tease and tantalise defenders will always invite dubious tackling. Robben is the reason fans pay hard-earned money to watch football matches – he is a supreme entertainer.

Beginning his senior career with local club Groningen in Holland, Robben impacted instantly, winning the club Player of the Year for the 2000–01 Eredivisie season. Signing for PSV Eindhoven in 2002, he won the Eredivisie at the first time of asking (2002–03) and won the Dutch Young Player of the Year Award. Robben played the game as I liked to do in village football, cutting in from the wing to score goals. Robben perfected the ploy from the right wing, coming inside to score some wonderful goals with his magical left foot, where my left foot, purely for standing on, meant I preferred to cut in from the left wing.

Alex Ferguson met Robben, expressing interest in signing the new Dutch wing wizard, but Robben felt Chelsea wanted him more. A broken metatarsal bone in a pre-season friendly with Roma delayed Robben's Chelsea debut. After finally debuting for Chelsea in November 2004, Robben enjoyed a fine first season at Stamford Bridge, being marginally pipped by Wayne Rooney for PFA Young Player of the Year. Robben suffered a series of injuries while at Chelsea. These meant he missed the 2005 League Cup Final against Liverpool – Chelsea won 3-2 after extra time, the devastating Didier Drogba among the scorers. Robben also missed Chelsea's successful title win, and the run to the Champions League semi-finals – this time the club lost 1-0 to Liverpool on aggregate.

Returning to fitness in 2005–06, Robben helped Chelsea win a second successive Premier League title, the first time the club achieved the feat. Coming on as a substitute for Claude Makélélé in the 2007 League Cup Final against Arsenal, Robben set up Drogba's winning goal. A knee injury hampered the 2006–07 season unfortunately. His first appearance upon returning from the injury came against Liverpool in the Champions League semi-final. Robben's penalty kick was saved by Pepe Reina as Liverpool won the penalty shoot-out. His final game for Chelsea came in the 2007 FA Cup Final. He replaced Joe Cole at half-time, only to be substituted himself by Ashley Cole as Chelsea triumphed over Manchester United 1-0 thanks to Drogba again.

Robben's three seasons at Chelsea were very successful, if injury-marred. He scored 15 goals in 67 Premier League games, winning the Premier League twice, the FA Cup in 2007, and the League Cup twice. Robben had his critics, who thought that he was prone to dive (I disagree), but he was always a joy to watch. Robben's move to Real Madrid proved relatively short-lived, a mere two season stop-over, scoring 11 times in 50 La Liga games. At Real, Robben was utilised as a left-winger or left-sided midfielder. In his first season in Spain 2007–08, Real won La Liga. A key player again in 2008–09, Robben's place came under threat when Real signed Cristiano Ronaldo and Kaka. Incoming club president Florentino Rodriguez sanctioned these signings. Robben left, purportedly against his will, signing for Bayern Munich for the 2009–10 season. Little wonder Europe's biggest clubs were clamouring for his signature – Robben has been synonymous with Bayern Munich's successes 2009–2020. Robben subsequently came back to haunt English clubs on the European stage.

If Robben was an unwilling participant in the move to Bayern Munich it didn't show. Bayern provided Robben with his foremost stage. The 'flying Dutchman' scored 99 goals in 201 Bundesliga games 2009–19. Against Manchester United in the 2009–10 Champions League quarter-finals Robben's volley was critical to Bayern's qualification for the last four. United won the second leg in question 3-2, but crucially failed to hold on to a 3-0 lead. Robben had also scored in both legs of the last 16 ties with Fiorentina. In the first leg of the semi-final against Lyon in Munich, won 1-0, Robben scored for Bayern again. He was fundamental to Bayern's appearance in the 2012 Champions League Final. Prior to this 2012 final Bayern claimed the Bundesliga and DFB Pokal double, the cup won 4-0 against Werder Bremen, Robben scoring the first goal from the penalty spot, one of 23 goals in 37 appearances in his first season with Bayern. On 25 May 2010, Robben won the Footballer of the Year Award in Germany, the first Dutchman to do so. Not bad for an unwilling transferee.

Robben missed the first half of the 2010–11 season after returning from international duty with a hamstring strain. In this 2011–12 Champions League season, Robben's penalty made the scoreline 3-3 against Real Madrid, enabling extra time and a penalty shoot-out victory. He ended the season with 19 goals in 36 appearances, but a fourth major cup final defeat in two years, namely a World Cup Final with Holland, two Champions League finals and a DFB Pokal final. Starting the 2012–13 season on the bench, Robben fought his way back into the team and ended the season with an assist and a goal as Bayern beat Borussia Dortmund 2-1 to win the 2013 Champions League Final – he also scored in both semi-final legs against Barcelona. Robben helped Bayern put Manchester United to the sword again in the 2013–14 Champions League quarter-finals, scoring in the 3-1 home victory (Bayern won 4-2 on aggregate). In the 2-0 extra time DFB Pokal win over Borussia Dortmund, Robben scored the first goal, the win completing his third domestic double with Bayern in five years. The goal made him the first player to score in three different DFB Pokal finals. He ended the season with 21 goals in 45 appearances.

When he scored against SC Paderborn in February 2015, Robben had netted against every single Bundesliga team he'd played against. Injuries blighted the next two seasons, although he still netted 16 times in 2016–17 in all games. In 2017–18 Robben became the most prolific Dutch goalscorer in Bundesliga history. His 11th career domestic league title (his seventh Bundesliga title) surpassed the legendary Johan Cruyff's ten. Robben ended a highly successful ten-year tenure with Bayern by winning another domestic title in 2018–19 – his eighth Bundesliga title. The DFB Pokal was won again, Bayern beating RB Leipzig 3-0. Robben, ostensibly, retired from senior football in July 2019 while at Bayern, but was tempted to return to his first club Groningen in Holland. He finally called it a day in July 2021, ending his professional career with 150 senior goals in 426 appearances. Injuries prevented his game total being nearer 600 appearances.

On the international stage Robben scored 37 times in 96 games for Holland. Ousting Germany from the second place in Group D at the 2004 Euros, Holland beat Sweden in the last eight, only to lose 2-1 to Portugal in the last four. In the opening game against Serbia and Montenegro at the 2006 World Cup Robben scored the winning goal as Holland won 1-0. Portugal prevented longevity in the competition, defeating the Dutch 1-0 in the last 16. Only used as a substitute in the 2008 Euros group match against France, the pace and trickery of Robben impacted immediately he entered the field in the second half. He assisted a goal for Robin van Persie, and then scored himself as Holland ran out 4-1 winners. The Dutch, looking impressive at this stage, also beat Italy 3-0, and Romania 2-0. Matters turned horribly wrong as Russia beat them 3-1 after extra time in the last 16. Starting the 2010 World Cup with a suspect hamstring, Robben scored against Slovakia in the 2-1 last 16 victory, also being named Man of the Match. A rare header helped Holland beat Uruguay 3-2 in the last four as Holland reached the final. Not even Robben's special talent could prevent the better team in 2010, Spain, winning the final.

Three straight defeats at the 2012 Euros sent Holland home early. Robben, substituted in the 2-1 reverse against Germany, took umbrage, thinking his individual skill could still win the game. I fully understand this thought process. Not playing to my potential in a village game when I was 20, I knew my place was under threat with the game poised at 1-1 in the 80th minute. I knew I was considered inconsistent at this time, but I always felt I could turn a game. Lucky to remain on the pitch, I scored a hat-trick in the last ten minutes. Robben has my sympathy on that occasion against Germany. At the 2014 World Cup, Holland topped a group containing Chile and Spain – the latter not qualifying after that glorious 2008–12 'invincible' spell. Holland shocked the Spanish team with a tremendous 5-1 victory, Robben scoring twice. Holland then beat Chile 2-0. Next Holland defeated Mexico 2-1 in the last 16, squeaking through the subsequent last eight game with Costa Rica 4-3 on penalties after a 0-0 draw. Holland couldn't repeat the feat in the semi-finals as Argentina won 4-2 on penalties after another 0-0 game.

Arjen Robben was the type of player who instilled fear into defences. A drop of the shoulder, a feint right or left, outstanding touch, swivel hips, all of those attributes made him a full-back's worst nightmare. When a winger is this quick and skilful, often the only way to stop him is to foul him. Defenders adopting this stance against the mesmeric Robben gave the Dutchman a bad name as he acquired a diving tag. I think he was often simply too good for his direct opponent.

On the left flank opposite Robben on this 2012 evening in Munich was the 81-times capped French international Franck Ribéry. Capable of playing with both feet, quick, skilful, a precision passer, Ribéry was one of the top European footballers of the last two decades. His formative years were largely spent in France, but his career club highlight came in his 273 Bundesliga game spell with Bayern Munich (86 goals) 2007–19.

Ribéry's early professional career was unsettled, struggling to settle at Boulogne, Brest and Metz in France; playing 14 games for Galatasaray in Turkey (winning the Turkish Cup) in 2005. Returning to France, joining Marseille, Ribéry began to settle, helping the Marseillais to two Coupe de France Cup Finals – both lost, the first 2-1 to Paris Saint-Germain (2006), the second on penalties to Sochaux after a 2-2 draw (2007). No trophies, but Ribéry's form and 11 goals in 60 Ligue 1 games earnt him a transfer to Bayern Munich for the 2007–08 season – and he was named French Footballer of the Year for 2006–07.

In his first season in Munich, Ribéry scored 16 goals, assisted 17, and helped Bayern win the domestic double. He scored three goals in the club's UEFA Cup run. Surprisingly, Bayern went down 5-1 on aggregate to eventual winners Zenit St Petersburg, a 4-0 drubbing in Russia their downfall. Ribéry scored the goal in the 1-1 draw in Munich. In the Champions League quarter-finals of 2008–09 Ribéry scored against Barcelona, but Bayern again lost 5-1 on aggregate. Bayern also lost their Bundesliga title to Wolfsburg. Tendonitis in his left knee spoiled the 2009–10 season for Ribéry, although upon returning to the team in the second half of the season he scored a crucial equalising goal in the Champions League quarter-finals as Bayern beat Manchester United on away goals. Sent off in the successful 4-0 aggregate win over Lyon (in the home first leg), Ribéry missed the 2010 Champions League Final (which Bayern lost 2-0 to José Mourinho's Inter Milan). Ribéry's consolation – if the description is appropriate when missing the premier European club final – came in scoring in Bayern's 4-0 DFB Pokal final win over Werder Bremen.

A feisty character, Ribéry came to blows with teammate Robben in the dressing room at half-time of the 2011–12 Champions League semi-final against Real Madrid in Munich. Ribéry had opened the scoring, and Bayern subsequently put Real out on penalties – but players at this stratospheric level are ultra-competitive, and differences of opinion are not uncommon. Ribéry scored in the DFB Pokal final against Borussia Dortmund, but Bayern were humbled 5-2 against a Robert Lewandowski-inspired side (he scored a hat-trick). Bayern exacted their revenge in beating Dortmund 2-1 in the 2013 Champions League Final, Ribéry assisting Robben's match-winning goal. Ribéry ended the 2012–13 season with the top assists in the Bundesliga (15) as Bayern won the treble. On 29 August Ribéry won the UEFA Best Player in Europe Award. He was third in the Ballon d'Or in 2013, behind only Cristiano Ronaldo and Lionel Messi, the two players who utterly dominated the award in the 2010s.

Upon ending his Bayern career in 2019, Ribéry had accumulated 24 titles with the club. His eighth appearance in the 2019 DFB Pokal final win over RB Leipzig is unmatched in German football history. Ribéry moved to Fiorentina in Italy for two seasons (five goals in 50 games), signing for newly promoted Salernitana, the Campania, southern Italy-based club in 2021.

Ribéry played 81 times for France 2006–14, scoring 16 goals. Debuting against Mexico in 2006, Ribéry did enough to be selected for the French 2006 World Cup squad. He scored as France beat Spain 3-1 in the last 16, but France lost out in the final 1-0 to Italy. France were unexpectedly eliminated in the group stages at the 2010 World Cup, even trailing behind the hosts South Africa. Injured shortly before the 2014 World Cup, he missed the tournament. An outstanding player in European club football for Bayern, it was Ribéry's misfortune to play for France at a time when the great Deschamps, Vieira, Petit period had passed and France's fortunes floundered.

Classified as a winger, Ribéry better personified the wide midfield role in modern football. Fast, tricky, but also a competitive player who liked a tackle, comfortable on the ball, a fine passer, Ribéry encapsulated all the characteristics of the perfect modern midfielder. Ribéry's versatility also allowed him to play in the centre of midfield if called upon.

Thomas Müller seems like the archetypal German footballer. He can play on either wing, but usually appears on the right as an attacking midfielder, and can even play as a centre-forward. Typically it's Müller's never-say-die attitude that make him the player he's been for the past decade and more. Müller's 30 career titles make him Germany's most decorated footballer.

Müller debuted for Bayern Munich in August 2008 under then manager Jürgen Klinsmann. The 2009–10 season was Müller's first full season, ending with a domestic double and a failed final attempt in the Champions League, lost 2-0 to Inter Milan. Müller ended the season with 19 goals in 52 games in all competitions. In a poll conducted by German sports magazine Kicker (primarily focusing on football) Müller was voted by his fellow professionals Best Newcomer of the 2009–10 Bundesliga season. The 2010–11 season saw Müller repeat his 19 goals in all competitions, but Bayern remained trophy-less. Müller's 83rd-minute header appeared to have won this 2012 Champions League Final, only for that man Drogba to equalise five minutes later.

Making up for the disappointment of the 2011–12 season, Bayern won the treble in 2012–13 under new manager Jupp Heynckes. In the semi-finals of the Champions League, Müller scored twice as Bayern routed Barcelona 4-0 in the first leg in the Allianz Arena. He also scored in the 3-0 win at the Nou Camp in the second leg. He didn't score in the triumphant 2-1 win over Borussia Dortmund in the final, but atoned by converting a penalty kick in the 3-2 DFB Pokal Final win over VfB Stuttgart. Müller's 23 goals in all competitions in this season were impressive given he is not an out-and-out striker. He scored eight goals in the 2012–13 Champions League campaign, another impressive feat. He scored a further eight goals in the 2013–14 DFB Pokal campaign, including Bayern's second goal in extra time against Borussia Dortmund in the final, won 2-0, adding another five goals in the Champions League.

In April 2015 Müller overtook Mario Gómez as Bayern's top scorer in Champions League history. He ended the season with 13 goals in the Bundesliga, and seven goals in ten Champions League games, although Barcelona with Xavi, Iniesta and Messi in their pomp surpassed Bayern 5-3 on aggregate in the semi-finals of the latter, Müller scoring in the second leg 3-2 win in Munich.

In the 2015–16 season Müller became the youngest player to win 50 Champions League matches in the game against Olympiakos of Greece, breaking Lionel Messi's previous record by 14 months. Bayern Munich are always there or thereabouts at the sharp end of the Champions League. Müller scored a 91st-minute equaliser to take Bayern into extra time against Juventus in the last 16. From near defeat, Bayern turned the match around to win 6-4 on aggregate. In the semi-finals against Atlético Madrid, Müller's penalty kick in the second leg in Munich was saved. It proved costly as Atlético won the tie on away goals. Müller scored twice as Bayern beat Werder Bremen 2-0 in the DFB Pokal semi-final. The final was won 4-3 on penalties against Borussia Dortmund, Müller converting his spot-kick. Müller ended the season with 20 Bundesliga goals, and eight more in the Champions League – he seems to be something of a European club game specialist. Thirty-two goals in all competitions made 2015–16 his most prolific season.

In 2016–17 new manager Carlo Ancelotti preferred the Spaniard Thiago Alcântara (later to shine at Liverpool) to Müller in his preferred role behind the strikers. Müller was even surprisingly used only as a substitute in important European games. 2017–18 brought about a revival in Müller's fortunes: eight Bundesliga goals and 14 assists in 29 games; 15 goals in 45 games in all competitions. You can't keep a good player down. In the 2018–19 season Müller won his eighth Bundesliga title with Bayern. Not letting up as he approached his 30s, Müller posted a record 21 assists in the Bundesliga in 2019–20. I found this an interesting facet of my own game when playing. Still quick, but less likely to score goals in batches as I had done in my early 20s, my linking play with other forwards improved markedly in my 30s. My co-striker in my last season (I was 37) scored 39 goals – I'd like to think I assisted approaching half of these.

Two goals for Müller against Barcelona in that remarkable 8-2 aggregate drubbing of Barcelona in the 2019–20 Champions League quarter-finals helped Bayern through to a final they won 1-0 against Paris Saint-Germain, Bayern's sixth Champions League win, and Müller's personal second. Müller won a ninth consecutive Bundesliga title in the 2020–21 season, his tenth overall. Now 32 years old he still managed to score 15 goals in all competitions. Remaining with Bayern in 2021 Müller had scored 137 goals in 415 Bundesliga games from 2008.

Müller's goal tally for Germany is none too tawdry either, 44 in 116 internationals by July 2022. Making his mark at the 2010 World Cup, Müller was the scourge of England with his runs from deep as Germany beat my home country with ease 4-1 in the last 16. Whether Frank Lampard's wrongly disallowed goal (the ball was at least a foot over the line) would have made a difference we'll never know, but the manner in which Germany dismantled a poor England team was nothing less than humiliating. Suspended for a handball offence after scoring against Argentina (4-0) in the last eight, Müller was unable to contribute as Germany lost 1-0 to Spain in the semi-final. Müller's five tournament goals made him joint top scorer with Wesley Sneijder of Holland, David Villa of Spain and Diego Forlan of Uruguay, but his three assists earned him the Golden Boot. Müller also won the 2010 World Cup Best Young Player award. In Germany's opening match at the 2014 World Cup Müller scored a hat-trick as Portugal were swept aside 4-0, earning the Man of the Match award. In winning Group G, Müller also scored the only goal for Germany against the USA. Müller scored the opener as Germany thrashed Brazil 7-1 in the semi-final. At the end of the tournament Müller had scored five goals again, this time earning the Silver Boot as the competition's second highest scorer behind Colombia's James Rodriguez (six). Müller helped Germany defeat Argentina 1-0 in the final, earning himself a place in the FIFA World Cup All-Star XI.

Astonishingly – or not, given their machine-like efficiency in penalty shoot-outs – Müller's failed penalty kick against Italy in the 2016 Euros quarter-finals (Germany still won through 6-5 on penalties) was his country's first missed penalty kick since Uli Stielike's at the 1982 World Cup. Eliminated by France in the semi-finals, Müller's well had run dry as he failed to score in the tournament. Again goalless at the 2018 World Cup, Müller couldn't prevent a lesser standard than usual Germany from elimination in the group stages. Beaten 2-0 – at last – by England in the last 16 at the delayed Euros 2020 tournament, Müller it was who almost broke English hearts again as he ran from deep but failed to beat Jordan Pickford. England's slender 1-0 lead looked fragile indeed at that point.

Müller's versatility with Bayern Munich and Germany make him one of his country's most successful players of recent times. His tall, lean, athletic frame make him a different prospect for defenders used to playing against either muscular forwards or pocket geniuses like Maradona or Messi. Müller's intelligence and excellent reading of the game make him a constant goal threat as a second or third striker. Müller has the Martin Peters knack of arriving in the penalty area at the right moment to score crucial goals. Hard-working, team-oriented, Müller defines his role in the team in German football as 'Raumdeuter' – 'space interpreter' or 'finder'. It's an apt description for a player who doesn't appear to offer serious skilful threat but seizes on the moment to score with alacrity.

Mario Gómez wasn't the best German centre-forward in living memory. Nor was he the worst. He couldn't match the explosive penalty box quality of Gerd Müller. Karl-Heinz Rummenigge may have been the best striker Germany had other than Gerd in the last 50 years. Gómez proved highly efficient as a main striker and goalscorer for Bayern Munich and Germany without possessing Rummenigge's mobility or Müller's goal-poaching nous.

Mario Gómez started professionally with VfB Stuttgart 2003–09, scoring 63 goals in 121 Bundesliga games; a one-in-two games ratio. VfB won the Bundesliga in 2006–07 with Gómez as their spearhead. A broken hand in March 2007, along with a torn ligament in his left knee halted his fine season, but returning in May 2007 Gómez came on as a substitute and scored immediately. VfB almost won the double, but lost the DFB Pokal Final to FC Nurmberg 3-2 after extra time. Gómez's performances earned him the German Footballer of the Year Award for 2007. The following season Gómez scored 19 goals in 25 appearances, second only to Bayern's Italian international centre-forward Luca Toni who scored 24. Continuing to rattle in the goals, Gómez, German born with a Granada, Andalusia, southern Spain father and a German mother, scored 24 goals in 32 Bundesliga games, and eight goals in ten UEFA Cup matches in his last season with VfB Stuttgart (2008–09).

Gómez's relentless consistency finally won him a four-year contract with his country's strongest club, Bayern Munich. Paired with Miroslav Klose in attack for Bayern, Gómez's impact with his new club was not instant. His career at Bayern lifted considerably in his second season in Munich, 2011–12. Losing 1-0 in Switzerland to a Basel side containing Granit Xhaka (later of Arsenal) and Xerdan Shaqiri (later of Liverpool), Bayern turned the tables in the return game. After Arjen Robben (two) and Thomas Müller put Bayern 3-0 up in Munich, Gómez proceeded to score four more as Bayern cruised through 7-1 on aggregate in this 2011–12 Champions League game. In the first leg quarter-final against Lyon Gómez scored again, his 11th Champions League goal of the campaign. Against Real Madrid in the semi-final Gómez netted his 12th goal of the campaign. He ended the 2011–12 season with 26 goals in 33 Bundesliga games and 13 Champions League goals in 14 games. An exceptional season.

An ankle operation after the 2012 Euros meant Bayern signed the excellent Croatian striker Mario Mandzukic to bolster their squad. Mandzukic ended up as the 2012–13 Bundesliga top scorer (15 goals in 24 appearances). Gómez, meanwhile, scrapped for his place, coming on as a 77th-minute substitute against Vfl Wolfsburg in the semi-finals of the DFB Pokal cup and scoring a six-minute hat-trick as Bayern ran out 6-1 winners. With Mandzukic injured, Gómez stepped in and scored as Bayern thumped Barcelona 4-0 on aggregate in the 2012–13 Champions League semi-finals. Only a substitute in the successful 2013 Champions League final against Borussia Dortmund, Gómez scored twice as Bayern defeated his former club VfB Stuttgart 3-2 in the DFB Pokal Cup Final. Gómez couldn't stop scoring, but unhappy at being second choice behind Mandzukic he decided to move on.

Moving to Italy to join Fiorentina, the Florence-based team, a knee injury spoilt his time there. Loaned to Besiktas in Turkey in July 2015 for a year, Gómez rediscovered his mojo, scoring 26 goals in the Turkish Super Lig, 28 goals in all competitions, finishing ahead of the prolific Samuel Eto'o at Antalyaspor. Besiktas won the Turkish Super Lig in Gómez's only season with the club. Due to internal unrest in Turkey, Gómez felt compelled to return to Germany for the 2016–17 season, signing for Vfl Wolfsburg. Wolfsburg competed at the wrong end of the Bundesliga table, but Gómez could not be faulted, scoring 18 goals in 37 games in all competitions. Gómez was named captain of Wolfsburg for the 2017–18 season, but his form dipped. Gómez rejoined first club VfB Stuttgart for the 2018–19 season, top scoring with seven goals, but this was a meagre total given his relentless scoring at Bayern Munich. Gómez's professional career ended fittingly, the striker scoring in his final match for Stuttgart, enabling the club a return to the Bundesliga after relegation.

Debuting for Germany against Switzerland in February 2007, Gómez scored the second goal in a 3-1 victory. In his second match he came on as a substitute against San Marino and scored twice. In the squad for the 2008 Euros, manager Joachim Low seemed unsure how to accommodate Gómez, Klose and Lukas Podolski in the same team. Low couldn't find the magic formula. Gómez wasn't hitting the buttons like he did in the Bundesliga and Germany eventually lost the final 1-0 to Spain. At the 2010 World Cup Gómez appeared in four games, all as a substitute, as Klose was preferred in the striking role. In the opening game of the 2012 Euros Gómez scored the only goal as Germany defeated Portugal 1-0. He then proceeded to score twice as Germany beat Holland 2-1. He didn't score in the third game against Denmark, but Germany again won 2-1. Greece were beaten 4-2 in the last eight, but Italy won a tight semi-final 2-1 with two goals from the enigmatic Mario Altobelli. Injured for the majority of the 2013–14 season, Low excluded Gómez from his 2013–14 World Cup squad.

Gómez's form at Besiktas earned him a recall for the Euro 2016 tournament. Selected for the first group game against Northern Ireland, Gómez scored the winner. In the last 16 win over Slovakia (3-0) Gómez scored again, becoming German's all-time European Championship leading scorer with five goals. Gómez played fitfully at the ill-fated 2018 World Cup in which Germany came bottom of a group containing Sweden, Mexico and South Korea. Post-tournament Gómez retired internationally, having scored 31 goals in his 78 appearances for Germany.

In all, Gómez scored 231 senior goals in 456 club games. I never thought his game matched up to the great German strikers, but one cannot dispute his goal-scoring record. Gómez was more like an old-fashioned English centre-forward who was efficient in meeting the crosses of Robben and Ribéry at Bayern Munich.

The best of Bayern's substitutes at this 2012 Champions league Final was undoubtedly the Croatian striker Ivica Olic. Signed from Hamburger SV in 2009, Olic built up a fine reputation with Dinamo Zagreb (16 goals in 27 league games), CSKA Moscow (35 in 78) and Hamburger SV (29 in 78). With Bayern 2009–12, Olic netted 13 times in 55 Bundesliga games. Olic scored in both 2010 Champions League quarter-final ties against Manchester United. In the semi-final against Lyon in the same season Olic scored a hat-trick. In this 2011–12 season, Olic scored twice in the quarter-finals against Olympique Marseille. Sadly for Olic he missed his spot-kick in the final penalty shoot-out against Chelsea, but Bayern fans loved Olic's commitment.

Chelsea have had more managers since Roman Abramovich's ownership of the club than one cares to remember. Pitched against the vastly experienced Jupp Heynckes for Bayern on this evening was former Chelsea player Roberto Di Matteo. Di Matteo was only ever seen as a stopgap by the Chelsea hierarchy, but what an interim manager he proved to be.

Capped 34 times for Italy 1994–98 (two goals), Di Matteo was a stylish player (style is synonymous with Italians) who went on to play 119 Premier League games for Chelsea after signing from Lazio of Rome in 1996. Di Matteo often scored key goals for Chelsea, like Didier Drogba – his strikes helped Chelsea win FA Cup Finals against Middlesbrough, 2-0 in 1997, and Aston Villa, 1-0 in 2000. In the 1998 League Cup Final Chelsea beat Middlesbrough 2-0 once more, Di Matteo scoring the second goal in extra time. He also scored in the semi-final against Arsenal won 4-3 on aggregate. He also played in the 1998 European Cup Winners Cup Final against VfB Stuttgart won 1-0 with Gianfranco Zola's goal.

Turning to management, Di Matteo's first role came as he replaced ex-England midfielder Paul Ince at MK Dons. Signing ex-Chelsea centre-forward Tore André Flo, Di Matteo took MK Dons to the Division 1 play-offs in 2008–09 where they lost to Scunthorpe United. Ironically, the talented Flo missed the decisive penalty kick in the penalty shoot-out. Di Matteo stayed just one season with the Dons, subsequently managing West Bromwich Albion for the next two seasons. In his first season at The Hawthorns Di Matteo took WBA back up to the Premiership after relegation in 2008–09, the club finishing second behind Newcastle United in the Championship in 2009–10, winning automatic promotion.

In June 2011, Di Matteo was invited back to Chelsea as assistant manager to André Villas-Boas. When Villas-Boas was sacked in March 2012 Di Matteo took over as caretaker manager for the remainder of the 2011–12 season. It always felt that Chelsea – and Abramovich – were looking for a higher profile manager than the relatively inexperienced Di Matteo. But what else can you do but win the Champions League in your first few months as manager? Tony Barton achieved the same feat in winning the 1982 European Cup with Aston Villa. Di Matteo's start as Chelsea manager was very impressive. Tottenham Hotspur were demolished 5-1 in the FA Cup semi-finals, Benfica were beaten in the Champions League quarter-finals. Barcelona were beaten by a dogged Chelsea performance in the Nou Camp (3-2 on aggregate) as Chelsea reached the Champions League Final. Di Matteo led Chelsea to FA Cup triumph, beating Liverpool 2-1 in the FA Cup Final. Whether by good fortune or not, Chelsea outlasted Bayern Munich to win the Champions League Final in the Allianz Arena, the home of their German opponents. Two major trophies in three months for the managerial novice Roberto Di Matteo. The rumour mill persisted despite these achievements that Di Matteo would step aside when the 'right' manager came along. Predictably, Di Matteo lost his job when Chelsea lost a Champions League match 3-0 to Juventus in Turin. Di Matteo had only been in the job eight months. To say he was desperately unfortunate is an understatement. Such is the merry-go-round nature of modern football management. Succeed and you are the bee's knees, fail in a couple of games and you are deemed surplus to requirements. Patience is not generally a characteristic of football clubs in the modern era – and certainly not evident at Chelsea in the last two decades.

THE FINAL

My memory informs me that Chelsea were lucky to win this match, Bayern bossing affairs for long periods, but unable to make superior possession count, for all the fabulous experience at their disposal. The Allianz Arena – a huge white state-of-the-art bowl, looking like a modernistic version of the archaic, but 'filled with memories' Maracana stadium in Rio De Janeiro, Brazil. The arena looked amazing from the TV overhead shots.

The game was goalless at half-time. Arjen Robben had a shot blocked by Petr Cech's legs, Thomas Müller volleyed wide when it looked easier to score. Bayern's goal came inevitably from Müller in the 83rd minute, arriving late to head down awkwardly past Petr Cech in the Chelsea goal, the ball entering the net via a post. Didier Drogba's headed equaliser was altogether more impressive, his movement excellent, his near post header from a Juan Mata corner-kick crashing past a helpless Manuel Neuer.

Bayern had the chance to win the game in the 105th minute. Drogba fouled Franck Ribéry in his own penalty area. It was a forward's foul – I always felt that when a forward tracks back he can be a liability in his own penalty area. Forwards simply lack defensive technique in these situations. Arjen Robben's hard, low left foot shot was saved brilliantly by the excellent Cech. Extra time couldn't separate the teams, Chelsea clinging on somewhat. Mata's penalty was saved by Neuer, giving Bayern the advantage. Philipp Lahm's penalty was too good for Cech, but Ivica Olic's left foot strike was the perfect height for Cech to save comfortably. Neuer stepped up to fire a penalty past Cech – cool indeed from one goalkeeper against another. Ashley Cole's penalty arrowed into the corner of the goal. Bastian Schweinsteiger stuttered deliberately before shooting from the spot, his kick beating Cech, but not the post as Cech parried it brilliantly. It was left to Drogba to send Neuer the wrong way and win the match for Chelsea.

Drogba stated afterwards that Chelsea suffered during the 120 minutes at the hands of a very good Bayern Munich team. Under the cosh for much of the match, Chelsea's immense team spirit carried them through, giving Di Matteo a storybook start to his managerial career.

2018 CHAMPIONS LEAGUE FINAL
Real Madrid 3 v 1 Liverpool

Jürgen Klopp has been magnificent since taking over as Liverpool manager in October 2015. This final came just too soon into Klopp's transformation of Liverpool, Real Madrid's vast experience at this level too much on the night. Liverpool started well enough, but ultimately Real's greater know-how, and the loss of talisman Mo Salah at the hands of a dubious challenge from Sergio Ramos told against Klopp's team.

Route to the Final
Liverpool came into the competition in the play-off round stage, defeating German club 1899 Hoffenheim 2-1 away and 4-2 at home. Liverpool's German midfielder Emre Can scoring twice at Anfield. Moving through to the group stages, Liverpool topped Group E from Sevilla in second place. It was not all plain sailing, firstly 2-2 at Anfield against the awkward Spanish team, whose Europa League record in the noughties and the 2010s is outstanding – six times winners. Roberto Firmino and Mo Salah scored for Liverpool, but Argentine forward Carlos Correa scored a 72nd-minute equaliser. In Russia, Liverpool could only draw 1-1 with Spartak Moscow, Philippe Coutinho equalising a goal from Spartak's Brazilian midfielder Fernando.

Finally Liverpool came good, a relentless attacking display that has become Jürgen Klopp's trademark dispatching Slovenian club Maribor 7-0 with goals from Firmino (two), Coutinho, Salah (two), Alex Oxlade-Chamberlain and Trent

Alexander-Arnold. Salah, Can and Daniel Sturridge were on the scoresheet in the return match against the Slovenians, Liverpool winning 3-0. Sevilla again proved obdurate opponents in Andalusia, a 3-0 lead given Liverpool by early goals from Firmino (two) and Sadio Mané whittled away in the second half by goals from French striker Wissan Ben Yedder (two) and 93rd-minute equaliser by Argentine midfielder Guido Pizarro. A very cosmopolitan outfit, Sevilla. Luckily Liverpool were rampant at Anfield against Spartak Moscow, winning 7-0 again with goals from Coutinho (three), Mané (two), Firmino and Salah, while Sevilla were surprisingly held to a 1-1 draw in Maribor.

Real Madrid could only finish second in Group H, behind a Tottenham Hotspur team who ultimately flattered to deceive. Apoel Nicosia of Cyprus were beaten comfortably at the Bernabeu 3-0, Cristiano Ronaldo (two) and Sergio Ramos the scorers. Real's second game brought a further three goals at the Westfalenstadion, Dortmund for Ronaldo (two) and Welsh wizard Gareth Bale. Real's 3-1 beating of Borussia Dortmund in the return saw Pierre-Emerick Aubameyang, Arsenal 2018–22, subsequently transferred to Barcelona, replying for the Germans. A Raphaël Varane own goal gave Tottenham the lead at the Bernabeu, Ronaldo's penalty saving Real's blushes in a 1-1 draw. Tottenham reserved their best performance of the group stage for the return home leg, Dele Alli (two) and Christian Eriksen scoring three goals that meant Ronaldo's 80th-minute reply was a mere consolation.

Apoel proved mere fodder for Real's array of attacking talents in Cyprus – although the Cypriots had earned a fine 1-1 draw in Dortmund in their previous game. Real won 6-0 with goals from Karim Benzema (two), Ronaldo (two), Luka Modric and Spanish defender Nacho. Aubameyang again found the net for Borussia Dortmund at the Bernabeu, Real scoring three times to run out 3-2 winners, Ronaldo, unsurprisingly, one of the scorers.

Tottenham, so impressive against Real, couldn't repeat their historic win when drawn against one of Europe's other great clubs, Juventus of Italy, in the last 16. They seemed to have set themselves up for another glory night at White Hart Lane by drawing 2-2 in Italy, but you don't write off the European giants. Son Heung-min's opener in north London was cancelled out by goals from Juve's two Argentine strikers Gonzalo Higuain and Paulo Dybala. Tottenham were a whisker from success under Maurico Pochettino, but the financial clout of the big clubs in England, Manchester City, Liverpool and Chelsea in particular, has cursed Tottenham to the role of bystanders at the head of the English Premier League.

Indeed Liverpool had no such problems in the last 16, seeing off Porto emphatically in Portugal's idyllic Douro River city to the tune of 5-0. Mané's hat-trick was the highlight, Salah and Firmino adding further goals. The goalless return at Anfield was an irrelevance. Manchester City, vying with Liverpool to repeat English club's heroics of the previous decade – Chelsea, Manchester United as winners 2012, 2008; Liverpool, winners 2005, beaten finalists 2007; Chelsea beaten finalist 2008; Manchester United beaten finalists 2009, 2011 – would surely offer Liverpool a sterner test in the last eight. Well, no, Jürgen Klopp's 'Gegenpressing' powerhouse of a team swept City aside at Anfield 3-0 with goals from Salah, Oxlade-Chamberlain and Mané. Gabriel Jesus's second-minute strike at the City of Manchester Stadium filled the sky blues with hope, but Pep Guardiola's team couldn't stem the red tide and Salah and Firmino won the match 2-1 for Liverpool with second-half goals. When Liverpool are on top of their attacking game under Klopp they are a joy to behold. A.S. Roma were Liverpool's semi-final opponents. At Anfield Liverpool appeared to have taken complete control of the ties, their 5-2 win with goals from Salah (two), Firmino (two) and Mané setting them up nicely for the return in the Stadio Olimpico. Subsequently Liverpool endured a torrid night in Rome. Mané opened the scoring to give the Reds a 6-2 cushion, but James Milner's own goal gave Roma an equaliser on the night. Gino Wijnaldum's 25th-minute goal made the tie scoreline 7-3. Then it all went pear-shaped for Liverpool as Bosnian striker and former Manchester City player Edin Dzeko and Belgian midfielder Radja Nainggolan (two) put the tie on a knife edge. Liverpool ran out 7-6 aggregate winners, but their frailty at the back would lead to the signing of the outstanding Dutch centre-back Virgil van Dijk after this 2017–18 Champions League campaign.

Real Madrid met another big spending-big city club in the last 16. Paris Saint-Germain have followed the Manchester City and Chelsea route of a top manager (Guardiola at City, Pochettino at PSG), top players from foreign shores, and huge investment from Saudi Arabian and Qatari owners. PSG as I write have yet to win the hallowed Champions League. Neither have Manchester City. Money can buy you the best players – but it is the best teams that win the Champions League. Real beat PSG 3-1 in Spain, Ronaldo (two) and the Brazilian left-back Marcelo (past his best in 2018) the scorers. Real also won the return tie, 2-1, with Ronaldo and Carlos Casemiro, the Brazilian midfielder, scoring. Edinson Cavani replied for PSG – the Argentine's impressive movement lighting up the Premiership at Manchester United as the 21st century entered its third decade. In the last eight, Real beat Tottenham's conquerors Juventus, 3-0 in Turin. Ronaldo, later to wear the famous black and white stripes of the Italian club, scored twice, Marcelo netting the third. In a surprise return match, Juventus turned the tables on Real, Mario Mandzukic (two) and French midfielder Blaise Matuidi giving Juve the chance to obtain a dramatic victory. Who should spoil the party but Cristiano Ronaldo with a 98th-minute penalty spot decider. How does a game of football last 98 minutes? If not through injury there is an awful lot of time-wasting going on.

In the semi-final, Real were taken all the way by Bayern Munich – hardly surprising. Real effectively won the tie in the Allianz Arena with goals from Marcelo (again, an impressive return from a waning player) and Marco Asensio. Joshua Kimmich had earlier given Bayern the lead. A third-minute goal from Kimmich at the Nou Camp raised Bayern's hopes of recovery, but French striker Karim Benzema swiftly turned the tie back in Real's favour with two goals. James Rodriguez second-half goal equalled the tie on the night, but Asensio's second half goal in Munich decided matters, Real winning through 4-3 on aggregate.

The Brazilian goalkeeper Alisson Becker may be Liverpool's best ever custodian – Pepe Reina, Jerzy Dudek and certainly Ray Clemence might argue that one, but the presence of Becker and van Dijk in Liverpool's defence have made a huge difference to the team. Unfortunately the solidity of Alisson was not present in Liverpool's side on this evening. Instead the German Loris Karius stood between the posts. Karius played only 29 Premier League games for Liverpool from 2016, spending more time on loan at Besiktas in Turkey (2018–20) and Union Berlin in Germany (2020–21). Spotted in a German national U-16 game, it was Manchester City, Liverpool's closest rivals of recent years, who signed Karius initially in July 2009. Karius played for City's U-18 and U-21 teams without making a full senior appearance with the club. Loaned out to Mainz in the German Rhineland Palatinate, Karius's nine clean sheets and two penalty saves saw him voted the Bundesliga's second-best goalkeeper behind only the impeccable Manuel Neuer. This form earned him his transfer to Liverpool in May 2016.

In the 2016–17 season Karius replaced Belgian international Simon Mignolet, but indifferent performances cost Karius his place. Klopp took Karius out of the firing line for a while, but Karius returned for the 2017–18 season. His performances against Manchester City and A.S. Roma in the quarter-finals and semi-finals of this Champions League campaign covered the spectrum: smart saves, rash decision-making and poor handling. Karius was at fault for the first and third goals against Real Madrid in this 2018 Champions League Final. His inexperience and questionable judgement cost him, as the previously patient Klopp would break the world record transfer fee for a goalkeeper to bring Alisson Becker to Anfield. Karius represented Germany at every age group U-16 to U-21, but has not played a full international – Neuer has been simply too consistent.

As an attacking full-back, Trent Alexander-Arnold has only one equal in English football: Manchester City's Kyle Walker. Walker's greater strength and ability to use his pace to cover any slips by Harry Maguire and John Stones have seen England manager Gareth Southgate select Walker as England's right-back, or as a right-sided defender of three ahead of the talented Alexander-Arnold. Why has Southgate persisted in experimenting with Alexander-Arnold as a right-sided midfielder? The deployment of the Liverpool starlet further upfield robs the player of his biggest weapon. Alexander-Arnold is the best crosser of a ball in the English game since David Beckham. For Liverpool, Alexander-Arnold uses the weapon relentlessly, assisting countless goals for his deadly strikers Mo Salah and Sadio Mané.

Like Karius for Germany, Alexander-Arnold has played for his country at every age level U-16 to U-21, but he has also played 17 senior games for England (August 2022), a total that will surely be added to considerably in coming years. Alexander-Arnold's prospects were highlighted at Liverpool from an early age, the youngster invariably captaining whatever age group he played in. Alexander-Arnold was singled out by Liverpool coaching staff at a half-term schools camp, aged only six. One to watch throughout his youth years at Anfield, Alexander-Arnold debuted in Liverpool's first team in a League Cup match against Tottenham Hotspur in October 2016. Completing 12 games in all competitions in 2016–17, Alexander-Arnold won Liverpool's Young Player of the Year Award. Regular right-back Nathaniel Clyne became injured in 2017–18, the door opening for Alexander-Arnold and another talented young defender Joe Gomez to replace him. Alexander-Arnold's European debut free-kick goal in the 2017–18 play-off round of the Champions League made him Liverpool's third youngest scorer in the competition behind Michael Owen and David Fairclough. Alexander-Arnold endured difficult one-on-one contests with Crystal Palace's Wilfred Zaha and Manchester United's Marcus Rashford in the Premier League, but succeeded in nullifying the gifted German left-winger Leroy Sane as Liverpool swept Manchester City aside 5-1 on aggregate to reach the semi-finals of this 2017–18 Champions League. At the end of this season Alexander-Arnold was voted Liverpool's Young Player of the Season for the second successive year. In starting the 2018 Champions League Final he became Liverpool's youngest European Cup Final participant. Pitted against Cristiano Ronaldo, the youngster did not disgrace himself.

In season 2018–19 Alexander-Arnold truly emerged, being selected for the PFA Team of the Year alongside Liverpool's other outstanding full-back Andrew Robertson, the immaculate Virgil van Dijk, and speedy goal machine Sadio Mané. In May 2019 Alexander-Arnold's 11th assist in the Premiership equalled the previous best record for a defender making goals. Not to be outdone, Robertson managed the same feat from the left flank. Alexander-Arnold's 12th assist on the final day of the 2018–19 season against Wolverhampton Wanderers made him the outright holder of the record, surpassing Robertson, Andy Hinchcliffe of Manchester City, Everton and Sheffield Wednesday, and Leighton Baines of Everton. He became the youngest player to play in two successive Champions League Finals since AC Milan's Christian Panucci as Liverpool finally won Europe's most coveted prize in 2018–19. Alexander-Arnold was also voted into the UEFA Champions League Team of the Season.

In late 2019 Alexander-Arnold was named in the 2019 UEFA Team of the Year. Matching his 12 assists from the 2018–19 season in 2019–20, Alexander-Arnold became the third youngest player to reach 25 Premier League assists behind Cesc Fàbregas and Wayne Rooney. Elevated company indeed. Covid-19 saw the Premier League suspended between March and June 2020. When the competition returned Liverpool confirmed their first Premier League title win in 30 years. An albatross had been removed from the necks of the club by this excellent new Liverpool team. On the penultimate day of the season, Alexander-Arnold reached 13 assists in a 5-3 win over Chelsea. This outstanding young defender won the 2019–20 inaugural Premier League Young Player of the Season, the PFA Young Player of the Year, and was voted into the PFA Team of the Year.

In December 2020, Alexander-Arnold became the youngest captain of Liverpool in European competition against the Danes of FC Midtjylland in a 1-1 draw. Later in the month he was selected in the 2020 FIFPRO Men's World XI alongside teammates Alisson, van Dijk, and new recruit Thiago Alcântara.

Gareth Southgate has yet to find a permanent place for this hugely talented footballer, but time is on his side, and Kyle Walker is nearly ten years older than Alexander-Arnold. It has been Southgate's fortune to be blessed with excellent full-backs Luke Shaw, Ben Chilwell and Kieran Trippier, but surely Alexander-Arnold's time will come. Utilised by Liverpool as a midfielder as a youth, he seemed to find his best position as a right full-back. Those sweeping crosses may be even better than David Beckham's. Alexander-Arnold's outstanding crossing and passing ability suit Liverpool's style. Can Gareth Southgate find a way to incorporate this rare talent into the England team?

Liverpool have been fortunate indeed to be able to play a pair of excellent full-backs in recent seasons. Scottish international captain Andrew Robertson is almost on a par with Alexander-Arnold for crosses and assists, and has arguably been more consistent than his younger teammate defensively. Robertson's professional career began in his native Scotland with Queens Park and Dundee United 2012–14 before transferring to Hull City in 2014. Robertson was named PFA Scotland Young Player of the Year for 2014. Robertson stayed three seasons with Hull, completing 99 league games for the Humberside club, impressing, but only mildly alluding to the player he has become with Liverpool and Scotland in the third decade of the 21st century. Robertson suffered two relegations with Hull City, a promotion back to the Premiership sandwiched in between.

Signing for Liverpool in July 2017, Robertson understudied Spanish left-back Alberto Moreno initially, but once established Robertson became the more consistent player. Robertson's engine seems enormous as he powers up and down the left flank for Liverpool. Some full-backs in the modern era have been good going forward but not so adept in the traditional art of defending. Robertson achieves both aspects consummately. Gary Neville, a Manchester United man to the core – and a Liverpool adversary – has called Robertson the best left-back in the world. In winning the 2019 Champions League 2-0 against Tottenham Hotspur, Robertson became the first Scot to win the Champions League since Manchester United's Darren Fletcher (who only appeared as a substitute) in the 2008 final against Chelsea, and the first Scot to be on the field in a winning team since Paul Lambert with Borussia Dortmund in 1997.

Scotland's reliance on the effervescent Robertson at the 2020 Euros was burdensome, Robertson looking the most likely Scottish player to score in their games, despite being a nominal left-back. He played as a captain should, inspiring his teammates, but he was often asked to do too much – or chose to take greater responsibility himself. Since 2014 Robertson has won 59 caps for Scotland, scoring three goals (August 2022).

Croatian defender Dejan Lovren played in the heart of Liverpool's defence on this night of May 2018. Lovren came from Southampton after a solid season on the south coast 2013–14. He played 131 Premier League games for Liverpool 2014–20 before transferring to Zenit St Petersburg in 2020. Lovren was an able centre-back for the club, but the star turn for Liverpool at the back in recent times has been his teammate on the night alongside him, Virgil van Dijk. One wonders what took English clubs so long in snapping up the cool, unflappable van Dijk from Glasgow Celtic and Southampton, his two previous clubs.

Born to a Dutch father and a Surinamese mother, van Dijk's early playing days began as a full-back. He only transferred to the centre of defence upon having a growth spurt when 17 years old. Celtic signed van Dijk from Groningen in June 2013. In his first season in Glasgow, van Dijk was named in the PFA Scotland Team of the Year, a feat achieved again in 2014–15. Van Dijk looked a cut above this level, his composed demeanour and goal threat when coming forward earmarking him for greater things. He won two consecutive Scottish

Premierships and the 2014–15 Scottish League Cup at Celtic.

Van Dijk moved to Southampton in September 2015 under Dutch compatriot Ronald Koeman. He helped Southampton reach the 2017 EFL Cup Final (formerly the League Cup), but an ankle injury kept him out of the 3-2 defeat to Manchester United. Liverpool signed van Dijk in January 2018, and the tall Dutchman became an instant cult hero at Anfield. Van Dijk went straight into Jürgen Klopp's constantly improving team and immediately became a leader on the pitch. He played 22 games in all competitions until the end of the 2017–18 season.

In April 2019 van Dijk was chosen alongside Sadio Mané, Alexander-Arnold and Robertson in the 2018–19 PFA Team of the Year. A week later he was named the PFA Player's Player of the Year. He was Man of the Match as Liverpool finally claimed the Champions League against Tottenham Hotspur in the 2019 final. In August 2019 he was named the UEFA Player of the Year, finishing above the apparently immoveable pair Lionel Messi and Cristiano Ronaldo.

A dubious challenge by Everton and England goalkeeper Jordan Pickford in the Merseyside derby in October 2020 left van Dijk with an anterior cruciate ligament injury to his right knee. The injury put paid to the rest of the 2020–21 season for van Dijk. The impact upon Liverpool's defence – especially as Joe Gomez was also absent through injury – was seismic. With several other players also sidelined, an injury crisis disrupted Liverpool's season, negating their impact in 2020–21.

Since 2015 van Dijk has appeared 47 times for Holland (August 2022). He has yet to win a trophy for his country, but Holland did reach the newly formed FA Nations League Final only to lose 1-0 to Portugal. For such a big man (six feet four inches) van Dijk is exceptionally good on the ball. Quick, strong in the air, but above all a calm presence in the heart of Liverpool's defence, his absence to the club in 2020–21 was crucial. Van Dijk's awareness on the pitch has heightened considerably since joining Liverpool.

If one had to be critical one might say that Liverpool's midfield on this night lacked a creative spark – a Philippe Coutinho perhaps. James Milner, Jordan Henderson and Georginio Wijnaldum gave Liverpool energy plus in the middle of the park, but none of them were playmakers in the mould of Luka Modric or Tony Kroos for Real Madrid. Liverpool's trio suited Jürgen Klopp's idea of 'Gegenpressing' down to a tee. Milner and Wijnaldum are better players than they are given credit for, and Henderson's game has improved substantially since his early days, but which of these three was going to unlock Real's experienced defence marshalled by their combative captain Sergio Ramos?

James Milner's service to Liverpool has been exceptional. Filling in at full-back or in either wide midfield position, Milner's lung capacity, determination and team ethic have made him an invaluable member of Jürgen Klopp's squad of the last seven years. An all-round sportsman of excellence at school, Milner played for Yorkshire Schools at cricket, was cross-country champion at his school and district champion at 100 metres two years in a row. Milner's parents were season ticket holders at Leeds United. Milner subsequently became a ball boy at Elland Road. The next step came in joining Leeds United's youth academy.

Milner's experiences with Leeds, Newcastle United and Aston Villa earned him a big-time transfer to Manchester City, where despite his consistency he was often a squad player, not a guaranteed first choice. Liverpool admired Milner's tenacity, signing him in 2015. In this 2017–18 Champions League campaign Milner assisted nine of Liverpool's goals en route to the final. Another player perhaps cursed by his versatility. Milner has never let Liverpool down, wherever he's been asked to play on the pitch.

Jordan Henderson, Liverpool captain, has been an inspirational leader under Klopp. Sunderland-born, Henderson joined his home city club's academy aged eight. He was loaned out to Coventry City for the latter part of the 2008–09 season, returning to Sunderland for the 2009–10 season when he permanently established himself at the club. Henderson won Sunderland's Young Player of the Year two years running, 2009–10 and 2010–11. He was a player on the radar of top clubs, but there was uncertainty about his ability to transition to the elite.

Liverpool signed Henderson in June 2011. Henderson's energy was never in question; his consistency back then was doubted. He played in two cup finals in his first season at Anfield, the League Cup won on penalties against Cardiff City, and the 2-1 FA Cup Final defeat to Chelsea. The incumbent manager Brendan Rogers almost sold Henderson to Fulham. Henderson rejected the idea and set about establishing himself as a first team regular at Anfield. Rogers' uncertainty about Henderson's quality was not shared by incoming manager Jürgen Klopp in 2015. Henderson's revived Liverpool career led to him being made captain. Since Klopp's arrival Henderson has been the manager's trusted lieutenant on the field of play – except when hindered by injuries. He captained the side throughout this 2017–18 Champions League campaign. By sheer force of personality and bloody-minded determination Henderson became vital to Klopp's new-look team. If one were to be critical, Henderson's goal return is scant, 29 scored in 325 Premier League games 2015–22. Henderson's persistence was rewarded in May 2019 when Liverpool lifted the Champions League trophy after beating Tottenham Hotspur 2-0.

Henderson has played 69 times for England to date (August 2022). Injuries have cost him as Gareth Southgate turned to younger midfield players of a similar style: West Ham's Declan Rice and Kalvin Phillips of Leeds United. Henderson's grit stood him in good stead again when named England Player of the Year in 2020, becoming the first England player to win the award at senior and U-21 level. This refusal to lie down may yet revive his international career, but now aged 31, it is difficult to see Southgate selecting him in front of the younger Rice and Phillips.

Jordan Henderson has been used as a box-to-box player in the mould of Bryan Robson, or as a defensive midfielder by Klopp. His passing has improved under the German management maestro. Not renowned for his creative forward passing, Henderson's game has become more complete in recent years. If only he could stay fit – and score more goals!

'Gino' Wijnaldum is another player whose overall ability is more than the sum of his parts. The Rotterdam-born midfielder played for local club Feyenoord 2007–11, transferring to PSV Eindhoven in June 2011. In his last season at PSV

(2014–15) he captained the club to their first Eredivisie title since 2008. Joining Newcastle United in July 2015, Wijnaldum played for a team who appear to have been in permanent transition in recent decades. The 'almost' glory years of Kevin Keegan's Newcastle United, the big-name strikers, Alan Shearer, Les Ferdinand, David Ginola et al from the 1990s a distant memory as Newcastle have fought relegation battles in the Premiership on a regular basis. Wijnaldum made his mark at St James's Park, scoring four goals in a 6-2 home win against Norwich City in October 2015. He ended the season as Newcastle's top scorer. With respect to Wijnaldum this speaks volumes about Newcastle's lack of a quality central striker. Despite Wijnaldum's contributions, Newcastle were relegated.

Wijnaldum returned to the Premiership, signing for Liverpool in July 2016. During the 2016–17 season Wijnaldum scored important goals against Manchester City and Arsenal, his most significant goal coming in the last game of the season against Middlesbrough, ensuring Liverpool's top-four finish and a place in the 2017–18 Champions League. Wijnaldum's goal against Roma in the 2017–18 Champions League semi-finals helped break the competition's record for total goals in a single campaign, Liverpool's 46 surpassing the previous best of 45 by Barcelona. Klopps' power-play approach has made Liverpool a side always worth watching – even if the style requires tremendous fitness levels – and could lead to injuries.

The 2018–19 Champions League semi-final second leg against Barcelona was one of THE greatest European football matches of recent years. 3-0 down from the first leg, Liverpool overcame the great Spanish team of Messi et al, 4-0. Wijnaldum came on as a second half substitute and scored twice in two minutes. Playing in 37 of Liverpool's Premier League games in 2019–20, Wijnaldum helped his team to a first top-flight title in 30 years. It had been a long, long time coming, and it felt like it was never going to happen after the near miss with the Gerrard-Suarez-Coutinho-Sterling-Sturridge team under Brendan Rogers. In June 2021 Wijnaldum, deemed surplus to Liverpool's requirements with Thiago Alcântara arriving from Bayern Munich, and Curtis Jones emerging, signed for Paris Saint-Germain, who purportedly offered the Dutchman twice the wage he might have earned if transferring to Barcelona. It is a mark of Wijnaldum's quality that two such esteemed European giants were fighting for his signature.

Curiously, Wijnaldum's scoring record with Holland is superior to his club record. With Liverpool, Wijnaldum scored 16 goals in 179 Premier League games. For Holland, Wijnaldum scored 26 goals in 86 internationals (August 2022). He scored against Brazil as Holland won the 2014 World Cup third place play-off 3-0. When Virgil van Dijk suffered his ACL injury in 2020, Wijnaldum was named Holland's captain. The Dutchman goes under the radar a little in teams like Liverpool and PSG with superstar strikers, but like Henderson is a key player in midfield who ensures the tempo of the game is managed in his team's interest.

Liverpool's three-pronged attack on this night have become the envy of many a top European club. Mohamed Salah plays mostly from the right flank, enjoying cutting into the penalty area to score goals. Salah is currently being touted by Jürgen Klopp as the best player in the world. With Messi and Ronaldo in the latter stages of their careers it's an argument difficult to disagree with. Only Kylian Mbappé suggests parity with Salah, and Salah's balance, quick feet, lightness of touch, and goal awareness make him the stand-out candidate with Mbappé's future at PSG uncertain.

Salah first caught the attention of English football supporters – and club coaches – when playing for Swiss side FC Basel 2012–14. In his first season at Basel, Salah shone against Tottenham Hotspur in the Europa League quarter-finals as Basel won 4-1 on penalties after a 4-4 draw. Tottenham struggled to contain the fleet-footed Egyptian. Chelsea managed him better in the semi-final, winning 5-2 on aggregate, although Salah scored at Stamford Bridge. Basel won the 2012–13 Swiss Super League by way of consolation. Qualifying for the 2013–14 Champions League, Basel beat Chelsea home and away in the group stages, but failed to reach the knockout stages. Salah scored in both games against Chelsea, including the winner in the 1-0 home win. Basel won the Swiss Super League for the fifth year running. Chelsea had seen enough to sign Salah in January 2014. Oddly, Salah failed to settle at Chelsea, scoring just twice in 13 Premier League games 2014–16, finding himself on loan to first Fiorentina, then Roma, in Italy. Salah's switch to Fiorentina in February involved the Colombian winger Juan Cuadrado moving to Stamford Bridge. Ironically Cuadrado also played 13 Premier League games for Chelsea 2015–17 – without scoring. Who is the more highly regarded player now?

Salah again tortured Tottenham in the 2015 Europa League group stages, his first Fiorentina European goal helping his team to a 3-1 aggregate victory. Fiorentina wanted a permanent deal for Salah, but the player refused, switching to Roma in 2015–16 on a further loan deal from parent club Chelsea. In March 2016 Salah twisted the knife against Fiorentina, scoring twice in a 4-1 win. Salah scored 15 goals in 42 games in all competitions for Roma, helping the team finish third in Serie A in 2015–16 behind winners Juventus and second placed Napoli. Salah was awarded Roma's Player of the Season. In the 2016–17 season Salah scored 19 goals in all competitions as Roma finished second in Serie A behind Juventus.

In June 2017, Salah transferred to Liverpool for a club record fee of £36.5 million. Salah had been a coming star, but nothing prepared Premier League teams for the astonishing impact on their hapless defences. Sometimes players find a natural fit, and Salah certainly found his at Anfield under Jürgen Klopp. Salah instantly scored on his debut in a 3-3 draw with Watford. On his 26th appearance, Salah became the second fastest player to reach 20 goals with Liverpool. The fastest was George Allan in 1895 (in 19 appearances), but one would suggest that Salah's achievement was greater in a modern game with highly developed, fit, technical defenders.

In March 2018 Salah scored four times in a 5-0 win over Watford. Thirty-six goals were accrued in 2017–18 with Liverpool, a total surpassing Lionel Messi and Harry Kane. Salah was the leading scorer in Europe's top five leagues: Serie A, the Bundesliga, La Liga, Ligue 1 in France and the Premiership. In April 2018 Salah scored in both legs of the Champions League quarter-finals against Manchester City – who'd been slight favourites to progress into the semi-finals.

In scoring twice against former club Roma in the 5-2 home first leg semi-final, Salah became the first African player to score ten goals in a Champions League campaign. His total of 43 goals in all competitions in 2017–18 surpassed previous totals of 36 by Robbie Fowler, and 33 by Fernando Torres (himself a major success at Anfield 2007–11) in a Liverpool debut season. Salah's 43 surpassed Roger Hunt's previous high of 42 in 1961–62 – at a higher, more sophisticated level surely. Only Ian Rush has scored more goals in a season for Liverpool (47 in 65 games 1983–84). Salah came to grief following the challenge by Sergio Ramos in the 30th minute of this 2017–18 Champions League Final, his left shoulder dislocated. The Egyptian FA made a statement saying Salah's presence at the 2018 World Cup would not be affected. They were wrong, as Salah's impact for his country in Russia proved minimal.

In 2018–19 Salah surpassed Rush, Fowler, Michael Owen, Hunt et al in becoming the quickest player in the history of the club to reach 50 goals, in 65 games. Salah's 50th Premier League goal in 72 games broke the record previously held by Torres. Salah's penalty kick gave Liverpool the lead in the 2-0 Champions League Final victory over Tottenham Hotspur in 2019.

In the Premier League season of 2019–20 Liverpool finally laid the ghost of the non-delivery of England's top-flight title for 30 years. Liverpool beat every other Premier League club during the course of the season, the first time the club achieved the feat in their 127-year history. In March 2020 Liverpool beat Bournemouth 2-1 (Salah opened the scoring) as the club recorded an English top-flight record of 22 consecutive home wins. Salah's 20th goal of the season made him the first Liverpool player to score 20 goals in all competitions at Liverpool in three consecutive seasons since Owen 2000–02.

In October 2020 Salah scored his 100th goal for Liverpool in all competitions in a 2-2 draw with Merseyside rivals Everton at Goodison Park. When reaching his 100th goal Salah was the fastest to reach the total at Liverpool purely in the top tier – Hunt and Jack Parkinson (1903–14) were quicker, but their totals came in Divisions 1 and 2 in the old league system. Salah's 100th Premier League goal came in a 3-0 away win against Leeds United in September 2021. His two goals in a 3-2 away win against Atlético Madrid in the Champions League group stages made him the first Liverpool player to score in nine successive games. The second of these goals took his Champions League total for Liverpool to 31, surpassing Steven Gerrard's 30. In his next game Salah scored a hat-trick at Old Trafford as Liverpool's explosive, high-powered attack tore Manchester United's defence to shreds, a shock 5-0 humbling the beginning of the end for the decent Norwegian manager and ex-Champions League hero for United (1999), Ole Gunnar Solsjkaer. Salah's three goals took him above Didier Drogba (104) as the top-scoring African player in Premier League history. They also constituted scoring in a tenth successive game for the club.

Salah has scored 47 goals in 85 Egyptian internationals to date (August 2022). His talismanic presence in his country's shirt is obvious – how they rued his lack of fitness in Russia at the 2018 World Cup. He has been unable to help Egypt win the African Nations Cup, having lost the final to Cameroon, then Senegal in recent times.

Klopp has been able to maximise Salah's goal potential by playing him closer to the goal, relying less on his wing trickery than at previous clubs Salah played at. Some of Salah's goals in the early part of the 2021–22 season were outstanding. He seems to have an ice-skater's balance in the penalty area; if his balance is exquisite, then his finishing is absolutely clinical – and defenders are unable to get near enough to him, his quickness of feet and mind enabling to steal away from them with ease. Salah is an incredible player, playing in a Liverpool team under Klopp whose style suits him perfectly. Salah had scored 118 goals in 180 Premier League games as I write.

Playing in a central role for Liverpool is another outstanding African forward, the Senegalese speedster Sadio Mané. Ostensibly on the left side of Liverpool's attack, Mané is more often than not in the centre, with Roberto Firmino flitting in the hole behind Salah and Mané. Extraordinarily, Klopp has since found two further exquisite strikers in the Portuguese Diogo Jota and the Colombian wide player Luis Diaz. As the 2022–23 Premier league season arrived, Klopp found a third in Darwin Nunez from Benfica. Astonishing! It is Liverpool's great fortune to have two such outstanding attacking full-backs in Alexander-Arnold and Robertson, allowing Salah and Mané to push further forward.

Mané, forbidden to play football by his Imam (mosque worship leader) father, left his home in Dakar, Senegal, aged 15 to pursue his football ambitions (his father died when Sadio was seven). As a 19-year-old, Mané played professionally for Metz in Ligue 2 in France in his first senior season, the team ending up being relegated to France's third tier, the Championnat National. In August 2012 Mané moved to Red Bull Salzburg, winning the domestic double of league and cup in his first 2012–13 season.

Ever ambitious, Mané forced a transfer to England in August 2014, signing for Southampton. It was quickly evident that Mané was destined for higher things. In Southampton's final home game of the 2014–15 Premier League season, Mané scored a hat-trick in 2 minutes and 56 seconds, beating Robbie Fowler's previous best of three in 4 minutes and 33 seconds against Arsenal in 1994. Mané ended his first Southampton season with 10 goals in 32 appearances in all competitions. In December 2015, Liverpool got a close look at Mané as he scored in 39 seconds in the League Cup quarter-final at the St Mary's Stadium. Undeterred, Liverpool eased through 6-1 on the night. Mané ended the 2015–16 season in style, scoring twice in a 3-2 Premier League win over Liverpool, concluding the campaign with five goals in five games, including a hat-trick against Manchester City. Mané netted 15 goals in all competitions in this season.

In June 2016 Mané signed for Liverpool for a £34-million transfer fee, becoming the most expensive African player in history at that time. Mané scored 13 Premier League goals in his first 2016–17 season with Liverpool, but it wasn't just his goals output that was crucial to the emerging force of Jürgen Klopp's Liverpool. Mané's pace, movement, and eagerness make him a constant threat in any opponent's penalty area. Although injured towards the end of the season, Mané won the club's Player of the Season Award in May 2017.

Liverpool's attack was explosive as the 2017–18 season began. Salah, Mané, Firmino and Philippe Coutinho were tagged 'The Fab Four' by the media in an obvious allusion to The Beatles. I was extremely disappointed when Coutinho departed for Barcelona mid-season. I felt Coutinho's touch and long-range shooting helped Liverpool come out of the wilderness after years of disappointment following their Champions League Final appearances in 2005 and 2007. Coutinho made it clear that Barcelona was a dream move for him. The little Brazilian's genius gone, Liverpool settled for a 'Fab Three' and how the trio of Salah, Mané and Firmino have lit up Anfield since 2017. When signing Diogo Jota, Klopp revived the idea of a Fab Four – the 2021 signing of Luis Diaz raised the spectre to opposing defences of a 'Fab Five'!

Mané attempted to rival Salah in scoring in six consecutive Premier League games in 2018–19 (following Owen, Torres, Salah and Luis Suarez). Two goals in the last 16 of the Champions League against Bayern Munich helped Liverpool in the quarter-finals in 2018–19. The two goals in Munich made Mané the club's record away scorer in the competition with seven. In scoring his 17th goal of the season against Fulham in a 2-1 win, Mané became the highest scoring Senegalese player in a single Premier League season, beating Demba Ba's previous record. The records kept tumbling: Mané was chosen for the 2018–19 PFA Team of the Year; he shared the 2018–19 Golden Boot for Premier League top scorer with Arsenal's Pierre-Emerick Aubameyang and teammate Salah, scoring 22 goals.

In January 2020 Mané was named the CAF African Footballer of the Year, only the second Senegalese to win the award – the other being El Hadj Diouf, another ex-Liverpool forward. Mané is the more complete player of the two, his pace, energy, and agility honed to perfection in Klopp's barnstorming Liverpool team. Liverpool won the Premier League in style in 2019–20, having been cruelly pipped at the post by Manchester City in 2018–19. With the majestic Virgil van Dijk out for the majority of the 2020–21 season, Liverpool floundered. Mané tested positive for Covid-19 in October 2020, the movement of players on international duty being called into question by Klopp and the British public in general. In September 2021 Mané scored against Crystal Palace in a 3-0 home win in the Premier League, becoming the first player to score in nine consecutive games against the same opponent in the top flight. In October Mané reached the same 100th Premier League goal tally as his African compatriots Mo Salah and Didier Drogba when scoring in a 5-0 away victory over Watford.

Mané was clearly one of the better players at the 2018 World Cup in Russia, but Senegal failed to qualify from the group stages, suffering elimination at the hands of Japan on a contrived fair play points system. Like Salah, Mané could not enable a triumph for his country in the 2019 African Cup of Nations, Senegal losing the final 1-0 to Algeria. Mané was still named in the Team of the Tournament.

Mané's pace from a standing start, his trickery, spatial awareness and explosive shooting make him a world-class striker. He is also an outstanding player in defending from the front. It has been suggested that Salah and he do not always play off the same page, but Klopp has managed the pair consummately, waiving any perceived personality clash for the good of Liverpool's cause. The result is that Liverpool possessed not one, but two world-class operators, two massive goal threats, two players feared at the top of European and world football. It came as something of a shock when Mané moved to Bayern Munich in the summer of 2022 after scoring 90 goals in 196 Premier League games for Liverpool.

Roberto Firmino completed Liverpool's attacking Fab Three. Firmino divides opinions, but his ability to link up with the front two of Salah and Mané, his capacity to knit attacks together, his work-rate, and team-first attitude, are highly valued by Klopp and all of Firmino's teammates. Liverpool's bench on the night included the unlucky Adam Lallana (injuries ensuring his Liverpool exit in 2020 to Brighton and Hove Albion), the German midfield international Emre Can and Dominic Solanke, a young striker who impressed with England in winning the 2014 European U-17 Championship in Malta. Solanke scored in the semi-final and final as England triumphed over Holland on penalties after drawing 1-1. Solanke has had to take the step down in order to gain regular football, but in 2021–22 he was top scorer for Bournemouth, the team winning promotion back to the Premier League.

Real Madrid and Barcelona may both have peaked in the 2000s and 2010s, neither club quite the force they were in the hallowed Ronaldo and Messi days. Yet in 2017 Real Madrid still represented an adversary proving too tough for Liverpool to break down. In defence, Sergio Ramos continued to be the sternest of opponents for even Salah and Mané; Frenchman Raphaël Varane alongside him would win a World Cup winner's medal the following year; Brazilian left-back Marcelo was arguably the finest attacking left-back in the world prior to this final.

In goal, Costa Rican custodian Keylor Navas won 12 titles with Real, including three consecutive Champions Leagues 2015–16 to 2017–18. Navas is considered the best goalkeeper in the history of the CONCACAF, the Confederation of North, Central American and Caribbean Association Football. Signed from Levante in 2014 by Real after making the most saves (267) of any keeper in La Liga in 2013–14, Navas won the 2014 CONCACAF Player of the Year, the first Costa Rican goalkeeper to do so. Navas acted as Real's first team goalkeeper for 2015–16 and 2016-17, winning the CONCACAF Player of the Year Award again in 2017. Navas's eight saves against Bayern Munich in the semi-final second leg of this 2017–18 Champions League ensured Real's progress to this final against Liverpool.

Navas won the 2017–18 UEFA Champions League Goalkeeper of the Season Award, ahead of Alisson Becker of Liverpool, and Juventus's stalwart Gianluigi Buffon, but still lost his place ultimately when Belgian keeper Thibaut Courtois signed for Real in August 2018. In September 2019 Navas signed for Paris Saint-Germain, the latest aspiring Champions League hopefuls ballasted by massive financial clout from Quatari wealth. In his first season with PSG (2019–20), Navas won the Coupe de France, beating Saint-Étienne 1-0 in the final. PSG added the Coupe de la Ligue Cup, beating Lyon 6-5 on penalties after a goalless draw. The Ligue 1 title followed, completing a domestic treble, but the quadruple was denied them in the 2020 Champions League Final, Bayern Munich winning through Kingsley Coman's goal.

Navas finds himself in competition again with the best goalkeeper at the 2020 Euros, Italy's Gianluigi Donnarumma, a six feet five inches colossus, threatening the Costa Rican's longevity with PSG, despite Navas's healthy start to his PSG career. When the best players are available, the wealthiest clubs stalk them and pounce. It seems Navas's athleticism and shot-stopping ability may be deemed insufficient in PSG's quest for the holy grail of the Champions League.

Raphaël Varane was one of the most accomplished players in his centre-back position at the 2018 World Cup. Signing for a Manchester United seemingly in permanent transition, Varane's personal injury problems and a loss of form in United's defence in general have left the jury out on whether the elegant Varane can make his mark in Manchester.

The Lille-born centre-back transferred to Real Madrid from Lens in 2011. A decade of continual success followed in the Ramos-Ronaldo-Modric-inspired team that fought tooth and nail with Barcelona for La Liga titles. Varane fended off competition with the Portuguese hard man Pepe to play 236 La Liga games for Real 2011–21. The six feet three inches Varane was named in the 2018 FIFPRO Mens World XI and the 2018 UEFA Team of the Year. A fine passer of the ball, Varane lacked Pepe's strength, but was arguably a better pure footballer.

Varane represented France at U-18, U-20 and U-21 levels before debuting for the senior French team against Georgia in a 2013 World Cup qualifying match, won by France 3-1. Didier Deschamps promptly selected Varane for his 2014 World Cup squad. Varane was out-thought and outfought by the experienced Mats Hummels in conceding the only goal of the game as Germany defeated France 1-0 in the quarter-finals. Varane, despite this blip, was short-listed for the tournament's Best Young Player Award. In October 2014, Varane took the captain's armband from Blaise Matuidi at half-time in the 3-0 win over Armenia. A thigh injury halted Varane's progress, preventing selection for the 2016 Euros. 2018 was Varane's time for redemption. Starting all seven of France's games he scored a headed first goal as France beat Uruguay 2-0 in the quarter-finals. Varane became a double champion in 2018 – World Cup and Champions League winner, repeating the feat of fellow countryman Christian Karambeu (1998), Brazilian Roberto Carlos (2002) and German player Sami Khedira (2014). It's no surprise that these other three double champions all played their club football for Real Madrid.

Varane's pace, technical prowess, and tactical awareness make him the ideal modern centre-back. Manchester United can only hope Varane can bring some of his success with Real Madrid to their club. Thus far it does not look promising. Varane has a 37-year-old Cristiano Ronaldo as a leader of the attack, but he doesn't have the guile of Luka Modric and Tony Kroos in United's midfield, or an experienced striker of the calibre of Karim Benzema as a striking teammate. Varane needs to be a senior leader at Old Trafford, aiding the progression of younger colleagues like Marcus Rashford.

Whether or not you approve of Sergio Ramos's tackling of Mo Salah in this 2018 Champions League Final, what is beyond question is the leadership skills of Real Madrid's captain on this night. Ramos is indelibly linked with 'Los Blancos', yet began his career with Seville in 2003 before transferring to Real in 2005. A mark of the esteem with which Ramos is held in world football is shown by his selection for the FIFA World XI 11 times, a record for a defender; his selection for the UEFA Team of the Year nine times, also a record for a defender; and his selection as La Liga's Best Defender five times. In addition to being a consummate defender, Ramos has also chipped in over the years with crucial goals for Real (72 in 469 La Liga games, November 2021), and 23 in 180, YES, 180 internationals for Spain as 2022 neared.

Playing 41 times for Sevilla in 2004–05, Ramos helped Seville qualify for the 2005–06 UEFA Cup, a competition the club went on to win, crushing Middlesbrough, captained by Gareth Southgate, 4-0 in the Philips Stadium, Eindhoven, Holland, without Ramos. Twenty-two-time trophy winner with Real Madrid, Ramos simply went on to a career with Real on an even grander stage. The young, long-haired, bandana-wearing Ramos filled in for Real in his first season as a defensive midfielder, as a right-back, or in his now accustomed central defensive role. An indication of Ramos's at-times rugged approach came with the first of a slew of red cards in his Real career. He has been sent off 24 times in the white shirt of Real! I'm not sure that you'd call Ramos a dirty player, but ultra-competitive, certainly.

A constant threat at set-pieces, Ramos headed two goals against Bayern Munich in the 2014 Champions League semi-finals in four minutes as Real humiliated Bayern 4-0 in Munich. Ramos's 93rd-minute header saved Real from defeat in the final, Real going on to win handsomely, 4-1, in extra time against fierce city rivals Atlético Madrid. Scoring again in the 2016 Champions League Final, Ramos became only the fifth player to score in two Champions League Finals along with Real's legendary striker Raul, Lionel Messi, Cristiano Ronaldo and Samuel Eto'o. Real won this one 5-3 on penalties after a 1-1 draw. In winning the 2016–17 Champions League Final, won 4-1 against Juventus at the Millennium Stadium, Cardiff, Real won their first La Liga and European Cup double since the 1957–58 season, a season featuring glittering strikers Ferenc Puskás, Alfredo Di Stéfano, and Francisco Gento.

Ramos captained Real for six seasons, lifting the Champions League trophy for a third successive season here in 2017–18 as captain of the club. Salah's dislocated shoulder and Loris Karius's concussion occurred after challenges with Ramos, although Ramos insists he was pushed into Karius by Virgil van Dijk. A free-kick goal against Real Mallorca in a 2-0 La Liga victory in 2019–20 took Ramos to 68 goals, the highest scorer in the competition for a defender, surpassing Ronald Koeman's 67. Ramos scored 11 La Liga goals in this season, the first centre-back to exceed ten goals since Fernando Hierro in the 1993–94 season. In June 2021 it was announced, inconceivably, that Ramos would leave Real. Ramos has now joined the Paris Saint-Germain bandwagon, the Paris club claiming Ramos has the body of a man ten years younger. The same claims have been made about Cristiano Ronaldo at Manchester United. Ramos and Ronaldo remain great players, but can they really defy old father time and compete with 20-somethings?

Ramos succeeded instantly with Spain, winning the 2004 Euro U-19 championship, beating Turkey 1-0 in the final. Ramos played for Spain at the 2006 World Cup as a right-back, replacing previous regular Michel Salgado, a Real teammate who retired internationally.

Ramos missed only one match (against Greece) in the group stages at the 2008 Euros. He played in every game at the 2010 World Cup. Spain won both tournaments, with Ramos exceptional at right-back in the latter, five clean sheets helping his country to glory. Both finals were won 1-0, the first against Germany, the second against Holland. This was the era of Spanish dominance, an era when opponents spent 90 minutes chasing shadows as Spain's possession-based game frustrated all who challenged their superiority. In Barcelona's Xavi and Iniesta, Spain had two players who kept the ball better than any other players taking the field over the last two decades. Spain's thrashing of Italy, 4-0, in the 2012 Euros Final ended a three-tournament spell where Spanish football appeared invincible.

The glory years ended in 2014 when Spain were eliminated at the group stage of the World Cup. At the 2018 World Cup, Spain topped their 'Group of Death', ahead of Portugal. In the last 16 Spain were defeated on penalties by hosts Russia. In 2019 Ramos became Spain's most capped player. He stands as Spain's equal eighth record goalscorer alongside the great Alfredo Di Stéfano. It's ridiculous as a defender that he has parity with one of the all-time creative players. Ramos has also overtaken Italy's Gianluigi Buffon as European football's most capped player.

Quick, technically competent, aggressive in the tackle, Ramos can supplement the attack with his fine passing and crossing. Ramos is also an expert dead-ball specialist, free kicks and penalties alike. Experts such as Carlo Ancelotti and Italy's defensive colossus Giorgio Chiellini rate Ramos as good a defender in world football as anyone over the last two decades. Praise indeed from Chiellini who embodied Italy's 'they shall not pass' defensive philosophy to the hilt at the 2020 Euros. A proper defender, Chiellini, and one would say the same of Sergio Ramos. Chiellini is a pure defender in the best Italian tradition. The extra benefit Ramos has given Real Madrid and Spain over the last two decades has come in the shape of crucial goals, a reflection of Ramos's intensity and desire in high-pressure situations.

The Brazilian left-back, Marcelo, is one of two outstanding players to hold down the position at Real Madrid in the modern era, the other being Roberto Carlos. Aged 18, Marcelo was named in the Brazilian Serie A Team of the Season while with first club Fluminense. Marcelo, like Ramos, has won 22 trophies with Real Madrid after joining them in 2007. Marcelo is another product of the game of futsal, the Brazilian equivalent of five-a-side football. I have always been a great advocate of the importance of this style of football, the way in which the necessity to keep the ball low and adopt good close control can enhance technique. Being of slighter than average build myself, the format certainly suited me.

Marcelo impacted immediately with Real Madrid in 2007–08, his swift running and attacking skills an extra weapon to his new team on the left. With Juande Ramos at the helm, Gabriel Heinze, the streetwise Argentinian left-back was preferred in defence in 2008–09, but Ramos used the attack-minded Marcelo as a left-midfielder on occasions. In 2009–10 future Manchester City manager Manuel Pellegrini took over from Juande Ramos, continuing to use Marcelo as a winger-cum-midfielder. José Mourinho came in, and somewhat surprisingly Marcelo adapted well to both defensive and attacking responsibilities. He would have been swiftly cast aside by the demanding Mourinho had he not heeded his defensive duties. Marcelo was now established as Real's first choice left-back.

In the 2013–14 Champions League Final against Atlético Madrid Marcelo did not start, but upon replacing Fabio Coentrao he made his mark, scoring the third goal in Real's 4-1 victory. Marcelo's appearances have been more sporadic in recent seasons; the feeling persists that he is better going forward than when called upon to defend. When Sergio Ramos left for Paris Saint-Germain for the 2021–22 season, Marcelo was named Real Madrid's club captain, the first foreign player to receive the honour since 1904. Marcelo has completed nearly 400 League games for Real since signing in 2007, scoring 26 goals to date (August 2022). Marcelo has played 58 times for Brazil, scoring six goals. I suspect with a little more defensive solidity his caps total would be nearer 100.

An exciting player to watch, Marcelo revels in the traditional Brazilian mould of flair players. He is the antithesis of modern Brazilian players who have become more 'team responsible'. Marcelo just loves to attack – he would have been perfect for the 1970 World Cup team with their emphasis on progressive attacking play. Marcelo's skills are almost entirely of the attacking variety – pace, close control, eye of the needle passing and crossing, an eye for goal. He is one of the best attacking left-backs seen in world football. Question marks hang over his defensive qualities.

The Brazilian defensive midfielder Casemiro anchored the Real midfield on this night; the gifted playmaker Tony Kroos, one of two in Real's midfield – English football can scarcely field one in midfield of home origin – took the left midfield slot. On the right was the only other European midfielder who could claim parity with the immaculate Xavi and Iniesta at Barcelona – Croatian magician Luka Modric. Modric, at five feet eight inches, looks slight and boyish on a football field. Behind this mask lies a steely competitor with silk in his football boots. Modric's touch and awareness of space have made him one of the great midfielders of his generation. Signing for Dinamo Zagreb, aged 16, the Zadar, Dalmatian coast-born Modric was winning senior titles in his teens. Playing for Dinamo 2003–08 Modric won three consecutive league titles – the Croatian Prva HNL – 2005–06, 2006–07, 2007–08. He also won the Croatian Cup in the two latter years. Modric was named the Prva HNL Player of the Year for 2007.

Modric moved to Tottenham Hotspur for a then-club record fee of £16.5 million in the summer of 2008. Premier League pundits thought Modric too lightweight in his early days at Tottenham. How he would prove them wrong. A knee injury hampered his initial progress in England. A fractured right fibula in 2009–10 further hindered Modric's impact at Tottenham.

The club's top-four finish in 2009–10 enabled Modric to showcase his burgeoning talent at a higher level, the 2010–11 Champions League, where future club Real Madrid gave them a football lesson in Madrid to the tune of 4-0. The home tie was also lost 1-0, seeing Tottenham eliminated by one of the great European clubs. Unsurprisingly, Cristiano Ronaldo scored in both legs. At the end of this season Modric was named Tottenham's Player of the Year. Chelsea made offers of £22 million, £27 million and £40 million for the twinkle-toed

Modric, chairman Daniel Levy refusing to listen to the haranguing of their new star player (along with Gareth Bale). Modric refused to play in the first match of the 2011–12 season, feeling Levy was denying him his rightful career progress. When he returned to the team, to his credit, Modric played as if he'd never been absent. There was no question of the Croatian reining in because of his unsettled situation.

Modric signed for Real Madrid – Chelsea left disappointed – in August 2012. A lack of pre-season training meant José Mourinho (then manager of this great club) did not start the gifted Croatian regularly initially. The presence of the experienced Xabi Alonso and German international Sami Khedira in the centre of midfield, and an in-form Mesut Ozil as the team's offensive midfield player, kept Modric on the sidelines. At the end of the 2012–13 season, Spanish sports newspaper Marca rated Modric the worst signing in La Liga. Difficult to please, Spanish journalists, but, unbowed, Modric won football followers of all constitutions over eventually. His form didn't pick up swiftly enough to stall Real Madrid's 2012–13 Champions League semi-final defeat to Borussia Dortmund as Robert Lewandowski ran riot in the first leg in Dortmund, scoring all of the German club's goals in a 4-1 rout. Played as a deep-lying playmaker in the second leg at the Bernabeu, Modric helped Real win 2-0, but the margin of victory fell narrowly short. By the end of the season Modric had completed the most passes of any player in a Real shirt, adding several long-range strikes to his growing catalogue of excellence.

With Carlo Ancelotti as manager, Modric became Xabi Alonso's regular midfield partner. Real reached the 2013–14 Champions League Final, astonishingly for the first time in 14 years, in May 2014 – there are no guarantees of being a European Cup finalist in this rarefied competition. It is truly the crème de la crème of European club football, previous status irrelevant when the competition comes from Barcelona, Bayern Munich and our own Liverpool and Manchester City. It was Modric's assist that enabled Sergio Ramos's last gasp equaliser in the 2014 Champions League Final against Atlético Madrid. Modric was voted into the UEFA Champions League Team of the Season; in addition to winning the La Liga Best Midfielder Award for 2013–14. Alonso departed, Modric forming a fine new fulcrum of the team for Real with German international Tony Kroos.

A thigh injury sustained in November 2014 was followed by strained ligaments in his right knee, wrecking the 2014–15 season for the mercurial Croatian playmaker. Those who doubted his influence were confounded as Real failed to win either La Liga or the Champions League in 2014–15 without him. He was still selected to the 2015 FIFPRO World XI.

The managerial merry-go-round continued, Ancelotti giving way to 'Rafa' Benitez, but Modric remained a key player in Real's midfield. Real won the Champions League, defeating Atlético Madrid once more in the 2015–15 final. Modric was named in both the Champions League and the UEFA Teams of the Season. He was then named in the UEFA Team of the Year for 2016. Modric again assisted a goal for Cristiano Ronaldo in the 2016–17 Champions League Final, a 4-1 victory against Juventus. Modric's standing in the world game had now reached a peak, his election to the Champions League Team of the Season and the

FIFA FIFPRO World XI a formality. Recognised now as a class act, Liverpool failed to nullify his impact in this 2018 Champions League Final. Modric was again included in the UEFA Team of the Year for 2017, and in the Champions League Team of the Season for the third consecutive year. The highest individual accolade, the Ballon d'Or for the best player in Europe finally came his way in 2018. Typically, the modest Modric cited the players he felt should have won the award in the previous decade and didn't: Xavi and Iniesta at Barcelona, the Dutchman Wesley Schneider. Real failed to win silverware in 2018–19, but Modric was again named (for the fifth year running) in the FIFPRO World XI.

Luka Modric starred in his teens for the Croatian U-15, U-17, U-18 and U-19 teams, progressing subsequently to the national U-21 team. His senior debut came against stern opponents Argentina in March 2006, Croatia winning the friendly international 3-2. In the 2008 World Cup qualifying group stages Croatia beat England at home 2-0, and at Wembley 3-2. England simply couldn't master the little magician who controlled the game in his effortless manner at Wembley, a game that cost Steve McLaren his short-lived manager's job. In scoring a penalty to give Croatia a 1-0 win against hosts Austria at the 2008 Euros, Modric became the youngest player to score for his country (22 years and 273 days). Croatia headed Group B, beating Germany in their next match 2-1, and Poland 1-0 in their final group game. Sadly for Croatia they could not beat Turkey in the last 16, Modric one of three Croatians to miss a spot-kick in a penalty shoot-out after a 1-1 draw. Modric was selected in the UEFA Team of the Tournament, only the second Croatian to receive the honour after Davor Suker.

Croatia's form did not hold, as they failed to qualify for the 2010 World Cup, finishing behind second-placed Ukraine. At the 2012 Euros Croatia went out in the group stages behind Italy and Spain. At the 2014 World Cup a 3-1 loss to Mexico prevented qualification from the groups once more. In the 2016 Euros, Portugal defeated the Croats 1-0 in extra time in the last 16.

The Croatian press expected more of a talented team and they finally delivered at the 2018 World Cup. Nigeria were beaten 2-0 in Croatia's first Group D match, Modric scoring a penalty and winning the Man of the Match Award. Press expectation proved too overbearing for Croatia's next opponents Argentina. It seemed the whole world willed Lionel Messi to lift the Jules Rimet trophy, but Croatia were having none of it, winning conclusively, 3-0. Modric, not Messi, won Man of the Match, clearly being the outstanding player on the field. Modric pulled the strings, dictated the tempo, and for good measure scored a stunning 25-yarder to put Croatia 2-0 up in the 80th minute. The Croatians made heavier weather of beating the 'weakest' team in the group, Iceland, winning 2-1 courtesy of a 90th-minute winner from the talented wide player Ivan Perisic. Denmark put up their customary spirited resistance in the last 16, Croatia only winning through 3-2 on penalties after a 1-1 draw. Modric remained calm enough to score a penalty in the shoot-out having missed one in normal time, revealing his unflappable nature. Man of the Match again against Russia in the last eight, it required another penalty shoot-out to vanquish hosts Russia. Modric won a third Man of the Match Award.

The semi-finals brought a Gareth Southgate youth-inspired England into confrontation with the combative Croats. Much was expected of Southgate's team who were finally delivering a brand of play suited to tournament football. Kieran Trippier scored a delightful free kick in the fifth minute and England seemed to be on their way to a first World Cup Final appearance since 1966. It has become something of a habit of Southgate's young team to sit on a lead, gradually conceding possession to their opponents instead of continuing to press up against them. Also England's better short-passing game of recent years under Southgate has given way to long balls as they desperately cling on to slender leads against quality teams (the same happened against Italy in the 2020 Euro Final). If England can play so smoothly for 45 minutes, comfortably keeping possession, can they not manage it for the full 90 minutes? This is the next step for Gareth Southgate's constantly evolving team.

Sadly for England they struggled to reinforce their first half superiority; Croatia strengthened their resolve, fought back into the game, masterminded by the maestro Modric. There was an air of inevitability about Ivan Perisic's 68th-minute equaliser; an even greater fear on the part of watching England fans of Mario Mandzukic's 109th-minute extra-time winner. Luka Modric ran the most miles of any player at the 2018 World Cup, and had the most dribbles and passes in the half of his opponents. Predictably, Modric was chosen for the 2018 Team of the Tournament. Modric could not repeat his magic in the final, a Kylian Mbappé-inspired France deservedly winning 4-2. It was a game too far for the stubborn Croatians. Modric, not to be totally denied, deserved to win the Golden Ball as the tournament's best player.

Slight of stature, Luka Modric compensates for his lack of physicality with the keenest of football brains. Calm when consternation surrounds him, Modric dictates play by eluding challenges with sleight of foot. His passing and shooting are outstanding. The Puppet Master, as this magician has been called, has lit up Tottenham, Real Madrid and Croatia's midfields of the past decade and more. His gifts are subtle, a delightful player to watch at all times, Luka Modric – unless you are an England supporter and remember his mastery of our national teams in 2007 and 2018!

Playing in the offensive midfield role in front of Modric, Casemiro and Kroos, Isco brought a different dimension to Real and Spain's teams. Born in the coastal Costa del Sol town of Benalmadena near Malaga in Andalusia, Isco played briefly for Valencia, before joining Malaga in 2011. Sixty-nine La Liga games and 14 goals late he progressed to one of the country's top two teams, Real Madrid, in 2013. He has played 239 La Liga games for Real, scoring 37 times (November 2021).

In December 2012 Isco won the Golden Boy Award for Best Young Player in Europe. He arrived at Real rich in promise. On his debut for Real in August 2013 Isco scored a winning header in a 2-1 win over Real Betis. He assisted the first goal. With Ancelotti preferring a 4-3-3 formation instead of Isco's preferred 4-4-2, regular starts eluded him in this first season, although he scored 11 goals. Isco played 30 times as Real won the 2016–17 La Liga title, but has since failed to secure a regular starting place. For Spain, Isco played 38 games 2013–19, scoring 12 goals. It seems if he plays he'll contribute goals, but at club and international level his selection depends on the system in place. He seemed set to make an important statement at international level when Spain won the 2013 European U-21 Championship in Israel, beating Italy 4-2 in the final, Isco scoring the fourth with a penalty – Liverpool's Thiago Alcântara scored a hat-trick. Yet Isco was omitted from Spain's Euro 2020 squad by Luis Enrique.

Isco is still only 29 as I write. Quick, skilful, an excellent dribbler, Isco is probably the antithesis of the modern Spanish footballer who wants to retain possession at all times. Isco looks to make things happen, but suffers for his individuality in the Spanish set-up. Iker Casillas predicted in 2015 that Isco would become Spain's most important player. It hasn't happened yet.

Karim Benzema won the 2004 European U-17 Championship, hosted by his home country France, 2-1 against Spain. Ex-Arsenal and Manchester City enigma Samir Nasri scored the winner. Benzema, unlike the talented but inconsistent Nasri, offered a constant attacking threat from the outset of his career. Benzema broke through at Lyon in a team including Michael Essien and Florent Malouda (future Chelsea stars), Sylvan Wiltord who'd been at Arsenal 2004–07, and the excellent defender Eric Abidal who would go on to play for Barcelona. Benzema came into a team who were in the midst of a six successive Ligue 1 title-winning run. He scored 43 goals for Lyon 2004–09 in 112 Ligue 1 appearances. Only when Malouda, Wiltord and John Carew departed ahead of the 2007–08 season was Benzema assigned the number 9 shirt. At the end of the season he was declared Ligue 1 Player of the Year, and was selected in the Ligue 1 Team of the Year.

In July 2009, Benzema signed for Real Madrid, his career truly taking off. The presence of Argentina scoring legend Gonzalo Higuain presented Benzema with an initial obstacle, but injury to Higuain gave the Frenchman a pathway into the first team. Emmanuel Adabayor arrived on loan from Manchester City in the 2010–11 season. Benzema's response: ten goals in eight matches. He finished the season with 26 goals behind only… Cristiano Ronaldo.

Advised by compatriots Laurent Blanc and Zinedine Zidane to attend a clinic where he underwent a weight reduction programme in Merano in the Southern Tyrol, Italy, Benzema never looked back. José Mourinho was given credit for Benzema's instant progression upon returning from Italy, but Mourinho admired the player's intent to improve himself. In December 2011 Benzema was named by France Football magazine French Player of the Year. In March 2012 Benzema surpassed Zidane as the top-scoring French player in La Liga history. La Liga was claimed by Real in this 2011–12 season, the club's first title in four years – Barcelona were making life very difficult for 'Los Blancos' at this time.

In December 2012 Benzema won France Football's French Player of the Year Award for the second consecutive year. Real continued to fight the Barcelona tidal wave, beating their old foes 2-1 in the 2014 Copa del Rey Final, Benzema assisting Angel Di Maria's opener – Gareth Bale scored the winner. It was Benzema's goal that won the Champions League semi-final first leg of 2013–14 against Bayern Munich, 1-0. Benzema, Bale and Ronaldo, dubbed the 'BBC', netted a season's total of 97 goals. Winning the French Player of the Year Award for a third time in December 2014, Benzema lay behind only Thierry Henry in securing this feat.

A regular starter again in 2016–17, Benzema helped Real win the La Liga/ Champions League double. He netted twice against Bayern Munich in the 2017–18 Champions League semi-finals, before scoring the first goal in this 2018 final against a well beaten Liverpool.

Ronaldo's departure to Juventus in July 2018 placed the onus on Benzema to be the club's main striker. He didn't disappoint, scoring 30 goals in all competitions in 2018–19. He reached 60 Champions League goals in a 2-1 away win over Ajax, only the fourth player to achieve the feat. Two goals against Galatasaray in a 6-0 scoreline in the 2019–20 season made him only the second player behind Lionel Messi to score in 15 consecutive Champions League seasons, and he became the third Real player to hit more than 50 goals in the competition. He ended the season with 27 goals in all competitions. After La Liga resumed after a three-month hiatus due to Covid-19, Benzema overtook the great Ferenc Puskás as Real's fifth all-time top scorer.

Remaining at Real Madrid, Benzema was rewarded with the vice-captaincy under Carlo Ancelotti for the 2021–22 season. He continued to break scoring records, overtaking Henry as the highest scoring Frenchman in club football. He also became the fourth Real Madrid player to score 200 plus goals in La Liga, after the genius Alfredo Di Stéfano, club legend Raul, and goal-scoring legend and 21st-century superstar Cristiano Ronaldo. Benzema had netted 219 La Liga goals in 415 matches as I write. A dependable source of goals, Karim Benzema.

For France, Benzema has netted 37 times in 97 internationals (August 2022). Not chosen in the 2004 European U-17 Championship Final win over Spain, Benzema became a regular at U-18 level. Like mentor Zinedine Zidane, Benzema has Algerian parentage, but opted to play for France – probably in the knowledge that he would win trophies with the multi-talented French team. In a tough group at the 2008 Euros, held in Austria and Switzerland, France drew 0-0 with Romania, lost 4-1 to Holland, and lost 2-0 to Italy. Benzema played in the first and third games, not chosen for the middle game after criticism of his performance. Despite disagreement with older players William Gallas and Claude Makélélé, Benzema remained in the starting line-up, but he was not chosen in France's preliminary 30-man squad for the 2010 World Cup.

Out of favour under Raymond Domenech, Benzema returned to the team under new coach Laurent Blanc. Blanc sought to build the attack around Benzema, the player repaying him with two assists as France beat Ukraine 2-0 at the 2012 Euros in the group stages. France finished behind England in Group D, but qualified in second despite losing 2-0 to Sweden. Two goals from Xabi Alonso saw France knocked out by Spain in the last 16. At the 2014 World Cup France beat Honduras 3-0, Benzema scoring twice, assisting the other. Benzema also scored in a 5-2 win over Switzerland. France reached a stage further this time, but Germany were their conquerors in the quarter-finals. Surprisingly, given his club form, Benzema was omitted from the squad at the 2016 Euros and the 2018 World Cup, the player feeling coach Didier Deschamps was being pressurised by outside factions. This meant Benzema played no part in France's 2018 World Cup triumph – Kylian Mbappé becoming France's new lauded striker. Included in the Euro 2020 squad after a five-year absence, Benzema scored twice against Portugal in a 2-2 draw at the tournament, and twice more as Switzerland surprised France in the last 16, knocking the World Champions out on penalties after a 3-3 draw. In the semi-final of the UEFA Nations League, Benzema scored France's opening goal as they defeated Belgium 3-2. He also scored the equaliser as France went on to defeat Spain 2-1 in the final. It seems those 2016 and 2018 omissions did indeed have a political ring to them. He was named Man of the Match in the final.

Strong, quick, two-footed, good in the air, always a threat in the penalty area, Benzema is the archetypal modern centre-forward. He also doesn't mind doing the dirty defensive side of being a number 9. His spatial awareness often gave Cristiano Ronaldo the freedom to be Real Madrid's frequent goal hero in their two-pronged attacking partnership.

Two outstanding teams on show in Kiev on this night, Real's perfectly formed, Liverpool's a work in progress at this juncture, although Klopp's team had shown enough since his arrival in 2015 to suggest they would be a European force again. Liverpool's high-pressing style, their explosive forwards and commanding new centre-back Virgil van Dijk promised much. Two outstanding figures in charge of the teams too – Jürgen Klopp, clearly a man who players respond to, swift to put an arm around a player he's pleased with; and Zinedine Zidane – the best player in Europe during his playing days, and a decent manager who sought on this evening to complete a hat-trick of consecutive Champions League Winners' medals as a manager. Two-time La Liga winner in 2016–17 and 2019–20, some think Zidane has had problems with certain players, but the statistics don't lie, and top players invariably look up to a manager whose own playing career was at least the match of theirs – or better.

THE FINAL
The first half was a curious affair, Real Madrid dominating possession, yet Liverpool creating the better chances. Cristiano Ronaldo blasted over the bar after a counter-attack on the right flank. The game turned against Liverpool when Sergio Ramos locked arms with Mo Salah to prevent the Egyptian escaping him; Salah fell awkwardly and left the field in tears with a dislocated shoulder. Ronaldo headed Isco's cross goalwards, Karius saved, but Karim Benzema netted the rebound. Ronaldo, marginally offside, prevented the goal standing

Liverpool took a surprise lead after the break when James Milner's corner kick from the right saw Dejan Lovren win a header in the penalty area. Sadio Mané was his customary lightning quick self in intercepting the ball as Keylor Navas came out and diverted the ball over the goalline. Karius's nightmare evening in goal for Liverpool then took a turn for the worse as he carelessly attempted to throw the ball across his own penalty area, his throw way too short, allowing Benzema a simple intercept that saw the ball trickle into the net. It was left to Gareth Bale, on as a 61st-minute substitute to execute a sensational bicycle kick that left the hapless Karius without hope of saving Real's second goal. Bale met Marcelo's right foot cross expertly, somehow finding the space between van Dijk and Milner, his effort soaring beyond Karius. Bale's subsequent 25-yarder was nothing more than hopeful, but Karius compounded his earlier error with another dreadful mistake, allowing the ball to slip through his fingers into the net. Two very soft goals conceded, Liverpool went from a position of hope to deserved defeat on the night. Bale, only on the pitch for half an hour, was declared Man of the Match, but the circumstances of Liverpool's defeat were very disappointing. They would make up for this non-show in 2019.

2018–19 CHAMPIONS LEAGUE FINAL
Liverpool 2 v 0 Tottenham Hotspur

Mauricio Pochettino created a brand of football at Tottenham not dissimilar to that of Jürgen Klopp's at Liverpool, built on a high-pressing style. Pochettino made Tottenham into a team that were competing regularly for a top four position in the Premier League in the 2010s. Spurs were there or thereabouts in the FA Cup and League Cup also under Pochettino, but just couldn't take the final step in winning silverware. A defence marshalled by Belgian centre-backs Toby Alderweireld and Jan Vertonghen eventually aged beyond trophy-winning hopes. Dele Alli emerged as a top-class England player for a short while; Christian Eriksen provided the class and creativity in midfield, while South Korean Son Heung-min and Harry Kane made for a potent striking pair. Liverpool, having reached the final for a second successive year, were in no mood for sentiment on this night, winning an anti-climactic final 2-0 after the 'miracle' of their 4-3 win over Barcelona in the semi-final after trailing 3-0 from the first leg.

Route to the Final
It was Tottenham's misfortune to find themselves in Group B of the group stages alongside two of European football's greatest clubs, Barcelona and Inter Milan. Barcelona proved untouchable, winning four and drawing two of their six games. The magician Lionel Messi scored a hat-trick in Barca's first game, a 4-0 drubbing of the Dutch team PSV Eindhoven. Tottenham's first game took them to the San Siro in Italy. Christian Eriksen gave them a 52nd-minute lead, only for Inter Milan to strike back in the 86th minute through Argentine striker Mauro Icordi, then win the match in the second minute of injury time with a goal by South American midfielder Matias Vecino. It didn't get any better for Tottenham in their second game when Barcelona came to town. Harry Kane and Eric Lamela gave the Spurs hope after two early goals from Philippe Coutinho and the Croatian midfield star (he's only a whisker behind Luka Modric) Ivan Rakitic, but two goals from Messi sealed a 4-2 victory for Barca at Wembley Stadium, Tottenham's temporary home while their pristine new stadium was being built.

Lucas Moura put Tottenham 2-1 up at the Philips Stadium against PSV Eindhoven, but Luuk de Jong's 87th-minute equaliser left Tottenham staring at an early exit from the 2018–19 Champions league competition. De Jong gave PSV a second-minute lead at Wembley, but two late goals from Kane revived Tottenham's interest in the competition. They still had it all to do in their last two games. An 80th-minute goal from Eriksen was enough to defeat Inter Milan 1-0 in their last 'home' game at Wembley. Ousmane Dembélé, the French international forward gave Barcelona a seventh-minute lead at the Nou Camp in Tottenham's last group game. Tottenham again seemed destined to leave the competition early until Lucas Moura netted an 85th-minute equaliser. Luckily for Tottenham, Inter Milan could only draw 1-1 against PSV Eindhoven in their last group game. With the same goal difference as Inter, but more goals scored, Tottenham luckily progressed to the knockout stages. Inter transferred to the Europa League – it was a hair's breadth margin.

Liverpool also qualified for the knockout stages in similarly tight fashion, losing Group C to Paris Saint-Germain, and pipping the Italians Napoli by dint of more goals scored and the same goals differential. There was no hint of the drama to unfold in Liverpool's first match at Anfield – unless you count a 92nd-minute winning goal from Brazilian forward Roberto Firmino as a close call. Daniel Sturridge gave Liverpool the lead, Belgian full-back Thomas Meunier scoring for PSG in the 40th minute, after James Milner's penalty kick made it 2-0. The electric Kylian Mbappé made it 2-2 in the 83rd minute, but Firmino's dramatic late goal won the match for Liverpool 3-2. The wealth of PSG's attacking talents were firmly in evidence in their second match against Red Star Belgrade, a hat-trick from Brazilian enigma Neymar, and further goals from Edinson Cavani. Angel Di Maria, and Mbappé saw the Serbians swept away 6-1.

Liverpool meanwhile lost 1-0 to the diminutive (five feet four inches) Lorenzo Insigne's 90th-minute goal for Napoli. It was then Liverpool's turn to crush Red Star at Anfield, 4-0, with goals from Firmino, Salah (two) and Mané. Intrinsically proud as a nation (a Yugoslav trait across the board), Red Star turned the tables on Liverpool in the return match in Belgrade, striker Milan Kavlov's brace sealing a 2-0 win that made qualification difficult for Liverpool, especially as the Reds then lost 2-1 to PSG at the Parc des Princes in Paris, Neymar scoring the winner. Victory was imperative in Liverpool's final home game, Mo Salah's 34th-minute strike enough to beat Napoli 1-0 and qualify Liverpool for the knockout stages and cast their opponents back into the Europa League.

The reason it is so hard to win the European Cup/Champion League comes down to the high quality of the very best teams in Germany, Spain, Italy and France. In recent years the competition has invariably been won by Bayern Munich, Real Madrid or Barcelona, when not won by an English club. Even outstanding clubs like Juventus and Paris Saint-Germain have found the competition a fingertip away from their grasp. English giants of the last decade, Manchester City, crushed German club Schalke 04 7-0 in the last 16 second leg, yet like PSG they await their first Champions League victory. PSG beat Manchester United 2-0 at Old Trafford, only to lose 3-1 to the Red Devils in Paris, two goals from Romelu Lukaku and a 94th minute Marcus Rashford penalty putting United through to the quarter-finals.

Tottenham Hotspur cruised through to the last eight, beating the Germans of Borussia Dortmund 4-0 on aggregate. Son Heung-min, Jan Vertonghen and Spanish striker Fernando Llorente giving Tottenham a 3-0 cushion to take to Germany. Kane's solitary goal in Germany sealed the 4-0 win. Llorente, an awkward opponent for centre-halves, only scored two goals in 36 Premier League games for Tottenham, but came good in European games. Two titanic games ensued in the last eight for Tottenham with Manchester City. City, spectacularly successful under Pep Guardiola, were favourites, but Son Heung-min's goal gave Tottenham a 1-0 first leg win at the sparkling new Tottenham Hotspur Stadium. At the City of Manchester Stadium the two teams put on an outstanding exhibition of attacking football, Spurs riding their luck. Raheem Sterling gave City a fourth-minute lead, only for Son Heung-min to score twice in the seventh and tenth minutes. Bernardo Silva equalised in the 11th minute. Sterling gave City the lead in the 21st minute – 3-2 to City. This breath-taking start was the quickest five goals in Champions League history. Sergio Agüero's 59th-minute goal put City 4-2 up, 4-3 on aggregate. Llorente, disappointing in league games, showed his European mettle by pulling a goal back in the 73rd minutes with a back-header. Son the South Korean international, was magnificent in the absence of the injured Kane as Tottenham squeaked through.

Tottenham's spirit rose another notch in the semi-final. Donny Von de Beek's goal won the first leg for Ajax 1-0 in London. The return tie at the Johan Cruyff Stadium in Amsterdam was only one of two astonishing come-back victories for the English participants in the 2018–19 Champions League semi-finals. Ajax went into the game having lost only once in 24 games. The precocious centre-back and captain for this young Ajax team, Matthijs de Ligt, gave Ajax a fifth-minute lead; Moroccan attacking midfielder Hakim Ziyech made it 2-0 on the night, seemingly putting the tie beyond Tottenham's reach. Only Ajax's inexperience cost them a tilt at Liverpool in the final. Lucas Moura scored twice in four minutes to keep the match alive for Tottenham in the second half. Still the tie seemed to be over until Moura scored his hat-trick goal six minutes into injury time to put Tottenham through on away goals. Ziyech hit the post for Ajax, Vertonghen hit the bar for Tottenham in a match that swung and swayed. De Ligt left in the summer transfer window for Juventus; midfield starlet Frenkie de Jong went to Barcelona.

Liverpool looked unlikely winners of their last 16 tie after a goalless draw with the mighty Bayern Munich at Anfield. As has often been the case, Liverpool's attackers proved too much for even the best defences, Sadio Mané the hero this time with two goals in the return in Munich. Joel Matip put through his own goal, but Virgil van Dijk's 69th-minute goal gave Liverpool an impressive 3-1 victory over the Germans. The last eight tie with Porto was, by contrast, a stroll for Liverpool. Naby Keïta and Roberto Firmino gave Liverpool a 2-0 cushion to take to Porto. At the Estadio de Dragao, Liverpool's attacking trio of Mané, Salah and Firmino scored a goal apiece. Van Dijk added a fourth. Porto could only reply with a goal from defender Eder Militao as Liverpool ran out 4-1 winners on the night, and comfortable 6-1 winners on aggregate.

The semi-final ties against Barcelona were among the best matches seen in the Champions League in recent years, especially the astonishing second leg at Anfield. I watched these matches at the home of a Liverpool-supporting cousin of mine. We were of one accord after the conclusive 3-0 home win for Barcelona at the Nou Camp. Barcelona were three goals better on the night, and even if Liverpool played the game of their lives (they did) at Anfield, a Barca attack containing Luis Suarez, ex-Liverpool star Philippe Coutinho, and the incomparable Lionel Messi, would surely score at Anfield. Downed by goals from Suarez and two from Messi in the last 15 minutes at the Nou Camp, Liverpool fully comprehended the massive threat posed by Barcelona. Yet they came out all guns blazing at Anfield.

Full-backs Trent Alexander-Arnold and Andrew Robertson not only supplemented the attack in their by-now requisite manner, but also blocked the high forward runs of Barca full-backs Jordi Alba and Sergio Roberto. Alexander-Arnold's quick thinking from a seventh-minute right-wing corner-kick has gone down in recent European football legend. Spotting Divock Origi on the corner of the six-yard box, his quickly taken corner-kick caught Barcelona completely unawares. A defender might argue that Barca were guilty of slack marking, but credit Alexander-Arnold for his presence of mind, his quick brain. Origi turned the ball into the net and Liverpool's mode for the evening was set, despite not being able to add any further first-half goals. Loaned out to Vfl Wolfsburg in Germany for the 2017–18 season, Origi was only playing because Firmino and Salah were injured. Xherdan Shaqiri, the Swiss international forward, only appeared for the same reason. It seems unthinkable now that Liverpool could have won this tie without the talents of Salah and Firmino.

An inspired second half substitution by Jürgen Klopp turned the tide for Liverpool, unexpectedly. The outstanding Robertson was unfortunate indeed to depart the field. I questioned the change at the time, but James Milner dropped back from midfield, and Dutchman Georginio Wijnaldum came on to score twice in two minutes. The scorers were unlikely ones for Liverpool, and it was Origi who scored again in the 79th minute. It seemed inconceivable at the time, but how Liverpool deserved their 4-0 win. Klopp set them up to attack Barcelona, to absorb the impetus of the Anfield crowd, playing on Liverpool's historic Anfield 'European nights' support. Liverpool were rarely threatened by Barcelona on the counter-attack. What a magnificent performance.

The hapless Loris Karius was loaned out first to Besiktas in Turkey, 2018–20, then to Union Berlin in Germany 2020–21. Replacing him in goal in this 2018–19 Champions League Final, returning from injury, was possibly the third best goalkeeper to ever play in the Premier League after Peter Schmeichel and Petr Cech, Alisson Becker. Indeed, in 2019 Becker was voted the Best FIFA Goalkeeper in the World. He began his professional career with the Porto Alegre based club Internacional in Brazil. In each of his four seasons with the club, Alisson won the Brazilian Serie A, the top flight in Brazil. He signed for A.S. Roma in 2016, initially understudying the Polish ex-Arsenal custodian Wojciech Szczesny, only becoming first choice when the Pole moved to Juventus. In 2018 Alisson became Jürgen Klopp's world transfer record goalkeeper, costing an initial £56.5 million. It's a tribute to Liverpool that the two goals let in against Roma in the 2017–18 Champions League semi-finals were the first goals conceded at home in the competition by Alisson.

In his first season at Liverpool Alisson won the Golden Glove, achieving 21 clean sheets in the Premier League – over half the season's fixtures. Alisson's performances against Barcelona at Anfield, and against Tottenham Hotspur in this Champions League Final, were equally impressive. Injured in March 2020,

Alisson was unable to take part as Liverpool were knocked out in the last 16 second leg match of the Champions League against Atlético Madrid. Liverpool finally winning the Premiership in 2019–20 after a 30-year wait, Alisson was instrumental in Liverpool's achievement. On 16 May 2021 Alisson came up for a 95th-minute corner kick taken by Trent Alexander-Arnold, met his teammate's assist with an emphatic header, the winning goal in a 2-1 win over West Bromwich Albion.

Selected to keep goal for Brazil in the 2018 World Cup, Alisson could not prevent his country's exit in the quarter-final at the hands of Belgium. Brazil found solace in winning the 2019 Copa America on home soil, beating Peru 3-1 in the final. It was the only goal Alisson conceded in the whole tournament. Alisson was awarded the Best Goalkeeper Award for his displays.

Quick off his line, Alisson is part of the modern sweeper-keeper movement so loved in today's football, citing Victor Valdés and Manuel Neuer as inspirations. Agile, athletic, a great shot-stopper, commanding on crosses into his penalty area, only his Brazilian compatriot Ederson at Manchester City compares with him in today's English game. Therein lies the nub for Alisson, who has played 51 times for Brazil (November 2021) – he has Ederson as a serious rival for the international jersey.

German-born centre-back Joel Matip standing six feet five inches, made a colossal partner to the six feet four Virgil van Dijk in the centre of Liverpool's defence. Matip signed from Schalke 04 to Liverpool in 2016. He played 194 Bundesliga games for Schalke. By August 2022 he had completed 126 Premier League games for Liverpool. Matip replaced Dejan Lovren from the 2018 Champions League Final. Matip's competition from Joe Gomez in partnering van Dijk tempered his regular starting games.

The Brazilian defensive midfielder Fabinho has become a crucial cog in Liverpool's team. Like compatriot Fernandinho at Manchester City, Fabinho is the glue that sticks the team together. Fabinho also provided useful cover as a centre-half for Liverpool when van Dijk was sidelined by Jordan Pickford's challenge in the Merseyside derby with Everton in 2020. Ostensibly, Fabinho began playing professionally with Fluminenese in Brazil, but spent his entire senior Fluminense career out on loan to Real Madrid Castilla (Real's second team) and Monaco in France. At Monaco, Fabinho played 233 games in all competitions, scoring 31 goals, winning Ligue 1 in 2016–17. After his stop-start beginnings, Fabinho signed for Liverpool in May 2018. In his first season with Liverpool he won this 2018–19 Champions League Final. A fine reader of the game, Fabinho has provided invaluable defensive cover from midfield for Liverpool, allowing the outstanding attacking full-backs Alexander-Arnold and Robertson to bomb forward and assist an already deadly Liverpool attack. Fabinho has not truly established himself in the Brazilian national team, playing 27 times for his country since 2015 (August 2022).

Lovren, Gomez, Alberto Moreno, James Milner, Adam Lallana, Alex Oxlade-Chamberlain, Xherdan Shaqiri, Daniel Sturridge,and Divock Origi gave Liverpool multiple defensive and attacking options from the bench, the latter coming on to seal victory for Liverpool with an 87th-minute goal. The semi-final and final of the 2018–19 Champions League have clearly been Origi's career highlights thus far. Origi, loaned out to VfL Wolfsburg in 2017–18, has appeared in 107 Premier League games for Liverpool, scoring 22 goals (August 2022); in the international jersey of Belgium he'd started 32 games during the same period, scoring three goals. A useful player, Origi remained on the fringes at Liverpool, and with his country, before AC Milan signed him for the 2022–23 season.

One look at Tottenham Hotspur's line-up for this 2018–19 Champions League Final fills me with sadness as age, loss of form and catastrophic ill health (Christian Eriksen) have left Tottenham Hotspur circa 2021–22 a mere shadow of the team challenging here (until the arrival of the dynamic Antonio Conte as manager). Mauricio Pochettino seemed to reach his personal management pinnacle here, but after defeating Inter Milan, Borussia Dortmund, Manchester City and Ajax en route to the final, they were second best in the Metropolitano Stadium, Madrid to Jürgen Klopp's inspired Liverpool team.

In goal for Tottenham, Hugo Lloris also captained the team. Lloris seemed an excellent acquisition for Spurs in his early years at White Hart Lane. Also captain of the French national team, Lloris's performances at Spurs have fluctuated in recent times, but the loss of the powerful Vertonghen and Alderweireld combination in front of him as both players advanced in years did not help Lloris's cause.

Lloris reached the Coupe de la Ligue Final in 2006 with Nice, losing the final 2-1 to AS Nancy. Moving to Lyon, Lloris won Ligue 1 Top Goalkeeper two years running. In his last season with Lyon, Lloris won the Coupe de France beating Quevilly 1-0 in the final. Teammates included Dejan Lovren, later of Liverpool, and Alexander Lacazette, later of Arsenal.

Signing for Tottenham Hotspur in the summer of 2010, Lloris played 25 times in his first season at the club, keeping nine clean sheets. Pochettino instilled a lesser level pressing game (than that of Klopp's 'Gegenpressing') to Tottenham. With a defence as solid as Tottenham had fielded for some time, Eriksen pulling the strings in midfield, and Harry Kane regularly among the Golden Boot contenders, Tottenham enjoyed several seasons in the 2010s where their style made them a treat to watch – yet trophies eluded them. They reached the 2014–15 League Cup Final, only to lose to a superior Chelsea side 2-0. Lloris was named captain by Pochettino for the 2015–16 season. This was the season that Tottenham really should have won the title, finishing five points behind surprise winners Leicester City, but ahead of Manchester City, Liverpool, Manchester United, Chelsea and Arsenal. The 2016–17 Premier League season saw Tottenham's new-found defensive solidity peak. The club's 26 goals conceded in the domestic league was a club record, Lloris keeping 15 clean sheets in the season.

From 2008 onwards Hugo Lloris has played 139 times for France (August 2022), captaining the team in recent years. Lloris was in goal for the 2005 U-19 European Championship-winning team in Northern Ireland, France beating England 3-1 in the final. Lloris starred as France controversially beat the Republic of Ireland over two legs to qualify for the 2010 World Cup (the hand of Thierry Henry, not the 'Hand of God'). Lloris captained France for the first time at Wembley in November 2010, aiding his country's 2-1 win over England. After several barren tournaments – the 2012 Euros, the 2014 World Cup, the 2016 Euros, France came good to win the 2018 World Cup in Russia, Lloris captaining the side. At the 2020 Euros, Switzerland surprisingly eliminated France in the last 16 on penalties – Lloris failed to save a single Swiss spot-kick. Renowned for his athleticism, agility and speed off his line, Lloris has also been accused of being inconsistent. Many an inconsistent goalkeeper has won the World Cup, incidentally.

Kieran Trippier, like a fine wine, improved with age. Part of Manchester City's youth system 2009–12, Trippier failed to break through to the first team, being loaned twice to Championship team Barnsley. Trippier signed for Burnley on a season-long loan 2011–12, the move becoming permanent in 2012, the player going on to win the club's Player of the Year Award for 2011–12. In season 2012–13 Trippier earned selection to the Championship PFA Team of the Year for the second consecutive season. Burnley finished second in the Championship, earning a return to the Premiership.

Trippier signed for Tottenham Hotspur in June 2015, but found his passage in the team blocked by Kyle Walker. Trippier was used in the club's Europa League games, but Tottenham were eliminated in the last 16. Replacing the injured Walker at right-back in the 2016–17 season, Trippier broke into the national team. Walker moved to Manchester City in the summer of 2017 and Trippier became a regular starter at Tottenham. The signing of Frenchman Serge Aurier in September 2017 jeopardised Trippier's place in the team again. Aurier, swift and athletic, lacked Trippier's defensive nous in my opinion. Injuries in 2018–19 marred Trippier's last season with Tottenham.

Moving to Atlético Madrid in July 2019 seemed to make Trippier a better player. Capable of playing effectively in either full-back position, he has filled in at left-back for England in recent times, looking better defensively than when at Tottenham. Atlético's defensive-minded set-up, and the impact of Argentine coach Diego Simeone have clearly done Trippier no harm. Trippier won La Liga with Atlético in 2020–21, Simeone's team breaking the Real Madrid/Barcelona monopoly, something that doesn't happen too often in Spain. A certain Luis Suarez top-scored for Atlético with 21 goals.

Trippier represented England U-18s, going on to be a key part of the team beaten in the U-19 European Championship Final 2-0 by hosts Ukraine. He also played for the national U-21s before making his senior debut against France in a friendly that England lost 3-2. An excellent performer at the 2018 World Cup in Russia, Trippier's free kick gave England false hope in the semi-final 2-1 extra-time defeat against Croatia. He was widely recognised as one of England's better players in the tournament, creating 24 chances in the games he partook in. Trippier had played 37 times for England by the end of 2021. Signed by Newcastle United in 2021–22, Trippier has returned to the Premiership.

The left-back on the night for Spurs, Danny Rose, appeared 29 times for England from 2016, having represented England at every level from U-16s through to the U-21s. Born in Doncaster, Rose started out with Leeds United's youth academy, but never made a first team appearance. His career reveals a succession of loan spells with Watford, Peterborough, Bristol City, Sunderland and Newcastle United. Only at Tottenham did Rose play regularly, and make his mark on a team, despite his obvious talent.

Rose's debut for Spurs was auspicious for two reasons: the opposition were Arsenal, and he opened the scoring in a 2-1 win with a thunderous volley, the goal winning the club's Goal of the Season. Harry Redknapp convinced Rose that only by playing at left-back, not left-wing, would Rose achieve international status. Rose was named in the PFA Team of the Year twice in succession in 2016 and 2017, but knee surgery in May 2017 dampened Rose's rise. Pochettino gone, Rose failed to find favour with new manager José Mourinho – many have trodden this path. Rose signed for Watford in June 2021, but failed to pull up trees at Vicarage Road. His well-publicised bouts of depression, along with racist barbs thrown at him and other black English players seem to have truly left a mark upon him.

The Belgian centre-backs, Toby Alderweireld and Jan Vertonghen both gave sterling service under Mauricio Pochettino. Vertonghen was the first to sign for Spurs in 2012, Alderweireld following his international teammate in 2015. Until time caught up with the pair, their excellence was crucial to improving Tottenham's defensive set-up in the 2010s. Vertonghen excelled at Ajax 2006–12, playing 220 games and scoring 28 goals in all competitions. He won two Eredevisie titles 2010–11, 2011–12, and two KNVB Cups (the equivalent of the English FA Cup, 2006–07 and 2009–10, beating AZ Aalkmar in the former 8-7 on penalties after a 1-1 draw, and Feyenoord 6-1 on aggregate in a two-legged final in the latter). A young Luis Suarez was already giving notice of his considerable talent, scoring a ridiculous 81 goals in 110 Eredivisie games for Ajax 2007–11. In his last season with Ajax, Vertonghen failed to capture the double as the Amsterdam team lost the KNVB Cup Final 3-2 to Twente Enschede.

Vertonghen's versatility made him crucial to Ajax's Eredivisie successes. Essentially a central defender, he could switch to midfield or left-back if called upon. He captained Frank de Boer's team in this last season of 2011–12, winning the Eredivisie Player of the Year. Manchester City, Arsenal and Newcastle were all linked with Vertonghen, but the Belgian went to Tottenham following assurances he would play as a central defender. Although sent off in a frustrating 2012 Europa League quarter-final against Basel (Mo Salah emerging as a new world star), Vertonghen's first season, 2012–13, ended with him being selected in the PFA Team of the Year. When Pochettino came to Tottenham in 2014–15, Vertonghen initially lost his place to the pairing of Younes Kaboul and Federico Fazio. He won his place back, helping Tottenham reach the 2014–15 League Cup Final, lost to Chelsea 2-0. Paired with compatriot Alderweireld in 2015–16, Tottenham looked the most secure defensively they'd been for many a year. A repeat showing in 2016–17 made Vertonghen one of the stand-out defenders in the Premier League. Thirty-six games in the Premier League in 2017–18 didn't suggest any imminent demise. Scoring and assisting in a 3-0 Champions League last 16 win over Borussia Dortmund from a left-wing back position suggested his continuing importance to the team. Suffering concussion in the semi-final against Ajax – after colliding with long-time colleague Alderweireld – Vertonghen had to wear a protective face mask upon returning to the field in Amsterdam. Vertonghen attributed his subsequent loss of form to the collision. From the outside it appeared Vertonghen had lost a little pace, but perhaps the collision impacted upon him more than he would have liked. This fine defender has since joined Benfica (2020). One hopes the collision had no lasting effects. He played 232 Premier League games for Spurs, scoring six goals.

Belgium have every reason to be thankful for his international contributions, Vertonghen having played 139 times for his country, scoring nine goals. Veertonghen's preference was always to play in the centre of defence, but the pairing of ex-Ajax teammate (also of Arsenal) Thomas Vermeulen and Manchester City's colossus Vincent Kompany saw Vertonghen often chosen at left-back for his country. Belgium have been seen as the coming team over the last decade, but like his club time at Tottenham, a 'golden generation' of players have been unable to maximize their opportunities.

Beaten 1-0 by Argentina in the last eight of the 2014 World Cup, Vertonghen's luck ran out again in the 2016 Euros as an ankle ligament injury prevented his selection in the quarter-final defeat to a plucky Welsh side inspired by Gareth Bale and Aaron Ramsey. At the 2018 World Cup, the Belgians (recently voted as the Number 1 team in the world) were lifted by Vertonghen's 69th-minute goal in a dramatic 3-2 victory over Japan, after trailing 2-0 in a thrilling match. The Belgians followed this up with an excellent 2-1 victory over Brazil in the last eight, the Brazilians unable to combat the advanced central midfield role of the influential Kevin de Bruyne of Manchester City. Belgium were everyone's favourite team it seemed, tipped to go all the way, but France were looking solid throughout their team, and Samuel Umtiti's solitary goal ended the Belgian dream in the semi-finals. Vertonghen's impact at Tottenham was substantial, but this sturdy defender with a ferocious shot left Tottenham in 2020 with only two runners-up medals, a scant reflection of his ability.

Toby Alderweireld's career almost mirrors that of Jan Vertonghen. Joining the Ajax youth academy in 2004, Alderweireld only established himself in the first team alongside Vertonghen in 2009–10 after Thomas Vermeulen moved to Arsenal. He stayed at Ajax until 2013, alerting the likes of Liverpool as his contract ran down. In September 2013 Alderweireld joined Atlético Madrid. His stay in Madrid was brief, although he appeared as an 83rd-minute substitute in the 2014 Champions League final against city rivals Real Madrid, experiencing the pain of being minutes away from a winners' medal, only to see Sergio Ramos equalise deep into injury time. Real than ran away with the game in extra time, to the tune of 4-1. A season-long loan at Southampton followed. The Saints wanted to buy Alderweireld, but Atlético held out for a sale to the highest bidder. That club was Tottenham Hotspur.

In his first two seasons with Spurs, 2015–16 and 2016–17, Alderweireld could do no wrong, forming with Vertonghen the best central defensive partnership seen at the club for decades. Alderweireld was selected in the 2015–16 PFA Team of the Year. Unfortunately, a hamstring injury incurred against Real Madrid in the Champions League in November 2017 kept him out of the side for several months. When about to return, Alderweireld aggravated the injury in training. He only returned to the squad in April 2018. One wonders whether the injury seriously hampered him thereafter. One of my sons, an excellent junior player, scarcely laced his boots in anger post-25 years old after a succession of hamstring injuries. Alderweireld regained favour in the 2019–20 season, but in July 2021, cowed by his injury and a subsequent loss of pace, Alderweireld signed for Qatar club Al-Duhail. Still only 32, one feels that if he could sprint full out, unhindered, Alderweireld would still be playing in the higher echelons of a European league.

Like Vertonghen, Alderweireld has played over 100 times for Belgium (121 appearances, five goals, August 2022). Alongside Vertonghen for his country, Alderweireld's best performance came at the 2018 World Cup, beaten by France in the semi-finals 1-0, Belgium claimed the bronze medal after beating England 2-0 in the third and fourth place play-off match, goals from Thomas Meunier and Eden Hazard earning the Belgians a merited third place as one of the tournament's brightest lights.

Set up by Pochettino in a 4-2-3-1 formation, the two defensive midfielders in Spurs' side on this evening were Harry Winks and Moussa Sissoko. Winks has played ten times for England (one goal), but has never truly established himself in the first 11 at Tottenham. Joining Tottenham's academy at the tender age of five, Winks has never known anything other than Tottenham Hotspur in his career. Debuting in 2016 for the first team, Winks's passing and link play make him a typical product of the Tottenham Hotspur system. Sadly for Winks, an ankle ligament injury incurred in a freak tumble in a dugout at Burnley in April 2017 ended his 2016–17 season prematurely.

Winks's performances in the 2017–18 season earned him a call-up to the England national team. Capped at every level from the U-17s to the U-21s, Winks's natural ability boded well for him. He missed the 2018 World Cup through injury. It now seems like a mountain for Winks to climb to get back into an England team playing with two deep-lying midfielders in Declan Rice of West Ham and Kalvin Phillips of Leeds United who are both in excellent form. Gareth Southgate's recent insistence on England playing a possession-based game akin to the best teams – Spain, Italy – ought to suit Winks's style, but the player continues to fight indifferent form with Tottenham, being linked with a move away from the club as I write.

Tottenham simply have not replaced the talented Christian Eriksen in a moderate midfield circa 2021/22. Moussa Sissoko gave the team strength, power and energy in the midfield area over 141 Premier League games 2016–21, but has since moved to Watford for the 2021–22 season. Good enough to start 71 internationals for World Champions France, Sissoko has been labelled inconsistent despite his power and muscular frame. Playing for Toulouse 2007–13, Sissoko completed 192 games, scoring 20 goals. Liverpool were reported to be interested in him. Tottenham expressed interest in signing him as early as 2009, Manchester City and Bayern Munich were also linked with the Paris-born, Malian-parented Sissoko, but it was to Newcastle in the north-east of England that Sissoko moved in January 2013.

In his home debut Sissoko endeared himself to the Toon Army with two goals in a 3-2 victory over Chelsea. Captain in the final games of the 2015–16 season, Sissoko was unable to prevent an ailing Newcastle side from being relegated to the Championship. Sissoko scored 11 goals in 118 Premier League games for Newcastle, but when Tottenham finally bid for him in August 2016, Sissoko moved south. Despite their prolonged interest in him, Sissoko hardly started a game in his first season under Mauricio Pochettino. In 2018–19 Sissoko broke into the team, playing 43 times in all competitions. Unfortunately for Sissoko it was his trailing arm that resulted in a penalty kick after only 22 seconds in this 2018–19 Champions League Final. A right knee ligament injury incurred in a New Year's Day match kept him out of the team until June 2020 when the Covid-19 delayed season restarted. In August 2021 Sissoko signed for Watford,

Whether injury was the reason for the transfer one can only wonder. Certainly Sissoko's powerful displays are not being replicated in the Tottenham team of 2021–22. Sissoko represented France at every level from U-16s to the U-21s. He scored his first international goal at the 2014 World Cup in a 5-2 win over Switzerland. In the final of the 2016 Euros Sissoko performed heroically as France lost 1-0 to Der's extra-time goal for Portugal. Injuries and loss of form cost him his place in the 2018 World Cup, named only on the stand-by list. This is another player who the watching football world waits to see if the rich promise of his youth can be revitalised.

Tottenham's three offensive midfielders on this night were Dele Alli, Christian Eriksen and the excellent South Korean Son Heung-min. The only one of this trio who is a nominal midfield player is the super-talented Dane Eriksen, who was so catastrophically taken from the field of play after collapsing in Denmark's opening game of the delayed 2020 Euros against Finland at the Parken Stadium, Copenhagen, in June 2021. This is a player I admired greatly at Tottenham. A proper playmaker, Eriksen supplied the bullets for Son Heung-min and Harry Kane; scored some marvellous free kicks, and generally dictated the tempo of play for Tottenham in his time with the club 2013–20. Eriksen was a joy to watch, a stylish player who initially appeared out of synch with the hurly burly 200 mph nature of the English game.

Born in Middelfart in central Denmark (you couldn't make that name up, could you?), Eriksen followed his father by playing for the local side Middelfart G & BK, a Danish third-tier team. This is where Eriksen spent his footballing years 1995–2005. In 2005 he joined Odense Boldklub, the first-tier club in the Danish Superliga. At Odense, Eriksen's technical abilities alerted Barcelona and Chelsea. He trialled at both clubs – and with Real Madrid, Manchester United and AC Milan. Choosing Ajax in Holland in 2008 instead, Eriksen believed his progress should be staggered, rather than throw himself in deep at a massive club. It was a shrewd decision.

Ajax manager at the time, Martin Jol – previously at Tottenham – ironically, compared Eriksen to Wesley Schneider and the imperious Michael Laudrup for his positional awareness and technical accomplishment. Eriksen played in the second leg of the KNVB Dutch Cup Final of 2009–10, a 4-1 win over Feyenoord, and by the season's end he'd debuted for Denmark on the international stage. He won the Danish Talent of the Year (Footballer of the Year) Award in 2010. Johan Cruyff also compared Eriksen to the stylish Laudrup brothers, Michael and Brian. Upon leaving Ajax in August 2013, Eriksen had won three consecutive Eredivisie titles with Ajax 2010–11 to 2012–13 and scored 32 goals in 162 games in all competitions.

There were teething problems for the slightly built Eriksen in his first 2013–14 season at Tottenham, but the Dane came good, scoring ten goals and assisting 13, winning the Danish Footballer of the Year and Tottenham's Player of the Season. It wasn't difficult to see why Eriksen won the latter award. This stylish, creative player was of a calibre Tottenham fans weaned on Jimmy Greaves, Alan Gilzean, Chris Waddle and Glenn Hoddle absolutely adored.

Eriksen's form continued to soar under new manager Mauricio Pochettino in the 2014–15 season. Eriksen credited Pochettino with improving the team's fitness. I have always felt that English football has over-egged the physicality and power side of the game at the expense of technique, but you can see how Pochettino felt the need to have a fitter, stronger team with sides such as Manchester City, Liverpool and Chelsea playing an ever-faster – and technical – game with improved emphasis on passing and ball retention. In January 2015 Eriksen scored twice in the League Cup semi-final 2-2 draw with Sheffield United to aid a 3-2 aggregate win. Tottenham failed to make the elusive final step, losing to the powerful Chelsea team 2-0 in the final. In winning the Danish Footballer of the Year Award in 2016 for the third successive year, Eriksen became the first Dane to do so. Tottenham finished the Premier League season in third place, qualifying for the 2015–16 Champions League.

Tottenham finished the 2016–17 season in second place in the Premier League, seven points behind champions Chelsea, but an impressive eight points clear of Pep Guardiola's Manchester City. Pochettino's Tottenham were getting closer and closer, but they couldn't get over the line and in 2022 the wait for the first trophy since 2008's League Cup win against Chelsea looks like going on for a while yet. Eriksen's eight goals and 15 assists for the season were bettered only by the precise passer Kevin de Bruyne (18 assists) at Manchester City. Eriksen also won Tottenham's Player of the Year for a second time.

In September 2017 Eriksen's 33rd Premier League goal surpassed the previous best total by a Dane in the Premier League (Nicholas Bendtner at Arsenal). There is no doubting that Eriksen, a superior player to Bendtner, deserved the accolade. Two goals in the quarter-finals of the 2017–18 FA Cup quarter-finals against Swansea City helped Tottenham through to a second consecutive FA Cup semi-final, but again they were deprived of a chance of silverware, this time Manchester United their conquerors 2-1. Dele Alli's early goal was cancelled out by replies from Alexis Sanchez and Ander Herrera. Eriksen was named in the PFA Team of the Year alongside teammates Harry Kane and Jan Vertonghen.

Eriksen scored in both legs of the 2018–19 Champions League group stages against Inter Milan. It was a portent – Inter would be his next club. On 31 March 2019, Eriksen became only the second player after David Beckham to provide more than ten assists in four successive Premier League seasons. He provided the assist for Son Heung-min's first ever goal at the newly christened Tottenham Hotspur Stadium in his 200th Premier League appearance in April 2019.

Important staging posts at Ajax and Tottenham achieved, Eriksen's career path seemed to follow natural progression. In January 2020 the Dane signed for Inter Milan. He debuted as a substitute for Alexis Sanchez in a 2-1 home victory over Fiorentina in the Coppa Italia quarter-finals. In August 2020 Inter played in the Covid-19 delayed 2020 Europa League Final, but Inter fell 2-3 to the consistent Spanish Europa League winners Sevilla. It was Romelu Lukaku's misfortune to score the own goal winner for Sevilla, off-setting his impressive performances with Inter. Lukaku befriended Eriksen, helping the Dane to overcome his settling-in difficulties, attributed to the language barrier.

In the 2020–21 Coppa Italia quarter-final against AC Milan, Eriksen came on with the score poised at 1-1. In the seventh minute of injury time he conjured up one of the wonderful free-kick goals Tottenham fans came to love to send Inter through to the semi-finals. Inter couldn't capitalise on the victory, losing 2-1 on aggregate to Juventus in the semi-finals. One of Italy's star players at the delayed 2020 Euros, Federico Chiesa, would score the winning goal in the final won by Juventus 2-1 against Atalanta. Inter Milan closed out the 2020–21 season by winning Serie A at the death, ending a nine-year run of Juventus title wins. He couldn't win the Premiership with Tottenham, but Eriksen claimed the equally hard-to-win Serie A in his first season with Inter.

A serious talent from a young age, Eriksen scored nine goals in 16 games for Denmark U-17s, being named Danish U-17 Talent of the Year in 2008 by the Danish FA. He went on to represent Denmark at U-18, U-19 and U-21 level. Making his debut against Austria in March 2010, Eriksen became the fourth youngest full international for Denmark, the youngest debutant since Michael Laudrup. There are many comparisons of Eriksen with the Laudrups. Michael may be the best Danish player I have ever seen, his calmness and technical ability making him one of the world's greatest players in the 1980s and 1990s. Failing to reach the last 16 at the 2010 World Cup, Eriksen played against Holland and Japan in the group stages, the youngest player in the tournament. Eriksen's star was burning brightly, and although Denmark lost a friendly 2-1 to England in February 2011, Eriksen was named Man of the Match.

Established as Tottenham's playmaker, Eriksen scored eight goals in the 2018 World Cup qualifying group stages as Denmark reached a play-off against the Republic of Ireland. A hat-trick against the Irish in a 5-1 romp at Dublin's Aviva Stadium – after the Irish had drawn 0-0 in Copenhagen, sent Denmark through to the 2018 World Cup proper. The hat-trick gave Eriksen a total of 11 goals in the qualifying rounds. Only Poland's Robert Lewandowski (16) and Portugal's Cristiano Ronaldo (15) bettered his total – and both are recognised strikers, not midfielders. Denmark qualified for the last 16 at the 2018 World Cup, Eriksen scoring in a 1-1 draw with Austria, but Croatia ended the Dane's interest in the tournament, 3-2 on penalties after a 1-1 draw, Eriksen one of three players to miss their spot-kicks. In his 100th match for Denmark, Eriksen converted a penalty kick as Denmark beat England 1-0 at Wembley in the 2020–21 UEFA Nations League competition.

It would have been a shock for any player to collapse on the field of play in a football match. Bolton Wanderers' Fabrice Muamba never played again after suffering a heart attack in the March 2012 FA Cup quarter-final against Tottenham Hotspur at White Hart Lane, but Eriksen's sudden collapse in the match against Finland at the Parken Stadium, Copenhagen, in the 2020 Euros seemed all the more poignant because of the wonderful displays he gave at Tottenham 2013–

2020. He was certainly one of my favourite players of the 2010s, his stylish contribution to Tottenham's midfield peppered with great strikes, free kicks and astute passing. Denmark's captain Simon Kjaer was swiftly on the scene, along with Leicester City goalkeeper Kasper Schmeichel. There was an awful delay while Eriksen received cardio-pulmonary resuscitation and defibrillation on the pitch before the match was suspended. An hour or so later, after Eriksen had been confirmed awake and stable at the Rigshospitalet in Copenhagen, the match resumed. Danish goalkeeping legend Peter Schmeichel criticised the decision to restart, UEFA feeling it was the safest option after apparently receiving Eriksen's blessing from hospital. The match ended 1-1, Denmark torn between wanting to win the match for Eriksen and playing the remainder of the match in a state of shock.

Noted as a classic number 10, Eriksen orchestrated Tottenham's midfield beautifully in his time at White Hart Lane. I couldn't help feeling he left prematurely – possibly another player to feel uncomfortable in a José Mourinho-coached team. His return with Brentford in 2021–22– and his reassuringly excellent form – has been the most heart-warming story of the season. A football match is always better for the presence of the gifted Christian Eriksen. The Danish manager of Brentford, Thomas Frank, gave Eriksen a chance to resume his career after medical all-clears, an opportunity denied him by Inter Milan and Serie A's stringent rules. Ambitions remaining, Eriksen has now signed up to the thankless task of attempting to resuscitate Manchester United's fortunes for the 2022–23 season.

On the left side of Tottenham's midfield on this evening in Madrid, Dele Alli shone brightly for several seasons under Mauricio Pochettino. The enigmatic Alli has since completely gone off the radar for England and in club football, yet his clever linking play and crucial goals earmarked him as one of Europe's great coming players in recent times. What on earth has gone wrong?

Born in Milton Keynes, Alli played for hometown club Milton Keynes Dons 2011–15, scoring 24 goals in 88 appearances in all competitions. He signed for Tottenham in February 2015, being loaned back to MK Dons for the remainder of the season. In his first two seasons at Tottenham, 2015–16 and 2016–17, Alli was named the PFA Young Player of the Year, and selected to the PFA Team of the Year. His fall from grace is difficult to comprehend. He netted ten Premier League goals in his debut (2015–16) season at Tottenham. Aged 19, his youth and inexperience told when he received a three-match ban for an off-the-ball incident, striking West Bromwich Albion midfielder Claudio Yacob. The skirmish acted as a precedent as Alli was then sent off for a dangerous tackle on Gent Midfielder Brecht Dejaegere as Tottenham were knocked out of the last 32 of the Europa League in the 2016–17 season, 3-2 on aggregate. Losing 1-0 away, Tottenham disappointingly drew 2-2 at Wembley Stadium in the return game. Tottenham's 'nearly men' also lost 4-2 in the FA Cup semi-final to old foes Chelsea, their nemesis at this time. Alli equalised for Tottenham to make it 2-2, but late goals from Eden Hazard and Nemanja Matic condemned Tottenham to defeat. In April 2018, Tottenham earned recompense by beating Chelsea at Stamford Bridge for the first time in 28 years, Alli scoring twice. Strangely, I remember the boot being firmly on the other foot back in the early 1970s. I recall a strong Chelsea team unable to beat the Tottenham side of Chivers/Gilzean/Mullery/Peters, a dank night game under floodlights circa 1971 ending in a 2-0 defeat for Chelsea, Martin Chivers scoring in injury time, is an abiding memory. In October 2018, Tottenham beat Chelsea 3-1 at home, Alli again scoring. The 2018–19 season ended unhappily for Alli, a hamstring injury ruling him out for two months at a time when his form was outstanding.

The same hamstring injury kept Alli out of the early games of the 2019–20 season. In November 2019 José Mourinho replaced Mauricio Pochettino as Tottenham manager. Mourinho reverted Alli to an attacking role behind Harry Kane after he'd been deployed as a conventional midfield player in latter years under Pochettino. Alli repaid Mourinho with three goals in his first three games under the Portuguese. A snapchat video making fun of the Asian influence on Covid-19 earned Alli another one-match ban by the FA, in addition to a £50,000 fine. One wishes this talented player would simply let his boots do the talking. Alli soon lost favour with Mourinho, the last season and a half frittered away, the player not displaying anything like the form he'd shown 2015–18. Alli's ability is unquestionable. He has represented England at every level from U-17s to U-21s, through to the national team. Debuting for the senior team against France at Wembley in November 2015, Alli beat teammate Hugo Lloris with a long range shot to complete a fine 2-0 win. 2-0 down against Germany in a friendly in Berlin, England revived to win 3-2, Alli named Man of the Match by BBC Sport. At the 2018 World Cup, Alli scored the second goal as England beat Sweden 2-0 to reach the semi-finals for the first time in 28 years. Alli won the free kick from which Kieran Trippier scored in the semi-final against Croatia, lost 2-1 after extra time. How could this form disappear almost completely in the following years? Gareth Southgate subsequently omitted him from his 2020 Euros squad.

For a period of time (2015–18), Alli looked like a class act, for England particularly. He played the role behind the main striker to a tee. If he has a fault it is that he likes to play the game on the edge. When not playing in that manner, Alli seems half the player. Some players have to play in this way. If Alli could temper this edge, play with controlled aggression, surely his international career is not yet over. He has 37 caps (three goals) for England (November 2021). His linking play made him a class act on the international stage for a while. Real Madrid were reportedly keen on signing him. He is still only 25 years old as I write, but has shown no form whatsoever in recent times, Everton and the substitutes' bench his latest home.

Son Heung-min is another player who is a joy to watch. It's a rare thing to see a professional footballer playing with a smile on his face, but Son appears to genuinely love the game. At Tottenham, Son became the top Asian goalscorer in Premier League history and Champions League history, and surpassed Cha Bum-Kun's 98 Bundesliga goals for Eintracht Frankfurt and Bayer Leverkusen 1979–1989, a European record for an Asian player. Football runs in Son's family, his father good enough to play for the South Korean B team. Son represented South Korea at the 2009 U-17 World Cup in Nigeria, his country qualifying for the knockout stages, finishing second in Group F behind Italy. Son didn't score against Italy as South Korea lost 2-1, but netted against Uruguay (3-1), and Algeria (2-0). South Korea beat Mexico 5-3 on penalties after a 1-1 draw in the last 16, before losing 3-1 to hosts Nigeria in the last eight, Son scoring his country's goal.

After his country's valiant attempt to win the U-17 World Cup, Son signed for Hamburger SV's youth academy in Germany. In his first season in the academy side Son scored nine goals in 18 games. His first senior league goal against 1. FC Köln made him the youngest Hamburg player to score in the Bundesliga, beating a record previously held by Manfred Kaltz, the legendary attacking right back. Playing at Hamburg until 2013, Son scored 20 Bundesliga goals in 73 matches. Signing for Bayer Leverkusen in June 2013, Son scored a hat-trick against former club Hamburger SV in November 2013. He ended the season with 12 goals in 43 matches. At the end of the 2014–15 season he'd scored 17 goals in 42 matches, totalling 21 Bundesliga goals in 62 Bundesliga matches with Bayer Leverkusen.

Upon signing for Tottenham Hotspur for £22 million in August 2015 Son became the most expensive Asian player in football history. Son took time to settle at Tottenham, but Mauricio Pochettino felt he was transformed come the 2016–17 season. In the Champions League, Son scored the only goal of the game as Tottenham beat CSKA Moscow in Russia, a notoriously tricky destination. Son scored 21 goals in all competitions in the 2016–17 season. He'd found his feet. In scoring his 20th Premier League goal in the 1-0 victory over Crystal Palace, Son overtook Manchester United's Park Ji-Sung as the top Asian scorer in Premier League history. In February 2019 Son was named Premier League Player of the Year at the London Football Awards. In the quarter-finals of the 2018–19 Champions League, Son's goal in the 1-0 victory over Manchester City became the first European competition goal at the new Tottenham Hotspur Stadium. The stadium's opening had been delayed, meaning Tottenham had to play their European home games at Wembley. The new stadium's opening was welcomed by Tottenham, but one wonders whether the money ploughed into its building meant a repeat of their North London rivals Arsenal's struggles after moving from Highbury to the Emirates Stadium. Son also scored the first Premier League goal at the new stadium in April 2019 in a 2-0 win over Crystal Place. Son's two goals in the return leg of the quarter-final Champions League tie with Manchester City helped Tottenham through to their first Champions League (European Cup) semi-final since 1962, the era of the 20th-century's first double-winning team – Blanchflower, Smith, Greaves et al.

In November 2019 Son ran from his own half leaving seven Burnley players trailing in his wake, an individual goal that eventually won the 2019–20 Premier League Goal of the Season. In scoring twice at Villa Park in a 3-2 win over Aston Villa, Son became the first Asian player to pass 50 goals in the Premier League. In the second match of the 2020–21 season, Son scored four goals in a 5-2 win over Southampton – all four goals assisted by a deeper-lying Harry Kane. To date (August 2022), Son Heung-min has scored an impressive 93 Premier League goals (at the end of the 2021–22 season he tied with Liverpool's Mo Salah as the league's Golden Boot winner with 22 goals) in 210 games.

Son Heung-min is a talisman for his country, South Korea, scoring 33 goals by August 2022 in 102 internationals. Indeed, the team relied heavily upon him at the last (2018) World Cup, in the way that Argentina have leaned on Lionel Messi. Son scored a breakaway goal in the 97th minute that sealed Germany's early dismissal from the 2018 World Cup. It wasn't enough to take South Korea through to the last 16 as they'd already lost their first game to Sweden 1-0.

Son Heung-min has proved to be an excellent buy for Tottenham Hotspur, his pace and trickery, and eye for goal a massive boost to the team. At times he has been omitted from the Tottenham team (a mistake in my book) if Tottenham opted to play a lone-striker system. Inevitably, Harry Kane got the nod in these circumstances, but it could be argued that Son's influence on Tottenham's attacking play has been just as important since his signing in 2015. His partnership with Kane has blossomed, each player happy to be the assister to the other.

Harry Kane has become one of English football's greatest goalscorers – he has a lot to live up to, the great Jimmy Greaves who made the art of goal-scoring look ridiculously easy; Alan Shearer in the Premier League at Southampton, Newcastle United and Blackburn Rovers. How many more goals might Shearer have scored had he transferred to Manchester United when Alex Ferguson expressed interest in him?

Harry Kane progressed in senior football via the long route, loan periods in his early Tottenham days including spells at Leyton Orient, Millwall, Leicester City and Norwich City. Kane played for Ridgeway Rovers in Chingford, East London, as a boy, the stamping ground of David Beckham, Everton's Andros Townsend, and Stoke City's Dwight Gayle. Expert ex-players such as the great Irishman Liam Brady – so stylish at Arsenal and Juventus – doubted Kane's potential as a boy, thinking him overweight and unathletic. Kane was released from the Arsenal youth academy, starting out in senior football with Watford in 2004. Tottenham swiftly took him on after an impressive display against them – but as a midfield player initially. Not until Kane had a growth spurt in his mid-teens did Tottenham take him on, Kane signing a scholarship contract in 2009. In 2009–10 he played 22 times for Tottenham's U-18 side, scoring 18 goals.

In July 2010 Kane signed a professional contract with Spurs, but spent from January 2011 to the end of the 2010–11 season on loan at Leyton Orient. He scored five goals in 18 matches, the move exposing him to the physicality of men's football in the lower tiers of the English Football League. In 2011–12, Kane and recent interim manager at Tottenham, Ryan Mason, spent the January to April 2012 period at Millwall on loan. Nine goals in 27 matches in all competitions earnt Kane Millwall's Young Player of the Year Award for 2011–12. In August 2012 Kane joined Norwich City on a season-long loan. A metatarsal injury prevented much game time at Norwich. Tottenham recalled him in February 2013, then loaned him out again to Leicester City for the remainder of the season. Kane helped Leicester reach the Championship play-off semi-finals of 2012–13, only to lose to Watford. Still not a regular at Tottenham in 2013–14 Kane scored in three consecutive games in April 2014, a sign that he was maturing into a proper centre-forward at the top level.

Kane's breakthrough season finally arrived in 2014–15, the player helping Spurs reach the League Cup Final, his team losing 2-0 to the streetwise Chelsea side 2-0, scorers John Terry and Diego Costa summing up the difference on the day, both players warriors who were prepared to go to war. Kane's consolation came in scoring 21 Premier League goals in this season, equalling a Premier League scoring record at Spurs shared by Teddy Sheringham, Jürgen Klinsmann and Gareth Bale. Kane was voted the PFA Young Player of the Year. He was named too alongside Costa in the PFA Team of the Year. He was again selected to the team in 2015–16 after scoring 25 goals to win the Premier League Golden Boot. In 2016–17 Kane was named in the PFA Team of the Year for the third consecutive season. In this season Kane's 29 Premier League goals also earned him a second successive Golden Boot.

Scoring 56 goals in all competitions for the calendar year 2017, Kane broke a seven-season monopoly of this feat achieved by world and European superstars Lionel Messi and Cristiano Ronaldo. For the fourth consecutive season Kane was selected to the 2017–18 PFA Team of the Year. Kane's goal in the 1-0 victory over Borussia Dortmund in Germany in the 2017–18 Champions league tie made him Tottenham's top scorer in European competitions with 24 goals. Unfortunately Kane began to be affected by hamstring injuries over the coming year. Returning to the team – and to better form – Kane won his third Golden Boot award in the 2020–21 season (23 goals), but at club level at least this was a new Harry Kane as he dropped deeper to supply countless assists for teammate Son Heung-min. The pair achieved the most assists for two players in a Premier League season, Kane also winning the Playmaker of the Season award with his 14 assists.

Kane has continued to be England's focal point in attack as a conventional centre-forward, but there is no doubt that his deeper-lying role at Tottenham has added another dimension to his game. In the run-up to the delayed 2020 Euros Kane was subject to intense media speculation, the theory being he would end up at Manchester City for the 2021–22 season. The move didn't materialise, with Tottenham chairman Daniel Levy's intransigence a factor, Levy insisting that Kane be sold for nothing less than a sky-rocketing sum of money. The upshot was a dip in Kane's form in the early part of the 2021–22 season, although he continued to score regularly for England. If Kane should stay at Tottenham he has the great Greaves's club record in his sight (220 goals in 321 games). Kane's total stood at 183 in 279 as the 2022–23 season approached.

Kane had scored 50 goals in 73 internationals for England (August 2022), passing Bobby Charlton's 49, and surpassing Jimmy Greaves's 44 – although Greaves scored his in only 57 internationals. Kane appeared at every age level for England from U-17 to U-21 level, totalling 17 goals. He reached the semi-finals of the 2012 U-19 European Championships with England, only to lose to Greece 2-1. Kane introduced himself in typical style to the senior team, appearing as a substitute for Wayne Rooney against Lithuania, scoring 80 seconds after entering play in a Euro 2016 qualifying match. Kane captained his country for the first time in a 2018 World Cup qualifier with Scotland at Hampden Park, scoring a critical injury time equaliser in the 2-2 draw.

At the 2018 World Cup, Kane's star was in the ascendancy, scoring both goals (including an injury-time winner) as England beat a defiant Tunisia 2-1. England then swept a weak Panama team aside 6-1, Kane scoring a hat-trick. Only Geoff Hurst (1966 versus West Germany) and Gary Lineker (1986 versus

Poland) had previously scored hat-tricks for England in tournament play. Kane's penalty against Colombia in the last 16 took his tally to six for the tournament in the 1-1 draw, England winning 4-3 on penalties, His six goals earned him the tournament's Golden Boot as World Cup top-scorer, the first English player to win the award since Lineker in 1986. Wayne Rooney's 53 goals currently make him England's all-time top-scorer, but it's only a matter of time before Kane supersedes his total.

In the 2020 Euro qualifying campaign, Kane scored 12 goals, scoring in every game. There was no let-up for England even if his club scoring form didn't match his international achievements. At the 2020 Euros, Kane continued to score regularly in important matches for England, although it was Manchester City's Raheem Sterling who put fear into the hearts of opponent's defences. Kane scored the second, conclusive goal as England beat Germany 2-0 in the last 16, added two more as England routed the Ukraine 4-0 in the last eight, and scored the winner in a nervy 2-1 semi-final win over Denmark. If England hadn't sat back on a 1-0 lead (for the second tournament in a row) Kane might have added to his four goals for the tournament, although wily Italian defenders Leonardo Bonucci and Giorgio Chiellini might have had a say in the matter. England lost the final 3-2 on penalties after a 1-1 draw, but should have been braver after Luke Shaw's early goal. Harry Kane, criticised in his youth for being technically behind others, has shown a Kevin Keegan-esque desire to make himself the very best player he can be. His technique now belies his slight lack of pace, and his awareness where to be in the penalty area speaks for itself in goals. Kane's desire to better himself through extra training is a huge credit to him, and in addition he has a true striker's propensity to shoot on sight. A player I once played with did this, scoring 54 goals in one season. He may not have possessed my pace or flair, but how I wish I'd just put the ball into the net as he did, instead of always attempting to score the perfect goal.

The two managers on the night, Mauricio Pochettino and Jürgen Klopp, have been among the best managers in the world over the last decade. Pochettino now oversees a team flooded with superstars at Paris Saint-Germain, while Klopp's 'Gegenpressing' has transformed Liverpool into a winning machine again, and although 'machine' could be interpreted unkindly, Liverpool have plenty of flair and individual skill among a fine team. The irony of this 2018–19 Champions League Final is that the intensity with which these two teams had played to reach the summit of European club football was sadly missing on the night, the match proving a bit of an anti-climax after the heroics of seeing off Barcelona and Ajax in epic semi-final ties.

THE FINAL

Liverpool, so impressive in their remarkable comeback from 3-0 down against Barcelona in their semi-final, were able to impose their superiority on this match without ever reaching the extraordinary heights set by Jürgen Klopp's team in recent years. Both teams were below par on the night. Whether the occasion got to the Tottenham players, or whether the two teams had simply exhausted themselves in their quest to reach this pinnacle, only the players know. What was unquestionable was that the game was an anti-climax. I only played in two finals in nearly 20 years of local football and I didn't do myself justice in either of them. Sometimes you can just try a little too hard. A little nervousness is acceptable as players feed off adrenaline, but this final didn't showcase what either of these two teams were truly capable of.

The die was cast for Tottenham in only the 24th second of the match. Moussa Sissoko handling the ball with an outstretched arm after Sadio Mané attempted a pass. Unfortunate I thought at the time, but Sissoko's arm was held too high. Mo Salah dispatched the penalty kick in his usual no-nonsense fashion. Hugo Lloris guessed the right direction, but Salah's kick carried too much power for him. Liverpool continued to press, Trent Alexander-Arnold drifting a 25-yarder wide, and fellow full-back Andy Robertson's rasping shot from the same distance was tipped over the bar by Lloris. In reply Christian Eriksen scooped his own 25-yarder high over the bar – it was unlike the talented Dane to be so technically deficient. Liverpool had the last chance of the half, James Milner driving the ball narrowly wide after a cute set-up by Salah and Mané.

The second half began as the first ended, Mané's pace and movement causing Spurs endless problems, the Senegalese international setting up Milner for another shot that whisked narrowly past a post. Delle Alli had the best two chances for Spurs. First he scooped a spiralling shot into Alisson Becker's arms, the ball slowing down to allow a comfortable save. Alli then headed over from close range, a missed chance that Spurs came to rue. Son Heung-min powered through the middle of the pitch, beating Liverpool's defence for pace, but the recovering Virgil van Dijk caught him, a long leg clearing the ball before Son could shoot. The effervescent Son tried with all his might to impact the game for Spurs. When Lucas Moura headed down, Son flicked the ball over the bar, but was offside anyway. Another Son shot was beaten away by Alisson, Moura's follow-up too tame. Eriksen's free kick from the left looked to be creeping under the bar, but the alert Alisson watched the flight of the ball all the way to tip the shot over. Liverpool substitute Divock Origi, a hero from the semi-final, had the last laugh. From a right-wing corner-kick, van Dijk's shot was blocked, Fabinho teed up Origi who drove the ball into the far corner of the goal from the left-hand diagonal of the penalty area.

Liverpool possessed the better players on the night: Andy Robertson was a huge influence on the game breaking forward to supplement the attack. Fabinho's calm control in midfield was taken for granted somewhat, but here there was no doubting his influence. For Tottenham, Harry Kane was very subdued. Liverpool were worthy winners. Tottenham didn't realise it at the time, but five years of near misses in semi-finals and finals, a second and third place in the Premier League in two title seasons they might have won, drew to an end here in 2019 at the Wando Metropolitano Stadium. Tottenham's story since this final has been of Pochettino being sacked, José Mourinho replacing him without success, and hopefully a revival under current manager Antonio Conte. It's a story of a fine team unwinding – Eriksen moving to Inter Milan, the ageing Vertonghen and Alderweireld gone from a once stern defence. A story of Harry Kane's frustration as Tottenham's form dwindled, and now a story of another fine, fiercely demanding manager in Conte (formerly successful with Chelsea) arriving to attempt to raise Tottenham's quality once more. There have been positive signs, but also a 2-1 defeat to MS Mura of Slovenia, the lowest ranked team in the newly-formed third tier UEFA European Conference League in a group match. The only way is up, as the song goes.

2021 CHAMPIONS LEAGUE FINAL
Chelsea 1 v 0 Manchester City

The 2020 Champions League Final had been contested by Paris Saint-Germain, seeking their first Champions League/European Cup Final victory, and one of the historic masters of the competition, Bayern Munich. Bayern's 1-0 victory prevented that first European summit success for PSG. The pattern prevailed in the 2021 final in Porto, Portugal. Manchester City's Saudi Arabian-backed wealth led the club to this final along with the astute stewardship of the 21st century's most prominent manager/coach, Pep Guardiola. Like PSG, City couldn't get over the line. Chelsea's new manager Thomas Tuchel, another advocate of high pressing in the modern game, led Chelsea to a third successive victory over Manchester City in the space of a few weeks. Before the game my feeling was that surely City wouldn't succumb to Tuchel's power play for a third successive match, but Chelsea's victory was thoroughly merited.

Route to the Final
Manchester City topped Group C by three points from Porto, the competition's hosts for the final of 2020–21. The two teams met at the City of Stadium in the first group stage match, City triumphing 3-1 with goals from Sergio Agüero (in his last season with the club), Ilkay Gündogan and Fernan Torres. City scored three times again in their second match, Torres, Gündogan and Raheem Sterling securing a 3-0 victory over Marseille in the south of France. The threes kept coming, Torres, Brazilian striker Gabriel Jesus and Portuguese full-back João Cancelo sealing a 3-0 home win over the Greeks of Olympiakos. Two late goals gave this match a slightly heightened impression. In the away tie in Greece, Phil Foden's goal was enough for City to win 1-0. A goalless draw with Porto followed. City completed the group with yet another 3-0 home win, Torres (in fine European competition form), Agüero and an Alvaro own goal the scorers. Again two late strikes created a slightly false impression. City have looked comfortable in the Champions League group games since 2012, only to founder against awkward opponents in the later stages of the competition.

Chelsea's quest for the holy grail of the Champions League started with a different type of manager, the German Thomas Tuchel, a disciple of the *'Gegenpressing'* style of play popularised by Jürgen Klopp, Mauricio Pochettino, and latterly in 2021 by another German coach at Manchester United, Ralf Rangnick. Rangnick lacked the players to carry out the system effectively. Chelsea topped Group E by one point from the splendid Spanish club Seville. The two teams could not be separated at Stamford Bridge in the opening game of the group, a goalless draw resulting. Chelsea made up for the indifference of their start by beating Russian club Krasnodar 4-0 in southern Russia, goals coming from Callum Hudson-Odoi, a Timo Werner penalty, Hakim Ziyech and Christian Pulisic. Werner scored twice, Tammy Abraham netting the other as Chelsea beat French club Rennes 3-0 in their second tie. Hudson-Odoi opened the scoring against Brittany-based Rennes in the return game. Forward Serhou Guirassy equalised with five minutes remaining, and it was left to 34-year-old substitute, French international centre-forward Olivier Giroud to steal the match for the Blues in the 91st minute, It was the next match where the evergreen Giroud truly shone. With Seville's passage to the knockout stages already secured, Giroud scored all four goals in Seville as Chelsea won 4-0 in a match that surely would have offered a different scoreline if qualification was an issue. Unsurprisingly, Chelsea coasted in their last match, drawing 1-1 with the hapless Russians of Krasnador, Jorginho's penalty goal almost an irrelevance.

Borussia Möenchengladbach provided scant resistance to the powerful Manchester City team in the last 16, both ties won 2-0 by City. With Covid-19 ravaging Europe, the matches were played a fortnight apart in the same Puskás Arena in Budapest, Hungary. The away game City won with goals from the Portuguese attacking midfielder Bernardo Silva and Jesus. Kevin De Bruyne and Gündogan sealed a second 2-0 victory a fortnight later in the home game. Hungary was deemed at the time to be one of the European nations with the least devastating outbreak of Covid-19, the damaging virus that ruled the lives of the world's populace after March 2020.

City similarly won through to the last eight with identical 2-1 victories against Borussia Dortmund of Germany. This time the ties took place at the home venues of the clubs, but without any supporters in attendance, as in Budapest in the last 16. At the City of Manchester Stadium, the outstanding De Bruyne gave the sky blues an early lead, only for German international forward Marco Reus to equalise in the 84th minute. Phil Foden, City's bright young English international starlet, only impacting fully on his team since the departure of the mercurial Spaniard David Silva, rescued City with a 90th-minute winner. At the Westfalenstadion, Dortmund, another hugely impressive English youngster, Jude Bellingham, a player mature well beyond his 18 years, gave Dortmund a 15th-minute lead. City played a patient game, Riyad Mahrez equalising with a 54th-minute penalty, Foden snatching the winner in the 75th minute. This looked like being City's year – at long last after a decade of trying – to win the 2020–21 Champions League, when the highly fancied French team Paris Saint-Germain, beaten finalists in 2019–20, were seen off 4-1 on aggregate in the semi-finals. De Bruyne and Mahrez replied to an early opener by Brazilian defender Marquinhos for PSG in Paris. In Manchester, City won 2-0 with a pair from the skilful Mahrez.

That City were not to win their much-cherished European summit title was down to the tireless work ethic and sheer bloody-mindedness and organisation instilled into Chelsea by the incoming German coach Thomas Tuchel. Chelsea had been beaten before by last 16 opponents Atlético Madrid, but under Tuchel the team tightened up in the manner of their notoriously defensively organised Spanish adversaries. Atlético coach, the Argentine master of defensive nous in Europe and the world over the last decade, Diego Simeone, found himself beaten at his own game by Chelsea. It was the Stamford Bridge outfit who didn't concede a goal in the two ties. The veteran Giroud came up trumps again with the only goal of Atlético's 'home' game in Bucharest, Romania. These were strange times, times that continue to feel awkward, devoid of reality, the reality of personal contact between supporters, times of fanatical club passion from blinkered, loyal fans whose attachment to their clubs was undying. The return game, held at an empty Stamford Bridge ground in south-west London, saw Ziyech give Chelsea a lead that was added to in injury time by Brazilian left-back Emerson Palmieri, the Blues running out 2-0 winners on the night, and 3-0 on aggregate.

Portuguese club Porto couldn't stem the new Chelsea tide under Tuchel in the last eight, Mason Mount and Ben Chilwell, two of the excellent young England internationals thriving under great coaching at Chelsea, and with national manager Gareth Southgate, notching goals in Portugal to seemingly render the tie meaningless. Porto didn't buckle in London, Chelsea couldn't score, and a 94th-minute goal by Iranian striker Mehdi Taremi for the Portuguese team saw Chelsea creep through to the semi-finals 2-1 on aggregate.

The mighty Real Madrid stood in Chelsea's way of a final appearance. American international Christian Pulisic opened the scoring at the Alfredo Di Stéfano Stadium in Madrid, the prolific French striker Karim Benzema equalising. Evenly poised at 1-1 at the Bridge, Chelsea raised their game substantially, beating Real 2-0 with goals from Werner and Mount putting them in the final.

City's goalkeeper on the night, the Brazilian Ederson, is virtually on a par with Liverpool's Alisson Becker. Ederson is a great shot-stopper, and part of the much-vaunted brigade of modern sweeper-keepers. Pep Guardiola, a great believer in building from the back, values Ederson as an extra outfield player, a keeper prepared, and willing to be the basis of his team's desire to play football starting from their own goalline. Ederson began his youth career at Sao Paulo before playing two years junior football with Benfica in Portugal. He played at second and third division level in Portugal with Ribeiro and Rio Ave before returning to Benfica for the 2015–16 season, winning the Portuguese Primeira Liga in his first full season. He helped Benfica reach the 2015–16 Champions League quarter-finals, where (no disgrace) his team lost 3-2 on aggregate to Bayern Munich.

Ederson joined Manchester City in June 2017, making an instant impact upon the team, replacing the less consistent Claudio Bravo as City's first-choice goalkeeper. In July 2020 Ederson received the Golden Glove Award for the most clean sheets (16) in the 2019–20 Premier League season. His excellent distribution from the back makes him key to Guardiola's favoured possession-based style of football. Quick, agile, decisive, Ederson can be excused for the odd gaff in losing possession at the back – it's the goalkeeper's lot. He's played just 18 times for Brazil since 2017 (August 2022). Many more caps may follow, if he can dislodge the outstanding Alisson Becker.

It was good to see England internationals playing in the defences of both teams on this night. Kyle Walker, at right-back for City, has become a regular starter in Gareth Southgate's England team, his pace a useful weapon for club and country, but particularly so for England where he's called upon to cover for two footballing centre-halves in Harry Maguire and John Stones. These two players are excellent technicians, but both are prone to the odd lapse, or in the case of Maguire, a little susceptible to pacy, tricky forwards. Walker had Stones alongside him for City on this night, but in Rúben Dias, the other centre-back for City he had a teammate bang in form, and playing more consistently than his English counterparts, Walker's international teammates. Walker too has suffered inconsistent form at times, but now in his 30s he appears to be a more rounded performer.

Kyle Walker started out with his home city club Sheffield United 2008–10, helping the club to a 2009 Championship play-off final which they lost 1-0 to Burnley, Walker becoming the youngest Sheffield United player to play at Wembley. He was loaned out to Northampton Town before signing for Tottenham Hotspur in July 2009. Loaned back to Sheffield United initially, he then spent loan spells with Queens Park Rangers and Aston Villa. When he finally established himself at Tottenham in the 2011–12 season he was awarded the PFA Young Player of the Year honour in April 2012, also being included in the PFA Team of the Year for 2011–12. Walker's form wavered at times at Tottenham, although he was named again in the PFA Team of the Year for 2016–17.

Since joining Manchester City in July 2017 Walker has become more consistent under the wise guidance of Pep Guardiola. He has won four Premier League titles with City in five years – sadly it looks like his decision to leave Tottenham was a good one. Walker has played 68 internationals to date (August 2022), usually as a right-back, but at the 2018 World Cup Gareth Southgate deployed him in a defensive three at the back with Stones and Maguire. Back at right-back for the 2020 Euros, Walker was selected in the Team of the Tournament as England succumbed on penalties to the wily Italians in the final at Wembley after the game ended 1-1.

John Stones might be the best footballing centre-half English football has produced in recent years – since Rio Ferdinand probably. Maguire may perceive himself as Stones's equal. Stones improved his defensive positioning under Guardiola, although lapses of concentration still cost him at times. Like Walker, Stones began his professional career with his hometown club, in this instance, Barnsley. He moved to Everton in January 2013, his form sufficient for Chelsea to make three bids for him that were rejected in 2015.

Stones instead stayed in the north, signing for Manchester City in August 2016. Since then it has been a constant struggle – one which to his eternal credit Stones has largely won – to hold down a regular starting place in Guardiola's multinational, multi-talented team. Stones's £47.5 million transfer made him the second most expensive transferring defender in football history, behind only David Luiz. Despite his travails at the club, Stones has recently signed a new five-year contract with City.

For England, Stones has represented his country at U-19, U-20, U-21 and senior level (58 caps, August 2022). At the 2018 World Cup, Stones scored twice in the 6-1 thrashing of Panama in the group stages. Guardiola clearly admires Stones, a ball-playing centre-half. He's the closest thing in English football to the great Franz Beckenbauer as a sweeper centre-half. Those occasional indecisions haunt him sometimes – but I would rather have a centre-back who can play rather than an out-and-out stopper. The misgiving? Stones and Maguire in the same defence for England might be regarded as a luxury.

Stones has the comfort of the excellent Portuguese central defender Rúben Dias alongside him at club level. Dias is only 25 as I write, but plays with a maturity and certainty well beyond his tender years. Since joining Manchester City from Benfica in September 2020, City have rediscovered the calmness at the heart of their defence that the great leader Vincent Kompany gave them for a decade. Voted the Primeira Liga's Best Young Player of the Year in 2017–18, Dias has swiftly cemented a place in the Portuguese national side. Dias has exhibited great leadership skills in his short time at City, bringing composure to the team's defence, winning the Football Writer's Footballer of the Year Award in his first full season, 2020–21. Dias was the first defender to win the award since Liverpool's Steve Nicol in the 1998–99 season. Dias also won Manchester City's Player of the Season and the Premier League Player of the Season, earning a triple haul of personal accolades in his first season in England. He's played 37 times for Portugal, having represented his country at U-16, U-17, U-19, U-20 and U-21 level (December 2021).

Dias has now displaced the ex-Southampton (currently at Lille in France) centre-back José Fonte for Portugal, playing alongside the experienced Pepe (ex-Real Madrid, latterly Porto). Winning the inaugural 2019 UEFA Nations League Final 1-0 against Holland, Dias was named Man of the Match. He was in the team at the 2020 Euros, although Portugal exited in the last 16, losing 1-0 to Belgium. Two-footed, excellent on the ground, composed, a natural leader with a keen sense of anticipation that allows him to intercept balls and stop attacks at source, Dias is already one of the world's best centre-backs.

Left-back, Ukrainian international (52 caps, eight goals, August 2022) Oleksandr Zinchenko, is one of his country's brightest stars, even if he goes under the radar a little in Manchester City's team of all talents. Zinchenko represented the Ukraine at U-16, U-17, U-18, U-19 and U-21 level before progressing to the senior national team. Signing for Manchester City in July 2016, Zinchenko found himself loaned out to PSV Eindhoven in Holland for the 2016–17 season. Returning to City for the 2017–18 season, Zinchenko had French international Benjamin Mendy and the experienced Fabian Delph for competition for the left-back spot. Poor form and injuries to this pair gave Zinchenko the chance to establish himself as City's first choice left-back. A solid acquisition for City, Zinchenko signed for Arsenal for the 2022–23 season.

David Silva having moved on, it has been left to England's great new hope Phil Foden, and the Portuguese attacking midfielder Bernardo Silva to step up to the plate. Bernardo Silva's form in the 2021–22 Premier League season suggested he was doing just that. Silva, Lisbon-born, plied his trade briefly with home city team Benfica, earning the accolade of the 2013–14 Segunda Liga (2nd Division) Breakthrough Player of the Year playing for Benfica B. He was loaned to Monaco in France for the 2014–15 season, earning a permanent move 2015–17. He ended his second 2016–17 season in the south of France with 11 goals and 12 assists in all competitions. Silva impressed in the knockout stages of the 2016–17 Champions

League. The City of Manchester Stadium became his new home in May 2017.

Silva played 53 games in all competitions in 2017–18, more than any other City player, helping City to a Premier League title with a record 100 points total and the EFL Cup (formerly the old Football League Cup). A further 51 appearances in the 2018–19 season reaped 13 goals and 14 assists in all competitions. Silva's influence in this season was crucial as City's outstanding Kevin De Bruyne missed large chunks of the year through injury. The loss of De Bruyne's obvious quality was negated by Silva's performances, City retaining their title. The five feet eight inches Silva was duly named as Manchester City Player of the Season, voted for by the club's fans, and was named in the PFA Team of the Year. Silva was apparently unsettled – could it be the incessant Manchester rain making the Portuguese pine for sunnier climes? Silva stayed, winning three consecutive Player of the Month awards. In the form of his life, the decision was a good one for City.

In August 2022 Bernardo Silva had played 166 Premier League games (29 goals) for City. For Portugal, Silva's tally thus far during the same period reads 70 caps, eight goals. Silva featured in all four games for Portugal at the 2018 World Cup, Portugal being eliminated in the last 16, 1-2 against Uruguay. Portugal won the inaugural 2018–19 UEFA Nations League Final on home soil, Silva winning the Player of the Tournament Award. Silva again appeared in all Portugal's 2020 Euros games, his country exiting against Belgium in the last 16. Silva's slight frame and excellent close control have enabled him to step effortlessly into the shoes of Spanish namesake David Silva at Manchester City.

Phil Foden has been touted as English football's best young player since Wayne Rooney exploded into the Premier League with the winning strike against Arsenal as a 16-year-old in October 2002. Foden's breakthrough as a teenager came at the same age, assisting England's winning of the FIFA U-17 World Cup. Foden won the Golden Ball award for Best Player in the tournament. His performance in the final was exceptional as England swept Spain aside 5-2, Foden scoring twice, his pace and trickery too hot for the Spanish to handle.

Phil Foden joined Manchester City aged four! Born in the Manchester satellite town of Stockport, Foden was always destined to play for City. Pep Guardiola raves about Foden's natural talent, but initially, despite being tagged with future superstar status, Foden's place in the team was blocked by the two outstanding Silvas, David and Bernardo, in addition to Kevin De Bruyne. I am all for quality foreign players raising the level of English football teams, but it's very frustrating when a player of Foden's class is held back. Guardiola argues that he's been mentoring Foden, introducing him into the first team piecemeal, rather than exposing him too soon to the rigours of senior football.

Aged 17, Foden became the youngest player to ever receive a Premier League winner's medal in the 2017–18 season. Foden scored his first Champions League goal (Manchester City and English football's youngest ever scorer) against Schalke 04 in the 7-0 home win in the last 16 of the 2018–19 campaign. In the 2019–20 Champions league group stages, Foden's assists total of six was beaten only by the incomparable Lionel Messi (seven). Foden won the Alan Hardaker Trophy (the ex-secretary of the English Football League and founder of the League Cup) as Man of the Match as City defeated Aston Villa 2-1 to win the League Cup. City bowed to Liverpool as champions of the 2019–20 Premier League season, but as a reminder to Liverpool that they would not take the slight lying down, Foden scored as City beat the new champions 4-0 in July 2020, the culmination of the Covid-19 disrupted season. Foden had begun to be accepted as a regular in the City team, scoring eight goals and providing nine assists in all competitions.

Liverpool's defence disrupted by injuries to Virgil van Dijk and Joe Gomez, Foden led an impressive victory at Anfield in February 2021, scoring and assisting as City ran out comfortable 4-1 winners. City and Foden were fizzing, the youngster assisting Riyad Mahrez's match-winner against Borussia Dortmund in the Champions League quarter-finals and scoring himself in both legs of the semi-finals against Paris Saint-Germain as City won 4-1 on aggregate. In May 2020–21 a third Premier League in four seasons was secured by City, Foden winning the Premier League Young Player of the Year and the PFA Young Player of the Year awards.

Understandable excitement surrounded Foden's impact on English football as he represented England at U-16, U-17, U-18, U-19 and U-21 levels, scoring 21 goals in the process. Foden debuted for the senior national team in a 1-0 away win in Iceland in the UEFA Nations League tournament in September 2020. In the return game at Wembley, Foden scored his first two senior international goals – his only international goals to date (August 2022). Blessed with the best crop of young players the country has had for a decade, Gareth Southgate has not yet made Foden a regular starter in the national team, but surely it's only a matter of time – and maturity – before Phil Foden's full repertoire of skills is unleashed on the best defences in world football. Foden is not especially quick, but his touch, technique and general football ability appear to make him a worthy successor indeed to the mini-marvel that was David Silva in the 2010s at Manchester City.

I have loved language all my life. I read avidly as a boy; my wife suffers the fact that I always have my head in a book, newspaper or magazine with exceptional grace. I have dabbled in Italian, Spanish, French, Norwegian, Greek, Portuguese/Brazilian, Mandarin and Finnish languages purely for travel/holiday purposes without gaining fluency in any of them. I love wordplay, learning about the derivation of words and language. Why is the German international midfielder's Ilkay Gündogan's surname pronounced Gund-o-wan? Specifically, because Gündogan has Turkish parents, although he was born in Gelsenkirchen, North Rhine-Westphalia, the largest urban area in Germany. Language is a constantly curious and wonderful thing, isn't it?

Gündogan helped Borussia Dortmund stem the irresistible tide in German football that is Bayern Munich in his time at Dortmund 2011–16. Having spent two seasons at IFC Nurnberg 2009–11 (48 Bundesliga appearances, six goals), Gündogan transferred to Borussia Dortmund in May 2011. In the semi-final of the DFB Pokal Cup in March 2012, Gündogan's 120th-minute goal took Dortmund into a final against Bayern Munich. With Polish super-striker Robert Lewandowski on fire in the final – he netted a hat-trick – Dortmund surprisingly won the Cup with a handsome 5-2 margin victory over Bayern, in so doing completing the double in the 2011–12 season, denying the great German team either trophy. Bayern exacted revenge in the 2012–13 Champions League Final, beating Dortmund 2-1 at Wembley, Gündogan netting a penalty for Dortmund, but the irrepressible Arjen Robben scored an 89th-minute winner for Bayern. In his last season with Dortmund (2015–16), Gündogan scored in a semi-final DFB Pokal shoot-out victory over Bayern once more. Dortmund then surprisingly lost the final to VfL Wolfsburg, a certain Kevin De Bruyne scoring in a 3-1 scoreline. Football is no respecter of reputations.

In June 2016 Gündogan signed for Manchester City, becoming Pep Guardiola's first signing for the club as new manager. In December 2016 Gündogan tore knee ligaments, missing the rest of the 2016–17 season. Returning to fitness, Gündogan enjoyed an especially fruitful 2020–21 season, ending the season as City's highest scorer in the Premier League with 13 goals.

Gündogan has won 60 caps, scoring 15 goals, for Germany (August 2022). A friendly match against Paraguay in August 2013, drawn 3-3, saw Gündogan leave the field with a back injury that would keep him out of Germany's successful conquest of the 2014 World Cup. Unlucky with injury, Gündogan was also ruled out of the 2016 Euros. He returned, selected for the subsequent 2018 World Cup and the 2020 Euros, although Germany's national team struggled to recapture the glory of the 2014 World Cup victory. Gündogan is a versatile midfielder, capable of playing the holding role in the midfield, capable also of being a playmaker or offensive midfielder. He has great energy, and scored crucial goals for City in the 2020–21 season. He just needs a little more luck with injuries.

Gündogan's teammate and conqueror in that 2015–16 DFB Pokal Cup Final, Kevin De Bruyne, has become one of the world's most complete midfield players of the last decade. His formative professional years were spent with Genk in his native Belgium 2008–12. After winning the 2010–11 Belgian Pro League at Genk, De Bruyne was on the radar of Europe's top clubs. Then came the move that Chelsea must rue did not work out for the club as De Bruyne has become the best forward-passing midfielder in world football. Others have kept possession better it could be argued – Xavi and Iniesta the obvious candidates – but no other midfielder in world football possesses De Bruyne's capacity to play the eye of the needle ball, to pace the ball with metronomic precision – and he's a useful goalscorer too.

De Bruyne signed for Chelsea in January 2012 but played only three Premier League games in two seasons at Stamford Bridge. In January 2012 De Bruyne was loaned out to Werder Bremen. José Mourinho assured De Bruyne he had a future with Chelsea upon returning to the Blues and De Bruyne returned to the club in July 2013. Despite assisting a goal in the opening game of the 2013–14 season as Chelsea beat Hull City 2-0, De Bruyne, unhappy at a lack of regular first team football, moved again in January 2014 to VfL Wolfsburg, feeling wanted in the Bundesliga.

De Bruyne had scored ten goals in 33 Bundesliga games for Werder Bremen. He followed this with 13 in 52 for VfL Wolfsburg. In January 2015 De Bruyne served notice of his quality, scoring twice in a 4-1 victory over Bayern Munich, Bayern's first Bundesliga defeat since April 2014. De Bruyne ended the 2014–15 season with ten goals and 21 assists, the latter a new Bundesliga record, VfL

Wolfsburg finishing second behind… Bayern Munich. He ultimately totalled 16 goals and 28 assists in all competitions, and won the 2015 Germany Footballer of the Year Award. It would be fair to say Kevin De Bruyne had arrived as a force in European and world football.

In August 2015 De Bruyne signed a six-year contract with Manchester City. His return to the Premier League announced a more rounded player than the one briefly seen at Chelsea 2012–14. De Bruyne's £55 million move made him the second most expensive transferee in British football history after the Argentine international Angel Di Maria's move to Manchester United in 2014 from Real Madrid. There is little doubt which player has made the biggest impact in Manchester and England. De Bruyne, when not injured, has been simply sensational for Manchester City, pulling the strings in midfield, playing penetrating passes with precision pace like no other player on the planet. Di Maria by comparison was disappointing, scoring only three times in 27 Premier League games, although he has revived his career in recent years at Paris Saint-Germain. Only a litany of injuries has prevented De Bruyne's impact at City being even greater.

In his first 2015–16 season, after an impressive start to life at City, a knee injury kept De Bruyne out for two months in the spring of 2016. Returning against Bournemouth in the Premier League on 2 April, he scored in a 4-0 win on the south coast of England. Four days later he opened the scoring at the Parc des Princes as City drew 2-2 in the Champions League quarter-finals. Ten days later he scored the winner as City beat PSG to confirm a 3-2 aggregate victory and advance to the semi-finals. Sadly, City couldn't maximise their fine result, losing by a solitary Fernando own goal in Spain against Real Madrid over two legs. Pep Guardiola praised De Bruyne's special qualities at the end of this season, his innate capacity to see everything clearly on a football pitch.

De Bruyne's consistent excellence in a City shirt earned him a new long-term contract in January 2018, keeping him (ostensibly, nothing is certain in top-level professional football) at the club until 2023. City's 3-0 defeat of Arsenal in the 2017–18 EFL Cup Final gave the club their first silverware under Guardiola. With 16 assists in the 2017–18 Premier League season, De Bruyne won the inaugural Premier League Playmaker of the Season award. He was also voted the Manchester City Player of the Season, winning selection to the PFA Team of the Year. A further injury to the same right knee in August 2018 during a training session put De Bruyne out of action for three months. Returning in October 2018 he once again injured the knee in a fourth round EFL cup tie against Fulham. Coming on as a substitute in the 2019 FA Cup Final against Watford, De Bruyne scored the third goal and assisted two more as City ran out rampant 6-0 winners. De Bruyne, only on the pitch from the 56th minute, won the Man of the Match award. City won the first English domestic treble of Premier League, FA Cup and EFL Cup for the 2018–19 season. De Bruyne's influence on Manchester City had become irresistible.

In the 2019–20 season he scored 13 goals, assisted 20 more (equalling Thierry Henry's previous record), won the Premier League Player of the Season, was named in the PFA Team of the Year, and won the PFA Player of the Year, the first

Manchester City player to achieve the feat. In April 2021, De Bruyne signed a new four-year contract with City, keeping him at the club until 2025 (all being well). De Bruyne scored at the Parc des Princes again as City beat Paris Saint-Germain 2-1 in the 2020–21 Champions League semi-final first leg. Two goals from Riyad Mahrez in Manchester sealed a comfortable 4-1 aggregate victory. City failed to win the trophy, denied by their 2021 nemesis club Chelsea. A nose bone and eye socket injury suffered in a collision with Antonio Rudiger in the final curtailed his Champions League final appearance, De Bruyne leaving the field after an hour.

De Bruyne had scored 57 Premier League goals in 207 appearances come August 2022, but it's his outstanding passing/assisting of goals that has made an even bigger contribution to his club since signing in 2015. Winner of the 2020–21 PFA Player's Player of the Year award, if De Bruyne stays fit silverware for City is all but guaranteed.

In 91 internationals for Belgium De Bruyne had scored 24 goals by August 2022. A major trophy eludes his country despite Belgium's recent No. 1 world ranking. Like winning the European Cup/Champions League, winning the World Cup or Euros is not a given when you have Brazil, Argentina, Germany, Italy, Spain, France for competition. Like his club, Manchester City, Belgium have not been able to attain the summit of football at international level.

De Bruyne has a Belgian father and a mother born in Burundi, Africa. Opting for Belgian international status, De Bruyne was capped at U-18, U-19 and U-21 level. He became a regular for Belgium in the 2014 World Cup qualifiers, scoring four goals. At the 2014 World Cup tournament De Bruyne scored in the last 16 as Belgium beat the USA 2-1 after extra time, only to lose to eventual finalists Argentina in the last eight 1-0. After routing Hungary in the last 16 of the 2016 Euros, Belgium came unstuck in losing surprisingly 3-1 to a passionate Welsh team in the quarter-finals. At the 2018 World Cup, De Bruyne was outstanding in an advanced false nine role as Belgium beat Brazil 2-1, scoring the winner, and winning the Man of the Match award. Once again the final hurdle could not be taken as France beat Belgium 1-0 in the semi-finals. In June 2021 at the delayed 2020 Euros, De Bruyne assisted the first goal and scored the winner as Belgium beat Denmark 2-1 in Group B. Belgium topped the group, but lost 2-1 to Italy in the last eight, De Bruyne playing after suffering an ankle injury in the last 16, 1-0 win over Portugal. That final victory, a World Cup or Euros trophy looks like eluding Belgium's talented golden generation in the same way England's Gerrard-Beckham-Lampard-Scholes-Ashley Cole-Terry generation failed to live up to their reputations internationally.

Kevin De Bruyne's unnerving precision passing help make him the best advanced attacking midfielder in world football over the last six or seven seasons. He also possesses a thunderous shot, and leads City and Belgium's counter-attacks with huge threat. Pep Guardiola believes he is the best midfielder in the world in 2022 – not bad for a Chelsea 'misfit'!

Strikers Raheem Sterling and Riyad Mahrez gave City great pace and variety in attack. Mahrez signed from Leicester City in 2018, not long after the Midlands club sensationally won the Premier League in 2015–16. Mahrez, along with Jamie Vardy, were Leicester's break-out players, Vardy having risen from semi-professional football; Mahrez an under-the-radar signing from Le Havre in France. Born in Sarcelles, a commune in the northern suburbs of Paris to an Algerian father and an Algerian/Moroccan mother, Mahrez could have represented France. Slight of build, Mahrez was initially overlooked by professional clubs. Only upon developing his considerable ball skills did Mahrez begin to attract attention. Mahrez trialled with St Mirren in Scotland, but left due to the bitingly cold weather. Instead he ended up in rainy Manchester!

In 2010 Mahrez joined Le Havre in the French Ligue 2, but was unimpressed with the defensive nature of the league. He could have no such qualms after joining a Leicester City side in 2013–14 whose attack grew substantially with his signing. Leicester's chief scout Steve Walsh was actually vetting Mahrez's teammate Ryan Mendes, but left the Le Havre game he'd been watching with a new target. In Mahrez's first season in the Championship, Leicester won the title, earning a return to the Premiership for the first time in ten years. The club's first season back in the top tier was a struggle, but winning seven of their final nine games was only the beginning of their miracles. Mahrez's four goals in 30 games didn't suggest Leicester had bought a new superstar player.

In the first three games of the 2015–16 season Mahrez gave notice that he had properly adapted to the Premier League by scoring four goals – the same total as the previous season in 27 less games! His hat-trick against Swansea City made him the first Algerian to score three in one match in the Premier League. By the season's end Mahrez had aided Leicester's shock Premiership title triumph, been named in the PFA Team of the Year, and won the PFA Player's Player of the Year award. No Algerian had previously won the Premier League. Mahrez was voted by BBC radio listeners the 2016 African Footballer of the Year, but with Leicester unable to repeat their 2015–16 form, the 2016–17 season proved something of an anti-climax. At least Mahrez shone in the Champions League, proving he was no flash-in-the-pan, as Leicester reached the quarter-finals, only losing out 2-1 on aggregate to Diego Simeone's tough as nails Atlético Madrid.

Mahrez, increasingly ambitious, attracted interest from Arsenal and Italian club A.S. Roma in the 2017–18 season, before a move to Manchester City fell through. He was subsequently criticised for a failure to train with Leicester as a result, although his teammates didn't turn against him. In July 2018 the move to Manchester City finally happened, his £60-million transfer making him the most expensive African player of all time. Mahrez cited the hope of winning the Champions League as his reason for pressing for the move. He played 14 Premier League games at City in 2018–19, sufficient to become only the second African player to win the Premier League with two clubs along with Kolo Touré (Arsenal, Manchester City). He began to find a way into the starting line-up in the following two seasons 2019–20, 2020–21, believing in himself after expecting a slow transition into a City team replete with international talents. Mahrez confirmed his importance to City in the Champions League semi-final of 2020–21, scoring the two goals as City defeated Paris Saint-Germain 2-0 in the second leg at the City of Manchester Stadium.

In 2013 Mahrez decided upon Algeria as his international country of choice, being called up to the 2014 World Cup squad. He played in Algeria's opening game of the tournament against Belgium, but played no further part as Algeria reached the last 16, losing 2-1 to Germany in extra time. It was the Germans' narrowest squeak as they went on to win the tournament. After several vain attempts to win the African Nations Cup, Algeria managed the feat for the first time since 1990 in 2019. Mahrez scored a 95th-minute winner in the semi-finals against Nigeria. Algeria went on to beat Senegal 1-0 in the final. Mahrez has scored 26 goals in 75 internationals, August 2022.

Mahrez's pace, balance and outstanding close control make him a formidable opponent for any defence. Steve Walsh saw in Mahrez a player with exquisite touch, a player who once exposed to the physical levels of English football, and increased fitness levels, could develop into a world-beating player. How Walsh has been proven right, Mahrez's 38 goals in 115 Premier League games (August 2022) supplemented by countless assists.

Raheem Sterling has become a crucial component in Gareth Southgate's young England team, his electric pace terrifying the world's sternest defences. It seems there's always a but with Raheem though. Many fans feel he doesn't score enough goals – and he's not an out-and-out striker in the mould of Harry Kane. Yet Sterling helped City win back-to-back Premier League titles in 2017–18 and 2018–19. In the latter season his form earned him the PFA Young Player of the Year and the FWA Footballer of the Year awards. In recent times Sterling has been left out of City's starting 11 on occasions by Pep Guardiola, but I feel this is as much to do with the multitude of attacking talents at Guardiola's disposal and modern-day squad rotation, as much as any serious dip in Sterling's form. Sterling has been at the forefront of the appalling trolling of black English players. As time has passed by he has become a justifiably outspoken critic of these so-called 'fans'. Frustrated at lack of game-time, Sterling eventually took the decision to move to Chelsea for the 2022–23 season.

In the age of ludicrously top-heavy international staffed top clubs, City could call upon Aymeric Laporte of Spain, Benjamin Mendy of France, Joao Cancelo of Portugal as defensive cover; Rodri of Spain and Fernandinho of Brazil to give the team defensive midfield cover; and Gabriel Jesus of Brazil, Sergio Agüero of Argentina (admittedly at the end of a sparkling career with the club) and Fernan Torres, the young Spanish striker, as attacking replacements.

Chelsea's goalkeeper, the Senegalese Edouard Mendy, has performed in inspiring fashion in the last couple of years, only to suffer the keepers' plague of inconsistency in the 2021–22 season. A human wall at times, Mendy's consistency was certainly sufficient to usurp the less consistent Spanish international Kepa Arrizabelaga from the first team.

Mendy played third division football in France for Cherbourg before progressing to Reims and Rennes higher up the French leagues. He almost quit football after being released by Cherbourg in 2014. Becoming a regular at Reims he helped the club win Ligue 2 in 2017–18, keeping 18 clean sheets in 34 games. In 2018–19 in the top tier, Mendy kept 14 clean sheets in 38 games. After signing for Rennes, Mendy kept nine clean sheets in a pandemic-shortened 24 league matches in the 2019–20 season.

In September 2020, Mendy signed for Chelsea. Mendy immediately emulated the great Petr Cech in keeping clean sheets in his first three Premier League games with Chelsea. In this 2021 Champions League Final Mendy became the first African goalkeeper to partake in the top tier European Cup Final since the Zimbabwean Bruce Grobbelaar appeared for Liverpool in 1985. Mendy's nine clean sheets in the 2020–21 Champions League campaign equalled the previous record set by Santiago Canizares for Valencia in the 2000–01 season and Real Madrid's Keylor Navas in 2015–16. Dominant and assertive in his own penalty area, Mendy has also been a strong vocal organiser of the Chelsea defence. Come August 2022 on the horizon Mendy had played 25 times for Senegal.

Chelsea opted for a fluid 5-2-2-1 formation on the night, with the athletic, solid Spaniard César Azpilicueta captaining the team. Alongside Azpilicueta were two tremendous exponents of defensive football, Brazilian icon Thiago Silva, and German strong man Antonio Rudiger. Silva signed for Chelsea as an experienced 36 years old. Now 37, and at an age where he would expect to be past his best, Silva has confounded his critics with his astute positional play and reading of the game.

Thiago Silva is a serial winner – the Copa do Brasil in 2007 with his native Fluminense in 2007; Serie A winner in Italy with AC Milan in 2010–11; Ligue 1 in France with Paris Saint-Germain in eight of his nine seasons in Paris – and a five-time Coupe de France winner. He didn't need to win the Champions League to prove his quality, but after being a runner-up against Bayern Munich in 2019–20 with PSG, he righted the wrong by winning the trophy in 2020–21 with Chelsea. Alessandro Nesta and Paolo Maldini at AC Milan claimed that Silva was a champion player with all the defensive attributes of the very best players in his position in the world. In the Serie A-winning season of 2010–11 Silva was voted the Milan Player of the Season. The Italian media also voted him the best defender in Serie A.

Money-rich Qatari-owned Paris Saint-Germain signed Silva in the summer of 2012, although Silva claimed to be happy with Milan. The trophies flooded in as PSG dominated French football for the next decade. Silva's time at Chelsea will only be short-lived, but he has categorically proven doubters wrong with his displays since signing in August 2020. To date (August 2022) Silva has played 107 times for Brazil. An unused substitute at the 2010 World Cup, Silva went on to captain his country at the 2014 World Cup, but did not play in the humiliating 1-7 drubbing by Germany in the semi-finals. The debacle showed that manager Luiz Felipe Scolari's loss of Silva to suspension due to an accumulation of yellow cards was critical. Silva's all-round game has led to his inclusion in his teams as a defensive midfielder at times, but it was his outstanding tactical intelligence that shone in the heart of Chelsea's defence 2020–2022.

Antonio Rudiger, the six feet three inches Berlin-born German international received plenty of acclaim for his tenacious performances in Chelsea's defence as the 21st century entered its third decade. There were many who doubted him initially at Chelsea, not least his manager before Thomas Tuchel, Frank Lampard, but recent displays earmarked by his tough-tackling, aggressive, no-nonsense style made him a target for other leading clubs in Germany and Spain.

Rudiger made his name with VfB Stuttgart, reaching the final of the DFB Pokal in 2014, only to lose 3-2 to Bayern Munich. He joined A.S. Roma on loan in August 2015, the move becoming permanent in the 2016–17 season. His time at Roma was typified by two red cards received in February 2017 against Villareal in a Europa League defeat, and against Lazio in a 3-1 Serie A reverse in April 2017. Rudiger always plays on the edge, a trait admired by professional managers and players alike.

In July 2017 Rudiger signed a five-year contract with Chelsea. He won the FA Cup in 2018, the Europa League in 2019 and this Champions League trophy in 2021. His competitive spirit has been there for all to see. He could have played for Sierra Leone, his mother's homeland, but from 2010–14 his choice of Germany was borne out by caps at U-18, U-19, U-20 and U-21 level. A torn anterior cruciate ligament in his right knee kept him out of the 2016 Euros, returning to help Germany win the final of the 2017 Confederations Cup held in Russia, 1-0 against Chile. Replacing first choice centre-back Mats Hummels (injured) against Sweden in the second 2018 World Cup group game, Rudiger helped his country win 2-1. In the final group game, the infamous 0-2 defeat to South Korea which saw Germany eliminated, Rudiger was not selected. At the 2020 Euros Rudiger was finally seen as a permanent fixture in Germany's defence, but he couldn't prevent the 2-0 defeat to England in the last 16. Rudiger departed for Real Madrid in the summer of 2022. Chelsea will miss his diligence and professionalism.

The two young 'wing-backs' for Chelsea, Reece James and Ben Chilwell, were part of the team's nominal five-man defence, but given license to roam further forward thanks to the vast experience of Azpilicueta, Thiago Silva and Rudiger covering behind them. Both players excel in foraging upfield, scoring many crucial goals over the last two seasons. James comes from a footballing family, his sister Lauren a forward for Chelsea womens' professional team. He trained with Chelsea aged six, moving to Fulham at seven years of age. Rejoining Chelsea, James captained the winning U-18 FA Youth Cup team in 2017–18 after turning professional in March 2017. He was loaned to Wigan Athletic in the Championship for the 2018–19 season, winning the club's Player of the Year award, and being selected for the Championship Team of the Year. James returned to Chelsea with a vengeance, firmly establishing himself from 2019–20, and making his mark for Gareth Southgate's England national team also. In November 2019 James became Chelsea's youngest ever Champions League scorer in the 4-4 draw with Ajax.

The sturdily built James offers pace and a trusty physical prowess to Chelsea and England's right flank. He represented England at U-18, U-19, U-20 and U-21 level before debuting in the senior team against Wales at Wembley as a second half substitute for Kieran Trippier. James's form in 2021 made him foremost in Southgate's thinking for England. His performances for Chelsea, where he has been an outstanding supplement for an at times ineffective attack, have been increasingly important to the team. In August 2022 James had been capped 13 times by England.

Ben Chilwell excelled as an attacking left-back first with Claudio Ranieri's Leicester City, although he didn't feature enough to win a Premier League winners' medal in Leicester's astonishing 2015–16 triumph. Ninety-nine Premier League games at Leicester 2015–20 saw Chilwell earmarked as an outstanding contributor to the team's attacking style under Brendan Rogers. Despite signing a new contract in October 2018, Chilwell decided to leave for Chelsea, doubtless anticipating greater things at the perennially successful south-west London club. Some thought Chilwell disloyal to Leicester. Ironically, Chilwell's goal in the 88th minute of the 2021 FA Cup Final against his former club was controversially ruled out, Youri Tielemans' goal deciding the match for Leicester. Chilwell started the 2021–22 season in fine fettle, becoming the first English player to score in four consecutive Premier League games since Frank Lampard in February 2013, but injury has since curtailed his progress at the club.

Named in England's 26-man squad for the 2020 Euros, Chilwell and teammate Mason Mount were required to self-isolate after close contact with Scottish youngster Billy Gilmour (another Chelsea teammate) after the 0-0 draw with Scotland at Wembley, a game that saw England sucked into the tribal warfare siege mentality of their opponents. A stylish player with a wonderful left foot, if Chilwell can allay troublesome injuries he may offer England a better attacking option than the 2020 Euros incumbent at left-back, Manchester United's Luke Shaw.

In front of Chelsea's fluid five-man defence sat two excellent, steadfast midfield players of great experience. Italy's Jorginho (outstanding in his country's 2020 Euros triumph) and Frenchman N'Golo Kanté are the best at what they do. Jorginho's lack of pace seemed to be detrimental to him after a bright start at Chelsea under Maurizio Sarri. What is unquestionable is that if Jorginho is given space he will dictate the tempo of his team with his metronomic passing.

Born in the southern Brazilian port and coastal town of Inibituba, Jorginho moved to Italy aged 15, beginning his professional career with Verona. Joining Napoli in 2014, Jorginho prospered under Sarri's stewardship at the club, winning the Coppa Italia in 2014, Napoli defeating Fiorentina 3-1. Sarri's employment as Napoli's manager saw Jorginho switched to a deep-lying role in midfield where his passing became crucial to Napoli's challenge for the Serie A title – although the team couldn't deny perennial winners Juventus.

It came as no surprise when Jorginho signed for Chelsea on 14 July 2018, the same day as Maurizio Sarri became the club's new manager. Where the chain-smoking Sarri paced the touchline anxiously in his short tenure as Chelsea manager, Jorginho patrols the spaces between the touchlines with great authority – but it wasn't always so. Jorginho's passing rate was exemplified when he completed 158 passes (a new club record) against Newcastle United in Chelsea's third Premier League game of 2018–19. He broke Chelsea's and Manchester City's Ilkay Gündogan's passing record in the sixth game of the campaign with 180 attempts. Jorginho ended the season winning the 2019 Europa League title as Chelsea humbled Arsenal 4-1 in the final.

For a while Premiership clubs seemed to have his number, cutting off his supply by closing him down quickly, exposing his lack of pace. To his credit, Jorginho persevered, returning to form with a vengeance in the 2021–22 season. In August 2021 Jorginho was named UEFA Mens' Midfielder of the Year, topping teammate Kanté and Manchester City's Kevin De Bruyne. In November 2021 he came third in the Ballon d'Or behind Lionel Messi and Robert Lewandowski. Unfussy, Jorginho's status is assured by his contribution to his team's dictation of play.

In November 2017, Italy lost 1-0 on aggregate to Sweden in a 2018 World Cup qualifier, meaning Jorginho's country failed to qualify for the tournament for the first time in 60 years. His consistency from the penalty spot came to the fore in the semi-finals of the 2020 Euros. After their contest with Spain ended 1-1 after 120 minutes, it was Jorginho's decisive penalty that put Italy into the final. In the final England started positively through Luke Shaw's second-minute goal, but tailed off in the second half as wily defensive campaigners Leonardo Bonucci and Giorgio Chiellini strangled the threat of Raheem Sterling and Harry Kane. Jorginho, the model of penalty consistency, this time missed his shoot-out kick, but with England missing kicks by Marcus Rashford, Jadon Sancho and Bukayo Saka (all shamefully trolled on social media), Italy triumphed 3-2 on penalties after the 1-1 draw.

At the 2020 Euros Jorginho was the most fouled player, he made the most interceptions (25) and completed the second most passes after Spain and Manchester City's Aymeric Laporte (the influence of the adherence to short passing under Pep Guardiola). Jorginho also covered the most ground of any player at the tournament. Predictably he was named in the Team of the Tournament.

Jorginho compensates for his lack of pace with high football intelligence, his positional play astute, and by withdrawing slightly from the higher midfield positions on the pitch he gives himself ample time to dictate the tempo of the game.

The relentless running and exceptional retrieval rate of Jorginho's fellow deep-lying midfielder in this Chelsea team, N'Golo Kanté, formed these two obdurate bedfellows at the base of the Blues midfield on the night. The higher positioned Mason Mount, freed by Jorginho and Kanté's stranglehold of the midfield was able to apply his underrated technique and incisive movement to great effect on Chelsea's left. Alongside Mount, in front of Jorginho, the less consistent, but on the night, match-winning Kai Havertz was one of two young German internationals appearing for Chelsea. An unusually tall (six feet three inches) player for an attacking midfielder, Havertz appears ungainly, but possesses deceptively good touch. Still only 23 upon writing, Havertz must have something about him as he is the youngest player to reach the milestone of 100 German Bundesliga appearances with Bayer Leverkusen. He was that club's youngest ever debutant and youngest ever goalscorer. In all, Havertz scored 36 goals in 118 Bundesliga games for Bayer Leverkusen,

In 2018–19 Havertz became the highest scoring teenager in the Bundesliga with 17 goals, finishing a narrow runner-up to Marco Reus in the German Footballer of the Year poll. Havertz scored in both ties as Leverkusen defeated Porto 5-2 on aggregate in the 2019 Europa League last 32. In the last 16 he scored a penalty against Rangers in Glasgow as Leverkusen came through 4-1 on aggregate. He also scored in the quarter-final against tougher opponents in Inter Milan, this time his goal only a consolation as Leverkusen were defeated 2-1.

Havertz signed for Chelsea in September 2020. The tall, languid youngster has endured a mixed start to his Chelsea career, but was on hand to score the only goal of this 2021 Champions League Final. It's early days for Havertz at Stamford Bridge, but he has already established himself as a regular starter for Germany, scoring eight goals in 28 internationals (August 2022). After scoring four goals against Belarus in an U-19 European Championship qualifier (and captaining the team), Havertz was elevated to Germany's full senior squad. At the 2020 Euros he scored against Portugal in a 4-2 win, and against Hungary in a 2-2 drawn group match that saw Germany through to their abortive 2-0 last 16 defeat against England. Havertz likes to play the false nine role (which he invariably does for Chelsea) in order to find space between the lines, in the hole behind the main striker. His height makes him extremely adept in the air. There is so much more to come from Kai Havertz.

The other young German in Chelsea's starting 11 joined the club with even greater expectation foisted upon him. A goal-scoring machine with RB Leipzig 2016–20 (78 goals in 127 Bundesliga games), the responsibility of being Chelsea's main striker weighed heavily upon him. At youth level for Germany Timo Werner was prolific (34 goals in 48 games from U-15 to U-21 level), but the young striker has failed to fulfil his remit at Chelsea, scoring just seven goals in 44 Premier League games. Any observer can see it is not for want of trying – indeed he may be trying too hard. With pace to burn, Werner, like Raheem Sterling at Manchester City, always frightens defences. A natural goalscorer for Germany, for the moment Werner's clinical striker's qualities have deserted him.

At first Werner became the youngest player to mark 50 appearances in the Bundesliga with VfB Stuttgart, soon to be overtaken by compatriot Kai Havertz. Only when joining RB Leipzig in June 2016 did Werner's stock rise substantially. Upon leaving Leipzig in June 2020 Werner totalled 95 goals in all competitions, hence the huge expectation upon his arrival at Stamford Bridge. It would appear Werner simply needs to dial down the energy when nearing goal. Many a lightning quick striker has failed in front of goal. Werner has at least scored the fastest goal in Champions League history after a mere 82 seconds against Russian club Zenit St Petersburg in December 2021.

Werner – nicknamed 'Turbo Timo' given his capacity to switch on the after-burners – has a better record with Germany, scoring 24 goals in 53 internationals (August 2022). He won the Golden Boot with three goals and two assists in the tournament-winning 2017 FIFA Confederations Cup team. He failed to score at the 2018 World Cup, and with his form dipping, didn't make his mark on the 2020 Euros, again failing to score. What is not in doubt is Werner's effort and team ethic, his hard-running style contributing to goals scored by his Chelsea teammates. It simply seems that he has been unable to score regularly himself in a Chelsea shirt (ten Premier League goals, August 2022). Linked with Real Madrid as I write, can Werner rediscover himself?

Who would the winning manager be? The Teutonic titan Thomas Tuchel of Chelsea or the god-given graceful Guardiola of Manchester City? Football's pragmatists have a habit of usurping upstarts with seemingly superior skill, and so it proved here in Portugal, Tuchel's organised Chelsea beating City for the third time in a month. At the time I thought Chelsea couldn't get lucky three times, could they? Organised, powerful, sticking to their manager's game plan, Chelsea were worthy winners ultimately.

THE FINAL
Manchester City – and Guardiola's undoing – was encapsulated by Guardiola's decision to go for all-out attack at the expense of either of his holding midfielders, Fernandinho or Rodri. It proved to be a costly mistake; Mason Mount soon broke clear of the City defence to set up Timo Werner for a tame shot that summed up the player's hapless form in front of goal. Kevin De Bruyne's slick ball gave Phil Foden the opportunity for an attempt with the outside of his boot that was blocked at the other end by the ever-hungry Antonio Rudiger. Chelsea broke the ice when Kai Havertz broke on to a fine through ball from Mount to round the onrushing Ederson and score. The closest City came to equalising was through Riyad Mahrez's hooked shot that narrowly cleared the crossbar in the second half. Tuchel shaped his team in a mere few months to be an exceptionally difficult outfit to play against. Why did Guardiola feel the need to tinker with his system on the night? It's something he's repeatedly done in his vain quest to win the Champions League with Manchester City.

2021–22 CHAMPIONS LEAGUE FINAL
Real Madrid 1 v 0 Liverpool

Again, as I concluded my writings, another British team reached the pinnacle of European Football: the Champions League Final. Under Jürgen Klopp, Liverpool have re-established themselves as one of European football's power-house clubs. This final brought together again the 2018 finalists, Real Madrid and Liverpool. Liverpool have strengthened considerably since 2018. The core of their team remained the same: the exciting full-backs Trent Alexander-Arnold and Andrew Robertson, the imperious centre-back, Virgil van Dijk, Jordan Henderson in midfield, the scintillating forwards Mohamed Salah and Sadio Mané. The latter two players' contracts are running out – perhaps Liverpool will have to evolve once more in coming seasons (yes, as Mané moved to Bayern Munich for the 2022–23 season). Klopp wisely played down any talk of revenge against Real Madrid, particularly in the light of the unfortunate circumstances in which danger-man Salah left the field four years ago. The 'bad guy' on that occasion, Sergio Ramos, left for French shores with Paris Saint-Germain. Surely Liverpool would have enough to win this time? No, actually, as Real became party-poopers again, all their experience brought to play to damn the dream of a second Liverpool Champions League in four years, and in winning, claimed their own 14th European Cup/Champions League. Real won the first five trophies 1956–1960, and in a neat twist they became the last winners of the competition in my book.

Liverpool showed only three changes from the starting 11 from their victorious 2019 final against Tottenham Hotspur. In defence, Paris-born to Malian immigrant parents, the towering six feet four inches Ibrahima Konaté offered Liverpool a powerful presence alongside Virgil van Dijk. Konaté played for Paris FC in Ligue 2 before joining Sochaux where he made only 12 senior appearances. He'd shown enough for upcoming German club RB Leipzig to take him on. In 66 appearances 2017–21 with Leipzig, Konaté displayed assets that saw Liverpool sign him, another cog in Jürgen Klopp's relentless Liverpool wheel.

In midfield the exquisitely talented Thiago Alcântara gave Liverpool an experienced, controlled midfield marshal of the ilk of former star Xabi Alonso. Thiago, Italian born, Spanish nationalised, joined Barcelona aged 14. Thiago is a four-time La Liga winner with Barcelona, and a seven-time Bundesliga winner with Bayern Munich. Another step up in class for Liverpool, it would seem. Thiago has also won 46 caps for Spain (June 2022). The other change for Liverpool came in attack, where the Colombian international left winger Luis Diaz (35 appearances, eight goals) brought a freshness and creative spark to the end of Liverpool's 2021–22 Premier League season, scoring four goals in 13 appearances.

Ramos gone, Real Madrid's defence might not offer such stubborn resilience in 2022, would it? Wrong. At right-back, Spanish international Dani Carvajal (29 caps, June 2022), didn't put a foot wrong all evening in this final. Carvajal has been with Real since 2013, appearing 223 times (August 2022). At centre-back for Real, the 24 years old Brazilian Eder Militao proved to be another irrititant to Liverpool. Born in Sao Paulo state, Brazil, Militao has appeared 63 times for Real (August 2022), becoming a major player in this season's Champions League. He has won 22 caps for Brazil since 2018 (August 2022).

As if Carvajal and Militao's performances on this night were not enough to spoil the party for Liverpool, they also faced one of European football's finest defenders of the last decade in Vienna-born David Alaba. Austrian Footballer of the Year eight times, including six consecutive wins 2011–16, Alaba proved his mettle with Bayern Munich 2010–21 in 281 appearances (22 goals). During this time he was named three times in the UEFA Team of the Year. Capped 94 times for Austria (14 goals, August 2022), Alaba was outstanding when my sons and I saw him against Italy in the 2020 Euros at Wembley.

In attack Real Madrid boasted the form striker in this season's Champions League in French international Karim Benzema, but it was the two young wide players who caught my attention on the night. Montevideo-born Federico Valverde has appeared 104 times, five goals) for Real since 2017. He was loaned out to Deportivo La Coruna 2017–18, but Valverde looked a perfectly-formed player on this evening with his hard-running style and positivity. Valverde had played 42 times for Uruguay (four goals) by 2022. On the other flank, the goalscorer on this evening, Brazilian left-winger Vinicius Junior, was a constant threat to Liverpool all evening. Only 21 years old, Vinicius didn't do enough apparently to convince former managerial legend Zinedine Zidane, but Carlo Ancelotti had no such qualms about Vinicius, and the young Brazilian repaid him handsomely. In 117 appearances for Real, Vinicius had scored 25 goals (June 2022), adding a single goal for Brazil in 14 caps to this tally. There would appear to be very much more to come from the sprightly Vinicius Junior.

THE FINAL

The Stade de France in Paris was the venue for this 2022 Champions League Final. The Parisian night air rang out before the game to the tune of 'You'll Never Walk Alone', the perennial anthemic favourite of Liverpool fans made famous by Gerry and the Pacemakers during my childhood in 1963. The kick-off was delayed by 37 minutes – at the time viewers were not aware of the seriousness of the delay. Only later would the world discover how close this final came to another Hillsborough or Heysel. Late arriving fans and poor French organisation were apportioned equal blame; fake tickets was another accusation by the French authorities, although this was later attributed to a glitch in the computer system wrongly reading the authenticity of the tickets. As with the Manchester United versus Villareal Europa League Final last year, I am able to stream this match for free on BT Sport on the internet.

Real went into the match full of confidence after defeating the cream of Europe from the last 16 onwards: Paris Saint-Germain 3-2 on aggregate in the last 16; Chelsea 5-4 on aggregate in the last eight; and Manchester City 6-5 on aggregate in the last four. In the same rounds Liverpool defeated Inter Milan 2-1 on aggregate; Benfica 6-4 on aggregate; and Villareal rather more comfortably by 5-2 on aggregate in the semi-finals.

Liverpool stalwarts Fabinho and Thiago Alcântara had been injured in recent games, but both were passed fit to play. The epitome of cool – Dutchman Virgil van Dijk, walked on to the pitch from the players tunnel, looking totally unflappable as usual. He had been rested by Jürgen Klopp after an injury scare. Manchester City had enough chances in the semi-final to have ensured another all-English final here. Surely Liverpool would be more clinical if allowed the same openings by Real Madrid? After the horrors of the Heysel Stadium in Brussels in 1985 when 39 people died, it was absolutely paramount that fans here were safely directed to the correct areas of the Stadium. Another disaster was only averted by the calm actions of Liverpool fans who remembered 1985 only too well – and the even more horrendous Hillsborough incident of 1989 where 97 people died.

Previous legendary strikers, Raul of Real Madrid and Ian Rush of Liverpool brought the Champions League trophy out on to the pitch. It was a nice touch that only half alleviated the chaos surrounding the stadium. Flares shot off into the night sky as the game finally began at 8.37 am. Karim Benzema's purple and green football boots were a reflection of football fashion circa 2022. The game has come a long way since 1956, the year of my birth. Real lined up with Gareth Bale, Eden Hazard and Isco only among the substitutes, match-winners and superstars all, but none considered consistent enough to start the game. Benzema, sturdy, but shorter than the towering centre-backs of Liverpool, van Dijk and Konaté, would make his statement on the night, his movement impressing even if for once he failed to score. As predicted in the press, Jordan Henderson doubled up with Trent Alexander-Arnold in an attempt to thwart the threat of Vinicius Junior on Real's left flank. Belgian goalkeeper for Real, Thibaus Courtois, the ex-Chelsea custodian, was quoted in the *Saturday Telegraph* as saying Real would win the trophy, "because they always win finals" – but surely this was a different Liverpool team to the one beaten 3-1 by Real in the 2018 final.

Immediately it was evident that the technical skills on show were on an altogether higher plane than those seen in last month's Europa League Final. Real looked a younger, pacier side than their teams of recent years, while retaining the wise older heads of Benzema, Luka Modric and Tony Kroos – they had a good balance in their side. Liverpool began by bossing possession, but it was startlingly obvious that Real Madrid offered a serious counter-attacking threat. Liverpool created the first serious chance of the game, Mo Salah's close range shot saved by Thiebaut Courtois. Sadio Mané set Salah up for another shot that was too close to the imposing Courtois. It was a healthy start for Liverpool, the roaming Colombian Luis Diaz on the left carrying on his recent Premier League form. Salah teed up Trent Alexander-Arnold for another shot that flew over the bar. The biggest opportunity of the match for Liverpool came when Mané fired a sharp shot that appeared to beat Courtois, the Belgian stopper getting the merest of fingertips to the ball to turn it on to the inside of a post. Only post-match is it evident what a brilliant save Courtois made. The ball rebounded back into play and Real survived. Salah desperately wanted to make amends for his aborted 2018 final appearance, but he was largely unable to affect the game. Diaz, Liverpool's most dangerous player, was involved in an intriguing battle with Dani Carvajal. The longer the game went on, the more the tide turned in favour of the determined Spaniard.

Alexander-Arnold whipped in one of his trademark crosses, but Salah's header lacked the pace to beat Courtois. The 35th minute: Liverpool had had eight attempts on goal, Real none. This only partially tells the story as Real stuck to their counter-attacking plan, Benzema and Vinicius Junior working a smart one-two that only failed due to Jordan Henderson's diligent covering. Thiago Alcântara, so brilliant at blind passes, shaping to go one way then passing the other, reminded me of Cesc Fàbregas in his pomp at Arsenal. A lovely turn by Mané after receiving the ball from Andrew Robertson was thwarted by the alert Eder Militao. From the corner-kick, Jordan Henderson fired wide. In the 42nd minute Real's counter-attacking potency almost broke the deadlock. Benzema escaped Robertson, Alisson Becker and Ibrahima Konaté made a hash of clearing the ball, and Benzema fired into goal. VAR was called into action. Benzema was given marginally offside in the second action in the goalmouth melee, not from his original run. Fabinho's touch on the ball suggested Benzema had been played onside. It's a let-off for Liverpool, the half ending goalless.

In the 46th minute Diaz dived and just failed to connect with another Alexander-Arnold cross. Fifty-minute statistics show the game had now evened up, and Real made the breakthrough in the 58th minute. Federico Valverde, hard-working and threatening all night, sped down the right side of the field, arrowing the ball beyond the backtracking Alexander-Arnold, and Vinicius Junior had the easiest of tap-ins. Real lead 1-0. Liverpool, largely dominant, creating more chances, now had it all to do. The frustration of the situation got to Fabinho, the Brazilian catching Valverde late and receiving a yellow card. Salah had gone off the boil; Mané was being shackled by the persistent Militao. Salah cut in from the right and bent a smart left-foot shot towards the far corner of the Real goal, but the inspired Courtois saw it all the way and saved. The lively Diaz came off, replaced by Diogo Jota. Jota almost impacted immediately, heading back across the goal for the onrushing Salah, but Courtois blocked his close range effort. Courtois, feted as the best goalkeeper in the word during his time at Chelsea, was an increasingly resistant barrier to Liverpool's dreams.

Benzema was giving a huge amount to his team, dropping deep to help his teammates in midfield and defence. Real had come into the game now, only a desperate tackle by Konaté stopped Vinicius Junior as he was about to unleash another shot. Liverpool tried with all their might to claw their way back into the game, Alexander-Arnold drilling the ball across the goalmouth, but Jota failed to divert the ball into goal. In the 75th minute Roberto Firmino joined the fray, replacing the tiring Thiago. Liverpool almost sleep-walked again when a free kick from the right culminated with a poor Casemiro lay-back. For all their dominance of play, it was another lucky escape for Liverpool.

Naby Keïta came on for Henderson as Liverpool's desperation increased. Eightieth minute: 19 goal attempts to two in Liverpool's favour, but they still trailed the wily Spanish side. The artful Firmino pulled a lovely diagonal ball back from the bye-line but Keïta slashed his shot wildly over the bar. Salah escaped on the right and shot right-footed, but Courtois deflected the ball wide for a corner-kick. Eighty-ninth minute: Modric came off, job done. There was five minutes injury time to play as Tony Kroos encouraged the Real fans to stoke up the atmosphere as Real won a rare corner-kick. Kroos, Modric and Benzema had used all their experience to retain the ball at all costs. Rafa Nadal, the great Spanish tennis champion, was spotted in the crowd, in a break from his pursuit of yet another French Open victory. Real, street-smart, triumph 1-0. Liverpool were not outplayed, but out-thought. The prophetic Courtois was clearly Man of the Match. Real won their 14th European Cup, their fifth in the last nine seasons. Carlo Ancelotti became the first manager to win the competition four times, twice with AC Milan, 2003, 2007, twice with Real 2014, 2022. He also won the trophy twice as a player for AC Milan in 1988–89 and 1989–90. Ancelotti also became the first manager to win five European League titles with Real in this season – the other clubs being AC Milan, Chelsea, Paris Saint-Germain, Real Madrid and Bayern Munich. Some manager.

The aftershocks of poor organisation by the French authorities rumbled on after this game for a week or two. On a financial note, the following morning's BBC news revealed that Real Madrid would net approximately £102 million for winning the Champions league; Liverpool as runners-up would net £98 million. Not a bad journey for the two teams, I would suggest, and one can see why this enduring competition has become so important to Europe's leading clubs, and why even finishing fourth in the Premier League is a branch on which English clubs fall over themselves to grasp.

Prologue

Pep Guardiola found to his cost that the Champions League – or the European Cup in its former guise – is the hardest club competition in the world to win. Even when playing football on the scale of Manchester City's wondrous teams of the last decade, there will always be Bayern Munich, Real Madrid, Barcelona, AC Milan, Inter Milan, Juventus et al waiting in the wings to tear down your dreams.

There are so many memories for me watching this competition – the indefatigable 'Lisbon Lions', Jock Stein's unlikely Glasgow Celtic winners of 1967; the fairytale ten-year quest of Sir Matt Busby and Bobby Charlton to assuage the horrors of the Munich air crash when Manchester United won the trophy the following year in 1968 (it didn't fully, nothing can counteract the tragic loss of young lives only a quarter-lived); the total football genius of the early 70s Ajax team of Cruyff, Neeskens and Krol; the stylish Franz Beckenbauer and explosive Gerd Müller of the mid-70s Bayern Munich; and then the superstar individuals of the 21st century, Barcelona's Lionel Messi and Real Madrid's Cristiano Ronaldo.

The emergence of a new super-fit footballing athlete has taken the cream of European competition on to ever-increasing heights. That's what makes the triumphs of the British clubs, Celtic, Manchester United, Liverpool, Chelsea so rare, so special. It's the best club competition in the world –with apologies to the South American equivalent, the Libertadores Cup – and you need a smidgen of luck and a team of either the greatest quality or a team ethic unmatched by any of your great rivals to win it.

Cheers to British football's triumphant and successful victors in the European Cup Winner's Cup, the UEFA Cup/Europa League, and the European Cup/ Champions League. It takes a titanic effort to win any of these competitions, and a humble approach in the manner of the fine Liverpool side of the late 1970s and early 1980s to realise that others in Europe have made strides that British clubs have to match or surpass. Arrogance is a common, nay, necessary trait in a top professional football player, but it should be tempered with humility. Managers like Bob Paisley at Liverpool and Alex Ferguson at Manchester United have shown that it never hurts to acknowledge that other European clubs have progressed – and they have in turn learned from this progression in the wonderful game of football.

Football is naturally a game of constant flux, transfers occurring even as I write these final words. What is indubitable is football's capacity to constantly entertain and arouse passion and discussion.

Printed in Great Britain
by Amazon

22994813R00306